SunOS 4.1 Command	SunOS 5.x (SVR4) Changes
df	Add the −k option to display output in a format similar to that of just the df command. The −t option now displays a full listing with totals, rather than reporting on the type of files.
diff	The −c takes no argument and assumes a default of 3. −C requires an argument giving the number of lines to display for each difference. The −S option requires that you add a space between the −S option and the name to specify (e.g., diff −S *name*).
dkinfo	Use the prtvtoc command to display similar results.
fastboot	Use the boot, reboot, or init 6 commands for similar results.
fasthalt	Use the init 0 command for similar results.
file	The -L option is no longer available. When you use the file *filename* command (if the file indicated by *filename* is a symbolic link), the file command tests the file referenced by the link, rather than the symbolic link itself.
find	The −ncpio *device* option, which wrote the current file on the device indicated by *device* in the cpio command's −c format, is no longer available.
fsck	Now specify most options after you specify the file system type.
grep	The -w option searches for the regular expression (as a word), if surrounded by \< and \>.
hostid	Use the sysdef -h command to display similar results.
hostname	Use the uname −n command to display similar results.
init	When you use the -a *n* option, the value of *n* can only be 1 or 2. You can no longer use the value 3. There is now no restriction to the argument −j, which previously could only be 1 or 2.
leave	The cron and at commands display similar results.
ln	The ln *target* command now removes the *target* if it already exists, provided you have the proper permissions. The −f option now forces files to be linked without displaying permissions, asking questions, or reporting errors.
lockscreen	Use the xlock command for similar results.
lpq	Use the lpstat command to display similar results.
lpr	Use the lp command for similar results.
lprm	Use the cancel command for similar results.

(Continued on inside back cover)

FOR EVERY COMPUTER QUESTION,
THERE IS A SYBEX BOOK THAT HAS THE ANSWER

Each computer user learns in a different way. Some need thorough, methodical explanations, while others are too busy for details. At Sybex we bring nearly 20 years of experience to developing the book that's right for you. Whatever your needs, we can help you get the most from your software and hardware, at a pace that's comfortable for you.

We start beginners out right. You will learn by seeing and doing with our **Quick & Easy** series: friendly, colorful guidebooks with screen-by-screen illustrations. For hardware novices, the **Your First** series offers valuable purchasing advice and installation support.

Often recognized for excellence in national book reviews, our **Mastering** titles are designed for the intermediate to advanced user, without leaving the beginner behind. A **Mastering** book provides the most detailed reference available. Add our pocket-sized **Instant Reference** titles for a complete guidance system. Programmers will find that the new **Developer's Handbook** series provides a more advanced perspective on developing innovative and original code.

With the breathtaking advances common in computing today comes an ever increasing demand to remain technologically up-to-date. In many of our books, we provide the added value of software, on disks or CDs. Sybex remains your source for information on software development, operating systems, networking, and every kind of desktop application. We even have books for kids. Sybex can help smooth your travels on the **Internet** and provide **Strategies and Secrets** to your favorite computer games.

As you read this book, take note of its quality. Sybex publishes books written by experts—authors chosen for their extensive topical knowledge. In fact, many are professionals working in the computer software field. In addition, each manuscript is thoroughly reviewed by our technical, editorial, and production personnel for accuracy and ease-of-use before you ever see it—our guarantee that you'll buy a quality Sybex book every time.

To manage your hardware headaches and optimize your software potential, ask for a Sybex book.

FOR MORE INFORMATION, PLEASE CONTACT:

SYBEX

Sybex Inc.
2021 Challenger Drive
Alameda, CA 94501
Tel: (510) 523-8233 • (800) 227-2346
Fax: (510) 523-2373

Let us hear from you.

alk to **SYBEX** authors, editors and fellow forum members.

et tips, hints and advice online.

ownload magazine articles, book art, and shareware.

Join the SYBEX Forum on ▣ **CompuServe**®

If you're already a CompuServe user, just type **GO SYBEX** to join the SYBEX Forum. If not, try CompuServe for free by calling 1-800-848-8199 and ask for Representative 560. You'll get one free month of basic service and a $15 credit for CompuServe extended services—a $23.95 value. Your personal ID number and password will be activated when you sign up.

Join us online today. Type **GO SYBEX** on CompuServe. If you're not a CompuServe member, call Representative 560 at **1-800-848-8199** .

SYBEX   (outside U.S./Canada call 614-457-0802)

Mastering
Solaris™ 2

BRENT D. HESLOP & DAVID F. ANGELL

San Francisco • Paris • Düsseldorf • Soest

SYBEX®

ACQUISITIONS EDITOR: Dianne King
DEVELOPMENTAL EDITOR: Gary Masters
EDITOR: Kimn Neilson
PROJECT EDITOR: Kathleen Lattinville
TECHNICAL EDITOR: Jeff Horan
BOOK DESIGNER/PRODUCTION ARTIST: Suzanne Albertson
SCREEN GRAPHICS: John Corrigan
TYPESETTER: Ann Dunn
PROOFREADERS/PRODUCTION COORDINATORS: Arno Harris and Catherine Mahoney
INDEXER: Ted Laux
COVER DESIGNER: Archer Design
COVER PHOTOGRAPHER: David Bishop
COVER PHOTO ART DIRECTION: Ingalls + Associates

SYBEX is a registered trademark of SYBEX Inc.

TRADEMARKS: SYBEX has attempted throughout this book to distinguish proprietary trademarks from descriptive terms by following the capitalization style used by the manufacturer.

SYBEX is not affiliated with any manufacturer.

Every effort has been made to supply complete and accurate information. However, SYBEX assumes no responsibility for its use, nor for any infringement of the intellectual property rights of third parties which would result from such use.

Library of Congress Card Number: 92-83942
ISBN: 0-7821-1072-X

Manufactured in the United States of America
10 9 8 7 6 5 4

To Kim for her love, patience, and understanding

B.D.H.

*To Frank Meritt Angell, who inspired me
before I even realized it*

D.F.A.

ACKNOWLEDGMENTS

MANY people at SunSoft were instrumental in the writing of this book. We owe a huge debt of gratitude to Bentley Radcliff, who helped supply us with the needed materials to make the transition from Solaris 1 to Solaris 2. Robert Saft was invaluable to this project. He graciously shared his time and advice to help us solve problems and improve this book. He deserves credit for many of the insights and tips in the chapter on customizing Solaris. We also would like to acknowledge Don Charles, who helped us get our Solaris 2 system up and running.

If we had to choose one person at SunSoft who really helped us make this book a reality, Doug Royer would be at the top of the list. Doug proved not only to be one of the most knowledgeable people about Solaris 2, he was, without a doubt, the most supportive. He put up with several late-night calls at his home and even made a special weekend trip to our office to help us. Doug also saved us hours of time by introducing us to XV (a shareware graphics program by John Bradley) that we used for all the figures in this book. Doug, thank you. Jeff Horan at SunSelect deserves a great deal of credit for his technical assistance and expertise. Jeff worked with us on our first book on SunOS, *Mastering SunOS,* and continues to be a lifesaver.

We also want to extend our appreciation to Ron Lee, who cheerfully explained many of the idiosyncrasies of Solaris 2 that had us scratching our heads. John Linton also deserves an honorable mention for his advice on how to improve this book. Stuart Marks deserves credit for helping us resolve problems related to capturing the screens used in the figures.

Thanks also to Karin Ellison and Kim Ingram for helping us with Solaris 2 for x86 information.

Outside of SunSoft we want to thank Larry Goodman for his help with the command reference and the use of his workstation. Kudos to Kimn Neilson for applying her superior copyediting skills to our text. Thanks also go to Kim Merry who helped us take and edit screenshots for several of the figures in this book. The new chapter on communications and networking would not have been possible without the support of Brian Fudge at Portal Communications Company. Brian helped us with questions about networking and communications and let us use a connection at Portal to test the accuracy of our text. Thanks go to Joe Ballard and Mike Cerni at Distributed Processing Technology (DPT) for making it possible to run Solaris 2 for x86 by providing us with a DPT Smartcache controller. This is the easiest controller card to install, and it has proven to be incredibly fast and dependable. A note of thanks to Sue Glassberg at UniPress Software Inc. for supplying us with XVision, the best product for working with the X Window System and Microsoft Windows we have seen. Thanks also go to David Newman at Island Graphics for supplying us with Island Write Draw and Paint.

At SYBEX, several people made writing this book an enjoyable experience. First off we want to acknowledge Dianne King, Acquisitions Editor, and Rudy Langer, Vice President and Editor in Chief, who gave us the opportunity to work on this exciting project. We are also grateful to Gary Masters, who besides giving us advice and encouragement, finagled the time we needed to finish this massive job. A warm thanks to Kathleen Lattinville, our project editor, who brought such a positive attitude to this project that we didn't mind working late into the night to make the deadlines. Thanks also to Barbara Gordon, Managing Editor. And many thanks to the entire production staff at SYBEX for their efforts in seeing this book through production.

Contents
AT A GLANCE

CONTENTS

PART THREE   **BEYOND THE FUNDAMENTALS**

CONTENTS

CONTENTS

INTRODUCTION

S

UN stands for Stanford University Network, a name given to a printed circuit board developed in 1981 that was designed to run the popular UNIX operating system. This board was instrumental in bringing UNIX to the desktop from its minicomputer roots and catapulting Sun Microsystems to dominance in the workstation market. Sun continues its leadership in the computer industry with Solaris 2.x, its new UNIX-based operating system. Solaris is a distributed computing environment from SunSoft (a subsidiary of Sun Microsystems) that includes the SunOS 5.x operating system and ONC+ networking, plus the OpenWindows graphical user interface. OpenWindows represents a new, friendly face for UNIX that rivals the ease of Microsoft Windows and the Macintosh computer. Solaris 2.x brings this new computing power to not only Sun workstations and Sun workstation clones, but extends the reach of the powerful UNIX operating system to Intel-based PCs with Solaris 2 for x86.

What Is Solaris?

Solaris 2.x is a multilayered operating system (see Figure 1 below) that includes SunOS 5.x, Open Network Computing, OpenWindows, and the DeskSet. At the core of Solaris is SunOS, the collection of programs that actually manages the system, which includes the kernel, the file system, and the shells. The next level of Solaris is its built-in ONC+ networking features, which allow for distributed computing. The top layer of the Solaris operating system is OpenWindows, the graphical user interface, based on OPEN LOOK and Sun's implementation of the X Window System. The following sections provide an overview of the components that make up Solaris.

SunOS

SunOS is a collection of UNIX programs that control the Sun workstation and provide a link between the user, the workstation, and its resources. The core programs manage the computer system and remain hidden from the user. The remaining programs are utility programs that provide the user with tools for working with SunOS.

UNIX was created by Ken Thompson and Dennis Ritchie at AT&T's Bell Laboratories to provide an environment that promoted efficient program development. AT&T later licensed UNIX to universities, and at the

FIGURE 1

The layers of Solaris

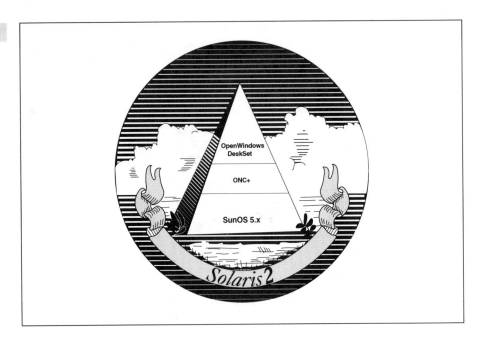

University of California at Berkeley it began a life of its own. Eventually the enhanced UNIX became known as Berkeley UNIX, or as it is more commonly called, BSD (Berkeley Software Distribution). Over time, UNIX matured into an easier to use, increasingly powerful operating system, incorporating such key features as portability, networking, security, and a friendly user interface.

SunOS has its roots firmly placed in the two most popular UNIX families: Berkeley UNIX (BSD) and AT&T's UNIX. Early versions of SunOS blended some of AT&T's UNIX with Berkeley UNIX and offered additional enhancements. AT&T and Sun Microsystems later worked together to create a new industry standard, AT&T UNIX System V Release 4, commonly known as SVR4. SunOS 5.x merges SunOS 4.1 and SVR4. Most of the new changes in SunOS come from SVR4. As a result, Solaris 2.x is based on SVR4 but contains a few additional BSD/SunOS features. To help in the transition from the old (largely BSD-based) SunOS to the new System V Release 4/SunOS 5.x, Solaris 2.x provides the BSD/SunOS Compatibility Package. This package is not covered in this book since these commands will eventually be removed from SunOS. The following sections briefly explain the major components of SunOS, including the kernel and file system, shell programs, and utility programs.

Kernel and File System

The *kernel* is the heart of SunOS; it resides in memory and manages the system's memory and hardware, such as terminals, printers, drives, and other devices. It schedules and terminates processes (programs being run) and keeps track of the file system and other important functions. The *file system* is integrated with the kernel and provides the organizing structure that stores your data. It enables you to organize files in a logical and structured manner, utilizing a hierarchical file system that allows related files to be grouped together in directories. These files are stored on a disk and organized into different levels with parent directories and subordinate directories called subdirectories, similar in structure to a family tree.

Shell Programs

A *shell* program (also called a *command interpreter*) manages the interaction of the user with the kernel. The shell first accepts, then interprets, and finally executes commands entered at the command-line prompt. There are three primary SunOS shells: the Bourne shell, the C shell, and the Korn shell. All three shells come with SunOS 5.x. The Bourne shell was developed by Steve Bourne for AT&T's UNIX. The C Shell was originally developed by Bill Joy as part of Berkeley UNIX. The Korn shell was developed by David Korn of AT&T Bell Laboratories as a response to the C shell. The Korn shell is noticeably more efficient than the C and Bourne shells because it has more built-in functions. However, many of the Korn shell commands are compatible with the C and Bourne shells. Because of the Korn shell's many benefits, and the fact that it is rapidly replacing the C and Bourne shells in popularity, this book focuses on the Korn shell.

Utility Programs

Beside the programs that transparently manage the computer system, SunOS 5.x includes over 300 UNIX utility programs. These utility programs allow you to perform a wide range of tasks from the command line, such as file management, text editing, sending and receiving electronic mail, performing calculations, and many other specialized functions. These utility programs share the same names as the commands used to execute them.

Distributed Computing

One of the key tenets of Sun Microsystems' computing philosophy is "The network is the computer." Solaris incorporates this philosophy by including built-in networking features clustered around the ONC+ (Open Network Computing) family of networking protocols and distributed services. ONC+ allows distributed computing so users can access everything on the network, including servers, printers, databases, and other resources, without having to know where it is, or what type of machine it resides on. To support distributed file systems, Solaris incorporates the Network File System (NFS) standard that was developed by Sun Microsystems to enable files and programs to be transparently accessed across a network.

Graphical User Interface

Solaris incorporates the OpenWindows graphical user interface to make working with SunOS substantially easier. OpenWindows includes on-screen objects that allow you to intuitively interact with UNIX without entering cryptic commands. In the OpenWindows environment, you use a mouse to work with icons, menus, and windows. OpenWindows is based on the OPEN LOOK graphical user interface, a set of standards for user interface design based on the X Window System. The X Window System is a network-independent, operating-system-independent graphical windowing system developed by MIT that has been adopted as an industry standard. The X Window System is sometimes referred to as X11. Solaris includes an impressive set of OpenWindows applications called the DeskSet that use the X Window System. These applications allow you to perform a wide variety of everyday tasks, such as managing files, editing text files, and sending email.

How This Book Is Organized

Mastering Solaris 2 explains how to work with Solaris using the graphical-based applications as well as using the traditional SunOS command-line prompt. This book provides a practical orientation supported by numerous step-by-step instructions that get you up and running quickly and efficiently.

Throughout this book you will find helpful tips, warnings, and notes that provide you with extra information. *Mastering Solaris 2* is organized into four parts. Part I, "Working with the OpenWindows DeskSet," explains working with all the applications in the OpenWindows DeskSet. In this part, you'll find detailed, hands-on instructions for performing everyday tasks using such DeskSet applications as the File Manager, the Multimedia Mail Tool, the Calendar Manager, the Audio Tool, and more. You'll also learn how to customize your OpenWindows environment to suit your needs.

Part II, "Working from the SunOS Command Line," explains how to work with SunOS and Korn shell commands. In this part, you'll learn essential SunOS commands that are used to navigate the file system, manage files, send and receive mail, and create, edit, format, and print documents. Expanding your SunOS skills, you'll learn how to master advanced commands and techniques, such as learning how to locate files, search for text within files, perform sort operations, use redirection, pipes, and filters, and manage multiple tasks.

Part III, "Beyond the Fundamentals," explains how to harness the power of Solaris. It shows you how to customize Solaris to suit your own needs and how to communicate across your network or around the world from your workstation. You'll learn system administration basics for working with hard disk drives, tape drives, CD ROMs, and floppy disks. It also explains how to use the OpenWindows-based Administration Tool to add users, workstations, and printers to your network.

Part IV, "Command Reference," provides a comprehensive, practical reference guide to SunOS and Korn shell commands. This handy alphabetical command listing provides syntax, description, and real-world examples for using commands, showing not just how, but when and why to take advantage of a command.

PART ONE

Working with the OpenWindows DeskSet

CHAPTERS

Getting Started with OpenWindows and the DeskSet

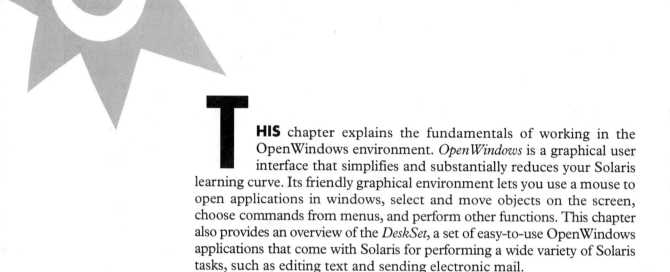

THIS chapter explains the fundamentals of working in the OpenWindows environment. *OpenWindows* is a graphical user interface that simplifies and substantially reduces your Solaris learning curve. Its friendly graphical environment lets you use a mouse to open applications in windows, select and move objects on the screen, choose commands from menus, and perform other functions. This chapter also provides an overview of the *DeskSet*, a set of easy-to-use OpenWindows applications that come with Solaris for performing a wide variety of Solaris tasks, such as editing text and sending electronic mail.

About OpenWindows and the DeskSet

The OpenWindows graphical interface rivals the ease of Microsoft Windows and the Macintosh computer, yet taps the power of UNIX. OpenWindows is based on the Open Look Graphical User Interface, a set of standards for user interface design. The background of the main Open-Windows screen is called the *Workspace*. The Workspace is the display area for objects such as windows, icons, and menus. It is analogous to a desktop that contains objects such as calculators, clocks, and file folders.

Solaris includes a set of default applications called the *DeskSet*. The DeskSet is a collection of basic applications for performing a wide range of tasks. These applications are also commonly referred to as *tools*. Each DeskSet application runs in its own window, and multiple applications can be run simultaneously. You interact with OpenWindows and DeskSet applications using the mouse, with the keyboard primarily used for entering text when needed. The following applications are included in the DeskSet:

- The Command Tool allows you easy access to the SunOS command line to enter SunOS commands.

- The Text Editor enables you to create and edit text files.

- The File Manager is a visual file management application for copying, moving, renaming, and deleting files and performing other file management tasks.

- The Mail Tool enables you to communicate with other users electronically. It includes features for sending and receiving messages as well as the ability to send and receive voice mail (when used in conjunction with the Audio Tool).

- The Calendar Manager allows you to create daily, weekly, monthly, and yearly calendars for upcoming appointments. It also lets you see the appointments of other users on the network for coordinating schedules.

- The Clock displays the current time, in either analog or digital form.

- The Calculator includes a financial and scientific calculator for performing both simple and complex calculations.

- The Print Tool allows you to easily manage your printing jobs.

- The Audio Tool lets you record and play audio files that contain recorded sounds.

- The Tape Tool provides a convenient way to back up or archive files onto a tape cartridge.

- The Binder allows you to connect a file to an application or icon so that you can start an application directly from the file.

- The Snapshot application lets you easily take snapshots of a part of the screen or the entire screen, print the image, and save the image to a file.

- The Icon Editor allows you to create your own icons which can be attached to files.

- The Performance Meter enables you to monitor many aspects of your system's performance, with either a graph or a dial meter.

- The Shell Tool lets you access the SunOS command line to enter commands.

- Demos includes a collection of special effects programs and utilities.

Logging into Solaris

NOTE   If you have already logged in and want to work with OpenWindows, skip to the section "Starting OpenWindows and the DeskSet."

The process of getting into Solaris to start OpenWindows is called *logging in*. Before you can log into Solaris to get to OpenWindows and the Desk-Set, you need an *account* set up by the *system administrator*, the person responsible for managing the system. In setting up your account, the system administrator instructs Solaris to accept you as a user and establishes certain parameters for your use of the system. You are then assigned a *user name*. Your user name identifies you to the system and usually consists of the initial letter of your first name and your complete last name.

After you have been assigned an account and a user name, you need to choose a password that you can enter at the prompt Solaris displays after you have entered your user name. Your *password* prevents the use of your account by unauthorized users. Pick a password that is easy to remember, yet not easily deduced by others. You can change your password at any time, as explained later. The following are requirements for selecting a password for the first time.

- A password must have at least six characters. If you use a password of less than six characters in length, Solaris prompts you to use a longer password.

- A password must contain at least two alphabetic characters and at least one numeric or special character, such as an &, +, −, @, !, %. A password can contain uppercase or lowercase letters.

- Your user name, with its letters reversed or moved around *cannot* be used as a password.

To log in, at the `login` prompt, type in your user name in lowercase characters and press Return. If you typed a wrong character and have not yet pressed Return, use the Delete key to erase the incorrect character and type the correct character.

N O T E If you enter a password more than three times that the system doesn't recognize, Solaris displays a message telling you there have been too many attempts and to try again later. This is a security feature to prevent unauthorized users from trying to guess a password.

After entering your user name, Solaris prompts you to enter your password. At the `password` prompt, type in your new password, then press Return. Your password will not be displayed as you type it. Solaris then logs you in and displays the system prompt, indicating that you are ready to start OpenWindows or enter SunOS commands.

System Login Messages

After you have logged in, you may see a *login message* displayed on your screen just before the system prompt. A login message usually displays information from the system administrator, such as a warning that the system will be shut down for maintenance. A message indicating that you have electronic mail from other system users may also appear. Some systems may prompt you to type **news** to display a news bulletin. For information on reading electronic mail messages, see Chapter 3, "The Multimedia Mail Tool Makes Mail Easy."

Changing Your Password

It is a good idea to change your password periodically in order to prevent unauthorized access to your files. Depending on how your system administrator set up your account, you may even be required to change your password at regular time intervals. The following are additional requirements for changing a password beyond those described earlier for entering your password for the first time.

- Uppercase and lowercase characters are not considered different by Solaris when changing a password.

- A new password must differ from the previous password by at least three characters.

The following steps explain how to change your password:

1. At the system prompt, type in the command `passwd` in lowercase characters and press Return. Solaris prompts you for your old password.

2. Type your old password and press Return. The system will not display the characters you type. The system will prompt you for your new password.

3. Type your new password and press Return. After you enter your new password, you will then be asked to retype your new password for verification.

4. Type your new password again and press Return.

Starting OpenWindows and the DeskSet

On some systems, OpenWindows comes up when you log in. If the system prompt (**$**) is displayed, you can start OpenWindows from the command line by typing

```
openwin
```

The Workspace appears with a default blue or gray background (depending on your screen type) and these DeskSet application windows appear on your screen (as shown in Figure 1.1):

- The `Console` window displays system messages. If a `Console` window does not appear on the Workspace, system messages will appear there instead, creating a cluttered screen. A new `Console` window can be opened and any system messages that appear on your screen can be removed by refreshing the Workspace, as explained in the "Workspace Utilities" section later in this chapter.

FIGURE 1.1

The default Open-Windows startup screen

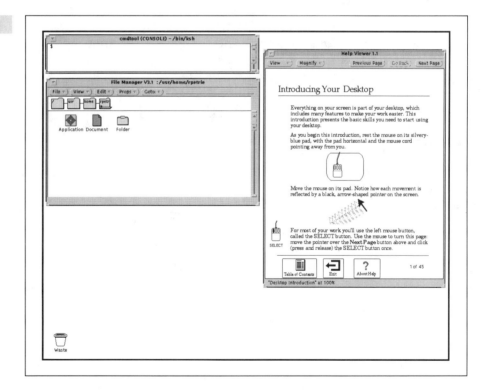

- The `File Manager` window is used to manage your files. The `Waste` (trash can) icon, which is part of the File Manager application, also appears on your screen.

- The `Help Viewer` window accesses information about Open-Windows and the DeskSet.

Using the Mouse

The mouse allows you to perform a variety of operations in OpenWindows by simply pressing a button. The arrow that appears on the screen pointing toward the upper left is the *pointer.* It changes location when you move the mouse. On most Sun workstations you must move the mouse on the metallic pad that accompanies your system. The key to mastering OpenWindows and the DeskSet is knowing where to move the pointer and which mouse button to push. Figure 1.2 shows the effects of each mouse button when used in OpenWindows. The following describes each mouse button and its related function.

FIGURE 1.2

Mouse button action

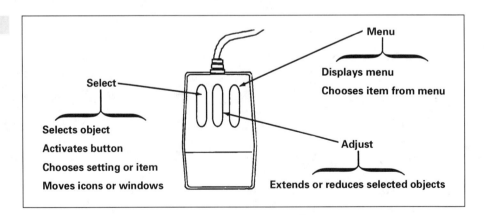

MOUSE BUTTON	FUNCTION
Left	Selects object, activates button, chooses setting or item, or move icons or windows. The left mouse button is also referred to as the *Select* button.
Middle	Extends or reduces selected objects. The middle mouse button is also referred to as the *Adjust* button.
Right	Displays menu or chooses item from menu. The right mouse button is also referred to as the *Menu* button.

N O T E If you are using a two-button mouse with Solaris for x86, the middle mouse button's function is obtained by simultaneously pressing the left mouse button and the Shift key on the keyboard.

The following describes the seven basic mouse actions performed in OpenWindows.

ACTION	DESCRIPTION
Point	Move the mouse to change the location of the pointer.
Click	Quickly press and release a mouse button.
Double-click	Quickly press and release a mouse button twice (without moving the mouse).
Press	Hold down a mouse button without moving the mouse.
Drag	Hold a mouse button down while moving the mouse.

ACTION	DESCRIPTION
Drag and drop	Hold a mouse button down while moving the mouse. When the on-screen object is over an area that accepts the object as input, release the mouse button to drop it.
Control-drag	Press the Control key on the keyboard and drag the mouse.

Pointer Indicators

The pointer also acts as an indicator of different actions occurring in the system. For example, when an application is busy, the pointer changes to a stopwatch to indicate that the application is busy and cannot accept input. The standard pointer is an arrow pointing up to the left.

Pointer Jumping

In most cases, you move the pointer by moving the mouse. However, in some cases, the pointer moves directly to a specific place on the screen automatically. This is called *pointer jumping* and is used to indicate the default response. Figure 1.3 shows an example of a pointer jumping to a button in a Notice.

FIGURE 1.3

Pointer jumping to a button in a Notice

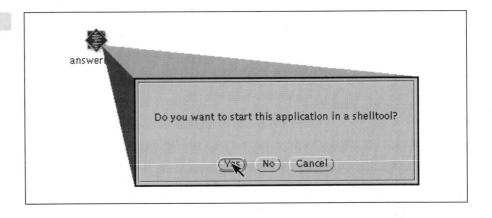

Working with Menus

A menu lists the choices that can be made from the Workspace or a Desk-Set application window. You can display a menu without making a selection by clicking the right mouse button with the pointer on the Workspace, a menu button, a window border, or the work area of a window. For example, moving the pointer to the top border of the `Help Viewer` window and clicking the right mouse button displays the `Window` menu. You can then click the right mouse button on a menu option to execute the command. Otherwise, the menu will remain displayed until you click or press any mouse button again.

Pressing and holding the right mouse button on the Workspace, a menu button, a window border, or the work area of a window displays the menu and lets you drag the pointer to highlight a menu option. When you release the mouse button, the menu option is activated. For example, pressing and holding down the right mouse button with the pointer on the top border of `Help Viewer` window displays the `Window` menu. Dragging the pointer to highlight the `Quit` option and releasing the mouse button activates the `Quit` command, which removes the `Help Viewer` window from the Workspace. Moving the pointer off the menu and releasing the mouse button removes the menu from the screen. Menus that are accessed by moving the pointer to any area of the Workspace, a window border, or the work area of a window are referred to as *pop-up menus*.

Menus in OpenWindows incorporate standardized features. Each option in a menu is called an *item*. A dimmed menu item indicates the item is not available. The direction of the arrowhead indicates where a menu will appear. An arrowhead pointing downward, such as on a menu button, indicates the menu will appear below the arrowhead. An arrowhead appearing to the right of a menu item indicates that a submenu of options will appear to the right of that item. To display a submenu, press the right mouse button and move the pointer to the arrowhead. To choose an item in a submenu, continue to move the pointer to highlight the item you want, then release the mouse button.

Choosing a menu item followed by an ellipsis (...) displays an application or pop-up window. For example, choosing the `Properties…` item in the `Workspace` menu displays the `Workspace Properties` pop-up window. Pop-up windows are explained later in this chapter.

Pinning a Menu to the Workspace

Many menus include a pushpin in the upper-left corner of the menu. You can use the mouse to push the pin, pinning the menu to the Workspace. You can open and pin a menu by pressing the right button to display the menu, dragging the pointer on top of the pushpin, then releasing the button. You can also click the right mouse button to display the menu, then click the right or left mouse button on the pushpin. Figure 1.4 shows a menu before and after pinning it to the Workspace. The menu remains pinned until you unpin it or you close the application. A pinned menu can be moved anywhere on the Workspace by moving the pointer to the menu header, pressing the left mouse button, and dragging the menu to its new location.

To unpin a menu or pop-up window, click the left mouse button on the pushpin or choose `Dismiss` from the `Window` menu by clicking the right mouse button with the pointer on the menu's header, the area above the line at the top of the menu. The `Window` menu can also be accessed by moving the pointer on any part of the menu's border and pressing the right mouse button. The `Window` menu is explained in detail later in this chapter.

Choosing the Default Menu Item

The default menu item is usually the first item listed in a menu and is encircled with a small black border (Figure 1.5). Most menus have default menu items. The default item is activated by clicking the left mouse button on the menu button or choosing just the menu item that accesses the default item in the submenu. In both cases, you save the extra step of having to display the menu or submenu.

FIGURE 1.4

A menu before and
after pinning it to the
Workspace

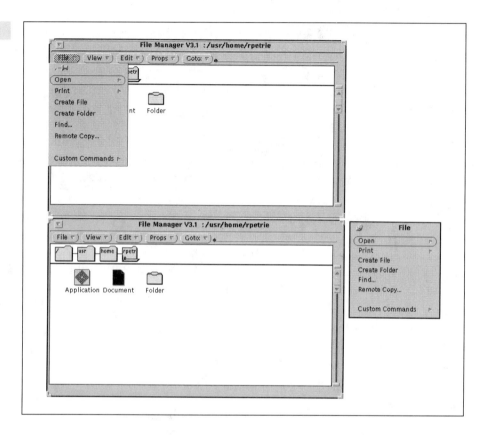

FIGURE 1.5

The default item in a
menu

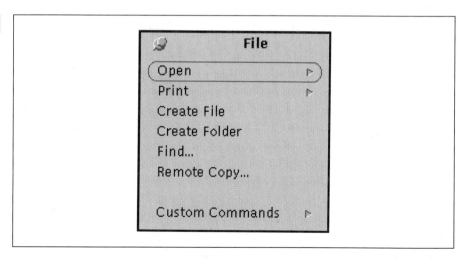

If you find that you frequently choose a menu item choice other than the default, you can define that item as the default item. To change the default choice, do the following:

1. Press the right mouse button to display the menu in which you want to change the default item.

2. Drag the pointer to highlight your new default menu item.

3. Press the Control key on your keyboard, release the right mouse button, then release the Control key.

The Workspace Menu

The Workspace menu is sometimes called the *root* menu because it is the primary menu you use to access applications and utilities. To display the Workspace menu, move the pointer anywhere on the Workspace background and press the right mouse button. The Workspace menu appears (Figure 1.6). To quit displaying the Workspace menu, move the pointer off the Workspace menu and release the right mouse button. The following describes the items displayed in the Workspace menu.

FIGURE 1.6

The Workspace menu

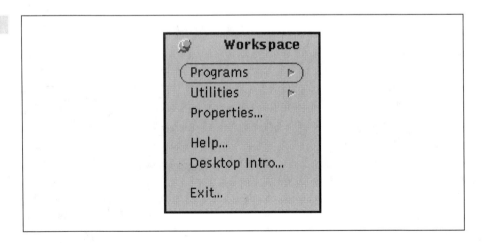

MENU ITEM	RESULT
Programs	Displays a submenu of DeskSet and other applications.
Utilities	Displays a submenu of services, including utilities for redisplaying (refreshing) the Workspace or windows, locking the screen, saving the Workspace layout, opening a new Console window, displaying a window's management menu, or displaying on-screen Function keys and their settings.
Properties	Displays a window containing settings for customizing your Workspace.
Help	Displays the help handbooks' Table of Contents in the Help Viewer window.
Desktop Intro	Displays the Desktop tutorial in the Help Viewer window.
Exit	Exits OpenWindows.

Starting a DeskSet Application

To start a DeskSet application, with the pointer on the Workspace menu and the highlight on the Programs item, drag the pointer to the right. The Programs submenu is displayed (Figure 1.7). You can pin the Programs submenu to the Workspace for easy access to your applications. Move the pointer to highlight the application item in the Programs submenu that you want to start and release the mouse button. The application appears on the Workspace as either an open window or as an icon.

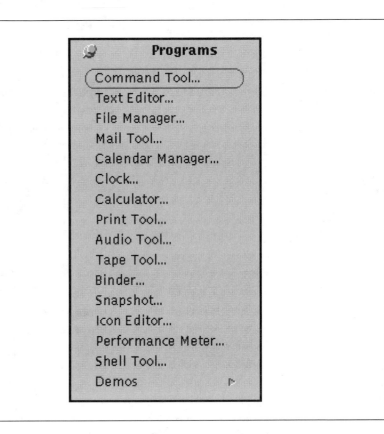

Working with Windows

All windows in the OpenWindows environment utilize a consistent interface. In other words, you perform the same tasks, such as opening or closing a window, using the same procedures, regardless of the application
window. Some applications use more than one window. For example, the
Mail Tool includes a *base window* that includes the main controls and also
has a secondary window for composing mail messages. In addition to application windows, there are *pop-up windows*, which are usually connected
to applications for changing settings. The following sections explain working with and managing windows on the Workspace.

The Parts of an Application Window

All application windows have similar features that make up the window. Figure 1.8 uses the DeskSet's `Text Editor` window to illustrate the parts of an application window. The following describes the main parts of the DeskSet's `Text Editor` window that are common to application windows.

WINDOW PART	DESCRIPTION
Window header	The wide stripe at the top of the window is called the window header. The contents of the header depend on the application you are using. The header typically tells you the name of the application associated with the window. If the application window contains a file, the path name for the file is usually included. You can access the `Window` menu by pressing the right mouse button with the pointer in the window header.
Control area	A region of a window where controls such as buttons, settings, and text fields are displayed.
Scrollbar elevator	The scrollbar elevator allows you to move (scroll) through the contents of a window using a mouse. You can also move the pointer to any part of the scrollbar and press the right mouse button to display the `Scrollbar` menu. The boxes at the ends of the scrollbar are cable anchors that allow you to move quickly to the beginning or end of a file by moving the pointer to a cable anchor and clicking the left mouse button.
Pane	The application window's work area.

FIGURE 1.8

The parts of the Text Editor window

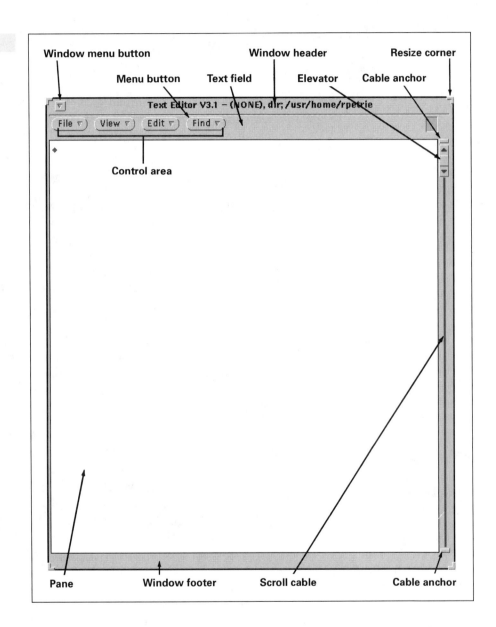

WINDOW PART	DESCRIPTION
Insert point	A symbol indicating where text or a command you type from the keyboard will appear in the window's pane. Some applications use a black triangle and others use a solid rectangle.
Menu button	Displays a menu when you click or press the right mouse button on the menu button. The button labels are command names. Menu buttons with an arrowhead beside the button label always have additional submenus layered underneath. An ellipsis (...) on a button indicates that a pop-up window will appear when you click on the button with the left mouse button.
Drag-and-drop target	The rectangle in the upper-right corner of the window's control area is a target (or source) for dragging and dropping files. The target's primary purpose is to act as a receptacle for loading files. Dragging an icon to the drag-and-drop target and dropping the icon (releasing the left mouse button) loads the selected file.
Resize corner	By moving the pointer onto any of the four resize corners and pressing the left mouse button, you can change the window to a new size, larger or smaller.

WINDOW PART	DESCRIPTION
Window menu button	This small triangle button in the upper-left corner of a window accesses the `Window` menu. When you click the right mouse button on the Window menu button, the `Window` menu appears with items for managing the window. Clicking the left mouse button on the Window menu button activates the default item from the `Window` menu, the `Close` item which allows you to easily close a window to an icon.
Window footer	This area at the bottom of the window displays messages and status information.

Using the Scrollbar

In most cases, the right side of a window displays a *scrollbar*. The scrollbar is made up of five major components: cable anchors, up arrow, drag box, down arrow, and the cable. Figure 1.9 identifies each of these parts of a scrollbar.

Pressing the left mouse button and dragging the drag box moves the contents up or down relative to the direction you drag the drag box. The following list explains how to use a scrollbar to move through a file.

MOVEMENT	ACTION
Beginning of a file	Place the pointer on the top cable anchor and click the left mouse button.
Bottom of a file	Place the pointer on the bottom cable anchor and click the left mouse button.

FIGURE 1.9

The parts of the
scrollbar

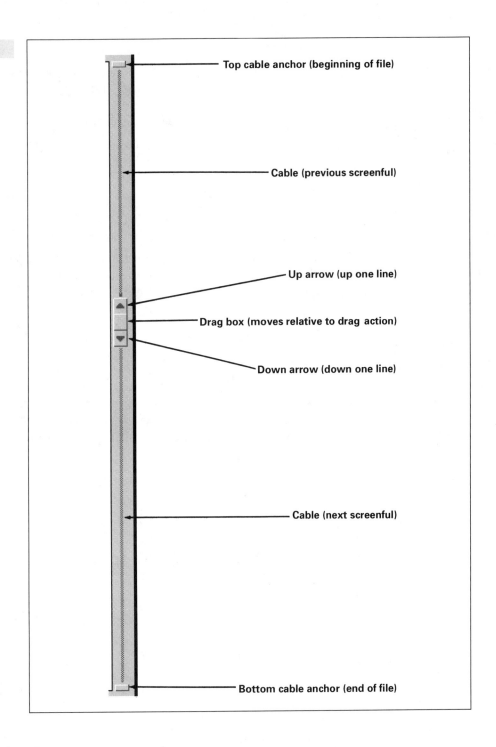

Top cable anchor (beginning of file)

Cable (previous screenful)

Up arrow (up one line)

Drag box (moves relative to drag action)

Down arrow (down one line)

Cable (next screenful)

Bottom cable anchor (end of file)

MOVEMENT	ACTION
Up a screen	Place the pointer on the cable between the top cable anchor and the Up arrow and click the left mouse button.
Down a screen	Place the pointer on the cable between the bottom cable anchor and the Down arrow and click the left mouse button.
Up one line	Place the pointer on the Up arrow and click the left mouse button.
Down one line	Place the pointer on the Down arrow and click the left mouse button.

The Scrollbar Menu

You can also use the **Scrollbar** menu to move to one of three locations in a window. To display the **Scrollbar** menu (Figure 1.10), move the pointer anywhere on the scrollbar and press the right mouse button. You choose the **Scrollbar** menu item by moving the pointer to highlight the item you want. The following explains the items in the **Scrollbar** menu.

FIGURE 1.10

The Scrollbar menu

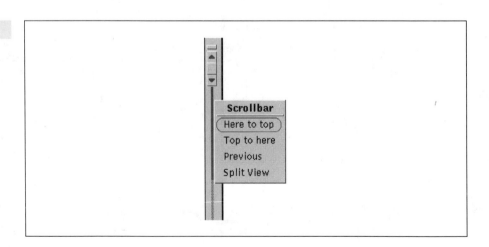

MENU ITEM	RESULT
`Here to top`	Moves the line where the pointer is located to the top of the text pane.
`Top to here`	Moves the text pane display towards the top of the file at a distance relative to the position of the pointer in the scrollbar.
`Previous`	Moves the text pane display to the position where you were located when you pressed a mouse button.
`Split View`	Creates another scrollable pane of the same document. A `Join View` item then appears in the `Scrollbar` menu, which is used to unsplit the last pane split.

Splitting a Window Pane

You can split a window pane into two or more parts, so you can work with different parts of a text file or file listing. Figure 1.11 shows a split `Text Editor` window pane. This allows you to have different vantage points for the same file or file listing from different panes. You can split a pane by dragging the top or bottom cable anchor, or by using the `Scrollbar` menu.

To split a pane using the cable anchor, move the pointer to the top or bottom cable anchor, press the left mouse button and drag the cable anchor to the position where you want to split the pane, then release the mouse button. To unsplit a pane, drag the cable anchor back to the top or bottom of the scroll bar.

To split a pane using the `Scrollbar` menu, move the pointer to the location on the scrollbar where you want to split the pane, press the right mouse button, then choose the `Split View` item.

FIGURE 1.11

FIGURE 1.11

A split Text Editor
window pane

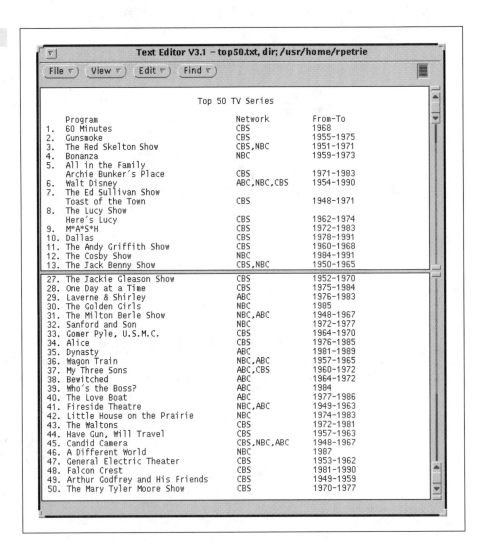

The Clipboard

The *clipboard* is a buffer, a storage place in memory that temporarily holds text or files during move or copy operations in or between application windows. Using an application's **Copy**, **Cut**, and **Paste** menu items automatically stores the selected information on the clipboard. Only one item or group of items is stored on the clipboard at a time.

WARNING   If you choose a cut or copy operation while information is stored on the clipboard, or you quit OpenWindows, the information in the clipboard is lost.

Pop-up Windows

A pop-up window is a different type of window than an application window. Any button or menu item followed by an ellipsis (...) displays a pop-up window. Pop-up windows provide controls for conveniently changing specific attributes of an application. Most pop-up windows have pushpins in the upper-left corner so you can pin the window to the Workspace. Figure 1.12 shows a typical pop-up window. When you quit an application window, its related pop-up windows are also removed from the Workspace.

FIGURE 1.12

A pop-up window

CM Appointment Editor: rpetrie@stv

Date: 03/29/93
Month / Day / Year

Start: ▽ 09:00   AM   PM

End: ▽ 5:00   AM   PM

What: Developer's Conference

Appointments

9:00 Developer's Conference
2:00 Round Table
3:30 Staff Meeting

Appt | ToDo | My Eyes Only

Alarm:
Beep	5 ▽ mins
Flash	5 ▽ mins
PopUp	5 ▽ mins
Mail	2 ▽ hrs

Repeat: ▽ Daily

For: ▽ 3   days

Mail To: rpetrie@stv

(Insert) (Delete) (Change) (Clear) (Restore Size)

Pop-up windows have an associated Window menu (Figure 1.13) that is similar to an application window's Window menu. Because a pop-up window *cannot* be closed to an icon, there is no Close menu item. To display a pop-up window's Window menu, place the pointer in the window header and click the right mouse button. The following explains the pop-up window's Window menu items:

MENU ITEM	RESULT
Dismiss	Provides you with options for quitting the current pop-up window or dismissing all pop-up windows.
Move	Allows you to reposition the pop-up window using the arrow keys.
Resize	Allows you to resize the pop-up window using the arrow keys.
Back	Moves the current pop-up window to the back of the window stack.
Refresh	Redisplays the contents of the pop-up window.
Owner?	Flashes the window header of the window that the pop-up window was started from and moves the application window of the associated application to the foreground of the screen.

FIGURE 1.13

The pop-up window's Window menu

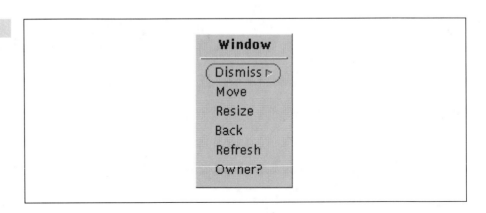

Types of Window Controls

In OpenWindows, there are standardized controls for working with settings in either application or pop-up windows. Figure 1.14 shows the different types of settings available in OpenWindows. You can navigate settings in a pop-up window by using the mouse, or you can press Return or the Tab key. The following list explains these window controls.

CONTROL	DESCRIPTION
Button	Displays menus or pop-up windows, or executes commands when you move the pointer onto them and click a mouse button.
Abbreviated menu button	Displays a menu of options.

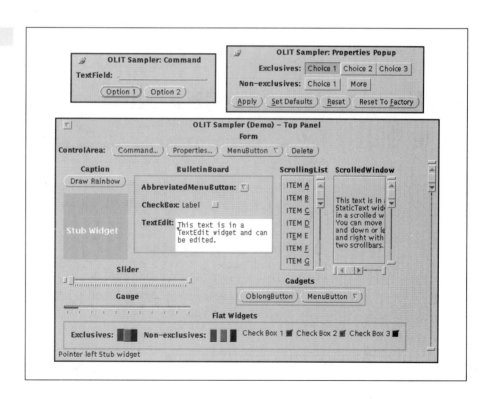

CONTROL	DESCRIPTION
Check boxes	Activates or deactivates settings by moving the pointer inside the check box and clicking the left mouse button.
Text field	Text input areas for entering text, such as specifying directories, files, or numeric settings. If a text field has more text than can appear in the field, a scrolling button automatically appears on the side of the text field where text is hidden. You can quickly delete all the text in any text field by triple-clicking the left mouse in the text field.
Numeric field	Text field with increment and decrement buttons for increasing and decreasing the value in the text field.
Scrolling list	List of options or settings that include a scrollbar. Scrolling lists include a **Scrolling List** pop-up menu that allows you to navigate and edit the list.
Exclusive setting	One setting can be chosen from a set of options.
Nonexclusive settings	Multiple settings can be chosen from a set of options.
Slider	Dragging the slider handle sets a value from a range of values.

The Active Window

Because there can be several windows open on the Workspace at once, OpenWindows must keep track of which window is currently active. To switch to a window and make it the active window, simply move the pointer to any location in the window you want active and click the left mouse button. An inactive window header lacks a 3-D effect or appears dimmed.

You can change the default setting for activating a window from clicking the mouse button to simply moving the pointer to anywhere in the window, as explained in Chapter 7, "Customizing the Workspace and Icons."

When a text application window, such as the Text Editor, is active, the insert point appears as a black triangle, indicating it is ready for you to enter text or a command. In some applications windows, such as the Shell Tool, a solid rectangle appears, indicating the window is active. A dimmed diamond or a hollow rectangle indicates the window is inactive.

The Window Menu

Moving the pointer onto the Window menu button, an icon, a window header, or the border of a window and pressing the right mouse button displays the `Window` menu. The `Window` menu provides you with items to manage the application window, such as opening, closing, or resizing a window to take up the full screen. Figure 1.15 shows the `Window` menu.

FIGURE 1.15

The Window menu

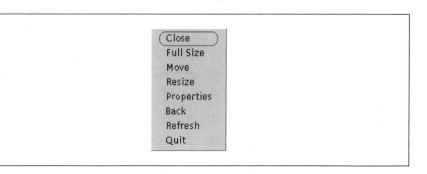

Closing and Reopening a Window

Closing an application window means reducing the window to an icon. The application is still active, but unavailable until you reopen it. Figure 1.16 shows the **Help Viewer** window closed to an icon. Every Open-Windows application window closes to an icon. The easiest way to close an application window is to move the pointer to the Window menu button (upper-left corner) and click the left mouse button to choose the default **Close** menu item. When you release the mouse button, the window shrinks to an icon.

FIGURE 1.16

The Help Viewer window closed to an icon

An application window can also be closed by moving the pointer to any part of the window header or the outside border of the window, pressing the right mouse button, then choosing the **Close** item from the **Window** menu.

To reopen a DeskSet application, place the pointer on top of the icon and double-click the left mouse button. The window is restored to the size it was when you closed it. You can also reopen the window by pressing the right mouse button on the icon to select it, then choosing **Open** from the **Window** menu.

NOTE

An alternative to using the mouse to open and close a window is to use the Open accelerator key on the left side of your Sun workstation keyboard. With the icon selected, press the Open accelerator key. This key acts as a toggle, so pressing it again with the pointer in an active window changes the window back into an icon.

Quitting a Window

The last menu item in the `Window` menu is `Quit`. Quitting is different from closing a window because the application is actually removed from the desktop. If you have unsaved changes, selecting `Quit` displays a confirmation Notice. The Notice usually contains two *buttons,* such as `Cancel, do NOT Quit` and `Discard edits, then Quit`. If the button outline is shown in boldface or a double outline surrounds the button, you can press Return to choose that choice; otherwise, you must move the pointer directly to the button you want to choose and click the left mouse button. If you want to quit the application and remove the icon or window from the Workspace, click the left mouse button or press Return, and the icon or window will disappear. Otherwise you can cancel the `Quit` operation by moving the pointer to the `Cancel, do NOT Quit` button and clicking the left mouse button.

Moving a Window

Windows and icons can be arranged anywhere on your screen, even on top of other windows or icons. When you move a window, an outline of it moves as you drag the pointer. This outline is known as a *bounding box.* To move a window, move the pointer to the window header of the window you want to move. Press the left mouse button and drag the bounding box to its new location. When you release the left mouse button, the window is moved to the location of the bounding box.

A less efficient way to move a window is choosing `Move` from the `Window` menu. To display the `Window` menu, press the right mouse button while the pointer is located in the window header, choose `Move`, then use the arrow keys to position the bounding box and press Return.

Moving Multiple Windows

Multiple windows can be selected as a group then moved together. For example, you might want to arrange several windows on the Workspace, then move the whole arrangement to a new location. Moving a group of windows involves selecting the group of windows you want, then moving them to the new location. You can select a group of windows by clicking the left mouse button on one window and the middle mouse button on each additional window or icon. You can also select a group of windows (and icons) by moving the pointer to any corner of the set of windows you want to group, pressing the left mouse button, then dragging the pointer diagonally to the opposite corner of the group and releasing the mouse button. After selecting a group of windows, place the pointer on the edge of one of the grouped windows, press the left mouse button, and drag the pointer to the new location. The group of windows moves to the new location. To ungroup the windows, click the left mouse button with the pointer anywhere in the Workspace.

Moving Windows to the Background

Windows (and icons) can be stacked up on your Workspace similar to the way you stack folders or papers on your desk. Anytime a window overlaps another window, the window in the background is inactive. You can switch between windows using the Window menu or by clicking the left mouse button on a window header or border.

To move a window that is in the background to the foreground, move the pointer to the window header or the border of the window you want and click the left mouse button. If the window is not available, move the foreground window to expose the window.

To move a window to the background behind another window, click the right mouse button on the window header or the border of the window you want. Choose the Back item from the Window menu. Figure 1.17 shows a Calendar window first in the foreground, then in the background.

FIGURE 1.17

The Calendar window in the foreground and background

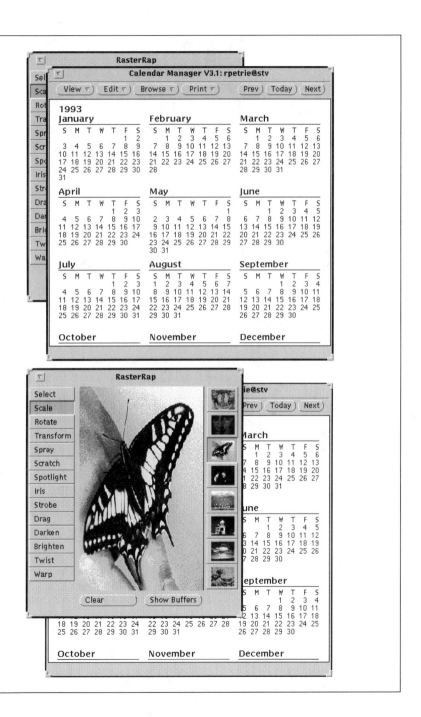

NOTE You can also move a window to the background or foreground by moving the pointer to the window you want to move to the foreground, then pressing the Front accelerator key on Sun workstation keyboards. This key acts as a toggle, so pressing it again sends the window to the background.

Resizing a Window

Moving the pointer to any of the resize corners of a window causes the arrow pointer to change to a target pointer. Pressing the left mouse button and dragging the target pointer allows you to change a window's height and width. The bounding box changes size when you drag the pointer, and the window changes to the size of the bounding box when you release the mouse button.

A window can also be resized by using the `Resize` item from the `Window` menu. To display the `Window` menu, press the right mouse button with the pointer in the window header. Choose `Resize`, use the arrow keys to stretch the bounding box to the size you want, and press Return.

You can resize a window so that it takes up the full height of the screen by moving the pointer to the window header or border, pressing the right mouse button, and choosing `Full Size` from the `Window` menu. Once you release the left mouse button, the window is resized to the height of your screen, and the `Full Size` item in the `Window` menu changes to `Restore Size`. To return to the normal size of the window, choose `Restore Size` from the `Window` menu.

Redisplaying a Window

Sometimes fragments of previous work appear in a window, or a portion of the window appears to have a section missing. Choosing `Refresh` in the `Window` menu clears and redraws the window.

Dragging and Dropping Files

The OpenWindows drag-and-drop feature enables you to easily transfer text or files between applications, or open applications on the Workspace. For example, you can drag icons representing files from the File Manager and drop them into other windows or icons to enter them as input for the application. A file icon can also be dragged and dropped on the Workspace to open the file and the application associated with it. To delete files, you can easily drag and drop unwanted files onto the `Waste` icon.

To drag and drop a file into an application window, move the pointer onto the icon you want to drag and drop. Select a file using the left mouse button, drag the file inside the application window's pane, and release the left mouse button. Releasing this button is known as dropping a file. The file is inserted or a message appears in the window footer explaining why the action was unsuccessful.

N O T E   Chapter 2, "Using the File Manager" explains how to use the drag-and-drop feature to manage files.

Drag-and-Drop Targets

OpenWindows includes another feature for dragging and dropping files into applications called a *drag-and-drop target*. The Print Tool, Audio Tool, Tape Tool, and Snapshot DeskSet applications have drag-and-drop targets. The target is a rectangle located in the upper-right corner of a window's control area. If you drag a document icon or a piece of text and drop it into a text pane that already contains a file, the document will be inserted in the location the icon was dropped. If you drop the icon on the drag-and-drop target, the document replaces the existing text.

Some file icons can be dragged out of the drag-and-drop target. For example, you can drag a loaded text file icon out of the Text Editor's drag-and-drop target and drag and drop it onto the Print Tool icon to print the file.

Getting Online Help

OpenWindows comes with two kinds of online help, Magnify help and help handbooks. Magnify help is for immediate information on any specified object, such as a menu item, control, or window. Help handbooks supply information about how to use DeskSet applications. Help handbooks are available in the `Help Viewer` window. These help handbooks are organized by topic.

Using Magnify Help

Magnify help allows you to get specific information about a particular window or menu. To get online help about a window or menu item, move the pointer to the item (such as a window or menu) that you want to know about, then press the Help key on the keyboard. (The Help key is only available on the Sun workstation keyboard.) A help pop-up window appears with information about the item. If there is more text than appears in the pop-up window, a scroll bar appears for scrolling through the additional text. Figure 1.18 shows a sample Magnify help pop-up window. If there is more information available on the topic in a help handbook, a `More` button appears at the bottom of the window. Clicking the left mouse button on the `More` button opens the `Help Viewer` window, with the appropriate topic appearing in the window. If there is no Magnify help available for the item you specified, a small pop-up window appears that tells you there is no help for that item. The pointer jumps to the `OK` button. Click the left mouse button to continue.

A Magnify help pop-up window is closed when you close or quit an application. If you want to close the Magnify help window before you close or quit an application, click the left mouse button on the pushpin in the upper-left corner of the Magnify help window.

FIGURE 1.18

A sample Magnify
help pop-up window

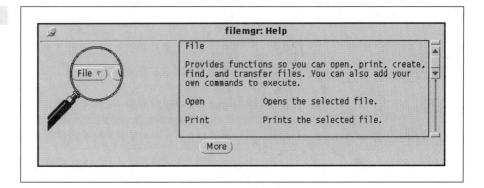

Using the Help Handbooks

The help handbooks include a tutorial and 15 additional help handbooks that provide information on working with the Workspace and DeskSet applications. Choosing **Desktop Intro** from the **Workspace** menu displays the first page of the tutorial in the **Help Viewer** window. This tutorial introduces and explains working with the Desktop. Choosing **Help** from the **Workspace** menu displays the Table of Contents for all the help handbooks in the **Help Viewer** window (Figure 1.19).

The help handbook can also be quickly accessed from any DeskSet application, icon, or menu by positioning the pointer over the area of interest, and pressing Shift, then Help on your keyboard. The **Help Viewer** window appears on the Workspace, displaying the appropriate handbook.

Using the Help Viewer Icons

The **Help Viewer** window uses standardized features to make navigating it easy. Handy icons located at the bottom of the **Help Viewer** window let you quickly return to the Table of Contents, display information about the Help Viewer itself, or exit the tutorial. Depending on your location in the Help Viewer window, one or more icons will appear at the bottom of the **Help Viewer** window. To choose an icon, you must double-click on it. The following describes each icon's function.

FIGURE 1.19

The help handbooks'
Table of Contents in
the Help Viewer
window

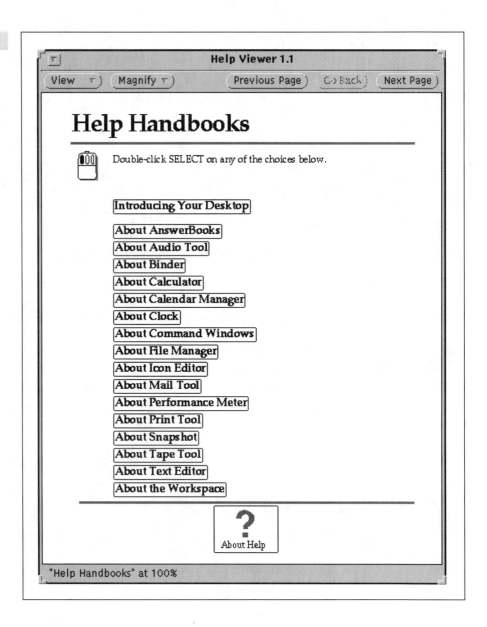

ICON	DESCRIPTION
About Help	Lets you view a description of how the help system works. Displays in all pages of the Help Viewer window.
Table of Contents	Displays the Table of Contents for the current help handbook. Appears after any first page of a help handbook.
Exit	Displays instructions on quitting the Desktop Introduction handbook. Appears only when the Desktop Introduction handbook is displayed.
More Handbooks	Displays the Table of Contents for all the help handbooks. Appears only on the first page of any help handbook.

Magnifying the Help Viewer Window

The Magnify menu contains items for changing the size of the Help Viewer window. By default, the Help Viewer window can be enlarged by 110% of its standard default size every time you click the left mouse button on the Magnify menu button, which chooses the default Larger item. Choosing Smaller shrinks the size of the Help Viewer window from any size larger than the standard size to no smaller than the standard window size. Choosing Standard returns the Help Viewer window to its default size.

NOTE An easier way to magnify the Help Viewer window than using the Magnify menu button is to use the resize corners to stretch the window smaller or larger.

You can temporarily adjust the size of the Help Viewer window by choosing Custom Magnification to display the Custom Magnification pop-up window. Drag the slider control to specify the size you want, then click the left mouse button on the Apply button.

Navigating a Handbook

When you display a particular help handbook, you can page through the handbook using the buttons at the top of the Help Viewer window. Clicking the left mouse button on these buttons enables you to move backward (the Previous Page button) and forward (the Next Page button) one page at a time. The Go Back button redisplays the last page viewed. If you viewed pages in various parts of a handbook or in different handbooks, choosing the Go Back button allows you to retrace your steps, one by one. These navigation features are also available in the View menu.

The Help Viewer window also incorporates a handy navigation feature called *hypertext links*. Any text in a handbook that has a black outline indicates you can double-click the left mouse button on the text to move to related information.

Closing or Exiting the Help Viewer Window

The Help Viewer window can be closed to an icon by clicking the left mouse button on the Window menu button in the upper-left corner of any handbook. You can also close the Help Viewer window by clicking the left mouse button with the pointer on the window header and choosing Close from the Window menu. To exit the Help Viewer window, choose Quit from the Window menu.

Workspace Utilities

The Workspace menu includes the Utilities submenu (Figure 1.20). This menu includes several useful utilities for working with Open-Windows and the Workspace, such as options that save your Workspace configuration and lock your screen to keep unauthorized users out of your system when you are away from your workstation.

FIGURE 1.20

The Workspace
Utilities submenu

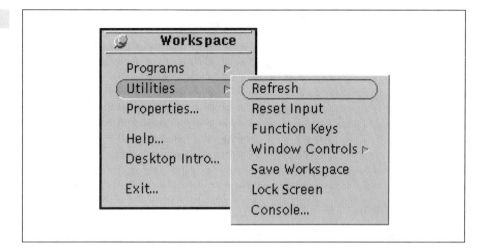

To open the `Utilities` submenu, press the right mouse button on the Workspace to display the `Workspace` menu. Drag the pointer to the `Utilities` item then to the right over the arrowhead to display the `Utilities` submenu. To choose an item, drag the pointer to the item you want and release the mouse button. The following sections explain these useful utility programs.

Refresh

Sometimes an application prints characters outside of a window, or leaves lines or other remnants from the window displayed after the window you quit is removed. For example, if you accidentally quit the `Console` window from the Workspace, there may be system messages printed on the Workspace. To redisplay the Workspace, choose `Refresh` from the `Utilities` submenu. The Workspace screen is redrawn.

Reset Input

If you're running several types of applications at once, you may occasionally find that characters you type in a window are garbled. This is because of an incompatibility between the way the different applications handle input data. The `Reset Input` item corrects the problem.

Function Keys

When you choose `Function Keys`, an on-screen display of the function keys on the keyboard (Figure 1.21) appears in a pop-up window at the bottom of the Workspace. Each function key on your keyboard appears as a button with a label of what the function key does. Placing the pointer on the function key and clicking the left mouse button is the same as pressing the key on your keyboard. The Function Key pop-up window can be pinned to the Workspace.

FIGURE 1.21

The Function Key pop-up window

NOTE
You must have the `Click Select` option (the default setting) set in the `Miscellaneous` category of the `Workspace Properties` pop-up window for the Function Keys utility to work properly, as explained in Chapter 7, "Customizing the Workspace and Icons."

Currently, the Function Keys utility is not supported by DeskSet applications. If the application you are working with supports the Function Keys feature, the key labels display each key's function. The function key labels are automatically updated when the pointer is moved to another application that supports the Function Keys feature.

Window Controls

The `Window Controls` item displays a submenu of items for performing basic window operations for any selected window or group of windows on the Workspace. It is especially useful for performing operations on multiple windows simultaneously, instead of using each window's `Window` menu.

These basic operations include opening, closing, resizing, and moving windows behind other windows. Pinning this pop-up window to the Workspace allows you to quickly manage the windows on the Workspace.

To change a single window or icon, simply select the window or icon by clicking the left mouse button on it, then choose an item from the `Window Controls` submenu.

To select a group of windows or icons before using an item from the `Window Controls` submenu, either click the left mouse button on one window and the middle mouse button on each additional window or icon, or press the left mouse button and drag the pointer diagonally across the Workspace. Any windows or icons inside the rectangle formed by the dragging motion will be included in the group. The following explains each item in the `Window Controls` submenu.

MENU ITEM	DESCRIPTION
Open/Close	Opens selected icons or closes selected windows.
Full/Restore Size	Increases the size of selected application windows to the full height of the screen. Clicking the left mouse button on the `Full/Restore Size` item a second time (without deselecting the group of windows) decreases the size of selected windows to their former size.
Back	Moves selected application windows to the back of another window or group of windows.
Quit	Quits selected application windows or icons.

Save Workspace

Choosing the `Save Workspace` item saves an arrangement of windows and icons on the Workspace other than the default configuration that appears when you start OpenWindows. You can save your Workspace configuration as often as you like.

To save the Workspace, first arrange the application windows and icons in the locations you want them to remain, and close any windows that you want to be closed to icons whenever you start OpenWindows. After choosing `Save Workspace`, a Notice appears informing you that the Workspace layout has been saved. Click the left mouse button on the `OK` button to continue. The next time you start OpenWindows, the windows and icons appear on the Workspace exactly as you saved them.

Lock Screen

If you want to leave your terminal unattended, you can lock your screen to protect your work and prevent anyone else from using your system. The `Lock Screen` item also activates a feature called a *screen saver* that displays a series of changing images. This protects your screen from characters or images burning into the screen surface. For information on changing the default screen saver, see Chapter 15, "Customizing Solaris."

To unlock your screen, press any key (other than F1 or Lock Caps) or click a mouse button. Solaris displays a message instructing you to enter your password to unlock your screen, as shown in Figure 1.22. After you enter your password, the message `validating login` appears. If you entered your password correctly, you are returned to your original screen.

Console

The `Console` window, by default, normally appears in the upper left corner of the Workspace after you start up OpenWindows. Its primary function is to display messages from the network, and inform you of system errors. You should keep the `Console` window open at all times for important messages. If the `Console` window (or icon) is not on the Workspace, system messages appear on the Workspace. To open a new `Console` window, choose the `Console` item.

FIGURE 1.22

The locked screen
message

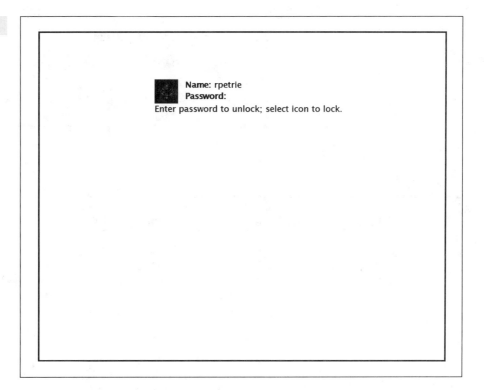

Name: rpetrie
Password:
Enter password to unlock; select icon to lock.

Exiting OpenWindows and the DeskSet

When you have finished using OpenWindows and the DeskSet, you can exit the OpenWindows environment by choosing Exit from the Workspace menu. Solaris displays a Notice that asks you to confirm if you want to exit, as shown in Figure 1.23. The pointer jumps to the Cancel button. Click the left mouse button with the pointer on the Exit button.

FIGURE 1.23

The Exit Notice

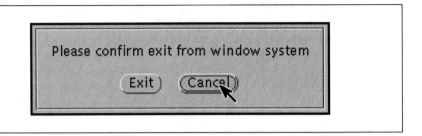

Logging Out of Solaris

After completing a Solaris session, it is important to *log out*. Otherwise, anyone who passes by your terminal can gain unauthorized access to your files. To log out of Solaris, first make sure the system prompt is displayed, then press Control-D or type

    exit

and press Return. The system will display the login screen again. If the system prompts you with the message `there are stopped jobs`, type `exit` again. For more information on logging out with stopped jobs, see Chapter 14, "Multitasking with SunOS."

CHAPTER

2

Using the File Manager

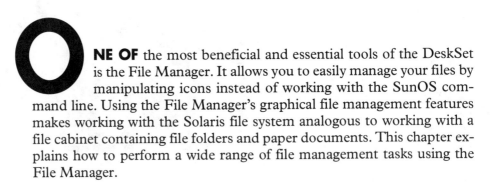

ONE OF the most beneficial and essential tools of the DeskSet is the File Manager. It allows you to easily manage your files by manipulating icons instead of working with the SunOS command line. Using the File Manager's graphical file management features makes working with the Solaris file system analogous to working with a file cabinet containing file folders and paper documents. This chapter explains how to perform a wide range of file management tasks using the File Manager.

An Overview of the Solaris File System

The File Manager is an easy-to-use tool for working with files and directories in Solaris. A *file* is a storage place for data or executable programs. Special files called *directories* contain indexes that are used to group and locate files. The File Manager uses a file folder icon to represent a directory and a single-page document icon to represent a text file. Other types of files, such as applications and picture files, have their own unique icons.

Solaris uses a hierarchical file structure, an inverted tree structure with the base of the tree at the top, similar to the structure of a family tree. The topmost directory of the tree is known as the *root* directory and is indicated by a slash (*/*). All other directories on your system branch out from the root directory. Although every directory, except the root directory, is a *subdirectory* of the root directory, a subdirectory is commonly referred to as a directory.

In keeping with the family tree analogy, directories in a hierarchical file structure are commonly referred to as *parent directories* and *child directories*. Any directory that has subdirectories is a parent directory and each subdirectory is a child directory of the parent directory that is above it.

Solaris relies on specific system directories to operate. In most cases, the system administrator organizes and restricts access to many of these directories. However, there are several important directories that you can work with using the File Manager. The following lists the main directories used by Solaris to store files and application programs.

DIRECTORY	DESCRIPTION
/export	Contains files you want to share with other users on the system.
/home	Contains home directories for all users on your system. The names of these home directories are usually based on user names, for example, /home/rpetrie.
/usr	A general purpose directory that contains several important subdirectories for users, including the openwin/bin directory, which contains OpenWindows application programs.
/bin	Contains SunOS program files or commands.
/tmp	Stores temporary files that can be deleted.

Starting the File Manager

By default, when you start OpenWindows, the File Manager window and its associated Waste icon, which is used for deleting files, appear on the Workspace (Figure 2.1). If the File Manager is not displayed on the Workspace, press the right mouse button anywhere on the Workspace to display the Workspace menu, then choose File Manager from the Programs submenu.

FIGURE 2.1

The File Manager and
Waste icons

To close the **File Manager** window to an icon, click the left mouse button on the Window menu button (the upside-down triangle in the upper-left corner).When closed, the File Manager displays a filing cabinet drawer icon with the name of the current directory appearing beneath the icon (Figure 2.1). When you quit the File Manager, the **Waste** icon is also removed from the Workspace.

An Overview of the File Manager Window

The **File Manager** base window consists of three main parts: the path pane, the control area, and the file pane, as shown in Figure 2.2. Each part of the **File Manager** window is described in the following sections.

Path Pane

The path pane displays your current location in the file system. A *path* is the route through directories that Solaris must follow to access a file. By default, the File Manager displays the path where you started Open-Windows as a series of connected folders in a straight line. The path displayed in the path pane shows only the folders for the directory and sub-directory that lead to the current folder, which is the folder that is open.

The path pane display can be changed to a tree display, which displays a hierarchical tree representation of directories in the file system (Figure 2.3). To change the path pane to a tree display, click the left mouse button on the **View** menu button. The **Show Tree** item in the **View** menu is the

FIGURE 2.2

The three main parts
of File Manager
window

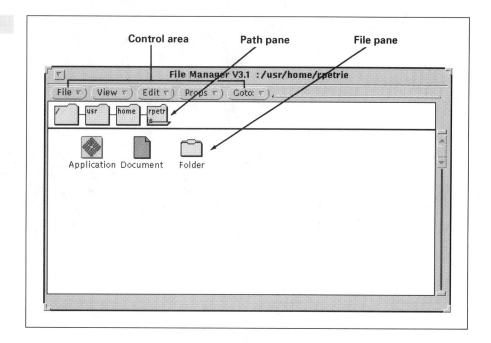

default item. Clicking the left mouse button on the View menu button
again switches you back to the path pane display.

Both the path and tree displays have associated pop-up menus. If you are
displaying the path, clicking the right mouse button in the path pane displays the Path Pane pop-up menu (Figure 2.4). If you are displaying the tree
display, clicking the right mouse button in the path pane displays the Tree
Pane pop-up menu (Figure 2.5). The default item in each pop-up menu
toggles to the other pane display.

Control Area

The control area of the File Manager window has five menu buttons:
File, View, Edit, Props, and Goto. To the right of the Goto button is a text
field for entering path names to find directories and files. Each of these
buttons displays menus that allow you to perform a variety of operations
on one or more selected files. Any of these menus can be displayed by
clicking or pressing the right mouse button on a menu button. The File,
View, and Edit menus have pushpins so you can pin them to the Workspace.

FIGURE 2.3

The File Manager displaying directories using the Show Tree item

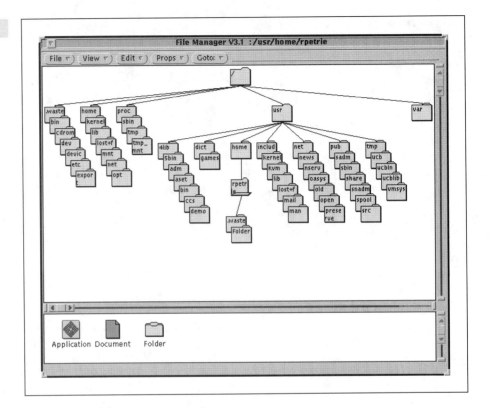

FIGURE 2.4

The Path Pane pop-up menu

FIGURE 2.5

The Tree Pane pop-up menu

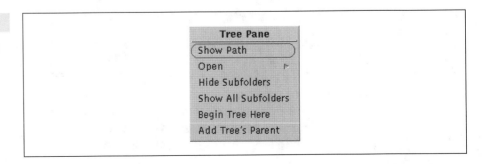

File Pane

The file pane is located directly below the path pane and displays the folders and files in the current directory. This area of the `File Manager` window allows you to navigate the file system and open folders and files. By default, folder and file icons are displayed in the standard size, but you can use smaller icons instead of the standard-size icons if you want to display more folder and file icons in the file pane. The file pane's elevator scrollbar lets you move up or down to display icons.

Folder and file icon names that cannot be completely displayed are followed by a "greater than" sign (>) to show that the full name is not displayed. If you want to see the complete file name, click the left mouse button on the icon name. The entire name is displayed in an editable text field.

The file pane can be split into two or more parts to allow you to view a file listing from more than one vantage point. To split the file pane, press the left mouse button on the top or bottom cable anchor, drag the cable anchor to where you want to split the pane, then release the mouse button. To unsplit a pane, return the cable anchor back to the top or bottom location you originally dragged it from. You can also split a pane by moving the pointer to where you want the pane split on the scrollbar, pressing the right mouse button, and choosing the `Split View` item from the `Scrollbar` menu. To unsplit the last pane split, choose the `Join Views` item from the `Scrollbar` menu.

The file pane provides a `File Pane` pop-up menu, which contains commands that are a subset of the commands you access from different menus in the File Manager's control area. To display the `File Pane` pop-up menu, press the right mouse button anywhere in the file pane. Figure 2.6 shows the `File Pane` pop-up menu.

File Manager Icons

Directories and files appear in the File Manager as icons. Different types of files are represented by different icons in the file pane. There are standard icons used by OpenWindows and DeskSet applications. If you are using a third-party application, its files may have unique file icons. The following are standard-size OpenWindows and DeskSet file icons.

FIGURE 2.6

The File Pane pop-up menu

File Pane

(Select All)

Cut
Copy ▷
Paste

Delete
Print ▷
Up

FILE TYPE	ICON
Directory file	 Folder
Text file	 Document
Raster file	 Snapshot.rs
Audio file	 Sound.au
PostScript file	 Picture.ps
Mail file	 Mail

FILE TYPE	ICON
Shell Script file	Script
DeskSet Application file	Application

Performing Basic Operations

The File Manager provides several ways to navigate the file system and perform file management operations such as copying, moving, deleting, and printing files. To open a single folder or file, double-click the left mouse button on the icon. The following methods can be used to perform file management operations on a single file or folder or on a group of files or folders.

- *Drag-and-drop icon(s)*. This is the easiest way to perform most file management operations. Dragging and dropping is performed by pressing the left mouse button on the file or folder icon you want, dragging the icon to any area that accepts the icon as input, and dropping it. You can drag icons onto the Workspace, application windows, window drag-and-drop targets, or other icons.

- *Select the icon(s) and choose a command from a menu*. For example, you can open selected files or folders by choosing `Open` from the `File` menu.

- *Select the icon(s) then press an accelerator key*. Accelerator keys are located on the left side of most Sun keyboards. For example, selecting a file and pressing the Cut accelerator key deletes the file.

Selecting Folders and Files Using the Mouse

When you drag and drop a single file or folder, it is automatically selected when you press the left mouse button on the icon. If you use a menu item or an accelerator key, or you want to drag and drop multiple folders or files, you must first select the file(s) or folder(s) you want before performing the operation.

To select a single file or folder, click the left mouse button on the file or folder you want. The icon turns black to indicate that the file or folder has been selected. You can then use the appropriate menu item or accelerator key to perform your file management task.

If you want to select multiple files or folders, click the left mouse button on the file or folder you want. Select additional files and folders by clicking the middle mouse button on the next file or folder you want. You can also select all the file and folder icons in the current folder by choosing **Select All** from the **File Pane** pop-up menu.

To unselect an icon, click the middle mouse button on a selected file or folder. Clicking the left mouse button in any blank area of the file pane unselects any selected files or folders in the file pane.

Another way to select multiple folders or files is by moving the pointer to any corner of a group of icons in the file pane you want to select, pressing the left mouse button, dragging the pointer diagonally to the opposite corner of the group, then releasing the mouse button.

Selecting Folders and Files Using the Keyboard and Wildcards

A file or folder, or a group of files or folders, can also be selected by moving the pointer to a blank area of the file pane and typing the name of the file you want to select. By naming files with the same character conventions, you can easily select a group of files.

The File Manager also supports the use of wildcards to select files and folders. *Wildcards* are special characters used to represent any single character or series of characters in a file or folder name. For example, to select a group of files ending with the letters `.rs` (a standard Raster file name extension), type `*rs` in the file pane. When you type the asterisk, the window footer displays the message `Building *`. After you type the letter `r`, the files containing the letter `r` are selected, and the message `Matching *r*` appears in the window footer. If a matching file is not found, the window footer displays a message telling you that it has not found any matching file names.

You can also use the question mark (?) wildcard character to represent any single character in a file or folder name. For example, you can type `hu?` to search for any file or folder that starts with hu followed by any character, such as hug, hub, and so on. You can use more than one question mark (?) in a file or folder name. For example, you can type `hu??` to search for any file or folder that starts with hu followed by any two characters, such as huge, hull, and so on.

Changing the File and Pane Displays

The File Manager allows you to change how icons are organized and displayed in the file pane and what folders appear in the path pane when you are using the tree display. The `View` menu button provides several items for specifying the organization and appearance of icons in the file pane. For example, file and folder icons can be sorted by their file size and displayed in a smaller size.

Because the tree display in the path pane can become extended as you navigate through the file system, the File Manager provides features for controlling which folders are displayed or not displayed. The following sections explain how to change the file and path pane displays.

Changing How Icons Are Displayed in the File Pane

The View menu (Figure 2.7) includes Icon items that let you display files and folders with standard-size icons. The List items in the View menu let you display the icons in a smaller size, so you can view more files and folders in the file pane and show more information about each file. The following describes the Icon and List items in the View menu.

NOTE

The Customize item in the View menu lets you perform additional changes to the display of files and folders in the file pane. For information on working with the Customize item in the View menu, see "Customizing the File Manager" later in this chapter.

FIGURE 2.7

The View menu

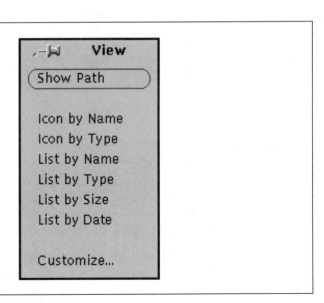

MENU ITEM	DESCRIPTION
`Icon by Name`	Displays standard-size folder and file icons sorted alphabetically.
`Icon by Type`	Displays standard-size icons grouped by file type. Folders are grouped first, followed by data files, then applications.
`List by Name`	Displays small folder and file icons sorted alphabetically by name in a multicolumn format.
`List by Type`	Displays small folder and file icons grouped by the file type in a multicolumn format. Folders are grouped first, followed by data files, then applications.
`List by Size`	Displays small file and folder icons in a multicolumn format sorted by file size in bytes, from largest to smallest.
`List by Date`	Displays small file icons in a multicolumn format sorted by date, from the newest file to the oldest.

Changing the Tree Display in the Path Pane

The `Tree Pane` pop-up menu displays items to selectively show all or part of the file system in the path pane when using the tree display. For example, using the `Tree Pane` pop-up menu, you can hide unwanted folders or display folders starting at a specific folder. Depending on which folder you have selected, one or more of the items in the `Tree Pane` pop-up menu are activated. The following explains the `Tree Pane` pop-up menu items that allow you to change the tree pane display.

MENU ITEM	DESCRIPTION
Hide Subfolders	Hides all subdirectory folders.
Show All Subfolders	Displays all subdirectory folders.
Begin Tree Here	Begins the tree display at the selected folder.
Add Tree's Parent	Displays the parent directory of the selected subdirectory.

Navigating the File System

The File Manager provides a collection of features for navigating the file system to find files. Navigating the file system using the File Manger involves opening folders and moving through the hierarchical structure of the file system to find files. In addition to navigating the Solaris file system folder by folder, you can also have the File Manager search the system to find files for you. The following sections explain working with the File Manager's navigation and file-searching features.

Opening Folders

To open a folder to view its contents, simply double-click on the folder icon either in the path pane or file pane. You navigate down the hierarchy of folders by double-clicking folders in the file pane. Double-click on the folder icon to the left of the open folder icon in the path pane to go back up to the parent directory. You can also move up to a parent directory by selecting a folder in the file pane then choosing Up from the File Pane pop-up menu. If you're using the tree display, the same folders remain displayed in the `Tree Pane`, even after you have moved up from the selected directory. The contents of the current opened folder appear in the file pane.

A folder can also be opened by selecting its icon in the file or path pane, clicking the left mouse button on it, and choosing `Open` from the `File` menu. The `Open` item is also available in the `Path Pane` or `Tree Pane` pop-up menus.

Opening Folders as Windows on the Workspace

The File Manager's file pane can display only the contents of the current folder. If you change to another folder, the contents of the previous folder are removed and the contents of the new folder appear. The File Manager allows you to open folders on the Workspace and keep the contents of multiple folders visible, regardless of which folder currently appears in the file pane. Opening folder windows on the Workspace makes it easier to perform file management tasks such as copying and moving files between folders.

To open a folder on the Workspace, drag and drop a folder or a selected group of folders onto the Workspace. A folder window contains the standard window features, including a scrollbar and `Window` menu for managing the window. You can resize the window by dragging the resize corners. Pressing the right mouse button in the file pane of the window displays the same `File Pane` pop-up menu that appears in the File Manager base window's file pane. Figure 2.8 shows several folder windows opened on the Workspace.

Using Goto to Navigate Directly to Files and Folders

When you know the path of the folder you want to open, or when you know the path and file name of a specific file you want to select, you can use the `Goto` text field to go directly to the folder or file. To use the `Goto`

FIGURE 2.8

Folders opened to
windows on the
Workspace

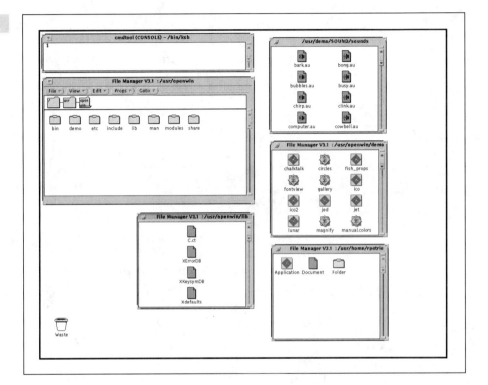

feature, click the left mouse button on the Goto text field then type the
path and folder or file name you want to select in the Goto text field. After
entering the path, press Return or click the left mouse button on the Goto
button. For example, to select a folder named **depositions** in the **/ex-
port/home/pmason** directory, type

        /export/home/pmason/depositions

in the Goto text field and press Return. When you enter a path and a folder
or file name, the folder or file appears selected in the file pane.

When you enter a path, the directory you specify becomes the current
directory, and its contents are displayed in the file pane. If you have
changed your location in the file system, click the left mouse button on
the Goto button, and the current directory will change to the directory
entered in the text field.

You can also use wildcard characters with the `Goto` text field to select groups of related files. For example, entering

```
practice/*.c
```

finds and highlights all files in the practice directory ending in `.c`.

Clicking the right mouse button on the `Goto` menu button displays a menu listing the home directory and the last nine directory paths you navigated to, whether or not you used the `Goto` text field. Figure 2.9 shows an example of the `Goto` menu. You can move to any of the directories listed in the `Goto` menu by choosing the item from the menu. Your home directory is always the default item in the `Goto` menu. Clicking the left mouse button on the abbreviated `Goto` menu button quickly returns you to your home directory.

Searching for Folders and Files

If you do not remember the exact name of the file or folder you want to find, choose `Find` in the `File` menu to locate the file or folder. Choosing `Find` displays the `Find` pop-up window (Figure 2.10) with controls that allow you to perform file searches based on a variety of file attributes. To find a specific file or group of files, fill in some or all of the text fields according to the type of search you want to perform. The following explains each setting in the `Find` pop-up window.

FIGURE 2.9

A sample Goto menu

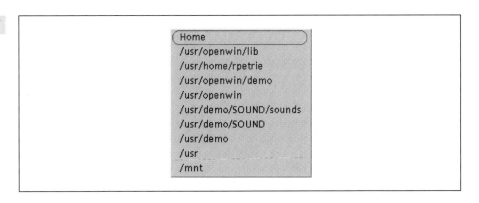

FIGURE 2.10

The Find pop-up window

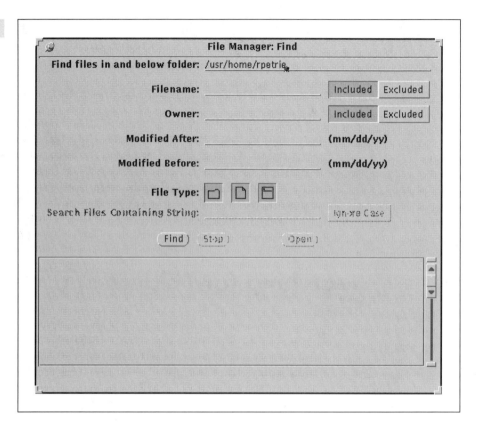

SETTING	DESCRIPTION
Find files in and below folder	Use this setting to specify where in the file system you want to start the search. The search begins in the folder you specify in this text field, and includes all subfolders.
Filename	Specifies a file name or pattern you want to match. Use the **Included** or **Excluded** setting to either include or exclude the file name or pattern you specified in the **Filename** text field.

SETTING	DESCRIPTION
Owner	Specifies searches for files by the owner of the file (file ownership is explained later in this chapter). Use the `Included` or `Excluded` setting to either include or exclude the owner specified in the `Owner` text field.
Modified After	Specifies searches for files with last modified dates after the date specified in this setting. Enter the date in the format indicated to the right, `mm/dd/yy` (month, day, year). `Modified After` and `Modified Before` entries can be combined to specify a range of file dates.
Modified Before	Specifies searches for files with last modified dates before the date specified in this setting. Enter the date in the format indicated to the right, `mm/dd/yy` (month, day, year). `Modified After` and `Modified Before` entries can be combined to specify a range of file dates.
File Type	Specifies whether you want to search all the files or only folders, document files, or application files. The mini-icons displayed in the `File Type` setting are the same icons that appear in the file pane when you choose a `List` item from the `View` menu.
Search Files Containing String	Specifies searches for files with a specific text content. This feature is active only if you restrict the search to document files in the `File Type` setting. Clicking on the `Ignore Case` setting removes any particular case specification from the search.

After filling in the fields to restrict the search, click the left mouse button on the `Find` button. If you want to cancel the search, click the left mouse button on the `Stop` button. When files that match the search criteria are found, their full path names are displayed in the scrolling list at the bottom of the `Find` window. Pressing the right mouse button in the scrolling list displays the `Scrolling List` pop-up menu, which contains items for managing entries in the scrolling list.

If more than one file is found, select the file you want from the scrolling list. When you select an item from the list, an outline appears around it and the `Open` button becomes active (changes to black). To open the file, click the left mouse button on the `Open` button. The file opens in the application window that the file is bound to. For example, if it is a text file, the file's contents appear in the `Text Editor` window.

Opening Files

Each DeskSet application's file in the File Manager is connected or bound to its related application so that when you open the file, you also open the application. In other words, opening a file means that the corresponding application is also automatically opened with the file you selected loaded in the application window. This OpenWindows feature is referred to as *binding* a file to an application. The *Binder* database, which is maintained using the DeskSet's Binder application, contains the information about each file and its corresponding application.

NOTE   Creating your own custom icons and working with the binder to connect them to an application using the DeskSet's Icon Editor and Binder applications is explained in Chapter 7, "Customizing the Workspace and Icons."

To quickly open a file, double-click the left mouse button on the file icon you want. You can also open an application without loading a file by double-clicking on the program icon. Another easy way to open a file is to drag and drop the file icon from the File Manager to the Workspace. Even though you can start an application by dragging it from the File Manager and dropping it onto the Workspace, you cannot quit the application by dragging and dropping it back onto the File Manager. You must use the application's `Window` menu's `Quit` item.

A file can also be opened by selecting the file icon you want, then clicking the left mouse button on the `File` menu button. This activates the default menu item in the `Open` submenu. You can select multiple files then open them using this method.

Dragging and Dropping Files to Other Applications

A file can be dragged and dropped onto another application outside the File Manager. The results of dragging and dropping a file onto another application depends on whether the file is dropped onto a window's drag-and-drop target, a window's work area, or an icon. Dragging and dropping a file onto a drag-and-drop target of an application window loads it into the application. Dragging and dropping a file onto a window pane inserts the file's contents into the application at the location of the pointer. When you drag and drop a file onto an icon, it loads the file into the application and opens the application window. If you drop an icon onto an application that has an inappropriate format, the move is not performed, and a message appears in the window footer informing you that the file is in an incorrect file format. For example, if you drag a file created with the Text Editor and drop it onto the Snapshot application window, the message `unrecognized file type` appears in the footer of the Snapshot window.

Creating Folders and Files

The `File` menu provides you with items to create folders or files. The file you create using the File Manager is a text file that when opened displays the file in the Text Editor. Working with text files in the Text Editor is explained in Chapter 4, "Using the Text Editor, Shell Tool, and Command Tool." When you create new files or folders, they are automatically added to the File Manager's path or file pane.

To create a folder, make sure you are located in the directory where you want to create a subdirectory. Press the right mouse button on the `File` menu button and choose `Create Folder`. An empty directory named `New-Folder` appears (Figure 2.11), highlighted and underlined with an active insert point at the end of the line. Subsequent new folders you create in the current session are numbered in sequence. To name the new folder, type the name you want (the new folder's text field is already selected), then press Return or click the left mouse button on the background of the file pane.

You create a file in the same way you create a folder, except that you choose `Create File` from the `File` menu. When you create a file, a file icon appears with the name `NewDocument` highlighted and underlined, and an active insert point at the end of the line. Figure 2.12 shows a new file icon. Subsequent new document files you create in the current session are numbered in sequence. To name the new file, type the name you want

FIGURE 2.11

A new folder icon

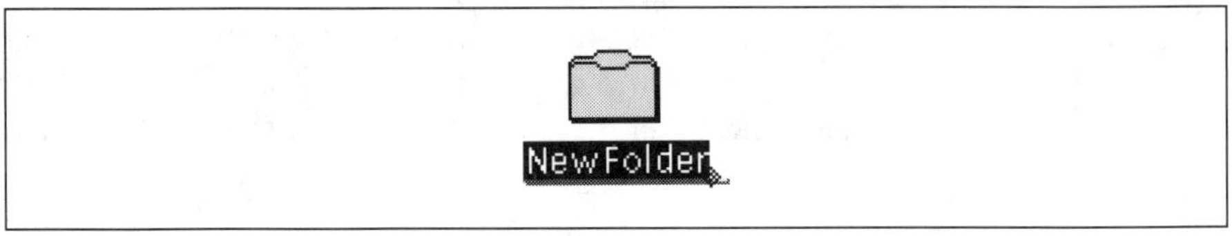

FIGURE 2.12

A new file icon

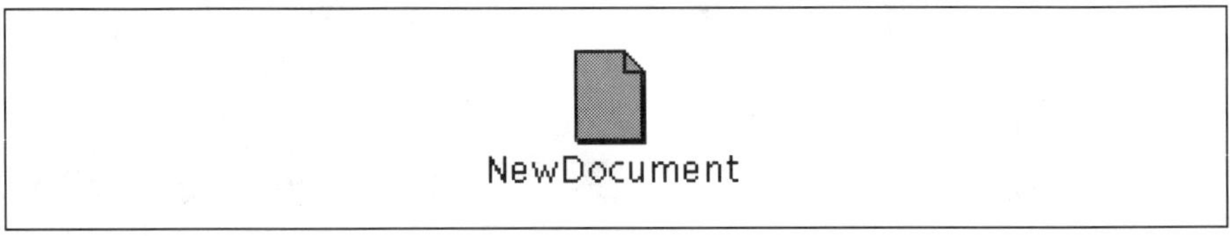

(the new folder's text field is already selected), then press Return or click the left mouse button on the background of the file pane.

NOTE Don't use spaces in your file or folder names. While the File Manager can handle spaces in file names, SunOS has trouble handling spaces when performing file management commands from the command line.

Changing Folder and File Names

To change the name of a new or existing folder or file, click the left mouse button on the folder or file icon. Then click the left mouse button on the file name. This selects the icon and displays the file or folder name highlighted and underlined with an insert point at the end. You can rename it by typing in a new name. When you are finished renaming the file or folder, press Return or click the left mouse button on the background of the file pane. The file or folder is sorted by the item specified in the `View` menu and displayed with its new name.

Deleting Files and Folders

The `Waste` icon is a holding tank for files you want to remove from the File Manager and permanently delete at a later time. Double-clicking on the `Waste` icon displays the `Wastebasket` window (Figure 2.13).

You can easily store files and folders you want to discard from the File Manager into the wastebasket by dragging and dropping them onto the `Waste` icon or the `Wastebasket` window. You can also select files and

FIGURE 2.13

The Wastebasket icon
and window

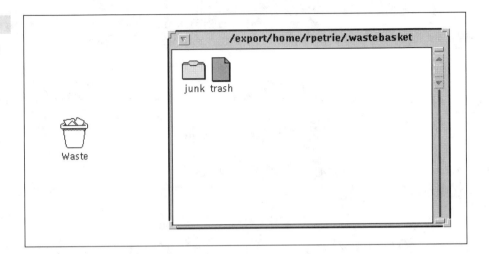

folders, then choose `Delete` from the File Manager's `File Pane` pop-up menu. If there are any files or folders in the wastebasket, overflowing papers appear in the `Waste` icon (Figure 2.13), or the file or folder icons appear in the `Wastebasket` window.

TIP

You can use `Undelete` in the `Wastebasket` **pop-up menu to restore any selected files and folders in the** `Wastebasket` **window back to their original location.**

Files remain in the wastebasket (even if you quit the File Manager) until you choose `Empty Wastebasket` for deleting all files and folders or `Delete` for selected files and folders from the `Wastebasket` pop-up menu (available in the `Wastebasket` window pane). Files you discard in the wastebasket are stored in a directory named `.wastebasket` in your home directory so that you can move them back to the File Manager if you change your mind. If the wastebasket file becomes full, a message warns you that you must empty the wastebasket before adding additional files.

To delete all the files and folders the `Waste` icon contains, do the following:

1. Double-click on the `Waste` icon to open the `Wastebasket` window.

2. Press the right button in the blank area of the file to bring up the `Wastebasket` pop-up menu.

3. Choose `Empty Wastebasket`. All the folders and files in the wastebasket are then permanently deleted.

To selectively delete individual files or folders stored in the `Waste` icon, do the following:

1. Double-click on the `Waste` icon to open the `Wastebasket` window.

2. Select the files you want to delete. Use the left mouse button to select the first file and the middle button for additional files. To unselect a file, click the middle mouse button on the selected file.

3. Press the right button in the blank area of the file pane to bring up the `Wastebasket` pop-up menu.

4. Choose `Delete` to permanently remove the files from the `Wastebasket` window.

If you quit the `Wastebasket` window, you can create a new one by selecting a file or folder in the file pane and choosing `Delete` from the `Edit` menu or the `File Pane` pop-up menu. A new wastebasket is created containing the file or folder you selected.

Deleting Files and Folders Using the Clipboard

The File Manager's `Edit` and `File Pane` menus also include a `Cut` item for removing selected icons. Using the `Cut` item removes the files or folders to the clipboard. The last item cut can be retrieved using `Paste` from either the `Edit` and `File Pane` menu. The `Wastebasket` pop-up menu also includes `Cut` and `Paste`, which remove and add selected files and folders.

Copying and Moving Files and Folders

Copying a file keeps the original file intact while making a copy of the file in the folder you specify. Moving a file copies the file to the new location then deletes the original file at the old location. The easiest way to copy or move files and folders is to drag and drop the file and folder icons.

TIP   Remember, you can open folders as windows on the Workspace to view the contents of each folder, which makes copying or moving files and folders easier.

To use the drag-and-drop method to move files and folders, simply drag the selected files and folders from the current folder in the File Manager to the folder where you want to move them, and release the left mouse button to finish the operation. You can display different folders by dragging and dropping them onto the Workspace. This makes copying and moving files between directories easier.

You can also copy files and folders by dragging and dropping them from the file pane onto folders displayed in the path pane. To copy one or more files, do the following:

1. Select the files you want to copy.

2. Hold down the Control key and press the left mouse button.

3. Drag and drop the files onto the target folder in the path pane, file pane, or folder window.

Whenever you perform a move or copy operation, a message appears in the window footer stating whether or not the copy or move action was successful.

Using the Clipboard to Copy and Move Files and Folders

The `Copy`, `Cut`, and `Paste` items are available in both the `Edit` menu and the pop-up `File Pane` menu. Using these items, you can *cut* or *copy* files and *paste* them into other folders or applications.

To copy a file using the clipboard, select the desired file then choose `Copy` from the `Edit` menu or the `File Pane` pop-up menu. To move a file using the clipboard, select the desired file then choose `Cut` from the `Edit` menu or the `File Pane` pop-up menu. Select the folder where you want to copy the file to then choose `Paste` from the `File Pane` pop-up menu in the File Manager's file pane or the file pane of a folder window on the Workspace.

WARNING Only one item or group of items is stored on the clipboard at a time. If you choose `Copy` or `Cut` while information is already stored on the clipboard, the previous information is lost. If you quit the File Manager or exit OpenWindows, the contents of the clipboard are lost.

The following steps explain how to copy or move a group of files using the clipboard.

1. Click the left mouse button on the first file you want to select and click the middle button on each additional file you want. The selected files are highlighted in black.

2. Press the right mouse button on the `Edit` menu button or in the file pane, which displays the `File Pane` pop-up menu. Choose `File` from the `Copy` submenu. Choose `Cut` if you want to move the files.

3. Change to the folder where you want to copy or move the files.

4. Press the right mouse button on the `Edit` menu and choose `Paste`.

TIP

If you are using a Sun workstation keyboard, you can save time when entering path and file names in text fields by using the Paste accelerator key. Select the file or folder icon that you want to insert the name of, press the Copy accelerator key, click on the text field where you want the file or folder name to appear, then press the Paste accelerator key. The full path and file name is pasted in the text field.

Using Accelerator Keys to Copy and Move Files and Folders

Another way to use the clipboard is to use the Copy, Cut, and Paste accelerator keys on the left side of the Sun workstation keyboard to copy or move file or folder icons. To use the accelerator keys, select the file(s) or folder(s) you want to copy or move, then press the Copy or Cut accelerator key. Move the pointer to where you want to copy or move the file(s) or folder(s) and press the Paste accelerator key.

Copying Files to Other Systems

The `Remote Copy` item in the `File` menu allows you to transfer copies of files between systems. You can copy between systems only if the permissions and ownership of directories and files allow you to perform the operation. For more information on permissions, see the "File and Folder Permissions" section later in this chapter.

NOTE If your system is using the Automounter, you don't need to use the remote copy feature. With the Automounter running, directories located on different machines appear to be part of the same system. You can use the standard methods for copying and moving files. For more information about using the Automounter, see Chapter 17, "System Administration Basics."

When you choose `Remote Copy`, the `Remote Copy` pop-up window appears (Figure 2.14). To transfer files from your system to another system, follow these steps:

1. Choose `Remote Copy` from the `File` menu. If you have selected files, your host name will be displayed in the `Source Machine` text field, and the file names will be displayed in the `Source Path` text field of the `Remote Copy` pop-up window.

2. Type the destination machine name in the `Destination Machine` text field. For example, type `mayberry`.

3. Type the destination path in the `Destination Path` text field. For example, `/export/home/bfife`.

FIGURE 2.14

The Remote Copy pop-up window

File Manager: Remote Copy

Source Machine:

Source Path:

Destination Machine:

Destination Path:

Copy

4. Click the left mouse button on the **Copy** button to initiate the copy process. While the transfer is in process, the **Copy** button displays the standard busy pattern.

Printing Files

There are sure to be times you want a printed copy of a document file. You can print files directly from the File Manager using **Print File** from the **File** submenu or the **File Pane** pop-up menu. Choosing **Print File** prints the selected file(s) using the default printer and print instructions from the application that is bound to the icon.

To print a file or group of files using **Print** from the **File** menu or the **File Pane** pop-up menu, do the following:

1. Select the file(s) in the file pane you want to print.

2. Press the right mouse button on the **File** menu button and choose **Print File** from the **Print** submenu.

N O T E

Files can also be printed by dragging the file icons from the File Manager and dropping them onto the Print Tool. For more information on working with the Print Tool, see Chapter 6, "Using the Print Tool, Audio Tool, and Other DeskSet Applications."

The **Custom Print** item displays the **Custom Print Properties** pop-up window (Figure 2.15). Using this pop-up window allows you change the default printing settings for printing a file. The **Print Method** setting allows you to enter SunOS commands for formatting and printing a file. Initially, the default File Manager print script is displayed as **cat $FILE | mp -lo | lp**. If you are using a PostScript printer, you may need to change the default script to read as follows:

```
cat $FILE | mp -lo | lp -T postscript
```

You can change the default print script permanently by using the **File Manager** menu item in the **Props** menu, as explained later in this chapter. See Chapter 13, "Formatting and Printing," for more information on formatting and printing commands to enter in the **Print Method** setting. The **Copies** setting lets you specify the number of copies of a file you want to print.

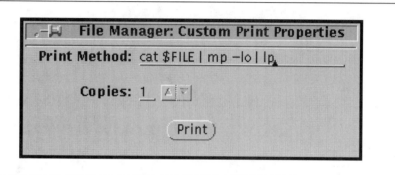

File and Folder Permissions

The Solaris security system is structured around permissions. Permissions determine which users can read, write, or execute files. Permissions can be changed for any file or folder you own (a file you created) or any file that the owner has given you permission to write to. Each folder and file in the file system has permissions assigned to it that can be changed to allow or restrict access.

You can change the permissions of files and folders using the **File Properties** pop-up window (Figure 2.16). To display the **File Properties**

FIGURE 2.16

The File Properties
pop-up window

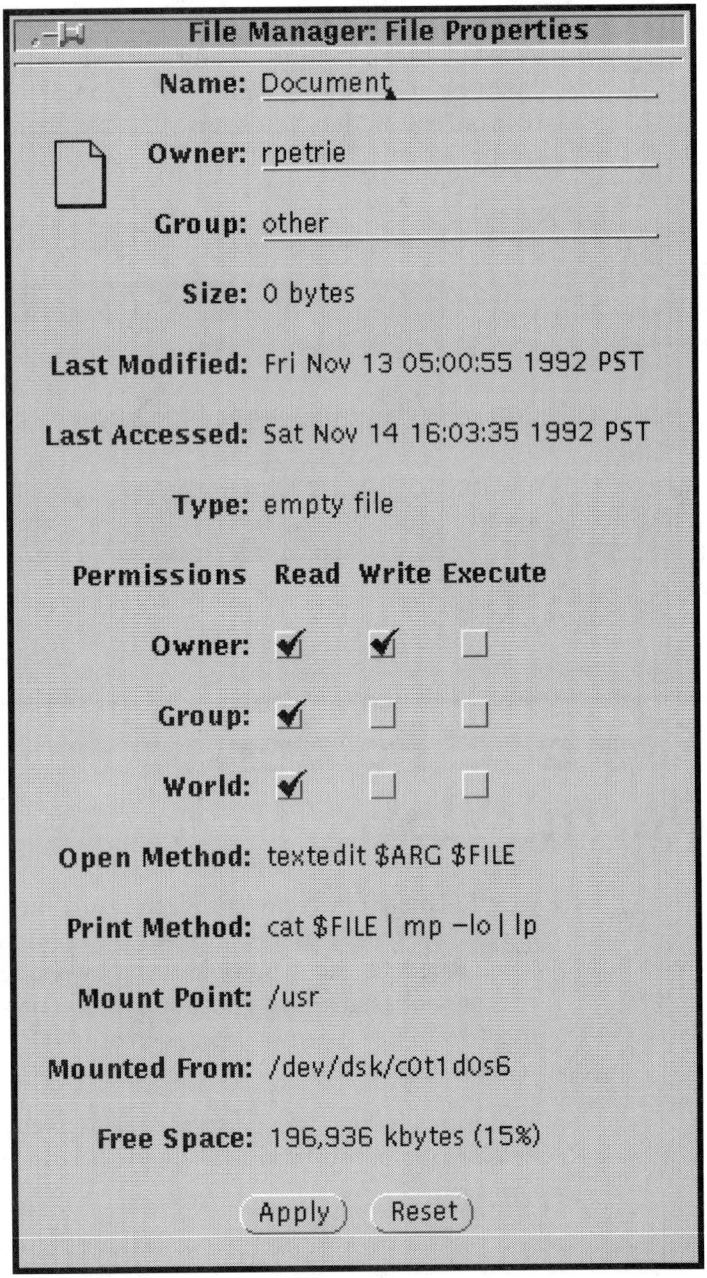

File Manager: File Properties

Name: Document

Owner: rpetrie

Group: other

Size: 0 bytes

Last Modified: Fri Nov 13 05:00:55 1992 PST

Last Accessed: Sat Nov 14 16:03:35 1992 PST

Type: empty file

Permissions Read Write Execute

Owner: ☑ ☑ ☐

Group: ☑ ☐ ☐

World: ☑ ☐ ☐

Open Method: textedit $ARG $FILE

Print Method: cat $FILE | mp −lo | lp

Mount Point: /usr

Mounted From: /dev/dsk/c0t1d0s6

Free Space: 196,936 kbytes (15%)

(Apply) (Reset)

pop-up window, first select the file or folder you want to change permissions for, then click the left mouse button on the **Props** button to choose the default **File** item. Remember, to make your permissions changes take effect, you must click the left mouse button on the **Apply** button.

Changing File and Folder Permissions

To change file or folder permissions, click the left mouse button on the boxes representing the permissions you want to change. The **Read**, **Write**, and **Execute** permission boxes are toggles that turn permissions on or off. If a box appears checked and you press the left mouse button on the check box, it then appears unchecked. The following explains the three types of permissions.

PERMISSION	DESCRIPTION
Read	Allows the authorized user to display the contents of the file or directory.
Write	Allows the authorized user to create or remove files and subdirectories from a folder or modify the file.
Execute	Allows the authorized user to change the directory, look at information about the files, or execute the file if the file is an executable program.

You can change read, write, and execute permissions for three types of users on the system.

USER TYPES	DESCRIPTION
Owner	The owner of the file or folder (usually the person who created the file or folder).
Group	The name of a specified group that can access the file.
World	All other users.

Changing Permissions for Groups of Files or Folders

The permissions of several files or folders can be changed at the same time. If you select more than one file, the file properties window shows those properties the selected files have in common. File or directory names and individual file or directory information are not displayed. You can change the permissions for the group of selected files the same way you change a single file, by clicking the left mouse button on the check boxes for the permissions you want to change to add or subtract.

Linking Files

Linking files allows several users to access a single file from different locations on the system, so there is one master file instead of many different copies or versions of the file. A *link* is a connection or pointer to a single file that allows access from more than one directory without having to move to the original directory where the file resides. When a file is linked, an icon appears in the directory where it is linked as though the file resides in that directory. Any editing changes you make to a file with links are reflected in all of the directories because there is really only one file.

Creating a Link

The Copy item in the File Manager's Edit menu or the File Pane pop-up menu allows you to create a link to a file using as a Link in the Copy submenu. To link a file, perform the following steps:

1. Select the file or files you want to link.

2. Press the right mouse button on the Edit menu and choose as a Link from the Copy submenu. The following message appears: Link these file(s) by opening the target folder and selecting 'Paste.'

3. Open the folder you want to add the link to.

4. Choose `Paste` from the `Edit` menu, the `File Pane` pop-up menu, or use the Paste accelerator key.

Once a link is established, the file's link information can be displayed using `File` from the `Props` menu. If you use a `List` item in the `View` menu, the linked file appears with an arrow pointing to the directory name that contains the file with which the file is linked. Figure 2.17 shows a linked file in **rpetrie**'s home directory.

T I P

If the display produced by your `List` item differs from Figure 2.17, activate the `Links` setting using the `Customize` item of the `View` menu.

FIGURE 2.17

A linked file displayed by using List by Type from the View menu

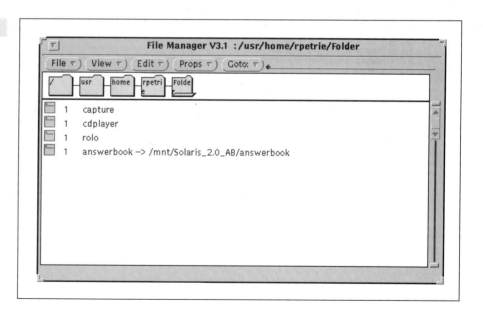

Removing a Link

To remove a link, select the file and choose **Delete** from the **Edit** sub-menu. Removing a link does not remove the original file. If you remove the original file without deleting the link, the icon for the link changes to display a broken chain, as shown in Figure 2.18.

FIGURE 2.18

A file icon representing a broken link

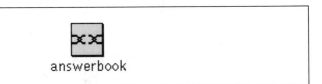

Customizing the File Manager

The File Manager provides three different pop-up windows to customize various features. Using the **Customize View** pop-up window, you can customize the way the file system is displayed in the file pane. The **Tool Properties** pop-up window provides a collection of settings for changing default File Manager settings, such as specifying a different default printer or instructing the File Manager to automatically delete any files placed in the wastebasket. The **Create Command** pop-up window allows you to create and store commonly used SunOS commands as menu items. The following sections explain how to work with these customizing features.

There are additional customizing options that affect the File Manager that are executed from the command line. Working with these File Manager customization settings is explained in Chapter 15, "Customizing Solaris."

Customizing the File Pane View

The `Customize` item in the `View` menu displays the `Customize View` pop-up window, as shown in Figure 2.19. The settings in this pop-up menu allow you to change the default setting for how the File Manager displays and sorts your files. To change a setting, click the left mouse button on the setting you want to change. This will toggle the setting on or off. When a setting is on, it appears highlighted or with a bold border. After making your changes, click the left mouse button on the `Apply` button. The following explains each of the `Customize View` pop-up window options.

OPTION	DESCRIPTION
Display Mode	The `Icon` setting displays the current directory's files using standard-size icons. The `List` setting displays smaller icons so you can display more information about each file, as determined by options in the `List Options` settings. The `Content` setting displays the contents of an icon and raster files (files that contain images). The images are not displayed to scale. Using the `Content` setting slows scrolling through the file pane because the images must be drawn to the screen each time to change the display. The default is the icon setting.

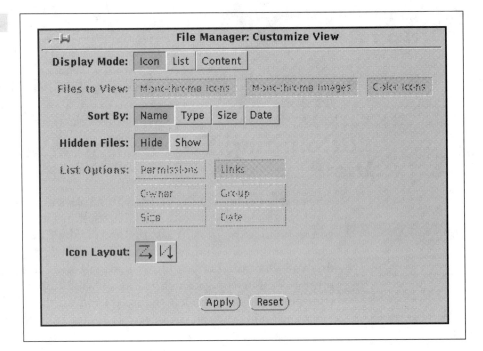

OPTION	DESCRIPTION
Files to View	Allows you to specify if icons appear in monochrome or color. This setting is only effective when the **Display Mode** is in the **Content** setting. You can choose from among three settings: **Monochrome Icons**, **Monochrome Images**, and **Color**. In most cases, the **Files to View** option is set with both monochrome settings on. The default monochrome settings speed up the display of icons and images.

OPTION	DESCRIPTION
Sort By	Allows you to arrange files in the file pane according to the option specified. The `Name` option sorts alphabetically by the file name. The `Type` option sorts files alphabetically by file type, with folders first, followed by document files, then by applications. The `Size` option sorts files by size, from largest to smallest. The `Date` option sorts the files in reverse chronological order, from the newest to the oldest file, based on the date the file was last modified. By default, the icons are sorted alphabetically by file names.
Hidden Files	Allows you to choose whether or not to display those files and folders ordinarily not displayed. Hidden file names begin with at least one period. Choosing the `Show` setting displays hidden files in the file pane. The default is `Hide`.
List Options	Allows you to choose how much information is displayed when you use the `List` option in the `View` menu. You can display one or more of the following options: `Permissions`, `Links`, `Owner`, `Group`, `Size`, and `Date`.
Icon Layout	Specifies whether icons wrap to the beginning of the next line or are displayed in a columnar format. The default is to wrap the icons to the beginning of the next row.

Using the Tool Properties Window

Choosing **File Manager** from the **Props** menu displays the **Tool Properties** pop-up window (Figure 2.20). This pop-up window provides you with options to customize how the File Manager displays and works with files and folders. Remember, after making changes in the **Tool Properties** pop-up window, you must click the left mouse button on the **Apply** button for the settings to take effect. These settings take effect immediately and are displayed in the **File Manager** window. The following list explains each of the options available in the pop-up window.

FIGURE 2.20

The Tool Properties pop-up window

File Manager: Tool Properties

Default Print Script: cat $FILE | mp —lo | lp

View Filter Pattern:

Longest Filename: 15

Delete: to wastebasket | really delete

Default Document Editor: texteditor | Other:

Apply | Reset

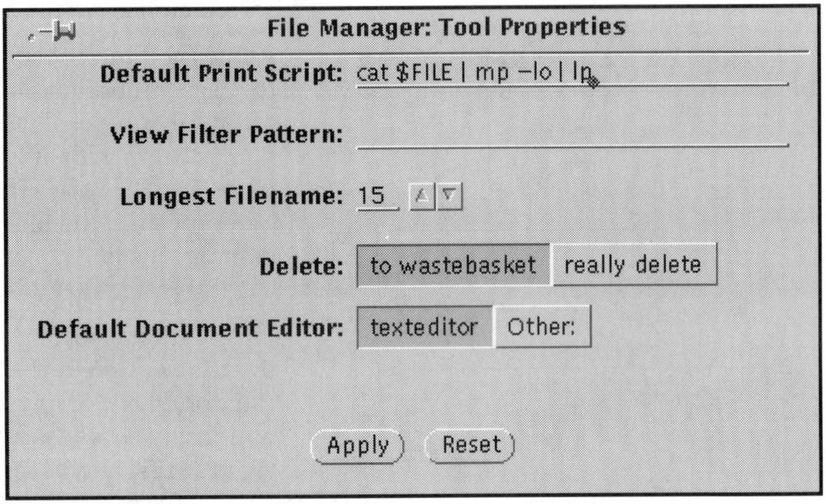

OPTION	DESCRIPTION
Default Print Script	Allows you to specify a print script for files that are printed using the `Print File` item in the File Manager's `File` menu that does not have a method defined by the DeskSet's Binder application. The print script shown in Figure 2.20 prints your files in landscape mode on your default printer, using the `mp` PostScript pretty-printer filter. The variable name `$FILE` acts as a placeholder for a file you select. If you are using a PostScript printer, you may need to change the print script to `cat $FILE	mp -lo	lp -T postscript`. The `-T postscript` argument specifies that you are using a PostScript printer. For more information on printing, see Chapter 13, "Formatting and Printing."
View Filter Pattern	Allows you to specify that only a certain type of file is displayed in the file pane of the File Manager. For example, entering `*.ps` lists all PostScript files that end with a `.ps`. The filter pattern used to filter files is always listed in the header of the window.
Longest Filename	Allows you to specify the number of characters that display for a file or folder name. You can type any number from 0 to 255 in this numeric field to choose how many characters of each file name are displayed in the file pane of the File Manager. The default is fifteen characters. The number of characters actually displayed for each file name may vary because the width of different fonts may vary.

OPTION	DESCRIPTION
Delete	Specifies whether or not a file is placed in the wastebasket or automatically deleted. The default **to wastebasket** option stores files you choose to delete in the waste-basket until you specify that they actually be deleted. The **really delete** setting instructs the File Manager to permanently delete a file. If you choose the **really delete** setting, the **Waste** icon will not appear the next time you log in because the File Manager will not hold files you want to delete.
Default Document Editor	Specifies the default editor the File Manager uses to display text data files not specifically bound to another application. The default setting is the DeskSet's Text Editor. Choosing the **Other** setting lets you specify a text editor; the default is the vi editor. If you want to specify an editor other than vi, you must type **shelltool**, followed by the name of the editor. Working with the vi editor is explained in Chapter 12, "Using the vi Editor."

Adding Commands to a Menu

NOTE

Working with the File Manager's custom commands feature requires that you have some working knowledge of working with SunOS commands. If you are not familiar with SunOS, see Part II, "Working from the SunOS Command Line."

The File Manager allows you to create and store commonly used commands. Once you have added the commands to the menu, you can use them at any time by choosing them from the `Custom Commands` menu. Figure 2.21 shows an example of the `Custom Commands` menu with custom commands created using the `Create Command` pop-up window.

To open the `Create Command` pop-up window, choose `Custom Commands` from the `File` menu, then from the submenu choose `Create Command`. The `Create Command` pop-up window appears (Figure 2.22). The scrolling list shows any custom commands that were created. You can use the items in the `Edit` menu (under the scroll list) to add, delete, and change the order of your custom commands.

The following steps explain how to add a new custom command in the `Create Command` pop-up window. This custom command allows you to move selected files to a directory you specify.

1. Click the left mouse button on the `New Command` button to activate and clear the settings below the scrolling list, if necessary. These settings are dimmed when you do not have a command selected in the scrolling list, or when you are not currently creating a new command.

FIGURE 2.21

Sample command items in the Custom Commands submenu

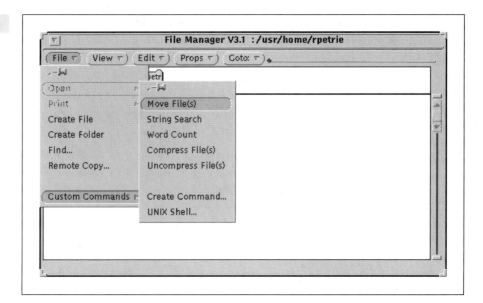

FIGURE 2.22

The Create Command
pop-up window

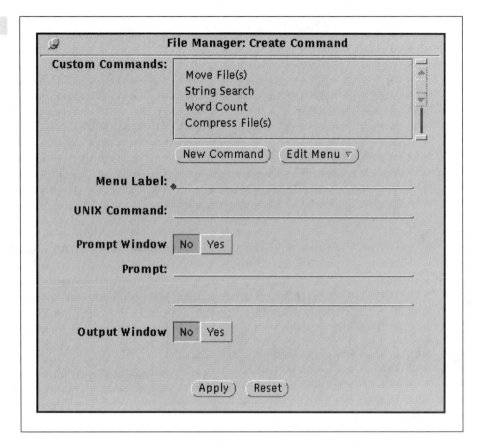

2. In the Menu Label text field, type the name for your custom command that you want to appear on the Custom Commands menu. The menu label should be descriptive enough to let you know what the custom command does. For this example, type

    ```
    Move File(s)
    ```

N O T E For information on working with the mv command, including setting arguments, see Chapter 9, "Navigating Directories and Working with Files."

3. Type the actual SunOS command in the UNIX Command text field. Adding $FILE or $ARG to the command creates a representation for the selected file(s) or special arguments (options) that you specify at the time you choose the command. For this example, type

```
mv $FILE $ARG
```

in the UNIX Command text field.

4. Change the Prompt Window setting to Yes. This causes the File Manager to display a prompt window for a command's arguments, if necessary, when executing the command. If you use a prompt window, when a custom command is chosen from the Custom Commands menu, a window is displayed with the prompt label. You use this pop-up window to type the command options.

5. In the Prompt field, enter the prompt that you want to display to instruct the user to enter argument and file variables. For example, in the previous example, you might use a prompt such as

```
Move Files to:
```

When you choose the custom command, a prompt window asks you to specify which directory to move the selected files to, as shown in Figure 2.23. If the command will produce output, such as a list of file names, change the Output Window setting to Yes. This causes an output window to be displayed when the custom command is chosen, where you can see the result of your command. In this case, there is no output.

6. Choose Apply to add the command to the Custom Commands submenu. Once you have added the command to the menu, you can use it at any time by choosing it from the Custom Commands submenu.

FIGURE 2.23

A sample prompt window

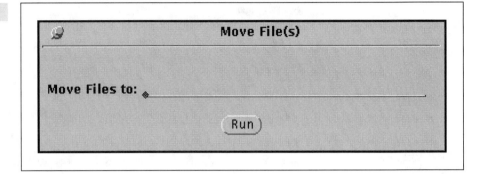

Editing a Custom Command

The `Edit Menu` button in the `Create Command` pop-up window displays a menu of options for copying, deleting, and moving commands in the `Custom Commands` submenu. To edit a command, first select the command in the list, press the right mouse button on the `Edit Menu` button, then choose the item you want to perform. For example, selecting a custom command and choosing `Cut` from the `Edit Menu` submenu removes the custom command from the `Custom Commands` submenu and stores it in the Clipboard. Selecting an item from the `Paste` submenu lets you move the custom command `Before` or `After` another custom command or to the `Top` or `Bottom` of the `Custom Commands` submenu.

The Multimedia Mail Tool Makes Mail Easy

THE DeskSet's multimedia Mail Tool, with its friendly graphical environment, is your gateway to communicating with other users, in the next office or around the world. It allows you to easily receive, write, send, and manage your electronic mail (commonly referred to as *email*), as well as attach files, such as audio and picture files, to your messages to make your point. This chapter explains Mail Tool fundamentals, as well as the rich collection of other features provided by the Mail Tool.

Starting the Mail Tool

To start the Mail Tool, choose `Mail Tool` from the `Workspace` menu's `Programs` submenu. The Mail Tool icon shows up on the Workspace. As shown in Figure 3.1, the icon for the Mail Tool appears differently depending on whether or not you have new mail, or if there is no old mail stored in your mail file. To open the Mail Tool from an icon to a window, double-click on the Mail Tool icon. The `Mail Tool Header` window appears (Figure 3.2).

FIGURE 3.1

The Mail Tool's icons

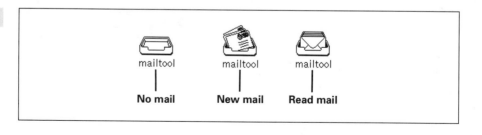

FIGURE 3.2

The Mail Tool Header window

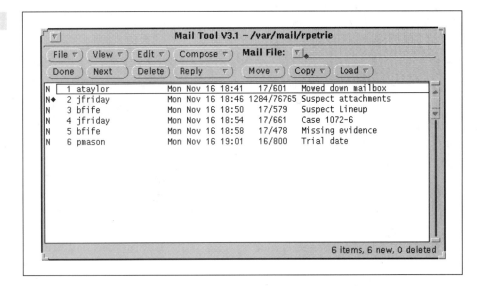

An Overview of the Mail Tool Header Window

The `Mail Tool Header` window is the base window that provides the main controls for the Mail Tool. Its headers pane displays the list of mail message headers and the status of your mail messages. Mail message headers provide information about the message such as the sender and subject. The headers pane contains a `Messages` pop-up menu (Figure 3.3) that includes some of the most frequently used Mail Tool menu items. To display the `Messages` pop-up menu, press the right mouse button anywhere in the headers pane. The `Messages` pop-up menu can be pinned to the Workspace.

The control area of the `Mail Tool Header` window has eleven menu buttons: `File`, `View`, `Edit`, `Compose`, `Done`, `Next`, `Delete`, `Reply`, `Move`, `Copy`, and `Load`. The first four buttons are the main buttons you use to store, view, edit, and send mail. The remaining buttons are custom buttons which can be used for quick execution of any item in the `File`, `View`, `Edit`, and

FIGURE 3.3

The Messages pop-up
menu

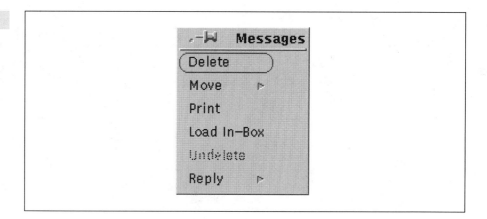

Compose menus. The mail file abbreviated menu button and the **Mail File** text field are used for storing mail messages. Changing the custom buttons and working with mail files is explained later in this chapter.

Receiving and Viewing Messages

Incoming messages are delivered to your electronic mailbox, a default mail file for all incoming messages, named **In-Box**. *Mail files* are special files that can contain multiple messages. As explained later in this chapter, you can create your own mail files. The Mail Tool periodically checks for new messages as specified from the **Mail Tool Properties** window. The default is every five minutes.

When messages are retrieved by the Mail Tool, their headers are displayed in the **Mail Tool Header** window. If the Mail Tool is closed to an icon, the icon changes to indicate new mail has arrived. In addition, any time you receive incoming mail, with the Mail Tool running on the Workspace, Solaris beeps.

Once mail message headers are in the **Mail Tool Header** window, you can select and open a mail message into a **View Message** pop-up window, which displays the contents of the message and shows file icons for any attachments to the message. A mail message *attachment* is a file of any type, such as a sound file generated from the Audio Tool or a Raster image file, that is sent along with the mail message. For example, a mail message might contain a picture and voice message attachment to provide the recipient with an illustration and voice mail. The following sections explain the fundamentals for reading your mail messages and any attachments.

NOTE

If you have a problem receiving your mail, contact your system administrator or see Chapter 17, "System Administration Basics."

Manually Checking Your Mail

While the Mail Tool checks your `In-Box` mail file automatically at specified time intervals, you can also manually check for any new messages. To check your mail manually, click the left mouse button on the `File` button in the `Mail Tool Header` window. The default `Load In-Box` item is activated. If you have new mail, the new mail message headers appear in the `Mail Tool Header` window or the Mail Tool icon displays letters with canceled stamps.

Mail Message Headers

The mail message headers displayed in the `Mail Tool Header` window list information about the mail message. In addition, status messages, displayed at the right side of the window footer, tell you the total number of messages in your `In-Box`, the number of new messages, and how many messages you have deleted. Each header has nine columns of information. The following explains each column:

- The status of the mail message: an arrow points to the current message, an `N` indicates that the message is new, a `U` indicates that the message is unread, a blank indicates that you have viewed the message, and a diamond indicates that an attachment was sent with the message.

- A message number indicating the order in which your messages were received.

- The electronic mail address of the sender of the message.

- The day of the week the message was sent.

- The month the message was sent.

- The date the message was sent.

- The time the message was sent.

- The size of the message. The first number indicates the number of lines in the message, and the second number indicates the number of characters in the message.

- The subject of the message, if the person who sent the message provided a subject line.

Selecting and Viewing Messages

A single mail message can be quickly displayed by double-clicking the left mouse button on the mail message header you want. A selected mail message header can also be displayed by pressing the right mouse button on the View menu and choosing Message. The mail message appears in a View Message pop-up window (Figure 3.4) on the Workspace. Once you have displayed a mail message, its New status is removed from the message header listing in the Mail Tool Header window, whether or not you actually read the message.

Once you open a single mail message in the View Message window, you can select and open additional mail message headers by double-clicking on the header name. The previous mail message in the View Message window is replaced with the new selected message. The number of the mail message is displayed in the header of the View Message pop-up window.

Choosing the Next item or Previous item in the Mail Tool Header window's View menu allows you to view the previous or next mail message listed from the one currently displayed. You can also click the left mouse button on the Next button to display the next mail message.

FIGURE 3.4

The View Message
pop-up window

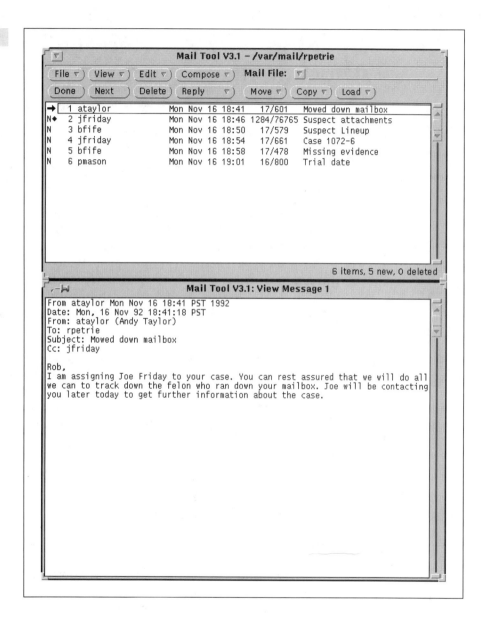

Opening and Viewing Mail Attachments

When you receive a mail message that contains one or more attachments, the `View Message` pop-up window displays a separate `Attachments` pane at the bottom, as shown in Figure 3.5. Attachments can be opened without moving them out of the Mail Tool. You can also open an attachment by moving it to the Workspace or any other application that accepts that type of file.

To open a mail message attachment, double-click the left mouse button on the attachment icon you want to open or drag and drop the attachment file icon onto the Workspace. The application bound to the attachment's file type is started, and the mail attachment is loaded into that application. For example, if you open a voice mail attachment created by the Audio Tool, the Audio Tool application window appears and the voice mail attachment is loaded. You can then work with the audio file using the Audio Tool.

A mail message attachment can also be opened by selecting the attachment and choosing `Open` from the `File` menu button at the top of the `Attachments` pane. Figure 3.6 shows a mail message with voice mail and picture attachments. For information on using the Audio Tool, see Chapter 6, "Using the Print Tool, Audio Tool, and Other DeskSet Applications."

Opening Multiple View Message Windows

Multiple mail messages can be opened, each appearing in a separate `View Message` window. To select multiple message headers in the `Mail Tool Header` window, click the left mouse button on the first message header then click the middle mouse button on each additional header you want to select. A mail message header can be unselected by clicking the middle mouse button on the mail message header. After selecting the messages, press the right mouse button on the `View` menu button and choose `Messages`. The `View Message` pop-up windows are displayed on top of one another in the numerical order of the messages listed (Figure 3.7).

FIGURE 3.5

The Attachments pane
in the View Message
window

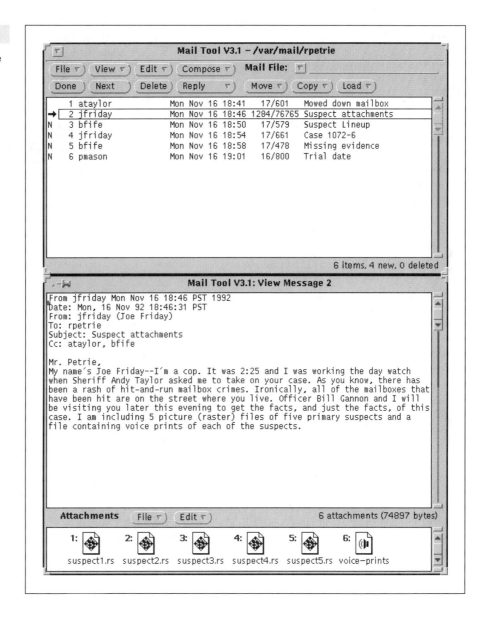

FIGURE 3.6

A mail message with voice and picture attachments

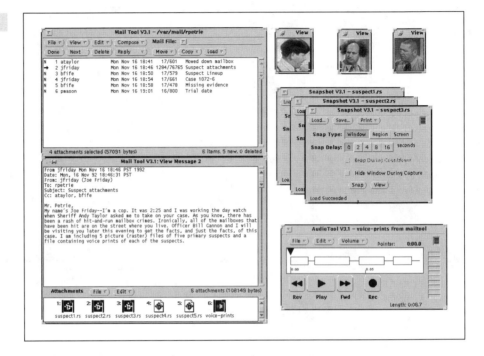

Viewing Messages with Full Headers

By default, the message header information appearing in the **View Message** window is in an abbreviated form. You can view messages with more information about the mail message appearing in the mail message header in the **View Message** window (Figure 3.8). For example, you can display information about the type of file and number of lines in the mail messages. The differences in the information that appears between the two displays are determined using the Mail Tool's **Properties** pop-up window.

To display a mail message with the full message header, first select the message in the **Mail Tool Header** window. Press the right mouse button on the **View** menu button, then choose **Full Header** from the **Messages** submenu.

FIGURE 3.7

Multiple messages
displayed

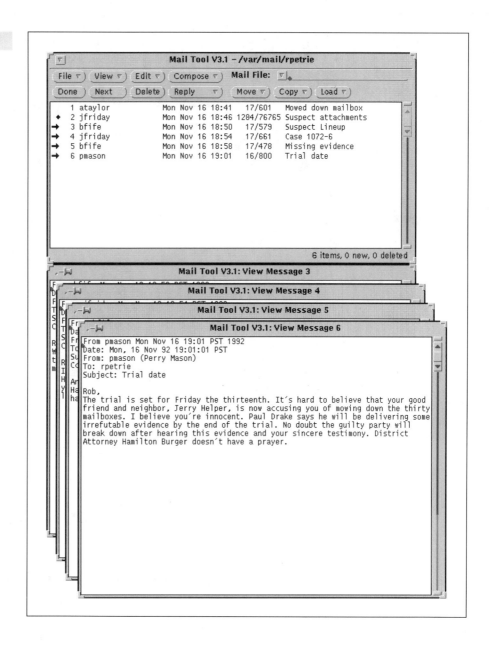

FIGURE 3.8

A full mail message header

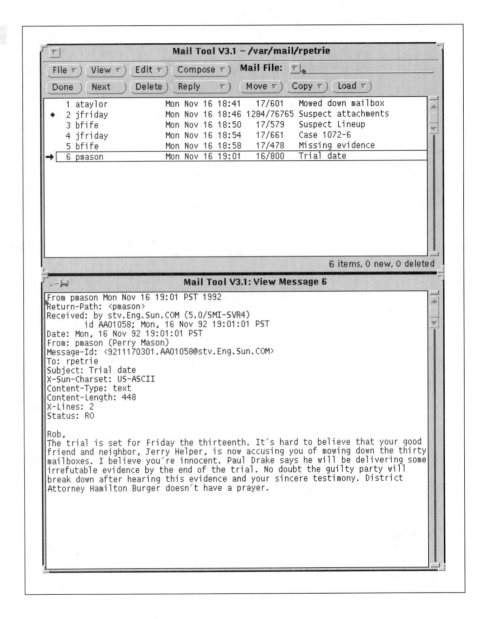

Saving Mail Tool Header Window Changes

If you attempt to quit the **Mail Tool Header** window after reading mail or after making any changes by using the **Quit** item in the **Window** menu, a Notice appears (Figure 3.9) informing you that changes have been made and prompting you for a confirmation. The following describes the options available in the Notice.

FIGURE 3.9

The Save Changes Notice

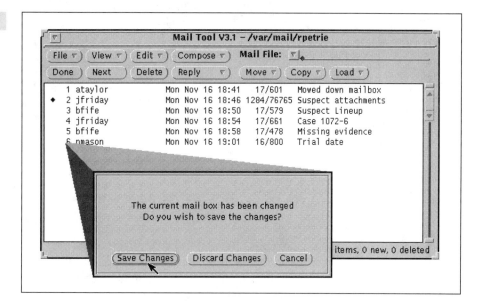

OPTION	DESCRIPTION
Save Changes	Saves any changes you have made and quits the Mail Tool, removing the icon from the workspace.
Discard Changes	Disregards changes you've made, restoring any deleted messages, and quits the Mail Tool, removing the icon from the Workspace.

OPTION	DESCRIPTION
Cancel	Aborts your request to quit the Mail Tool.

Changes can also be saved as you work by either using the `Save Changes` or `Done` item in the `Mail Tool Header` window's `File` menu or clicking the left mouse button on the `Done` button in the control area. The `Save Changes` item saves changes made in the Mail Tool without closing the `Mail Tool Header` window. The `Done` item or button closes the `Mail Tool Header` window and saves any changes.

Composing and Sending Messages

To create and send mail messages, use the Mail Tool's `Compose Message` window (Figure 3.10). The `Compose Message` window allows you to create mail messages using standard text editor functions. You can also add attachments to your mail messages, such as audio and image files.

The `Compose Message` window operates independently from the `Mail Tool Header` window. An opened `Compose Message` window can be closed to an icon for later use or you can keep the `Compose Message` window open while the `Mail Tool Header` window is closed to an icon. You can open several `Compose Message` windows at one time to reply to or compose several messages simultaneously. Once you have opened a `Compose Message` window, you can use it to write and send mail messages without having to reopen the `Mail Tool Header` window.

To display a `Compose Message` window, click the left mouse button on the `Compose` menu button in the `Mail Tool Header` window. The `Compose Message` window appears. When you close the `Compose Message` window without sending the message you are composing, its own icon (Figure 3.10) appears on the Workspace.

FIGURE 3.10

The Compose Message
icon and window

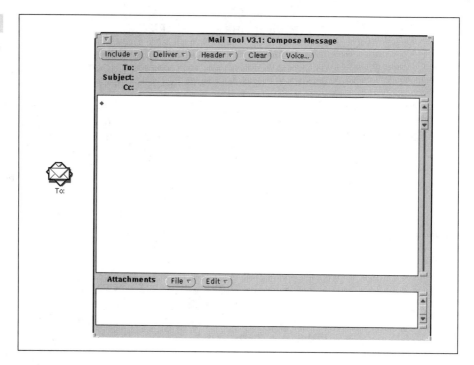

An Overview of the Compose Message Window

The **Compose Message** window has its own set of controls, which are displayed as five buttons in its control area: **Include**, **Deliver**, **Header**, **Clear**, and **Voice**. The following explains what each menu provides.

MENU BUTTON	DESCRIPTION
Include	Provides choices that allow you to include selected messages as part of the message you are composing and also provides you with a set of templates for creating different types of messages. This menu also includes an option that brings up the Attachments pane, which allows you to include attachments with your message (such as a voice file).

MENU BUTTON	DESCRIPTION
Deliver	Provides choices for how the Compose Message window behaves once the message is delivered.
Header	Provides choices for the number and type of text fields provided to create the message header.
Clear	Clears the contents of the Compose Message window and the Attachments pane.
Voice	Starts the Audio Tool, which lets you create audio files to attach to mail messages.

Just below the control area are three text fields: To, Subject, and Cc. These text fields allow you to include the addresses of the users you want to send your mail message to, the subject of the message, and the addresses of any users you want to send carbon copies of the mail message to. The text pane of the Compose Message window is where you type the contents of the message you want to send. The Attachments pane of the Compose Message window allows you to easily attach other files to your messages. It includes File and Edit menu buttons, which contain items for moving, copying, renaming, and deleting attachments.

An Overview of Mail Addresses

Before you send a mail message to a user, make sure you know the user address of the person you want to send your message to. The user address includes the user name and the name of the machine. The format for entering a user address is *username@machinename*. If the user is located on your system (sharing the same server), you don't need to add the machine name to the address.

Solaris includes a database system known as *alias mapping* that simplifies identifying users on the system. Alias mapping allows you send mail to users on other machines by just typing their user name without having to add the machine name. If you don't know the user name of the person you want to send a mail message to, see Chapter 11, "Electronic Mail and Messages," for information on using the `who`, `finger`, and `rusers` SunOS commands, which you can enter in the `Command Tool` or `Shell Tool` windows. Working with the `Command Tool` or `Shell Tool` windows is explained in Chapter 4, "Using the Text Editor, Shell Tool, and Command Tool."

Creating and Sending Mail Messages

Creating a mail message involves entering several standard items—including the user or users you are sending the message to, the subject of the message, and any user or users you want to send a carbon copy of the mail message—then entering the message text.

The `To` text field in the `Compose Message` window is where you enter the email address of the user or users you want to send the mail message to. To enter more than one email address, separate each address with a space. The `Subject` text field is an optional field, but entering information helps recipients identify what your message is about from the header listed in their `Mail Tool Header` window. The `Cc` (Carbon Copy) text field allows you to send a copy of the mail message to users other than those specified in the `To` text field. You can also send a blind carbon copy to another user so that the recipient does not know that the carbon copy was sent. To add the Blind Carbon Copy header for a message, choose the `Add Bcc` item from the Header menu in the `Compose Message` window.

You can create an *alias* that allows you to create your own distribution list containing a group of user email addresses. Then instead of typing a list of user email addresses that you frequently send mail to each time in either the `To` or `Cc` text fields, you can just enter the alias name. The Mail Tool automatically enters the group of user email addresses. Creating aliases is explained later in this chapter.

The area for entering your mail message text in the `Compose Message` window is a standard text pane that includes the `Text Pane` pop-up menu (Figure 3.11). This menu provides you with the standard text editing features that are available in the DeskSet's Text Editor, which is explained in Chapter 4 "Using the Text Editor, Shell Tool, and Command Tool." To

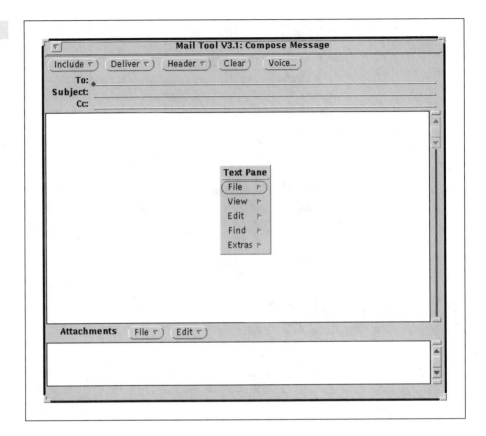

display the **Text Pane** pop-up menu, press the right mouse button anywhere in the text pane.

The following steps explain how to create and send a mail message.

1. If a **Compose Message** window is not displayed, click the left mouse button on the **Compose** menu button. The **Compose Message** window is displayed.

2. Click the left mouse button on the **To** text field to set the insert point. Type the address or series of addresses you want to send your mail message to. If you type more than one address, separate each with a space.

3. Move the insert point to the `Subject` field and type the subject of your message.

4. Move the insert point to the `Cc` field. Type the addresses of all those whom you want to receive a carbon copy of the message, if any.

5. Click the left mouse button in the `Compose Message` window's text pane to set the insert point in the text pane.

6. Type in your mail message. Pressing the right mouse button in the text pane displays the standard `Text Pane` pop-up menu. The `Edit` submenu lets you cut, copy, and paste text.

7. When you have finished composing the message, click the left mouse button on the `Deliver` button. The message is delivered and the `Compose Message` window is removed from the Workspace.

The `Deliver` menu button offers three additional items besides the default `Quit window` item, which removes the `Compose Message` window after sending a mail message. The `Close window` item closes the `Compose Message` window to an icon after sending a mail message. The `Clear message` item clears the `Compose Message` window after sending a mail message. The `Leave message intact` item leaves the message in the `Compose Message` window after sending the mail message.

Adding Attachments to Messages

Just as you can receive mail messages with attachments that can be files of any type, you can also add attachments to your outgoing mail messages. Attachments can be easily added to a mail message by dragging and dropping the file from the File Manager onto the `Attachments` pane of the `Compose Message` window. You can also drag and drop files or documents from the Text Editor or any other application that supports dragged and dropped files.

By default the `Attachments` pane is displayed at the bottom of the `Compose Message` window; if it is not, choose the `Show Attachments` item from the `Compose Message` window's `Include` menu.

A mail attachment can also be added to a mail message using the `Add Attachment` window. Click the left mouse button on the `File` button at the top of the `Attachments` pane. The `Add Attachment` pop-up window is displayed, as shown in Figure 3.12. Type the directory name containing the file to be attached in the `Add Attachment Directory` text field, and type the name of the file in the `File Name` text field. Click the left mouse button on the `Add` button, and the file is added to the `Attachment` pane.

FIGURE 3.12

The Add Attachment pop-up window

When you send a mail message with attachments, the receiver will see an `Attachments` pane at the bottom of the `View Message` window. The user can open the attachments by using the `Open` item in the `File` menu.

Including Other Messages in a Message

Other mail messages can be included in the mail message you are currently working on by using the `Include` menu button in the `Compose Message` window. The Include menu includes two items that allow you to specify how an included mail message is distinguished from the text you have entered in the mail message. The `Bracketed` item distinguishes a mail message by enclosing the message between dashed lines identifying the beginning and end of the included message, as shown in Figure 3.13. The `Indented` item displays a greater-than sign (>) preceding each line of an included text message, as shown in Figure 3.14. The greater-than sign is referred to as an *indent* character. A different indent character can be specified, as explained later in this chapter. The following steps explain how to include another mail message in the mail message currently displayed in a `Compose Message` window.

FIGURE 3.13

An included mail
message using the
Bracketed item

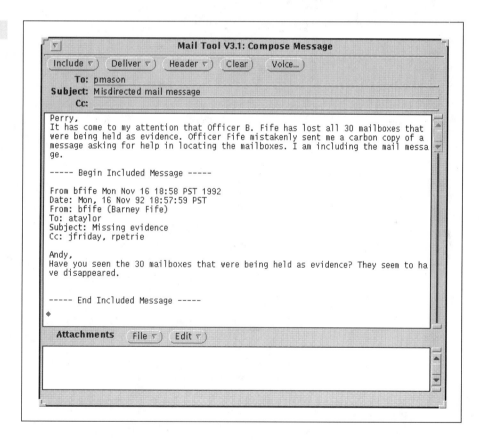

1. Open the mail message you want to include in the mail message
   currently opened in a `Compose Message` window.

2. Position the insert point at the location you want to insert the included mail message in the `Compose Message` window containing
   the mail message you want to add the mail message to.

3. Press the right mouse button on the `Include` menu button in the
   `Compose Message` window containing the mail message you want
   to insert the mail message into then choose `Indented` or `Brack-
   eted`. The entire mail message is entered into the mail message at
   the location of the insert point.

Replying to a Message

Choosing `Reply` from the `Compose` menu automatically displays a `Compose Message` window, places the sender's address in the `To` text field, and places the subject of the mail message sent to you in the `Subject` text field of your reply message. The `Reply` submenu offers four choices for sending replies.

ITEM	RESULT
To Sender	Adds the name of the sender of the original message to the `To` field.
To All	Fills in the `To` and `Cc` fields with all the names in the selected message's text fields, including the originator of the message.
To Sender, Include	Fills in the `To` text field and puts a copy of the text of the original message into the `Compose Message` window pane.
To All, Include	Adds all the names from the original message to the `To` and `Cc` text fields, and puts a copy of the text of the message into the `Compose Message` window pane.

To reply to an individual message or to a group of messages, click the left mouse button on the `Reply` button or follow these steps:

1. Select the message header or headers that you want to answer by pressing the left mouse button on the first header and the middle mouse button on each additional header.

2. Press the right mouse button on the `Compose` menu and choose one of the four items from the `Reply` submenu. A `Compose Message` window is opened for each selected header.

Using Drag-and-Drop with the Mail Tool

You can drag mail messages from the `Mail Tool Header` window and drop them onto other applications. You can also drag and drop selected text or files from other applications onto the Mail Tool's `Compose Message` window to be included as text.

Single or multiple headers can be selected in the `Mail Tool Header` window and dragged to other DeskSet applications. When you drag a mail header, the entire mail message is moved along with it, including any mail attachments. The message headers can be dragged and dropped onto the File Manager, Text Editor, Print Tool, Calendar Manager, or any other application that accepts files via drag-and-drop. To drag and drop a copy of a mail message, select the message header, then drag it to the destination you want and drop it. A document object moves with the pointer to show that you are dragging a text file. When you select multiple headers, a group of three document objects is dragged with the pointer.

Managing Your Messages in the Mail Tool Header Window

The following sections explain Mail Tool features for managing and printing your mail messages in the `Mail Tool Header` window. To help you manage your messages, you can sort your messages, find specific messages by defining a search criteria, delete and undelete messages, and print messages directly from the `Mail Tool Header` window.

Sorting Message Headers

Mail messages in the `Mail Tool Header` window can be sorted by information contained in the mail message header. To sort mail message headers, choose an item in the `Sort By` submenu in the `View` menu (Figure 3.15). Immediately after you choose a sorting item, the message headers are redisplayed, sorted according to the item you selected. The following describes each sorting item available in the `Sort By` submenu.

FIGURE 3.15

The Sort By submenu

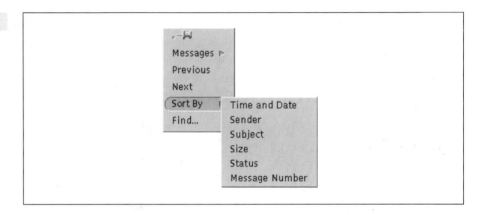

ITEM	DESCRIPTION
Time and Date	Sorts messages by receipt date and time with the most recently received messages at the bottom.
Sender	Sorts messages alphabetically by the name of the sender. This is useful for grouping together all messages from a particular person. Uppercase characters appear before lowercase characters in the alphabetical search.
Subject	Sorts messages alphabetically by mail message subjects. Uppercase characters appear before lowercase characters in the alphabetical search.

ITEM	DESCRIPTION
Size	Sorts messages by the size of the messages, from smallest to largest.
Status	Sorts messages by the read status of the messages. This puts the messages you have read first, the unread messages next, and the new messages last. This is useful to group together all unread mail after you read your messages in nonsequential order.
Message Number	Sorts messages by the message numbers assigned by the Mail Tool for each message.

Finding Messages

You can search through your messages using a number of different criteria to find a single message or group of messages. For example, you can find messages with a particular subject, or messages sent by a specific person. To find messages, choose Find from the View menu. The Find Messages pop-up window appears (Figure 3.16), which includes four text fields for entering search criteria. Searches can be based on information in a single field or combination of fields. The text fields do not distinguish between uppercase and lowercase characters and can match partial words and phrases. The following describes each setting in the `Find` pop-up window:

SETTING	DESCRIPTION
From	Searches the messages by the sender name. You don't need to type a complete sender name to find a match.
To/Cc	Searches for messages sent to an address or alias either directly or by Cc list.
To	Searches only for messages sent directly to an address; does not search for carbon copies.
Cc	Searches only for messages sent as carbon copies to an address or alias.
Subject	Searches for messages by subject.

After you fill out the search criteria text fields, click the left mouse button on one of the `Find` buttons located at the bottom of the `Find Messages` pop-up window. The `Find Forward` button selects the next message header that matches the specified information. The `Find Backward` button selects the previous message header with the specified information. The `Select All` button selects all message headers with the specified information. A status message displayed in the footer of the `Find Messages` window tells you how many messages are selected. The `Clear` button empties all text in the `Find Message` pop-up window's text fields.

Deleting Messages

Deleting messages that you no longer want from the `Mail Tool Header` window is easy. You can use the drag-and-drop method, the `Delete` button, or the `Delete` item from the `Edit` menu or `Messages` pop-up menu. To delete messages using the drag-and-drop method, select the mail message(s) you want, then drag and drop the mail message headers onto the

`Waste` icon or `Wastebasket` window. Remember, a file is not deleted from the `Wastebasket` window until you actually specify that the file be deleted.

To delete messages from the `Mail Tool Header` window using the `Delete` button or item, do the following:

1. Select the headers for messages you want to delete. Click the left button to select the first message, then click the middle button on each subsequent message to either add it to the group or remove it if it is already selected.

2. Click on the `Delete` button or choose the `Delete` item from either the `Edit` or `Messages` pop-up menu. The selected messages are deleted, and the status message in the footer reflects the current state of your `Mail Tool Header` window.

Undeleting Messages

If you deleted a message using the `Delete` item from either the `Edit` menu or `Messages` pop-up menu, and you have not chosen the `Save Changes` or `Done` items from the `File` menu, or the `Done` button, the deleted messages remain available for you to undelete. When no deleted messages are available, the `Undelete` item in the `Edit` or `Messages` menu appears dimmed.

NOTE

Remember, if you deleted a message by dragging and dropping the header to the `Waste` icon or `Wastebasket` window, and you have not deleted the file, the file is still available in the `Wastebasket` window.

To undelete all the deleted messages, choose `Undelete` from the `Messages` pop-up menu or the `Edit` menu. You can also selectively undelete messages, as follows:

1. Choose `From List` in the `Edit` menu's `Undelete` submenu. The `Undelete` pop-up window appears, displaying a list of messages you have deleted since you last saved changes in the Mail Tool (Figure 3.17).

2. Select the headers you want to undelete. Click the left mouse button on the message header you want to undelete. Select additional message headers by clicking the middle mouse button on the message header. To unselect a message header, click the middle mouse button on the mail message header.

3. Click the left mouse button on the `Undelete` button in the bottom of the `Undelete` pop-up window.

FIGURE 3.17

The Mail Tool Undelete pop-up window

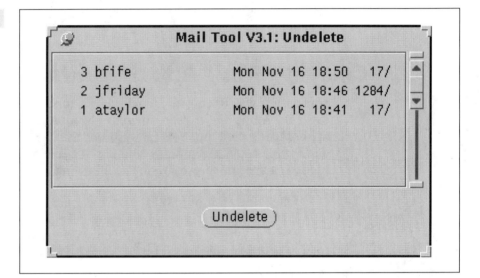

Printing Messages

Mail messages can be printed directly from the `Mail Tool Header` window using the `Print` item from the `File` menu or `Messages` pop-up menu. To print messages, first select the headers for the messages you want to print, then choose the `Print` item from the `File` menu or the `Messages` pop-up menu. The message is printed to the default printer for your system. The way to customize how your messages are printed is explained later in this chapter. Mail messages can also be printed by dragging and dropping messages from the `Mail Tool Header` window to the Print Tool's drag-and-drop target.

Working with Attachments

The Mail Tool allows you to manage mail message attachments from either the `Mail Tool Header` or `Compose Message` window. You can copy an attachment to store the file separately from the mail message, as well as rename or delete an attachment.

Copying Mail Attachments

The easiest way to copy an attachment is to simply drag and drop it into the File Manager or any other application that accepts files of the attachment's file type. You can also use the `Export Attachment` pop-up window to copy attachments to a specific directory. To copy an attachment to a specific directory, do the following:

1. Click the left mouse button on the attachment you want to copy. The attachment is then highlighted. To copy more than one attachment at a time, click the middle mouse button on each additional attachment that you want to copy.

2. Press the right mouse button on the `File` button at the top of the `Attachments` pane and choose `Copy Out`. The `Export Attachment` pop-up window is displayed.

3. In the `Export Attachment` pop-up window, type the name of the directory to which you want to copy the attachments in the `Directory` text field, and click the left mouse button on the `Export` button.

Renaming Mail Attachments

An attachment file can be renamed using the standard file name conventions used in the File Manager. You can only rename one attachment at a time. Follow these steps to rename a mail attachment in the `Attachments` pane:

1. Click the left mouse button on the attachment you want to rename. The attachment is highlighted.

2. Press the right mouse button on the `Edit` button at the top of the `Attachments` pane and choose `Rename`. The `Rename Attachment` pop-up window is displayed.

3. Type the new attachment name in the `Name` text field.

4. Click the left mouse button in the `Rename` button. The attachment file in the `Attachments` pane is renamed.

Deleting Mail Attachments

The easiest way to delete a mail attachment is to drag and drop the attachment icon from the `Attachments` pane to the `Waste` icon or `Wastebasket` window.

To delete a mail message attachment using the `Delete` item from the `Attachments` pane's `Edit` menu, click the left mouse button on the first attachment you want to delete. If you want to delete more than one attachment, click the middle mouse button on each additional attachment. Press the right mouse button on the `Edit` button at the top of the `Attachments` pane and choose `Delete`. The selected attachment or attachments are deleted from the mail message. You can use the `Undelete` item to restore the most recently deleted attachment.

Forwarding Mail

If you receive mail that you want to send to another user, you can forward it by selecting the mail message or messages and using the `Forward` item in the `Compose` menu of the `Mail Tool Header` window. When you forward a mail message, a `Compose Message` window opens, with the selected message appearing in the text pane and the subject field filled in. You can then forward the mail message by specifying the recipient of the forwarded message in the To text field. A carbon copy of the message can also be sent to another user by entering the person's name in the field labeled Cc.

Vacation Mail

When you are away from your terminal for an extended period of time, you can use the Mail Tool's Vacation feature to notify anyone sending you mail that you are not available to read it. When a user sends you a message, your Mail Tool automatically sends the user a reply indicating you are not available to read the message.

To display the Vacation Setup pop-up window, choose the Start/Change item from the Vacation submenu in the Mail Tool Header window's Compose menu. The default Start/Change item is chosen from the Vacation submenu and the Vacation Setup window appears (Figure 3.18).

You can edit the message template in the Vacation Setup pop-up window in the same way you edit messages in the Compose Messages window. The "$SUBJECT" string in the message text automatically extracts the subject from the message sent by the sender and includes it as part of the Vacation item's reply message.

To start the vacation reply message, click the left mouse button on the Start button. The word Vacation is displayed in the header of the Mail Tool Header window to remind you that Vacation mail is turned on. Incoming messages are stored in your In-Box and are readily available when you return to the office.

Once you've activated the Vacation mail feature, the Stop item on the Vacation submenu is available and becomes the new default setting. To stop Vacation mail, choose the Stop item from the Vacation submenu. If you decide you don't want to activate Vacation mail, choose Dismiss from the Window pop-up menu.

FIGURE 3.18

The Vacation Setup
pop-up window

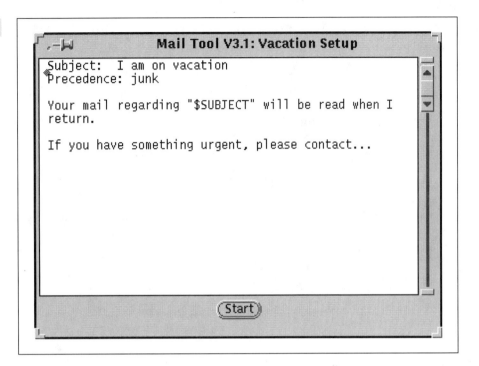

Mail Tool V3.1: Vacation Setup

```
Subject:  I am on vacation
Precedence: junk

Your mail regarding "$SUBJECT" will be read when I
return.

If you have something urgent, please contact...
```

(Start)

Using Mail Tool Templates

The Mail Tool allows you to use template files to create boilerplate messages of frequently used text such as a standard office memo. Each template is a text file that you can create using the DeskSet's Text Editor application, then add as an item on the **Templates** submenu of the **Compose Message** window's **Include** menu. Chapter 4, "Using the Text Editor, Shell Tool, and Command Tool," explains how to create a text file using the DeskSet's Text Editor. The Mail Tool includes a Calendar template, which inserts text information that can be added to the recipient's appointment calendar using the DeskSet's Calendar Manager application. To add a template to the Mail Tool, you use the Mail Tool's

Template Properties pop-up window, as explained in the "Template Properties" section later in this chapter.

To use a template as a basis for a mail message, press the right mouse button on the **Include** menu button in the **Compose Message** window and choose the template item you want from the **Templates** submenu. The template is inserted into the **Compose Message** window pane at the location of the insertion point. Figure 3.19 shows a sample template inserted in the **Compose Message** window text pane.

FIGURE 3.19

A sample template in the Compose Message window

```
Mail Tool V3.1: Compose Message

( Include ▾ )  ( Deliver ▾ )  ( Header ▾ )  ( Clear )  ( Voice... )

      To:
 Subject:
      Cc:

          ** Calendar Appointment **

          Date:    |>mm/dd/yy<|
          Start:   |>hh:mm pm<|
          End:     |>hh:mm pm<|
          What:    |>line 1<|
                   |>line 2<|
```

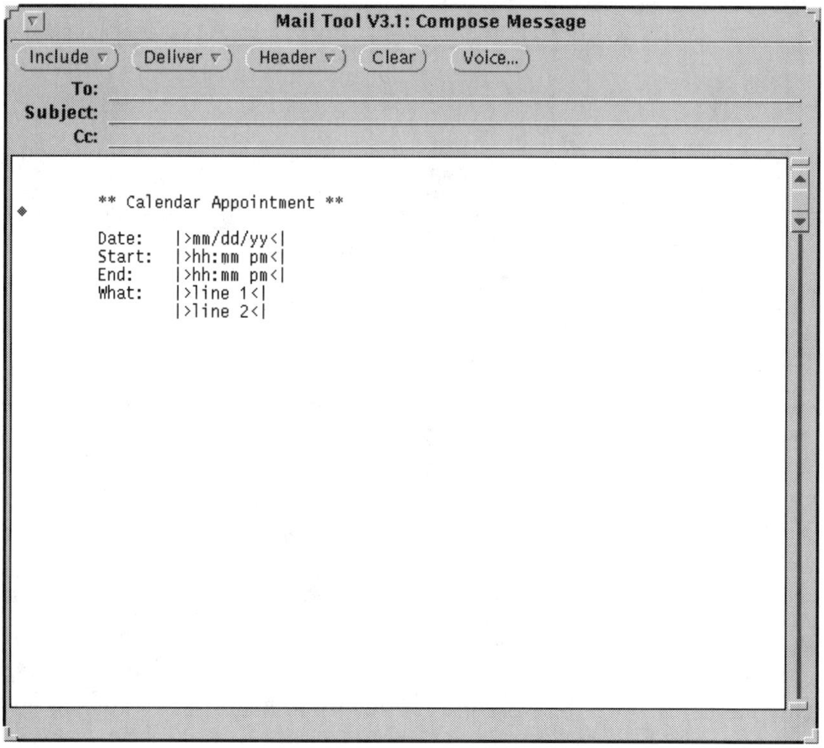

Working with Mail Files

As explained earlier, the `In-Box` is the default mail file (`/var/mail/user-name`) that receives and stores your incoming messages. Over time the `In-Box` becomes full of messages. While you can delete messages, it is better to save mail messages to another mail file. A mail file is a special file used by the Mail Tool for storing messages. Mail files allow you to store multiple messages in a single file. If you view a mail file outside of the Mail Tool, it looks like a single file with multiple messages appended to one another. When you view a mail file using the `Mail Tool Header` window, each separate message header is displayed in the header pane in the same way as messages from the `In-Box`. You can view, edit, delete, and respond to each message in any mail file in the same way you do for messages in the `In-Box`. The following sections explain how to manage your messages using the Mail Tool's mail file management features.

Specifying a Default Mail File Directory

By default, mail files are stored in your home directory. To keep your home directory organized, specify a new default mail file directory using the `Mail Filing Properties` window. To specify a new default directory for your mail files, do the following:

1. Choose `Properties` from the `Edit` menu in the `Mail Tool Header` window. The `Mail Tool Properties` pop-up window appears.

2. Choose `Mail Filing` from the `Category` menu (the abbreviated menu button in the upper-right corner of the window). The `Mail Filing Properties` window appears (Figure 3.20).

3. Enter the path for the directory where you want to store your mail files in the `Mail File Directory` text field. Unless a full path is specified, the directory you specify is considered a subdirectory of your home directory. In most cases, you want to create the directory in your home directory.

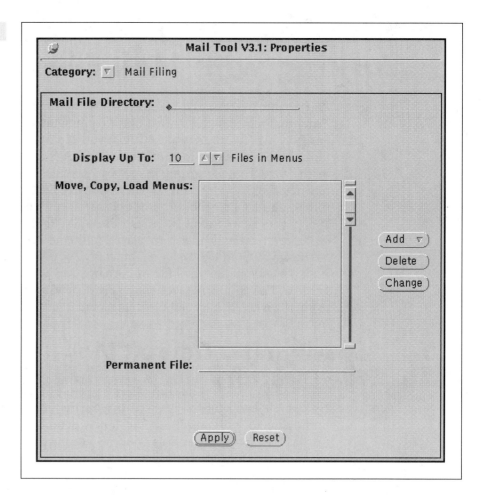

4. Click the left mouse button on the `Apply` button. If the directory
   name you specify does not exist, a Notice is displayed asking if
   you want to create the directory.

5. Click the left mouse button on the `Apply Changes` button.

The Mail Files Pop-up Window

The `Mail Files` pop-up window allows you to create, view, delete, and
rename mail files, and add messages to a mail file. To open the `Mail Files`

pop-up window (Figure 3.21), choose `Mail Files` from the `File` menu. The `Mail Files` pop-up window includes four menu buttons for working with mail files: `Save`, `Load`, `Create`, and `Edit`.

The scrolling list in the `Mail Files` pop-up window allows you to navigate directories and mail files in your default mail file directory. The scrolling list's first entry is your `In-Box` mail file. All files are indicated with a mailbox icon to the left of the name. If any folders are in the default mail file directory, they are listed after `In-Box` mail file with a folder icon appearing to the left of the folder name. Any additional files in the current directory are displayed after any subdirectories in the mail files scrolling list.

To navigate the `Mail Files` pop-up window's scrolling list, you can double-click on the folder icon to display any subdirectories and mail files in that directory. If you are in a subdirectory, the first entry in the list is

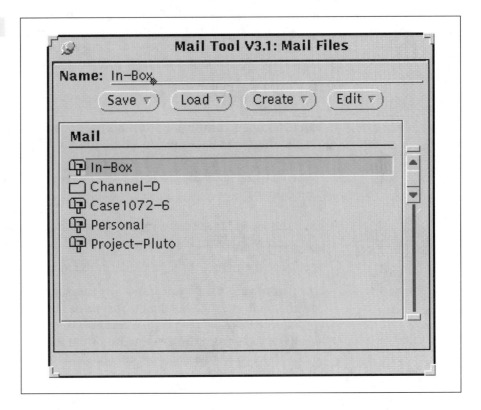

FIGURE 3.21

The Mail Files pop-up window

..(Go up 1 level). Press the right mouse button in the scrolling list to display the Scrolling List pop-up menu. If you are scrolling through a long list, choose the Locate Choice to return to the last selected file or folder.

Creating a New Mail File and Saving Messages in Mail Files

There are two ways to create a mail file and save messages to it. The easiest way is to use the Mail File text field in the Mail Tool Header window. In this procedure, you cannot create a new mail file without copying or moving messages. However, you can create a new mail file without having to copy or move mail messages by using the Mail Files pop-up window. To create a new mail file using the Mail File text field and copy or move multiple messages into it, do the following:

1. Type the name of the new mail file in the Mail File text field. For example, typing epistles will create a mail file named epistles.

2. Select the mail message headers from the Mail Tool Header window to move or copy to the new mail file.

3. Click the left mouse button on the Move or Copy button. The selected messages are moved or copied to the new mail file.

To create a new mail file using the Mail Files pop-up window, follow the steps below:

1. Choose Mail Files from the File menu in the Mail Tool Header window. The Mail Files pop-up window appears.

2. Type the name of the mail file in the Name text field.

3. If you want to copy or move any messages to the mail file, select the mail message headers from the Mail Tool Header window and choose Move Message into Mail File or Copy Message into Mail File from the Save menu in the Mail Files pop-up window. The selected messages are moved or copied to the new mail file.

Creating an Empty Mail File or Mail Files Directory

You can create subdirectories for storing mail files in the default mail directory or create a new, empty mail file using the `Mail Files` pop-up window, as follows:

1. Choose `Mail Files` from the `File` menu in the `Mail Tool Header` window.

2. Type the name of the new mail file or the new subdirectory in the `Name` text field. If you want to create a subdirectory to an existing directory listed in the `Mail Files` pop-up window's scrolling list, double-click on the folder name in the list to open the directory.

3. Choose either the `Mail File` or `Directory` item from the `Create` menu. The new mail file or directory is created and added to the scrolling list.

Saving Messages to an Existing Mail File

Additional mail messages can be added to a mail file at any time by using either the `Mail File` abbreviated menu button and the `Move` or `Copy` buttons in the `Mail Tool Header` window, or using the `Mail Files` pop-up window. To add messages to an existing mail file using the `Mail Tool Header` window, do the following:

1. Choose the name of the mail file to which you want to copy or move mail messages from the `Mail Files` menu by pressing the right mouse button on the abbreviated `Mail File` menu button. The mail file name appears in the `Mail File` text field.

2. Select the mail message headers in the `Mail Tool Header` window.

3. Click the left mouse button on the `Move` or `Copy` button. If there are messages already in the mail file, the newly added messages are appended to the existing messages.

To add messages to a mail file using the `Mail Files` pop-up window, do the following:

1. Choose the `Mail Files` item from the `File` menu in the `Mail Tool Header` window. The `Mail Files` pop-up window appears.

2. Click the left mouse button on the mail file name in the scrolling list.

3. Select the mail message headers to be moved or copied to the new mail file from the `Mail Tool Header` window.

4. Choose `Move Message into Mail File` or `Copy Message into Mail File` from the `Save` menu in the `Mail Files` pop-up window. The selected messages are moved or copied to the new mail file.

Loading Mail Files in the Mail Tool Header Window

Any mail file can be loaded into the `Mail Tool Header` window so you can work with its contents. By loading a mail file into the `Mail Tool Header` window you can perform all the tasks that you can with the `In-Box` messages, such as deleting, printing, and sorting messages. In addition, loading a mail file into the `Mail Tool Header` window allows you to move or copy messages from it to another mail file specified in the `Mail File` text field or using the `Mail Files` pop-up window.

You can load mail files using three different methods: using the `Mail File` text field and `Load` button in the `Mail Tool Header` window, using the `Mail Files` pop-up window, or dragging and dropping mail files from the File Manager to the `Mail Tool Header` window.

To load a mail file into the `Mail Tool Header` window using the `Mail Files` pop-up window, do the following:

1. Choose `Mail Files` from the `File` menu in the `Mail Tool Header` window. The `Mail Files` pop-up window appears.

2. Double-click on the mail file name that you want to load from the scrolling list. The mail message headers in that mail file will appear in the **Mail Tool Header** window. You can double-click on another mail file to display its mail headers in the **Mail Tool Header** window, replacing the previous mail file's contents.

To load a mail file into the **Mail Tool Header** window, do the following:

1. Press the right mouse button on the **Mail File** abbreviated menu button and choose the mail file you want to view. The mail file name appears in the **Mail File** text field.

2. Click the left mouse button on the **Load** button. All the messages saved to that mail file appear, as mail headers, in the **Mail Tool Header** window.

A mail file can be loaded from the **Mail Files** pop-up window or by dragging and dropping a mail file from the File Manager to the **Mail Tool Header** window. A mail file icon appears as a stack of envelopes in the File Manager's file pane, as shown in Figure 3.22. To load a mail file from the

FIGURE 3.22

Mail file incons in the File Manager's file pane

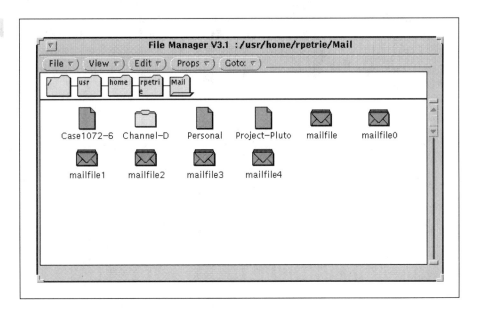

File Manager, do the following:

1. With the File Manager window open, navigate to the default mail file directory in your home directory.

2. Press the left mouse button on the mail file icon and drag it to the `Mail Tool Header` window's headers pane. The pointer changes to a target.

3. Drop the mail file icon onto the `Header` pane. The message headers in the mail file appear.

Managing Your Mail Files

You can empty a mail file, rename it, or delete it with the `Edit` menu of the `Mail Files` pop-up window. To empty, rename, or delete a mail file, you need to first select the mail file in the scrolling list in the `Mail Files` pop-up window. You can only work with one file at a time in the `Mail Files` pop-up window. If the mail file is in a subdirectory below the one displayed on the scrolling list, double-click the left mouse button on that subdirectory to display it. If the mail file is in a directory higher up from the one displayed in the scrolling list, double-click the left mouse button on the (`Go up 1 level`) folder item until the mail file you want is in the scrolling list. When the mail file is in the scrolling list, click the left mouse button on the mail file to select it.

To delete a mail file, select the mail file in the scrolling list. Then choose `Delete` from the `Edit` menu. The Mail Tool asks you to confirm that you want to delete the mail file. Click the left mouse button on the `Delete Mail File` button to delete the mail file.

To empty a mail file, select the mail file in the scrolling list. Then choose `Empty` from the `Edit` menu. The Mail Tool asks you to confirm that you want to empty the mail file. Click the left mouse button on the `Empty Mail File` button to empty the mail file.

To rename a mail file, select the mail file in the scrolling list, type the new name in the `Name` field, then choose `Rename` from the `Edit` menu.

Customizing the Mail Tool

The **Mail Tool Properties** pop-up window allows you to customize a wide variety of the Mail Tool's settings. To display the **Mail Tool Properties** window, choose **Properties** from the **Edit** menu. The **Mail Tool Properties** window appears (Figure 3.23).

FIGURE 3.23

The Mail Tool Properties pop-up window

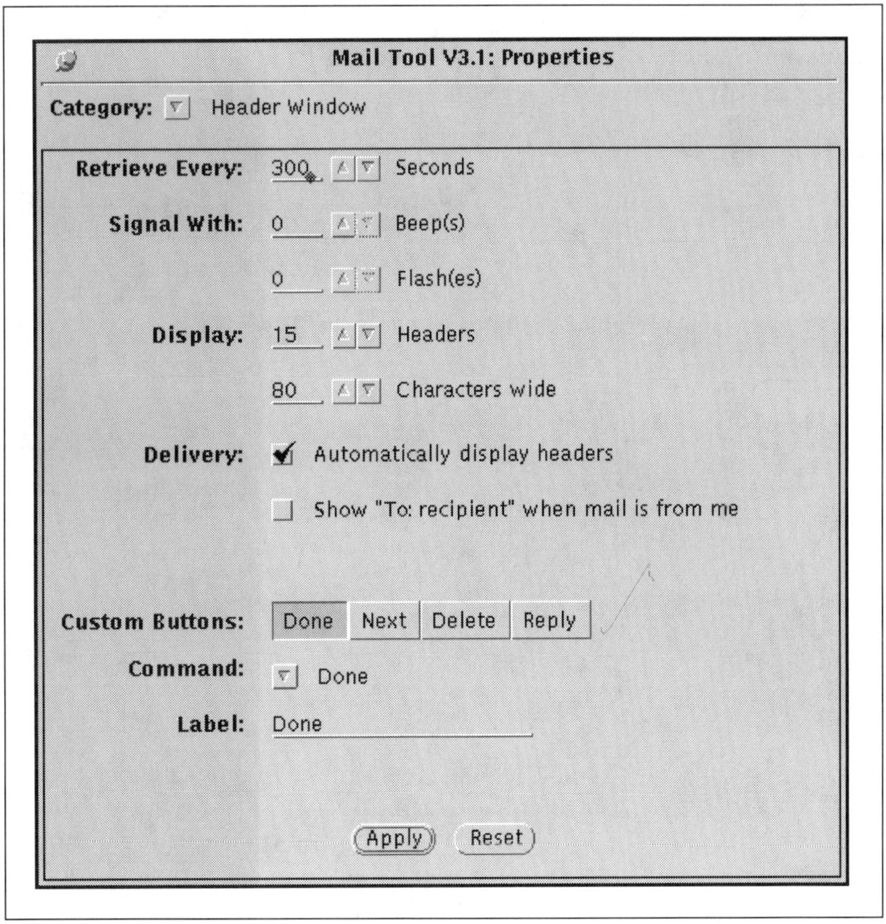

To display the menu that lists the categories of properties you can customize, click the right mouse button on the **Category** menu button. The **Category** menu (Figure 3.24) lists seven items: **Header Window**, **Message Window**, **Compose Window**, **Mail Filing**, **Template**, **Alias**, and **Expert**. Each of these menu items displays a pop-up window containing buttons and text fields for setting the category properties. To display the **Category** menu and choose a category item, press the right mouse button on the **Category** menu button and choose the category you want to change.

FIGURE 3.24

The Category menu

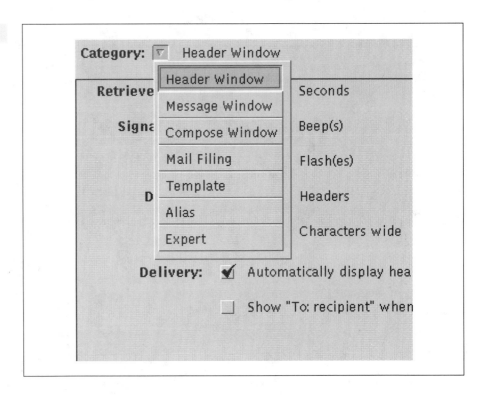

To save changes you make in any category window, click the left mouse button on the **Apply** button. If you want to cancel any changes you made, click the left mouse button on the **Reset** button. The properties window returns to their previous settings. But please note, if you click on the **Apply** button, you cannot reset your settings. If you make changes in any of the categories and attempt to leave the category without clicking the **Apply**

button, a Notice appears prompting you to save your changes. Click the left mouse button on the `Apply Changes` button to save your changes.

Header Window Properties

The `Header Window Properties` window is the default category that appears when the `Mail Tool Properties` window is opened (Figure 3.23). It allows you to change settings for the `Mail Tool Header` window. These settings include how often the Mail Tool checks for new mail, the way you are notified when new mail arrives, and whether headers are automatically displayed for new mail messages. You can also define the custom buttons that appear in the bottom row of the control area in the `Mail Tool Header` window, using the `Custom Buttons`, `Command`, and `Label` settings, as explained in the next section. The following explains the remaining settings in the `Mail Tool Properties` window.

SETTING	DESCRIPTION
`Retrieve Every`	Determines how often new mail is automatically retrieved. The default value is 300 seconds, or 5 minutes. To increase or decrease the number of seconds between mail checks, type a number in the numeric field or click the left mouse button on the appropriate scroll button to the left of the field.
`Signal With`	Determines how the Mail Tool signals that new mail has arrived. The `Beep(s)` setting causes the Mail Tool to beep the specified number of times when there is incoming mail. The `Flash(es)` setting causes the Mail Tool icon or the `Mail Tool Header` window to flash when there is incoming mail. To increase or decrease the number of beeps or flashes that signal the arrival of mail, type a number in the numeric field or click the left mouse button on the appropriate scroll button.

SETTING	DESCRIPTION
Display	The `Headers` setting determines how many headers are displayed in the `Mail Tool Header` window. The `Characters` setting determines the width of all Mail Tool panes and windows. To increase or decrease the number of headers to display or the number of characters wide, type a number in the numeric field or click the left mouse button on the appropriate scroll button.
Delivery	The `Automatically display headers` setting determines if the Mail Tool automatically displays or does not display the headers of incoming messages in the `Mail Tool Header` window. If you do not choose this option, the Mail Tool does not display headers for incoming messages unless you specifically request them by choosing `Load In-Box` or `Save Changes` from the `File` menu. If the `Show "To: recipient" when mail is from me` setting is checked, the header of the message sent to you will display who you sent the message to instead of your email address.

Customizing Mail Tool Buttons

The first four buttons on the second row of the `Mail Tool Header` window are custom buttons. These buttons can be changed to any of the items in the `File`, `View`, `Edit`, or `Compose` menus. If these menus contain items that you frequently use, you can change your custom buttons to easily access those items.

The `Custom Buttons` settings (`Done`, `Next`, `Delete`, and `Reply`) indicate the current four custom buttons that appear in the control area of the `Mail Tool Header` window, from left to right.

The `Command` abbreviated menu button provides a menu of all of the available commands from the `File`, `View`, `Edit`, and `Compose` menus (Figure 3.25). The first column in the `Command` menu displays all of the choices available from the `File` menu, the second column displays the choices from the `View` menu, the third displays the choices from the `Edit` menu, and the last column displays the choices from the `Compose` menu.

If space allows, the selected menu item name automatically becomes the custom button label. The `Label` text field allows you to change the label of a custom button.

FIGURE 3.25

The Command menu

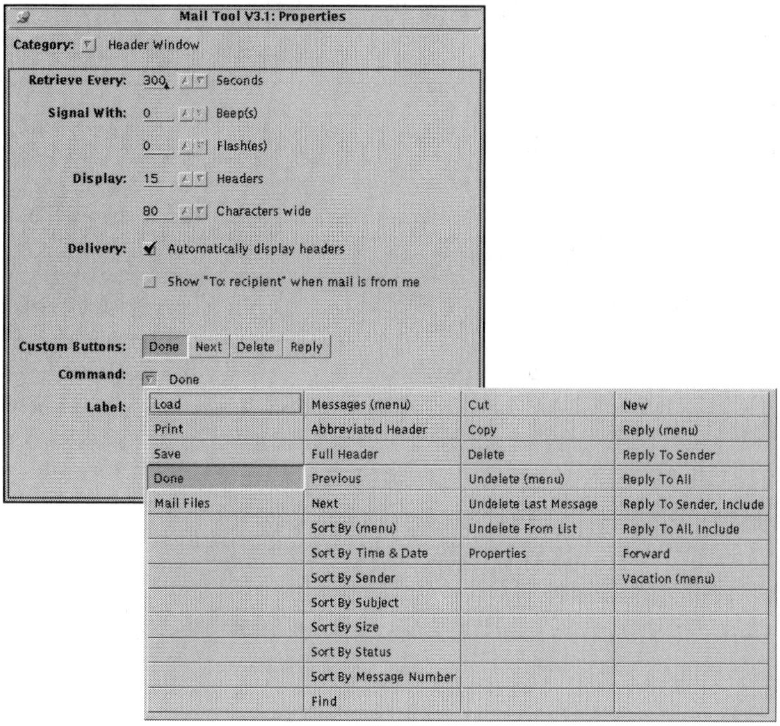

The following steps explain how to change a custom button.

1. Display the **Header Window Properties** window, if it's not already displayed.

2. Click the left mouse button on the **Custom Buttons** setting that you want to change.

3. Click the right mouse button on the **Command** menu button and click the left mouse button on the new command.

4. If you want, enter a new label for the selected command in the **Label** text field.

5. Click the left mouse button on the **Apply** button to change the custom button in the **Mail Tool Header** window. The changes are reflected in the current Mail Tool. Figure 3.26 shows new custom buttons appearing in the control area of the **Mail Tool Header** window.

FIGURE 3.26

New custom buttons added to the Mail Tool Header window

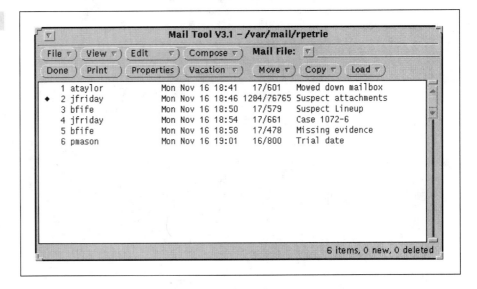

Message Window Properties

The **Message Window Properties** window, shown in Figure 3.27, allows you to define the number of lines in the **View Message** pop-up window text pane, use a different print script for printing messages, and determine the information *not* displayed when viewing a message with abbreviated headers. The following explains the settings in the **Message Window Properties** window.

FIGURE 3.27

The Message Window Properties pop-up window

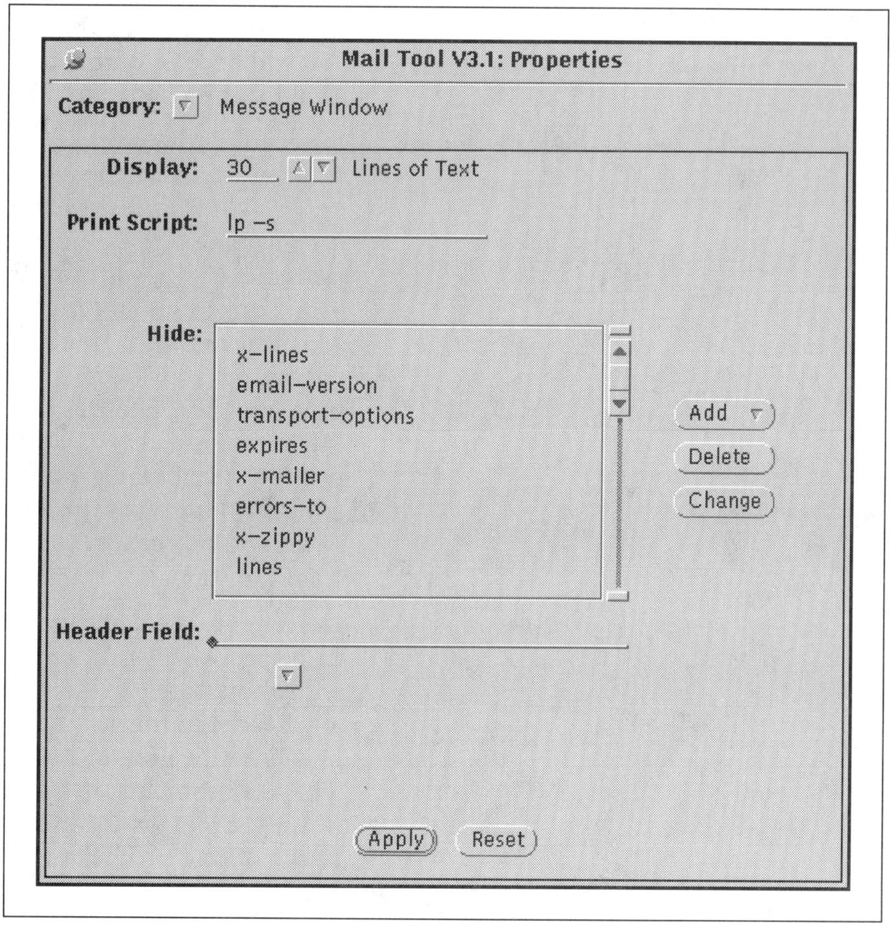

SETTING	DESCRIPTION
Display	Determines the number of lines of text displayed in each **View Message** window text pane. The default setting is 30 lines of text. To increase or decrease the number of lines, type a number in the numeric field or click the left mouse button on the appropriate scroll button. After you click the left mouse button on the **Apply** button to change this field, you will need to quit and restart the Mail Tool for this change to take effect.
Print Script	Determines the print script used to print your messages when you choose the **Print** item from the **File** menu or the **Header** pane pop-up menu. For example, if you want to use the same print script used in the File Manager, which prints with a fancy border containing your name and the current time and date, enter `cat $FILE	mp -lo	lp`. If you are using a PostScript printer, specify the printer type by adding `-T postscript` argument to the `lp` command (`cat $FILE | mp -lo | lp -T postscript`).
Hide	Determines which headers are not displayed when you view your messages with abbreviated headers. You can add any header to this list by typing the header in the **Header Field** text field. The **Add** submenu lets you place the header **Before** or **After** the currently selected header. The **Delete** button removes the selected headers, and the **Change** button allows you to edit the selected header's text typed in the **Header Field** text field.

SETTING	DESCRIPTION
`Header Field`	Allows you to add any header to the `Hide` scrolling list.

Compose Window Properties

The `Compose Window Properties` window, shown in Figure 3.28, allows you to customize several settings for the `Compose Message` window. The `Included Text Marker` text field specifies the characters that precede each line of an included text message. These are referred to as indent characters.

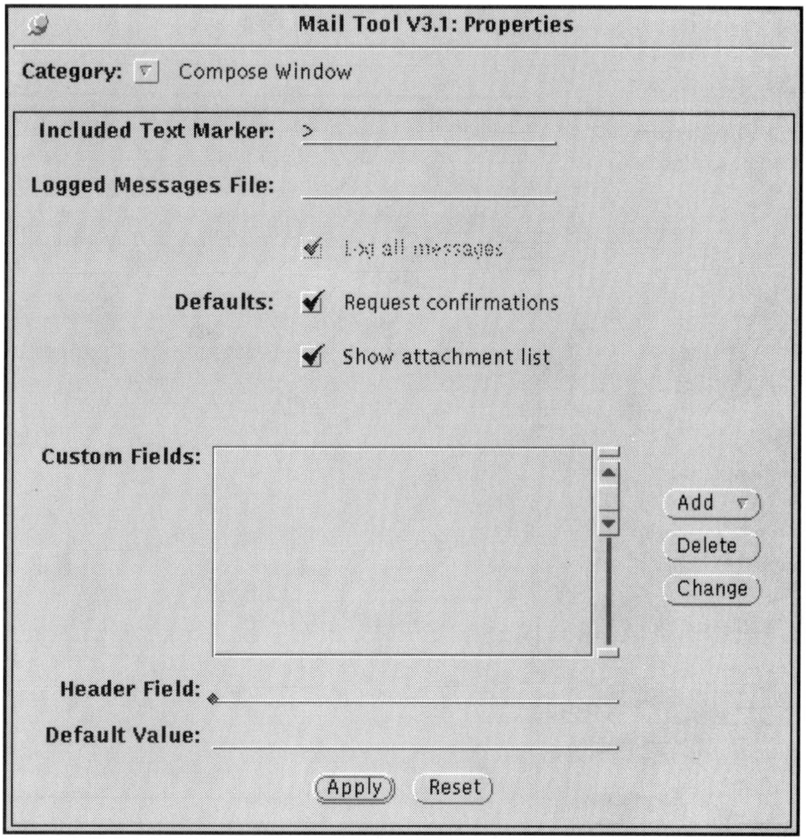

Mail Tool V3.1: Properties
Category:
Compose Window
Included Text Marker:
>
Logged Messages File:
Log all messages
Defaults:
Request confirmations
Show attachment list
Custom Fields:
Add
Delete
Change
Header Field:
Default Value:
Apply
Reset

FIGURE 3.28

The Compose Window Properties pop-up window

The default is a greater-than sign (>). This puts the greater-than sign character at the start of the included message when you choose `Indented` from the `Include` menu of the `Compose Message` window. A different indent character can be specified by typing a new character in the `Included Text Marker` text field.

The `Logged Messages File` text field allows you to specify the name of a log file to log outgoing mail messages. If a log file is specified, the `Log` check box appears on the `Compose Message` window, as shown in Figure 3.29. When the `Log` check box is checked on your `Compose Message` window, the message is logged into the log file when it is sent. The log file lists who the message is from, the recipient of the message, the character set used to create the message, the number of characters and lines contained in the message, and the entire message. Use the `Log all messages`

FIGURE 3.29

The Log check box in the Compose Message window

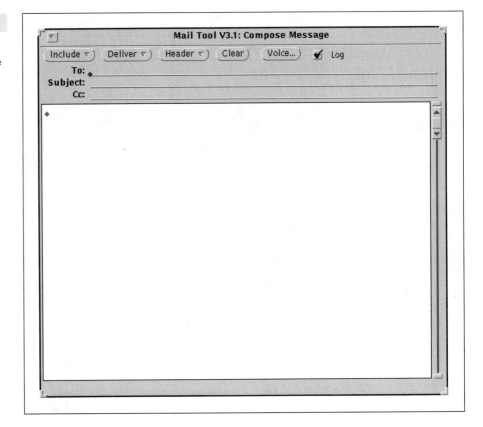

setting in the `Compose Window Properties` window to determine whether the `Log` check box in the `Compose Message` window is checked by default.

The `Defaults` setting's `Request confirmations` option determines if a Notice is displayed prompting you to confirm an operation or save any changes made in the following situations:

- When you have text or attachments in the `Compose Message` window and you choose the `Clear` button.

- When you have text or attachments in the `Compose Message` window and you quit the window.

- When you have made changes to a message in the `View Message` window, and you then display a new message, unpin the `View Message` window, or receive new incoming mail.

WARNING

If the Request Confirmations setting is not checked, any editing changes in the `View Message` window are automatically incorporated without notification. If you remove or change the `From` header of a message, your mail file will be corrupted and the message appended to the previous message in the mail file.

By default, a `Compose Message` window includes a pane at the bottom of the text area where you can add attachments to your message. If you rarely use attachments, you can use the `Show Attachment List` setting to specify whether the attachment pane is shown or not shown. If you turn off the default `Show Attachment List` setting, you can display the attachments pane on an as-needed basis by choosing `Show Attachments` from the `Include` menu.

Creating Custom Header Fields

The header of the `Compose Message` window always has `To`, `Subject`, and `Cc` header fields. A custom header field can be added to the `Header` menu in the `Compose Message` window by adding it to the `Custom Fields` scrolling list in the `Compose Window Properties` window. The following are some helpful predefined headers you can add to the headers menu.

HEADER FIELD	DEFAULT VALUE	DESCRIPTION
Precedence	junk	If the mail system cannot send a message with this header, no notices are sent to inform you that the message was not deliverable. This header can help keep mail notifications from cluttering up your mail file. However, it also keeps you from being informed that you entered an incorrect email address.
Reply-To	username @machinename	When you reply to a message containing this header, the reply is sent to the user specified instead of the sender of the message.
Return-Receipt-To	*yourusername* *@yourmachinename*	Similar to registered mail, adding this header informs the mail system to send you a transcript of the message after the message you sent is received. This header is useful for verifying that messages are received.

Any other custom headers you enter are added as text. The custom header is displayed in the header area of the **Compose Message** window. Figure 3.30 shows custom headers added to the **Header** menu in the **Compose Message** window. The following explains how to add the Return-Receipt-To header to the **Header** menu:

1. Type Return-Receipt-To in the **Header Field** text field in the **Compose Window Properties** window. A colon is automatically added to the end of the added text field.

2. Type your user name in the **Default Value** field.

FIGURE 3.30

The Header menu with custom header items

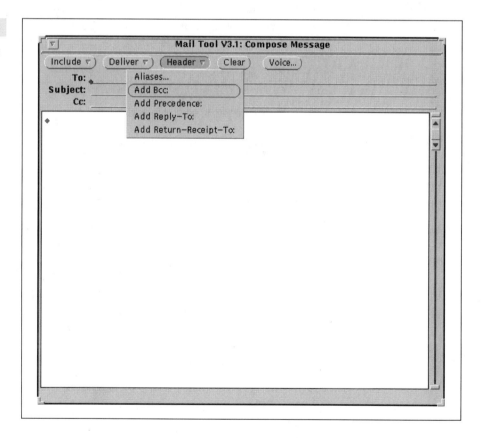

3. Click the left mouse button on the **Add** button. If you have other custom header fields displayed in the **Custom Fields** scrolling list, you can specify where you want to place the new custom header. Click the left mouse button on the custom header in the list you want your new entry before or after. Press the right mouse button on the **Add** button and choose either **Before** or **After**.

4. Click the left mouse button on the **Apply** button. The changes become effective immediately, adding the custom field to the **Header** menu of the **Compose Message** window.

To change a custom field, click the left mouse button on the item in the **Custom Fields** scrolling list, type the new values in the **Header Field** and **Default Value** text fields, click the left mouse button on the **Change** button, then click the left mouse button on the **Apply** button.

To delete a custom field, click the left mouse button on the item in the scrolling list, choose the **Delete** button, and click the left mouse button on **Apply**.

Mail Filing Properties

The **Mail Filing Properties** window (Figure 3.31) specifies where your mail files are stored and allows you to customize menus in the **Mail Tool Header** window. As explained earlier in this chapter, the **Mail File Directory** text field allows you to specify the directory where mail files you create are stored. Unless a full path name is specified, the directory will be located in your home directory. In most cases, it is recommended you store your mail files in your home directory or a subdirectory of your home directory to make backup of your files easier. If the directory name you specify does not exist, after you choose the **Apply** button, a Notice will be displayed asking you if you want to create the directory.

The **Move**, **Copy**, and **Load** menus in the **Mail Tool Header** window display up to ten of the most recently accessed mail files. You can change the maximum number of files in menus by changing the **Display Up To** setting of the **Mail Filing Properties** window. To increase or decrease the number of items displayed in these menus, type a number in the numeric fields or click the left mouse button on the appropriate arrow button to the left of the field.

FIGURE 3.31

Mail Filing Properties
pop-up window

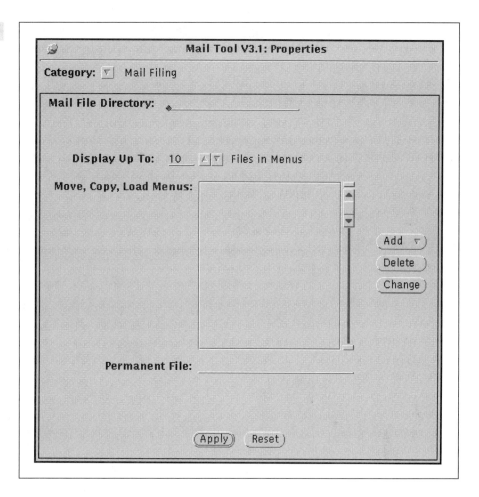

When you first start a new Mail Tool application, the Move, Copy, and Load menus are empty. Mail files are added to these menus as you access the mail files. You can specify mail files that you always want to appear at the top of these menus by adding them to the Move, Copy, Load Menus scrolling list setting.

To add any mail file to the list, type the name of the mail file in the Permanent File text field, then click the left mouse button on the Add button. If you already have mail files listed, select the mail file in the scrolling list that you want the new mail file to be listed before or after and choose Before or After from the Add submenu. The Delete button removes the currently selected mail file, and the `Change` button changes the currently selected mail file to the mail file typed in the `Permanent File` text field.

Template Properties

The Mail Tool allows you to use template files to create boilerplate messages of frequently used text such as a standard form letter. Each template is a text file that you create outside the Mail Tool. For example you can create a template using the DeskSet's `Text Editor`. Once you create a template, you use the `Template Properties` window (Figure 3.32) to add

FIGURE 3.32

The Template Properties pop-up window

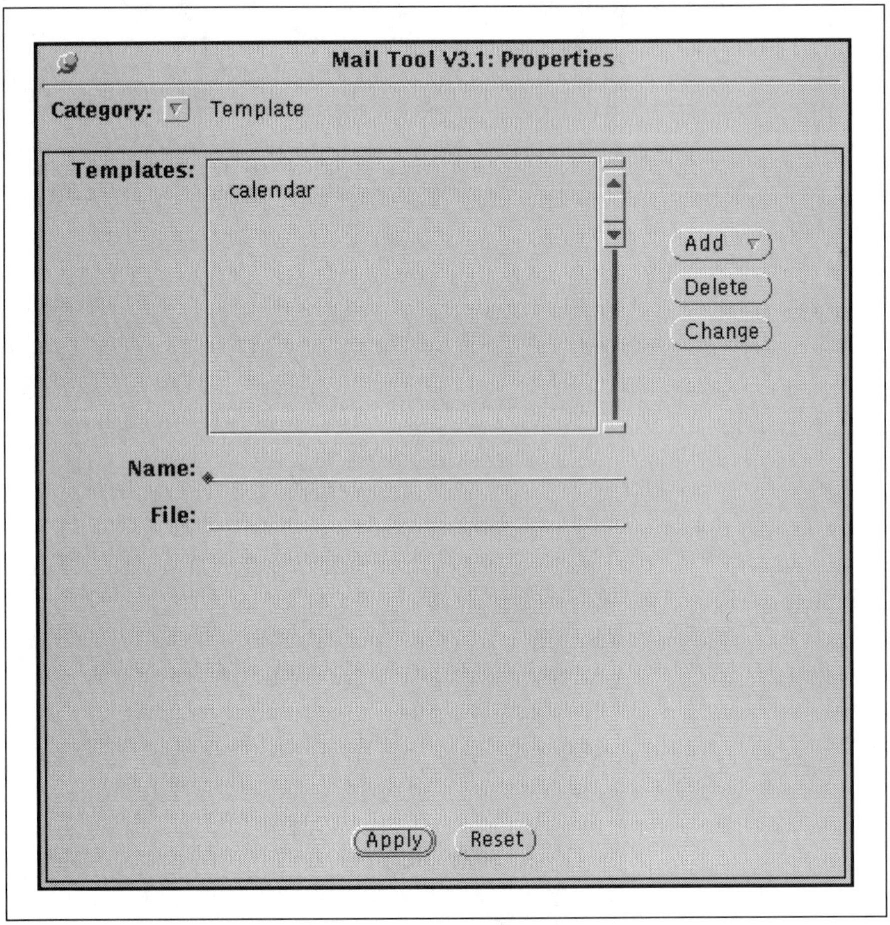

it as an item on the `Templates` submenu of the `Compose Message` window's `Include` menu. The following steps explain how to add a template to the `Templates` submenu in the `Compose Message` windows `Include` menu using the `Template Properties` window.

1. In the `Name` field in the `Template Properties` window, type the name of the template that you want displayed as an item in the `Include Templates` submenu of the `Compose Message` window.

2. Click the left mouse button in the `File` field and type the path and name of the file containing the template text. If the file is in your home directory, you can just enter the file name.

3. Press the right mouse button on the `Add` menu button and choose `Before` or `After`. If you select the `Before` item, the template name is inserted at the beginning of the templates list. If you select the `After` item, the template name is appended to the end of the list.

4. Click the left mouse button on the `Apply` button. The new template is placed in the scrolling list and added to the `Include Templates` submenu.

To delete a template name from the `Templates` submenu, first display the `Template Properties` window and click the left mouse button on the item in the scrolling list. Click the left mouse button on the `Delete` button.

Alias Properties

The `Alias Properties` window (Figure 3.33) allows you to create mail distribution lists of groups of users that you want to send a mail message to. Instead of repeatedly typing a list of names in the `To` or `Cc` text field, you only need to type the name you gave the alias in the `To` field in the `Compose Message` window. The alias name is replaced with the email addresses of all the users assigned to the alias.

The following explains how to create an alias that has more than one email address.

1. Type the alias name in the `Alias` text field in the `Alias Properties` window.

2. Type the email address of each person in the **Address** text field. Separate each name with a comma or a space.

3. Click the left mouse button on the **Add** button. If you have other **Aliases** displayed in the **Custom Fields** scrolling list, you can specify where you want to place the new custom header. Click the left mouse button on the custom header in the list you want your new entry before or after. Press the right mouse button on the **Add** button and choose either **Before** or **After**.

4. Click the left mouse button on the **Apply** button.

To change an alias, click the left mouse button on the item in the **Aliases** scrolling list, type the new value in the **Aliases** and **Addresses** text fields, click the left mouse button on the **Change** button, then click the left mouse button on the **Apply** button.

FIGURE 3.33

The Alias Properties
pop-up window

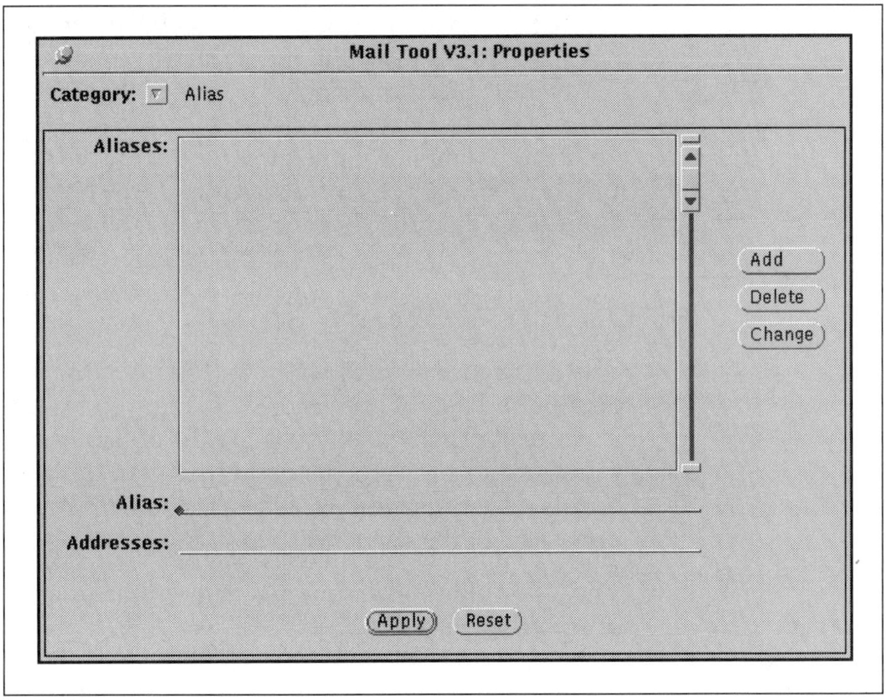

To delete an alias, click the left mouse button on the alias name in the **Aliases** scrolling list, choose the **Delete** button, and click the left mouse button on **Apply**.

Expert Properties

The **Expert Properties** window (Figure 3.34) includes settings that determine what happens when you choose the **To All** and **To All, Include** items from the **Compose** menu's **Reply** submenu in the **Compose**

FIGURE 3.34

The Expert Properties
pop-up window

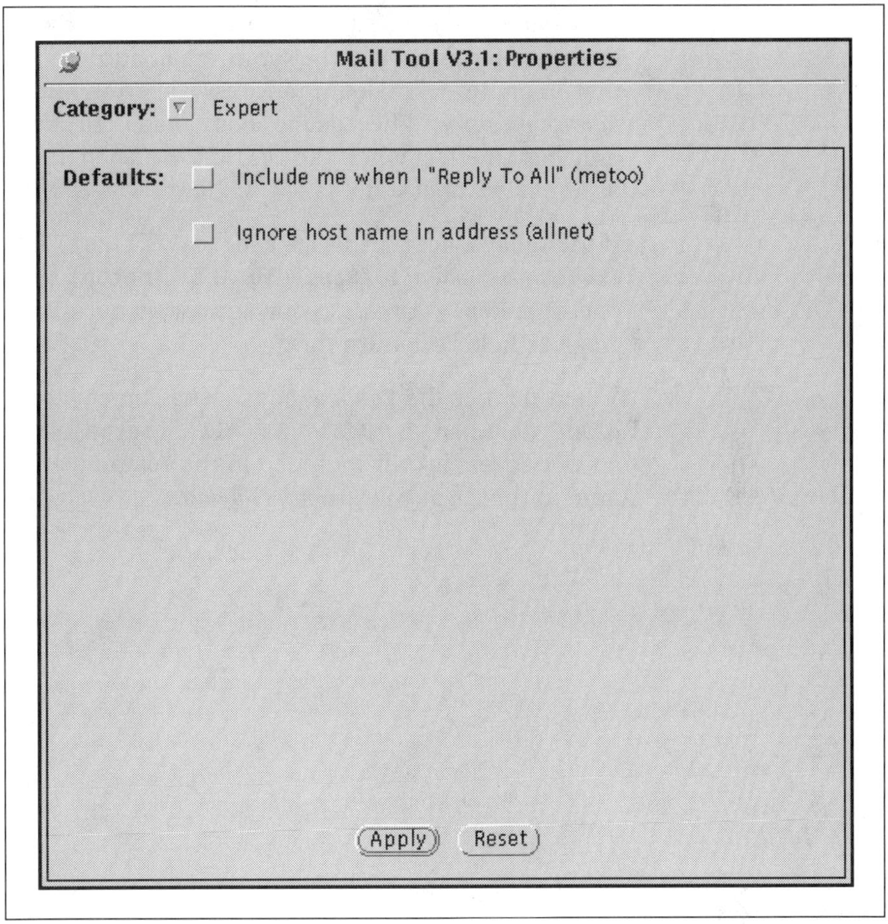

Mail Tool V3.1: Properties

Category: ▽ Expert

Defaults: ☐ Include me when I "Reply To All" (metoo)

☐ Ignore host name in address (allnet)

(Apply) (Reset)

`Message` window. These settings only apply when your email address appears in the `To` or `Cc` field's list of messages you are replying to.

If, when you do a Reply to All, the `Include me when I "Reply To All"` `(metoo)` setting is checked, and your email address appears in the `To` or `Cc` field, you will also receive the reply. Your email address is recognized in all forms that include your login address, such as *yourusername@machine* and *yourusername@host,* where "machine" is the name of your machine and "host" is the name of any host that is not your machine.

If the `Include me when I "Reply To All"` `(metoo)` setting is not checked, the message header of your reply depends on the `Ignore host name in` `address (allnet)` setting. The `Ignore host name in address (allnet)` setting determines whether your email address is recognized in all forms that include your login address, or only in the form of *youruser-name@machine.* The `Ignore host name in address (allnet)` setting only has an effect when the `Include me when I "Reply To All" (metoo)` option is *not* checked.

If the `Ignore host name in address (allnet)` setting is checked and the `Include me when I "Reply To All" (metoo)` setting is not checked, and you do a `Reply to All`, your address is not included in any form in the `To` or `Cc` fields of your reply.

When neither the `Ignore host name in address (allnet)` nor the `Include me when I "Reply To All" (metoo)` settings are checked, your email address is only included in the `To` and `Cc` fields of the `Reply to All` item in the form *yourusername@host.*

Using the Text Editor, Shell Tool, and Command Tool

THE DeskSet's Text Editor is an easy-to-use ASCII text editor that provides a friendly alternative to the SunOS vi editor. The Shell Tool and Command Tool let you easily access the SunOS command line without leaving the OpenWindows environment. Both tools are terminal emulators that allow you to work with the vast constellation of SunOS commands, which are explained in Part II, "Working from the SunOS Command Line." Because the DeskSet's Text Editor, Shell Tool, and Command Tool use similar commands, they are covered together in this chapter. In addition, this chapter also explains the DeskSet's `Console` window and the popular `xterm` window.

The Text Editor

The Text Editor simplifies creating and editing text files. It provides a friendly environment for working with text files. You can use the Text Editor to create text files as you would a word processor, or you can create programs to perform SunOS tasks. Once you create a text file using the Text Editor, you can easily cut and paste text directly between it and any other text pane in the DeskSet, such as the `Compose Message` window of the Mail Tool.

The Text Editor Window

The `Text Editor` window (Figure 4.1) has a control area that contains menu buttons and a text pane where you compose and edit text. The header of the `Text Editor` window always displays the path and the name of the file you are editing or the word `NONE` if you have not yet named your file. When you have made editing changes or have not yet saved a file, the word `edited` is displayed in parentheses following the file name. If you close the `Text Editor` window to an icon and you have created a new file but have not saved it, the icon displays the words `NO FILE`.

The rectangle located in the upper-right corner of the control area of the `Text Editor` window is the drag-and-drop target. You can drag text files directly from the File Manager to the drag-and-drop target to load them into the Text Editor or you can insert text or another text file into the

FIGURE 4.1

The Text Editor window and the Text Pane pop-up menu

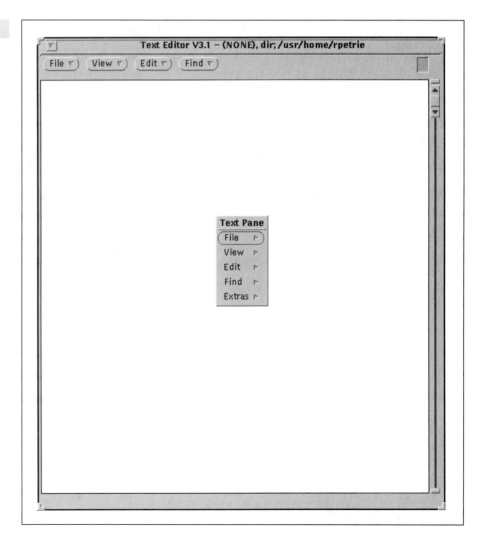

currently opened file by dragging and dropping a file in the Text Editor's text pane.

The control area of the `Text Editor` window has four menu buttons: `File`, `View`, `Edit`, and `Find`.

- The `File` menu includes items that allow you to load, save, merge, and clear text files.

- The `View` menu provides items for changing the position of the insert point, changing the portion of the file displayed in the text pane, and changing the Text Editor's line wrap feature.

- The `Edit` menu includes items for copying, moving, deleting, or undeleting text.

- The `Find` menu provides you with items to locate and replace any text selection in the text pane.

The text pane is the area in which you compose and edit your text. Placing the pointer inside the text pane and pressing the right mouse button displays the Text Editor's `Text Pane` pop-up menu. The `Text Pane` pop-up menu includes the same items as the menu buttons displayed in the Text Editor's control area, as well as an `Extras` submenu. The `Extras` submenu provides additional editing items, as explained later in this chapter. Figure 4.1 shows the `Text Editor` window and the `Text Pane` pop-up menu.

Starting the Text Editor and Loading Files

To start the Text Editor, press the right mouse button with the pointer anywhere in the Workspace to display the `Workspace` menu. Choose the `Text Editor` item from the `Programs` submenu. The `Text Editor` window appears on the Workspace. Move the pointer inside the text pane and click the left mouse button to activate the window. The insertion point appears as a black triangle, indicating the Text Editor is ready for you to enter text.

If you want to open the `Text Editor` window and load an existing file at the same time, move the pointer on the document file's icon in the File Manager and double-click the left mouse button. A `Text Editor` window is opened and the file is automatically loaded.

Loading Files Using the Drag-and-Drop Method

You can "drop" document file icons onto the `Text Editor` window's drag-and-drop target to *load* files into the Text Editor. Dragging and dropping a document file icon on the Workspace loads the document in the `Text Editor` window. You can also drop document file icons directly into the Text Editor pane to *insert* the file into an existing text file in the `Text Editor` window. Where you drop a document file determines how the `Text Editor` loads the file. If you want to open an existing file in the `Text Editor` window, drag the file icon to the drag-and-drop target (the rectangle located at the upper-right corner of the control area), and release the mouse button. If you want to insert the selected file into a file already loaded in the `Text Editor` window, drop the selected document file icon where you want the new text inserted.

Loading a File Using the File Menu

Another way to load a file into an open `Text Editor` window is to use the `Load File` item in the `File Menu` to display the `Load` pop-up window (Figure 4.2). To load a file using the `File` menu's `Load File` item, in the `Directory` text field, type the complete directory path and press Return. Type the name of the file you want to load in the `File` text field. Click the left mouse button on the `Load File` button. The file is loaded in the `Text Editor` window.

FIGURE 4.2

The Load pop-up window

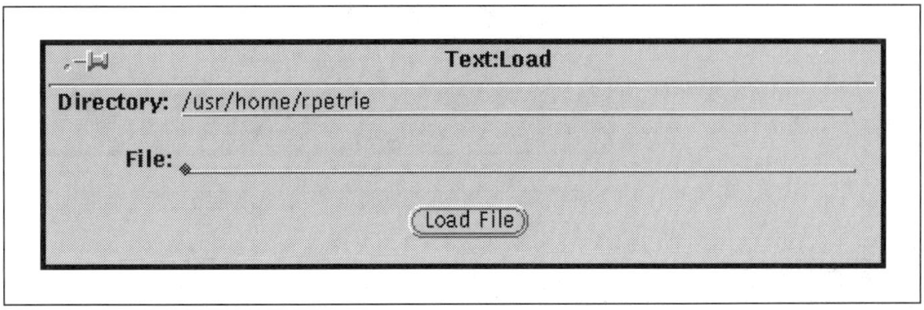

```
 ,-|+|                          Text:Load
Directory: /usr/home/rpetrie _____
     File: _____
                        ( Load File )
```

Saving a New or Existing Text File

If NONE is shown as the file name, click the left mouse button on the File menu button. This is the same as choosing the File menu's Store as New File item to display a Store pop-up window (Figure 4.3), so you can store the new file. To save the file, in the Directory text field, type the directory path and press Return. If you do not specify a directory, the Text Editor uses the current directory. In the File text field, type the name that you want for the file. Click the left mouse button on the Store as New File button to save the contents of the Text Editor pane.

Once you have named your file, the Text Editor icon shows the first ten characters of the file name. When the file has been edited and you have not saved changes, the file name is preceded by a > symbol. Figure 4.4 shows an example of a named and edited file Text Editor icon.

The Save Current File item in the File menu saves changes to a named and edited file. Use the Save Current File item to save the contents of the Text Editor pane that has previously been saved. Remember that the name of the file is always displayed in the Text Editor's window header followed by the directory path name.

FIGURE 4.3

The Store pop-up window

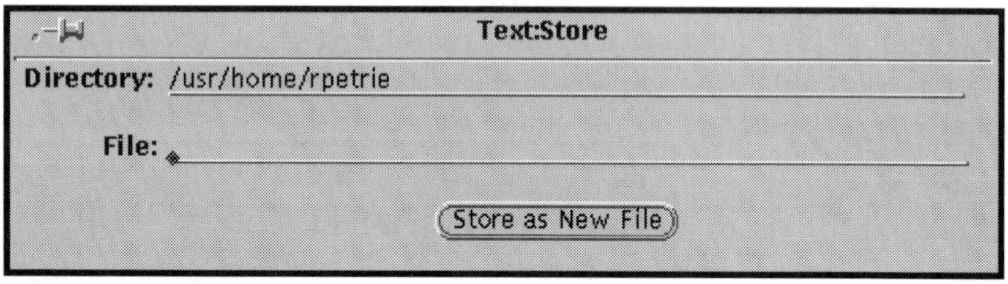

Text:Store

Directory: /usr/home/rpetrie

File:

(Store as New File)

FIGURE 4.4

Text Editor icon of an edited, named, but not saved, file

>sunspot

Entering and Selecting Text

Entering text is as easy as pointing to the location in the text pane where you want to add text, clicking the left mouse button then typing your text. By default, the Text Editor wraps at the word closest to window border.

You can easily select text in the Text Editor, so you can perform a variety of editing tasks such as copying or deleting. Selected text is highlighted in reverse video (white on black). If you type a character, the highlighted text is deleted and replaced with the typed character. The following list explains different methods of selecting text in a text pane.

SELECTION	OPERATION
Word	Double-click the left mouse button on the word you want to select.
Line	Click the left mouse button three times on the line you want to select.
Block of text	Click the left mouse button to set the insert point at the beginning of your text selection, move the pointer to the end of the selection, then click the middle mouse button.
Entire document	Click the left mouse button four times anywhere in the document.

You can also make a selection smaller by moving the pointer into the highlighted text where you want to end the selection and clicking the middle mouse button. Reducing a selection may not always work exactly as you expect because the adjustment depends on the method of the original selection and the starting position of the insert point.

Controlling the Position of the Insert Point

You can move the insert point anywhere in a text file by using the scrollbar to navigate to any location in the file then clicking the left mouse button.

You can also use the View menu, which provides three items for controlling the position of the insert point in a text file, or you can use the navigation keys on the numeric keypad on your keyboard.

The following describes the three items in the View menu used for controlling the position of the insert point.

ITEM	RESULT
Select Line at Number	Moves the cursor to the line number you specify. You can move the insertion point to any line in your text file by choosing the Select Line at Number item to display the Line Number pop-up window, as shown in Figure 4.5. Type the number of the line that you want selected, and click the left mouse button on the Select Line at Number button. The text on the specified line is selected, and the insertion point is moved to the beginning of the next line.
What Line Number?	Displays the line number of the selected text. The What Line Number? item allows you to locate the line number where the selected text begins. The line number is displayed in a Notice. When there is no current selection in the Text Editor window, the notice box displays an error message instead of a line number.
Show Caret at Top	Moves the insert pointer to the third line from the top of the *next* pane of text.

You can also use the keyboard to move the insert point to different positions in your text file. The following describes how to use keys to move the insert point.

FIGURE 4.5

The Line Number
pop-up window

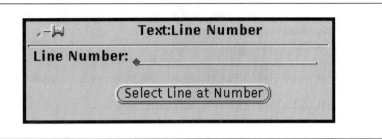

KEY	MOVES THE INSERT POINT
← or Control-B	One character to the left
→ or Control-F	One character to the right
Control-, (comma)	One word to the left
Control-. (period)	To the end of a word
Control-A	To the start of a line
Control-E	To the end of the line
↑ or Control-P	Up one line
↓ or Control-N	Down one line
Home or Shift-Control-Return	To beginning of text
End or Control-Return	To end of text

Copying, Moving, and Deleting Text

The **Edit** menu and the text pane's **Edit** submenu provide you with standard editing functions to copy, move, and delete text. Figure 4.6 shows the **Edit** menu and the text pane's **Edit** submenu. You can also perform any edit operations using the accelerator keys on the left side of most Sun keyboards. These keys are used in conjunction with the clipboard. The *clipboard* is a storage place in memory for selected text to be copied, moved, or deleted.

Only one selection can be stored on the clipboard at a time. If something is already on the clipboard and you perform a copy or cut operation, the contents of the clipboard are overwritten with the new information.

FIGURE 4.6

The Edit menu and the Edit submenu of the Text Pane pop-up menu

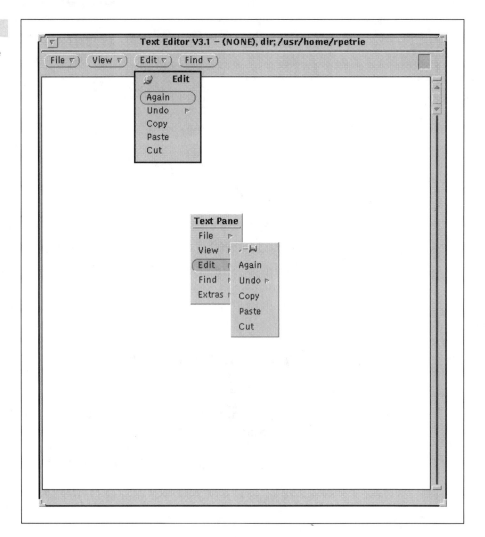

Copying a Text Selection

Select the text you want to copy. After you select the text, press the right mouse button on the **Edit** menu button and choose **Copy**. A copy of the selected text is stored on the clipboard. If you select the **Copy** item without first selecting text, a Notice will appear indicating that you must make a text selection. Once a text selection is copied, move the insertion point to where you want the copied text and choose **Paste** from the **Edit** menu.

The **Text Pane** pop-up menu and accelerator keys (on the left side of most Sun keyboards) allow you to perform the same copy operations. The **Text Pane**'s pop-up **Edit** submenu includes **Copy** and **Paste** items, which work in the same way as the **Edit** menu's **Copy** and **Paste** items. The Copy accelerator key on a Sun keyboard is identical to choosing the **Copy** item from an **Edit** menu. You can also copy text by pressing Diamond-c. If you are using another type of Sun keyboard, the Copy key is labeled L6 and the Paste key is labeled L8.

Copying Text Using the Drag-and-Drop Method

You can use the drag-and-drop method to copy selected text within the same file or to any location in the DeskSet environment that accepts ASCII text. The following explains the drag-and-drop method of copying text.

1. Select the text to be copied.

2. With the pointer on the selected text, press the Control key then press and hold down the left mouse button. Once you press the left mouse button, release the Control key. A Text Duplicate pointer appears, as shown in Figure 4.7. The first several characters of the selected text are displayed inside the rectangle.

3. Drag the pointer to the location where you want to copy the text (either within the Text Editor pane or anywhere on the DeskSet that accepts ASCII text), then release the left mouse button.

FIGURE 4.7

The Text Duplicate Pointer

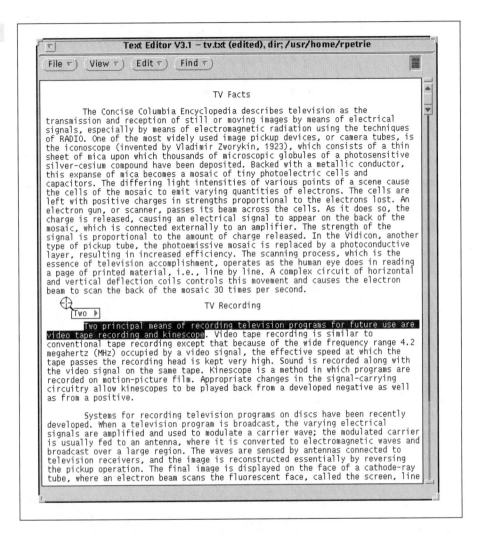

The Text Duplicate Pointer

Deleting or Moving a Text Selection

There is no Delete item in the **Edit** menu or the text pane's **Edit** submenu; instead you use **Cut** to delete text. To delete text, simply select it then choose the **Cut** item from either the **Edit** menu or the text pane's **Edit** submenu. You can also use keys on your keyboard to perform a variety of text deletions. The following describes the keys and the text they delete.

KEY	DELETES
Backspace	Character to the left of the insert point.
Control-w	Word to the left of the insert point.
Shift-Control-w	Word to the right of the insert point.
Control-u	To the beginning of the line.
Shift-Control-u	To the end of the line.

The process of moving a selection is similar to the copying process, only instead of using the Copy item, you choose the Cut item from the Edit menu. The Cut item removes the selected text and stores it on the clipboard. Once text is stored on the clipboard, you can select the Paste item to move the text from the clipboard to its new location.

The Text Pane pop-up menu and the accelerator keys (on the left side of your keyboard) allow you to perform the same move operation. The Text Pane's pop-up Edit menu also provides Cut and Paste items, which work identically to the Cut and Paste items in the control area's Edit menu. The Cut and Paste accelerator keys on a Sun workstation keyboard are identical to choosing the Cut and Paste items from an Edit menu. You can also paste text by pressing Diamond-V. On some Sun keyboards, the Cut key is labeled L10 and the Paste key is labeled L8.

Repeating or Undoing Edits

You can repeat the last editing action that changed your text by selecting the Again item from either the Edit menu or the Text Pane pop-up menu. To choose the Again item from the Edit menu, click the left mouse button on the Edit menu button. You can also press the Again (L2) key to repeat the previous operation.

If you make a mistake and want to undo either the last editing action or all editing actions since you last saved your file, use either the Edit menu or the Text Pane pop-up menu by pressing the right mouse button and choosing the Undo item. You can undo the last editing action or all editing actions by choosing the Undo Last Edit or Undo All Edits items from the Undo submenu (Figure 4.8). If you are using a Sun keyboard, you can also press the Undo (L4) key to undo a previous operation.

FIGURE 4.8

The Undo submenu of the Edit menu

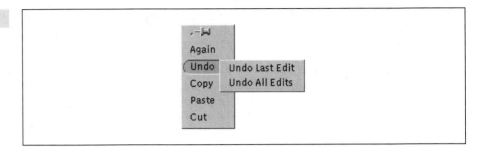

Clearing the Text Pane

If you want to clear the text pane of a window, use the `File` menu's `Empty Document` item. This clears the contents of the current text pane. If you have made editing changes and have not saved them, a Notice is displayed, asking you to confirm or cancel the operation. The Notice says `The text has been edited. Clear Log will discard these edits. Please confirm.` Click the left mouse button on the `Confirm, discard edits` button.

Splitting the Text Editor Pane

The Text Editor pane can be split into two or more panes so that you can view and edit different parts of a text file at the same time. The file itself is not split, so any editing changes you make in one view are reflected in the other views as well.

To split the Text Editor pane, drag the top or bottom cable anchor of the vertical scrollbar to the position where you want to split the Text Editor pane. To remove the split pane, return the cable anchor back to the top or bottom cable anchor where you originally dragged it from, and release the left mouse button. You can also split the Text Editor pane by dragging the vertical scrollbar's drag box down to where you want to split the pane, pressing the right mouse button on the drag box, and choosing the `Split View` item. To remove a split pane, choose the `Join Views` item from the `Scrollbar` pop-up menu.

Merging Files

The `File` menu's `Include File` item displays the `Include` pop-up window (Figure 4.9). The `Include` pop-up window allows you to merge two or more text files. To merge a file with the file in the text pane, type the directory in the `Directory` text field and the name of the file that you want to include in the `File` text field, then click the left mouse button on the `Include File` button. The file is inserted at the insert point in the text pane.

You can also drag and drop a text file from anywhere on the Workspace to merge it with a file in the Text Editor. Drag the file icon to the spot in the text pane where you want the text inserted and release the mouse button.

Changing the Line Wrap Mode

The `View` menu's `Change Line Wrap` item provides you with a submenu listing three choices for line wrapping: `Wrap at Word`, `Wrap at Character`, and `Clip Lines`. The most commonly used wrapping method is to wrap at the end of words. If you choose `Clip lines`, the beginning of each line that ends with a Return is displayed. If you choose the `Wrap at Character` item, lines wrap at the closest character before the window's border.

Finding and Replacing Text in the Text Editor

The **Find** menu allows you to search for specific text strings, special characters, and delimiters. Using the **Find** menu's **Find and Replace** item, you can either search for text or search for *and* replace text. If the text string you want to search for is displayed in the Text Editor pane, you can select it before activating the **Find and Replace** item. The selected string is automatically displayed as the string you want to search for. To activate the **Find and Replace** item, click the left mouse button on the **Find** button. The Text Editor displays the **Find and Replace** pop-up window, as shown in Figure 4.10.

FIGURE 4.10

The Find and Replace pop-up window

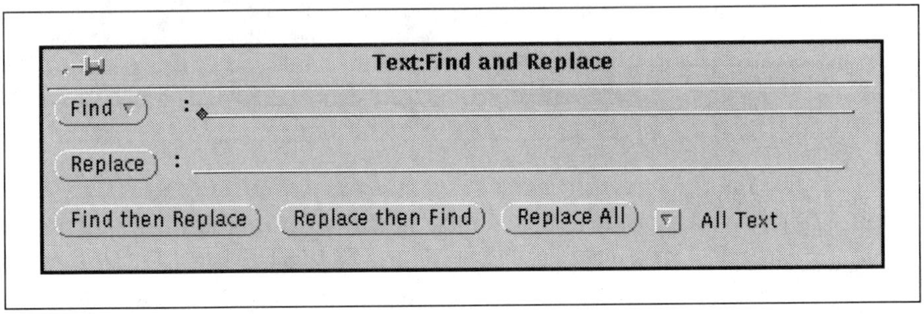

If you selected text before choosing the **Find and Replace** item, that text is displayed in the **Find** text field; otherwise, enter the text you want to search for.

If you only want to search ahead in the file for text, but not replace the text, leave the **Replace** field blank and click the left mouse button on the **Find** button. If you want to search backwards, press the right mouse button on the **Find** button and choose the **Backward** item.

To search and replace text, enter the text string you want to search for in the **Find** text field and the replacement string in the **Replace** text field. Click the left mouse button on the **Replace** button to search and replace the specified text. You can delete the text in the **Find** text field by leaving the **Replace** text field blank.

The buttons at the bottom of the `Find and Replace` pop-up window combine these find and replace operations: `Find then Replace`, `Replace then Find`, `Replace All`, and `All Text`. The following explains each of the `Find and Replace` pop-up window buttons:

ITEM	RESULT
Find then Replace	Searches for the next occurrence of the text string entered in the `Find` text field of the `Find and Replace` pop-up window, and replaces the matching text with the text entered in the `Replace` text field of the `Find and Replace` pop-up window.
Replace then Find	Replaces currently selected text (even if the text is different than the text in the `Find` text field) with the text in the `Replace` text field then searches for the next occurrence of the text in the `Find` text field.
Replace All	Replaces every occurrence of the text in the `Find` text field with the text in the `Replace` text field.
All Text	Specifies whether you want the find and replace operations to apply to the entire document or remain restricted to only the text between the insert point and the end of the document.

Searching for Selected Text

You can also search the file for another occurrence of a selected text string by using the `Find Selection` item in the `Find` menu in the Text Editor's control area. This item only *finds* selected text; it does not replace it. To find a text selection, select the text you want to search for, press the right mouse button on the `Find` button, then choose the `Find Selection` item. If you want to search forwards, release the mouse button. If you want to search backwards, choose the `Backward` item from the `Find Selection` submenu. The first match of the selected text in the file is then high-lighted. On Sun workstation keyboards you can use the keyboard to find selected text. Press Find (L9) to locate selected text to the right of the insert point. Press Shift-Find (L9) to locate selected text to the left of the insert point.

Searching for Delimiters

A *delimiter* is any character or combination of characters used to separate one item or set of data from another. For example, many databases use commas to delimit one field from another. You might think of a period as a type of delimiter used to separate sentences. The `Find Marked Text` item in the `Find` menu allows you to search for and highlight text between a matched set of delimiters. You can also insert or remove a matched set of delimiters. Eight types of delimiters are provided as items in the `Find Marked Text` pop-up window, as shown in Figure 4.11.

FIGURE 4.11

The Find Marked Text pop-up window

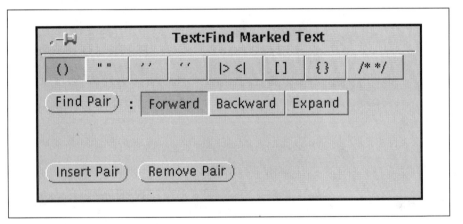

The `Forward`, `Backward`, and `Expand` buttons in the `Find Marked Text` pop-up window allow you to search for text between two or more sets of matched delimiters, such as two sets of matched parentheses (( )). When matched sets of delimiters are placed within another set of delimiters, they are referred to as *nested delimiters*. To select text within a set of nested delimiters, make sure the insert point precedes the delimiters you want to locate and do the following:

1. Choose `Find Marked Text` from the Text Editor's `Find` menu button. The `Find Marked Text` pop-up window is displayed.

2. Click the left mouse button on the type of nested delimiters that surround the text you want to locate.

3. Click the left mouse button on the `Forward` button.

4. Click the left mouse button on the `Find Pair` button.

Figure 4.12 shows the results of using the `Forward` setting and `Find Pair` button to select text and delimiters. Figure 4.13 shows the result of clicking the `Find Pair` button (using the `Forward` setting) three times to select text within two nested sets of matching delimiters. Figure 4.14 shows the result of changing to the `Expand` setting and clicking the left mouse button on the `Find Pair` button.

Inserting and Removing Delimiters

To surround selected text with delimiters, first select the text that you want to delimit then select a delimiter pair setting in the `Find Marked Text` pop-up window. Click the left mouse button on the `Insert Pair` button. The matching delimiters will surround your selection.

To remove the delimiters, click the left mouse button on the `Remove Pair` button. Be sure that your selection includes the delimiters specified in the delimiter settings. Otherwise, a notice box will appear telling you that the operation is aborted because the selection does not include the indicated pair.

Finding and Replacing Fields

The characters |> and <| act as text field delimiters, which indicate fields in a SunOS file. You can search forward through text from the insert point to find the text of each field and select the text using the `Replace |>field<|` item. Displaying the `Replace |>field<|` submenu provides you with three items explained below.

FIGURE 4.12

Using the Forward
setting and the Find
Pair button to select
text and delimiters

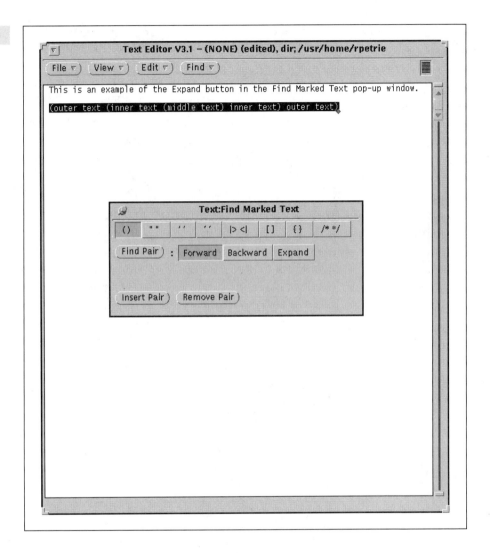

FIGURE 4.13

Using the Forward setting and clicking the Find Pair button three times to select text within two nested sets of matching delimiters

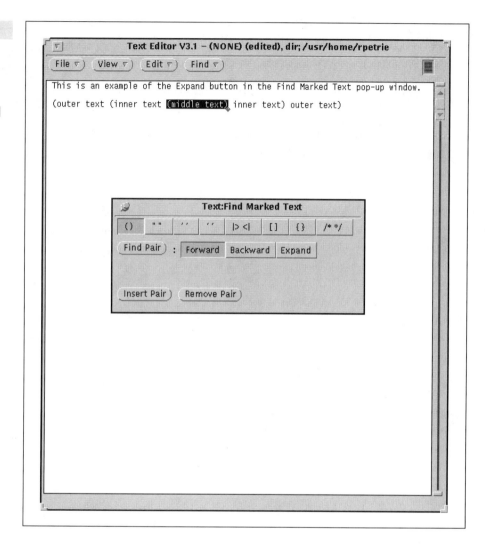

FIGURE 4.14

Using the Expand setting and clicking the left mouse button on the Find Pair button

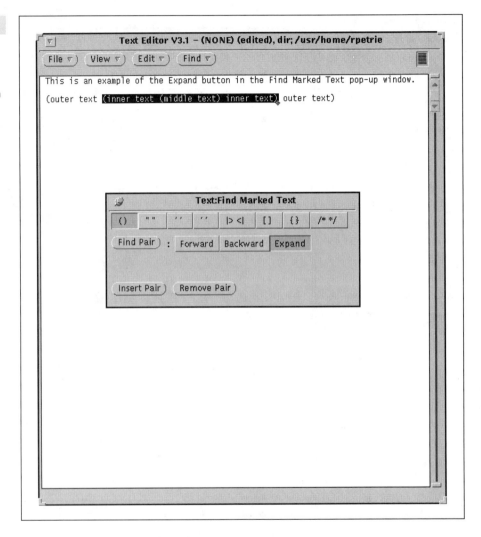

ITEM	RESULT
Expand	Searches in both directions and selects the entire field and its delimiters.
Next	Searches forward from the insert point and selects the next field.
Previous	Searches backward from the insert point and selects the previous field.

The Text Pane's Extras Pop-up Submenu

The text pane's `Extras` pop-up submenu (Figure 4.15) provides you with six items that allow you to format, indent, change the case of text, sort specified fields, insert brackets, or replace slashes. The following describes each of the items in the `Extras` submenu.

ITEMS	RESULTS
Format	Divides text into lines of not more than 72 characters. The `Format` item fills and joins lines, but it does not split words between lines.

FIGURE 4.15

The Text Pane pop-up menu's Extras submenu

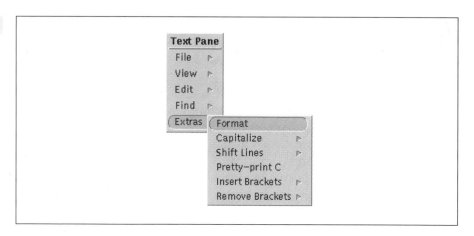

ITEMS	RESULTS
Capitalize	Changes the case of selected text from lowercase to uppercase (abcd **ABCD**), uppercase to lowercase (**ABCD** abcd), or capitalizes the first letter of every word in selected text (abcd -> Abcd).
Shift Lines	Inserts or removes a tab character at the beginning of each line in a selection. Choosing the Right item moves the selected lines to the right one tab stop. Selecting the Left item moves the selected lines one tab stop to the left.
Pretty-print C	Formats the selection to standard C program listing specifications.
Insert Brackets	Inserts matched parentheses, brackets, curly brackets, or quotation marks (( ), [ ], { }, or " ").
Remove Brackets	Removes matched parentheses, brackets, curly brackets, or quotation marks (( ), [ ], { }, or " ").

The Shell Tool

The Shell Tool is a command interpreter that accepts, interprets, and executes SunOS commands. Figure 4.16 shows the Shell Tool window. The pane of the Shell Tool window is referred to as a *terminal emulator* pane, which means that working in it is the same as working from a command prompt at a terminal. The text insertion point of the Shell Tool is indicated by a rectangle that appears as an outline when inactive and as a solid black block when active. To activate the insert point, move the pointer inside the Shell Tool window. If the insert point does not change to a solid block, click the left mouse button. After typing a SunOS command and pressing Return, the command is executed. For example, type the ls command and press Return while in the Shell Tool window to list the files in the current directory.

The Shell Tool's Term Pane Pop-up Menu

Pressing the right mouse button with the pointer in the text pane of the Shell Tool displays the Shell Tool's Term Pane pop-up menu (Figure 4.17).

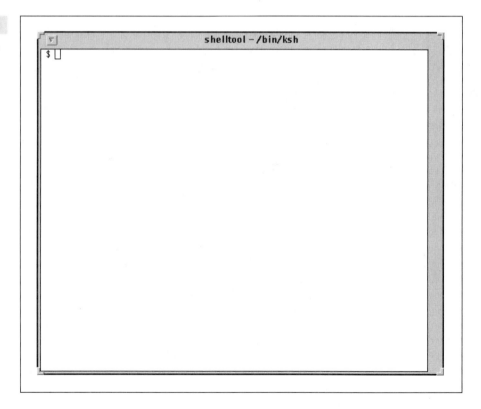

FIGURE 4.17

The Shell Tool's Term
Pane pop-up menu

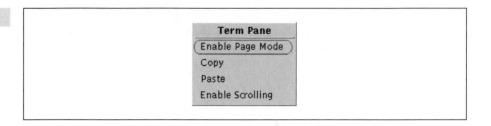

The four items in the `Term Pane` pop-up menu, include:

* `Enable Page Mode`, which displays text one pane of text at a time.

* `Copy`, which copies selected text from the Shell Tool window to the clipboard.

* `Paste`, which inserts the contents of the clipboard into a Shell Tool window.

* `Enable scrolling`, which turns the Shell Tool into a Command Tool.

Each of these items is described in the following sections.

Viewing Text in the Shell Tool

The `Enable Page Mode` item of the Shell Tool's `Term Pane` pop-up menu controls the scrolling of the screen so that you see only one paneful of text at a time. For example, if you have a directory listing that is longer than one pane, and you enter the `ls` command while `Enable Page Mode` is activated, the first paneful is displayed, and the pointer turns to a stop sign, as shown in Figure 4.18, indicating that the pane has stopped scrolling. To resume scrolling the contents of the Shell Tool, press the Space bar.

The `Enable Page Mode` item is replaced with the `Disable Page Mode` item when activated. If the `Disable Page Mode` item is activated, text scrolls without stopping until it reaches the end of the text to be displayed.

FIGURE 4.18

A partially scrolled
Shell Tool pane

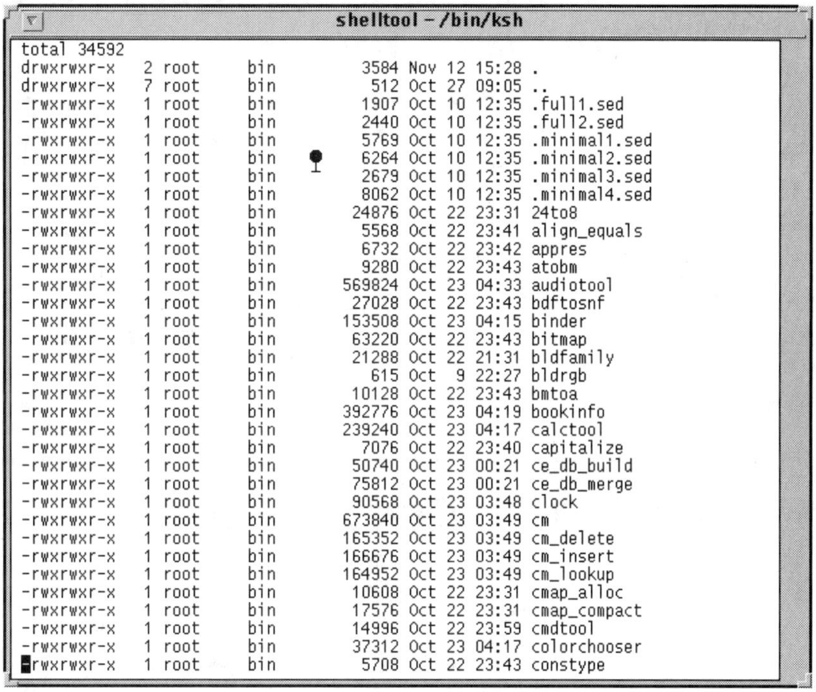

```
                          shelltool – /bin/ksh
total 34592
drwxrwxr-x   2 root      bin         3584 Nov 12 15:28 .
drwxrwxr-x   7 root      bin          512 Oct 27 09:05 ..
-rwxrwxr-x   1 root      bin         1907 Oct 10 12:35 .full1.sed
-rwxrwxr-x   1 root      bin         2440 Oct 10 12:35 .full2.sed
-rwxrwxr-x   1 root      bin         5769 Oct 10 12:35 .minimal1.sed
-rwxrwxr-x   1 root      bin         6264 Oct 10 12:35 .minimal2.sed
-rwxrwxr-x   1 root      bin         2679 Oct 10 12:35 .minimal3.sed
-rwxrwxr-x   1 root      bin         8062 Oct 10 12:35 .minimal4.sed
-rwxrwxr-x   1 root      bin        24876 Oct 22 23:31 24to8
-rwxrwxr-x   1 root      bin         5568 Oct 22 23:41 align_equals
-rwxrwxr-x   1 root      bin         6732 Oct 22 23:42 appres
-rwxrwxr-x   1 root      bin         9280 Oct 22 23:43 atobm
-rwxrwxr-x   1 root      bin       569824 Oct 23 04:33 audiotool
-rwxrwxr-x   1 root      bin        27028 Oct 22 23:43 bdftosnf
-rwxrwxr-x   1 root      bin       153508 Oct 23 04:15 binder
-rwxrwxr-x   1 root      bin        63220 Oct 22 23:43 bitmap
-rwxrwxr-x   1 root      bin        21288 Oct 22 21:31 bldfamily
-rwxrwxr-x   1 root      bin          615 Oct  9 22:27 bldrgb
-rwxrwxr-x   1 root      bin        10128 Oct 22 23:43 bmtoa
-rwxrwxr-x   1 root      bin       392776 Oct 23 04:19 bookinfo
-rwxrwxr-x   1 root      bin       239240 Oct 23 04:17 calctool
-rwxrwxr-x   1 root      bin         7076 Oct 22 23:40 capitalize
-rwxrwxr-x   1 root      bin        50740 Oct 23 00:21 ce_db_build
-rwxrwxr-x   1 root      bin        75812 Oct 23 00:21 ce_db_merge
-rwxrwxr-x   1 root      bin        90568 Oct 23 03:48 clock
-rwxrwxr-x   1 root      bin       673840 Oct 23 03:49 cm
-rwxrwxr-x   1 root      bin       165352 Oct 23 03:49 cm_delete
-rwxrwxr-x   1 root      bin       166676 Oct 23 03:49 cm_insert
-rwxrwxr-x   1 root      bin       164952 Oct 23 03:49 cm_lookup
-rwxrwxr-x   1 root      bin        10608 Oct 22 23:31 cmap_alloc
-rwxrwxr-x   1 root      bin        17576 Oct 22 23:31 cmap_compact
-rwxrwxr-x   1 root      bin        14996 Oct 22 23:59 cmdtool
-rwxrwxr-x   1 root      bin        37312 Oct 23 04:17 colorchooser
-rwxrwxr-x   1 root      bin         5708 Oct 22 23:43 constype
```

Copying and Pasting Text in the Shell Tool

Before you can copy and paste text, you must select the text you want to copy. You select text by moving the pointer to the beginning of the text you want to copy and clicking the left mouse button. Move to the end of the text and press the middle mouse button. Once you have selected the text, press the right mouse button to display the Term Pane pop-up menu then choose the Copy item. The selected text is copied onto the clipboard. If you don't select any text before selecting Copy, a notice box appears, indicating that you must first make a text selection. Move the insertion point to the location where you want to paste the text. Display the Term Pane pop-up menu and choose the Paste item.

Turning the Shell Tool into a Command Tool

The `Enable Scrolling` item in the `Term Pane` pop-up menu allows you to turn the Shell Tool into a Command Tool. The Command Tool provides more editing capabilities than the Shell Tool, as explained later in this chapter. When you choose the `Enable Scrolling` item, the tool name at the top of the Shell Tool window remains the same, but the Shell Tool now functions like a Command Tool. The Command Tool's `Term Pane` pop-up menu will appear instead of the Shell Tool's. To return to the Shell Tool, choose the `Disable Scrolling` item from the `Scrolling` submenu.

The Command Tool

The Command Tool is an enhanced Shell Tool with the added features of the standard Text Editor pane. The `Command Tool` icon looks the same as the `Shell Tool` icon. When opened, however, the `Command Tool` window (Figure 4.19) displays a scrollbar elevator and a different pop-up menu than the Shell Tool.

In addition to the same `Edit`, `Find`, and `Extras` items of the standard text editing pop-up menu, the Command Tool's `Term Pane` pop-up menu (Figure 4.20) has three additional items: the `History`, `File Editor`, and `Scrolling` submenus.

Working with the History Log File

The Command Tool automatically keeps track of commands you have typed in the Command Tool window for the current session in what is referred to as a *history log*. You can save this list of commands to a file, so you can choose a command from a list instead of entering it each time.

FIGURE 4.19

The Command Tool window

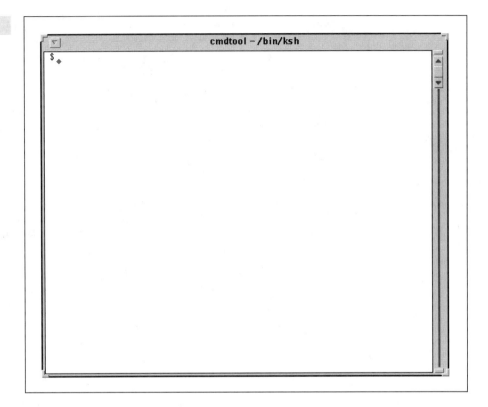

FIGURE 4.20

The Command Tool's Term Pane pop-up menu

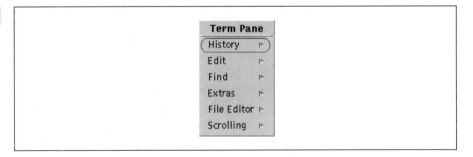

Repeating commands using the history log is explained in Chapter 10, "Improving Your Command Line Productivity." The `Term Pane` menu's `History` submenu provides items for saving and modifying the history log.

The **Mode** item determines whether the history log can be edited within the Command Tool. If you set the **Mode** item to **Read Only**, you cannot edit text in the Command Tool's terminal pane. However, you can still save the log to a file and edit that file using the **File Editor** item in the Command Tool's **Term Pane** pop-up menu. If the **Mode** item is set to **Editable**, you can edit text anywhere in the Command Tool's terminal pane, using the editing items on the **Term Pane** pop-up menu.

The **Store log as new file** item allows you to save the current history log to a file. The **Clear log** item clears the current history log. This resets the Command Tool history log as if you just started the Command Tool application. If the history log file has been edited, a Notice appears indicating that you've made changes and asks you to confirm the discard of your edits. Click the left mouse button on the **Confirm, discard edits** button to complete the discard operation or click on the **Cancel** button to return to the Command Tool without discarding the history log file's contents.

Saving the History Log to a File

The **Store log as new file** item allows you to save the current history log to a file. This history log file can be treated in the same way you would any other text file. You can edit it and save it again or drag and drop it from the File Manager onto a **Text Editor** window. The following steps explain how to save the current history log to a file.

1. In the Command Tool text pane, press the right mouse button to display the **Term Pane** pop-up menu.

2. Choose the **Store log as new file** item from the **History** submenu. The **Store** pop-up window is displayed.

3. In the **Directory** field, type your complete home directory path, then press Return.

4. In the **File** field, type the name under which you want to save the history log file.

5. Click the left mouse button on the **Store as New File** button.

Displaying a Text Editor Pane

The `File Editor` item in the `Term Pane` menu determines whether a Text Editor pane is displayed. To display the Text Editor pane in the `Command Tool` window, press the right mouse button to display the `Term Pane` pop-up menu and choose the `Enable` item from the `File Editor` submenu. The `Command Tool` window is then split into two panes: a Command Tool pane and a text editor pane, as shown in Figure 4.21. This Text Editor pane is the same as the pane that appears in the Text Editor window and includes the `Text Pane` pop-up menu. To remove the Text Editor pane, choose the `Disable` item in the `File Editor` submenu.

FIGURE 4.21

The Command Tool
with the Text Editor

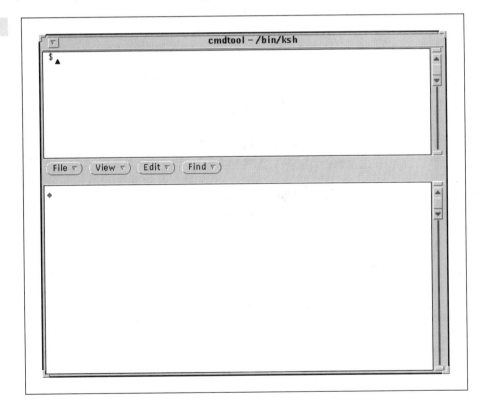

Turning the Command Tool into a Shell Tool

You can disable the editing capabilities of the Command Tool so that it appears and acts like a `Shell Tool` window by displaying the Command Tool's `Term Pane` pop-up menu and choosing `Disable Scrolling` from the `Scrolling` submenu. This item nearly doubles the performance of a `Command Tool`; when the scrolling feature is disabled, the window doesn't demand the overhead processing required to store commands. Choosing the `Disable Scrolling` item from the `Scrolling` submenu causes the Command Tool's `Term Pane` pop-up menu to appear the same as that of the `Shell Tool` window. To return to the original Command Tool `Term Pane` pop-up menu, choose the `Enable Scrolling` item.

The Console Window

A `Console` window is opened automatically whenever you start Open-Windows. The `Console` window is a special Command Tool that displays error and system messages for Solaris and some applications. If you accidentally quit a `Console` window, you can choose the `Console` item from the `Workspace` menu's `Utilities` submenu to open a new `Console` window.

It is not recommended that more than one `Console` window be open at a time since it is easy to miss important messages if you do not pay attention to which `Console` window is active. If no `Console` window is open, messages are displayed in large type at the bottom of the screen.

The xterm Window

One of the many layers of Solaris is the X Window System. The `xterm` window is not a part of the DeskSet, but a popular X window terminal emulator that comes with the X Window System and is included with Solaris. The `xterm` window is more versatile for copying and pasting text than the Shell Tool or Command Tool. It also lets you change font sizes, and display the window in reverse video using menus. The `xterm` program is usually stored in the `/usr/openwin/bin` directory.

To open an `xterm` window from the Shell Tool or Command Tool, enter

```
xterm -sb &
```

The `-sb` specifies opening the `xterm` window with a scrollbar. The `&` starts the program in the background, freeing up your Shell or Command Tool for additional commands. Figure 4.22 shows an example of an `xterm` window.

The xterm Window Menus

There are three menus available for working with the `xterm` window. All these menus are accessed by pressing the Control key on your keyboard

FIGURE 4.22

An xterm window

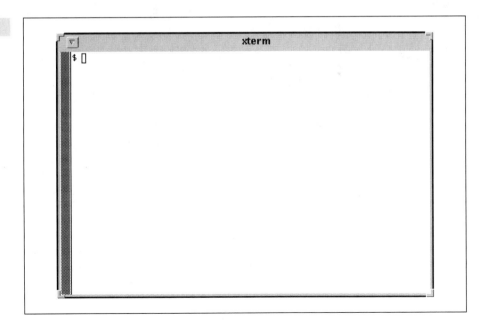

and pressing a mouse button. The following lists the key combinations used to display each of the three xterm menus:

KEY COMBINATION	DISPLAYS
Control and the left mouse button	Main Options menu.
Control and the middle mouse button	VT (video terminal) Options menu.
Control and the right mouse button	VT Fonts menu.

Figure 4.23 shows each of these menus. The following sections explain the most common operations and menu items for working in the xterm window.

FIGURE 4.23

The xterm Window menus

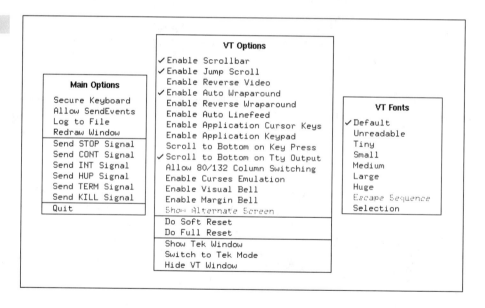

Scrolling the xterm Window

The highlighted area in the scrollbar is known as the *thumb*. The thumb reflects the amount of text stored in memory. By default, the last 64 lines are stored in memory. As more text is entered, the size of the thumb decreases. To scroll the text in an `xterm` window, move the pointer to the scrollbar. The pointer changes to a doubleheaded arrow. The extent of text scrolled depends on the position of the cursor in the scrollbar. The following explains how to use the mouse to scroll through text in an `xterm` window.

MOUSE BUTTON	ACTION
Middle	Scrolls text in direction of the cursor. To continue scrolling in a particular direction, keep the middle button pressed.
Left	Scrolls down the window.
Right	Scrolls up the window.

Selecting, Copying, and Pasting Text

The `xterm` window allows you to select and copy text within the same or other windows. The method of selecting text is similar to selecting text in a Shell or Command Tool. The last text selected replaces the previous text selection. The following lists ways to select text in the `xterm` window.

MOUSE ACTION	RESULT
Double-click	Selects the current word.
Triple-click	Selects the current line.
Drag the pointer to the end of the text	Selects a section of text.

To change the amount of text selected, move the pointer to the location where you want the text selection to end. Click the right mouse button. You can also press the right mouse button and drag the pointer to the location where you want to end the text selection. To copy a selection of text, simply select the text you want to copy, move the pointer to the `xterm` window in which you want to paste the text, and press the middle mouse button.

Logging an xterm Session

Just as you can log your commands in a history log using the Command Tool, you can create a log file for `xterm` window commands. To send your commands to a log file, press the Control key and the left mouse button and highlight the `Log to file` item in the `Main Options` menu. A check mark appears next to the `Log to file` item. All the `xterm` window output is now sent to a file named `XtermLog.pid`. The *pid* indicates the `xterm` program's Process ID number. The file is usually created in the directory that the `xterm` program was started from. You can enable logging to the default log file from the command line by adding `-l` to the `xterm` command. To designate a file to store your terminal log, start the `xterm` program with the `-lf filename` argument, where *filename* is the name of the log file. The following example starts an `xterm` window with a scrollbar, enables logging, and writes to the file named `xtermlog`:

```
xterm -sb -l -lf xtermlog
```

Displaying the xterm Window in Reverse Video

Displaying a window in reverse video (white on black) causes less eye strain. The VT menu lets you display the `xterm` window in reverse video. To change the current X window to display in reverse video, press Control and the middle mouse button and drag the highlight to the `Enable Reverse Video` item. To return to the previous display choose the `Enable Reverse Video` item again.

Changing the Size of Fonts in the xterm Window

Pressing the Control key and the right mouse button displays a menu listing fonts that you can change for the current xterm window. You can choose from one of the following font sizes:

Default

Unreadable

Tiny (5x8)

Small (6x10)

Medium (8x13)

Large (9x15)

Huge (10x20)

NOTE For more information on customizing the xterm window, such as changing to a specific font size and changing xterm window colors, see Chapter 15, "Customizing Solaris."

Get Organized with the Calendar Manager

THE Calendar Manager is a handy appointment scheduler and reminder application that allows you to organize and plan your time on a daily, weekly, monthly, or yearly basis. It lets you easily schedule appointments then automatically reminds you of the upcoming appointments. The Calendar Manager also lets you enter and manage tasks using a ToDo list. Using the Calendar Manager, you can also enter appointments in a group of users' calendars and automatically notify the group of users via email. This chapter teaches you how to harness the powerful time-management features of the Calendar Manager.

Starting the Calendar Manager

To start the Calendar Manager, choose `Calendar Manager` from the `Workspace` menu's `Programs` submenu. The Calendar Manager icon appears on the Workspace, which displays the current month and date (Figure 5.1). To open the Calendar Manager icon to a window, double-click the left mouse button on the Calendar Manager icon. The `Calendar Manager` window appears, as shown in Figure 5.1.

FIGURE 5.1

The Calendar
Manager icon and the
Calendar Manager
window

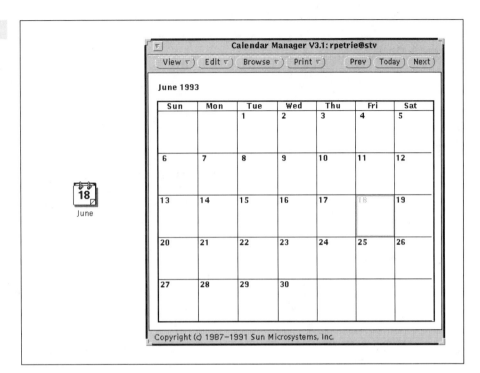

The Calendar Manager Window

The `Calendar Manager` window's default display shows the current month. The current day has a double border, or if you are using a color system, the border is the color of the window. The default display can be changed to show day, week, or year calendars. Any appointment entries for dates in the month view are displayed, although the information is usually clipped to accommodate the size of the date box. Each line in a date box is used for separate appointment text. The `Calendar Manager` window can be enlarged to view more text in a date box, or you can quickly display the day view to see your appointment information in more detail, as explained later in this chapter.

To see more appointment information in the month view, use one of the resize corners to stretch the window vertically or horizontally. You can also choose `Full Size` from the `Window` menu to expand the calendar view to the full size of your screen's height then use one of the resize corners to stretch the window horizontally.

The control area of the `Calendar Manager` window includes four menu buttons:

- The `View` menu lets you view a calendar, appointment list, or ToDo list by day, week, month, or year. It also provides a feature to search for specific appointments or ToDo list items.

- The `Edit` menu contains commands for entering and editing appointments or ToDo list items, specifying a different time zone, and customizing the Calendar Manager.

- The `Browse` menu contains commands to display single or multiple calendars, schedule group appointments, and add other users' calendars to your Calendar Manager.

- The `Print` menu allows you to print calendar views, appointment lists, and ToDo lists for any day, week, month, or year.

In the upper-right corner of the control area are three navigational buttons that allow you to quickly browse through the preceding or following time unit of the calendar view currently displayed. For example, with the `Month` view displayed, clicking the left mouse button on the `Prev` button displays the previous month's calendar. Clicking the left mouse button on the `Next` button displays the next month's calendar. Clicking the left mouse button on the `Today` button returns you to the current month with the current day selected.

The Four Views of the Calendar Manager

Four different calendar views, Day, Week, Month, and Year, are available in the Calendar Manager. The Day view (Figure 5.2) is useful for viewing in detail any appointment or ToDo list information scheduled for a particular day. The Week view (Figure 5.3) displays a weekly calendar based

FIGURE 5.2

The Day calendar view

on either the default current week or the week that includes the date you selected. The Week view displays an hourly box schedule with appointment times shaded. The Month view displays appointments from a monthly perspective. The Year view (Figure 5.4) displays a yearly calendar for any year from 1970 through 1999. The Year view does not display any appointment information.

FIGURE 5.3

The Week calendar view

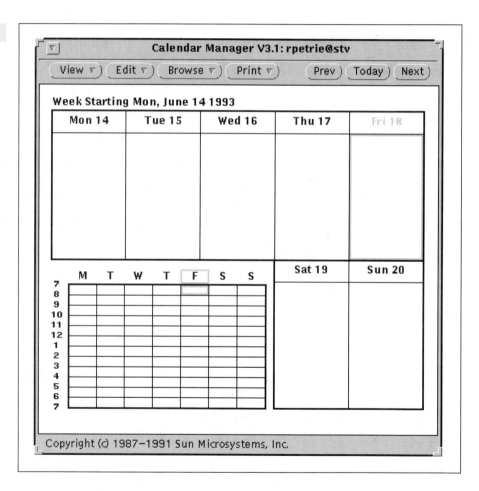

FIGURE 5.4

The Year calendar view

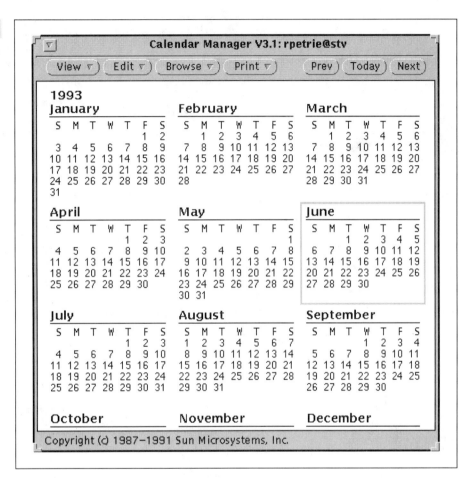

The Appointment List and ToDo List Views

In addition to displaying your schedule for a day, week, month, or year, you can also display pop-up windows of all your appointments and ToDo list items for a particular day, week, month, or year. Appointments are entered into any calendar view by using the CM Appointment Editor pop-up window. Appointments entered into any of the calendar views are also displayed in the other calendar views. Working with the CM Appointment Editor pop-up window is explained later in this chapter. Figure 5.5 shows a day calendar view displayed along with the appointment and ToDo lists for that day. An appointment list displays all the appointments for a particular time period, while a ToDo list displays all the ToDo items for a particular time period. To help you keep track of tasks that need to be accomplished, the ToDo list includes check boxes in which you can check off an item by clicking the left mouse button on the check box. To erase a check mark, click the left mouse button on the check box containing the check mark.

Navigating the Calendars and Lists

Several methods are available to navigate calendar views and their associated appointment or ToDo list views. To change calendar views with the View menu, press the right mouse button on the View menu button to display the View menu. If you want to display a calendar view, choose the calendar view item you want from the View menu. If you want to display a corresponding calendar view's appointment or ToDo list, choose Appt List or ToDo List from the appropriate calendar view's submenu.

FIGURE 5.5

A day calendar view with appointment and ToDo lists

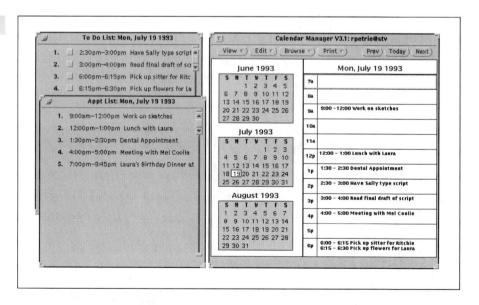

The Calendar Manager provides shortcuts to navigate between the `Day`, `Week`, `Month`, and `Year` calendar views. To display the `Week` view from the `Month` view, click the left mouse button directly on the number of the day within any date box. From the `Week` calendar view, you can display a `Day` view by clicking the left mouse button on the date for the day you want in any of the seven available date boxes.

You can also navigate to a specific day, week, or month by selecting it from the currently displayed calendar view, then using the appropriate calendar view item in the `View` menu. To access the `Week` view from the `Month` view, click the left mouse button on any day of the week you want, then choose the `Week` item from the `View` menu. The `Week` view is displayed with the day you selected outlined with a double line or a colored border. To access the `Day` view from the `Month` view, click the left mouse button on the date you want in the `Month` view, then click the left mouse button on the `View` menu button. Regardless of the view you're displaying, clicking the left mouse button on the `View` menu displays the selected `Day` view.

Entering Appointments and ToDo Items into the Calendar Manager

The `CM Appointment Editor` pop-up window (Figure 5.6) is used to enter appointments and ToDo list items into the Calendar Manager. It allows you to enter and set various parameters for your appointments. For example, you can choose the method the Calendar Manager uses to remind you of an appointment, such as beeping or sending an email message. Any appointment or ToDo list item entered using the Appointment Editor is available in all calendar views.

To display the `CM Appointment Editor` pop-up window, double-click the left mouse button on the day you want in either the `Week` or `Month` view. For the `Day` view, double-click the left mouse button on the starting hour of your

FIGURE 5.6

The CM Appointment
Editor pop-up window

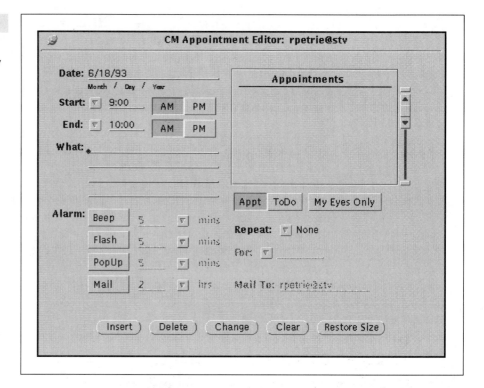

appointment. Clicking the left mouse button on the `Edit` menu button also displays the `CM Appointment Editor` pop-up window for the day you selected in either the `Week` or `Month` view or the hour for the `Day` view.

The CM Appointment Editor Pop-up Window Settings

The initial display of the `CM Appointment Editor` pop-up window is full size, meaning all the settings are displayed. Clicking the left mouse button on the `Restore Size` button displays an abbreviated `CM Appointment Editor` pop-up window, as shown in Figure 5.7. The abbreviated `CM Appointment Editor` pop-up window does not display the settings that allow you to set reminder alarm controls. To restore the `CM Appointment Editor` pop-up window to the full size, click the left mouse button on the `Full Size` button.

FIGURE 5.7

The abbreviated CM
Appointment Editor
pop-up window

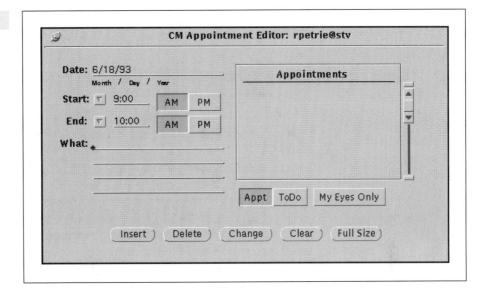

The following describes all the settings that appear in the full size CM
Appointment Editor pop-up window.

- The Appointments scrolling list displays either the appointments or
  ToDo list items scheduled for the day that is currently displayed in
  the Date field.

- The Date text field displays the selected date. Changing the date
  entry in the Date text field changes the settings to display the information for the new date.

- The Start and End text fields allow you to set the time of the
  appointment. You can choose a time from the abbreviated menu
  buttons to the left of the text field. When you set the starting time,
  the Appointment Editor automatically inserts an ending time of
  one hour later. The AM and PM settings let you specify whether the
  hour is a.m. or p.m.

- The What text field provides a description of your appointment.
  Your description is not limited to the displayed space of this field;
  if your description is longer than the displayed space of the What
  text field, a scroll button appears on the side(s) of the text field

where there is hidden text. Clicking the left mouse button on the scroll button scrolls through the hidden text.

- The `Appt` and `ToDo` settings under the `Appointments` scrolling list establish whether your entry is an appointment or a ToDo list item. The `My Eyes Only` setting allows you to hide your appointment or ToDo list item from other users that have permission to browse your calendar.

- The `Alarm` field includes four reminder settings: `Beep`, `Flash`, `PopUp`, and `Mail`. The `Beep` setting reminds you of an upcoming appointment with a beeping alarm sound. The `Flash` setting causes your calendar window or icon to flash to remind you of an upcoming appointment. The `PopUp` setting displays the `Reminder` pop-up window (Figure 5.8), to remind you of your upcoming appointment. The text field to the right of each reminder setting determines the advance time before being reminded for an upcoming appointment. The default is 5 minutes. The `Mail` reminder setting allows you to send the appointment reminder via email to yourself or any users on the system. The `Repeat` abbreviated menu button and `For` text field allow you to specify regularly repeated scheduled appointments. Reminder settings can be combined; for example you can use a pop-up window and send an email message.

- The `Insert`, `Delete`, and `Change` buttons enable you to enter, delete, or change an appointment or ToDo list entry. The `Clear` button clears any text in the `What` text field and resets the `Date`, `Start`, and `End` to their default settings.

FIGURE 5.8

The Calendar Reminder pop-up window

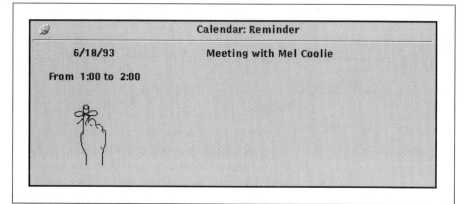

- The `Full Size` button displayed in the abbreviated `CM Appointment Editor` pop-up window displays the full size `CM Appointment Editor` pop-up window. The `Restore Size` button, displayed in the full size `CM Appointment Editor` pop-up window, returns the window to its abbreviated size.

Creating an Appointment or ToDo List Entry

To create an appointment or ToDo list entry, first double-click on the day you want the appointment set for in the `Week` or `Month` view, or the hour in the `Day` view. A day can also be selected after displaying the `CM Appointment Editor` pop-up window by entering the exact date you want in the `Date` text field. With the `CM Appointment Editor` pop-up window displayed, follow these steps to enter a new appointment or ToDo list item:

1. If you want to change the date in the `Date` field, first delete the current date entry. Enter the date for the new appointment in any of these formats: mm/dd/yy (11/22/92), m/d/y (1/4/92), or month day, year (August 15, 1992).

2. If the entry is a ToDo item, click the left mouse button on the `ToDo` button under the `Appointments` scrolling list. Choosing the `My Eyes Only` button prevents other users from viewing your appointment or ToDo item.

3. Press the right mouse button on the `Start` abbreviated menu button to display an hour menu, as shown in Figure 5.9. You can choose an hour item or from one of three 15-minute intervals within each hour. Each hour has a submenu that lists these intervals as `00`, `15`, `30`, and `45` minutes. You also need to choose the correct a.m. or p.m. setting for your appointment. When you set a start time, the end time is automatically set to one hour later. If the appointment is shorter or longer than an hour, set a different end time, choosing the time item you want from the `End` abbreviated menu button. Times can also be entered in the `Start` and `End` text fields. Choosing the `All Day` item automatically sets `Start` to 12:00 a.m. and `End` to 11:59 p.m.

FIGURE 5.9

The hour items for the
Start submenu

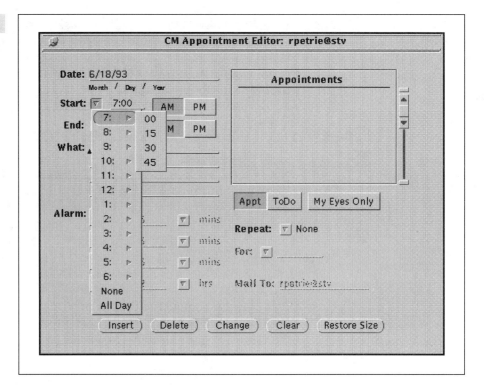

4. Click the left mouse button in the What text field to set the insert
   point. Type the appointment or ToDo list information; you can
   use up to four lines. Each line can be up to eighty characters in
   length. If the text is longer than the space in the What text field, a
   scroll button appears to the right or left of the text field to indicate
   that there is hidden text. Click the left mouse button on a scroll
   button to scroll through the hidden text.

NOTE

Be as descriptive as possible about the entry in the first
line of the What text field. The Calendar Manager
includes a feature that lets you search your appointment
and ToDo list entries based on text in the first line of the
What text field.

5. Choose an `Alarm` setting if you want to be reminded of your appointment. Click the left mouse button on the `Alarm` setting you want. The selected settings and the corresponding advance time fields are displayed in boldface. To change the default time for the specified `Alarm` setting, click the left mouse button on the setting's text field to set the insert point, and enter the time interval you want. You can specify minutes (the default), hours, or days by pressing the right mouse button on the corresponding advance-time abbreviated menu button to the right of the text field and choosing the time unit you want. If you choose the `Mail` setting, make sure you enter the email address in the `Mail To` text field.

6. If you want the appointment repeated regularly, press the right mouse button on the `Repeat` abbreviated menu button and choose the desired time interval: `None, Daily, Weekly, Biweekly, Monthly,` or `Yearly`. When you select a `Repeat` setting (other than the default `None`), the `For` menu button and text field are activated. The `For` setting allows you to specify the time frequency of the `Repeat` setting. For example, if you choose the `Daily` setting, you can set the number of days between recurring appointments. You can choose the time frequency using the `For` abbreviated menu button or you can enter your own number in the `For` text field.

7. After you have finished entering the information for the appointment or ToDo list item, click the left mouse button on the `Insert` button. The appointment is added to the scrolling list in the `CM Appointment Editor` pop-up window as well as to the current calendar view. The `CM Appointment Editor` pop-up window remains displayed, allowing you to enter another appointment or ToDo list item.

8. To quit the `CM Appointment Editor` pop-up window, click the left mouse button on the pushpin or choose `Dismiss` from the `Window` menu.

Deleting Existing Appointments or ToDo List Items

Appointments and ToDo items are constantly being changed or canceled, so the Calendar Manager makes it easy to remove a scheduled appointment or a ToDo list item from your calendar. To delete an existing appointment or ToDo list item from your Calendar Manager, follow these steps:

1. Double-click on the day containing the appointment or ToDo list item you want to delete in the **Week** or **Month** view, or the hour in the **Day** view. The **CM Appointment Editor** pop-up window is displayed.

2. Click the left mouse button on the appointment or ToDo item in the scrolling list you want to delete. The appointment or ToDo entry is highlighted and its information is displayed in the appropriate settings. The user name of the person who scheduled the appointment is displayed in the window footer.

3. Click the left mouse button on the **Delete** button. The appointment or ToDo list item is deleted from both the scrolling list and the calendar view and appointment or ToDo list view. If you select an appointment with a **Repeat** setting, when you click the left mouse button on the **Delete** button, a Notice is displayed (Figure 5.10) asking you if you want to delete the appointment for one or all dates or cancel the operation. Click the left mouse button on the **This One Only** button if you only want to delete the repeating appointment for the selected date. Click the left mouse button on the **All** button if you want to delete all repeating appointments regardless of the date.

FIGURE 5.10

The Delete
Appointment Notice

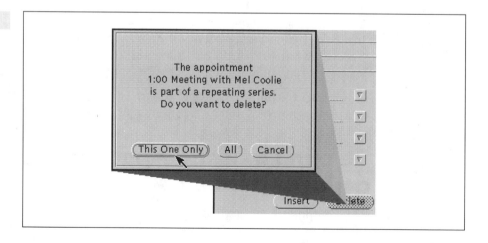

Changing Existing Appointments or ToDo List Items

Making changes to an existing appointment or ToDo item is performed in a similar way as creating a new appointment or ToDo item. The following steps explain how to make changes to existing appointments or ToDo items using the CM Appointment Editor pop-up window.

1. Double-click on the day that contains the appointment or ToDo list item you want to change in the Week or Month view, or the hour in the Day view. The CM Appointment Editor pop-up window is displayed.

2. Click the left mouse button on the appointment or ToDo item in the scrolling list you want to change. The appointment or ToDo entry is highlighted and its information is displayed in the appropriate settings. The user name of the person who scheduled the appointment is displayed in the window footer.

3. Edit any information for that appointment or ToDo list item.

4. Click the left mouse button on the Change button. If you made changes to an appointment with Repeat settings, a Notice appears asking if you want to change the appointment for the selected date only or for all dates that the appointment or ToDo item appears. Click the left mouse button on the This One Only button if you only want to delete the repeating appointment for the selected date. Click the left mouse button on the All button if you want to delete all repeating appointments regardless of the date.

Finding a Calendar Appointment

If you want to find an appointment, but you cannot remember the exact time it was scheduled, you can use the Calendar Manager's CM Find pop-up window (Figure 5.11). The CM Find pop-up window allows you to

FIGURE 5.11

The CM Find pop-up window

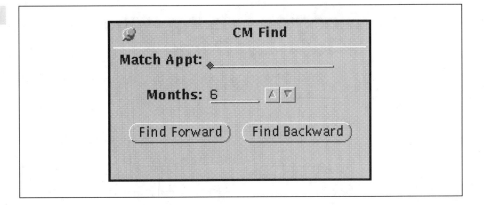

search for matching text in the appointment's What text field. To display the CM Find pop-up window, choose Find from the View menu.

The Match Appt text field is where you type text to match text entered in the first line of the appointment's What field. The text that you type can be either upper- or lowercase. Clicking the left mouse button on the Find Forward button searches forward for the number of months specified in the Months text field, starting with the currently displayed month. Clicking the left mouse button on the Find Backward button searches backward for the number of months specified in the Months text field, starting with the currently displayed month.

Printing Calendar Views, Appointment Lists, and ToDo Lists

The Calendar Manager allows you to print daily, weekly, monthly, and yearly calendars, appointment lists, and ToDo lists. The printed calendar views, appointment lists and ToDo lists match their screen counterparts. The `Print` menu provides settings for each calendar view along with a submenu for printing the respective calendar view's appointment and ToDo lists. The `CM Properties` window includes settings for changing the default printer settings, as explained later in this chapter.

The following explains how to print calendar views, appointment lists, and ToDo lists.

CALENDAR VIEW	PRINTING PROCEDURE
Day	To print the currently displayed day calendar view, click the left mouse button on the `Print` menu button. To print either the appointment list or ToDo list for the current day, press the right mouse button on the `Print` menu button, then choose `Appt List` or `ToDo List` from the `Day` submenu.
Week	To print the currently displayed week calendar view, press the right mouse button on the `Print` menu button and choose the `Week` item. To print the appointment or ToDo list for the currently displayed week, choose `Appt List` or `ToDo List` from the `Week` submenu.
Month	To print the currently displayed month calendar view, press the right mouse button on the `Print` menu button then choose the `Month` item. To print either the appointment or ToDo list for the currently displayed `Month`, choose `Appt List` or `ToDo List` from the `Month` submenu.

CALENDAR VIEW

Year

PRINTING PROCEDURE

To print the currently displayed year calendar view, press the right mouse button on the `Print` menu button and choose one of the two `Year` items. The `Year` item allows you to print two different calendars, the standard and alternate calendars. The standard year item, labeled (`Std`) is similar to the on-screen calendar, as shown in Figure 5.12. The alternate year item, labeled (`Alt`), prints the year calendar with each day denoted by a small box, as shown in Figure 5.13. To print either the Appointment or ToDo list for the currently displayed year, press the right mouse button on the `Print` menu button and choose `Appt List` or `ToDo List` from the `Year` submenu.

Working with the Multi-Browser Window

The Calendar Manager's `CM Multi-Browser` pop-up window lets you overlay the calendars of many users at one time to show the times when each user is busy, so you can coordinate appointment schedules. Once you find a convenient meeting time for the group, you can then use the `CM Multi-Browser` pop-up window to add an appointment to every user's calendar and send each user a mail message about the appointment.

The `CM Multi-Browser` pop-up window also allows you to add other users' calendars to your `Browse` menu. Adding users' calendars to your `Browse` menu allows you to view their calendars in the same way you view your own. In order to schedule appointments to another user's calendar or add another user's calendar to the `Browse` menu, you must have permission to use that user's calendar, as explained later in this chapter.

FIGURE 5.12

Printed standard year view

1993

06/25/93 02:38 AM

rpetrie@stv

January
S	M	T	W	T	F	S
					1	2
3	4	5	6	7	8	9
10	11	12	13	14	15	16
17	18	19	20	21	22	23
24	25	26	27	28	29	30
31						

February
S	M	T	W	T	F	S
	1	2	3	4	5	6
7	8	9	10	11	12	13
14	15	16	17	18	19	20
21	22	23	24	25	26	27
28						

March
S	M	T	W	T	F	S
	1	2	3	4	5	6
7	8	9	10	11	12	13
14	15	16	17	18	19	20
21	22	23	24	25	26	27
28	29	30	31			

April
S	M	T	W	T	F	S
				1	2	3
4	5	6	7	8	9	10
11	12	13	14	15	16	17
18	19	20	21	22	23	24
25	26	27	28	29	30	

May
S	M	T	W	T	F	S
						1
2	3	4	5	6	7	8
9	10	11	12	13	14	15
16	17	18	19	20	21	22
23	24	25	26	27	28	29
30	31					

June
S	M	T	W	T	F	S
		1	2	3	4	5
6	7	8	9	10	11	12
13	14	15	16	17	18	19
20	21	22	23	24	25	26
27	28	29	30			

July
S	M	T	W	T	F	S
				1	2	3
4	5	6	7	8	9	10
11	12	13	14	15	16	17
18	19	20	21	22	23	24
25	26	27	28	29	30	31

August
S	M	T	W	T	F	S
1	2	3	4	5	6	7
8	9	10	11	12	13	14
15	16	17	18	19	20	21
22	23	24	25	26	27	28
29	30	31				

September
S	M	T	W	T	F	S
			1	2	3	4
5	6	7	8	9	10	11
12	13	14	15	16	17	18
19	20	21	22	23	24	25
26	27	28	29	30		

October
S	M	T	W	T	F	S
					1	2
3	4	5	6	7	8	9
10	11	12	13	14	15	16
17	18	19	20	21	22	23
24	25	26	27	28	29	30
31						

November
S	M	T	W	T	F	S
	1	2	3	4	5	6
7	8	9	10	11	12	13
14	15	16	17	18	19	20
21	22	23	24	25	26	27
28	29	30				

December
S	M	T	W	T	F	S
			1	2	3	4
5	6	7	8	9	10	11
12	13	14	15	16	17	18
19	20	21	22	23	24	25
26	27	28	29	30	31	

Year view by Calendar Manager

FIGURE 5.13

Printed alternate year view

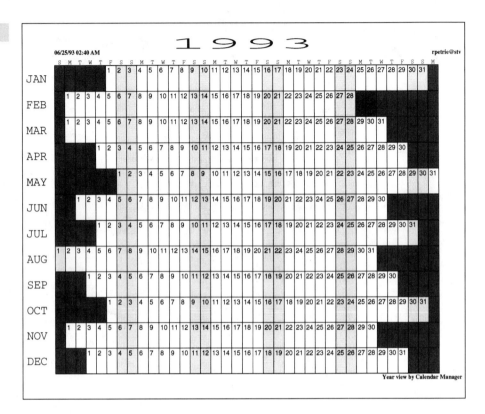

Year view by Calendar Manager

The *Multi-Browser* Window

To activate the CM Multi-Browser window, click the left mouse button on the Browse menu button. The CM Multi-Browser window appears, displaying the week time chart that includes the day you selected (Figure 5.14). The CM Multi-Browser window can be closed to an icon for added convenience (Figure 5.14). When you quit the Calendar Manager, the CM Multi-Browser window or icon is also removed. The CM Multi-Browser window includes the following controls:

- The Schedule button displays the CM Browser editor pop-up window, which is similar to the CM Appointment Editor pop-up window.

FIGURE 5.14

The CM Multi-Browser window and icon

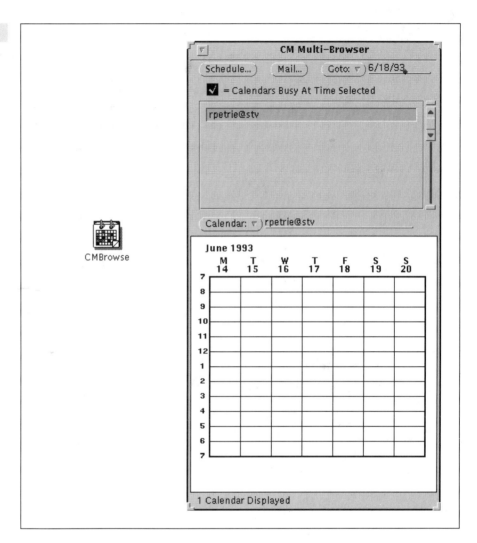

- The **Mail** button displays the Calendar Manager's **Compose Message** window for sending mail to notify users of your appointment scheduling.

- The **Goto** menu lists items to change in the Multi-Browser calendar display in order to show a different week or month.

- The Multi-Browser calendar list shows all the user names available in your `CM Multi-Browser` pop-up window. Each entry is the email address of the user.

- The `Calendar` menu button and text field allow you to add, delete, select, deselect, and sort the user names listed in the Multi-Browser calander list. Pressing the right mouse button in the Multi-Browser calendar list displays the `Calendar` pop-up menu, which is the same menu as the `Calendar` menu button.

- The Multi-Browser calendar display area displays any number of user calendars in an overlay manner to show a composite schedule. The number of calendars displayed in the calendar display area is noted in a message line in the bottom-left corner of the `CM Multi-Browser` window, directly below the calendar display area. The Multi-Browser only shows the times when each user is busy. To view the actual contents of a user's calendar, you need to choose the user name from the `Browse` menu, as explained later in the chapter.

Adding a User's Calendar to the Multi-Browser

In order to work with another user's calendar, you must first add it to the Multi-Browser calendar list. This scrolling list displays all of the calendars that are available to be browsed. These user names are also displayed as individual items in the Calendar Manager's `Browse` menu. New calendars are displayed on the `Browse` menu in the order in which you enter them in the Multi-Browser calendar list.

You must have browse permissions for each user's Calendar Manager, which are determined by the respective user, in order to work with the other users' calendars. The Calendar Manager does not confirm the validity of the user name nor the browse permissions for that calendar when you enter the user name in the calendar list. The Calendar Manager does check for such information when you select the calendar in the Multi-Browser calendar list, or when you choose the calendar from the `Browse` menu.

To add a user's calendar to the `Browse` menu:

1. Click the left mouse button on the `Browse` menu button. The `CM Multi-Browser` window appears.

2. Click the left mouse button on the `Calendar` text field to set the insert point and type in the user's login name, followed by @, then followed by the user's host machine name (for example, `ataylor@mayberry`).

3. Press the right mouse button on the `Calendar` menu button and choose `Add Calendar`. The calendar is added to the Multi-Browser calendar list and `Browse` menu.

You can sort the list of users in the Multi-Browser calendar list by choosing the `Sort List` item from the `Calendar` menu. The `Sort List` item sorts the user email addresses in alphabetical order.

Deleting a User's Calendar from the Multi-Browser

You can easily delete a user's calendar from the Multi-Browser calandar's list. If the `CM Multi-Browser` window is not open, click the left mouse button on the `Browse` menu button. Click the left mouse button on the user's name you want to delete as it appears in the calendar list. More than one user name can be selected by clicking the middle mouse button on each additional user's name. You can also type the user name of the user you want to delete in the `Calendar` text field. Choose the `Delete Selected` item from the `Calendar` menu. The selected user names are deleted from the Multi-Browser.

Determining an Appointment Time

When you open the `CM Multi-Browser` window, the week shown in the Multi-Browser calendar display is determined as follows:

- If the current view is the `Day` or `Month` view, the week containing the currently selected day is displayed.

- If the current view is the `Week` view, the current week is displayed.

- If the current view is the `Year` view, the first week of the currently selected month is displayed.

The Multi-Browser displays the days of the week and their corresponding dates at the top of the calendar display. On the left side of the calendar display are the one-hour blocks of appointment times. The 7 a.m. to 7 p.m. setting reflects the default `Day Boundaries` setting for the Calendar Manager, which can be changed using the `CM Properties` window.

The gray areas of the calendar indicate the times the selected users have scheduled appointments. If several calendars are being displayed, the gray blocks vary in shade. Darker blocks indicate that more users are busy during that time slot. There are up to three shades of gray, so a time slot when four people are busy does not appear any darker than a time slot when three people are busy. The white areas indicate times in which none of the selected users are busy.

The `Goto` menu provides several items for changing the Multi-Browser's Week display. Choose the `Prev Week` or `Next Week` item to display the previous or next week. Choose `This Week` to display the week of the day currently selected in the `Calendar Manager` window. Choose the `Prev Month` or `Next Month` to display a week one month before or after the current week. You can type any date in the `Goto` text field then click the left mouse button on the `Goto` button. The date can be entered in one of the following formats:

`mm/dd/yy` or `m/d/yy` (for example, 1/15/92 or 10/5/92)

`month day, year` (for example, June 30, 1992)

The following steps explain how to find free time slots for scheduling an appointment for a group of users.

1. Choose the `CM Multi-Browser` window by clicking the left mouse button on the `Browse` menu. Make sure that the calendars for all of the attendees are in the Multi-Browser calendar list.

2. Click the left mouse on each user name you want in the Multi-Browser calendar list. You can choose `Select All` from the `Calendar` menu to select every user name.

3. If the week you want is not currently displayed, use the `Goto` menu or enter the week you want in the `Goto` text field.

4. When all of the calendars are selected and overlaid, find an un-shaded block of time for the meeting. This represents a time when everyone is available.

5. If there is no time slot available on all the selected calendars, select a time slot that is lightly shaded and look at the selected user addresses in the Multi-Browser calendar list. If a user has an appointment scheduled for the selected time, a check mark appears to the left of the user's address, as shown in Figure 5.15. If you decide that a user does not have to be at the meeting, you can deselect that person's user name by clicking the left mouse button on it in the calendar list.

Scheduling an Appointment for a Group of Users

Once you have found a mutually convenient time, you can use the `CM Browser editor` pop-up window to mark the appointment in the calendars of all of the users. Remember, the user must give you permission (using the `Insert Setting` permission, which is explained later in this chapter) to add appointments to his or her calendar. Clicking the left mouse button on the `Schedule` button in the `CM Multi-Browser` pop-up window displays the `CM Browser editor` pop-up window (Figure 5.16). You can also double-click the left mouse button on the desired appointment time in the overlaid calendar area to display the `CM Browser editor` pop-up window.

The `CM Browser editor` pop-up window includes the same `Date`, `Start`, `End`, and `What` settings as the `CM Appointment Editor` pop-up window. The `Appointments` scrolling list displays appointments for all of the calendars selected in the `Calendars` scrolling list, at the time selected in the `CM Multi-Browser` window. When you select an appointment on the `Appointments` scrolling list, the appointment information is displayed in the `Date`, `Start`, `End`, and `What` text fields. The author of the selected appointment is displayed at the bottom-left corner of the `CM Browser editor` window.

FIGURE 5.15

The CM Multi-Browser
list showing busy users

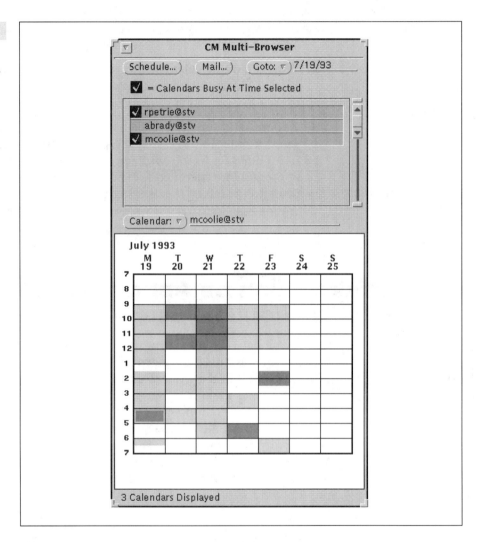

To schedule an appointment for a group of users, double-click the left mouse button on an available time slot for the new appointment, or select the time slot then click the left mouse button on the **Schedule** button. The **CM Browser editor** pop-up window is displayed. The **Date, Start,** and **End** text fields are automatically filled in and the selected calendars are listed in the **Calendars Insert Access** scrolling list.

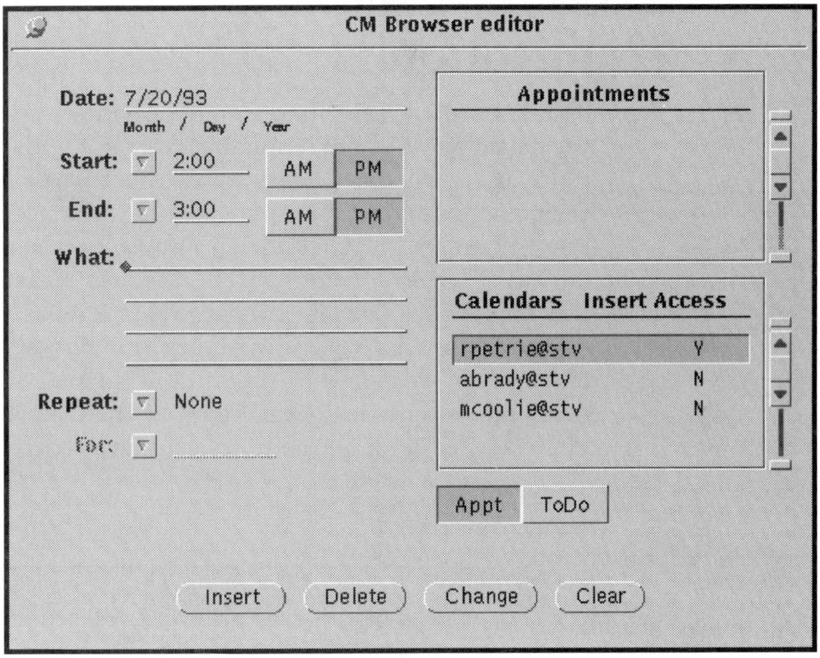

FIGURE 5.16

The CM Browser
editor pop-up window

If you have Insert Access permission (that is, permission to enter an appointment into that user's calendar), indicated by a `Y` in the `Calendars Insert Access` scrolling list, that calendar is automatically selected. If you do not have Insert permission, an `N` is displayed and the calendar is not selected. If any of the selected calendars has an appointment at the selected time, that appointment is displayed in the `Appointments` scrolling list, which is located just above the `Calendars Insert Access` list.

Fill out the new appointment information and click the left mouse button on the `Insert` button to add the appointment to the selected calendars. If the `Insert Access` column displays an `N`, you will need to send a mail message or contact that user to tell them to add the appointment to his or her calendar.

Sending a Mail Appointment Notification

The Multi-Browser's mail facility provides a convenient way to notify all the participants of a meeting that you have updated in their calendars and notify users who have not given you access to insert the appointment into their calendar. To display the Calendar Manager's `Compose Message` window (Figure 5.17), click the left mouse button on the `Mail` button in the `CM Multi-Browser` window. The `Compose Message` window is similar to the Mail Tool's `Compose Message` window, as explained in Chapter 3, "The Multimedia Mail Tool Makes Mail Easy." The information from the `CM Browser editor` pop-up window's `Date`, `Start`, `End`, and `What` text fields are automatically entered into the `Compose Message` window. The email addresses of all the users you have scheduled for the appointment

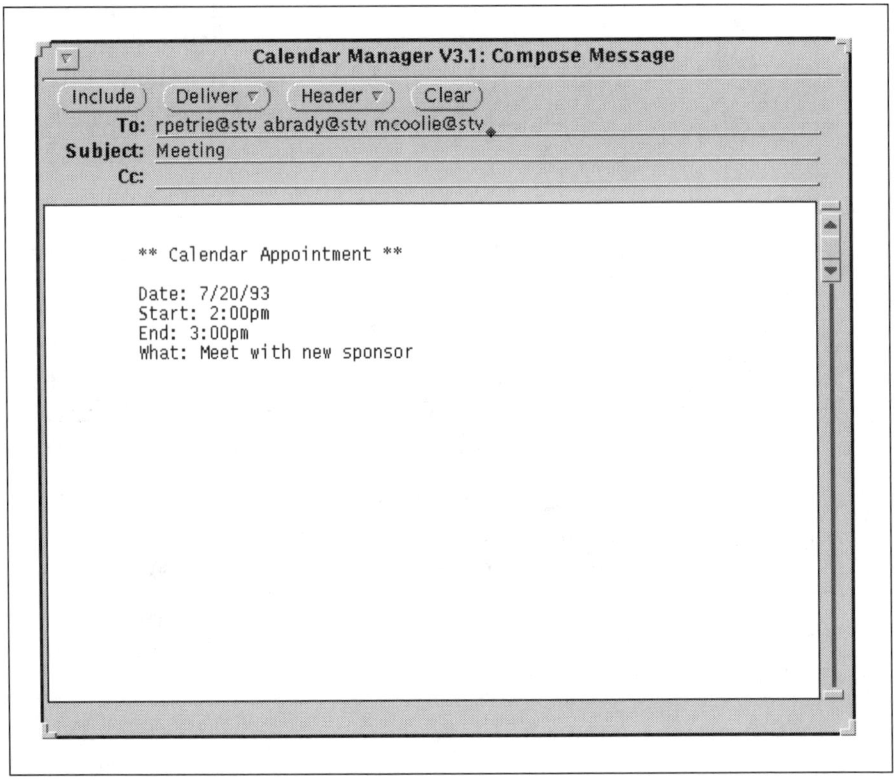

FIGURE 5.17

The Calendar Manager's Compose Message window

Calendar Manager V3.1: Compose Message

Include   Deliver ▽   Header ▽   Clear
To: rpetrie@stv abrady@stv mcoolie@stv
Subject: Meeting
Cc:

```
** Calendar Appointment **

Date: 7/20/93
Start: 2:00pm
End: 3:00pm
What: Meet with new sponsor
```

are displayed in the To text field, even if you were denied access to insert the appointment into a user's calendar. The default entry in the Subject text field is "Meeting," which you can change. The following steps explain how to send mail using the Calendar Manager's Compose Message window.

1. Before you send mail messages, make sure you have selected the recipient's user name in the CM Multi-Browser window. In the CM Browser editor pop-up window, make sure that you have filled in the Date, Start, End, and What fields for the appointment, and click the left mouse button on the Insert button.

2. Click the left mouse button on the Mail button in the CM Multi-Browser window to display the Compose Message window.

3. If you want to change the Subject field text or any text in the Compose Message window, click the left mouse button on any text area and edit the text.

4. Click the left mouse button on the Deliver button to send the mail message to the users listed in the To text field.

The mail message is sent in a format recognized by the Calendar Manager, so mail recipients can quickly add the appointment to their calendars, if it wasn't automatically added, by dragging the mail header to their Calendar Manager and dropping it anywhere on the window.

Browsing Another User's Calendar Using the Browse Menu

Once a calendar has been added to your Browse menu, you can display or edit the appointments for that user (depending on the access permissions that user has given you) by choosing the calendar from the Browse menu.

To choose a user's calendar from the **Browse** menu, press the right mouse button on the **Browse** menu button and choose the user's name you want. The user's calendar displays in your Calendar Manager in the same way as yours. If you do not have browse access for that user, you cannot see or edit that user's appointment information, but a scheduled appointment will appear as an **Appointment** entry for the specified time, as shown in Figure 5.18.

FIGURE 5.18

Browsing a user's calendar in the Week view without browsing permission

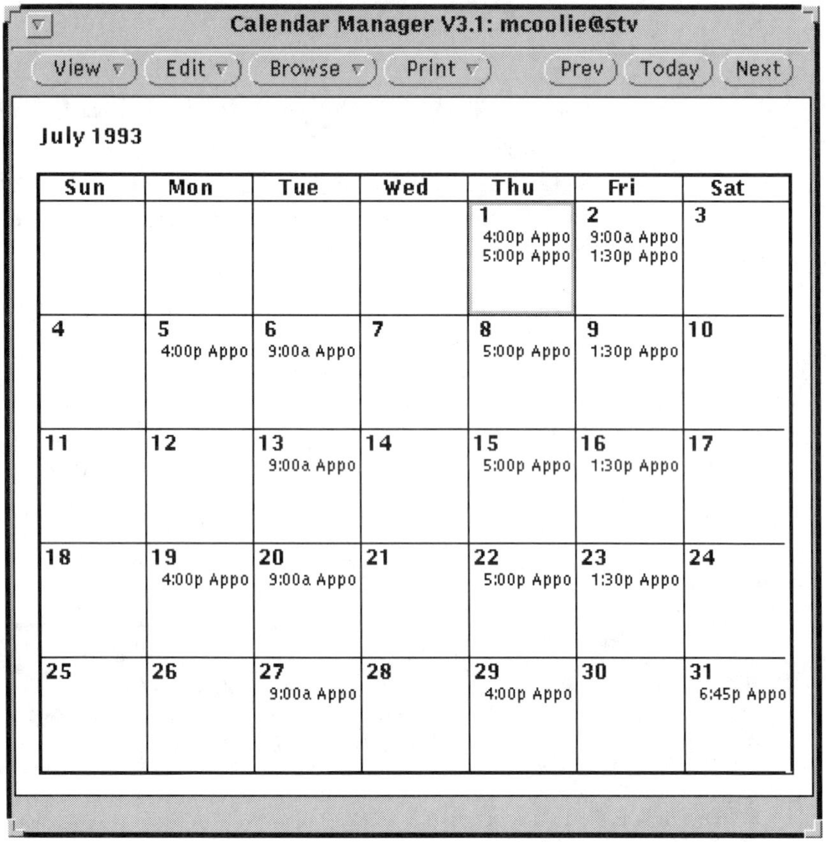

Calendar Manager V3.1: mcoolie@stv

(View ▽) (Edit ▽) (Browse ▽) (Print ▽)   (Prev) (Today) (Next)

July 1993

Sun	Mon	Tue	Wed	Thu	Fri	Sat
				1 4:00p Appo 5:00p Appo	**2** 9:00a Appo 1:30p Appo	**3**
4	**5** 4:00p Appo	**6** 9:00a Appo	**7**	**8** 5:00p Appo	**9** 1:30p Appo	**10**
11	**12**	**13** 9:00a Appo	**14**	**15** 5:00p Appo	**16** 1:30p Appo	**17**
18	**19** 4:00p Appo	**20** 9:00a Appo	**21**	**22** 5:00p Appo	**23** 1:30p Appo	**24**
25	**26**	**27** 9:00a Appo	**28**	**29** 4:00p Appo	**30**	**31** 6:45p Appo

Setting the Calendar Manager Time Zone

When you browse another user's calendar, the Calendar Manager adjusts the times to your time zone. For example, if you are on the west coast of the United States, and you are browsing the calendar of someone on the east coast, a 9:00 a.m. appointment appears as 6:00 a.m. to you. This is an important feature when using the Multi-Browser, because it ensures that all users' calendars are in synch. If you are only browsing a single calendar, however, you might want to view the appointments in their native time zone. To change the time zone for the currently displayed calendar, press the right mouse button on the `Edit` menu and choose the `Time Zone` item you want from the `Time Zone` submenu (Figure 5.19). Notice there are several time zones with their own submenus, such as the `US` item. If you change your own time zone in order to browse another calendar, make sure to change it back to your native time zone when you are done.

Customizing Your Calendar Manager

The Calendar Manager's `CM Properties` pop-up window allows you to customize the Calendar Manager's settings. To display the `CM Properties` pop-up window, press the right mouse button on the `Edit` menu and choose the `Properties` item. The `Category` menu initially shows the `Editor Defaults` settings, which are currently displayed in the `CM Properties` pop-up window (Figure 5.20). The `CM Properties` pop-up window provides five groups of settings: `Editor Defaults`, `Display Settings`, `Access List and Permissions`, `Printer Settings`, and `Date Format`. To choose a group of settings in the `CM Properties` pop-up window, click the right mouse button on the `Category` button and choose the

FIGURE 5.19

The Time Zone
submenu

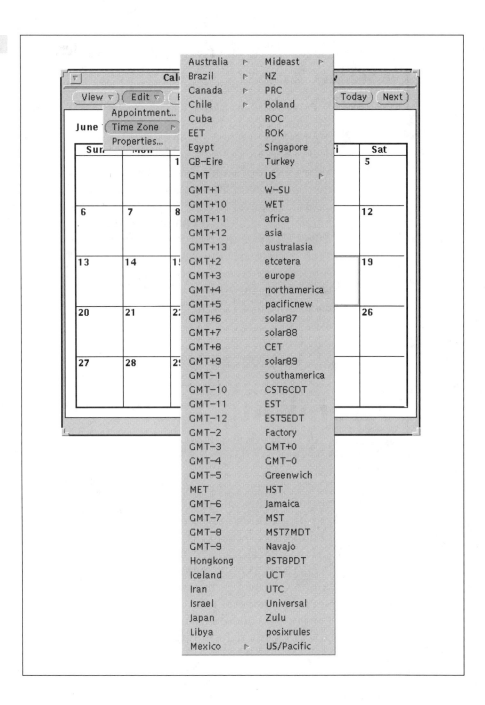

settings you want. There are three buttons at the bottom of the CM Properties pop-up window, regardless of which category is selected:

- The Apply button saves the changes made to the current CM Properties window. If you attempt to exit the CM Properties window after making changes without choosing the Apply button, a notice box appears requesting you either save or discard your changes, as shown in Figure 5.21.

- The Reset button restores the original properties settings to the current CM Properties window you had before you made changes in the current session.

	CM Properties

Category: ▽ Editor Defaults

Alarm:

Beep	5	▽	mins
Flash	5	▽	mins
PopUp	5	▽	mins
Mail	2	▽	hrs

Mail To: rpetrie@stv

(Apply) (Reset) (Defaults)

FIGURE 5.21

The CM Properties notice box

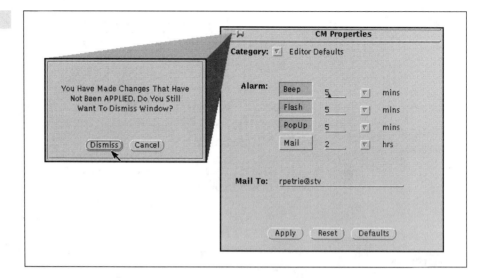

• The `Defaults` button restores the default settings for the current `CM Properties` window.

Changing Appointment Alarm Defaults

The `Editor Defaults` settings allow you to specify which of the four available `Alarm` settings are selected when you activate the `CM Appointment Editor` pop-up window. To select one or more `Alarm` settings, click the left mouse button on each `Alarm` setting you want. To enter a new time, click the left mouse button on the appropriate text field to set the insert point and type in a new number. To change the default time unit setting for an `Alarm` setting, press the right mouse button on the corresponding `Alarm` setting abbreviated menu button and choose the time unit item you want. You can also change the default `Mail To` text field entry, which specifies the email address for the `Mail` reminder setting. After making changes to the `Editor Defaults`, click the left mouse button on the `Apply` button, and the new defaults are saved and activated immediately.

Changing Display Settings

The `Display Settings` category lets you change the range of hours available for the `Start` and `End` fields in the `CM Appointment Editor` pop-up window, the `CM Multi-Browser` calendar display, and the `CM Browser editor` pop-up window. For example, if your normal working hours are 9 a.m. to 5 p.m., you would select 9 a.m. as your `Start` boundary and 5 p.m. as your `End` boundary.

The hour display for the Calendar Manager can be changed from the default `12 Hour` setting to a `24 Hour` setting using the `Hour Display` control. The `Default View` setting allows you to change the default calendar view when you activate the Calendar Manager application. The `Default Calendar` text field lets you specify the default user name you want to display in your Calendar Manager.

To change to the `Display Settings` settings (Figure 5.22), choose the `Display Settings` item from the `Category` menu. To change the Day Boundaries setting, follow these steps:

1. Press the left mouse button on the slider bar.

2. Drag the slider bar to the left or the right. Note that the time changes as you drag the slider. The pointer remains locked onto the slider as long as you keep the left mouse button pressed.

3. If you simply want to add or subtract an hour, click the left mouse button on the right (to increase the time) or on the left (to decrease the time) of the slider.

4. Once the Day Boundaries have been set, click the left mouse button on the `Apply` button to save your settings. The changes take effect immediately.

As explained earlier in this chapter, the `Month` view is displayed by default when you open the Calendar Manager. You can change this default view to `Day`, `Week`, or `Year`. To change the default view, click the left mouse button on the `Default View` setting you want, then click the left mouse button on the `Apply` button. The change takes effect the next time you activate the Calendar Manager.

FIGURE 5.22

The Display Settings
category

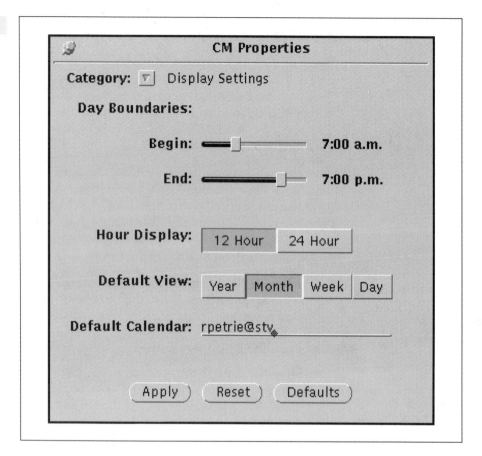

Specifying Who Can Browse and Change Your Appointments

The Access List and Permissions category in the Category menu lets you specify who may browse or change your appointments. Choosing the Access List and Permissions item displays the Access List and Permissions category window (Figure 5.23). The scrolling list displays a list of everyone who has access to your calendar. The default entry in the scrolling list, world, allows all users to browse your calendar and view your appointments, as indicated by the B (Browse) to the right of world.

FIGURE 5.23

The Access List and
Permissions CM
Properties pop-up
window

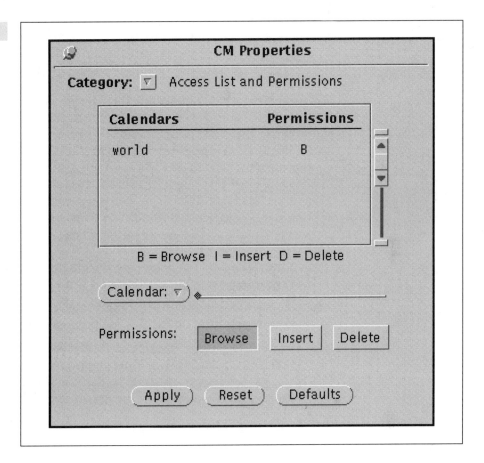

Three types of permissions can be establish for each user. The available permissions are:

Browse   Displayed as **B** in the scrolling list, the
                       Browse permission allows the user to
                       read your appointments.

Insert   Displayed as **I** in the scrolling list, the
                       Insert permission allows the user to add
                       new appointments into your calendar.

Delete   Displayed as D in the scrolling list, the
                          Delete permission allows the user to
                          delete appointments from your calendar.

You can combine any or all of the three permissions. If you give more permissions to the world entry than you give to an individual, that individual will still have the world permissions. If you delete the world entry from the access list, only the users you specifically add will be able to access your appointments. To give a user the ability to read, edit, and change appointments, you must give the user Browse, Insert, and Delete permissions. That user then has full permission to read appointments, insert new appointments, and delete or modify existing appointments. The following steps explain how to add a user to the access list:

1. In the Calendar text field, type the email address (such as, ataylor@mayberry) of the user you want to add.

2. Choose the permissions you want to give the user by clicking the left mouse button on the desired permissions.

3. Click the left mouse button on the Calendar menu button to add the user to the access list. You can also use the Add Calendar item from Calendar pop-up menu to add the user by pressing the right mouse button anywhere in the access scrolling list pane.

4. Click the left mouse button on the Apply button to save your changes.

To delete a user from the access list, select the user name in the scrolling list by clicking the left mouse button on the user name you want to delete, then choose the Delete Calendar item from the Calendar menu.

To change existing permissions for a user already on the access list, choose the user name from the scrolling list. Select the new permissions you want to give the user, then choose the Add Calendar item from the Calendar menu.

Changing the Default Printer Settings

You can change the default printer settings from the `Printer Settings` category window. To display the `Printer Settings` category window, choose the `Printer Settings` item from the `Category` menu. Figure 5.24 shows the `Printer Settings` category window with the default settings.

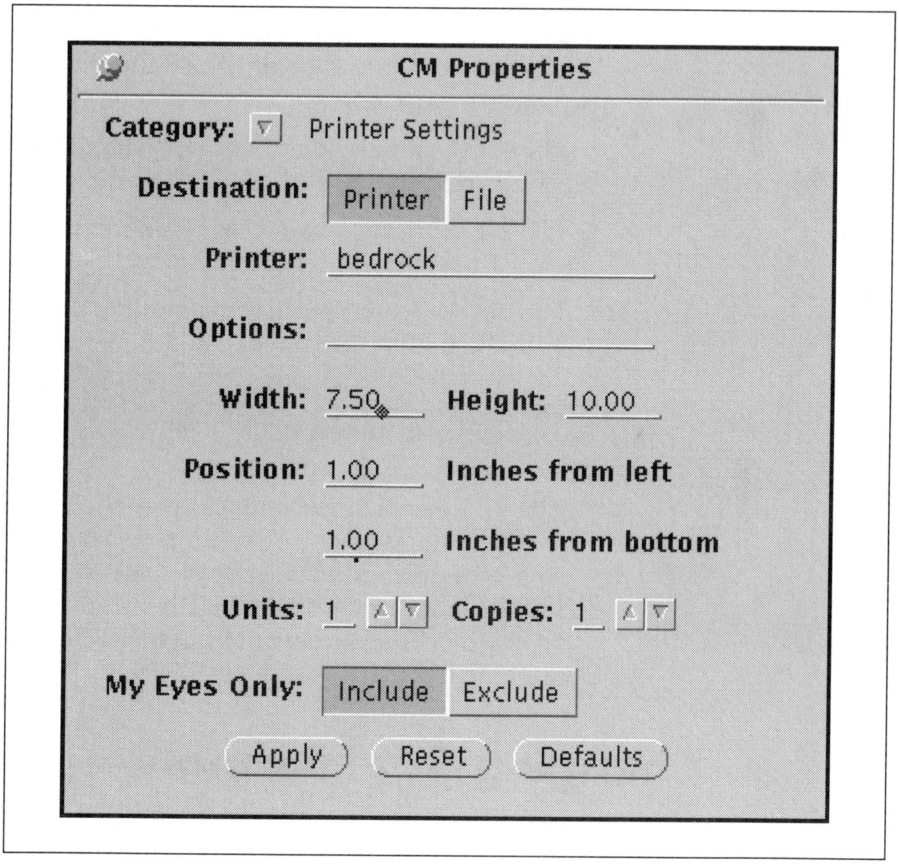

FIGURE 5.24

The Printer Settings CM Properties pop-up window

You can specify the following settings in the `Printer Settings` category window:

- The `Destination` setting specifies whether you want the Calendar Manager `Print` menu output sent to a printer or to a file. If the `Destination` setting is set to `Printer` (the default), the `Printer` and `Options` fields are displayed. If the `Destination` setting is set to `File`, the `Printer` and `Options` fields are replaced by `Directory` and `File` fields. The `Printer` field specifies the printer name and the `Options` field allows you to type in SunOS print commands to customize your printer defaults. The `Directory` and `File` fields allow you to type in the directory and file name of the file that you want to print to.

- The `Width` and `Height` fields allow you to specify the size of the printed output.

- The `Position` settings `Inches from left` and `Inches from bottom` specify the margins for printed output.

- The `Units` setting specifies the number of calendar view units from the selected day, week, month, or year calendar view to print. For example, when a day view is printed, the unit is `Days`.

- The `Copies` setting specifies the number of copies you want to print.

- The `My Eyes Only` settings allows to include or exclude printing any appointments or ToDo list items you have specified as for your eyes only. Choosing the `Include` setting allows them to be printed in an appointment or ToDo list. Choosing the `Exclude` setting blocks these entries from being printed in an appointment or ToDo list.

Changing Date Formats

The `Date Format` category (Figure 5.25) determines how the date in the `CM Appointment Editor` window is displayed. To display the date format set of controls, choose the `Date Format` item from the `CM Properties` window's `Category` menu. The `Date Ordering` settings determine the order in which the month, day, and year appear in the Appointment Editor's `Date` field. The `Date Separator` setting determines what separates each element of the date. To change the defaults, click the left mouse button on the settings you want, then click the left mouse button on the **Apply** button.

FIGURE 5.25

The Date Format CM Properties window

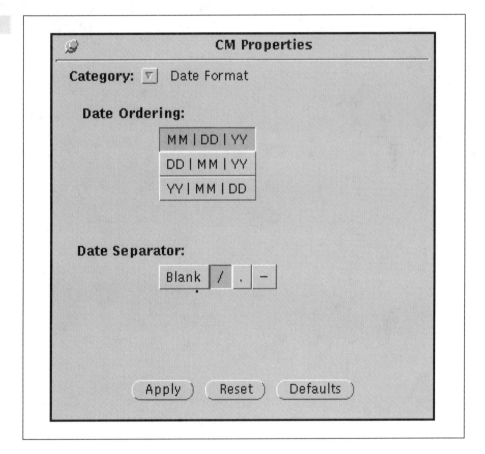

Using the Print Tool, Audio Tool, and Other DeskSet Applications

TO **EXTEND** your mastery of the DeskSet, this chapter covers these DeskSet applications:

- The Print Tool, which prints your files.

- The Audio Tool, which allows you to create and edit sound files.

- The Snapshot application, which allows you to take pictures of part of or the entire screen.

- The Clock, which displays the current time and date.

- The Performance Meters, which allow you to monitor the performance of your system.

- The Calculator, which enables you to perform mathematical calculations.

- The Tape Tool, which allows you to read and write files to and from a tape cartridge or archive file.

All the applications in this chapter can be started in the same manner as other DeskSet applications—by displaying the **Workspace** menu then choosing the application item from the **Programs** submenu.

The Print Tool

The Print Tool makes printing easy by providing you with a friendly user interface that lets you send files to the printer. Figure 6.1 shows the **Print Tool** window and Print Tool icon. The name of the active printer is displayed at the bottom of the Print Tool icon. The Print Tool allows you to specify the printer you want to use, the number of copies you want to print, and the file format of the file you want to print.

FIGURE 6.1

The Print Tool window
and icon

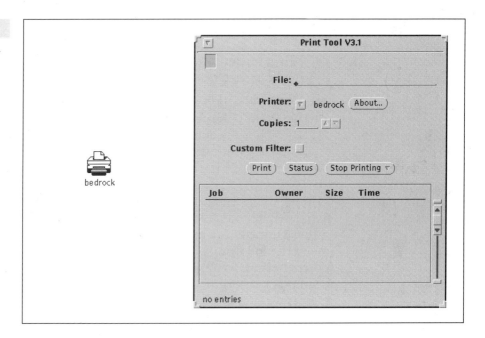

Printers are often in high demand in a networking environment because multiple workstations are usually connected to a small number of printers. To keep things running smoothly, Solaris normally feeds printing jobs to printers on a first-come, first-served basis. A *print job* is a term for a file sent to be printed as hard copy (on paper). Print jobs are sent to a *print queue*, which stores the printing jobs in memory in the order they are received. The status of your print jobs in the print queue can be quickly displayed in the `Print Tool` window, and specific or all print jobs stopped.

Printing a File

The Print Tool allows you to print an ASCII file using the default printer by either dragging and dropping files from the File Manager or typing the file name of the file to be printed in the `File` text field. You can also drag and drop a mail message header from the Mail Tool or the contents of a `Text Editor` window into the Print Tool for printing.

To print a file using the drag-and-drop method, follow the steps below.

1. Select one or more files from the File Manager, or one or more mail message headers from the Mail Tool header pane.

2. Drag and drop the selected files or mail message headers onto the `Print Tool` window's drag-and-drop target. The file names are automatically entered in the `File` text field, the files are loaded into the print queue, and a message indicating the status of your print request is displayed in the footer of the window.

To print a file using the `Print Tool` window's `File` text field, type the complete path name of the file in the `File` text field. Click the left mouse button on the `Print` button to send your file to the print queue. In turn, one of the following printing status messages is displayed in the window footer: `Printing filename`, which indicates that your print request is printing, or `(n)Print Job(s) Submitted*`, which indicates your print request is waiting in a queue to be printed.

If you want to print more than one copy, enter the number of copies you want to print by typing a number in the `Copies` text field, or click the left mouse button on the arrow (increment/decrement) buttons.

Choosing Another Printer

The Print Tool automatically displays the default printer. Other printers available to you are listed in the `Printer` menu. You can display information that your system administrator has included about a printer by clicking the left mouse button on the `About` button.

To choose another printer, press the right mouse button on the `Printer` abbreviated menu button to display the Printer menu, then choose the name of the printer you want. The name of the printer you choose is displayed to the right of the `Printer` menu button.

Checking the Print Queue Status

Clicking the left mouse button on the `Status` button lets you view a list of print jobs in the print queue. When there are no entries, the message `no entries` is displayed at the bottom of the window. When there are entries in the print queue, the list of all the jobs for that printer (not just your jobs) is displayed in the scrolling list in the `Print Tool` window, as shown in Figure 6.2. Pressing the right mouse button in the scrolling list displays the `Scrolling List` pop-up menu.

Stopping Printing Jobs

The Print Tool allows you to stop printing all your jobs in the job queue by choosing the `All Print Jobs` item from the `Stop Printing` menu. To stop specific printing jobs, follow the steps below:

1. Click the left mouse button on the `Status` button to display jobs in the print queue.

2. Click the left mouse button on the name of the job in the scrolling list you want to stop. To stop more than one job at a time, click the middle mouse button on the additional jobs you want to stop.

3. When you have selected the jobs you want to stop, click the left mouse button on the `Stop Printing` button.

Adding a Custom Print Tool Filter

When the file you are printing has a print filter added, the filter format is automatically chosen when you drop a file on the Print Tool or type its file name in the `File` text field and click the left mouse button on the `Print` button. For example, when you print a raster image, such as a Snapshot file, a raster filter automatically filters the image file into instructions that the printer can understand. If you are printing a file that does not have a filter bound to it, such as an ASCII text file that includes `troff` formatting commands, you need to send the file through the `troff` filter so the file

FIGURE 6.2

The Print Tool window
with print jobs listed in
the scrolling list

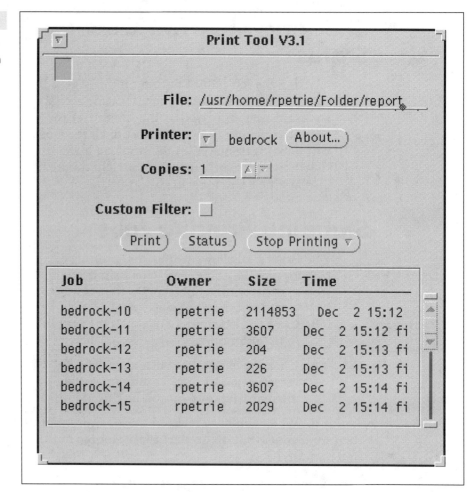

will print correctly. Chapter 13, "Formatting and Printing," explains
working with troff formatting commands.

To print a file using a filter, click on the Custom Filter check box. A check
appears in the Custom Filter check box along with a text field. In the text
field, type any command line print script. This text field accepts three variables. The $FILE variable substitutes the name of the specified file in the
print script. The $PRINTER variable substitutes the name of the printer cur-
rently selected in the Print Tool. The $COPIES variable substitutes the
number of copies currently specified in the Copies text field. For example,

to print a file containing `troff` commands to a PostScript printer, enter the following in the `Custom Filter` text field:

```
troff filename | dpost | lp -Tpostscript
```

This specifies that the file contains `troff` commands and sends the file to the `dpost` filter to convert the `troff` commands into PostScript instructions.

Using the mp PostScript Filter

Solaris includes a special PostScript printer filter to spruce up your standard output. The `mp` filter is included as the default custom filter for the File Manager and the Mail Tool. Both these tools use the following script:

```
cat $FILE | mp -lo | lp
```

The `-l` argument instructs the printer to print the file in landscape mode. The `o` argument identifies the format of the file as an ordinary ASCII file. If you are printing a PostScript file to a PostScript printer, you may need to add the `-Tpostscript` argument to the `lp` command as follows:

```
cat $FILE | mp -lo | lp -Tpostscript
```

The `-Tpostscript` argument specifies that the type of file you are printing is in a PostScript format.

Figure 6.3 shows a sample of the output using the `mp` filter. You can add arguments to the `mp` filter to print files in a format for use with personal organizers. For example, adding the `-f` argument to the `mp` command formats the output for use with a Filofax personal organizer, `-tm` formats the file for use with the Time Manager, and `-ts` formats the file for use with the Time/System International personal organizer.

The Audio Tool

The Audio Tool allows you to add a multimedia dimension to DeskSet environment. It provides features for recording, playing, editing sound files, and controlling your workstation's audio configuration parameters.

Listing for Robert Petrie   Sun Jun 20 02:34:41 1993   Page 1

```
# @(#)README   1.4    92/10/21 SMI

This directory hierarchy contains the sources and executables for demo
applications, a prototype audio programming library, and a set of
pre-recorded audio sound samples. Manual pages for the demo programs
are located in section 6: Games and Demos.

Note that the principal audio record/playback utility is AudioTool,
provided with the OpenWindows DeskSet applications (refer to the
DeskSet User's Guide and the audiotool(1) manual page).

Some of the XView demo programs contain spot help information. To obtain
spot help, set the HELPPATH environment variable to include the directory
in which the files are located. For example:

    % setenv HELPPATH "$HELPPATH:/usr/demo/SOUND/help"

The following is an overview of the contents of /usr/demo/SOUND:

/usr/demo/SOUND/bin        demo program executables
/usr/demo/SOUND/help       spot help files for the demos
/usr/demo/SOUND/include    header files for the prototype audio library
/usr/demo/SOUND/lib        libaudio.a, the prototype audio library
/usr/demo/SOUND/man        manual pages for libaudio functions
/usr/demo/SOUND/sounds     sample sound files
/usr/demo/SOUND/src        source code for the demo programs

Demo programs
-------------
soundtool(6)
    This is a prototype audio record/playback tool. It demonstrates
    many of the features of the audio programming interface. Since
    it the XView application, is written to obey the constraints
    of the XView toolkit and to issue only asynchronous I/O requests.
    Because it also attempts to keep an oscilloscope display synchronized
    during play and record, it is far more complex than most audio
    applications need to be. However, it serves as a demonstration of
    the real-time audio capabilities of the SPARCstation.

gaintool(6)
    This is a prototype audio control panel. It illustrates the ability
    to control various aspects of the workstation audio configuration
    outside of particular audio applications. For instance, since play
    volume may be controlled from the panel, it is not necessary for all
    audio applications to provide an output volume control themselves.

    Gaintool also has a property sheet (activated from a menu over the
    main panel) that displays complete status information for the audio
    device. This information can be useful for debugging audio programs.

Radio Free Ethernet
    Radio Free Ethernet is a suite of programs that allow broadcasting
    and receiving audio over the network. The receiver and transmitter
    (radio_recv and radio_xmit) are command-line programs that are
    controlled by window programs (radio and xmit). The command-line
    programs may also be invoked by shell scripts or through the cron(1m)
```

Listing for Robert Petrie   Sun Jun 20 02:34:41 1993   Page 2

```
    facility. See the About Sound document for a general overview of
    this demo.

radio(6)
    Radio is the window-based tool for the radio receiver. The interface
    is similar to that of a car radio.

xmit(6)
    Xmit is the window-based tool for the radio transmitter. When running
    xmit for the first time, a radio station name must be entered in the
    Station configuration panel before transmission can be started.

radio_recv(6)
    Radio_recv is the command-line radio receiver program (normally invoked
    by the radio program).

radio_xmit(6)
    Radio_xmit is the command-line radio transmitter (normally invoked by
    the xmit program).

Prototype audio programming library
-----------------------------------
    A preliminary audio programming library, libaudio.a, is provided.
    Manual pages for the functions in libaudio.a are located in
    /usr/demo/SOUND/man/man3. Header files for libaudio.a are in
    /usr/demo/SOUND/include/multimedia.

Sound files
-----------
    Some sample sound files are located in the /usr/demo/SOUND/sounds
    directory. sample.au contains guidelines in setting the recording
    volume level. The other files include sample sound effects and
    telephone control tones.

Building the demos from source code
-----------------------------------
    Source code is provided for all demo programs. Before attempting to build
    the demo programs from source, ensure that the OpenWindows, SPARCompilers,
    and Devguide (Version 3.0.1 or later) products are installed in your system.
    (Note that Devguide must be purchased separately.) Refer to the system
    installation manual for instructions on installing these products.

    Be sure to set the GUIDEHOME environment variable to the directory where
    Devguide is installed. Header files are included from $(GUIDEHOME)/include
    and libraries are linked from $(GUIDEHOME)/lib.

    To build the demo programs, do the following:

        % cd src
        % make

    To install them in /usr/demo/SOUND/bin, type:

        % make install
```

FIGURE 6.3

A sample of output using the mp filter

Before you can record anything, two additional pieces of hardware are needed: a microphone and an audio input/output adapter cable. The microphone can be any commercial variety that can be plugged into the audio I/O adapter cable. The adapter cable is part of the Sun workstation accessory package that comes with most Sun workstations. You can listen to audio output through a connected headphone or an externally powered speaker that is plugged into the headphone jack of the input/output adapter cable.

NOTE

If you are using Solaris 2 for x86, you need to have installed a supported sound board, such as the Sound Blaster Pro, to work with the Audio Tool.

The Audio Tool Window

The `Audio Tool` window uses a common tape recorder metaphor for working with sound files. Figure 6.4 shows both the Audio Tool window and icon. The `File` menu provides items for managing sound files. The `Edit` menu includes items for editing sound files, such as cutting and pasting sounds. The `Volume` menu provides items for adjusting the play and record volumes.

FIGURE 6.4

The Audio Tool window and icon

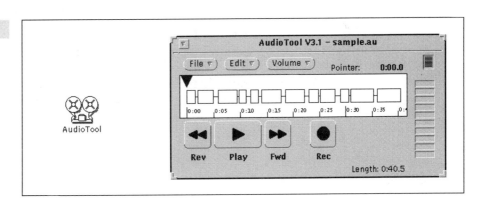

The display canvas area displays recorded sound graphically. Recorded information is represented with rectangle-shaped boxes that contain bands of sound, and silence is shown as a thin, flat horizontal line, as shown in Figure 6.4. Interval marks are displayed under the sound graph to measure recorded sound.

The four buttons located at the bottom of the window (`Rev`, `Play`, `Fwd`, and `Rec`) function like standard controls on a tape recorder. The drag-and-drop target allows you to drag sound files into the `Audio Tool` window. The `Level` meter, the boxes below the drag-and-drop target, graphically display the level of sound coming from the recording.

Loading Sound Files

There are several audio files included with Solaris, which are stored in the `/usr/demo/SOUND/sounds` and `/usr/openwin/lib/locale/C/help/handbooks/sounds` directories. Double-clicking the left mouse button on a sound file icon in the File Manager activates the Audio Tool and begins playing the recording.

A sound file can also be loaded into the Audio Tool using the drag-and-drop method. Dragging and dropping a sound file onto the drag-and-drop target loads the file into the Audio Tool, replacing any file currently in the Audio Tool. Dragging and dropping a sound file into the display canvas appends the sound file to any sound file already in the Audio Tool.

A sound file can also be loaded into the Audio Tool by clicking the left mouse button on the `File` menu to choose the default `Load` item. The `Load File` pop-up window appears (Figure 6.5). Select the file you want from the scrolling list and click on the Load button at the bottom of the window to load the file. Alternatively you can enter the directory path and file name of the sound file you want to load in the `Name` text field and click the left mouse button on the `Load` button.

FIGURE 6.5

The Load File pop-up window

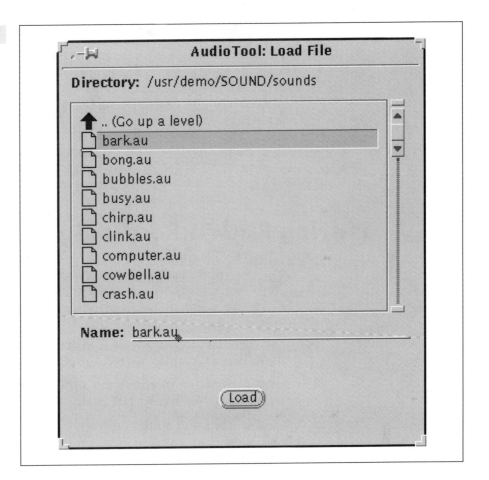

Recording a Sound

Recording a sound file in the `Audio Tool` window is similar to using a tape recorder. With the `Audio Tool` window displayed, make sure your microphone is turned on, and perform the following steps.

1. Click the left mouse button on the `Rec` button. The messages `Recording` and `Length` (elapsed time) are displayed in the status information area at the bottom of the Audio Tool window. The `Rec` button changes to a `Stop` button.

2. Record your sound or message.

3. To stop recording, click the left mouse button on the **Stop** button.
The recording is stopped and your recorded sounds are displayed
as boxes and lines in the **Display** canvas. You can append or record
over a recording by repositioning the cursor in the display canvas
and repeating steps 2 and 3.

The Audio Tool's status information is displayed below the recording
control buttons and the length of the sound file information is displayed
under the **Rec** button.

Playing Back a Recording

Playing back a recorded sound in the **Audio Tool** window is easy. With the
recorded sound displayed in the display canvas, do the following:

1. Click the left mouse button on the **Rev** (reverse) button or click
the left mouse button with the pointer at the beginning of the
recording in the display canvas. You can position the pointer at any
location in the recording to start the playback at that location.

2. Click the left mouse button in the display canvas. The **Play** position pointer is displayed at that position.

3. Click the left mouse button on the **Play** button. The recording is
played on your workstation's speaker, headphones, or external
speaker. The **Play** button changes to a **Stop** button, on which you
can click the left mouse button to stop the playback.

Saving Sound Files

To save a new sound file, choose the **Save** item from the **File** menu. The
Save File pop-up window appears (Figure 6.6). Enter the directory path
for the file and click on the **Save** button or press Return. In the **File Name**
text field, enter the file name for the sound file. Click the left mouse button on the **Save** button. An audio file icon (Figure 6.7) now appears in
the directory where you saved the audio file.

FIGURE 6.6

The Save File window

FIGURE 6.6

The Save File window

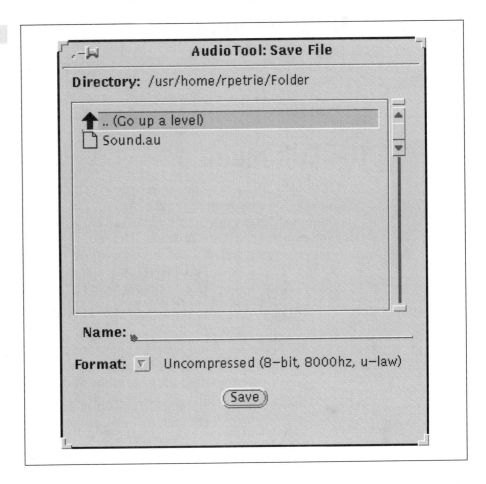

FIGURE 6.7

An Audio Tool file icon

Audio.au

If you're working on a sound file that has already been saved previously by choosing Save from the File menu, you can save it with another file name by choosing the Save As item from the File menu. This displays the same Save File pop-up window as displayed when first saving a file. The top center of the window displays the name of a sound file, along with its status.

The Edit Menu

The Edit menu provides standard editing commands for working in the Audio Tool window. If the editing command is dimmed, the use of that command is not available for the operation being performed. The following explains the items in the Edit menu.

ITEM	DESCRIPTION
Again	Repeats the last Edit menu command.
Clear	Removes the displayed sound data from the display window. If the sound data has not been saved before choosing the Clear item, a Notice prompts you to confirm the discard of your unsaved edits.
Undo	Reverses the effect of the last editing command issued. A submenu provides the Undo Last and Undo All commands. The Undo Last command reverses the previous edit. The Undo All command restores all edited changes to their original status.
Redo	Reverses the effects of the Undo command. A submenu provides the Redo Last and Redo All commands. The Redo Last command restores the previous edit. The Redo All command restores all edited changes.
Cut	Removes the current selection from the sound file and places it in the clipboard. You can cut segments from the same file or other sound files.

ITEM	DESCRIPTION
Copy	Copies the current selection and places it in the clipboard without modifying the original sound file. You can copy segments from the same file or other sound files.
Paste	Pastes information currently stored in the clipboard (as a result of previous `Copy` or `Cut` commands) into any active sound file.
Delete	Displays a submenu of four deletion items. The first, `Selection`, removes the current selection from your sound file directory. The `Unselected` item removes all but the selected portion of the sound file. `All Silence` deletes all silent pauses from the sound file. The last item, `Silent Ends`, deletes any silence that occurs at the end of a sound file.
Select All	Selects the entire sound recording in the display canvas.

Pressing the right mouse button in the display canvas displays the `Display` pop-up menu (Figure 6.8). All the items in this menu, with the exception of the `Reset pointer` item, are also available in the `Edit` menu.

FIGURE 6.8

The Display pop-up menu

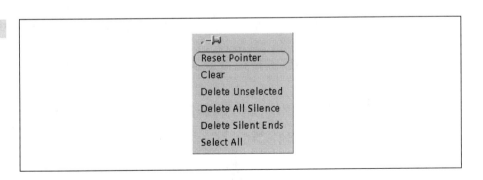

Editing a Sound File

Editing a sound file is similar to editing text in a text editor. You can copy, move, and delete sound data in the display canvas. Any time you move the pointer to the display canvas, the cursor becomes a thin vertical line. The position of the cursor is indicated by the cursor location status message in the upper-right corner. If you click the left mouse button while in the display canvas, the position pointer (an upside-down triangle located at the top of the display canvas) is displayed and its location is noted at the Pointer status message.

The following steps explain how to edit a sound file:

1. Load the sound file into the Audio Tool window.

2. Click the left mouse button at the beginning of the sound segment you want to edit in the display canvas. You can choose the Reset pointer item from the display canvas pop-up menu to move the pointer to the beginning of the display canvas.

3. Click the middle mouse button at the end of the sound segment you want to edit.

4. Press the right mouse button on the Edit menu button and choose either the Cut or Copy item. If you want to delete the selected sound data, choose the Delete item.

5. To copy or move the selected sound segment, move the cursor to the new position for the segment and click the left mouse button. The position pointer is displayed at the location.

6. Press the right mouse button on the Edit menu and choose the Paste item. The sound segment is pasted at the cursor's location.

Inserting a Sound File into Another Sound File

You can insert a sound file to an existing sound file in the Audio Tool window by using either the drag-and-drop method or the Include File item in the File menu. To insert a sound file using the drag-and-drop method, move the cursor in the display canvas to the location where you want to insert the sound file, and click the left mouse button. Drag and drop the sound file icon you want to insert on the display canvas.

To insert a sound file into an existing sound file in the `Audio Tool` window, first move the cursor in the display canvas to the location where you want to insert the sound file, and click the left mouse button. Choose the `Include File` item from the `File` menu to display the `Include File` pop-up window. In the scrolling list, select the file you want to insert in the `Audio Tool` pop-up window, and click the left mouse button on the `Include` button.

Customizing the Audio Tool

Choosing the `Properties` item menu in the `Edit` menu displays the Audio Tool's `Properties` window (Figure 6.9). The following list explains each control:

CONTROL	DESCRIPTION
Auto Play on Load	Instructs the Audio Tool to automatically play a file when it is loaded. The default setting is checked.
Auto Play on Selection	Automatically plays back any portion of a recorded sound selected in the display canvas. The default setting is unchecked.
Confirm before clear	Determines whether a warning message is displayed when you choose the `Clear` item from the `Edit` menu.
Silence Detection	Silence in the Audio Tool is identified by a straight line, and sound is identified by boxes. Unless this setting is checked, the Audio tool does not differentiate between sound and silence, so silence and sound are indistinguishable in the display canvas.

FIGURE 6.9

The Audio Tool's
Properties window

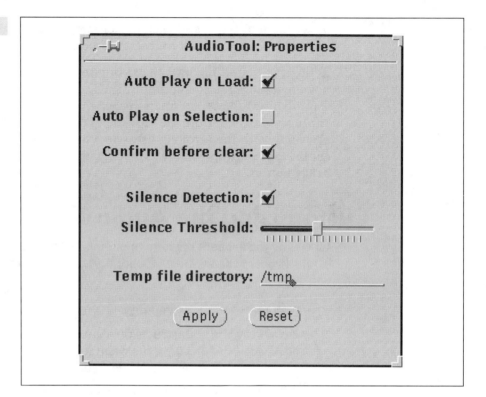

CONTROL	DESCRIPTION
Silence Threshold	Changes the degree with which silence is measured. It adjusts the sensitivity to pauses, determining when a pause should be interpreted as silence. Dragging the slider to the right decreases the sensitivity to short pauses, thus decreasing the number of sound-and-silence segments. Dragging the slider to the left increases the sensitivity to short pauses, thus increasing the number of sound-and-silence segments.

CONTROL	DESCRIPTION
`Temp file directory`	Lets you determine where temporary sound files are placed when working with the Audio Tool.

Clicking the left mouse button on the `Apply` button saves all the changes you make in the `Properties` pop-up window. Clicking the left mouse button on the `Reset` button before pressing the `Apply` button resets the most recent changes to their previous settings.

The Play Volume Pop-up Window

Choosing the `Play` item from the `Volume` menu displays the `Play Volume` pop-up window (Figure 6.10). The `Play Volume` pop-up window controls the volume of the audio input and output, and whether the audio output goes to the speaker or jack.

The `Play Volume` setting allows you to control the output volume to the internal workstation speaker. The `Monitor Volume` setting allows you to control the adjustment of the audio input signal. The `Spkr/Jack` control switches between your workstation's internal speaker and the external headphone jack. The default setting is `Spkr`, which sends the audio output to your workstation's speaker. The `Pause Play` button suspends and resumes all audio output from the Audio Tool.

FIGURE 6.10

The Play Volume pop-up window

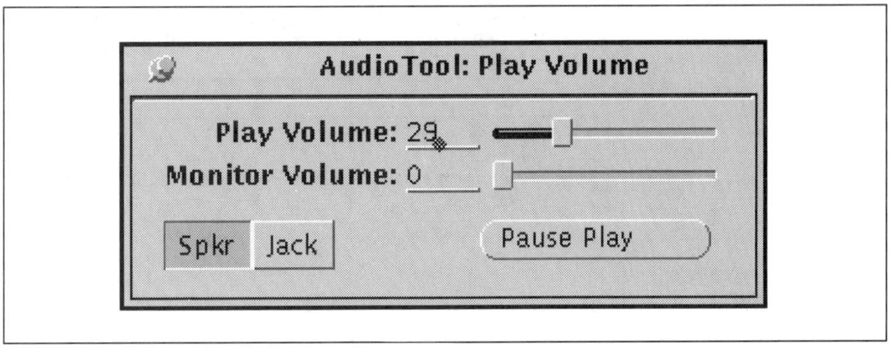

The Record Volume Pop-up Window

Choosing the `Record` item from the `Volume` menu displays the `Record Volume` pop-up window (Figure 6.11). The `Record Volume` pop-up window allows you to adjust the volume during recording using the `Record Volume` setting.

The `Auto-Adjust Record Volume` button sets the recording level to a programmed level adjustment, whereby the input sound data is scanned to determine its loudness. An input sensor meter is displayed on the window to show peaks and lows in the sound input. Once the volume is automatically adjusted, consistent loudness for each input device is set to an optimum signal level. If a microphone is connected to the audio input jack, adjustments can be made to voice input by selecting the `Auto-Adjust Record Volume` button. Speaking into the microphone in a normal tone until the process is complete automatically adjusts the voice input level.

FIGURE 6.11

The Record Volume
pop-up window

The Snapshot Application

The Snapshot application allows you to take color, gray-scale, and black-and-white snapshots of a region (a section of the screen), a window, or the entire screen. These snapshots are created and stored as raster files. *Raster files* store a picture as a matrix of dots. When you use the Snapshot application on a monochrome monitor, the images created are always black and white. When you take snapshots on a color monitor, the images are always in color, unless you are running OpenWindows in black-and-white mode. Some applications can handle black-and-white snapshots but cannot handle gray-scale or color snapshots. The **Snapshot** window and icon are shown in Figure 6.12. The following explains the controls in the **Snapshot** window.

FIGURE 6.12

The Snapshot window and icon

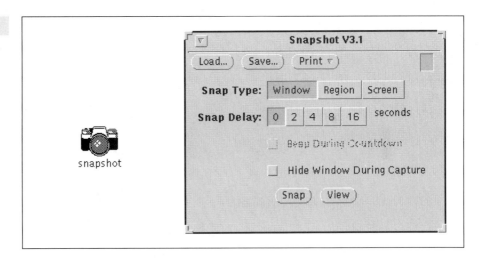

CONTROL	DESCRIPTION
Load button	Displays the **Load Options** pop-up window to allow you to load Snapshot files.

CONTROL	DESCRIPTION
Save button	Displays the Save Options pop-up window to allow you to save a snapshot to a file.
Print button	Lets you print your snapshots or displays the Print Options pop-up window to customize your printer settings.
Snap Type	Defines the area of the snapshot. The Window setting takes a snapshot of a single window. The Region setting takes a snapshot of part of the screen. The Screen setting takes a snapshot of the entire screen.
Snap Delay	Determines the time period between initiating the snapshot and taking it. The timer is especially useful if you are taking snapshots of menus that you must display after you start the snapshot. When the Snap Delay setting is set to 0 seconds, the snapshot is taken immediately. When the Snap Delay setting is set for more than 0 seconds, the Beep During Countdown setting becomes active and can be set.
Beep During Countdown	Activating the Beep During Countdown setting starts a bell beep each second between the time when you initiate the snapshot and when it is taken. Clicking the left mouse button on the Beep During Countdown setting acts as a toggle, setting it on or off.
Hide Window During Capture	Allows you to hide the Snapshot window when you're taking a snapshot of the screen.

CONTROL	DESCRIPTION
Snap	Activates the Snapshot application to take a snapshot.
View	Allows you to view the current snapshot in the `View` pop-up window.

Taking a Snapshot of a Window

To take a snapshot of a window, make sure the window or icon you want to capture is completely visible and not partly obscured by overlapping windows (unless you want to include them in the snapshot), and follow the steps below:

1. Make sure the `Snap Type` is set to `Window` in the `Snapshot` window. Set the `Snap Delay` and `Beep During Countdown` settings if you want to use them. When you have the `Snap Delay` set and are taking snapshots of windows or icons, Snapshot records the window position when the snap is initiated. However, if you move the window before the snapshot is completed, you may not get all the information you wanted in the window snapshot.

2. Click the left mouse button on the `Snap` button. A message appears in the window footer: `SELECT–Select Window. ADJUST or MENU–Cancel. SELECT` refers to the left mouse button. `ADJUST` refers to the middle button. `MENU` refers to the right mouse button. The `Snap` button appears shaded, indicating that it is waiting for you to select a window.

3. Click the left mouse button on the header of the window you want to snap to take the snapshot. To cancel the operation, click either the middle mouse button or the right mouse button. When the snapshot is complete, a message is displayed in the footer of the snapshot window indicating whether the snapshot succeeded or not. You can view the snapshot by clicking the left mouse button on the `View` button.

4. Click the left mouse button on the `Save` button. The `Save Op-tions` pop-up window is displayed, as shown in Figure 6.13. In the `Directory` text field, type the name of the directory to which you want to save the file. Type the file name for the snapshot in the `File` text field.

5. Click the left mouse button on the `Save` button in the `Save Op-tions` pop-up window.

FIGURE 6.13

The Save Options
pop-up window

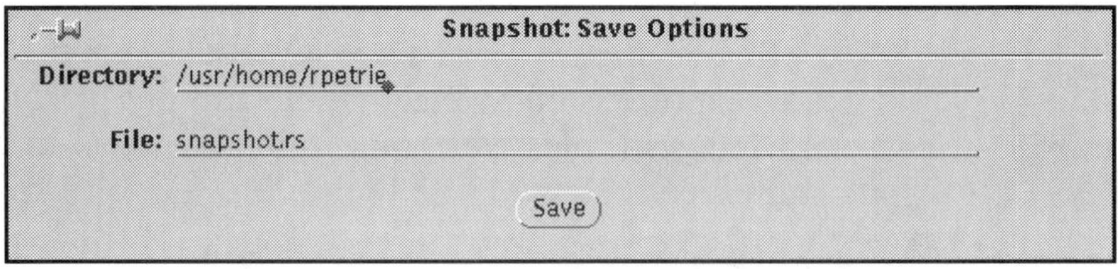

Taking a Snapshot of a Region

Snapshots of any rectangular area of the screen you specify can be taken using the `Region` button. Before taking a snapshot of a region of the screen, make sure the screen is displaying the windows or icons you want to capture, and perform the following steps:

1. Click the left mouse button on the `Region` setting in the `Snapshot` window. Set the `Snap Delay` and `Beep During Countdown` settings if you want to use them.

2. Click the left mouse button on the `Hide Window During Capture` setting if you need to.

3. Click the left mouse button on the `Region` button. A message appears in the window footer: `SELECT–Position Rectangle`, `ADJUST–Snap Image`, `MENU–Cancel`. `SELECT` means to click the left mouse button. `ADJUST` means to click the middle mouse button. `MENU` means to click the right mouse button.

4. Move the pointer to the top left corner of the region you want to define and press the left mouse button. Drag the pointer to define the rectangular region to be included. A bounding box is displayed. Release the left mouse button. An outline of the snapshot region is displayed.

5. Click the middle mouse button. Snapshot takes the snapshot of the boxed region of the screen and displays a message in the Snapshot window footer indicating whether the snapshot was successful. If you want to cancel the snapshot, click the right mouse button. You can view the snapshot by clicking the left mouse button on the `View` button.

6. Click the left mouse button on the `Save` button. The `Save Options` pop-up window is displayed. Type the name of the directory in which you want to save the file in the `Directory` text field. Type the file name for the snapshot in the `File` text field.

7. Click the left mouse button on the `Save` button in the `Save Options` pop-up window..

Taking a Snapshot of the Screen

Taking a snapshot of the entire screen is the easiest type of snapshot to take; however, it takes longer and requires more disk space to store. Unless you need a snapshot of the entire screen, it is recommended you use `Window` or `Region`. To take a snapshot of the entire screen, make sure the screen is set up in the configuration you want and follow these steps:

1. Click the left mouse button on the `Screen` setting. Set the `Snap Delay` and `Beep During Countdown` settings if you want to use them.

2. Click the left mouse button on `Hide Window During Capture` unless you want the `Snapshot` window in the screen shot.

3. Click the left mouse button on the `Snap` button. After the snapshot is taken, a status message informing you whether the snapshot was successful or not is displayed in the window footer. You can view the snapshot by clicking the left mouse button on the `View` button.

4. Click the left mouse button on the `Save` button. The `Save Op-tions` pop-up window is displayed. Type the name of the directory in which you want to save the file in the `Directory` text field. Type the file name for the snapshot in the `File` text field.

5. Click the left mouse button on the `Save` button in the `Save Op-tions` pop-up window.

Viewing a Snapshot

The Snapshot application allows you to view a snapshot file at any time. You can use either the drag-and-drop method or use the `Load` button. To display a snapshot using the drag-and-drop method, drag a snapshot file from the File Manager and drop it onto the `Snapshot` window's drag-and-drop target. Click the left mouse button on the `View` button. The `View` pop-up window appears, displaying the selected file. Once the `View` pop-up window is displayed, you can view other snapshot files by dragging and dropping one file at a time onto the `Snapshot` window's drag-and-drop target.

To display a snapshot using the `Load` button, click the left mouse button on the `Load` button. The `Load Options` pop-up window is displayed. Type the name of the directory and the snapshot file you want to load in the `Directory` and `File` text fields. Click the left mouse button on the `Load` button. In the `Snapshot` window, click the left mouse button on the `View` menu. The `View` pop-up window is displayed (Figure 6.14), showing the contents of the snapshot file. To view a snapshot immediately after taking it, simply click the left mouse button on the `View` button. If you are using a black-and-white monitor, Snapshot automatically converts a copy of gray-scale or color images to black and white so that they can be displayed. The file itself is not changed.

Only one snapshot at a time can be viewed, unless you load and use multiple snapshot applications. When the `View` pop-up window is displayed, and you type a new snapshot file name in the `File` text field and click the left mouse button on the `View` button, the `View` window is cleared and automatically resized to match the size of the second snapshot file.

The View pop-up window displaying a snapshot

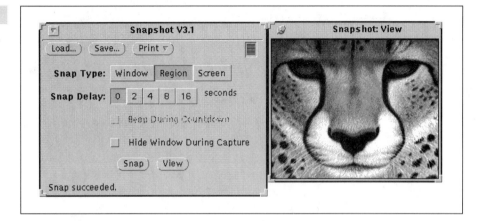

Printing a Snapshot

Snapshot files can be printed by clicking the left mouse button on the `Print` button. If you want to change the default printing settings, press the right mouse button on the `Print` button and choose the `Options` item. The `Print Options` pop-up window is displayed (Figure 6.15). This window allows you to change your printer settings for Snapshot. The following explains the controls in the `Print Options` window.

CONTROL	DESCRIPTION
Destination	Allows you to designate whether a snapshot is sent to a printer or to a file. When `Printer` is selected, use the text field to specify which printer you want to use. When `File` is selected, the `Directory` and `File` text fields are displayed.
Printer	Allows you to specify another printer.
Orientation	Determines the orientation of the printed image on the page. The `Upright` setting prints a portrait image. The `Sideways` setting prints a landscape image.

FIGURE 6.15

The Print Options pop-up window

	Snapshot: Print Options
Destination:	Printer | File
Printer:	bedrock
Orientation:	Upright | Sideways
Position:	Center | Specify
	0.25 Inches from left 0.25 inches from bottom
Scale to:	Actual Size | Width | Height | Both
	Width: 8 inches Height 10 inches
Double Size:	no | yes ✔ Monochrome Printer
	(Print)

CONTROL	DESCRIPTION
Position	Controls the position of the snapshot on the printed page. The **Center** setting centers the printed snapshot. You can specify the left and bottom margins for the printed image by choosing the **Specify** setting. This activates the **Inches from left** and **Inches from bottom** text fields, which have default values of .25 inch.

CONTROL	DESCRIPTION
Scale to	The default `Actual Size` setting prints the snapshot in the actual size of the displayed snapshot. You can specify the width of the printed snapshot by choosing the `Width` setting and typing a value, either a whole number or decimal, in the `Width` text field. The snapshot is scaled to the width you select. You can also specify the height of the printed snapshot by choosing the `Height` setting, and typing a value in the `Height` text field. When you choose the `Both` setting, both the `Width` and `Height` text fields are activated, allowing you to specify the width and height dimensions for the snapshot.
Double Size	Choosing the `Yes` setting allows you to double the size of the snapshot.
Monochrome Printer	Unless you are using a color printer, keep the `Monochrome Printer` setting checked.
Print	Clicking the left mouse button on the `Print` button prints the specified file.

Once you change the settings in the `Print Options` pop-up window, they are recorded and used each time you click the left mouse button on the `Print` button until you exit or quit the `Snapshot` window.

The Clock Application

The Clock application displays an analog clock icon that shows the current time of day (Figure 6.16). When you open the Clock icon, the same clock is displayed in the pane of a window. The `Clock` window (Figure 6.16) has a header and resize corners to make the clock image larger or smaller.

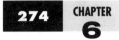
FIGURE 6.16

The Clock icon and window

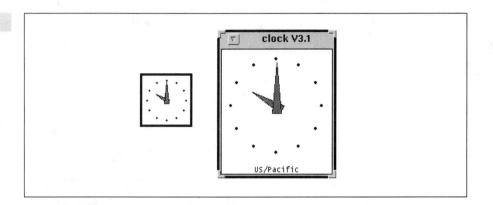

NOTE

Solaris also includes two X clock applications that display analog clocks. To display the square X clock in a Shell or Command Tool, enter `xclock &`. To display the circular X clock in a Shell or Command Tool, enter `oclock &`.

Customizing the Clock

The Clock can be customized using the settings in the `Clock Properties` window. To display the `Clock Properties` window, press the right mouse button in the Clock pane to display the `Clock` pop-up menu (Figure 6.17), then choose the `Properties` item. The following explains the controls in the `Clock Properties` pop-up window.

CONTROL	DESCRIPTION
Clock Face	The `digital` setting displays in the `Clock` window as a digital clock (Figure 6.18). The default `analog` setting displays a traditional clock face in the `Clock` window. The Clock icon always displays an analog clock, regardless of the `Clock Face` property setting.

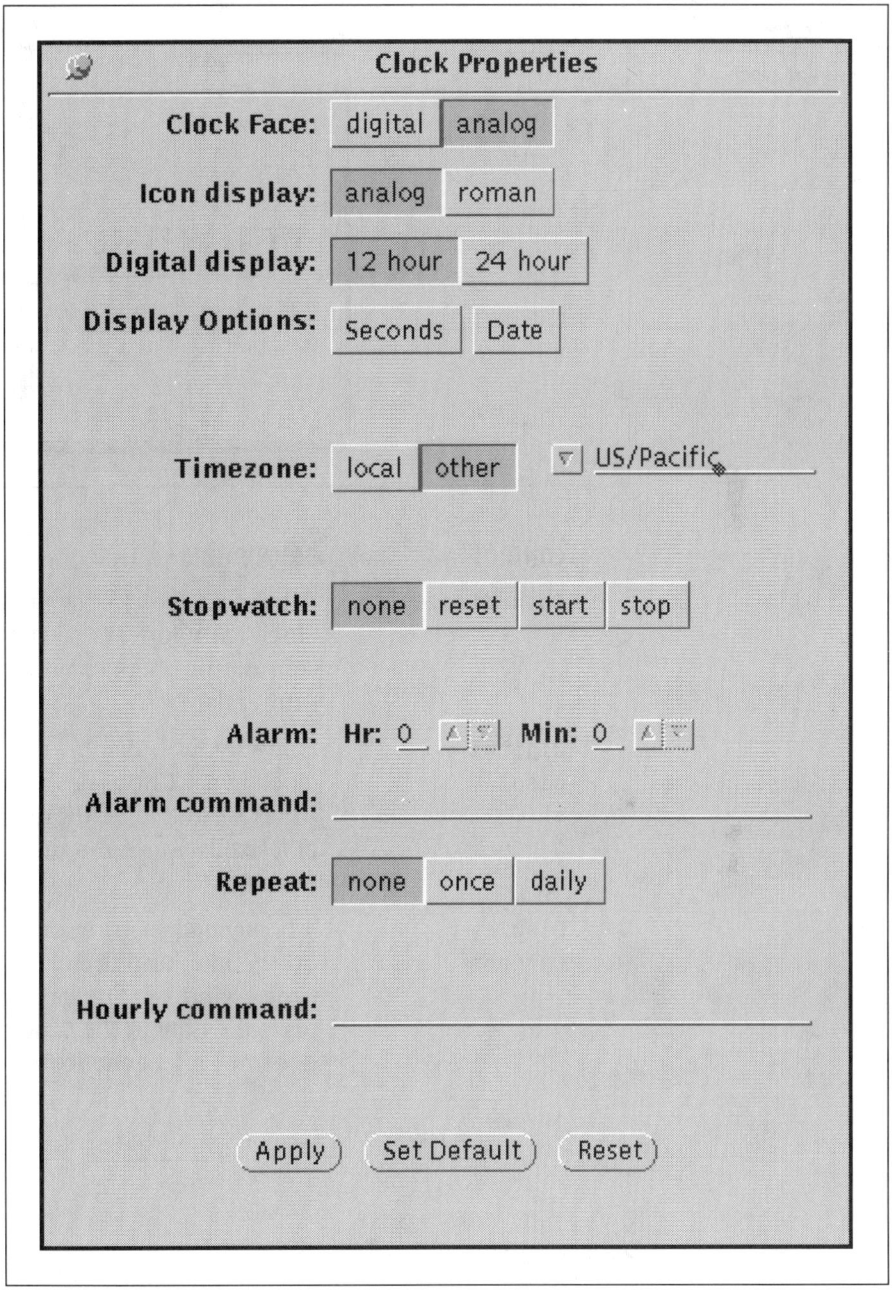

FIGURE 6.17

The Clock Properties
pop-up window

Clock Properties		
Clock Face:	digital	analog
Icon display:	analog	roman
Digital display:	12 hour	24 hour
Display Options:	Seconds	Date
Timezone:	local	other ▽ US/Pacific
Stopwatch:	none	reset start stop
Alarm:	Hr: 0 △▽	Min: 0 △▽
Alarm command:		
Repeat:	none	once daily
Hourly command:		
(Apply) (Set Default) (Reset)		

FIGURE 6.18

The digital clock

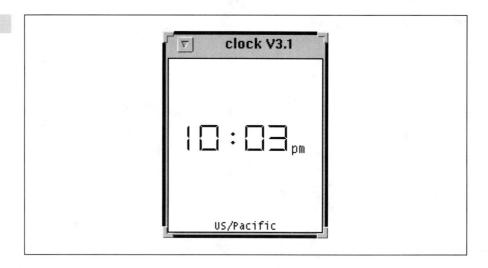

CONTROL	DESCRIPTION
`Icon display`	Allows you to choose whether the clock icon appears with dots representing numbers or with roman numerals.
`Digital display`	Allows you to display the digital clock in a 12-hour or 24-hour (military time) format. The digital 12-hour clock tells you if the time is a.m. or p.m.
`Display Options`	The `Seconds` setting displays seconds on the icon and the clock face in the `Clock` window. The `Date` setting displays the date in the `Clock` window but does not affect the icon display.

CONTROL	DESCRIPTION
`Timezone`	Allows you to display the time of a different time zone. By default, the time is displayed in your local time zone. You can set the clock to a different time zone by pressing the left mouse button on the `Other` setting to display the Timezone abbreviated menu button. Clicking the right mouse button on the Timezone abbreviated menu button displays a list of available time zones (Figure 6.19) so you can choose the time zone you want.
`Stopwatch`	The `reset` setting allows you to turn the clock display into a stopwatch. Using the `digital` setting in the `Clock Face` setting makes the stopwatch easier to read. To start the stopwatch, click the left mouse button on the `start` setting. To stop the stopwatch, click the left mouse button on the `stop` setting. The stopwatch settings take effect immediately, unlike the other settings, which take effect when you click the left mouse button on the `Apply` button.
`Alarm`	Allows you to specify the time for an alarm. You must specify the time, using a 24-hour format.

FIGURE 6.19

The Timezone submenu

CONTROL	DESCRIPTION
`Alarm command`	Enter the command that you want to take place at the alarm time in the `Alarm command` text field. If you don't specify a command, the Clock application will beep. If your workstation has audio capabilities, you can set the clock to crow like a rooster by entering `ksh -c "cat /usr/demo/ SOUND/sounds/ rooster.au > /dev/audio"`.
`Repeat`	Allows you to specify whether the alarm should be triggered just one time or daily at a given time. The alarm will not be triggered as long as the `Repeat` setting is `none`.
`Hourly command`	If you want a command to repeat hourly, type that command in the `Hourly` command text field. For example, you can enter `ksh -c "cat /usr/demo/SOUND/sounds/ rooster.au > /dev/audio"` to have the clock crow like a rooster on an hourly basis.

The `Set Default` button determines if the changes you make in the `Clock Properties` pop-up window will appear in each new clock you start. Unless you choose the `Set Default` button, the changes made in the `Clock Properties` pop-up window are not saved after the current Open-Windows session.

The Performance Meter

The DeskSet environment provides ten different Performance Meters that can be used to monitor various aspects of your system. One meter or a combination of meters can be run (displayed) at the same time. To display a Performance Meter, choose the `Performance Meter` item from the `Programs` submenu of the `Workspace` menu. The default `cpu Performance Meter` window is displayed in the size of a typical icon (Figure 6.20). Closing the performance meter window to an icon displays a graph icon, as shown in Figure 6.20.

FIGURE 6.20

An open and closed
Performance Meter

The Performance Meter Pop-up Menu

You can quickly change to another performance meter from any `Performance Meter` window using a `Performance Meter` pop-up menu (Figure 6.21). To display the `Performance Meter` pop-up menu, press the right mouse button in any `Performance Meter` window. The pop-up menu includes the ten Performance Meter items and a `Properties` item for customizing the Performance Meter. Choose the type of performance monitor you want to change to. The following is a brief description of what each of the items on this menu monitors.

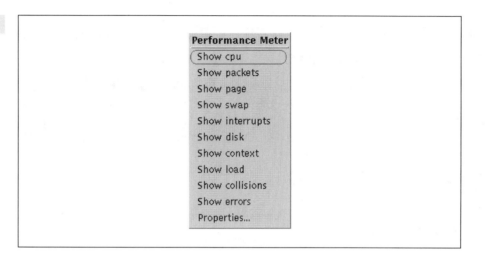

ITEM	MONITORS
Show cpu	Percent of CPU being used.
Show packets	Number of ethernet packets per second. (*Ethernet packets* are units for transmitting messages over a network.)
Show page	Paging activity in pages per second.
Show swap	Number of jobs swapped per second.
Show interrupts	Number of job interrupts per second.
Show disk	Disk traffic in transfers per second.
Show context	Number of context switches per second.
Show load	Average number of runnable processes over the last minute.
Show collisions	Number of collisions per second detected on the ethernet.
Show errors	Number of errors per second on receiving packets.

Customizing Performance Meters

The last item in the **Performance Meter** pop-up menu, **Properties**, allows you to customize the features of a Performance Meter. Choosing the **Properties** item displays the **Properties** pop-up window, as shown in Figure 6.22. The following explains the settings in the **Properties** pop-up window.

FIGURE 6.22

The Properties pop-up window

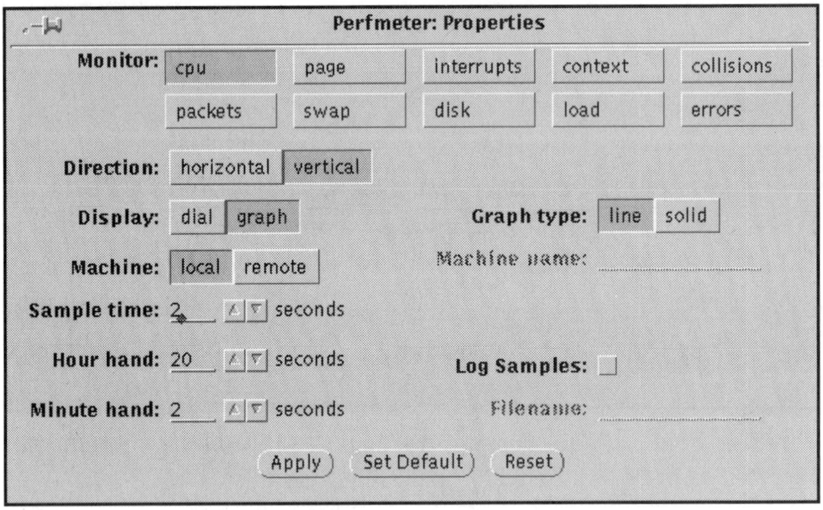

SETTING	DESCRIPTION
Monitor	Choosing one of the **Monitor** settings and clicking the left mouse button on the **Apply** button is the same as choosing one of the same items from the **Performance Meter** pop-up menu.

SETTING	DESCRIPTION
Direction	Determines if multiple Performance Meters are displayed side by side (horizontally) or stacked on top of one another (vertically).
Display	Determines if the Performance Meters are displayed as dials or as graphs. The `graph` setting is the default setting. Figure 6.23 shows a performance meter using a dial display.
Graph type	Choose the `line` setting to display a single line graph, and `solid` to display a solid graph.
Machine	Allows you to monitor the performance for your own machine (`local`, which is the default) or for another machine (`remote`) on the network. If you select the `remote` setting, the `Machine name` text field is activated to accept the name of the machine you want to monitor.

FIGURE 6.23

A performance meter using the dial display

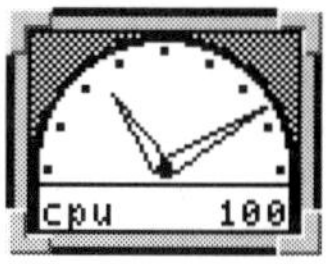

SETTING	DESCRIPTION
Sample time	Allows you to change the frequency with which the meters are updated and units measured by the Hour hand and the Minute hand settings. The short needle, referred to as an *hour hand*, tracks average performance over a twenty-second interval, and the long one, referred to as the *minute hand*, tracks current performance over a two-second interval. The type of performance being measured is shown in the lower-left corner of the icon and its maximum value is shown in the lower-right corner.
Log Samples	Lets you save and examine individual samples. Samples are saved in the file typed in the filename text field. If no file is specified, then samples are saved in a file in your home directory called perfmeter.logxxx, where xxx is replaced by a unique identifier. If you use the Log Samples, do not leave the performance meter running for a long period of time. The perfmeter.logxxx file can increase in size and leave you with little or no disk space.

Clicking the left mouse button on Set Default saves your Performance Meter settings for use in each new Performance Meter you start. If you change the values of any of the performance meter properties, you need to click the left mouse button on the Apply button to record the changes. Pressing the left mouse button on the Reset button returns all settings to the system defaults.

The Calculator

The Calculator is designed to perform a wide variety of mathematical functions. It provides financial, logical, and scientific functions. It looks and works in much the same way as many hand-held calculators. The Calculator allows you to use decimal, binary, octal, or hexadecimal numbers, as well as scientific notation. It has ten different memory registers in which numbers can be easily stored, retrieved, and replaced. In addition, the Calculator allows you to store functions you create in a menu.

The `Calculator` window and icon are shown in Figure 6.24. The buttons of the calculator are the controls that activate its functions. It has six rows of eight buttons, some arranged as buttons within other buttons, to emulate a typical calculator. Buttons that have a menu mark (the upside-down triangle) display menus when you press the right mouse button on them.

FIGURE 6.24

The Calculator window and icon

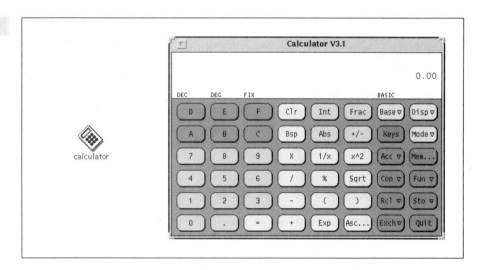

NOTE Solaris also includes the X calculator. To start the X calculator program in a Shell Tool or Command Tool, enter xcalc &. For more information on using the X calculator, enter xman & in a Shell or Command Tool.

Performing Simple Calculations

While the DeskSet Calculator is a powerful financial, logical, and scientific calculator, it also allows you to perform simple arithmetic operations such as addition, subtraction, division, and multiplication. To perform a numerical operation, such as adding two numbers together, follow the steps below:

1. Click the left mouse button on the number you want to enter. Numbers can also be entered using the keyboard. The number is entered in the calculator's display in the upper-right corner.

2. Click the left mouse button on the operation button you want; for example, move the pointer to the plus sign (+) to add a number. Operators can also be entered using the keyboard.

3. Click the left mouse button on the next number in the equation.

4. Click the left mouse button on the equal sign (=). The result is displayed in the Calculator display area.

Modes of Operation

The Calculator has four modes of operation: Basic, Financial, Logical, and Scientific. The area above the Base key displays the current mode. To change modes, press the right mouse button on the Mode button and choose the mode you want.

Number Bases

Binary, octal, decimal, and hexadecimal number bases can be set using the **Base** button in the top row. Pressing the right mouse button on the **Base** button displays the menu of number bases. Drag the pointer to a number base item and release the right mouse button. The numeric keypad changes to display those numbers appropriate to the number base mode you chose. The following list gives a brief description of each of the calculator's number bases. Figure 6.25 identifies the binary, octal, decimal, and hexadecimal keypads.

FIGURE 6.25

The binary, octal, decimal, and hexadecimal keypads

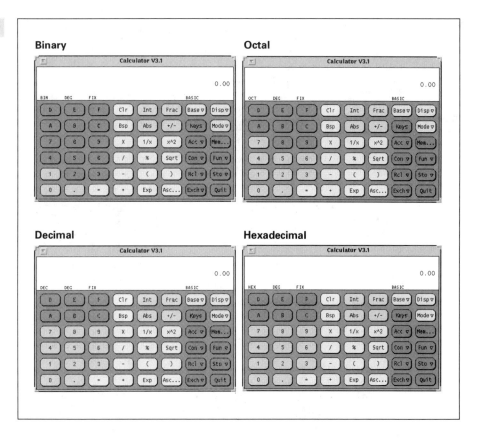

NUMBER BASE	DISPLAYS
Binary	Base 2, displays the digits 0 and 1.
Octal	Base 8, displays the digits 0 through 7.
Decimal	Base 10, displays the digits 0 through 9.
Hexadecimal	Base 16, displays the digits 0 through F.

Changing the Display Type

Normally the Calculator displays numbers in fixed-point notation. The Disp button lets you change the type of numeric display to engineering or scientific display. The Calculator display shows the notation type. Because the default is Fixed point notation, FIX is displayed in the Calculator display. To change to engineering or scientific display, press the right mouse button on the Disp button and choose the Engineering or Scientific item.

Miscellaneous Functions

The following list describes other helpful Calculator function keys:

KEY	DESCRIPTION
Clr (Clear)	Clears the value from the display.
Bsp (Backspace)	Removes the rightmost character from the current display and recalculates its value.
Acc (Accuracy)	Chooses the number of digits of precision used in the Calculator display and the memory registers.
Exp	Starts exponential input. Any numbers entered after you choose Exp are displayed exponentially. If no numerical input has occurred, a mantissa of 1.0 is assumed.

KEY	DESCRIPTION
Quit	Quits the Calculator.
Keys	Toggles the display of the keys to show the keyboard equivalents for mouseless operation of the Calculator.

Memory Registers

The Calculator has ten memory registers that can store and retrieve values for calculations. Registers are a handy way of storing calculation results for future computations. These memory registers can be accessed using the following keys:

MEMORY REGISTER	DESCRIPTION
Exch (Exchange registers)	Exchanges the value shown in the current display with a selected register number from the Exchange pop-up menu.
Mem (Memory)	Displays a pop-up window showing the values (in the current base and accuracy) of the ten memory registers.
Sto (Store)	Stores the current value in the memory register number you choose from the pop-up menu.
Rcl	Retrieves a value from the memory register number you choose from the pop-up menu.

The following steps explain how to store and retrieve register values.

1. Press the left mouse button on the number you want to store as a register value. The number appears in the Calculator's display area.

2. Press the right mouse button on the Sto (store) button at the far right, in the fifth row of keys, and choose the register you want to store the number in. The number is now in the register you selected.

3. Click the left mouse button on the `Mem` (memory) key, the second key in the top row, to view the stored register value.

4. To retrieve the register value you just stored, press the right mouse button on the `Rcl` button and choose the register value you want to retrieve. The value is displayed in the Calculator display.

User-Defined Functions

The Calculator allows you to enter your own set of constants and define your own functions using the `Con` (constant) and `Fun` (function) keys. Each of these keys contains a menu. Choosing the first item on the menu displays a pop-up window that lets you enter the name of a constant or a function and its value. Once you enter the number by clicking the left mouse button on the button at the bottom of the pop-up window, the number and its name are displayed as an item on the pop-up menu. To use the constant or the function, choose the appropriate item from the pop-up menu. The numbers you enter are stored in a file named `.calctoolrc` in your home directory. To edit or delete items from the `Constant` or `Functions` menus, you must edit the `.calctoolrc` file using the Text Editor or any other ASCII text editor. The following example describes how to create a function that determines the circumference of a circle.

1. Click the left mouse button on the `Fun` key (in the upper-right corner). The `Enter Function` pop-up window is displayed.

2. Enter a number to identify your function in the `Function no` text field and press Return. The insert point moves to the `Description` text field.

3. Enter a descriptive name (such as `circum`) for your function and press Return to move the insert point to the `Value` field.

4. Type a function in the `Value` field. For example, to create a function to determine the circumference of a circle, enter `3.14159 d *`.

5. Click the left mouse button on the `Enter Function` button to store the new function in your `.calctoolrc` file and add it to the `Functions` menu.

6. Press the right mouse button on the Fun (Function) key and choose the 3.14159 d * [circum] item, which displays 3.14. The next number you enter will be applied to the function.

7. Enter a number using the mouse or the keyboard to indicate the diameter of the circle you want to determine the circumference of, and either press Return or click the left mouse button on the = (equals) key.

Number Manipulation Operators

The Calculator provides the following number manipulation operators:

KEY	DESCRIPTION
Int	Returns the integer portion of the currently displayed value.
Frac	Returns the fractional portion of the currently displayed value.
Abs	Returns the absolute value of the currently displayed value.
+/−	Changes the arithmetic sign of the currently displayed value or the exponent being entered.
x	Returns the factorial of the currently displayed value.
1/x	Returns the current value of 1 divided by the currently displayed value.
x^2	Returns the square of the currently displayed value.
%	Calculates a percentage (determined from the next number entered) of the last number entered.
Sqrt	Returns the square root value of the currently displayed value.
Asc	Displays the ASCII value of a character.

The Financial Calculator

Choosing the `Financial` item from the `Mode` key pop-up menu, displays the `Financial Mode` pop-up window, as shown in Figure 6.26. The financial functions retrieve needed information from the memory registers. For example, in order to determine the amount of a loan payment, you must enter the amount of the loan, the interest rate, and the term of the loan. You store this information in the appropriate memory registers before you click the left mouse button on the financial function button.

The following describes each financial function and the memory register settings for each function.

FUNCTION	DESCRIPTION	EXCHANGE REGISTER SETTINGS
Ctrm	Computes the number of compounding periods it will take an investment of present value to grow to a future value, earning a fixed interest rate per compounding period.	*Reg. 0:* Periodic interest (*int*) rate. *Reg. 1:* Future value (*fv*) of the investment. *Reg. 2:* Present value (*pv*) of the investment.

FIGURE 6.26

The Financial Mode
pop-up window

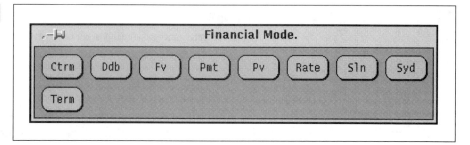

FUNCTION	DESCRIPTION	EXCHANGE REGISTER SETTINGS
Ddb	Using the double-declining balance method, Ddb commutes the depreciation allowance on an asset for a specified period of time.	*Reg. 0:* Amount paid for asset. *Reg. 1:* Salvage value of asset at end of life. *Reg. 2:* Useful life of an asset. *Reg. 3:* Time period for depreciation allowance.
Fv	The Fv function computes the future value of an investment based on a series of equal payments, earning a periodic interest rate over the number of payment periods in a term.	*Reg. 0:* Amount of each payment. *Reg. 1:* Interest rate. *Reg. 2:* Number of payments.
Pmt	Computes the periodic payment of a loan. Most installment loans are computed like ordinary annuities, in that payments are made at the end of each payment period.	*Reg. 0:* Amount of the loan. *Reg. 1:* Periodic interest rate of the loan. *Reg. 2:* Number of payments.

FUNCTION	DESCRIPTION	EXCHANGE REGISTER SETTINGS
Pv	The Pv function computes the present value based on a series of equal payments discounted at a periodic interest rate over the number of periods in the term.	*Reg. 0:* Amount of each payment. *Reg. 1:* Periodic interest rate. *Reg. 2:* Number of payments.
Rate	The periodic interest rate returns the periodic interest necessary for a present value to grow to a future value over the specified number of compounding periods in the term.	*Reg. 0:* Future value. *Reg. 1:* Present value. *Reg. 2:* Number of compounding periods.
Sln	The straight-line depreciation function divides the depreciable cost (actual cost less salvage value) evenly over the useful life of an asset. The useful life is the number of periods, typically years, over which an asset is depreciated.	*Reg. 0:* Cost of the asset. *Reg. 1:* Salvage value of the asset. *Reg. 2:* Useful life of the asset.

FUNCTION	DESCRIPTION	EXCHANGE REGISTER SETTINGS
Syd	The sum-of-the-years'-digits depreciation accelerates the rate of depreciation so that more depreciation expense occurs in earlier periods than in later ones. The depreciable cost is the actual cost less salvage value. The useful life is the number of periods, typically years, over which an asset is depreciated.	*Reg. 0:* Cost of the asset. *Reg. 1:* Salvage value of the asset. *Reg. 2:* Useful life of the asset. *Reg. 3:* Period for which depreciation is computed.
Term	The Term function computes the number of payment periods in the term of an ordinary annuity that are necessary to accumulate a future value earning a specified periodic interest rate.	*Reg. 0:* Amount of each periodic payment. *Reg. 1:* Future value. *Reg. 2:* Periodic interest rate.

Logical Functions

When you choose the Logical item from the Mode menu, the Logical Mode pop-up window is displayed, as shown in Figure 6.27. The Logical Mode Calculator provides the following logical functions.

FIGURE 6.27

The Logical Mode
pop-up window

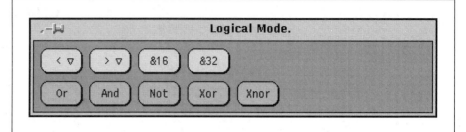

LOGICAL FUNCTION	DESCRIPTION
< (range 1 through 15)	Shifts the displayed binary value the designated number of places to the left.
> (range 1 through 15)	Shifts the displayed binary value the designated number of places to the right.
&16	Truncates the number displayed to return a 16-bit, unsigned integer.
&32	Truncates the number displayed to return a 32-bit, unsigned integer.
Or	Performs a logical OR operation on the last number and the next number entered, treating both numbers as unsigned long integers.
And	Performs a logical AND operation on the last number and the next number entered, treating both numbers as unsigned long integers.
Not	Performs a logical NOT operation on the current displayed value.
Xor	Performs a logical XOR operation on the last number and the next number entered, treating both numbers as unsigned long integers.

LOGICAL FUNCTION	DESCRIPTION
Xnor	Performs a logical XNOR operation on the last number and the next number entered, treating both numbers as unsigned long integers.

The Scientific Calculator

Choosing the `Scientific` item from the `Mode` menu displays the `Scientific Mode` pop-up window (Figure 6.28). The `Scientific Mode` pop-up window provides the following trigonometric functions.

KEY	DESCRIPTION
Trig	Displays a menu of trigonometric bases: `Degrees`, `Radians`, or `Gradients`. The current trigonometric base is indicated in the Calculator display.
Hyp	Sets or unsets the hyperbolic function flag. This flag affects the `Sin`, `Cos`, and `Tan` trigonometric functions.
Inv	Sets and unsets the inverse function flag. This flag affects the `Sin`, `Cos`, and `Tan` trigonometric functions.

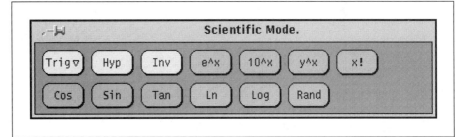

KEY	DESCRIPTION
e^x	Returns *e* raised to the power of the currently displayed value.
10^x	Returns 10 raised to the power of the currently displayed value.
y^x	Raises the last number entered to the power of the next number entered.
x!	Returns the factorial of the currently displayed value.
Cos	Returns the trigonometric cosine, arc cosine, hyperbolic cosine, or inverse hyperbolic cosine of the current value, depending on the settings of the Hyp and Inv flags. The result is displayed in the current units (degrees, radians, or gradients).
Sin	Returns the trigonometric sine, arc sine, hyperbolic sine, or inverse hyperbolic sine of the current value, depending on the setting of the Hyp and Inv flags. The result is displayed in the current units (degrees, radians, or gradients).
Tan	Returns the trigonometric tangent, arc tangent, hyperbolic tangent, or inverse hyperbolic tangent of the current value, depending on the settings of the Hyp and Inv flags. The result is displayed in the current units (degrees, radians, or gradients).
Ln	Returns the natural logarithm of the currently displayed value.
Log	Returns the base 10 logarithm of the currently displayed value.
Rand	Enters a random number (0 through 1) in the Calculator display.

Customizing the Calculator

You can change the appearance of the calculator. Pressing the right mouse button anywhere in the Calculator (other than on a button) displays the `Calculator` pop-up menu. Choosing the `Properties` item displays the `Calculator Properties` pop-up window, as shown in Figure 6.29. The following explains each of the Calculator settings.

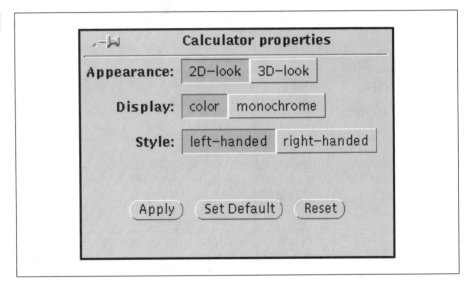

SETTING	DESCRIPTION
Appearance	Sets the calculator to display with two-dimensional or three-dimensional buttons.
Display	Sets the display to color or black and white.

SETTING	DESCRIPTION
Style	Changes the calculator keyboard layout. The left-handed setting is the default, with the numeric keys on the left side of the calculator. The right-handed setting moves the numeric keys to the right side of the Calculator keyboard. Figure 6.30 shows the calculator using the right-handed setting.

FIGURE 6.30

The Calculator using the right-handed setting

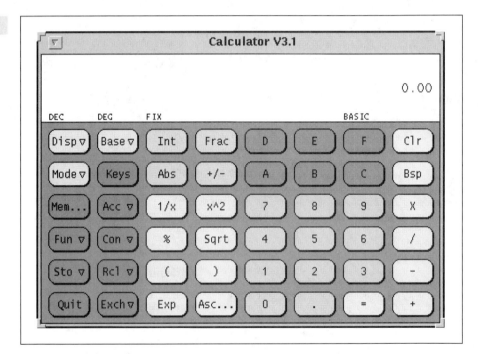

The Set Default setting saves your Calculator property settings, so the next time you start a calculator, the new Appearance, Display, and Style settings are applied. Be sure to click the left mouse button on the Apply button to apply your changes. If you make a mistake before pressing the Apply button, you can return to your original settings by clicking on the `Reset` button. If you want to return to the Calculator default settings, click on the `Set Default` button.

The Tape Tool

The Tape Tool lets you list files from a tape cartridge or an archive file that has been archived using the `tar` command. The Tape Tool cannot read tapes that have been written to using the `cpio` command. Working with `tar` and `cpio` commands are explained in Chapter 17, "System Administration Basics."

The `Tape Tool` window and icon is shown in Figure 6.31. You can drop files onto the `Tape Tool` window or onto the tape tool icon to select a file for archiving. The Tape Tool icon changes to display a unrewound tape, indicating the files have not been archived. Using the Tape Tool, you can read some or all of the files from a tape or archive file into the directory that you specify. You can write files or directories that you specify onto a tape cartridge or into an archive file.

FIGURE 6.31

The Tape Tool window and icon

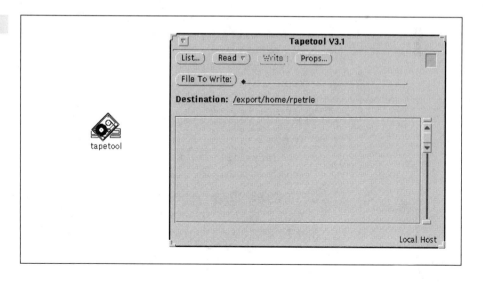

The `List`, `Read`, `Write`, and `Props` menu buttons provide controls for listing, reading from a tape, writing to a tape, and setting Tape Tool properties. The `File To Write` button and text field allow you to type in the
names of the files that you want to write to tape. After typing in the name
of a file to write, press Return or click the left mouse button on the `File
To Write` button. The scrolling list displays a list of the files you specify
by typing file names or by dragging and dropping icons from the File
Manager onto the drag-and-drop target.

The `Destination` field allows you to specify where in your file system files
are put when they are read from the tape. The default destination is your
current working directory. If the files on a tape have a complete path (absolute path), the files are always put in the directory specified on the tape,
regardless of what you type in the `Destination` field.

Viewing and Editing a List of Files on a Tape

By clicking the left mouse button on the `List` button, you can view a list
of files from a tape or archive file in the `Tape Contents/Files to Read`
pop-up window (Figure 6.32). Once the files are listed in the `Tape Con-
tents/Files to Read` pop-up window, you can edit the list to remove files
you do not want to retrieve. The following explains how to view and edit
a list of files from a tape or archive file in the Tape Tool window.

1. If you're viewing a list of files from a tape, insert the tape in the
   tape drive.

2. Click the left mouse button on the `List` button to display the
   `Tape Contents/Files to Read` pop-up window. This pop-up
   window displays a list of files on the tape in the scrolling list,
   and messages are displayed in the footer of the window telling
   you how many files have been found.

3. To select files to retrieve or remove from the list, click the left
   mouse button on each file you want. To select all the files in the
   scrolling list, press the right mouse button to display the `Read
   Functions` pop-up menu. Drag the mouse pointer to the `Select
   All` item and release the right mouse button.

FIGURE 6.32

The Tape
Contents/Files to Read
pop-up window

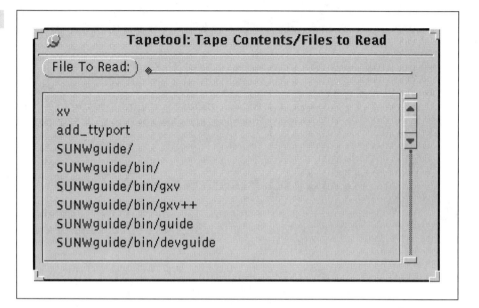

4. If you want to delete the selected files, press the right mouse button in the scrolling list and choose the **Delete Selected** item. If you inadvertently delete a file, you can place it back on the list by typing the file name in the **File To Read** text field, then pressing Return or clicking the left mouse button on the **File To Read** button. After editing your list, the Tape Tool will read only the selected files from the tape or archive file.

Writing Files to a Tape

Writing files to a tape copies the files you specify onto a tape cartridge. The following explains how to write files to a tape:

1. If you want to store files so they can be copied to a different directory than the one where they were originally stored, choose the **All** option in the **StripPath** setting in the Tape Tool's **Properties** window and choose Apply.

2. Select and drag files from the File Manager to the **Tape Tool** window's drag-and-drop target. You can also type the name of a directory or an individual file in the **File To Write** text field, and press Return or click the left mouse button on the `File To Write` text field.

3. Check the tape cartridge to be sure that it is not write-protected, and insert it into the tape drive.

4. Click the left mouse button on the `Write` button. If you receive an error message, such as `/dev/rmt/0 I/0 error`, make sure that your tape drive is on.

Reading Files from a Tape

The `Read` menu provides three items— `Selected`, `Entire List`, and `Entire Tape` —for reading files from the tape or archive files to the directory specified in the `Tape Tool` window.

After listing and selecting the files you want to retrieve, choose the `Selected` item from the `Read` menu to copy the files to the destination directory specified in the `Destination` text field. When you have not listed the contents of a tape, choosing the `Selected` item displays the `Tape Contents/ Files to Read` pop-up window without a listing. If you know the names of specific files that you want to retrieve, you can type a name in the `File To Read` text field, then press Return or click the left mouse button on the `File To Read` button to add them to the list.

Choosing the `Entire List` item from the `Read` menu reads the entire list of files from the `Tape Contents/Files to Read` pop-up window. While the files are being read, messages are displayed in the footer of the `Tape Tool` window, indicating the percentage of the files that have been read. As the files are read, they are removed from the `Tape Contents/Files to Read` pop-up window. When the process is complete, a message is displayed in the footer of the `Tape Tool` window telling you how many files were read. If there are a large number of files, it may take several minutes for the files to be copied to your system.

Choosing the `Entire Tape` item from the `Read` menu copies all of the files on the tape to the destination directory without displaying the `Tape Contents/Files to Read` pop-up window.

WARNING When you read files that have a path name in front of them, that path is always used as the destination.

Customizing the Tape Tool

You can customize the Tape Tool by using the `Properties` pop-up window (Figure 6.33). To display the `Properties` pop-up window, click the left mouse button on the `Props` menu button. After changing any setting, click the left mouse button on the `Apply` button (located at the bottom of the window) to save the changes. These changes remain in effect *only* until you quit the Tape Tool. Clicking the `Reset` button restores all your changes to the default settings.

The `Device` text field lets you identify the tape drive on your system. The most common device identifiers for a tape drive are `/dev/rmt/0` and `/dev/rmt/1`. You can also specify a file name in this field if you want to read or write files to and from one big archive file instead of to and from a tape cartridge.

The `Host Name` text field allows you to identify the name of the workstation where the reading or archiving of files is to take place. The default is your local host name.

The `Write` settings allow you to specify how you want to write files to a tape. You can choose none, some, or all of the settings listed. The following lists and describes each setting:

SETTING	RESULTS
No SCCS	Excludes all SCCS directories. SCCS stands for Source Code Control System. SCCS directories contain different revisions of source code for programs. Unless you are backing up directories containing source code for programs, leave this setting off.

FIGURE 6.33

The Properties pop-up
window

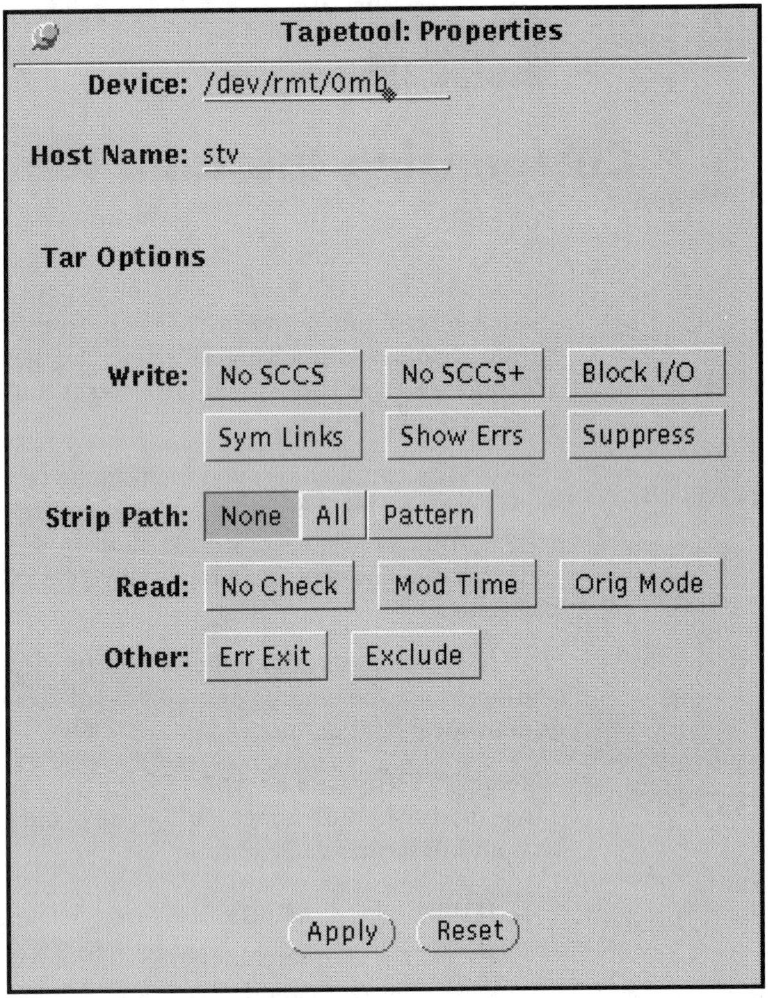

Tapetool: Properties

Device: /dev/rmt/0mh

Host Name: stv

Tar Options

Write: | No SCCS | No SCCS+ | Block I/O |
| Sym Links | Show Errs | Suppress |

Strip Path: | None | All | Pattern |

Read: | No Check | Mod Time | Orig Mode |

Other: | Err Exit | Exclude |

(Apply) (Reset)

SETTING	RESULTS
No SCCS+	Excludes all SCCS directories, files with a suffix `.o`, and files named `errs`, `core`, and `a.out`. Unless you are backing up directories containing source code for programs, leave this setting off.
Block I/O	Specifies a blocking factor for better through-put. When you click the left mouse button on this setting, a text field is displayed in which you can type the blocking factor you want the Tape Tool to use. In most cases, you leave this setting alone and use the default.
Sym Links	Follows symbolic links to archive the linked files.
Show Errs	Displays error messages if all links to archived files cannot be resolved.
Suppress	Suppresses information showing owner and file modes for portability.

The `Strip Path` settings allow you to choose whether you want selected files to be stripped completely of their path names, to use complete path names, or to use a specific path name. Clicking the left mouse button on the `Pattern` setting displays a text field in which you can type the name of a path to use for all files.

The `Read` settings allow you to specify how you want to read files from a tape. The following explains each of the settings:

SETTING	RESULTS
No Check	Ignores directory checksum errors.
Mode Time	Keeps the Tape Tool from resetting the modification time of files that it reads from the tape.
Orig Mode	Restores the named files to their original mode, ignoring the default `umask` setting of **2**.

The `Other` setting `Err Exit` instructs the Tape Tool to exit the operation as soon as an error is encountered. The `Exclude` setting lets you specify a file name that contains a list of files and/or directories that you want to exclude from reading from the tape. This setting can be useful when the tape contains many files and you want to retrieve all but a few of them.

CHAPTER

7

Customizing the Workspace and Icons

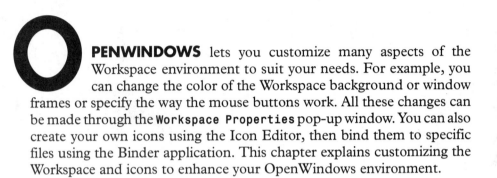

OPENWINDOWS lets you customize many aspects of the Workspace environment to suit your needs. For example, you can change the color of the Workspace background or window frames or specify the way the mouse buttons work. All these changes can be made through the `Workspace Properties` pop-up window. You can also create your own icons using the Icon Editor, then bind them to specific files using the Binder application. This chapter explains customizing the Workspace and icons to enhance your OpenWindows environment.

Using the Workspace Properties Window

The `Workspace Properties` pop-up window allows you to customize a number of Workspace settings. To open the `Workspace Properties` pop-up window, choose the `Properties` item from `Workspace` menu. The `Properties` pop-up window appears (Figure 7.1). The `Workspace Properties` pop-up window includes five property categories on a monochrome system and six categories on a color system. To view the property categories menu, click the right mouse button on the `Category` abbreviated menu button. Figure 7.2 shows the Category menu for a color system.

Changes you make using the `Workspace Properties` pop-up window are stored in the `.Xdefaults` file. This file contains all properties set for your Workspace. You can make additional modifications to the Workspace and DeskSet applications by manually editing the `.Xdefaults` file, as explained in Chapter 15, "Customizing Solaris."

FIGURE 7.1

The Workspace
Properties pop-up
window

After making changes to the properties, you apply them by clicking the left
mouse button on the **Apply** button. Although each category has its own
Apply button, you only need to click the left mouse button on one **Apply**
button after making changes to any Workspace properties category. For
example, you can make changes in the **Color** category, then make changes
in the **Mouse Settings** category and apply the changes for both categories
by clicking the left mouse button on the **Apply** button in the **Mouse Settings** category. The following sections explain each category of property
settings.

FIGURE 7.2

The Category menu

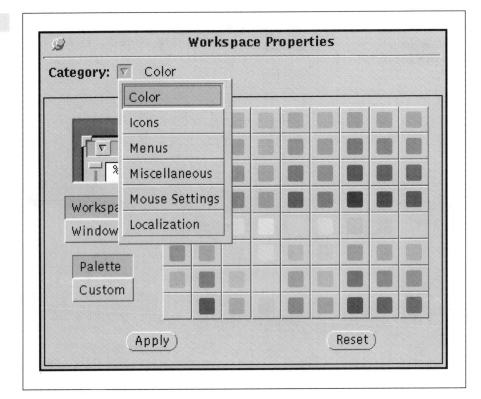

Setting Colors for the Workspace and Windows

If you have a color monitor, you have the option to modify the default colors for the Workspace and windows. When you open the Workspace Properties pop-up window, by default the Color category appears, as shown in Figure 7.2. You can modify the colors of the Workspace or windows by choosing from a palette of premixed colors or by mixing your own colors. The inset area located above the buttons displays a sample of the current color choice for either the Workspace or windows. The following steps explain how to change the Workspace and window colors using the palette in the Workspace Properties window.

1. Click on the **Windows** button to change the color of windows, or go to step two if you want to change the Workspace.

2. Click the left mouse button on the new color you want from the palette. The inset displays the current color choice.

3. Click the left mouse button on the **Apply** button to apply the new color. A Notice appears telling you that changes will be made to the **.Xdefaults** file (Figure 7.3).

4. Click the left mouse button on the **Yes** button. The Workspace or application windows change to the new color.

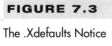

FIGURE 7.3

The .Xdefaults Notice

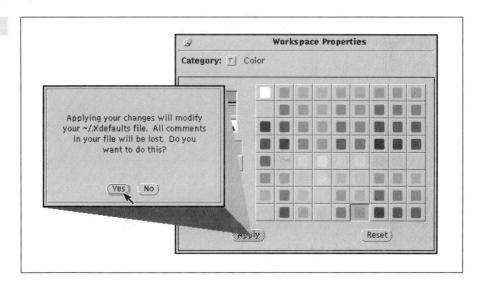

You can also create your own colors using the custom color palette. Click the left mouse button on the **Custom** button to replace the color palette with **Hue**, **Saturation**, and **Brightness** slider controls (Figure 7.4). To create a custom color, move the sliders as you watch the inset at the upper-left corner of the window. The following explains the three custom color settings.

- The **Hue** setting allows you to choose a gradation of color from the range of primary colors: red, green, and blue.

FIGURE 7.4

The Custom Color
Palette

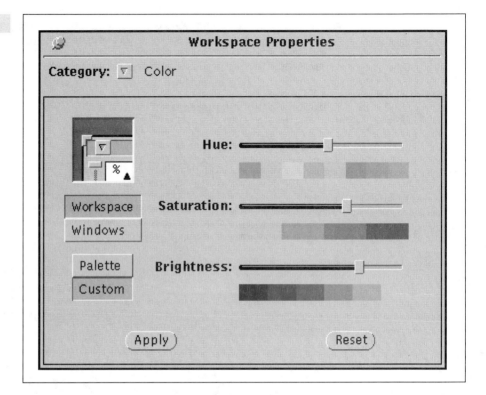

- The **Saturation** setting allows you to specify the deepness or richness of the color.

- The **Brightness** setting affects how much light is filtered into a color.

After creating your custom color, click the left mouse button on the **Apply** button, then click the left mouse on the **Yes** button in the Notice window. The changes you have made to the **Color** category will take place immediately.

Setting Default Locations for Icons

When you close a window to an icon on the Workspace, by default the icon appears at the bottom of the Workspace. You can change the default location where icons are placed on the Workspace by doing the following:

1. Press the right mouse button on the category abbreviated menu button and choose the `Icons` item. The `Icons` category appears (Figure 7.5).

2. Click the left mouse button on the appropriate `Location` setting: `Top`, `Bottom`, `Left`, or `Right`.

3. Click the left mouse button on the `Apply` button. The .Xdefaults Notice appears.

4. Click on the `Yes` button.

FIGURE 7.5

The Icons category

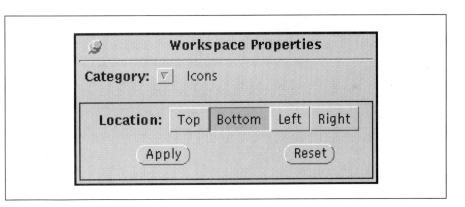

Changes to the `Icons` category take effect when you start a new application. Icons already displayed will not change location.

Changing Menu Settings

Choosing the Menus category enables you to change how you operate menus, including setting the distance you need to drag the mouse to the right to display a submenu, and determining whether the default menu item is chosen automatically when you click the left mouse button on a menu button.

The drag-right distance is the distance that you must move the pointer to the right before a submenu is displayed. This distance is measured on the screen in *pixels* (picture elements). The number of pixels available corresponds to the resolution of the monitor. Standard resolutions for most Sun monitors are 1152 by 900 and 1600 by 1280 pixels. The default pixel length for the drag-right distance is 100 pixels. Changes you specify in the Menus category take effect immediately.

NOTE

If you are using Solaris 2 for x86 the standard resolution is 1024 by 768.

To modify the drag-right distance, follow these steps:

1. Press the right mouse button on the Category abbreviated menu button and choose Menus. The Menus category appears (Figure 7.6).

FIGURE 7.6

The Menus category

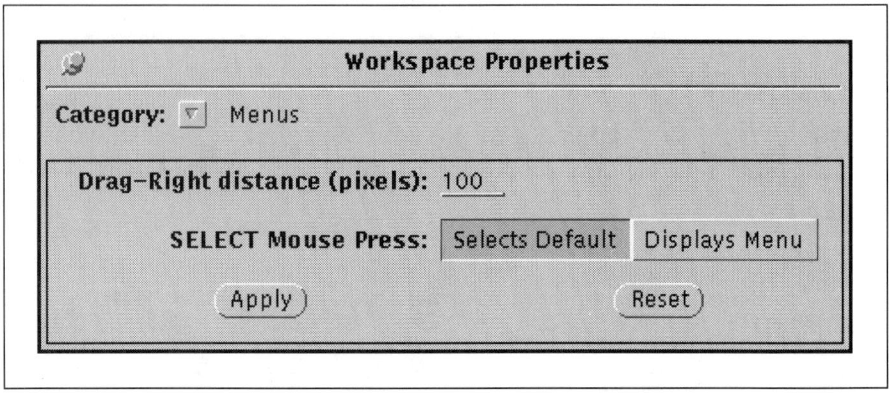

2. Enter the drag-right distance in the `Drag-Right distance` (`pixels`) text field. The higher the value, the more distance you need to drag the pointer.

3. Click the left mouse button on the `Apply` button. The .Xdefaults Notice appears.

4. Click on the `Yes` button.

The `SELECT Mouse Press` setting determines whether the default menu item is chosen automatically when you click the left mouse button on a menu button or if the menu is presented for you to make a choice. The default setting, `Selects Default`, specifies that the default menu item is automatically chosen when you click the left mouse button on the menu button. The `Displays Menu` setting specifies that when you click the left mouse button on the menu button, the menu is displayed instead of the default menu item being executed. This means you need to click the left mouse button again to choose a menu item. Changes to the `SELECT Mouse Press` option do not take effect on any applications that are already opened, but they do take effect on any applications you open after changing the `SELECT Mouse Press` setting.

Changing Miscellaneous Settings

The `Miscellaneous` category allows you to change three settings: `Beep`, `Set Input Area`, and `Scrollbar Placement`. To change these settings, choose the `Miscellaneous` category from the `Workspace Properties` menu. The Miscellaneous category appears, as shown in Figure 7.7. The following explains each setting in the `Miscellaneous` category.

SETTING	DESCRIPTION
Beep	`Always` (the default setting) specifies whether your system beeps for all application-generated beep actions, such as errors in the `Console` window. `Notices Only` beeps only when a Notice is displayed. `Never` specifies no beeps.

FIGURE 7.7

The Miscellaneous
category

SETTING	DESCRIPTION
Set Input Area	Click SELECT (the default setting) specifies that you must click the left mouse button on the window to make it the active window. The Move Pointer setting lets you simply move the pointer into the window to make the window active.
Scrollbar Placement	Specifies whether scroll bars are displayed at the right and left of the pane. This setting applies to all scrollable application windows on the Workspace. The default is the Right setting.

TIP

Changing the Set Input Area to the Move Pointer setting makes working with multiple windows much easier than using the Click SELECT setting.

Changes made to the `Miscellaneous` category take place immediately after you apply them using the `Apply` button. However, the scroll bar changes do not affect application windows that are already on the Workspace.

Customizing Mouse Settings

The `Mouse Settings` category contains pointer jumping controls for scroll bars and pop-up windows, as well as a setting for changing the time interval between double-clicks of mouse buttons. To change these settings, choose the `Mouse Settings` category from the `Workspace Properties` menu. The `Mouse Settings` category appears, as shown in Figure 7.8. The following explains the settings in the `Mouse Settings` category window.

SETTING	DESCRIPTION
Scrollbar Pointer Jumping	Determines whether or not you want the pointer to move along the scroll bar elevator during scrolling actions. When the box is not checked, pointer jumping is disabled, so the pointer remains in a fixed position as the scroll bar elevator moves.

FIGURE 7.8

The Mouse Settings category

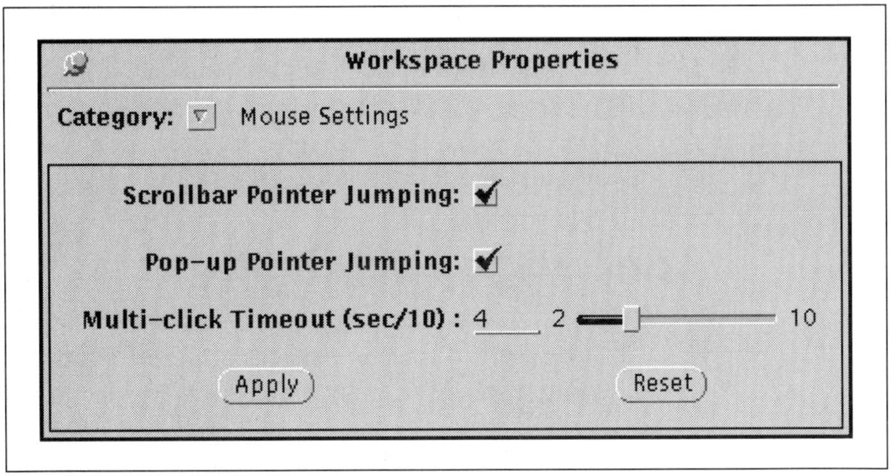

SETTING	DESCRIPTION
Pop-up Pointer Jumping	Determines whether or not you want the pointer to jump into a pop-up window automatically when it comes up. If this setting is chosen, the pointer jumps to the default choice whenever a pop-up window is displayed. When the box is not checked, the pointer does not jump to the default button in the pop-up window, but remains where it was when the pop-up window appeared.
Multi-click Timeout (sec/10)	Specifies how many tenths of a second can elapse between successive clicks on a mouse button before the first click is ignored. This affects how quickly you must double-click the left mouse button, for example, when you start an application from an icon. To set the multiclick time, you can either type in the number of tenths of a second in the numeric field, or you can drag the slider with the pointer.

Changes to the Scrollbar Pointer Jumping and Pop-up Pointer Jumping check boxes do not take place in applications already on the Workspace, but they do take effect when you open an application window. The Multi-Click Timeout option takes effect immediately in all applications. To make the changes take effect in already open applications you can quit then restart them, or restart OpenWindows.

Language Localization

If your system was installed with an OpenWindows localization CD, you have access to various European locales in addition to the basic U.S.A. setting. If your system was not installed with the OpenWindows localization CD, English is the only available language. The Localization category (Figure 7.9) of the Workspace Properties window provides you with controls for specifying an input and display language, as well as time,

FIGURE 7.9

The Localization category

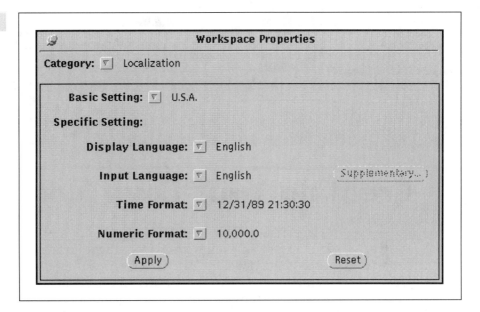

date, and numeric formats for different locales. If your system is not installed with an OpenWindows localization CD, these settings only reflect your system's language, date, and time format. For those systems that allow locale specifications, changes will apply when you start a new application. It will not affect applications that already opened. The following describes each setting in the `Localization` category.

SETTING	DESCRIPTION
Basic Setting	Specifies the name of the country or native language of the user interface. Specific setting choices listed below in the `Localization` category will vary depending on the basic locale setting.
Display Language	Specifies the language in which messages, menu labels, button labels, help files, etc., are displayed.
Input Language	Specifies the language to be used for input in application windows.

SETTING	DESCRIPTION
Time Format	Specifies the format for time and date.
Numeric Format	Defines the numeric format or placement of the comma and decimal point.

Creating Your Own Icons

The DeskSet's Icon Editor allows you to create your own icon images. You can also modify an existing icon image and save it with a new name in your home directory. The directory /usr/openwin/share/include/images contains many icon image files that you can modify and save in your home directory. Once you create a new icon, you can bind it an application and data file using the Binder application. Working with the Binder application is explained later in this chapter.

To start the Icon Editor, press the right mouse button on the Workspace to display the Workspace pop-up menu, then choose Icon Editor from the Programs submenu. The Icon Editor window appears on the Workspace. Figure 7.10 shows the Icon Editor window and icon.

The Icon Editor window's control area contains the File, View, Edit, Properties, and Palette menu buttons. The Preview area, located above the canvas to the right of the drawing controls, allows you to preview how the icon you are creating in the canvas pane of the Icon Editor window will look. The controls that you use to draw an image in the canvas appear to the left of the preview area. The drawing mode choices include tools for drawing and editing an image and adding text to an image. The Fill choices, below the Edit and Properties buttons, allow you to fill in a square or circle with a pattern. The Color choices allow you to choose between creating black-and-white or color images. The Move buttons allow you to adjust the position of the drawing on the canvas.

FIGURE 7.10

The Icon Editor icon and window

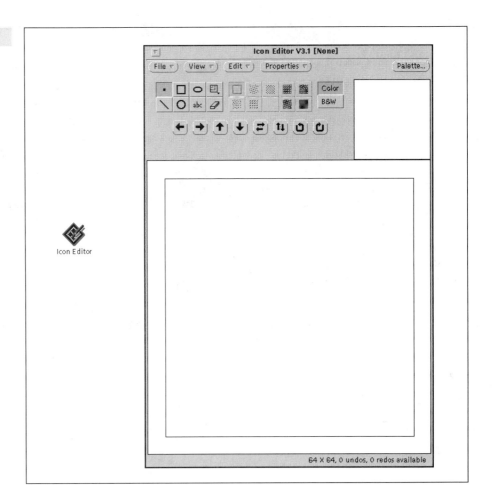

Color Control

You can create color or black-and-white icons by choosing the **Color** or **B&W** setting. The **Color** setting is not available if you are working with a black-and-white monitor. When the **Color** setting is selected, you can draw using any of the colors provided on the **Color Chooser** pop-up window, which appears when you click the left mouse button on the **Palette** button. Working with this pop-up window is similar to working with the color setting window described in the section "Setting Colors for the Workspace and Windows," earlier in this chapter.

NOTE

If you change your icon from color to black and white, the colors will not be restored when you switch back to color. If you inadvertently switch from color to black and white, use the Undo item on the Edit menu to restore the color.

When the B&W setting is chosen, the Palette button on the Icon Editor header changes to display only Black and White settings. When Black is selected, your icon is drawn with a black pen. When White is selected, your icon is drawn with a white pen. If the icon you are creating is in color when you select B&W, the icon is converted to a black-and-white image.

Drawing Controls

The drawing controls (Figure 7.11), provide you with the tools for drawing an image. The following explains the available drawing mode choices.

FIGURE 7.11

Drawing controls

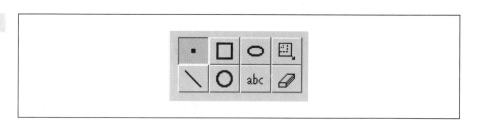

MODE	RESULT
Point	Click the left mouse button to insert one black pixel at the spot of the pointer on the canvas. Point to a black pixel and click the middle mouse button to turn the pixel from black to white.

MODE	RESULT
Line	Draws a line one pixel wide. To draw a line, position the pointer at one end of the line, press the left mouse button, drag the pointer to the other end of the line, and release the left mouse button. If you are in B&W mode, a white line can be drawn in the same way by selecting the White option in the upper right-hand corner of the Icon Editor window.
Square	Draws open or filled squares (or rectangles) using any of the fill patterns from the Fill area. Position the pointer at the top left corner, press the left mouse button, drag the pointer to the bottom opposite corner of the square or rectangle, and release the left mouse button.
Circle	Draws open or filled circles using any of the fill patterns from the Fill area. Position the pointer at the center of the circle and press the left mouse button, drag the pointer to the outside radius of the circle, and release the left mouse button.
Ellipse	Draws open or filled ellipses using any of the fill patterns from the Fill area. Position the pointer at the center of the ellipse and press the left mouse button, drag the pointer to the outside radius of the ellipse, and release the left mouse button. If you define a horizontal or vertical line, the ellipse is interpreted as a straight line.

MODE	RESULT
Text	Displays a pop-up window that allows you to type text to be displayed in your icon. Working with text is explained later in this chapter.
Region	Defines a rectangular region of the canvas that you can move, flip, or rotate by clicking the left mouse button on any of the Move buttons that are displayed directly above the canvas.
Eraser	Allows you to erase any pixels on the canvas by moving the pointer to the canvas, clicking the left mouse button, and dragging the eraser cursor over the areas you want to erase. Only the pixel under the front tip of the eraser is erased.

Fill Choices

The Fill choices (Figure 7.12) allow you to choose one of ten fill patterns to fill in squares, circles, ellipses, or irregular shapes with the specified pattern. To create and fill squares, circles, or ellipses, first choose a Fill option from the Fill choices area *before* using the draw mode. *You cannot fill previously drawn squares, circles, and ellipses.*

The first Fill choice, an open square, allows you to create an outline (unfilled) of the shape selected in the mode menu. Pressing the left mouse button and dragging the pointer defines the area of the square, circle, or ellipse. When you release the left button, the area you defined is filled with

FIGURE 7.12

Fill choices

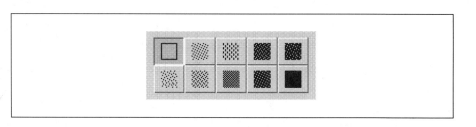

the pattern you specified. The other options represent patterns, from white to black, that create filled squares, circles, or ellipses.

Move Buttons

The series of eight move buttons in the Drawing Controls area (Figure 7.13) allow you to position the drawing on the canvas, or to move a region within the canvas. The first move buttons (left, right, up, and down arrows) in the Drawing Controls area adjust the position of the entire drawing or a region of the drawing in the canvas one pixel in the direction indicated.

FIGURE 7.13

The Move buttons

W A R N I N G   If you move part of the image off the canvas, the pixels are cropped from the image and are not restored when you move the image in the opposite direction.

To move a defined region of your image, select the `Region` option from the mode menu, indicated by intersecting dimmed rectangles. To select a region, move the pointer to the left corner of the region you want to move, press the left mouse button, and drag the pointer to the bottom right of the region you want to affect. A bounding box indicates the selected region. Release the left mouse button and the region is selected.

To move the selected region or the entire drawing, click the left mouse button on one of the four arrow buttons. Each click will move the drawing one pixel in the designated direction. The fifth and sixth buttons in the row of the move buttons flip the image on the canvas or a defined region from left to right or top to bottom. The right two buttons rotate the image or a defined region 90 degrees in the direction of the arrow.

WARNING   If you move part of the image over existing pixels, the pixels are removed from the image. Choose Undo from the Edit menu to restore the deleted pixels.

Adding Text to an Icon

Adding text to an icon is a simple operation. First choose `Text (abc)` from the Drawing Controls area and the `Text` pop-up window is displayed (Figure 7.14). To add text to the canvas, do the following:

1. Click the right mouse button on the `Font` abbreviated menu button and choose the font you want to use. Figure 7.15 shows the `Font` menu.

2. Click the right mouse button on the `Weight` abbreviated menu button and choose the weight (degree of bold) for the font you want to use.

3. Click the right mouse button on the `Style` abbreviated menu button and choose the font style you want to use.

FIGURE 7.14

The Text pop-up window

```
 ┌─╗                    Icon Editor: Text
    Text: ◈_____

   Font:  ▽   avantgarde ( itc )

 Weight:  ▽   book

  Style:  ▽   oblique

   Size:  ▽   default
```

FIGURE 7.15

The Font options of the
Text pop-up window

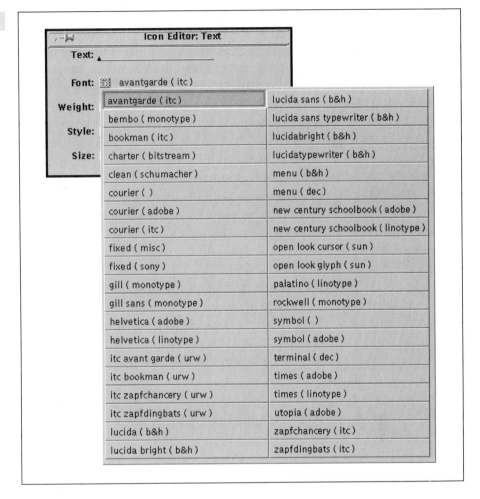

4. Click the right mouse button on the **Size** button and choose the font size you want.

5. Click the left mouse button on the **Text** text field and type the text you want to add to your icon.

6. Move the pointer onto the canvas and press the left mouse button to insert your text in the icon. A rectangle is displayed that shows the size of the text to be inserted. You can drag the rectangle anywhere within the canvas to position it.

7. When the rectangle is positioned correctly, release the left mouse button. The text is added to the canvas. White text can be typed on a dark background in the same way by selecting the White option. Once you have added text to the canvas, it can be edited as you would any other part of the image.

Editing Icons Using the Edit Menu

The Edit menu (Figure 7.16) provides you with seven editing items: Undo, Redo, Clear, Cut, Copy, Paste, and Invert. These editing items are also available in the Edit pop-up menu, which is displayed by clicking or pressing the right mouse button anywhere in the canvas.

You can undo up to seven of your last actions by choosing the Undo item. The status line at the bottom of the Icon Editor window informs you of the number of undos and redos available. After choosing Undo, you can then choose Redo to repeat the original action, which restores the canvas to its condition before you chose Undo. The Clear item allows you to erase the entire canvas. No warning Notice is displayed, since you can easily choose the Undo option to restore the contents of the canvas.

You can use the Cut, Copy, Paste, and Invert items in conjunction with the Region mode to move, copy, or invert selected regions of an icon. When you choose the Cut item, the current region is removed from the icon and placed on the clipboard. If you don't have a region currently

FIGURE 7.16

The Edit menu

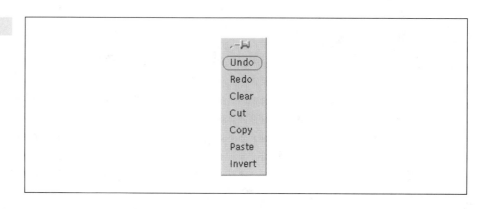

defined, the entire icon is deleted and placed on the clipboard. The `Copy` item copies the current region on the clipboard. Before choosing the `Paste` item, position the pointer so the upper-right corner of the copied or cut image matches the upper-right corner of the current region. If you use the Paste key from the keyboard, the contents of the clipboard are placed so that the upper-right corner is at the center of the icon. The `Invert` item simply inverts a black-and-white image. Black pixels become white and white pixels become black.

Displaying a Grid in the Canvas

Clicking the left mouse button on the `View` menu button activates the `Grid On` item, which allows you to display a grid background for your canvas. Figure 7.17 shows an example of the canvas with the grid turned on. The grid is useful for aligning and centering all or parts of the icon. You can toggle the grid on and off by clicking the left mouse button on the `View` menu button. When the grid is turned on, the `View` menu item changes to `Grid Off`.

Working with the Properties Menu

The `Properties` menu contains the `Format` and `Size` items. The `Format` item allows you to choose the format in which your icon file is saved. The `Format` submenu includes four format choices: `XView Icon`, `X Bitmap`, `Color X Pixmap`, and/or `Mono X Pixmap`.

In most cases you will save your icon images in the `XView Icon` format. A color image can also be saved as a color X Pixmap image. However, this type of icon can only be used for some XView applications. Save the icon as an XView icon if you want to display your icon in the File Manager by binding it to an application or data file using the Binder. If your icon is black and white, it can be saved as a regular XView icon, as an X Bitmap, or as a Monochrome X Pixmap image. You can save the icon as an X Bitmap if you want to include it in a C program.

FIGURE 7.17

The Icon Editor with
the Grid item activated

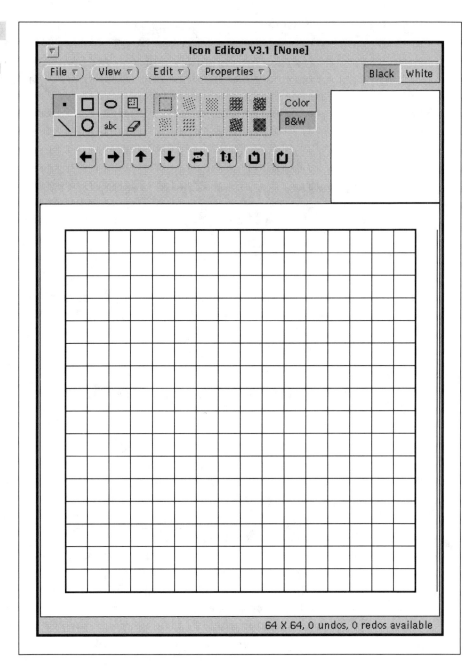

The `Properties` menu's `Size` submenu provides five icon-sizing options based on pixel measurements. The size for icons that appear in the File Manager window is 32 by 32 pixels. The `32` (`File manager Icon`) item is the default. If you need to create an icon for an application, choose the `64` (`Tool Icon`). This creates an icon that is 64 by 64 pixels, the standard size of an application icon on the Workspace. The other canvas sizes are 48 by 48 pixels, 16 by 16 pixels, and 128 by 128 pixels.

If you change the size of the canvas when an icon file is loaded, or load an icon into a different canvas size, the file is read from the upper-left corner. Larger images are cropped to fit the existing size of the canvas. The canvas can be changed to a larger size without losing data as long as you do not move the image. If you move the image, data outside the canvas is lost.

Saving an Icon File

To save an icon for the first time, click the left mouse button on the `File` button. A Notice appears informing you that no file was specified. Click the left mouse button on the `Continue` button. The `File` pop-up window appears, as shown in Figure 7.18. Type the name of the directory in which you want to store your icon in the `Directory` text field and the file name in the `File` text field. Press the right mouse button on the `Save` button and choose `XView` to save the icon. If you want to save an icon with a new or different file name, choose the `Save As` item from the `File` menu. The `File` pop-up window is displayed.

FIGURE 7.18

The File pop-up window

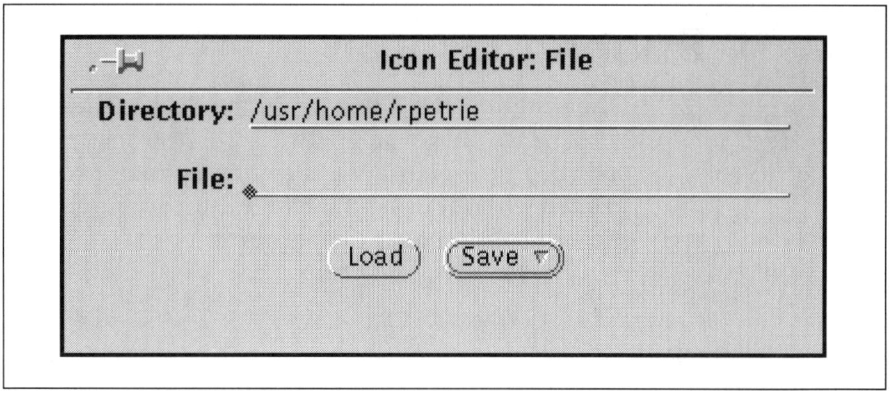

Icon Editor: File

Directory: /usr/home/rpetrie

File:

(Load)   (Save ▽)

In most cases, you will want to save your icon as an `XView Icon` so you can display your icon in the File Manager by binding it to an application or data file using the Binder, as explained later in this chapter. If your icon is in color, it can be saved as a `Color X Pixmap` image, which can be used for some XView applications. If your icon is black and white, you can also choose to save the icon as an `X Bitmap` or a `Mono X Pixmap` image.

Loading an Icon File

You can easily load an existing icon file by dragging it from the File Manager and dropping it onto the Icon Editor's canvas or onto the Icon Editor's preview window. The icon file appears in the `Icon Editor` window, as shown in Figure 7.19. An icon file can also be loaded by clicking the left mouse button on the `File` menu button, which displays the `File` pop-up window. Type the directory path in the `Directory` text field where you want to load the file from. Type the file name you want for your icon image file in the `File` text field. Click the left mouse button on the `Load` button to load the file into the canvas.

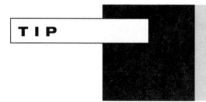

TIP

The DeskSet and supplementary icons are stored in `/usr/openwin/share/include/images` directory. These icons can used as a basis for creating your own custom icons.

Printing an Icon

Choosing the `Print` item from the `File` menu displays the `Print` pop-up window, as shown in Figure 7.20. You can print your icon image to a specified printer or a file. Printing an image to a file allows the file to be printed without using the Icon Editor application. The following explains the controls in the `Print` pop-up window.

FIGURE 7.19

An icon file icon in the
Icon Editor window

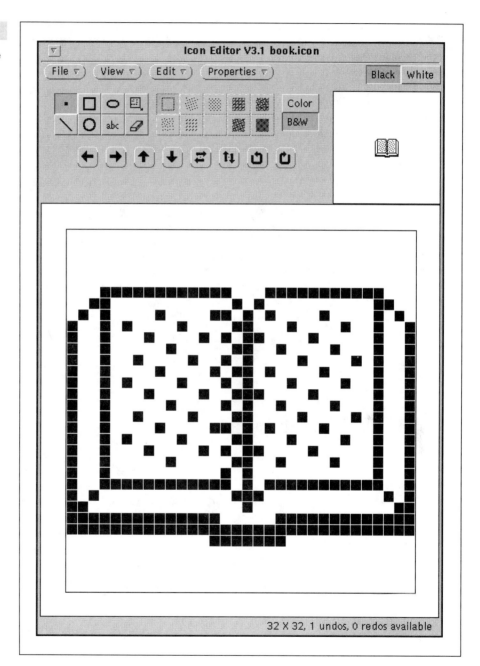

FIGURE 7.20

The Print pop-up window

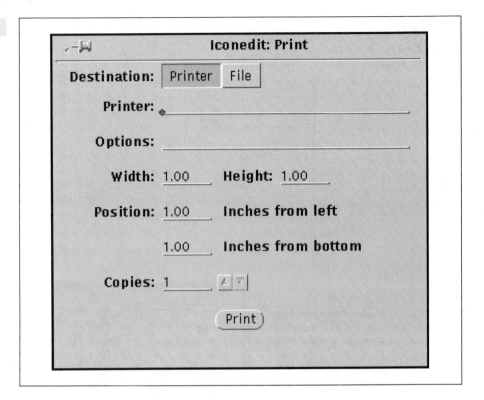

CONTROL	DESCRIPTION
Destination	Determines the destination of the printed output, which can be either a printer or a file. The default setting is Printer. If you choose the File setting, the Printer and Options settings change to Directory and File settings so that you can enter the path and file name of the file you want to print to.
Printer	Specifies the printer name.
Options	Allows you to type in SunOS commands that allow you to customize your printer option defaults.

CONTROL	DESCRIPTION
Width	Specifies the width of the printed image in inches.
Height	Specifies the height of the printed image in inches.
Position	The `Inches from left` specifies the left margin of the printed image. The `Inches from bottom` specifies the bottom margin of the printed image.
Copies	Specifies the number of copies. You can enter the number in the text field or click the left mouse button on the increment or decrement buttons to choose a number.
Print	Executes the printing of the current image in the canvas.

Using the Color Chooser Palette

If you're using the Icon Editor to create new icons for the File Manager, you should create black-and-white icons. You can use the Binder to specify foreground and background colors for your File Manager icons. However, you can create multicolor icons if you have a color workstation, and you can save them in a Color X Pixmap file format to be used with your own X applications.

If you want to create a color icon, select the `Color` choice button in the drawing controls area or click the left mouse button on the `Palette` button to display the `Color Chooser` pop-up window. The current color that the Icon Editor will use for drawing is displayed in the upper-left corner of the palette. The two colors at the top right of the palette are your Workspace and window colors, as defined in the `Workspace Properties Color` category window. The following explains how to use any of the colors displayed in the `Color Chooser` palette for the Icon Editor.

1. Click the left mouse button on the color you want in the `Color Chooser` palette. The selected color is highlighted and displayed in the `Color Chooser` preview area (the large square to the left of the palette).

2. Click the left mouse button on the `Apply` button to record the color change.

3. Move the pointer back to the Icon Editor to draw your icon with the chosen color. The pointer changes to the selected color as a reminder of the color you are drawing with.

Binding an Icon

The Binder application allows you to bind icons to files. It can also bind colors, applications, open methods, and print methods to files. A *binding* is a connection between file types and elements such as applications to be started when a file is opened, print scripts, or icons that the File Manager, Print Tool, Mail Tool, and other DeskSet applications use to display and operate on files. Because the DeskSet applications come with a default set of bindings, in most cases you will only need to use the Binder to bind customized icons to applications or files, or change the application used to open a file, or change the print script used to print a file. However, you may want to use the Binder to change the way particular files are displayed in the File Manager or other DeskSet applications, or to change the application used to open or print a file.

The Binder Window

To start the Binder application, press the right mouse button on the Workspace and choose the `Binder` item from the `Programs` submenu. Figure 7.21 shows the `Binder` window and icon. The `Binder` window has a control area, a scrolling list of Binder entries, and buttons at the bottom that you use to add a new binding or to modify or delete an existing binding. The Binder control area includes four menu buttons. The following explains each of these menus.

The Binder Window
and icon

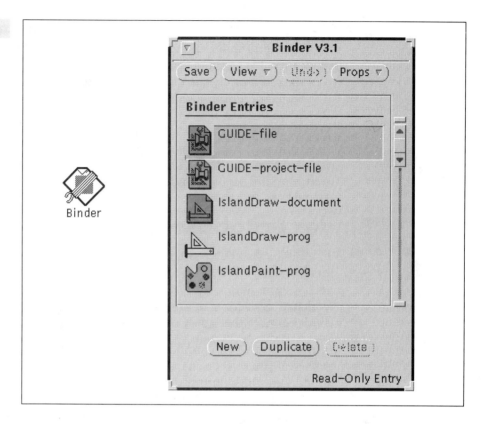

- The **Save** menu allows you to save your changes to the Binder database. The **Save** button replaces the standard **File** menu button because it is the only file operation used by the Binder.

- The **View** menu allows you to determine which Binder entries you want to display.

- The **Undo** menu allows you to undo the last operation. The operations that are undoable are the **New**, **Duplicate**, and **Delete** buttons at the bottom of the Binder window.

- The Props button allows you to display the properties of the selected Binder entry. There are two components for each Binder entry: Icon properties, which determine how a file is displayed and operated on by the DeskSet applications, and File Type properties, which determine which files are bound to the icon.

The scrolling list in the Binder window displays the bindings stored in three different databases: a network database, a system database, and a personal user database. The New, Duplicate, and Delete buttons at the bottom of the Binder window are used to work with Binder entries.

Binder Databases

The Binder databases are used by all applications in the DeskSet environment to determine how to display, print, and open any file. The network and system databases consist of the Binder entries shared by many workstations across the network. Your private database consists of the Binder entries that apply only to you.

In most cases, you cannot modify system or network (shared) database entries. If you select a shared network or system database entry, a message appears in the window footer of the Binder window telling you the selected entry is a read-only entry. The first time you run the Binder application, all your bindings will be system or network entries. If you want to customize a system or network entry, you can copy it to your personal database, then modify the user entry. When you add a new binding, it will be added as a personal Binder entry.

Viewing Binder Entries

The View menu allows you to determine the Binder entries displayed in the Binder window scrolling list. The All Entries item allows you to display a merged list of all private, system, and network entries. If you copy a system or network entry to your personal user database, only your personal version of the entry is displayed in the merged list. The Shared Entries item allows you to display all the system and network entries. The Personal Entries item displays only your entries.

Binder Entry Properties

Each Binder entry in the `Binder` window's `Binder Entries` scrolling list has associated properties, such as the application the entry is bound to or how the file is printed in the DeskSet environment. There are two types of properties associated with each Binder entry: Icon properties and File Type properties. The Icon properties include settings to determine how files of a particular type are displayed by DeskSet applications such as the File Manager, and what happens when files of that type are opened or printed. The Binder entry's File Type properties include defining the set of files that are bound to the icon. The `Props` menu button includes two items, `Icon` and `File Types`, for accessing pop-up windows that display the properties for the selected icon.

The Icon Properties Window

Selecting an entry in the `Binder Entries` scrolling list, then clicking the left mouse button on the `Props` menu button displays the Icon category `Properties` window (Figure 7.22) with the Icon properties for the selected icon. Clicking the left mouse button on the plus sign (+) button at the lower right of the `Properties` window, expands the window to display the full set of properties, as shown in Figure 7.23. You can shrink the window back down to the smaller size by clicking the left mouse button on the minus sign (−) button at the bottom of the expanded window. The following explains the controls in the expanded Icon category `Properties` window.

CONTROL	DESCRIPTION
Icon	Shows the current icon and Binder database entry name. You can use the text field to modify the entry name.

FIGURE 7.22

The Icon category
Properties window

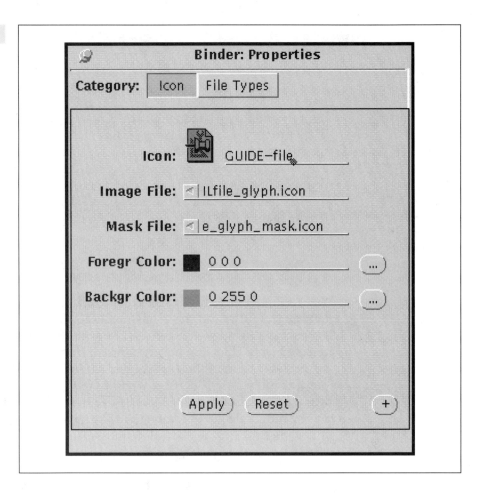

CONTROL	DESCRIPTION
Image File	Displays the path of the 32-by-32 pixel (XView format) icon that is bound to the current entry. This is the standard icon size displayed by the File Manager, Mail Tool, and other applications in the DeskSet Environment. The icon is displayed in the **Binder** window's **Binder Entries** scrolling list and the **Icon** field of the **Properties** window.

CONTROL	DESCRIPTION
`Mask File`	Displays the path of an icon color mask. A *color mask* defines the region of the icon to which the background color is applied. Think of a color mask as a background overlaid on top of your icon that indicates where the background color should be applied. If no icon mask file is specified, the entire icon is colored with the background color. For example, Figure 7.24 shows the icon and the icon mask for the `Audiotool-prog` Binder entry. The image in the Icon editor on the left is the icon image that determines the outline of the icon. The image in the Icon editor on the right is the icon mask that determines the icon area that will be colored with the background color.

NOTE

For a list of color settings, see the table in Chapter 15, or open the text file `rgb.txt` located in the `/usr/openwin/lib` directory.

FIGURE 7.23

The expanded Icon category Properties window

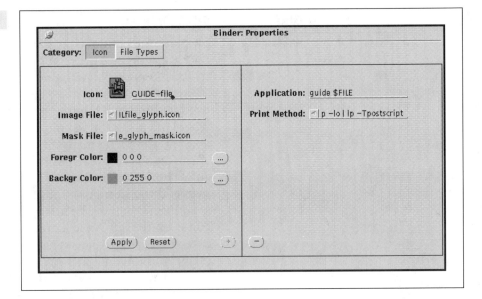

FIGURE 7.24

The Audiotool icon and Audiotool icon mask

CONTROL	DESCRIPTION
`Foregr Color`	The foreground color is the color that the icon itself is drawn with in the File Manager and other DeskSet applications. If no value is given for this field, the foreground color is black. If you want to pick a new foreground color, click the left mouse button on the button to the right of the `Foregr Color` field to display the `Color Chooser` pop-up window. This is similar to the window that you used to change the Workspace and window colors. Alternatively, you can type three numbers in the `Foregr Color` field to indicate the amount each of red, green, and blue in the foreground color. Color saturation values range from 0 through 255; for example, 255 0 0 represents a solid red color. The zeros represent the amount of green and blue in the color.
`Backgr Color`	The background color is the color that the icon is colored with in the File Manager and other DeskSet applications. If no value is given for this field, the background color is white. If you want to pick a new background color, click the left mouse button on the button to the right of the `Backgr Color` field to invoke the `Color Chooser` pop-up window. Alternatively, you can type three numbers in the `Foregr Color` field to indicate the amount each of red, green, and blue in the background color. Color saturation values range from 0 through 255; for example, 0 255 0 represents a solid green color. The zeros represent the amount of red and blue in the color.

CONTROL	DESCRIPTION
Application	Defines the application that is invoked whenever any file, defined by the current binding, is opened in the File Manager, Mail Tool, or other applications.
Print Method	Defines how a file is printed. If no print method is specified, the default print method of the application the file is being printed from is used.

The File Types Properties Window

By default, the Properties pop-up window displays the Icon category settings for the selected Binder entry. Clicking the left mouse button on the File Types category button displays the File Types category settings in the Properties pop-up window for the selected Binder entry, as shown in Figure 7.25. You can display the File Types category Properties window from the Binder window by choosing the File Types item from the Props menu.

Clicking the left mouse button on the plus sign (+) button at the lower right of the Properties window, expands the window to display the full set of properties. Figure 7.26 shows the expanded File Types Properties window. You can shrink the window back down to the smaller size by clicking the left mouse button on the minus sign (−) button at the bottom of the expanded window. The following explains the controls in the File Types category Properties window.

The File Types
category Properties
window

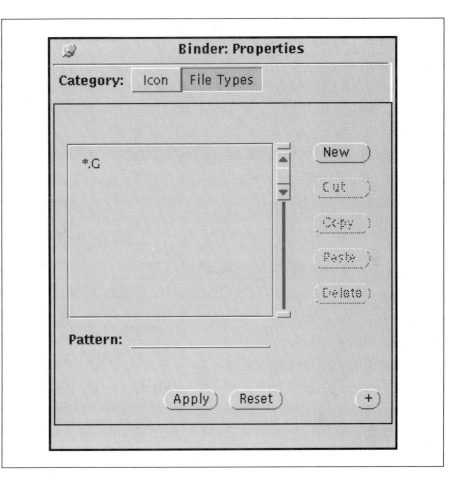

The expanded File Types category Properties window

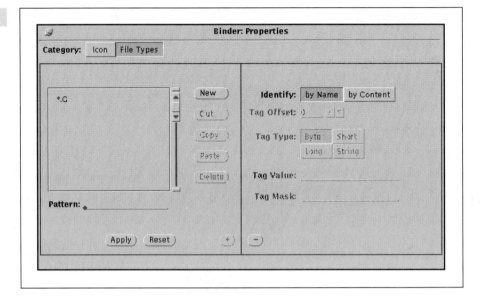

CONTROL	DESCRIPTION
File Types scrolling list	Each entry in the File Types scrolling list defines how a file, or group of files, is recognized by DeskSet applications. You can think of each entry in the File Types scrolling list as a class of files that consists of one or more files. Each class of files in this scrolling list (each File Type entry) is bound to the Icon properties of the current Binder entry. If you have two identical File Type entries in your Binder database, only the first one that the Binder reads is used. The first Binder entry to use the File Type entry is not necessarily the first Binder entry in the **Binder** window's scrolling list.

CONTROL	DESCRIPTION
`Pattern`	Modifies the name of a File Type entry. If the files are to be identified by a pattern, this pattern must be the name of the binding entry. If the currently selected File Type is identified by content, the `Pattern` text field is dimmed and unavailable. When there are no items selected in the scrolling list, you can type a pattern in the `Pattern` text field and press Return to create a new File Type entry.
File Types Properties buttons	The `New`, `Cut`, `Copy`, `Paste`, and `Delete` buttons to the right of the scrolling list allow you to create, delete, copy, and move entries in the File Types scrolling list. The `New` button creates a new File Type entry. Clicking the left mouse button on the `New` button creates a new entry in the scrolling list using the default name `unnamed_1`. If you create another new entry without renaming the first new entry, it is named `unnamed_2`. The `Cut` button allows you to remove the currently selected File Type entry and temporarily store it on the clipboard. The `Copy` button allows you to copy the currently selected File Type entry onto the clipboard. The `Paste` button allows you to add the File Type entry that is on the clipboard to the current Binder entry. The `Delete` button allows you to remove the File Type entry from the current Binder entry. The `Delete` button is inactive if the current Binder entry is a read-only entry. Deleting a Binder entry does *not* delete its File Type entry.

CONTROL	DESCRIPTION
Identify	Determines how the current class of files (the selected File Type entry) is recognized by DeskSet applications. A class of files is recognized either by name or by content. The default by Name setting recognizes files with names matching the text entered in the Pattern text field. For example, the File Type entry *.ps matches all the files that end with .ps. These are PostScript files, and they are displayed in the DeskSet environment with the postscript-file icon displayed in the Binder window's scrolling list. The asterisk (*) in the pattern means "match any file name here." The by Content setting recognizes files by matching file contents with the information entered in the Pattern field.

If the by Content setting is activated, files are recognized by matching file contents instead of the file name. The four settings, Tag Offset, Tag Type, Tag Value, and Tag Mask define what the file contents should be in the current File Type. In most cases, you will only use the default Tag Offset, the String Tag Type setting, and Tag Value settings. The following briefly explains each of the by Content settings. |
| Tag Offset (numeric field) | Determines the starting position in the file (counting from 0) where the file contents should be matched. The default value is 0. The value 0 starts matching the contents at the first character of the file. A byte offset of 1 would start matching the contents at the second character of the file, 3 the fourth character, and so on. |

CONTROL	DESCRIPTION
Tag Type	Determines the type of value that is to be matched in the file contents. The settings include **Byte**, **Short**, **Long**, or **String**. Most files are ASCII files consisting of the **String** data type (characters). A **Byte** type is a one-byte numerical value, a **Short** is a two-byte numerical value, and a **Long** is a four-byte numerical value. For example, to identify a file that begins with the word "project," choose the **String** setting.
Tag Value	Determines what to look for in the file contents. The **Tag Value** entry must be of the type defined in the **Tag Type** setting. In most cases, you will set the **Tag Type** setting to **String** and enter the text you want to match in the **Tag Value** text field. For example, enter "project" to match all files that begin with the text string "project."
Tag Mask	This optional field defines a mask value for **Byte**, **Short**, or **Long** data types. If a mask value is defined, a logical AND operation is performed on the **Tag Value** and the **Tag Mask** to determine the match value (the contents to be matched). The **Tag Mask** field is primarily intended for programmers developing applications to be integrated into the DeskSet Environment.

Binding an Icon to a File

Before you can bind an icon to a file, you first need to have created a 32-by-32 XView icon image. If you want to define the background area to apply a background color, you must also have created a mask file. Once you have created an icon, you can bind an icon image to a file by following the steps below.

1. Click the left mouse button on the **New** button at the bottom of the **Binder** window. The new entry **unnamed_1** appears in the Binder Entries scrolling list and in the Icon category **Properties** window, as shown in Figure 7.27.

2. Replace the name in the **Icon** text field with the name you want for the new Binder entry and press Return. This name will only appear in the binder; it is not a part of the icon. For example, you might enter "book-file" to identify that the icon indicates a text file associated with a book project.

3. Type the path and file name of your XView icon in the **Image File** text field and press Return.

4. If you want to specify a color mask (the area of the icon to be colored) you must have created another icon file that matches the size of your icon image to specify the area to apply the background color for the icon. Triple click in the **Mask file** text field to select the default entry, and enter the mask file name in the **Mask File** text field, then press Return. If you do not specify an icon mask file, the entire image appears in the background color.

FIGURE 7.27

The unnamed_1 entry appearing in the Icon category Properties window

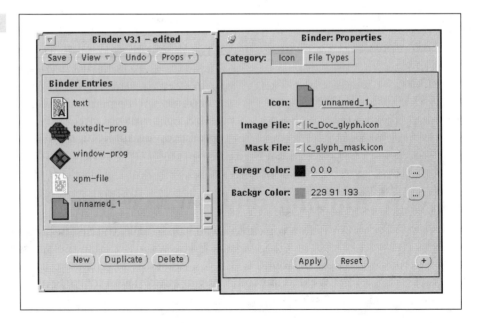

5. If you are using a color monitor, you can click on the buttons next to the `Foregr Color` text field and the `Backgr Color` text field to display the `Color Chooser` pop-up window. You can then select foreground and background colors for your icon. Be sure to click on `Apply` in the `Color Chooser` pop-up window to apply your selected colors.

6. Click the left mouse button on the + button in the lower left-hand corner. If you are defining the icon for an application other than the Text Editor, enter the application name in the `Application` text field. You can also define how a file prints by entering a print script (a series of print commands) in the `Print Method` text field. If you do not specify a print method, the print method of the application the file is being printed from is used.

7. Choose the `File Types` setting from the `Category` setting at the top of the `Properties` window. The `Properties` window now displays the File Types properties.

8. With the default `by Name` setting activated, type the file name pattern that you want to match in the `Pattern` text field. For example, to apply the icon to all files ending with the extension `.bk`, type `*.bk` in the `Pattern` text field and press Return.

9. Click the left mouse button on the `Apply` button to apply the icon file type and file type properties to your new binder entry.

10. Click the left mouse button on the `Save` button in the `Binder` window to save the new Binder entry in your personal database.

11. Choose `Close` from the Window menu to close the Binder to an icon.

12. Save a file using the file name pattern you indicated in step 8. Be sure that the file is not an empty file, or the new icon may not appear in the File Manager. In some cases, you must restart the File Manager or DeskSet application that your icon applies to. Figure 7.28 shows icons in the File Manager that match the file names ending with `.bk`.

FIGURE 7.28

A bound icon displayed in the File Manager window

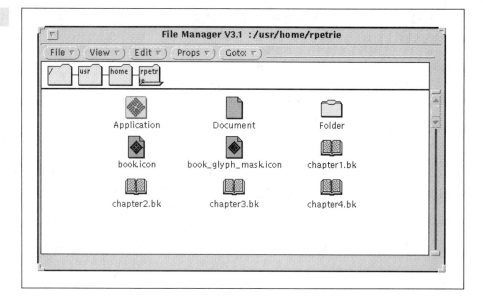

Deleting a Binder Entry

If you delete a Binder entry, the File Type entry associated with it is not deleted. If you want to delete the File Type entry, make sure to delete it from the File Type scrolling list before you delete the Binder entry. To delete the File Type entry, select the Binder entry in the base window scrolling list, display the File Type **Properties** window, select the entry or entries in the File Type scrolling list, and click the left mouse button on the **Properties** window's **Delete** button.

To delete a Binder entry, select the entry in the **Binder** window's scrolling list, and click the left mouse button on the **Delete** button. Then click the left mouse button on the **Save** button. Remember, the **Delete** button is dimmed and inactive if the currently selected entry is a system or network read-only entry.

Changing a Binding

To change a binding, select the entry in the `Binder` window's scrolling list, then modify the Icon and File Type properties fields that you want to change. If the binding that you want to change is a read-only entry, you can select the entry then click the left mouse button on the `Duplicate` button to make a private copy of the entry. You can then modify your private copy of the Binder entry. For example, suppose you want to change the color that the File Manager uses to display document files. Follow these steps:

1. Select the entry `default-doc` in the `Binder` window's scrolling list. A status message in the bottom-right corner of the Binder indicates that this is a read-only entry.

2. Click the left mouse button on the `Duplicate` button to copy the entry to your user database. A new Binder entry is created called `unnamed_1`, with all the same Icon properties as the original `default-doc` Binder entry. You can modify this new entry.

3. Rename the new Binder entry `default-doc`. This will put an entry called default-doc in your personal Binder database. This personal entry will take precedence over the system or network entry of the same name. If you later create a second user entry named `default-doc`, only the first entry you created will be recognized.

4. Change the background color to the new desired color. You can either type in the new RGB (red/green/blue) values in the `Backgr Color` text field, or click the left mouse button on the `Backgr Color` button to display the Color Chooser.

5. Click the left mouse button on the `Apply` button to update the icon name and color in the new Binder entry.

6. Click the left mouse button on the `Save` button in the `Binder` window. This updates your database to include the new Binder entry. Now when you view the merged Binder databases (the `All` item in the View menu), your personal entry will replace the shared entry

of the same name. If you want to use the shared entry again, simply delete the personal entry. The next time you start a new File Manager application, the color specified in your new personal entry will be used to display documents.

7. Choose `Quit` from the Window menu to quit the Binder.

N O T E

Changing the background of a default folder (`default-dir`) or document (`default-doc`) can change the background color of other icons.

PART TWO

Working from the SunOS Command Line

CHAPTERS

CHAPTER

8

Getting Started with the SunOS Command Line

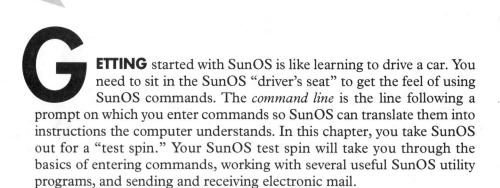

GETTING started with SunOS is like learning to drive a car. You need to sit in the SunOS "driver's seat" to get the feel of using SunOS commands. The *command line* is the line following a prompt on which you enter commands so SunOS can translate them into instructions the computer understands. In this chapter, you take SunOS out for a "test spin." Your SunOS test spin will take you through the basics of entering commands, working with several useful SunOS utility programs, and sending and receiving electronic mail.

Logging into SunOS

N O T E

If you have already logged in and want to work with SunOS commands in a Command Tool or Shell Tool window in the OpenWindows environment, skip to the section "Entering SunOS Commands."

The process of getting into SunOS is called *logging in*. Before logging into SunOS, you need an *account* set up by a *system administrator*, a person responsible for managing the system. In setting up your account, the system administrator instructs SunOS to accept you as a user and establishes certain parameters for your use of the system. When your account is established, you are assigned a user name. Your *user name* identifies you to the system. A common format for user names is the initial of your first name and your complete last name. Once you've been assigned an account and a user name, you are ready to log in.

After you have been assigned an account and a user name, you need to choose a password that you can enter when the system prompts you to after you have entered your user name. Your *password* prevents the use of your account by unauthorized users. Pick a password that is easy to remember, yet not easily deduced by others. You can change your password any time, as explained later. The following are requirements for selecting a password for the first time.

- A password must have at least six characters. If you use a password of less than six characters in length, the system prompts you to use a longer password.

- A password must contain at least two alphabetic characters and at least one numeric or special character, such as a &, +, −, @, !, or %. A password can contain uppercase or lowercase letters.

- Your user name, with its letters reversed or moved around, *cannot* be used as a password.

To log in, at the `login` prompt, type in your user name in lowercase characters then press Return. If you typed a wrong character and have not yet pressed Return, use the Delete key to erase the incorrect character, then type the correct character.

N O T E

If you enter a password more than three times that the system doesn't recognize, the system displays a message telling you there have been too many attempts and to try again later. This is a security feature to prevent unauthorized users from trying to guess a password.

After entering your user name, the system prompts you to enter your password. At the `password` prompt, type in your new password, then press Return. Your password will not be displayed as you type it. If your password is correct, the system logs you in and displays the system prompt, indicating that you are ready to start OpenWindows or enter SunOS commands.

System Login Messages

After you have logged in, you may see a *login message* displayed on your screen just before the system prompt. A login message usually displays information from the system administrator, such as when the system will be shut down for maintenance. A message indicating that you have electronic mail from other system users may also appear. Some systems may prompt you to type news to display a news bulletin. For information on reading electronic mail, see Chapter 11. For information on reading news messages, see Chapter 16.

Changing Your Password

It is a good idea to change your password periodically in order to prevent unauthorized access to your files. Depending on how your system administrator set up your account, you may even be required to change your password at regular time intervals. The following are additional requirements for changing a password beyond those described earlier for entering your password for the first time.

- Uppercase and lowercase characters are not considered different by Solaris when changing a password.

- A new password must differ from the previous password by at least three characters.

The following steps explain how to change your password.

1. At the system prompt, type in the command passwd in lowercase characters and press Return. Solaris prompts you for your old password.

2. Type your old password and press Return. The system will not display the characters you type. The system will prompt you for your new password.

3. Type your new password and press Return. After you enter your new password, you will then be asked to retype your new password for verification.

4. Type your new password again and press Return.

The SunOS Shells

A *shell* is the interface between you and SunOS; it translates commands you enter from the keyboard for the operating system. The system prompt is SunOS's way of saying it is ready and waiting for a command. How your SunOS prompt appears depends on which shell your system is using. The *Bourne shell* and *Korn shell* usually use the dollar sign ($) as the system prompt symbol. The Bourne shell is the standard shell for SunOS. However, your system may be using the *C shell*, which displays a percent sign (%) as its prompt. A system prompt may incorporate a system host name (also known as the name of the *file server*, the central computer on the network that enables you to access files throughout the system) followed by the system prompt. This is displayed as

```
bookware$
```

NOTE Most of the examples in this book will not include the system prompt. Just be aware that this prompt will be displayed on your screen as you follow the exercises presented here.

The Korn shell, Bourne shell, and C shell all come with SunOS. Previously the Korn shell had to be purchased separately. The Korn shell uses a simpler syntax and performs commands faster than the C shell. In addition, the Korn shell provides many of the convenient features of the C shell. It is also compatible with the Bourne shell (the default), so any Bourne shell command will run using the Korn shell. New users will benefit from the Korn shell because it provides features for easily editing and repeating commands that are not available in the Bourne shell. Because of the Korn shell's many benefits and the fact that it is rapidly replacing the Bourne shell in popularity, this book focuses on using the Korn shell. If you're not already using the Korn shell, at the system prompt, enter

```
ksh
```

NOTE Any Bourne shell command will run using the Korn shell.

Entering SunOS Commands

When you type in characters at the system prompt, you're entering characters into an area of memory called the *command-line buffer*. Pressing Return instructs SunOS to *execute* the command by accepting the contents of the command line in the buffer and processing it. The command line uses a simple standard *syntax* (rules governing the structure of a command line). Command lines can contain simple one-word commands or more complex commands that include *arguments*. Arguments modify commands and may be *options*, *expressions*, and *file names*. For example, adding a file name after a command identifies the file to be affected by the command. In SunOS you add an option to a command by typing a space then a hyphen before the first option letter. Options and expressions will be explained when commands that use them are introduced.

Keep in mind that the terms *commands* and *programs* are used interchangeably in SunOS because the names of the individual programs that make up the operating system are also the commands used to execute them. The general format for SunOS commands is as follows:

```
Command Option(s) Expression(s) Filename(s)
```

WARNING Keep in mind that SunOS is *case sensitive*, meaning that it treats lowercase and uppercase characters as two distinct character types.

Correcting Mistakes

There are several keyboard commands you can use to correct mistakes in the command line. The key combinations vary depending on how your system administrator has set up your system and account. Pressing the Delete key allows you to erase characters from the command line right to left. To erase an entire command line (as long as you haven't pressed Return), press Control-u. If you incorrectly type in a command and press Return, SunOS gives you an error message, such as `Command not found`. You can then retype the command. However, if you have typed in the wrong command, SunOS may execute a program you do not want to run. To terminate an executed program, press Control-c.

Useful SunOS Programs

SunOS contains over 300 utility programs that perform a wide variety of functions. To familiarize yourself with the SunOS environment, try running the utility programs described in this section. These programs enable you to display the date and time, display a calendar, perform simple mathematical calculations, establish who is using the system, echo text entered at the command line, and list and repeat commands you have entered previously. For more information on these and other SunOS commands, see Part IV, "Command Reference."

Displaying the Date and Time

To display the current date and time, type `date` at the system prompt, then press Return. SunOS uses a 24-hour clock and gives the time to the second. For example, SunOS might display the current date and time as

```
Tue Jan 30 10:52:35 PST 1999
```

Displaying a Calendar

The `cal` command displays a calendar on your screen for the month and year specified. Typing `cal` then pressing Return displays the calendar for the current month. You can enter arguments to the `cal` command to specify a particular month and year. There must be at least one space between the command and argument. The year can be in the range from 0 to 9999 A.D. The months are numbered 01 to 12, though you can use a one- or two-digit number for single-digit months, such as 5 or 05 for the month of May. To display the calendar for just one month of any year, enter

```
cal month_number year
```

To see the calendar for October 1999, enter

```
cal 10 1999
```

SunOS displays the calendar for October 1999 as follows:

```
    October 1999
 S   M  Tu  W Th   F   S
                   1   2
 3   4   5   6  7   8   9
10  11  12  13 14  15  16
17  18  19  20 21  22  23
24  25  26  27 28  29  30
31
```

Entering the command

```
cal 1999
```

displays the entire calendar for the year 1999.

Performing Simple Calculations

The `bc` program converts your computer into a handy desktop calculator. To start up the calculator program, type

```
bc
```

The `bc` command does not display a command prompt to let you know it has started. It simply waits for you to type your calculations. You can use standard operators to perform your calculations (plus +, minus –, multiplication *, and division /). To terminate the bc program, press Control-d. Type the calculation you want to perform. For example, the symbol recognized as the multiplication operator by bc is the asterisk (*), so entering

```
7*7
```

and pressing Return displays the result of the multiplication operation

```
49
```

In order to perform division operations with decimal places, you need to set the number of decimal places. The scale setting instructs bc how many decimal points to use in the division operation. To set the scale to two decimal places and divide 1 by 2, enter

```
scale=2
1/2
```

When you press Return, bc displays

```
.50
```

Press Control-d to return to system prompt.

Who Is Using the System?

SunOS is a multiuser system, which means more than one person can use the system at any one time. The who and finger commands are useful if you need to know a user's login name to send mail but only know their real name.

The who command lists the people logged into the system at that moment. The list contains user names, which terminals are being used, and the date and time each user logged in. To execute the who command, enter

```
who
```

SunOS displays a listing of current system users of your host machine. If your user name was rpetrie, the system might display

```
rpetrie    pts/06    Aug 30    11:35
bfife      pts/10    Aug 30    09:02
plane      pts/11    Aug 29    15:06
```

If you are working on a terminal other than your own, you may want to see the name that you are working under, or you may have access to more than one user name and want to remind yourself which name you used to logged in. To display information only about yourself simply enter

```
who am i
```

The **finger** command provides more detailed user information than the **who** command. Depending on what your system administrator has directed this command to display, it may list a user's full name, user name, terminal location, idle time, home directory, and more. To execute the **finger** command, enter

```
finger
```

SunOS then displays a **finger** command listing, such as

```
Login      Name   TTY Idle    When      Where
rpetrie    Rob Petrie         pts/06    12    Tue 10:30 NewRochelle
bfife      Barney Fife        pts/10    0     Wed 12:55 Mayberry
plane      Patty Lane         pts/11    20    Wed 15:06 Brooklyn
```

Echoing Text

The **echo** command is one of the simplest of SunOS commands. It displays on your screen whatever you type as its argument. The **echo** command can be very beneficial for displaying messages to yourself or other users. This command is frequently used when writing shell scripts, which are collections of commands stored in a file that can be run as a single program. To see just how the **echo** command displays text, enter

```
echo Is this the department of redundancy department?
```

when you press Return the **echo** command displays

```
echo Is this the department of redundancy department?
Is this the department of redundancy department?
```

The **echo** command prints on the line below the prompt, however you can move to the next line by adding the letter n followed by a backslash (\) and enclosing the text using single (') or double (") quotation marks. The backslash is used to identify the n as a special instruction for the **echo** command to perform, and the quotes or double quotes protect the backslash from being mistaken for text. For example, entering

```
echo "line 1 \nline 2 \nline 3"
```

displays

```
echo "line 1 \nline 2 \nline 3"
line 1
line 2
line 3
```

The **echo** command includes additional options for controlling how the message is displayed. By adding "\c", you can force **echo** to display on the same line. By adding \07 you can sound a warning bell. You can also add more than one option to the **echo** command. For example, entering

```
echo To beep "\07"or not to beep "\c"
```

beeps and displays the following

```
To beep or not to beep $
```

Displaying and Repeating Commands

The Korn shell stores a list of previously issued commands that can be redisplayed on your screen using the **history** command then reexecuted from the list. This timesaving feature speeds up the task of reentering commands. By default, **history** remembers the last 128 commands and displays the last 16 commands. To see a list of the previous 16 commands that have been captured by the **history** command, type **history** at the system prompt, then press Return. You can display additional commands by entering the following:

```
history  -n
```

The letter *n* indicates the number of commands you would like to display. For example, entering

```
history  -20
```

instructs the Korn shell to display the last 20 executed commands. You can also list a range of previously executed commands by entering **history** and separating the beginning and the ending number with a space.

Remember, you can check the numbering of the last 16 commands by entering `history`. To display commands 3 through 6, enter

```
history 3 6
```

For example, if you have entered each of the commands discussed in this chapter in the order in which they were introduced, entering `history 3 6` would produce this list:

```
3 cal 1999
4 bc
5 who
6 finger
```

The history list is dynamic, which means that it changes as you enter more commands at the system prompt. The commands issued first are the first to scroll off the list. You can reexecute any command in the `history` command list. To reexecute the last command in the list, type `r` at the system prompt and press Return. To execute any command in the list, type `r n` and press Return, where n is the number of the command in the list. For example, typing `r 3` and pressing Return executes the third command in the `history` command list `cal 1999`.

Clearing the Screen

The more commands you enter, the more cluttered your screen becomes. The `clear` command lets you easily wipe your screen clean. To clear the screen so the cursor appears in the upper-left corner, simply enter

```
clear
```

Sending and Receiving Electronic Mail

SunOS's mail program allows you to send mail messages, called *electronic mail* or *email*, to other users on the network and receive electronic mail in return. Whenever you log in, SunOS checks the system mailbox. If any mail is addressed to your user name, you may see the message **you have mail** displayed on your screen. You can then display a listing of your mail messages and read your mail or ignore the mail message prompt and read your mail at any time later. You can send mail messages to other users whether they are online or not.

Reading Your Mail

If you get a message notifying you that you have mail, someone has sent you a mail message through the SunOS mail system. In order to read your mail, at the system prompt enter

```
mail
```

The system displays postmark message headers, followed by the `mail` program prompt, as shown below.

```
From buddy Thu Jul 23 14:17 PDT 1992
Date: Thu, 23 Jul 92 14:17:12 PDT
From: buddy (Buddy Sorrell)
Message-Id: <9207232117.AA00233@abradyshow>
Content-Length: 53

Rob,
Can we use Mel's bald head for the bowling ball sketch?
Buddy

?
```

The question mark (?), at the end of the message, prompts you for a filing disposition for the current mail message. Typing an asterisk * displays a complete list of disposition commands. The following describes the most common options for disposing and saving mail messages.

OPTION	DESCRIPTION
Press Return	Display the next mail message and save this mail message so it will still be there next time mail is read.
d	Delete the current mail message and display the next mail message.

OPTION	DESCRIPTION
s *filename*	Save the current mail message in *filename* (where *filename* is a file name you enter to store the message) and display the next mail message.
q	Quit reading mail; unread mail is available next time you execute the mail command.
x	Exit and abort the mail program; any mail messages that you deleted are restored.

Sending Mail

You send mail by specifying the user name of the person or persons you want to receive the mail after the `mail` command. You can use the `who` or `finger` command as explained earlier in this chapter to find a user's name if you don't know it. When you send mail to another user, it is stored in the recipient's electronic mailbox, and that person is notified that they have mail. To send mail to another user, at the system prompt, type `mail` *username*, then press Return. To send the same mail message to multiple users, separate each user name with a space. Type in the text of your mail message. If you want to create a new line, simply press Return at any point. If you decide you want to cancel your mail message, press Control-c. When you've finished entering your mail message text, press Return to move the cursor to a new line, then press Control-d. The mail program sends your mail message and the system prompt returns you to your screen.

Getting Help with SunOS Commands

SunOS includes the reference documentation for all SunOS commands, called *man pages* (short for manual pages). These man pages are not written for the beginning user. However, using man pages can come in quite handy when you have forgotten the syntax of a command or you want on-line help with a command from the command line. The man pages include a brief description, the command syntax, available options, system files that are referenced by the command, and lists related to commands. The man pages conclude with any known problems and limitations of a command. The `man` command uses the syntax

    man *command*

where *command* is the name of the command you want help with. For example, to get more information on the `mail` command, enter

    man mail

The `man` command displays only one screenful of text at a time and the percentage of the pages displayed. To continue displaying man pages, press the Spacebar or the Return key. To quit displaying the man pages, enter q.

Command Summary

The following lists the commands covered in this chapter and their functions.

COMMAND	RESULT
`bc`	Performs simple calculations.
`cal`	Displays calendar for month or year specified.
`clear`	Clears the screen.
`date`	Displays current time and date.
`echo`	Displays the text that follows the `echo` command.
`finger`	Lists detailed information about users currently on the system.
`history`	List commands previously executed.
`mail`	Allows user to read or send electronic mail.

COMMAND	RESULT
man	Displays manual pages for a command.
r	Reexecutes the last command (Korn shell only).
who	Lists users currently logged into system.
who am i	Lists information about the user currently logged into system.

Navigating Directories and Working with Files

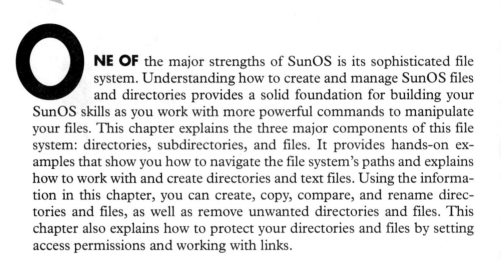

ONE OF the major strengths of SunOS is its sophisticated file system. Understanding how to create and manage SunOS files and directories provides a solid foundation for building your SunOS skills as you work with more powerful commands to manipulate your files. This chapter explains the three major components of this file system: directories, subdirectories, and files. It provides hands-on examples that show you how to navigate the file system's paths and explains how to work with and create directories and text files. Using the information in this chapter, you can create, copy, compare, and rename directories and files, as well as remove unwanted directories and files. This chapter also explains how to protect your directories and files by setting access permissions and working with links.

An Overview of the SunOS File System

SunOS uses a hierarchical file structure, an inverted tree structure similar to the structure of a family tree, with the base of the tree at the top. A *file* is a "container" that holds text or programs. *Directories* are files that contain indexes to aid SunOS in locating files. It's helpful if you think of directories as file cabinets and files as file folders containing the information that you want to access. That is, though directories really only contain indexes to files, you can think of them as actually containing the files themselves.

The topmost parent directory of the tree is known as the *root* directory and is indicated by a slash (/). The root directory contains files and *subdirectories*. Although every directory except the root directory is a subdirectory, subdirectories can be referred to as directories. In other words, the term subdirectory and directory are often used interchangeably. Your system may have a directory called **home** that contains home directories for all users. The names of these individual home directories are usually based on the names of the users.

Types of Directories

SunOS relies on specific system directories to operate. In most cases, the system administrator organizes and restricts access to these directories. The following list explains the primary types of directories that exist on a SunOS system.

DIRECTORY	DESCRIPTION
/ (root)	The first slash represents the top of the file system, or the root directory.
/bin	This is the binary files directory, which contains the SunOS program files or commands. For example, the commands you entered in Chapter 8 were executed from the **bin** directory.
/dev	This is the device directory, which contains files that support such devices as the screen, the mouse, and the disk drives.
/etc	This directory is used by the system administrator for machine-specific system maintenance. For example, the /etc/shadow file is used to keep user passwords in a file inaccessible to anyone except the system administrator and certain trusted programs.
/export	The /export directory contains files and file systems that a file server shares with other workstations on the network.

DIRECTORY	DESCRIPTION
/home	The /home directory contains user home directories. In some cases, user home directories are found in the /export directory so they can be accessed from other workstations on the network.
/kernel	The /kernel directory contains the program UNIX, which is also known as the *kernel*. The kernel is the heart of SunOS; it manages the system's hardware, and schedules and terminates processes.
/sbin	The /sbin directory contains programs for system administration.
/tmp	Temporary files are stored in this directory and are either periodically removed by your system administrator or deleted when you reboot your computer.
/usr	This is a general purpose directory that contains several important subdirectories for users. For example, /usr/bin contains many of the SunOS command programs, and /usr/share/man contains the online manual pages.
/var	This directory is maintained by the system administrator. It contains information that varies from machine to machine. For example, users' mail files are stored in the /var/mail directory.

Navigating Directories

When you want to move to another directory, enter the **cd** (change directory) command followed by the name of directory you want to move to.

The following sections describe more fully the **cd** command and explain additional techniques that you can use to move quickly through the file system. They also cover absolute and relative path names, on-screen displays of your current working directory, and shortcuts for returning to your home directory.

Navigating with Path Names

Every file has a path name. A *path name* tells SunOS which paths to take to find a specific directory or file, and so is similar to an address on a letter because both give specific directions for a final destination. You change from one directory to another by invoking the **cd** command with a path name. A path name consists of a directory name or series of directory names separated by slashes (**/**). For example, **/usr** indicates the directory **usr**, which is a subdirectory immediately below the root directory (indicated by the forward slash). There are two types of path names: absolute and relative.

Navigating with Absolute Path Names

You can construct the path name of a file by tracing a path from the root directory to the directory where the file resides. An *absolute path name* always begins with a slash (**/**) and lists the file name after the final slash. For example, **/export/home/srogers/letter** is the absolute path name for the file **letter** in the directory **/export/home/srogers**.

Navigating with Relative Path Names

Unless you specify an absolute path name by beginning the path name with a slash, SunOS assumes you are using a relative path name. A *relative path name* describes a path that starts from the directory in which you're currently working. In other words, relative path names trace the path from the working directory to the desired file or directory. Relative path names save you the time of typing in a complete, or absolute, path name to access a directory or file beneath the directory you are currently located in. For example, in the directory **/export/home/srogers**, the command

```
cd reports
```

moves you to the subdirectory **/export/home/srogers/reports**.

Moving to Your Home Directory

Your *home directory* is the directory that was created for you when you first logged into the system. Every user is assigned a home directory. Entering the `cd` command by itself moves you directly to your home directory. If you're using the Korn shell, the tilde character (~) can be used as a shortcut for typing in the entire path name for your home directory. For example, typing `cd ~/reports` moves you to the `reports` subdirectory of your home directory. You can also access another user's home directory by following the tilde character with the person's user name. For example, `cd ~mcooley` moves you to Melvin Cooley's home directory. Adding a plus sign to the tilde (~+) is the same as typing the absolute path name of the working directory. Adding a minus sign to the tilde (~+~−) is the same as typing the absolute path name of the directory you were previously in.

Displaying the Working Directory

The *working directory* is not a fixed directory but the directory in which you are currently located. A useful SunOS command is `pwd`, which prints (displays) on the screen the name of your working directory. When you use the `ls` command with the `-a` option to list the contents of a directory, SunOS may indicate the working directory path name as a single dot (.).

Moving to a Parent Directory

The *parent directory* is the directory located one level above your working directory. You can specify the path name of the parent directory of your working directory with two consecutive periods (..). For example, entering `cd ..` moves you up one directory level. The following example prints the working directory before and after moving up a directory level using the double-dot shortcut. If entering the `pwd` command displays

```
/export/home/srogers
```

issuing the command `cd ..` then issuing the `pwd` command displays

```
/export/home
```

Working with Directories

Now that you know how to use absolute and relative path names, you can use several helpful commands to conveniently and strategically organize your files. Your ability to perform actions on a given file is governed by the type of access you have to that file. The type of access you have is controlled by *permissions* settings.

- *Read* permission allows you to view or copy the contents of a file.

- *Write* permission enables you to add or delete directories.

- *Execute* permission allows you to move into a directory and execute programs.

In most cases, if you try to move, copy, or remove a file for which you don't have these permissions, SunOS will respond with a `Permission denied` message. Permissions are covered in detail later in this chapter.

Listing a Directory's Contents

The `ls` command by itself lists the contents (directories and files) of the working directory. You can also specify a directory after the `ls` command to get a listing for that directory. For example, `ls /export/home/srogers` lists the files for the directory `srogers` no matter which directory you're using. There are a number of arguments the `ls` command can accept to display different information.

OPTION	RESULT
-1	Lists subdirectories and files with each entry on a separate line.
-a	Lists all subdirectories and hidden files (special system files that have a file name beginning with a dot or a period).
-c	Lists files by creation/modification time.

OPTION	RESULT
-F	Lists and flags directories with a slash (/), executable files with an asterisk (*), and symbolic links—used primarily by programmers—with an at sign (@). Text files appear without a flag.
-g	Shows the group ownership of a file in a long listing but omits the actual owner.
-l	Displays a long listing of the contents of the directory.
-m	Merges a listing of the contents of the directory into a series of names separated by commas.
-o	Shows the ownership of a file in a long listing but omits the group name.
-R	Recursively lists the contents of each sub-directory under a specified directory. Each subdirectory name is followed by its relative path name and a listing of the contents of that subdirectory until SunOS reaches the last level of the hierarchical structure.
-r	Reverses the order of listing to display a reverse alphabetical directory listing.
-t	Lists a directory sorted by time in order of newest to oldest files.
-u	Lists subdirectories and files according to file access time.

To help you quickly identify the different directories, files, and programs (executable files), enter the ls command with the -F option, ls -F. When you enter ls -F, a directory listing such as this one appears on your screen:

```
Desktop* examples/     info*  memo
clients  final    mail/  textfile
```

Below is a sample listing produced by `ls -l`.

```
-rw-r--r--  1   rpetrie staff   1094  Dec  1   17:08   clients
drwxr-sr-x  2   rpetrie staff   0     Nov  9   19:52   Temp
-rw-r--r--  1   rpetrie staff   0     Dec  1   17:08   info
drwxr-sr-x  2   rpetrie staff   512   Jan  30  19:52   mail
```

The different components of this listing are explained in the "Listing File and Directory Permissions" section later in this chapter.

Creating a Directory

The `mkdir` command creates directories. By creating a directory you are making the equivalent of a file drawer where you can keep related files. Before creating a directory, make sure you are in your home directory by typing `cd` and pressing Return. Enter `mkdir` followed by the name you want to give your new directory. For example, in the directory `/export/home/srogers`, entering

```
mkdir reports
```

creates the subdirectory `/export/home/srogers/reports`. If you attempt to make a new directory with a directory name that already exists, the message `mkdir: failed to make directory "reports"; File exists` appears. In order to create a directory outside your home directory, you must have write and execute permissions in the parent directory.

Copying a Directory

You can duplicate the contents of any directory using the `cp` (copy) command and the `-r` (recursive) option. This guarantees that all files and subdirectories of the source directory are duplicated. For example, in the directory `/export/home/felix`, issuing the command `cp -r portfolio record` copies all files and subdirectories from the `portfolio` directory to the directory named `record`, where `record` and `portfolio` are subdirectories of `/export/home/felix`. If the directory to which the copies are supposed to be sent doesn't exist, the `cp` command first creates it, then copies the files and directories to the new directory. If the directory to which the copies are supposed to be sent already exists, any files already there are overwritten. To allow you to avoid mistakenly overwriting existing files, use the −i (interactive) option. This option causes SunOS to ask if you really want to overwrite files in a directory that already exists. Pressing any key other than y causes the `cp` process to terminate.

As with many SunOS commands, you can use more than one option with the `cp` at a time. When you use multiple options you only need to precede the list of options with a single hyphen. For example, if you enter `cp −ir portfolio record`, the −i causes SunOS to ask if you really want to overwrite the existing files in `record`. Press y, and the −r (recursive) option then copies all the files and subdirectories of the `portfolio` directory to the `record` directory until SunOS reaches the last level of the hierarchical structure.

You can maintain the original modification times and permission modes of files and directories by using the −p (preserve) option. If you don't use the −p option, the files are assigned the current date and default permission modes. To interactively and recursively copy the contents of the directory `bozo` to the directory `clone`, while preserving the original modification times and permission modes, enter

```
cp -ipr /bozo /clone
```

WARNING Beware of a recursive copy that doesn't specify files to be copied, such as `cp -r source source/backup`. This copy command can ruin your day by recursively creating new `backup` subdirectories and copying files until it fills the entire file system.

Removing a Directory

You can delete a directory using the remove directory command, `rmdir`. The directory that you want to remove cannot be the working directory (the directory in which you're located). To remove a directory with `rmdir`, the directory needs to be empty; that is, it cannot contain any subdirectories or files. When removing subdirectories from your current directory, remember that you can refer to subdirectories using the shorthand convention of relative path names. For example, to remove the empty subdirectory `reports` from your current directory, simply enter `rmdir reports`. Adding the `-i` option causes SunOS to ask if you want the directory to be removed before SunOS deletes the directory. If you attempt to remove a directory that isn't empty, SunOS displays the message `rmdir: directoryname: Directory not empty`.

To remove directories that contain files or subdirectories, use `rm` with the `-r` (recursive) option, which deletes all existing files and subdirectories, then removes the directory. To interactively remove a directory and its contents, enter the command `rm -ir directory_name`. You can force files to be removed without SunOS displaying permissions, asking questions, and reporting errors by adding the `-f` (force) option; for example, `rm -rf directoryname`.

WARNING

Be careful when using the `-r` and `-f` options. All subdirectories are permanently deleted when you use these options. Before removing a directory, use the `ls` command with the `-a` (all) option to guarantee that the directory doesn't contain subdirectories or files that you'll later need. Then use the `rm` command with the `-ir` options to ensure you don't accidentally remove needed directories and files.

Working with Files

Manipulating files is the essence of SunOS. SunOS provides commands to perform just about any operation on a file you can imagine. The following section only scratches the surface in explaining the most essential commands and options you can use when working with files, such as displaying a file's type or contents, or copying, renaming, moving, or removing files. In many ways, working with files is similar to working with directories. Most of the commands you use with directories are the same as the commands you use with files.

Listing Files

The command for listing files is the same as that for listing the contents of a directory. You can list the files for any directory by following the `ls` command with the absolute or relative path name and any of the `ls` options. If the directory is empty and you use `ls -a` to list all your files, a single period (.) indicating the current directory and two consecutive periods (..) indicating the parent directory are displayed.

Determining File Types

If you enter `file` followed by a file name, SunOS lists that file's *type*, such as ASCII text, program files, or directory. For example, issuing the command

```
file clients
```

causes SunOS to display

```
clients: ascii text
```

indicating that clients is an ASCII text file. If the file is a program file, the command also lists the language it was written in and any pertinent information about the file.

File Name Conventions

A file name must be unique in the directory where it resides. File names can be up to 256 characters long, but it is recommended that you keep them under 14 characters to save time entering them. You can assign a file any name you want, provided you avoid using special characters such as `*?<>!/\`. Remember, SunOS is a case-sensitive operating system, so you need to enter the file name exactly as you created it in order to use it again. File names that begin with a period (.) indicate special hidden files that are used by the system and do not appear when you use `ls` by itself to list the files. But you can use a period anywhere else in a file name and it will not become a hidden file.

Be careful when naming files. To create file names that are easy to remember and don't conflict with SunOS's special characters, it is best to restrict file names to letters, digits, underscores, and periods (except as the first character). Don't create a file name that contains a nonprinting character, or a *control character*, by pressing a Control-key combination, such as Control-a. Although in most cases SunOS would substitute the control character with a question mark on screen, a file name with nonprintable characters can make that file inaccessible.

Creating a File

There are several ways you can create a file. You can use a text editor, such as vi, to create a file, use the `cat` command, or use the `touch` command to create an empty file. The `cat` command is an abbreviation of *concatenate*, which means to link or connect in a series. To create a file with the `cat` command, type `cat > filename`, where *filename* is the name you want your file to have. After typing the name for your file and pressing Return, you can begin entering the text you want your file to contain. When you are finished entering the text, press Control-d. For example, to create a file using the `cat` command, type in the following:

```
cat >myfile (press Return)
My first text file. (press Return)
(press Control-D)
```

The greater-than sign (>) is a *redirection operator* that channels your text into the file `myfile`. Control-d signals the end of the text that is to be put into the file. If you accidentally type `cat` without a redirection symbol or a file name, press Control-d to exit the `cat` command.

Creating an Empty File

The `touch` command is usually used to change the time and date of a file. It is also an easy way to create an empty file. When you first start working with files, you may want to create files with the `touch` command to practice copying, moving, and removing files. The `touch` command uses the following syntax:

```
touch filename
```

If *filename* is the name of an existing file, the date and time of the file is updated to the current time and date. If no existing files match the *filename* argument, the **touch** command creates an empty file with the name indicated by the *filename* argument.

Displaying the Contents of a File

Once you've created a file, you can look at its contents by entering the **cat** command followed by the file name. If you misspell the name of the file you want to view, SunOS displays the file name you typed followed by the message **cat: Cannot open file**. If the file contains more lines than the screen can display, the beginning text scrolls off the screen, leaving only the last screen of text visible. The following key combinations are useful in this situation:

Control-s	Temporarily halts scrolling
Control-q	Resumes scrolling
Control-c	Cancels scrolling

You can display more than one file in sequence on the screen by typing in the names of all the files you want to see after **cat**, making sure to separate the file names with a space. For example, **cat doc1 doc2** displays the contents of the file **doc1**, followed by the contents of the file **doc2**.

NOTE

Many SunOS files are binary files that contain instructions only the computer can understand. When you try to display these files, they appear as text resembling what you might find in a cartoon balloon to indicate cursing.

The following options are available when using the `cat` command:

OPTION	RESULT
-e	Displays a $ character at the end of each line. The -e option is ignored unless used with the -v option.
-s	Causes `cat` to suppress messages if the file does not exist.
-t	Displays tab characters as ^I and formfeed characters as ^L. The -t option is ignored unless it is used with the -v option.
-v	Lists control characters.

Copying Files

You copy files with the `cp` command. To copy one of your files, type `cp` and the name of the file to be copied, and the file name you want to copy this file to. For example, `cp rocky smooth` copies the file `rocky` to a file with the name `smooth`, leaving `rocky` intact. Unless you use the -p (preserve) option to record the original modification time and permission modes, the file is created with the current date and default permission modes. (Permission modes are explained later in this chapter.) When copying files, use the -i (interactive) option to ensure that the target name for the copy doesn't already exist. That way if the file does exist, SunOS inquires if you really want to overwrite the existing file. Pressing any key other than y causes the copying process to terminate. You can also copy more than one file. To copy two or more files at once, list all the files after the command `cp`, making sure you separate each file name with a space. For example, to interactively copy the files **onefile twofile** to their parent directory, enter

```
cp -i onefile twofile ..
```

If the file names exist in the parent directory, SunOS asks you, one file at a time, whether or not to overwrite the existing file. Pressing any key other than y aborts the copy process for that file, and SunOS then asks if you want to overwrite the next existing file.

Moving and Renaming Files

Moving a file and renaming a file both use the same command, mv (move). To move a file, type mv followed by the name of the file you want to move, then type the directory you want to move the file to. If you want to rename a file, type mv followed by the file name you want to rename, then type the new name. For example, the command mv sunrise sunset changes the file name sunrise to sunset. The mv (move) command deletes the original file after copying the file and moving it to its new location. Use the -i option to ensure that you don't move a file to another file that already exists and overwrite the text there. You can't rename more than one file at a time. You can, however, move several files at one time by listing all the files you want to move before the destination directory and separating each file name with a space. For example, if you are in Perry Mason's home directory, entering the command

```
mv letter1 letter2 memo letters
```

moves the files letter1, letter2, and memo to the letters subdirectory of pmason.

Removing Files

The rm command deletes one or more files. To remove a file you need to have write permission in the directory that contains the file as well as in the file itself. If you don't have write permission for the file, and you created the file, SunOS asks you whether or not to override the permissions feature and remove the file. To remove more than one file, list all the files you want to delete and separate each file name with a space. The command rm junk trash removes the files junk and trash from the working directory. The rm -i (interactive) option prompts you with the question rm: remove filename: (y/n)?. Type y to remove the file; any other response will cause SunOS to ask if you want to remove the next file in an argument list or, if you only have one file in the list, aborts the removal process. You can force files to be removed without displaying access permissions or having SunOS ask questions or report errors by using the -f (force) option. To remove all the files and subdirectories in the current directory, use the rm -r (recursive) option.

WARNING Be careful using the −r and −f options. Files and subdirectories are permanently deleted when you use these options. When removing files, use the −i option to ensure you don't accidentally remove the wrong files.

Listing and Changing Permissions

Because SunOS allows users to share the file system, it protects files and directories by defining types of users and access permission modes. Every file and directory has three types of users and four types of access permission modes. By changing permission modes, you can selectively share files and directories with some or all of the people on the system.

Listing File and Directory Permissions

By adding the -l (long) option to the **ls** (list) command, you can list permissions information about files. Entering **ls -l** displays a long format for your directory listing. This option can be used alone or in conjunction with the other options. This next example shows a listing of files using the -l (long) and -a (all) options with **ls** (**ls -al**), followed by an explanation of each of the file attributes from left to right.

```
drwxrwxrwx   7   rpetrie staff   2560   Dec 1   17:00   .
drwxrwxrwx   7   rpetrie staff   512    Dec 1   17:00   ..
-rw-r--r--   1   rpetrie staff   1094   Dec 1   17:08   clients
-rw-r--r--   1   rpetrie staff   0      Dec 1   17:18   info
drwxr-sr-x   2   rpetrie staff   512    Jan 30  19:52   mail
-rw-r--r--   1   rpetrie staff   1094   Dec 1   17:28   memo
drwxr-sr-x   2   rpetrie staff   512    Jul 4   12:26   temp
-rw-r--r--   1   rpetrie staff   179    Mar 1   10:35   test
-rw-r--r--   1   rpetrie staff   1327   Mar 1   15:00   textfile
```

COLUMN	DESCRIPTION
Permissions	Permissions are displayed in the *permissions list*, which is the first ten characters in the listing. The first character that appears in the leftmost column indicates the file type (regular, directory, or device). The remaining nine characters in the series specify the permission modes for the three types of users: yourself (owner), group, and others (three characters for each user type).
Links	The number that follows the first ten characters lists the number of files and directories linked to that file. Links are covered later in this chapter.
Owner	The user name of the person who created or owns the file.
Group	Users can be organized into groups. This enables members of a particular department to share access to files and directories. There can only be one group associated with a file or directory.
Bytes	The size of the file (a byte equals one character).
Date	The date and time the file was created or last modified.
File name	The name of the file or directory.

File and Directory Types

The first character in the permissions list indicates the file type. The most common types of files are referred to as *standard* files and are indicated by a hyphen (−). A directory is identified by the letter **d**. Outside your home directory you are likely to encounter other types of files. Here are some of the characters used to identify these types of files on the system.

CHARACTER	DESCRIPTION
-	Indicates that the file is a standard file.
b or c	Indicates that the device is a special device file.
d	Indicates that the file is actually a directory or subdirectory.
1	Indicates that the file is actually a symbolic link used to link one file with another. Symbolic links are discussed later in the chapter.
p	Indicates that the device is a special file.

Types of Permissions

There are seven types of permissions you can assign to your files or directories. By assigning different permissions, you can limit the access others have to that directory or file. Here is a list of the seven permission modes and the characters that represent them in a permissions list.

CHARACTER	DESCRIPTION
r	The read privilege allows a user to list the contents of the directory or file. The read permission is also necessary to copy a file from one location to another.
w	The write permission allows a user to change the contents of a file or directory. This permits a user to create, append, and remove existing files.
x	The execute permission allows a user to execute a file. The ability to search through directories is also a function of the execute permission. A directory can be read from or written to, but unlike a file, it can't be executed. When applied to a directory, the execute access permission allows you to search through and list the contents of the directory.

CHARACTER	DESCRIPTION
-	The no access permission is also referred to as the protection mode. It prevents a user from reading, writing to, or executing a file.

Ownership of Files

File access is defined for four types of users: owner, group, and all others. The following lists descriptions for each of these three types of ownership, and also includes examples of permissions modes.

TYPE OF USER	DESCRIPTION
Owner	This refers to the creator of the file or directory. The first three characters after the file type character list the types of permissions available to the owner. For example, a permissions list beginning with -rw- indicates the owner has read and write permissions but not execute permission.
Group	Each user is a member of a group defined by the system administrator. The fifth, sixth, and seventh characters in the list indicate the permissions available to users who are in the same group as the owner. For example, a file beginning with -rw-r-- indicates that group members have read, but not write or execute permissions. To find out which group or groups you belong to, enter the command groups.
Others	This means all other users. The third set of three characters after the file type lists the types of permissions available to users who are not members of the same group as the owner. For example, a file with -rw-r----- permissions indicates that users outside the owner's group have no access to the file.

TYPE OF USER	DESCRIPTION
All	Incorporates all three: owner, group, and others.

Changing Permission Modes

The owner of a file controls which users have permission to access and work with that file. You use the `chmod` command to change the permission modes of a file or directory. The permission modes of a file can only be changed by the person who created the file or by someone who has *super-user* privileges (additional access to files beyond those of a normal system user); usually this is your system administrator.

There are two forms of the `chmod` command you can use to change file and directory permission modes: the symbolic form and the numeric form.

Changing Permission Modes Using Symbolic Notation

The format for changing permission modes with symbolic notation is as follows:

```
chmod class(es) operation permission(s) filename(s)
```

Use the following abbreviations to identify the class for which you want to change permission modes:

u	User
g	Groups
o	Others
a	All

You then use operators to assign r for read, w for write, and x for execute permission modes. The following shows abbreviations for the possible arguments that can be added to the `chmod` command to assign, add, or remove permissions from a file using symbolic notation. If you omit class, the setting is applied to all three classes (user, group, and others).

CLASS	OPERATIONS	PERMISSIONS
u User (owner)	= assigns a permission	r read
g Group	+ adds a permission	w write
o Others	- removes a permission	x execute
a All		

The following example lists **chmod** commands to assign the file named **populace** read, write, and execute permissions for all classes of users and to remove all permissions for everyone but the user (owner) of the file named **restricted**.

```
chmod a=rwx populace
chmod go-rwx restricted
```

The command

```
chmod a=rx testfile
```

changes the mode of **testfile** so that it can be accessed and read but not written to by all users on the system. It's important to note that if you use = and do not specify all types of permissions (that is, if you omit r, w, or x), the permissions for the omitted types will be turned off. You can also change permissions for multiple files, provided you want them to have the same access permissions. You must separate the file names with a single space.

The following combines several aspects of **chmod**:

```
chmod u=rw, o=r redfish bluefish
```

This command

- allows the owner of the files **redfish** and **bluefish** to read and write to them.

- allows everyone else to read (but not write to) these files.

- prevents everyone, including the owner, from executing the files (because x was not specified).

Changing Permission Modes Using Numeric Notation

To assign permissions using numeric notation, you enter numbers to specify the permissions you want. If you enter only one number after `chmod`, that permission will apply to the other's class. If you enter two numbers, the first number will specify permissions for the group and the second will set the permissions for others. If you enter three numbers, the first number will set the owner's permissions, the second number will set group permissions, and the third number will apply to all others. The following lists the numeric values that can be used to change permissions.

VALUES	PERMISSIONS	DEFINITION
7	rwx	read, write, execute
6	rw–	read, write
5	r–x	read, execute
4	r––	read only
3	–wx	write and execute
2	–w–	write only
1	––x	execute only
0	–––	no access

To change modes using numeric notation, enter the `chmod` command followed by the numbers indicating the mode you want to assign to each class of user. For example, entering `chmod 750 fugu` indicates that the file named `fugu` can be read, written to, and executed by the owner, because the first number indicates the owner's permission mode is equal to 7. The next number, 5, indicates that the file can be read and executed by a member of the owner's group. The last number, 0, indicates there are no permissions for others on the system.

Here are two other examples of using the `chmod` command to change permissions mode:

```
chmod 64 project
```

assigns both read and write permissions to the group with access to the file `project` and assigns only the read permission to all other users. (Since only two numbers were entered after `chmod`, no permissions were assigned to the owner.)

```
chmod 544 document
```

assigns read and execute permissions for the owner of the file `document` and only read permission to both the group and all others.

Creating and Removing Links to Files

A *link* is a directory entry that acts as a pointer to locate files. In SunOS, you can create different names for a single file (that is, you can create additional links) by using the `ln` (link) command. For example, if you and another member of your group are both working on a file, you can have the file listed (under the same or different names) in both of your home directories. This ensures that two different versions of a file don't exist and also saves disk space. When you list files using the list command with the `-l` option, `ls -l`, the number displayed between the permissions modes and the file owner's name indicates the number of links to that file. In the following file listing, the file named `unite` has two links and `sole` has one.

```
-rw-r--r--  2  tcleaver  1024  Apr  1  19:05  unite
-rw-r--r--  1  tcleaver   256  Apr  1  19:35  sole
```

NOTE

If two users are working on a linked file simultaneously, only the user who first accessed the file will be able to write to it.

Creating a Link

When you create a file, SunOS places the file name in the appropriate directory and creates a link, or pointer, that points to the file so SunOS can locate it. Anytime you remove a file, the link is broken and the pointer is removed from the directory. Each file has at least one link, but other links can be created. To create a link to a file, you must have execute permission for the directory in which you want to create a link. The syntax for the link command is as follows:

```
ln pathname\filename pathname\otherfilename
```

The `ln` command makes a file available from the directory in which you created the link. Once a file has been linked, it can be referenced without a path from that directory. If you wanted to link the file **chip** with the file **dale**, you would enter

```
ln chip dale
```

If the file originally named **chip** is the only file in the directory, entering `ls -l` would display

```
-rw-r--r--      2jfriday     lapd    23     May  5    12:35     chip
-rw-r--r--      2jfriday     lapd    23     May  5    12:35     dale
```

Removing a Link

Using the remove command, `rm`, to delete a file removes a single link. For instance, entering

```
rm dale
```

removes the link to the file **chip** created in the previous example. If a file has more than one link, you can remove one file name and still access the file from the other link. Once a file is down to a single link, however, the next time you use the `rm` command specifying that file, it is removed.

Command Summary

The following lists the commands covered in this chapter and their functions.

COMMAND	RESULT
..	Moves user to parent directory of working directory.
~	Changes working directory to user's home directory.
cat	Creates a file and displays a file's contents.
cd	Allows user to change directories.
chmod	Allows user to change permission modes of a file or directory.
cp	Copies contents of directories and files.
file	Lists file type of a given file.
ln	Creates links between files.
ls	Lists directories and files.
mkdir	Creates directories.
mv	Moves and renames files.
pwd	Prints the working directory on screen.
rm	Removes files and links to files.
rmdir	Removes directories.

CHAPTER

10

Improving Your Command-Line Productivity

THIS chapter equips you with a variety of helpful commands, tips, and techniques to improve your command-line productivity. The commands in this chapter are the building blocks that enable you to control SunOS rather than having SunOS control you. A great deal of this chapter exploits the command-line features of the Korn shell. It includes additional information on repeating and editing commands, and explains pattern matching, stringing together commands using pipes, filtering information from files using a variety of filter commands, and redirecting output and input.

Getting the Most from the Command Line

Using the Korn shell, you can perform multiple commands in the same command line, and list and repeat commands from your command history list. The Korn shell also includes commands for modifying command-line entries to quickly fix commands incorrectly entered. These Korn shell features allow you to perform an assortment of operations with only a few keystrokes.

Performing Multiple Commands

To place more than one command on the command line, separate each command with a semicolon (;). When two or more commands are separated by a semicolon, they are treated as if they were sequentially entered on separate lines. For example, typing `cd; pwd; ls -la` and pressing Return brings you to your home directory, displays the directory name, and displays a long listing of all the files in that directory. You can continue a command line onto the next line by using the backslash (\). For example, typing

```
cd; pwd; ls -la ; more file1\
```

and pressing Return displays

```
>
```

The greater than sign (>) indicates you can still continue to enter commands. When you press Return, the commands on both lines are executed.

Listing Command Line Entries

In Chapter 8 you learned how to use the `history` command to display a list of past commands. Adding -1 to the `fc` command lists previously executed commands. For example, entering

```
fc -l -7
```

lists the last seven commands and their numbers, and entering

```
fc -l 10 15
```

lists commands 10 through 15 in the history command list. You can also list a previously executed command line by adding the name of the command after the -1 option. To list the last **cat** command line and all subsequent commands up to the present command, enter

```
fc -l cat
```

Using the `fc` command with the -1n option, you can display the command list without the numbering that is displayed using the -1 option. You can use an editor to edit a group of commands by using the -e option followed by vi and the beginning and ending lines of the history list that you want to edit. For example, entering `fc -e vi 10 15` displays the command lines 10 through 15 in the vi editor and also runs the commands when you exit vi. Working with the vi editor is explained in detail in Chapter 12, "Using the vi Editor."

Reexecuting and Changing Command-Line Entries

The r command allows you to edit and reexecute commands. You can reexecute a previously executed command line by adding the first letter of a command line after the r command. To reexecute the last **cat** command line, enter

```
r c
```

If you make a mistake in a command line, use the r command to replace the incorrect text and reexecute the command. This is also extremely beneficial for changing long command lines and replacing the entire command line. For example, if you entered

```
cp file1 fle2 file3 file4 /export/home/rpetrie/work; cd; ls -l f*
```

enter

```
r fle2=file2
```

to correct the spelling of the file **fle2** to **file2**. You can also replace text and reexecute a command in the command list. For example, entering

```
r report=letter m
```

reexecutes the last command that begins with the letter m and replaces the report to letter.

Matching Patterns

Several facilities are built into the shell to help you locate files using special characters called *metacharacters* or *wildcard* characters. Wildcard characters are analogous to the joker card in card games, where the joker can be any card. These characters can be used to indicate one character of a file name or parts of file names.

File Name Wildcards

The special characters used most often for pattern or wildcard searches are the question mark (?) and the asterisk (*). The ? represents any single character. Entering the command `ls letter?` lists all files beginning with the word `letter` and ending with one additional character, such as `letter1` and `letterA`.

The asterisk character (*) matches any series of characters. Issuing the `ls` command followed by a single asterisk, `ls *`, lists every file in the working directory, except for hidden files. Entering the command `ls b*` lists every file beginning with the letter `b`, for example, `bard`, `beta`, `botany`, and `business`.

Character Class

Another way to search for files is to use the character-class option. A single character, or a *string* (a sequence of text characters) enclosed in brackets, is known as a *character class*. When you use brackets, you're instructing the Korn shell to match any character within the brackets. For example, `ls [Aabc]*` matches all file names beginning with an uppercase `A` or lowercase `a`, `b`, or `c`. You can also indicate a range of alphabetical characters by separating the beginning and ending range with a hyphen. For example, `ls [A-Z]*` matches all file names that begin with an uppercase alphabetical character, `ls [a-m]*` matches all file names that begin with lowercase alphabetical characters ranging from `a` through `m`, and `ls [1-9]` matches any numbers ranging from one to nine. You can match any character not enclosed in brackets by preceding the character with an exclamation point. For example `ls [!a-m]*` matches all file names that *do not* begin with lowercase alphabetical characters ranging from `a` through `m`.

Korn Shell Pattern-Matching Features

The Korn shell includes additional pattern-matching features. By using special metacharacters followed by patterns within parentheses, you can match a variety of different text and number patterns. The *(pattern) format matches any occurrences of the pattern within parentheses. Using the *(pattern) format you could find all files that begin with s by entering `ls *(s*)`. Multiple patterns can also be given, but they must be separated with a | character. For example entering

```
ls *(s*|t*)
```

displays all files beginning with the letter **s** and the letter **t**, such as `scratch`, `songs`, `temp`, and `totals`.

The `?(pattern)` format matches any occurrences of pattern. The following example matches and lists all file names that consist of only two or three letters:

```
ls ?(??|???)
```

The `+(pattern)` format matches one or more occurrences of the pattern within the parentheses. To list files containing `old` or `draft`, enter

```
ls *+(old|draft)*
```

The `!(pattern)` format matches anything except the pattern within the parentheses. To match any string that *does not* end with a `.c` or `.h` file name extension, enter

```
ls !(*.c|*.h)
```

Working with Filters

Filters are commands that accept text as input, transform it in some way, then produce text as output. For example, the **sort** command is a filter that sorts a file in alphanumeric order. Filters send their output to the screen by default, but the standard output can be redirected to files or system devices, as explained later in this chapter. Figure 10.1 shows a simple example of how a filter might process text.

FIGURE 10.1

An example of a filter
processing text

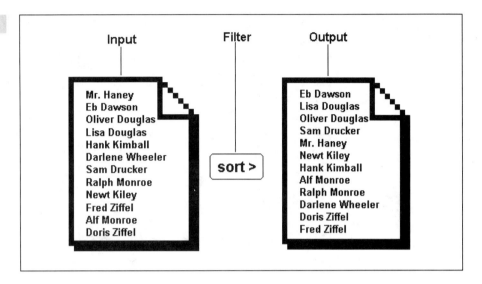

Filters for Displaying the Contents of a File

The `cat` command is an excellent vehicle for viewing the contents of a small file, but if the file is several pages long, it is easier to control how the text is displayed by using one of the many SunOS filter commands. Using a filter, you can display the contents of one or more files one screen of text at a time or display only the beginning or ending portion of a file. The following sections explain how to use filter commands to control the display of the contents of any text file.

Displaying a Long File One Screen at a Time

A convenient way to look at a long file is to use the `more` filter. The `more` filter simply transforms text into screen-sized blocks so the text of a file can be displayed one screen at a time. To use the `more` command, type `more filename(s)`, where `filename(s)` indicates the file or files you want to display. If you want to display multiple files, remember to separate each file name with a space. For example, `more doc1 doc2` displays the contents of `doc1`, followed by the contents of `doc2`, one screenful of text at a time.

To display the next screenful of text, press the spacebar. As you view a file using the more filter, the percentage of text that has been displayed is listed at the bottom of the screen in parentheses. To exit the more filter, type q.

Once you have started the more filter and the screen has stopped scrolling, you can display a specific number of lines at a time by typing in the number and pressing the spacebar or Return. For example, typing the number 5 and pressing the spacebar displays the next five lines of the file. You can change the display size by typing the number of lines you want the screen to show followed by d or Control-d. You can scroll back one page by pressing Control-b. If you are displaying a large file, backward scrolling can be excruciatingly slow.

Displaying the First or Last Lines of a File

If you want a quick look at the beginning or ending of a file, use the head or tail filters. The head filter displays the top 10 lines of a file by default. For example, head jaeger lists the first ten lines of the file named jaeger. Adding a minus sign followed by a number before the file name lists that number of lines from the top of the file. For example, head -12 jaeger lists the top twelve lines of the jaeger file.

The tail filter shows the tail end of a file. If you issue the tail filter without an option followed by the name of the file you want to view, tail lists the last ten lines of the file. You can change this display length by adding a hyphen and the number of lines you want displayed before the file name. For example, tail -20 stocks displays the last twenty lines of the file named stocks.

Finding Files by File Names

SunOS is a large file system. If you are working in several directories, it is easy to misplace a file, but you can discover where a file is located by using the find command. The find command searches for files that meet conditions you specify, starting at the top of the current or specified directory and automatically searching each subdirectory. A condition could be a file name matching a specific pattern, a file owned by a specific user or belonging to a specific group, or a file that has been modified within a specific time frame. The more specific your criteria, the narrower the field search becomes. The syntax for the `find` command is

```
find directory options
```

The `find` options create a criterion for selecting a file. To see which files within your home directory and its subdirectories end in the letter **s**, type

```
find ./ -name '*s' -print
```

The following explains each part of the preceding command-line entry.

`./`	Indicates that the search should begin at the top of the current directory. Remember the period is the symbol that specifies your working directory and the front slash begins the search at the highest directory.
`name *s`	Instructs `find` to find all file names ending with the letter **s**. If wildcards are used, as in this example, the file name character string and wildcard characters must be surrounded by single quotation marks.
`-print`	Indicates that you want the results to be displayed on your screen.

The following lists options that can be added to the `find` command to locate files.

OPTION	RESULT
`-exec command "{ } \;"`	Applies any command you specify to the files `find` calls up.
`-group groupname`	Finds files belonging to the specified group.
`-mtime n`	Selects files that have been modified in the last *n* days.

OPTION	RESULT
-name *filename*	Finds files that have names matching the character string you specify in single quotes.
-newer *filename*	Finds files that have been modified after the file specified.
-user *username* or *user ID number*	Selects files belonging to the user indicated.

You can reverse the meaning of an option by inserting a backslash (\) and an exclamation point before the option. The backslash is referred to as an *escape character*. It indicates that the special character or symbol following it has a different meaning than its normal meaning. In this instance, the exclamation point after the backslash indicates that SunOS should select files for which the option does *not* apply. For example, the command

```
find .\! -name 's*' -print
```

finds file names in the working directory and any subdirectories that *do not* begin with the letter **s**.

You can also use **find** to execute commands on the files it finds by adding the following option:

```
-exec command '{}' \;
```

For example, you can use **find** to locate and remove files that are named consistently. If the names of the files you want to remove begin with the string **junk** (such as **junk1**, **junk2**, and **junk3**), the following command line finds and removes them from the current directory:

```
find . -name 'junk*' -exec rm '{}' \;
```

Remember that a single period (.) refers to the working directory.

Finding Files by Text in a File

The **grep** command is a powerful pattern-searching command that locates text in files. You can have **grep** search for an exact string of text, or you can use wildcards and brackets to broaden the search pattern. You must tell **grep** which files it should search. The most basic **grep** syntax is

```
grep string filename(s)
```

If **grep** only searches through one file, it will simply display any lines that contain the search string. If it searches more than one file, it will display the matching lines and also tell you the names of the files in which they occur.

Within a search string, a period (.) matches any single character in the same way the question mark (**?**) is used in file name substitution. For example, the command **grep .s namelists** preceded by a character (any character) in the file **namelist**. The equivalent of the asterisk wildcard is a period preceding an asterisk (**.**). For example, the **grep 't.*' testfile** command locates every line in **testfile** containing the letter **t**. Note that the letter **t** and * wildcard character must be put in quotes.

A caret (^) instructs the pattern to match only the beginning of the line. The command **grep ^v** matches any line beginning with the letter **v**. A search string followed by a dollar sign (**$**) matches only those lines with that expression at the end of the line. For example, **grep s$ slist** displays all lines ending with the letter **s** in the file named **slist**. The command **grep ^v$** matches any line in which **v** is the only character.

Use double (") or single (') quotes to surround text that contains spaces. For example, if you use **grep** to search all files for the phrase **good work**, you would enter **grep 'good work'** and the name of the file to search. If you did not use the quotes, **grep** would only search for **good** and would consider **work** to be a file name.

Bracketed lists and ranges work just as they do for file name substitutions. For example, grep '[JE]' namelist, where the file namelist contains the names Jane, Judy, Elroy, and George, displays Jane, Judy, and Elroy but not George. Note that you must place quotation marks around the search string when you use brackets this way.

The characters &, !, $, ?, ., ;, and \ need to be preceded by a backslash when you want them to be treated as ordinary (literal) characters.

The following shows the characters that can be used to match or escape characters using the grep command.

CHARACTER	MATCHES
^	The beginning of a text line.
.	Any single character.
[ ]	Any character in the bracketed list or range.
[^]	Any character not in the list or range.
*	The preceding character or expression.
.*	Any characters.
\	Escapes special meaning of next character.
$	Any matching characters at the end of a line.

Using Options to Tailor grep's Output

There are several options that you can use to change the grep command's output to better fit your needs. The most useful of these are explained below. When you employ these options, use the following syntax:

```
grep option(s) string filename(s)
```

OPTION	RESULT
-v	Displays all lines that *do not* contain the search string.

OPTION	RESULT
-l	Causes **grep** to display only the names of any of the specified files that contain the search string. Does not display the lines that contain the search string.
-c	Causes **grep** to display the number of lines that contain the search string. If more than one file contains the string, displays the names of these files and the number of matching lines in each.

Spell-Checking a File

The **spell** command is a filter that checks an entire text file for words that do not match any of the words in the system dictionary. To check the spelling of a text file, type **spell**, followed by the name of the file you want to spell-check. If the spelling program hasn't been loaded into your system, SunOS displays the message **spell: command not found**. The **spell** command produces a list of words that don't match the entries in the SunOS online dictionary. For example, entering the command **spell brochure**, where **brochure** is a file than contains misspellings of the words **travel**, **oasis**, and **cruise**, displays the following results:

```
cruize
osais
travl
```

The **look** command lets you list words in SunOS's online dictionary that begin with the letters you enter. To use the **look** command, type **look** and the first few letters of a word for which you want to check the spelling.

Counting Words in a File

Another helpful filter for working with text files is the wc (word count) command. The wc command counts and displays the number of lines, words, and characters in a file. You can use these options with wc:

OPTION	RESULT
-l	Counts lines only.
-w	Counts words only.
-C	Counts characters only.
-c	Counts bytes only.

The following shows the results of using wc on a file named jumbo.

```
1625 2805 50545      jumbo
```

This indicates there are 1625 lines, 2805 words, and 50,545 characters in jumbo.

Comparing Text Files

Once you have copied a text file, you can use the diff command to ensure that the files are exactly the same. The diff command displays line-by-line differences between a pair of text files. You can check to make sure that a file has been copied using the ls command, but the diff command is helpful if you have two copies of a file and can't readily determine the differences between them. Entering the command

```
diff file1 file2
```

causes SunOS to display the differences between file1 and file2. If no differences are found, the prompt is redisplayed without a message. Use the diff3 command to display the differences between three files, such as diff3 file1 file2 file3. The following example shows the result of using diff on two files beginning with the same first line but with differences in the next three lines of text. The line containing numbers and an alphabetical character indicates the number of the lines and type of edits needed to make both files identical. If the letter a appears, it indicates that text needs to be appended. The letter d indicates text needs to be deleted. The letter c indicates text needs to be changed. In the following example, the first line indicates that lines 2 through 4 of `file1` need to be changed to match lines 2 through 4 of `file2`. The less-than signs (<) identify the differing lines in `file1`. The greater-than signs (>) identify the differing lines in `file2`.

```
diff file1 file2
2, 4c2,4
< line 2 in file1 contains the word incongruous
< line 3 in file1 contains the word disparate
< line 4 in file1 contains the word different
---
> line 2 in file2 contains the word analogous
> line 3 in file2 contains the word similar
> line 4 in file2 contains the word corresponding
```

Sorting a File

One of the most often used SunOS filters is the **sort** command. You can alphabetically sort the contents of a file in ascending order by issuing the **sort** command followed by the file name to be sorted. The **sort** command sorts lines in a file and displays the sorted list on your screen. To sort a file, you need to specify an output file using the −o (output) option. For example, to sort a list of customers in a file named **clients** and store the output in a file name **sclients**, enter

```
sort -o sclients clients
```

NOTE

Make sure the output file has a different name from the file you are processing. For example, if you are sorting a file called `clients`, do not send output to a file of the same name. This wipes out the original file before the information is sorted. Because the sorted clients information is directed into a file, it does not appear on the screen as it would if you simply typed `sort clients`. You can easily examine the `clients` file using the `cat` or `more` commands.

Selecting a Sort Field

The sort command begins numbering fields with the number zero. The second string of characters is considered field number one. The **sort** command allows you to sort by characters other than those at the beginning of a line. For example, say you have a file named **clients** in which you keep the following list of clients:

```
Buddy Sorrell
Melvin Cooley
Jerry Helper
Alan Brady
Sally Rogers
```

If you entered the command **sort clients**, the file would display on your screen sorted alphabetically by the first names of the clients. To sort the file by the last names, you have to specify which field to perform the sort on. *Fields* are character strings separated by spaces. The file **clients** contains two fields. The first field (field 0) comprises the first names and the second field (field 1) comprises the last names. The numbering scheme used with fields is illustrated in Figure 10.2.

NOTE

Remember that the sort command begins numbering fields with the number zero. The second string of characters is considered field number one.

To specify where a sort begins, use this syntax:

```
sort +fieldnumber filename
```

The plus sign (+) followed by the field number indicates the field on which the sort begins. If you wanted to sort your list of clients by their last names, you would enter

```
sort +1 clients
```

where the number 1 specifies that the sort be performed on the field containing the last names. The output of this command, the sorted list, will then appear on the screen. Most likely you will want to save the sorted list

FIGURE 10.2

The numbering scheme of fields in sorts

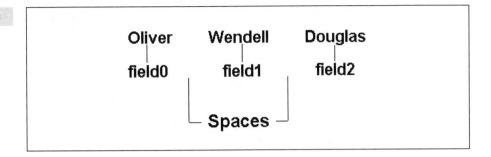

to another file, in which case you will have to enter a command such as this:

```
sort +1 -o clients1n clients
```

Here the output of sort, the sorted list of `clients`, is sent to a new file named `clients1n`.

In some instances, it is inconvenient to use spaces as field separators. For example, if your list of clients also included the name Dick Van Dyke and you tried to use the previous command to sort the list by last name, **sort** would only recognize Van and not include Dyke in the sort criteria. Of course, this would not affect the outcome of the sort on the current list, but if the file also contained the names Ella Vance, Jack Vance, and Jerry Van Heusen, it would cause problems. Fortunately, you can change the field separator to another character with the -t*c* option, where *c* is used to identify the new field separator. To add an option to the **sort** command, follow this general syntax:

```
sort option(s) +fieldnumber filename
```

If you inserted a symbol, say a colon, between the first and last names on your list and you specified the colon as the new field separator, you could sort by first or last names without worrying about spaces affecting the sort.

With the **sort** command you can sort on any range of characters you want as long as you specify where you want the sort to begin and end. This means you must indicate both the field number and character number to begin and end on. Use the following syntax to perform a sort on a specific range of characters:

```
sort option(s) +fieldnumber.characternumber
-fieldnumber.characternumber filename
```

Here the plus sign (+) indicates which field and character number to start the sort on and the minus sign (–) indicates which field and character number to end the sort on.

TIP   Remember, the first character in a field is numbered 0.

Let's say you added the amount of revenue of each client to the `clients` file. Your list might look like this:

```
Alan Brady:$1000.00
Buddy Sorrell:$4500.00
Jerry Helper:$250.00
Melvin Cooley:$500.00
Sally Rogers:$600.00
```

To produce a list of clients in order of lowest to highest revenue, enter

```
sort -o revenue -t: -n +1.1 -1.6 clients
```

Here the `-t:` indicates that the colon serves as the field separator, separating the list into two fields: names of clients and revenue. The `-n` (numeric) option allows you to sort in ascending numerical order. The `+1.1` specifies that the sort begin with the second field (field 1) and second character of the field (character 1), or at the first number after the dollar sign. The `-1.6` indicates that the sort ends with the sixth character (character 7) of the second field. The following output of the command is then sent to the file `revenues`:

```
Jerry Helper:$250.00
Melvin Cooley:$500.00
Sally Rogers:$600.00
Alan Brady:$1000.00
Buddy Sorrell:$4500.00
```

The following list reviews some of the options you can use with `sort`:

OPTION	RESULT
-f	Causes `sort` to ignore case when performing a sort. Otherwise the sort is performed according to ASCII number.
-n	Instructs `sort` to sort in numerical order.
-r	Produces a list sorted in reverse order (see next section).
-tc	Indicates the fields are separated by c. In the previous example the fields are separated by the colon (:) character.

Reverse Sorts

When you sort a file containing a field of numbers you may want to sort the file in descending numeric order to see the fields with the largest amounts first. Suppose you want to select the top three clients with the largest revenue from `revenue`. You can sort the file in reverse numeric order using the -r (reverse) and -n (numeric) options to produce a highest-to-lowest listing, then use the `head` command to select the top three entries. By using a pipe to combine the `sort` and `head` commands, you can get a list of the top three clients in the `revenue` file. Pipes are explained later in this chapter. Entering

```
sort -t: -r -n +1.1 -1.6 revenuelhead -3
```

displays

```
Buddy Sorrell:$4500.00
Alan Brady:$1000.00
Sally Rogers:$600.00
```

Combining, Grouping, and Controlling Commands

The more you work with SunOS the more likely you will want to combine and control multiple commands. The Korn shell includes a variety of sequential control structures, so you can connect and control how commands are executed. For example, you may want to substitute part of a command line with the output of a command, feed the output of a command in directly as input to another command, or you may want to conditionally execute a group of commands. The following sections explain how to feed the output of one command into another, control the execution of a group of commands, and control whether or not a command is executed.

Command Substitution

The Korn shell lets you substitute the output from one command to form part of another command. This is known as *command substitution*. To substitute the output of one command, place the command within *back quotes*. The shell executes the command inside the back quotes and uses the output to form the input for the preceding command not included in back quotes. (Do not confuse the back quote with an apostrophe. A back quote (`) is usually on the same key as the tilde (~) next to the Return key. Also, do not confuse the back quote with the single quote mark found on the same key as the double quote mark.) Using command substitution, you can remove all files containing the word **paid** by entering

```
rm `grep -l paid *`
```

The shell executes the **grep** command then performs the **rm** command using the list of file names generated by the **grep** command within the back quotes.

The Korn shell also lets you use a different format for command substitution: $(command). Any commands can be used inside the parentheses, including pipes, redirection operators, and wildcards. Pipes are explained in the following section. To use the Korn shell's command substitution to inform you of the date, begin a new line, and inform you of the name of the working directory, enter

```
echo Today is $(date) '\n'Your working directory is $(pwd)
```

When you press Return, the screen appears similar to the following:

```
Today is Mon June 19 13:25:58 PDT 1992
Your working directory is /export/home/rpetrie
```

Combining Commands

One of the most useful features of the shell is the *pipe* (|). The pipe is used to feed the output from one command into another. The pipe (|) key is to the right of the F12 key on most Sun keyboards. A set of commands strung together is called a *pipeline*. Pipes have a wide variety of uses. You can string together multiple commands with pipes, as long as the command line does not exceed 256 characters.

Piping is a convenient alternative to a multiline command. Because a pipe passes output from one command to the input of another, instead of having to store data into temporary work files and perform several operations, you can join commands together so that output from one is used as input for another. For example, the command ls -l |more allows the user to view a long directory listing page by page. You can even connect groups of commands this way.

In addition to using pipes for file processing, you can pipe commands to simplify daily SunOS operations. For example, suppose you want a quick list of all the files you have changed today in your home directory. You can pipe the output of a long directory listing (ls -l) into grep and produce a list of files matching today's date. For example, if today is July 19, you can obtain a list of files using the following:

```
ls -l | grep 'Jul 19'
```

The listing produced might look something like this:

```
-rw-rw-rw-  1    rpetrie staff   1640 Jul   19   03:09  project
-rw-r-xr--  1    rpetrie staff   64   Jul   19   10:10  style
-rwxr-xrw-  1    rpetrie staff   256  Jul   19   12:07  clients
```

Grouping Commands

When you combine several commands on the same line, you can use parentheses to group them. Grouping commands starts up a new copy of the shell to execute the commands. Using parentheses to perform a group of commands, you can change directories and execute one or more commands, after which the shell returns to the original shell and directory. For example, to change to the directory named **docs**, make a subdirectory named `finished`, move and rename (`mv`) an existing file named **draft1** to a file named `report` in the `docs/finished` directory, enter

```
(cd docs; mkdir finished; mv draft1 finished/report)
```

The **cd** command applies only to the group of commands within the parentheses. If you enter the **pwd** command you will find that you are still in the same directory as you were before issuing the group of commands.

Controlling Command Execution

The Korn shell includes logical operators for controlling command execution. The double ampersand (**&&**) operator is sometimes called a logical AND operator. Separating two commands with the **&&** operator executes the command following the **&&** operator only if the previous command was successfully executed. For example, entering

```
grep 'Birth of Venus' artwork && echo The Birth of Venus was found
```

displays the message `The Birth of Venus was found` only if the **grep** command finds the text string `Birth of Venus` in the file named `artwork`.

Separating two commands with double vertical bars (II) is the opposite of using double ampersands; each command is executed only if the preceding command fails. The II operator is sometimes called a logical OR operator. For example, if you enter the command

```
grep 'Mona Lisa' artwork || grep 'Water Lilies' artwork
```

and **grep** fails to find **Mona Lisa** in the file named **artwork**, the Korn shell executes the second **grep** command, which looks for the text string **Water Lilies**.

NOTE Using the && and || to control command execution only works with two commands; you cannot add additional commands to the same command line using the semicolon (;).

Redirecting Output and Input

When you execute commands, the results are displayed on your screen. The screen is considered to be the *standard output*. A command normally gets information from the keyboard, which is referred to as *standard input*. You can control standard input and output and redefine where information is sent once a command has processed it. For example, you can store the output of commands into files for review or editing. You can send output from one command into another and further process the data, such as formatting text to be sent to a printer.

Redirecting Output to a File

The greater-than symbol (>), also known as "to," redirects output from commands into a specified file rather than to the screen. For example,

```
ls -a > myfiles
```

sends the output of the **ls -a** (list all) command to a file named **myfiles**. When you redirect output to a file, because the output is redirected to the target file, it isn't displayed on the screen. Specifying a target file automatically creates the target file with the name you specify (if a file with that name does not exist). Using the Korn shell, you can save a command line to a file. The following example saves the last five commands to a file named `viewme`:

```
fc -ln -5 > viewme
```

Anytime you want to view the saved command line, simply use the `cat` command to display the contents of `viewme`.

Protecting Existing Files from Redirection Output

If you use > to redirect output to a file that already exists, the contents of that file will be overwritten. For example, `cat file1 > newfile` redirects the contents of `file1` to `newfile`, overwriting the contents of `newfile` if that file already exists. You can prevent redirecting output to an existing file by setting the `noclobber` option as follows:

```
set -o noclobber
```

If you attempt to redirect output to an existing file, a message displays informing you that the file already exists. You can still overwrite an existing file even if noclobber is set by adding a pipe (|) after the >. For example, entering `ls -l >| fileout` overwrites `fileout` even if `noclobber` is set. To automatically protect files with the `noclobber` setting when you first log in, see Chapter 15, "Customizing Solaris."

WARNING When you use > to redirect output to a file that already exists, the contents of that file will be overwritten unless the `noclobber` option is set.

Adding Text to an Existing File

Two greater-than symbols in succession can be used to append text to the end of an existing file. This append feature is useful for keeping running logs or for accumulating information in a single file. The command

```
cat clients >> newclients
```

appends the file `clients` to a file named `newclients`.

Using Files as Input to Commands

Just as you can redirect the output of a command, you can also have a file or device provide input to a command. The less-than sign (<), referred to as "from," redirects the standard input of a command.

Input redirection is valuable for the few commands that don't use file name arguments. For example, the command

```
mail dobie < reply
```

mails the contents of the file `reply` to `dobie`. Another command that reads from a file instead of the terminal is the `tr` (translate) command. The following example sends the file `filei` to the `tr` command and translates all lowercase i's displayed on the screen to uppercase I's.

```
tr i I < filei
```

Redirecting the Standard Error

When a command performs without problems, it produces results as standard output to your screen. When a command encounters a problem, it uses a different channel to send error messages, or diagnostic output, to the screen. *File descriptors* identify open files to running commands. The Korn shell automatically assigns file descriptor 0 to standard input for reading, and file descriptor 1 to standard output for writing. File descriptor 2 identifies a standard error. By using file descriptor 2 before the redirection sign (`2>`), you can redirect the standard error output to a file for later review. For example,

```
cat testfile 2> errorfile
```

redirects the standard output and standard error to the file named `error-file`. If `testfile` doesn't exist, `errorfile` contains the error message:

```
cat: cannot open testfile
```

Command grouping lets you redirect the standard output to one file and the standard error output to another. For example, enter

```
(cat testfile > stdoutfile) 2> errorfile
```

The `cat` command output is redirected to the `stdoutfile` file and any error messages are sent to the file named `errorfile`.

You can also redirect error messages to the system wastebasket file. This file is located in the device directory and named `null` (`/dev/null`). Any output you redirect to this file disappears, so you can send output here when you don't want it displayed. The following lists and explains redirection commands with examples.

COMMAND	FUNCTION	EXAMPLE
>	Redirects the standard output.	`cat file1 > file2`
2>	Redirects the standard error.	`cat file1 2> errorfile`
>>	Appends the standard output to the file.	`cat file1 >> file2`
2>&1	Redirects the standard output to file1 and the standard error to file2.	`(cat file > file1) 2>file2`
<	Redirects the standard input.	`tr a A < filea`

Redirecting Combined Commands

When you want to redirect the output of a group of commands, enclose the group of commands in parentheses. An example of the output of grouped commands being sent to a file instead of the screen might appear as follows:

```
(ls -l | grep 'Jul 19') > todaysfile
```

You can combine any number of commands this way to consolidate output into a single file. Output from grouped commands can also be piped to other commands. For example, typing

```
(ls -l | grep 'Jul 19') | lp
```

prints the listing. Not all SunOS commands accept standard input, which means you can't pipe information into them. You can, however, pipe information into the **lp** (printing) command, because this command accepts standard input.

Directing Data to More Than One Place

Like pipes, the **tee** command is a term borrowed from the plumbing trade to describe a single pipe that splits into two directions. The **tee** command splits output into two or more separate destinations. As the **tee** stores data in a file, it also displays the output on the screen or channels it to another selected destination. This ability to split output is useful in many situations. For example, you can use it to send a sorted list to two files instead of one, or to view the list on the screen while simultaneously saving the data in a file. The command

```
sort clients|tee sclients
```

displays the sorted information on the screen as well as sending the sorted clients file to the file named sclients. Be aware that the **tee** command overwrites files. If you have a file named **userfile** and entered

```
who|tee userfile
```

the **tee** command displays a listing of who is using the system and overwrites the existing file named **userfile**. If the file does not exist, the **tee** command creates **userfile** and sends the output of the **who** command to the file.

 **WARNING**   The tee command overwrites files without any warning.

If you use the -a option, tee appends the data into an existing file. For instance, the command

```
ls -l|tee -a userfile
```

displays a long directory listing and also adds this listing to the existing file userfile.

Useful SunOS Filters

The following lists useful SunOS filters, some of which were covered in earlier chapters. While they primarily use examples of filters processing files, keep in mind that filters can just as easily handle input from the keyboard or other commands.

COMMAND	PURPOSE OF FILTER	EXAMPLE
cat	Displays a file.	cat file1
	Creates a file from information typed at the keyboard.	cat > newfile
	Merges two or more files.	cat file1 file2 > file3
echo	Displays a message on the screen.	echo 'Hi SunOS'
grep	Searches a file or group of files for information you specify.	grep 'Clients' file1

COMMAND	PURPOSE OF FILTER	EXAMPLE
head	Displays the beginning lines of a file.	head file1
more	Displays one or more files, one screen at a time.	more longfile
sort	Sorts a file.	sort clients
	Sorts and merges multiple files.	sort clients prospects > contacts
tail	Displays the final lines of a file.	tail prospects
tee	Duplicates output to a file in addition to displaying output on the screen.	sort comm I tee temp
	Sends output to two files at once.	cat file1 I tee register log
tr	Translates one character or group into characters for another.	tr a b < temp
wc	Lists the number of lines, words, and characters in a file.	wc temp

Command Summary

The following lists the commands covered in this chapter and their functions.

COMMAND	RESULT
r	Repeats the last command.
r fle=file	Substitutes specified text and reexecutes last command.
r *n*	Repeats the command with the corresponding number in the history list.
r character(s)	Repeats the last command that matches the character string specified.
>	Redirects output.
>>	Appends text to the end of an existing file.
2>	Redirects standard error output.
<	Redirects input.
		Takes command output and channels it into another command.
clear	Clears the screen.
diff	Compares and displays differences between files.
find	Locates files.
grep	Searches for specified patterns in text files.
head	Displays top lines of a file.
history	Lists commands previously used.

COMMAND	RESULT
look	Lists all the words from the system dictionary that begin with the characters the user specifies.
more	Displays text one screenful at a time.
sort	Sorts files.
spell	Checks a text file for words that do not match those in the system dictionary.
tail	Displays last lines of a file.
tee	Sends output to two destinations.
tr	Changes characters in a text file.
wc	Counts the number of lines, words, and characters in a file.

CHAPTER

11

Electronic Mail and Messages

ONE OF SunOS's most useful features is its ability to send and receive electronic mail and messages. *Electronic mail* allows you to send and receive mail, including files, to and from other users, whether they're logged on or not. *Electronic messaging* allows you to interactively communicate with other users who are currently logged in. In this chapter, you'll learn how to receive, send, and manage your electronic mail using the `mailx` program. You'll also learn how to communicate with other users online using the `talk` and `write` commands, and how to view system news messages.

Overview of SunOS's Electronic Mail

Using SunOS's `mailx` program is similar to sending mail through the post office. When you send an electronic letter, the `mailx` program, like the post office, delivers your letter directly to the recipient's mailbox. The user login and machine name serve as the unique address of every user on the system. Each user on the system has a mailbox to receive electronic mail. This mailbox is usually a file with the same name as your login name, located in the `/var/mail` directory. Depending on how your system is set up, when someone on the system sends you mail, SunOS notifies you that you have mail in your mailbox. Once you've read your mail, thc `mailx` program automatically stores these letters in a special storage file called `mbox`, which is located in your home directory. When you execute the `mailx` program, it displays its own unique prompt, the question mark symbol (**?**). After executing the `mailx` program, a working buffer is created in memory, where all tasks you perform within `mailx`, such as moving and deleting mail messages, are temporarily stored. These changes are stored to disk only when you quit the `mailx` program.

Receiving Mail

When you log in, your incoming mailbox, */var/mail/username*, is checked for new mail. If there are any new letters, SunOS displays the message **you have mail** on your screen. If mail is sent to you while you're on the system, at the next SunOS prompt you are notified with the same message. SunOS checks your mailbox every few minutes to see if you have received mail. The time between these checks may vary, depending on how your system administrator has set up your account. You can choose to read your mail immediately after notification by SunOS or at a later time.

Listing Your Mail

To begin reading your mail, type `mailx` at the system prompt. If you don't have any mail, the `mailx` program displays the message, `No mail for` *username*. If you do have mail, the `mailx` program displays a list of mail headers from your */var/mail/username* file followed by the `mailx` program prompt, as shown below.

```
mailx version 5.0 Mon Feb 15 00:20:20:58 PDT 1993  Type ? for
help.
"/var/mail/rpetrie": 3 messages 2 new 1 unread
 >N  1 plane   Mon Jan 25 16:51   20/619   Date tomorrow
  N  2 pmason  Wed Jan 20 15:55   19/610   Trial briefs
  U  3 bfife   Tue Dec 15 09:08   12/281   Lost my job
?
```

New letters are indicated by N, as shown in the first column above. The U (Unread) status indicates the letter was new but was not read before quitting the `mailx` program previously.

The > located to the far left of the first header in the list indicates the current letter. The current letter is either the first new letter in your mailbox or the last letter you read. The following list describes the information provided in each of the columns from left to right in the mail headers list:

COLUMN	DESCRIPTION
Mail letter status	Status of a letter in the mailbox.
Mail letter number	Number order in which the letter was received (you can use this number to specify a letter).
Sender	User name of the person who sent the letter.
Time sent	Date and time the letter was sent.
Size	Number of lines and number of characters in the letter (lines/characters).
Subject	Subject of the letter.

If you have numerous letters in your mailbox, the header list may not show all of your mail headers. Instead, it displays one screenful of mail headers at a time. You can display the next screenful of mail headers with the command

z

To display the previous screenful of mail headers, enter

h-

Anytime you want to redisplay the mail headers list, enter

h

Reading Your Mail

After you've displayed the mail headers list, there are several ways to read the mail in your mailbox. The easiest way is simply to press Return. The current letter, indicated by the greater-than sign (>), is displayed. To continue reading your letters one by one, press Return again after each letter. When you've reached the end of the letters, `mailx` responds with the message `At EOF` (end of file), meaning `mailx` couldn't find any more mail letters in your mailbox.

NOTE   Remember that if you enter q to quit `mailx`, the letters you have read are moved to your `mbox` file.

Another way to read your mail is to type the message number at the `mailx` prompt (?). Letter numbers are displayed in the second column of the mail headers list. For example, if you want to read mail letter number 2, type 2 at the `mailx` prompt. The `mailx` program then displays the mail letter number 2:

```
Message 2:
From pmason Wed Jan 13 15:55 1993
From pmason (Perry Mason)
Subject: Trial briefs

Just a reminder, we need those trial briefs this week.
```

TIP   Another way to read a letter that is longer than a single screen is to save it as a file (explained later in this chapter), then use the `more` command.

If a letter is longer than the screen, it quickly scrolls down your screen. You can use Control-s to freeze the screen and Control-q to unfreeze it. You can check to see if a letter is longer than the screen by noting the number of lines in the size column of the mail headers list.

Replying to Mail

When you read your mail, `mailx` allows you to send a reply to the originator of any letter. Use the r (reply) command to quickly send a reply to the original sender of a letter. For example, to send a reply to the creator of mail message number 2, type r 2 at the `mailx` prompt. The `mailx` program responds with

```
To: pmason
Subject: Re: Trial briefs
```

The subject line of the reply will automatically hold the subject of the original letter, preceded by `Re:`. You can then type in your reply. When you complete your reply, press Return to place the cursor on a blank line, and press Control-d. Depending on how your system administrator has set up your mail account, the `mailx` program may then ask if you want to send any "carbon copies" by displaying a `Cc:` prompt. If you don't want to send duplicates of the reply to other users, simply press Return. The reply is sent to the author of the original letter. If you want to send a copy of the letter to another user, enter the user's name and address at the `Cc:` prompt, for example *username@machinename*.

Deleting Mail

After you've read or replied to mail letters, you may want to delete them rather than have them saved in your `mbox` file. You can delete the last letter you read by typing `d` at the `mailx` prompt. By typing `h` (header) you can verify that the letter was deleted. You can delete specific letters by typing `d` followed by the letter number. For example, typing `d 3` deletes letter number 3. If you want to delete multiple letters, separate each letter number with a space; for example, if you wanted to delete letters 1 and 3, type `d 1 3`. You can also delete a range of letters. For example, to delete letters 2, 3, and 4, type `d 2-4`. Keep in mind that deleted mail files are permanently removed when you quit `mailx` with the `q` command. To cancel deletions, simply exit `mailx` using the `x` command.

Undoing a Mail Deletion

If you accidentally delete a message, you can restore the message using the `u` (undelete) command. To undo the last delete command, type `u` at the `mailx` program prompt immediately after the deletion. If you deleted multiple messages using the delete command, for instance, typing `d4-7` to delete messages 4 through 7, you can undelete each message by typing `u` followed by the message number; for example, `u6`, `u5`, and so on.

Getting Help in the mailx Program

You can request help by entering a question mark (?) at the `mailx` prompt (?). Entering ? displays a list of available mail program commands with descriptions, as shown below.

alias, group user	declare alias for user names
alternates user	declare alternate names for your login
cd, chdir [directory]	chdir to directory or home if none given
!command	shell escape
copy [msglist] file	save messages to file without marking as saved
delete [msglist]	delete messages
discard, ignore header	discard header field when printing message
dp, dt [msglist]	delete messages and type next message
echo string	print the string
edit [msglist]	edit messages
folder, file filename	change mailboxes to filename
folders	list files in directory of current folder
followup [message]	reply to message and save copy
Followup [msglist]	reply to messages and save copy
from [msglist]	give header lines of messages
header [message]	print page of active message headers

help,?	print this help message
hold, preserve [msglist]	hold messages in mailbox
inc	incorporate new messages into current session
list	list all commands (no explanations)
mail user	mail to specific user
Mail	mail to specific user, saving copy
mbox [msglist]	messages will go to mbox when quitting
next [message]	goto and type next message
pipe,| [msglist] shell-cmd	pipe the messages to the shell command
print, type [msglist]	print messages
Print, Type [msglist]	print messages with all headers
quit	quit, preserving unread messages
reply, respond [message]	reply to the author and recipients of the msg
Reply, Respond [msglist]	reply to authors of the messages
save [msglist] file	save (appending) messages to file
Save [msglist]	save messages to file named after author
set variable[=value]	set variable to value
size [msglist]	print size of messages
source file	read commands from file
top [msglist]	print top 5 lines of messages
touch [msglist]	force the messages to be saved when quitting

undelete [msglist]	restore deleted messages
undiscard, unignore header	add header field back to list printed
unread, new [msglist]	mark messages unread
version	print version
visual [msglist]	edit list with $VISUAL editor
write [msglist] file	write messages without headers
xit, exit	quit, preserving all messages
z [+/−]	display next [last] page of 10 headers

[msglist] is optional and specifies messages by number, author, subject, or type. The default is the current message.

Quitting the mailx Program

There are two commands for leaving the mailx program: the q (quit) command and the x (exit) command. The q command

- Moves the letters you have read from your mailbox (/var/mail/ *username*) and saves them in a file named mbox in your home directory.

- Saves any changes you've made to letters in your mailbox, such as deleting letters.

- Quits the mailx program, and returns you to the system prompt.

If you have any unread mail in your mailbox, mailx displays a message similar to the following

```
Saved 3 messages in /export/home/rpetrie/mbox
Held 2 messages in /var/mail/rpetrie
```

The x (exit) command leaves the `mailx` program but doesn't save any changes you made to mail in your mailbox, such as deleting a letter. It also doesn't move any letters you have already read into the `mbox` file.

The Mail Storage File

When you read a letter, it is marked to be moved to another file for storage. The default file name for this secondary mail file is `mbox`, and it is located in your home directory. Letters remain in the `mbox` file until you remove them. This mail storage file enables you to read your mail and store mail for reference at a later date, leaving your mailbox (`/var/mail/`*username*) uncluttered.

Managing the Mail Storage File

When you want to access mail in your secondary mail storage file, `mbox`, use the `mailx` command with the `-f` option as follows:

```
mailx -f mbox
```

Your screen then displays a headers list similar to the headers list displayed when accessing your mailbox `/var/mail/`*username,* except the status of each message is replaced with the letter O. You can read, save, or delete letters using the same commands as you did when you used the `mailx` command without the `-f` option.

Holding Mail

To prevent letters from being automatically moved to your `mbox` file after reading them, you can use the `hold` command. The `hold` command instructs the `mailx` program to keep the letter(s) you have read in your `/var/mail/`*username* file after quitting `mailx` so that you can refer to the letter at a later time. Suppose you want to hold the last letter you've read; type `hold` at the `mailx` prompt. As with deleting letters, you can hold single or multiple letters, or a range of letters. For example, to hold letter number 3, type `hold 3` at the `mailx` prompt. If you wanted to hold multiple letters, such as letters 1 and 3, type `hold 1 3`. To hold a range of letters—for example, letters 2, 3, and 4—type `hold 2-4` at the `mailx` prompt. The hyphen (-) separates the beginning and end of the range of letters to be held.

Saving Letters as Files

You may want to save a letter as a file for editing or printing. To save the last letter you've read, including the header, into a file in your working directory, at the mail prompt (`?`) type

    s *filename*

Until you quit the `mailx` program, the letter `s` appears in the status column, indicating the message has been saved. In addition, you can save any letter by specifying its number from the mail headers list, as follows:

    s 4 filename

You can also save several letters in the same file at the same time. For example, to save letters 2, 4, 5, and 6 in a file, at the `mailx` prompt, type

    s 2 4-6 filename

You can also save a letter to a file using the `w` (write) command. This command is almost identical to the `s` (save) command, except it doesn't put the letter header into the file. Saved letters are marked in the mail headers list with the letter S. When you leave the `mailx` program using the `q` (quit) command, the marked letters are deleted from your mailbox (`/var/mail/username`) and saved in your `mbox` file.

Saving and Copying Letters in Folders

When you work with mail stored in files, you need to type the full path name in order to access the file. Saving and copying your mail to a mail folder, instead of separate files, saves time and keeps your mail files better organized. Folders are special files that are stored in a folder directory. Using a mail file automatically keeps your mail files together in the same directory, where they are easily accessible without typing long path names.

To use folders, you must first create a folder directory using the `mkdir` command. For example, if you wanted your folder directory to be called **messages**, you would create the directory messages as follows:

```
mkdir messages
```

You then need to use a text editor, such as vi, to edit the `.mailrc` file in your home directory (which contains `mailx` options) and set the folder directory path. Edit the "set folder" variable to include the full path name of your newly created folder directory. For example, you might enter

```
set folder=/export/home/rpetrie/messages
```

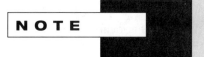

N O T E   For more information on setting `mailx` variables in the `.mailrc` file, see Chapter 15, "Customizing Solaris."

Saving Mail in Folders

You use the same commands to save or copy letters into folders as into files, except that the folder name is preceded by a plus sign (+) instead of a path name. The + tells `mailx` that the folder is to be kept in the folder directory. For example, to save message 3 to a folder called **memos**, at the `mailx` prompt type

```
s 3 +memos
```

`mailx` interprets this command as meaning save letter 3 into the `/messages/memos` directory. (If the folder doesn't already exist, `mailx` creates it.) To copy the letter into a folder, type

```
? c 3 +memos
```

If your mail account is set up to prompt you for carbon copies, you can send copies of your letters directly to a folder. To send a copy directly to a folder, simply type the folder name in either the **Cc:** or the **Bcc:** field. How to set up your mail account to prompt for carbon copies is explained later in this chapter.

Working with Mail in Folders

Working with mail in folders is similar to working with mail stored in files. To specify that the message is stored in a folder instead of a file, use the + sign. For example, if you want to read the letters stored in the **memos** folder, type

```
$ mailx -f +memos
```

This command starts **mailx** in the folder you specified. Only headers for the letters in the file or folder are displayed. Select a letter to read by typing its number at the **mailx** prompt and pressing Return. You can also work on mail folders within the **mailx** program. To display a list of your folders, at the **mailx** prompt, type

```
folders
```

To switch from your mailbox to a folder, or from one folder to another, type the command

```
folder +foldername
```

where *foldername* is the name of the folder you want to use. To return to the previous folder, type

```
#
```

An Overview of Sending Mail

You send mail with the **mailx** command by specifying the user name of the person or persons you want to receive a letter. You can use the **who**, **finger**, or **rusers** command to find a user's address if you don't know it. When you send mail to another user, it is stored in the recipient's electronic mailbox, and that person is notified that they have mail.

Who Is Using the System?

The who, finger, and rusers commands are useful if you need to know a user's login name but only know his or her real name. If the users you want to send mail to are logged into the same file server, you can address them using just their user names.

The who command lists the users logged into the system using the same file server at that moment. The list contains user names, identities of terminals being used, and the date and time each user logged in. Below is a listing produced by entering who.

```
wcleaver tty06  Jul 3 10:30
dreed    tty15  Jul 3 12:55
ataylor  tty19  Jul 3 12:56
```

The finger command provides more detailed user information than the who command. Depending on what your system administrator has directed this command to display, it may list a user's full name, user name, terminal number, idle time, home directory, and more. Idle time is the length of time in minutes since the last SunOS command was issued. When you enter the finger command, SunOS displays a listing of current system users, such as the following:

```
Login    Name          TTY   Idle  When
wcleaver Ward Cleaver   06    12    Fri 10:30
dstone   Donna Stone    15    0     Fri 12:55
ataylor  Andy Taylor    19    20    Fri 12:56
```

Listing Users on a Network

To find out who's logged in on other computers within your local network, use the rusers command. The rusers command by itself lists the machine name of each computer on the network, followed by the users currently on that computer. For example, entering rusers might display a listing similar to the one below. The left column lists the machine names.

```
mayfield     wcleaver
hilldale     dstone
mayberry     ataylor
```

If the person you want to send mail to is on a different computer on the same local network, you need to use both the user name and a machine name, separated by the at symbol (*username@machinename*).

If you know the relevant machine name but can't remember the specific user's name, enter `rusers` followed by the machine name to display user names for that specific computer. You can also add to `rusers` the `-1` (long) option, which lists the user name, machine name, terminal name, date and time the user logged on, idle time, and the name of the machine on which the user logged in. For example, entering `rusers -1 mayberry` might display

```
ataylor  mayberry:console    Jul   3    11:00    12
bfife    mayberry:ttyp0      Jul   3    11:46    03 (sitcom)
```

Sending Mail

Once you've established the user name and the machine name (if needed) of the person you want to send mail to, you can use the following four simple steps to send them electronic mail.

SunOS has a special system database that includes a feature known as *alias mapping*. Alias mapping simplifies identifying users on a system. If your network supports this feature, you can send mail to users on other machines using just their user name.

1. If the person you want to send a letter to is using the same machine, at the system prompt type `mailx` *username*, then press

Return. If the person is on another machine, type `mailx` *user-name@machinename*. If you are already in the `mailx` program, you can simply type `m` followed by the user name of the person you want to send a letter to. To send the same letter to multiple users, separate each user name with a space. The `mailx` program then prompts you for the subject of the letter.

2. Type in the subject of your letter at the `Subject:` prompt, then press Return.

3. Type in the text of your letter. If at any point you want to create a new line, simply press Return. Remember, even though a sentence may wrap on your screen, it is not considered a line until you press Return. Each line of text can be up to 256 characters long. If you exceed 256 characters on your system, your screen may freeze up and you will have to abort the letter by pressing Control-c twice.

4. When you've finished entering your text, press Return to move the cursor to a new line, then press Control-d to end your letter. You can also type a period and press Return to end your letter. Either way, the message `EOT` (end of text) appears. Depending on how your system administrator has set up the `mailx` program, it may then display the `Cc:` (carbon copy) prompt. If this is the case, you can then enter the names of other users to whom you want to send copies of the letter. To specify more than one user, separate each user name with a space. When you are finished entering user names, or if you don't want to send any copies to other users, press Return to send your letter. As the `mailx` program delivers your mail, it displays several status lines similar to the following:

```
$ ataylor@mayberry...  Connecting to mayberry via ether...
Trying 129.144.65.110...  connected.
220 mayberry.Eng.Sun.COM Sendmail 5.0/SMI-SVR4 ready at Thu 26
Aug 93 17:02:31 PDT

>>> HELO bookware.Eng.Sun.COM
>>> MAIL From:<rpetrie@bookware>
250 mayberry.Eng.Sun.COM Hello bookware.Eng.Sun.COM, pleased to
meet you
250 <rpetrie@bookware>...Sender ok
RCPT To:<ataylor@mayberry>
>>>DATA
354 Enter mail, end with "." on a line by itself
>>> .
```

```
250 Mail accepted
>>> Quit
221 mayberry.Eng.Sun.COM delivering mail
ataylor@mayberry... Sent
```

Aborting a Letter

If at any point you change your mind about sending a letter, press Control-c to abort the letter. The `mailx` program displays the message (`Interrupt -- one more time to kill letter`), asking you to press Control-c again to confirm aborting the letter. If you decide not to abort the letter, continue entering your text.

Undeliverable Mail

When you send a letter with an incorrect address through the postal service, it's either returned to you or ends up in a dead letter office. The SunOS mail system works much the same way. If you've created your letter and pressed Return, and have specified an incorrect user name, SunOS responds with the message *username*... User unknown, and the letter is returned to your mailbox (`/var/mail/username`). When you enter the `mailx` command again, the header states that you have returned mail, similar to the following example:

```
N 1 Mail Delivery Subs Wed Jul 3 12:55 19/61 Returned mail: User
unknown
```

When you view the returned letter, it will appear similar to the following returned mail message:

```
Message 1:
From dstone Fri Jul  3 12:53:21 PDT 1992
Date: Fri, 2 Jul 93 12:53:21 PST
From: Mailer-Daemon (Mail Delivery Subsystem)
Subject: Returned mail: User unknown
To: dstone

----- Transcript of session follows -----
550 wardcleaver... User unknown

----- Unsent message follows -----
Return-Path: <dstone>
Received: by hilldale (5.0/SMI-SVR4)
 id AA00305; Fri, 2 Jul 93 12:53:21 PDT
```

```
Date: Fri, 2 Jul 93 12:53:21 PDT
From: dstone (Donna Stone)
Message-Id: <9002060053.AA00305@hilldale.>
Errors-To: dstone
To: wardcleaver
Subject: hot water
Content-Length: 4

Meet me at the water fountain at 4:45.
```

The `mailx` program also sends this information without the letter's text to a person who is designated as the *postmaster* on your system. This person is usually the same as your system administrator. When a letter is interrupted by pressing Control-c or cannot be delivered as in the previous example, the file is also sent to a file named `dead.letter` in your home directory.

Sending Files Using mailx

If you have a file with information that you want to accompany a letter, such as a letter requesting payment and a file containing a list of outstanding invoices, you can mail the contents of a file as though it were a letter using the following command syntax:

```
mailx username < filename
```

The *username* is the name of the user you want to send the file to, and *filename* is the name of the file you want to send. For example, `mailx pmason < invoice` redirects the contents of the file named `invoice` to `pmason`'s mailbox.

When you send a file using the redirection symbol (<), `mailx` doesn't prompt you for a subject. If you want to add a subject line to the file, use the `-s` option followed by the text you want added as the subject. If the subject contains spaces, surround your subject text with quotation marks. The following is an example of adding a subject to a redirected file:

```
mailx -s "Outstanding 1993 invoices" pmason < invoice
```

Adding Carbon Copies

You can specify that a carbon copy of a letter is sent to other users. The `mailx` program even lets you send blind carbon copies so the recipient of your letter doesn't know that you sent a carbon copy to another user. In most cases, the system administrator sets up mail accounts by inserting the line

    set askcc

in a hidden `mailx` configuration file named `.mailrc`. If this line doesn't exist, you can add it to the `.mailrc` file using any text editor. Once this line is added to your `.mailrc` file, the `mailx` program will prompt you with the carbon copy `Cc:` prompt to enter any users you want to send a carbon copy to after `mailx` displays the subject prompt. If you want to send multiple carbon copies, separate each address with a space. Another way to send carbon copies is to use the ~c and ~h tilde escape commands, which are explained in the following section.

Using Tilde Escape Commands

During the composition of a letter, that is, while you're entering the text of a letter, you can use tilde escape commands to perform a variety of functions. A *tilde escape* command usually consists of the tilde character (~) followed by a single character and possibly an argument. If you want to add a literal tilde to your letter, type two tildes in succession; only one tilde appears in your letter. The following lists some helpful tilde escape commands:

COMMAND	RESULT
~! *command*	Escapes to perform a SunOS command.

COMMAND	RESULT
~?	Displays a helpful list of tilde escape commands and brief explanations.
~.	Simulates Control-d or a period on a separate line to mark the end of the file (**EOF**).
~:*mailcommand*	In the **mailx** program, performs the indicated mail command.
~b *username(s)*	Adds user name(s) to a blind carbon copy (**Bcc**) list. This is similar to the carbon copy (**Cc**) list, but the names in the **Bcc** list aren't shown in the header of the letter.
~c *username(s)*	Adds user name(s) to the carbon copy (**Cc**) list.
~d	Reads the contents of **dead.letter** file in your home directory into the letter.
~f *messagenumber*	Inserts message indicated by *messagenumber*.
~h	Displays, one at a time, the header lines **Subject**, **To**, **Cc**, and **Bcc**. You can delete any header text by using the Back Space key; then enter any new text.
~m *messagenumber*	Inserts the text from the specified letters into the current letter.
~p	Prints the current letter to the screen.
~q	The equivalent of pressing Control-c twice. If the body of the letter is not empty, the partial letter is saved in the **dead.letter** file.

COMMAND	RESULT
~r *filename*	Reads text from *filename* into your letter.
~s *subject*	Changes the contents of the subject line to *subject*.
~t *name(s)*	Adds the specified name(s) to the To: list.
~v *filename*	Writes the letter text into *filename* without adding the header information.
~w *filename*	Writes the letter text into *filename* without adding the header information.
~x	Exits similar to ~q but doesn't save the letter in the dead.letter file.

Using Electronic Messages

There are three kinds of electronic messages: interactive, broadcast, and system. Interactive messages let you communicate with another person who is currently using a terminal on your machine or using another machine on your local network in a way that is similar to talking on a telephone. Broadcast messages are for important announcements for all current users of a system, such as an announcement that the system will be down for maintenance. System messages are the only messages that will be displayed for users who log on after the message was generated.

Talking with Other Users

The talk command is an interactive way of sending messages. You can use talk to communicate with other users who are currently on the system.

To find out who is currently on the system, issue the **who** command. To talk to another user, enter

```
talk username
```

where *username* is the person on the system you want to talk to. If a user is on another computer in a network, enter the command **talk** *username* **@***machinename* where *machinename* is the name for the computer they're using. After entering this command, **talk**'s interactive screen appears and displays the message **No connection yet** until **talk** connects with the other user's machine. If you incorrectly enter the user name, or the other person isn't on the network, **talk** displays the message: [**Your party is not logged on**].

If the person you want to talk to is logged on, **talk** connects your computer or terminal with the other user's computer or terminal, displays a line across the middle of your screen, and notifies you that it is still contacting the other user with the message [**Waiting for your party to respond**]. While this message is displayed on your screen, the other user's screen displays a message similar to the following:

```
Message from Talk_Daemon@bradybunch at 01:11 ...
talk: connection requested by wcleaver@mayfield
talk respond with: talk wcleaver@mayfield
```

While the user is being notified that you want to talk, another message informs you that it is "ringing" the other user as follows:

```
[Ringing your party again]
[Ringing your party again]
```

The other person confirms that they want to be connected by typing in the user name and machine name, as displayed in the last line of the **talk** notification message.

```
talk wcleaver@mayfield
```

If the other user is busy or simply doesn't respond, then you can type Control-c to exit **talk**. If the other user responds, you will see the message [**Connection established**].

Now both users can type messages on the screen at the same time. The messages you send appear on the upper half of the screen. The other user's messages appear in the lower half of the split screen as shown below.

```
[Connection established]


Ward, how ya doin?
Eddie Haskell and Wally invited my kids to a party at your house
last week and they had a great time.
```

```
That's interesting, Mike, because June and I were in Mexico last
week.
```

The message you type appears on the other user's screen as you type it. You can correct any misspellings on a single line, but once you press Return, the line is sent. (Remember, even though a sentence may wrap on your screen, it is not considered a line until you press Return.) When either party wants to finish talking on the network, they can press Control-c to abort the `talk` program.

Writing Messages

The `write` command limits you to writing messages to only those users using terminals connected to the same computer as you. The `write` command doesn't use the entire screen like the `talk` command. To use the `write` command to send a message to another user, type `write` followed by the user name of the person you want to send the message to. The `write` command then displays the cursor on the next line without the prompt so that you can enter your message text. After typing the message text and pressing Return, the message is sent to the other user. The other person receives notification of the message directly below the command line, similar to the following:

```
Message from plane@brooklyn on ttyp3 at 11:58
When did you want that financial report?
```

If the other person wants to write you back, he or she can type `write`, followed by your (the receiver's) user name, press Return, and begin his or her reply message. The two users can then continue to send messages back and forth without reentering the `write` command. To stop conversing using the `write` command, type Control-d to end the session. When either user presses Control-d, the letters `EOT` (end of text) appear, indicating the end of the conversation. The other user must also press Control-d to get the system prompt back.

Broadcasting Messages

The `wall` (write to all) command allows you to broadcast messages to every user on your system. These messages should be reserved for important messages only, such as when the system is going to be down for maintenance. To broadcast a message to everyone, type `wall` then press Return. You can then enter the message you want to broadcast. Press Control-d and your message is sent immediately to everyone who is currently logged in.

WARNING Refrain from using `wall` unless your message is so important that everyone on the system should see it.

System Messages

Messages sent to you automatically (and possibly generated) by the SunOS system itself, such as error messages or a message informing you that you have mail, are known as *system messages*. If you are not logged on when such a message is sent, it will still appear when you do log on. The system administrator can also create system messages. The most common message of this type is the *message of the day*. This is an important or general interest message sent to all users of a system when they log in.

Another way that the system administrator can post announcements to you is by informing you that you should run the `news` command when you first log in. For example, after logging in, a message similar to the following may appear:

```
Type "news" TO READ news: framemaker
```

Enter the `news` command to display the title of the current news item and its time and date. Only the news items that you have not viewed before are displayed. To read a news message you have already viewed, add the -a (all) option. By using the -n (name) option, you can display the names of the current news items. For example, entering

```
news -n,
```

displays a line similar to the following:

```
news: framemaker party sunsoft downtime
```

To display news about when the system will be down for maintenance, enter

```
news downtime
```

If you just want to know how many current news messages exist, use the -**s** (sum) option. This displays any current news items that exist, without displaying their names or contents.

Command Summary

The following lists the commands covered in this chapter and their functions.

COMMAND	RESULT
?	Displays a list of available mail commands (at the mail prompt).
d	Deletes letters (at the mail prompt).
h	Displays mail headers list once in the mail program (at the mail prompt).
hold	Holds letters in the user's mail file (at the mail prompt).
mailx	Takes user into the `mailx` program and displays mail headers from the user's mail file.

COMMAND	RESULT
news	Displays news messages, such as announcing new programs available to the network and when the system will be down for maintenance.
q	Moves read letters to mbox, saves changes to letters, then exits the mailx program (at the mail prompt).
r	Mails a reply to sender of a letter (at the mail prompt).
rusers	Lists the machine name of each computer on the network.
s	Saves letters as files (at the mail prompt).
talk	Allows user to communicate interactively with another user.
u	Restores deleted letters (at the mail prompt).
wall	Allows user to broadcast messages to every user on your system.
write	Sends a message to another user without using the entire screen.
x	Exits the mailx program without saving changes (at the mail prompt).

CHAPTER

12

Using the vi Editor

THE vi editor (pronounced vee-eye) is a powerful, all-purpose file editor that edits everything from simple text files to complex program files. This editor provides an extensive collection of commands, many with overlapping functions, that can easily overwhelm new users. The purpose of this chapter is to provide you with a firm grasp of essential vi commands for editing and file management.

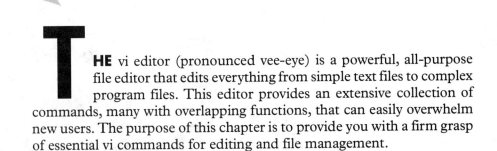

NOTE vi's command-driven structure can be a demanding environment for creating and editing simple text files, such as memos and letters. The DeskSet's Text Editor application is a considerably easier way to create and edit text files.

About vi

The vi (visual editor) program is a screen editor designed to display a text file one screen at a time. Early versions of UNIX forced users to work with line editors that only displayed one line at a time. While vi provides features for creating text documents, vi does not process text with the same ease associated with most commercial word processing software packages. For instance, vi cannot produce formatted printouts by itself. Instead, vi depends on the **nroff** and **troff** programs to format documents created or modified with vi before printing them. The **nroff** and **troff** programs are covered in Chapter 13. However, you can print files created or modified in vi using the SunOS **lp** command, which prints the text just as you see it on the screen.

Starting vi

To create or modify a file using vi, type `vi` *`filename`* at the system prompt, then press Return. For example, entering

```
vi evidence
```

executes vi and creates the new file, `evidence`. The following shows the last lines of the vi screen displayed with this file. The tilde (~) indicates empty lines.

```
~
~
~
~
~
~
~
~
"evidence" [New file]
```

If you want to execute vi with an existing file, such as a file named `tes-timony`, enter

```
vi testimony
```

The resulting screen display might look something like the example below:

```
OK. I admit it.
I hid the gun.
I did not want my niece to go to the chair.
~
~
~
~
~
~
~
"testimony" 3 lines, 67 characters
```

You can start vi without specifying a file name by simply entering `vi`. Later you can give your new file a name when you exit vi. A file name can be up to 256 characters in length and can include any characters except special characters (such as - * ? < > /).

The Status Line

The line at the bottom of the screen is called the *status line*. The status line shows the file name and the number of lines and characters in the file, as shown in the previous example. If you start vi to create a new file without a file name, no status line is displayed. Once you fill the screen with text, or move the cursor to the end of the file, the status line disappears. You can bring up the status line by pressing Control-g, which displays a new status line such as this:

```
"testimony" [Modified] line 2 of 3 --66%--
```

Command and Insert Modes

There are two modes of operation in vi, the command mode and the insert mode. The *command mode* allows you to enter commands for performing a wide range of vi functions, such as cursor movement and editing operations. The *insert mode* allows you to enter text into a file and is activated within vi by typing i while in the command mode. The vi program doesn't indicate which mode you're in, but pressing Esc always places you in the command mode.

The Command Mode

You start vi in the command mode. Most vi commands consist of one or two letters and an optional number, with uppercase and lowercase versions that usually perform related but different functions. For example, typing x deletes the character at the cursor, while typing X deletes the character preceding the cursor. You don't need to press Return after entering most vi commands. However, commands preceded by a colon do require you to press Return after the command. For example, to use the command :q! to quit vi and abandon changes, you must press Return after typing the exclamation point.

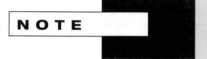

You don't need to press Return to enter a vi command unless it is preceded by a colon.

Undoing a Command

If you enter an incorrect vi command, you can undo it by typing u immediately after entering the command. (The insert mode command is an exception; if you mistakenly enter this command, press Esc to return to the command mode.) For example, if you've mistakenly deleted a line, immediately type u, and your deleted line is restored. You can also undo your last undo command. Typing U undoes all edits on a single line, as long as the cursor remains on that line. Once you move off a line, you can't use the U command for that line. The u command can be used to undo the U command.

Repeating the Previous Command

Any time you repeat the same editing command, you can save time duplicating the command by typing the repeat command (.) while in command mode. To repeat a command, position the cursor where you want to repeat the command and type a period (.). Keep in mind that you can only repeat the last command you executed, and that this command doesn't work with cursor movement or scrolling commands.

The Insert Mode

You leave the command mode and enter the insert mode by typing i (insert) while in the command mode. Typing i allows you to begin entering text at the cursor location. Characters you type subsequently appear to the left of the cursor and push any existing characters to the right. Remember, if you try to type a command while you're in the insert mode, the command characters are inserted as text. Press Esc any time you want to exit the insert mode and enter another command. The vi editor offers several other insert command options discussed later in this chapter.

Exiting vi

When you're creating or editing a file, you're actually working on a copy of the file that is stored in a *work buffer*, an area temporarily set aside in memory. Any changes you make to a file using vi only affect the file in the buffer until you instruct vi to save your file to disk. In other words, your edits don't affect your original file until you save your work. You can exit vi and abandon any changes you've made simply by not saving the contents of the work buffer. To quit vi, you must be in the command mode.

Exiting vi and Saving Changes

To save your changes to a file and quit vi, press Shift-ZZ while in command mode or type :x, then press Return to save your file and exit vi. Entering the command :w writes (saves) the buffer contents to the disk but doesn't exit vi.

WARNING Use :w frequently during a work session to prevent losing your work in the event of a system crash or failure.

If you started vi without a file name, type :w, followed by a new file name to save your work to file. If you attempt to exit and save a new file you haven't named, vi responds with the message `No current filename`. You can also quit vi and save both an old version of a file and a new version of a file with your new edits. For example, if you made changes to a file originally named `evidence`, you can save your edits to a different file called `evidence.new` by typing the command

        :w evidence.new

then pressing Return. Your old version of the file, `evidence`, remains unchanged, and the new file, `evidence.new`, contains your changes.

If you don't have a write permission for the file you've edited, when you use the Shift-ZZ command to exit vi and save the file, SunOS displays the message, `filename File is read only`. Enter `:w` with a different file name to save your file changes to disk. If you don't have write permission in the working directory, vi may still not be able to write your file to disk. Enter the `:w` command again, this time using a path name and a new file name in your home directory in place of the existing file name. For example, type

        :w /usr/evidence/temp

Exiting vi and Abandoning Changes

You can quit vi without saving your changes by typing `:q!` then pressing Return. Entering `:q` and pressing Return quits vi if you haven't made any edits to the file; otherwise, vi prompts you with the message

        No write since last change (:quit! overrides)

In this case, you can use the appropriate command to save your changes or abandon them. Type `:x` to exit vi and save changes or `:q!` to exit without saving your changes.

Recovering Text after a System Crash

If the system crashes while you're editing a file with vi, you can recover text that was not saved to disk before the crash. After the system is restored and you have a system prompt, type

        vi -r *filename*

where *filename* is the name of the file you were working on when the system crashed. The displayed file reflects the changes you made, but did not save, before the system crash. Use the :**w** (write) command immediately to save the salvaged copy of the work buffer to disk. You can then continue to edit the file.

Units of Text in vi

As you will see, many vi commands affect specific units of text, such as characters, words, lines, sentences, and paragraphs. To improve your productivity using vi commands, it's helpful to understand how vi defines these units of text. The following explains vi's defined units of text.

UNIT	DESCRIPTION
Character	Whatever is stored in a single byte. The letter **a** is a character, a space is a character, and a tab is also considered a character.
Word	A string of one or more characters separated on each side by a punctuation mark, space, tab, digit, or newline character (Return). A word can also be defined to include adjacent punctuation marks. These punctuated words are separated by the space, tab, or newline (Return) characters only.
Line	A string of characters separated by a newline character (Return). A line can be more than the width of a line of text displayed across your screen.

UNIT	DESCRIPTION
Sentence	A string of characters that ends at a period, exclamation point, or question mark, followed by two spaces or a newline (Return) character. If only one space follows the period, exclamation point, or question mark, vi doesn't recognize it as the end of a sentence.
Paragraph	A group of one or more lines of characters preceded and followed by a blank line. Two newline (Return) characters in a row create a blank line in the text, which vi considers as the division between two paragraphs. A paragraph can be a single line or up to 45 lines.

Cursor Movement

There are vi commands to move the cursor up, down, left, or right; forward or backward by units of text, such as characters, words, sentences, or paragraphs; and through an entire file. However, you can't move the cursor below a tilde (~), which indicates a line without text or hidden control characters, such as for spaces, tabs, or returns. Keep in mind that all movement commands are executed in command mode.

With most cursor movement commands you can specify the number of times you want the cursor movement repeated. You can't use a repeat factor on any control commands, such as Control-d, which scrolls the screen down, or on any commands that position the cursor at a specific point on the screen. The following lists vi editor movement commands.

COMMAND KEY	CURSOR MOVEMENT
spacebar	Right (forward) one character position.
l	Right (forward) one character.
h	Left (backward) one character.
+	First character of next line.
−	First character of previous line.
↓	Same position in line below.
↑	Same position in line above.
j	Down to same position in line below; moves left to last position if line below is shorter.
k	Up to same position in line above; moves left to last position if line above is shorter.
w	Forward to first letter of next word or punctuation mark.
W	Forward to first letter of next word.
b	Backward to first letter of previous word or punctuation mark.
B	Backward to first letter of previous word.
$	End of current line.
0	Beginning of current line.
Return	Forward to beginning of next line.
(	Back to beginning of current sentence.
)	Ahead to beginning of next sentence.
{	Back to beginning of current paragraph.
}	Ahead to beginning of next paragraph.
H	Left end of top line on screen.
M	Left end of middle line on screen.
L	Left end of lowest line on screen.

COMMAND KEY	CURSOR MOVEMENT
G	Last line in work buffer.
*n*G	Move to line number *n*.
Control-d	Down half screen.
Control-u	Up half screen.
Control-f	Down almost a full screen.
Control-b	Up almost a full screen.
Control-e	Scroll down one line at a time.
Control-y	Scroll up one line at a time.
\<Return>	Scroll up or down a screen while leaving cursor on same line.

Moving by Characters and Words

The arrow keys provide the easiest method for moving the cursor through a file one character at a time. You can also use the keys h, j, k, and l as follows:

h	left
j	down
k	up
l	right

Adding a repeat factor multiplies the movement factor accordingly. For example, typing **7** before pressing the right arrow key moves the cursor seven characters to the right.

Typing the **w** command moves the cursor forward one word at a time, treating symbols and punctuation marks as words. Typing the **W** command moves the cursor forward one word at a time, ignoring symbols and punctuation. To move backward one word at a time, type the command **b**. This command also treats symbols and punctuation marks as words. Typing **B** moves the cursor backward one word at a time, ignoring symbols and punctuation marks. You can multiply the movement effects of the **w**, **W**, **b**, or **B** commands by entering a repeat factor before the command. For example, typing **3w** moves the cursor forward three words; typing **6B** moves the cursor back six words, ignoring punctuation marks.

Moving by Lines, Sentences, and Paragraphs

Typing + while in command mode moves the cursor to the next line's first character; typing – moves the cursor to the first character of the previous line. You can also use the up or down arrow keys to move through lines and add repeat factors to multiply their effect.

Typing $ moves the cursor to the end of the current line. To move the cursor to the beginning of the current line, type **0**.

N O T E Remember, in vi a line isn't necessarily the same length as the visible line (usually 80 characters) that appears on the screen.

You can move to the beginning of the current sentence by typing an open parenthesis (( ). Typing a close parenthesis ( )) moves the cursor to the beginning of the next sentence. You can move back to the beginning of the current paragraph by typing an open curly bracket ({), or ahead to the beginning of the next paragraph with a closed curly bracket (}). You can use repeat factors with any of these commands. If there is a sequence of blank lines, the cursor moves to the beginning of the first blank line.

Moving within a Screen Display

You can move the cursor to certain positions on the screen. Typing **H** moves the cursor to the home position in the upper-left corner of the screen. Typing M moves the cursor to the beginning of the middle line of the screen. Typing L moves the cursor to the beginning of the last line on the screen. You can't add a repeat factor to any of these commands.

Scrolling through a File

Several useful commands for scrolling through a file are provided by vi. Pressing Control-u scrolls up half a screen at a time. Pressing Control-d scrolls down half a screen at a time. To move up or down one screen at a time, press Control-f to see the next screen, and press Control-b to see the previous screen. To scroll down one line at a time, press Control-e. To scroll up one line at a time, press Control-y.

If you want to scroll the screen up or down, but you want the cursor to remain where it is on the current line, use the z command. Pressing z, then Return, moves the current line to the top of the screen. Typing z. moves the current line to the center of the screen. Typing z- moves the current line to the bottom of the screen.

Line Numbering and Line Movement

In vi, each line in a file is assigned a sequential line number. Line numbers, by default, are not displayed. They can be displayed on the screen by entering the command

```
:set nu
```

Line numbers are displayed in vi as shown in the example below:

```
1  OK. I admit it.
2  I hid the gun.
3  I did not want my niece to go to the chair.
~
~
~
~
~
~
~
~
"testimony" 3 lines, 67 characters
```

Only lines that include text are assigned numbers. Blank lines, those starting with the tilde character (~), are not numbered. These line numbers appear on the screen for convenience only and do not become part of your file. You can also display the current line number in the status line by pressing Control-g, which displays the current line number, the total number of lines in the file, and the percentage of the total lines of the file above the current line position.

Using the G (Goto) command, you can move directly to any line containing text. For example, typing 44G moves the cursor to the beginning of line forty-four. Typing G without a line number moves the cursor to the last line of the file. Entering : *n*, where *n* is the specified line number, also moves the cursor to that line number in your file.

Editing Commands

There are four basic editing functions performed in vi.

- Inserting text in insert mode.
- Deleting text.
- Changing and replacing text.
- Cutting (or copying) and pasting text from one place to another in your file.

Most vi editing commands can also be combined with movement commands and repeat factors to further improve your productivity.

TIP

Remember, you can save time duplicating an edit command by using the repeat command. Simply position the cursor where you want to repeat the command and type a period.

Cleaning Up the Screen

Once you start making extensive changes to your file, the screen can get cluttered with leftover command symbols before vi redraws your screen. *Redrawing* a screen means updating the screen to reflect your changes and removing command symbols that have been executed. The vi editor doesn't automatically redraw your screen when you make changes, but instead redraws your screen periodically. You can redraw your vi screen at any time by pressing

```
Control-1
```

Inserting and Appending Text

In vi, there are several commands to insert text into your file. All of these commands are executed from insert mode. To enter the insert mode, first position the cursor at the location you want to insert text, then type **i** while in the command mode. You are now ready to begin entering text at the cursor location. The characters you type appear to the left or before the cursor position and push any following characters to the right. You can press Return to create a new line at any point while you are entering text.

Another way to enter the insert mode is by typing **a** for the append command. Characters you type after using the **a** (append) command are inserted to the right of the cursor. While in the command mode, you can insert a new line in your text by typing the **o** (open) command, which opens a new line below the cursor and automatically puts you in the insert mode. Typing **0** opens a new line above the cursor for text.

To leave the insert mode and return to the command mode, press Esc. The following lists vi insert mode commands.

COMMAND KEY	ACTION
i	Before cursor.
I	Before first nonblank character on line.
a	After cursor.
A	At end of line.
o	Opens a line next line down.
O	Opens a line next line up.
Esc	Quits insert mode.

Deleting Text

The vi editor provides a complete set of delete commands. Delete commands are performed in the command mode. After executing a delete command, vi remains in the command mode. Keep in mind that the u (undo) command, as explained earlier, is particularly useful in undoing deletion commands. The following lists and explains vi editor delete commands.

COMMAND KEY	DELETION
x	Character at cursor.
X	Character before cursor.
dw	To end of word.
dW	To end of word, including punctuation.
db	To beginning of word.
dB	To beginning of word, including punctuation.
d Return	Two lines, current and following.
dd	Entire line cursor is on.
d0	From cursor to the beginning of line.
d$	From cursor to the end of line.

COMMAND KEY	DELETION
d)	To end of sentence.
d (	To beginning of sentence.
d }	To end of paragraph.
d {	To beginning of paragraph.
dL	To last line on screen.
dH	To first line on screen.
dG	To end of the file.
d1G	To beginning of the file.

Deleting Characters and Words

Use the x command while in the command mode to delete a single character. Typing x deletes only the character the cursor is positioned on, unless you use a repeat factor. Typing X deletes the character before the cursor. You can delete multiple characters by typing the number of characters you want to delete before the command. For example, typing 10x deletes ten characters forward, starting with the character *at* the cursor; typing the command 8X deletes eight characters backward, starting with the first character *following* the cursor.

To delete units other than characters, type d, usually in combination with an argument that specifies the unit to be deleted. To delete a word, first position the cursor on the first or last character and type dw. If you want to delete a word, including any adjacent punctuation, type dW. You can include a repeat factor in these delete commands to delete a number of words. The number is placed following the d but preceding either the w or b, such as typing d4w to delete four words forward.

Deleting Lines and Sentences

Typing dd deletes the line where the cursor is currently located. If you type d, then press Return, vi deletes the entire line and the line following it. To delete more than two lines, precede the first d with the number of lines you want to delete. For example, typing 12dd deletes twelve lines down, starting with the current line.

You can also delete a part of a line. Typing d$ deletes from the cursor to the end of a line. Typing d0 deletes from the beginning of the line to the cursor. To delete a sentence from the cursor to the end of the sentence, type d). To delete a sentence from the cursor to the beginning of the sentence, type d(.

Placing the cursor at the very beginning or end of a sentence, then using the appropriate sentence deletion command, deletes an entire sentence. For example, typing d) with the cursor at the very beginning of the sentence deletes the entire sentence. As with other delete commands, you can add repeat factors to delete more than one sentence at a time. For example, typing d4) with the cursor located at the very beginning of a sentence deletes that entire sentence and the following three sentences.

Deleting Paragraphs and Other Sections of Your File

As with deleting sentences, placing the cursor at the very beginning or end of a paragraph and typing the appropriate delete command deletes the entire paragraph. To delete from the beginning of a paragraph to the cursor, type d{. To delete from the cursor to the end of the paragraph, type d}. You can also use the repeat factor to delete multiple paragraphs. For example, typing d3} with the cursor at the beginning of a paragraph deletes all of the current paragraph along with the two following paragraphs.

You can delete parts of your vi file displayed on your screen. Typing dH deletes text from the line the cursor is located on to the very top of the screen. Typing dL deletes text from the line the cursor is on down to the very last line on the screen. Typing dG deletes text from the line the cursor is on to the end of the file. Typing d1G deletes text from the line the cursor is located on to the very beginning of the file.

Changing and Replacing Text

The vi editor provides two commands to change text, the c (change) command and the r (replace) command.

- The change command combines the functions of deleting and inserting text in one command.
- The replace command allows you to overtype existing text.

Invoke both commands while in the command mode.

When you enter a change command, specify the text that will be replaced. The end of this text is then marked with a $ (the cursor location marks the beginning of the text to be changed). You then overtype the marked text, then press Esc to complete the deletion and effect the change. Your changes can be shorter or longer than the marked text that will be deleted. You can use the change commands to change words, lines, sentences, and paragraphs. As with most vi editing commands, you can add repeat factors to change commands. The following lists vi editor change and replace commands.

COMMAND	CHANGE OR REPLACEMENT
cw	To end of word.
cW	To end of word, including punctuation.
cb	From beginning of word to cursor.
cB	From beginning of word, including punctuation, to cursor.
cc	Current line.
c$	From the cursor to the end of the line.
c0	From the cursor to the beginning of the line.
c)	From the cursor to the end of the sentence.
c(	From the cursor to the beginning of the sentence.

COMMAND	CHANGE OR REPLACEMENT
c}	From the cursor to the end of the paragraph.
c{	From the cursor to the beginning of the paragraph.
r	Replaces character at cursor.
R	Replaces characters until Esc is pressed.

Changing Words, Lines, Sentences, and Paragraphs

To change a word, type the command **cw**. The **cw** (change word) command instructs vi to delete the word at the cursor location and insert new text. You can change multiple words by adding a repeat factor for the number of words you want to change. For example, typing **c3w** allows you to change three words forward from the cursor.

To change an entire line, type the command **cc**, which marks the line and places you in the insert mode to begin entering replacement text. When you are finished entering text, press Esc. It doesn't matter where the cursor is located on the line; **cc** deletes the entire line of text and replaces it with the text you entered before pressing Esc. You can also use a repeat factor to change multiple lines. For example, typing **7cc** marks the current line and the six following lines for deletion, then places you in the insert mode to begin replacing the lines.

You can remove part or all of a sentence or paragraph and enter the insert mode by using the commands **c)** (from the cursor to the end of the sentence), **c(** (from the cursor to the beginning of the sentence), **c}** (from the cursor to the end of the paragraph), and **c{** (from the cursor to the beginning of the paragraph). As with other change commands, you can also use repeat factors with sentence or paragraph change commands.

Replacing Text

The **r** (replace) command allows you to overtype a single character. You can multiply the effects of this command by typing the number of characters you want to affect before it. For example, typing **8r** allows you to replace eight characters forward from the cursor. Typing R is particularly useful because it allows you to overtype characters until Esc is pressed.

Changing Case in Command Mode

To change the case of a character without leaving command mode, position the cursor on the letter whose case you want to change and type ~. The case of the letter changes, and the cursor moves to the next character. You *can't* add a repeat factor or an argument, such as w for a word, to the tilde command (~).

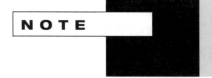

N O T E You can use the ~(tilde) command to change the case of any letter because it changes both lowercase letters to uppercase and uppercase letters to lowercase.

Joining Two Lines

You can merge shorter lines to form a longer line using the J (join) command. For example, to join two lines, first position the cursor anywhere on the first line, then type J to merge the line below it. You can also add a repeat factor to merge consecutive lines into one line and use the repeat command (.) to repeat the join command. To join these three lines

```
OK. I admit it.
I hid the gun.
I did not want my niece to go to the chair.
```

type 3J, which results in the following:

```
OK. I admit it. I hid the gun. I did not want my niece to go to
the chair.
```

Cutting and Pasting Text

Cutting and pasting text means you mark pieces of text, *yank* (copy) them, then *put* (paste) them at another location. The vi editor performs cutting and pasting tasks by storing the yanked (or deleted) text in buffers, which are areas set aside in memory to store text. There are two types of buffers for cutting and pasting text, the general buffer and named buffers. The *general buffer* stores only the last text manipulation you performed in memory. Because so many commands use the general buffer, such as delete and change commands, vi provides a way to create your own buffers for storing and retrieving text. These are called *named buffers*. Don't confuse the general buffer with the work buffer, which holds your entire file in memory until you save it to disk.

NOTE The u (undo) command always uses text placed in the general buffer as its source.

Using Named Buffers

You can establish up to 26 named buffers of your own, designated by lowercase letters ranging from **a** to **z**. These named buffers can store deleted, yanked, or changed text. You specify text stored in a named buffer by including a double quotation mark (**"**) and the name of the buffer before the delete, yank, or change command. For example, typing the command

    "z3dd

with the cursor at the beginning of a sentence deletes five sentences and stores them in a buffer named **z**. To retrieve the text stored in the **z** buffer, you can use the **p** (put) command, which is explained after the following section.

Using a lowercase buffer name when instructing vi to save text to a named buffer *replaces* any text you have previously saved in that buffer. Using the uppercase version of a buffer name *appends* text you save to that buffer. For example, if you have text saved in a buffer named **z**, saving additional text by specifying **Z** in the command appends this text to the existing text in the buffer named **z**. You can use this technique to collect separate lines in your file and use the uppercase name to place them together in a named buffer. Named buffers work as temporary buffers that are only active during your vi work session for a particular file.

WARNING The contents of all named buffers will be erased if you quit vi or log out.

Copying Text Using Buffers

To copy text from one location to another in your file, you use the y (yank) command. Yank commands copy a specified unit of text into the general buffer or a named buffer, leaving the original text in place. To paste the yanked text, move the cursor to the location you want to copy the yanked text, then use the p (put) command. The put command is explained below. The following lists available yank commands. Each yank command puts the specified text into the general buffer unless you specify a named buffer.

COMMAND	TEXT YANKED
yw	From the cursor to end of word.
yW	From the cursor to end of word including punctuation.
yb	From the cursor to beginning of word.
yB	From the cursor to beginning of word including punctuation.
yy	Current line.
y Return	Two lines, current and following.
Y$	From the cursor to end of a line.
y0	From the cursor to beginning of a line.
y)	From cursor to end of sentence.
y(	From cursor to beginning of sentence.
y}	From cursor to end of paragraph.
y{	From cursor to beginning of paragraph.
yG	To end of file.

Retrieving Text from Buffers

The p (put) command by itself retrieves text from the general buffer into your file. If the contents of the general buffer are characters or words, typing p puts them *after* the character the cursor is located on. Typing P puts characters or words *before* the character the cursor is located on. If the general buffer contains lines, sentences, or paragraphs, typing p inserts the contents below the line, sentence, or paragraph the cursor is located on. Typing P inserts lines, sentences, or paragraphs from the general buffer into the line, sentence, or paragraph above the cursor. If your named buffer contains different units of text, such as a word and line, the put command places the buffer's text according to which unit of text was placed into the named buffer last. You can specify a named buffer to use with the put command. For example, typing the command "tz puts the contents of buffer tz after the cursor in the appropriate location, depending on what units of text the buffer contains.

Inserting Text from Another File

With vi you can read the contents of another file into the file you're currently working on using the :r (read) command.

```
:r filename
```

The read command inserts the contents of *filename,* starting on the line after the cursor position in the current file. For example, suppose your user name is pmason and you are editing the file evidence and want to read in a file called testimony from another directory. To read the file testimony into the file evidence, first position the cursor one line above where you want the new data inserted in evidence. In the command mode, enter

```
:r /home/pmason/testimony
```

The entire contents of the file testimony are read into your file evidence.

You can also combine the read command with a SunOS command to read the results of a SunOS command into your file. For example, entering

```
:r! date
```

will read the system's date information into your file.

Searching vi Files

Two powerful tools are provided by vi for searching through your files for specified strings of characters—the search command and the global replacement command. Search commands search your file for a specified pattern. When a match is found, you can make changes, then search for the next occurrence of the string. Global replacement commands search your file for a specified pattern and automatically replace it with another pattern you specify.

WARNING A forward search continues until the end of the file and a backward search continues until the beginning of the file. If you begin in the middle of a file, the entire file will not be searched.

Searching vi Files for Patterns

Search commands search your file for a pattern match, which means vi searches for a string of characters that matches your specified text. To search forward through a file, type the forward slash character (/) while in command mode, followed by the pattern you want to search for. For example, type

```
/SunOS
```

then press Return. This instructs vi to search forward through the file to find the first occurrence of the pattern SunOS. Typing a question mark before the search pattern, as in the following

```
?SunOS
```

then pressing Return searches backward through your file for the specified pattern. If no match is found after executing a search command, the message `Pattern not found` is displayed in the status line. When a search command locates the first occurrence of a pattern, you can then perform an editing task such as changing or deleting the pattern. Typing n continues the search to find the next occurrence of a pattern in the same direction. Typing N changes the direction of the search. The following lists vi search commands.

COMMAND	RESULT
/*pattern* <Return>	Searches forward in file.
?*pattern* <Return>	Searches backward in file.
n	Finds next pattern in same direction.
N	Find next pattern in opposite direction.

Global Replacement

The vi editor provides a powerful tool for searching and replacing incorrect text entries. With one command you can automatically replace a string of characters, such as a misspelled word, wherever it occurs in the file. The global replacement command syntax is

```
:%s/oldpattern/newpattern/
```

Once a global replacement command is entered, vi checks each line of a file for a given pattern. When the pattern is found, vi automatically replaces the old pattern with the new pattern you've specified. Suppose you wanted to search through your file and find each occurrence of the word Harry and change it to Larry. Type

```
:%s/Harry/Larry
```

then press Return. The vi editor searches through the entire file for each occurrence of Harry and replaces it with Larry. If vi doesn't find any matches, it responds with the message `Substitute pattern match failed`.

Setting vi Parameters

You can adapt vi to your preferences for a vi work session by setting vi parameters. The vi editor offers a number of parameter options. You can list these options on your screen by typing the command

`:set all`

then pressing Return. The list shows the options available and their current status. You can set vi parameters to perform such functions as automatically inserting Returns, displaying line numbers, and displaying invisible characters such as tabs and end-of-line characters. To set a parameter while you're using vi, type `:set` followed by the option you want to change. For example, you can instruct vi to display line numbers by typing `:set nu` and pressing Return. To change back to the original set option, type `no` before the option. For example, typing the command

`:set nonu`

then pressing Return now instructs vi *not* to display line numbers. The following lists several useful set command options.

OPTION	RESULT
`set all`	Displays the complete list of options, including options that you have set as well as vi's default settings.
`:set wrapmargin=`*n*	Specifies the size of the right margin used to wrap text as you type, and saves manually entering Return after each line. A typical value for *n* is 10 or 15.

OPTION	RESULT
`:set nu`	Displays line numbers of a file.
`:set ic`	Specifies that pattern searches should ignore case.
`:set window=x`	Sets the number of lines shown in the screen window, where x is the number of lines.
`:set list`	Displays invisible characters, with tabs displayed as `^I` and the end-of-line characters (Returns) displayed as `$`.

Using SunOS Commands in vi

You can temporarily exit vi to execute SunOS commands, such as checking your mail, then return to your vi work session without having to quit vi. Typing the command `:sh` while in vi returns you to the SunOS system prompt. You can then execute other SunOS commands. When you want to return to vi, at the system prompt enter

```
exit
```

Save Time When Starting vi

There are several options available when starting vi beyond the basic `vi filename` start-up command. You can start up vi, open an existing file, then have the cursor move to a particular line in the file by typing

> `vi +n filename`

where *n* is the number of the line on which you want the cursor to be placed. You can also start up vi, open an existing file, and move the cursor to the last line of the file by typing `vi +` *filename*. The start-up command

> `vi +/pattern filename`

opens a file and positions the cursor at the first occurrence of a particular text pattern. For example, typing `vi +/fired letter` opens up the file `letter` and places the cursor at the first character of the line containing the word `fired`.

Command Summary

The following lists the commands covered in this chapter that are not contained in the earlier tables.

COMMAND	RESULT
.	Repeats previous command.
Control-l	Redraws screen.
:q!	Quits vi and abandons changes.
Shift-ZZ	Quits vi and saves changes.
vi	Allows user to enter vi.
:w	Saves buffer contents without quitting vi.

Formatting and Printing

IN THE last chapter, you worked with vi to create and edit text files. In this chapter, you learn how to use the `nroff` and `troff` formatting programs to enhance the appearance of your printed files. With the `nroff` and `troff` programs you can perform a wide range of formatting tasks from boldfacing a single word to changing your entire document's page layout. This chapter also teaches you how to use essential commands for performing basic formatting tasks. In addition, SunOS's printing commands and options are explained to provide you with a variety of ways to print your files.

An Overview of Formatting

SunOS provides several tools for formatting documents. The `nroff` and `troff` text formatting programs are two of these. One of the early text formatting commands in SunOS was named `roff`, which comes from the phrase to "run off" a document, used when a person wanted to format and print a document. The `nroff` command, which stands for "newer roff," is used primarily with line printers—printers that print one line of text at a time in a single style of typeface. The `troff` program is an adaptation of `nroff` for typesetters and laser printers. These printers can print a page at a time and change typeface size and styles, commonly referred to as *fonts*. Because of the prevalence of laser printers, this chapter focuses on using the `troff` text formatting program.

Adding Formatting Requests to a File

Before you can use `nroff` or `troff`, you must insert requests in the document you want to format. A *request* is simply a formatting instruction embedded in the text of the document to be formatted. You insert requests in a file with a text editor, such as vi, placing a request on a blank line above the text you want formatted.

Using Macros to Format a File

Certain types of documents may need extensive formatting, and could require you to insert many requests in the text. Instead of repeatedly typing the same commands, use macros to save time in formatting your documents. For our purposes, we will define a *macro* as a sequence of `nroff` or `troff` requests. Macros are distinguished from `nroff` and `troff` requests by case—macros use uppercase letters. In SunOS, these macros are grouped together in *macro packages*. This chapter explains how to use `troff` and some of the macros for formatting documents that are found in the `-ms` macro package. You format text with macros the same way as with `nroff` and `troff` requests. Use a text editor to insert the macro above the text you want to format.

Viewing and Printing Formatted Documents

Once you exit the text editor and return to the system prompt, you can view the document by entering

```
ntroff -ms filename | more
```

The `-ms` indicates that the macros embedded in your file belong to the `-ms` macro package. If you are not using `-ms` macros, you can exclude the `-ms` option.

To print a document containing -ms macro requests, use this general syntax:

```
troff -ms filename | lp -d destination
```

The nroff or troff program then formats your text according to the embedded requests. The lp command sends the formatted file to the printer specified by destination. If you are not using -ms macros, you can exclude the -ms option. The embedded requests will not appear on the printout.

When you filter a document that contains troff requests, it produces output in the ditroff format, which are instructions for the printer. If you are using a PostScript printer that doesn't recognize and convert the ditroff printing instructions into PostScript printing instructions, you may need to filter the document using the dpost filter. The dpost filter is stored in the /usr/lib/lp/postscript directory. To use the dpost filter you need to use the pipe to send the output from the troff command to the dpost filter, then use the pipe to send the filtered document to the lp command. Adding the -T postscript argument to the lp command indicates that the document you are printing is in a PostScript format. You must include the entire path name of the dpost filter or add the path to the PATH setting in your .profile file. For example, if you have not added the path to the dpost filter to your .profile file, enter

```
troff -ms filename | /usr/lib/lp/postscript/dpost | lp -T
postscript -d destination
```

If you add the /usr/lib/lp/postscript directory to your PATH setting, as explained in Chapter 15, "Customizing Solaris," you can simply enter the following:

```
troff -ms filename | dpost | lp -T postscript -d destination
```

Character Formatting

If you're using a laser printer or a typesetter, use troff requests and -ms macros to print characters in different fonts (both sizes and styles). The following explains the troff commands that allow you to use different fonts, such as italic and bold. You can use some of these requests, such as the underline request, with `nroff`, but `nroff` ignores requests for fonts it can't handle. In other words, `nroff` doesn't change the size or style of your font. This section also explains how to insert special characters, such as a bullet or a copyright symbol, using `nroff` and `troff`.

Italicizing Text

The `.I` macro is used to indicate italics. Italics are commonly used to set off a foreign word or expression or to indicate titles of books or magazines, as shown in the following example.

```
To inquire how the editors liked the manuscript for
.I
Les Miserables,
.R
Victor Hugo composed the following letter, quoted here in its en-
tirety: "?." The publisher responded: "!."
```

The text when printed then appears as follows:

> To inquire how the editors liked the manuscript for *Les Miserables,* Victor Hugo composed the following letter, quoted here in its entirety: "?." The publisher responded: "!."

If you use the `.I` macro with `nroff`, italicized characters are converted to underlined characters.

Underlining Text

To underline a word in a sentence, use the `.UL` macro; use the `.R` (roman) macro to stop underlining and return to a normal typeface. Unlike most formatting requests, the `.UL` request requires you to put the word to be underlined on the same line as the `.UL` request. You can also underline a certain number of words using the `nroff` request `.ul` n, where n is the number of words to underline. Unfortunately, neither `nroff` and `troff` provides a way to underline spaces between multiple words. The following is an example of underlining a single word in a text file.

```
The word "bug" in the slang expression "Don't bug me" comes from
the West African word
.UL bagu
.R
,meaning to annoy.
```

The text, when printed, appears as follows:

The word "bug" in the slang expression "Don't bug me" comes from the West African word <u>bagu</u>, meaning to annoy.

Boldfacing Text

Boldface is used to emphasize words or set headings apart from other text. To boldface text, use the `.B` macro; use the `.R` (roman) macro to return to normal roman typeface. The `.B` macro doesn't work with some line printers. For example

```
.B
Warning to all Personnel:
.R
Firings will continue until morale improves.
```

results in the printout

Warning to all Personnel: Firings will continue until morale improves.

Changing the Size of a Font

A laser printer or typesetter lets you print fonts in different sizes, measured in points. A *point* is $1/72$ of an inch. The default point size is 10 points. If you're using a laser printer or a typesetter, you can change the size of your font by using a few simple macros. The `.LG` macro makes the font two points larger. The `.SM` macro makes a font two points smaller, and the `.NL` macro returns your font to the normal size. To change the font size to a 12 points, enter

```
This text will print using a 10-point font.
.LG
This text will print using a 12-point font.
```

Inserting Special Characters

Not all the characters you can print are on your keyboard. The `nroff` and `troff` programs let you print a variety of characters not available on your keyboard by simply inserting a special code in your document. The following lists the most commonly used special characters that you can add using the standard fonts. Notice that the backslash escape character is used to identify the character code.

CHARACTER	CODE	DESCRIPTION
—	`\(em`	Em dash
–	`\(hy`	Hyphen
•	`\(bu`	Bullet
½	`\(12`	One-half
¼	`\(14`	One-quarter
→	`\(->`	Right arrow
←	`\(<-`	Left arrow
↑	`\(ua`	Up arrow
↓	`\(da`	Down arrow
|	`\br`	Boxed rule
¢	`\(ct`	Cent sign
®	`\(rg`	Registered
©	`\(co`	Copyright
°	`\(de`	Degree
´	`\(aa`	Acute accent
`	`\(ga`	Grave accent

Formatting Lines

To the nroff and troff programs, a file is only a stream of words. Both programs ignore the line breaks you made when you pressed Return while creating or editing a file. Instead nroff and troff format text by filling the lines to fit in the margins. This process is called *line filling*. When they encounter a space at the beginning of a line, they interpret the space as a line break, stop filling the current line, and begin a new line.

Filling and Justifying Lines

The -ms macro package by default inserts spaces between words to make lines end with a flush right margin; this is commonly known as *justification*. To produce a nonjustified (ragged) margin, use the request .na (nonadjusted). To return to a right margin justification alignment, add the request .ad. Look at the following example to see the effects of using .na and .ad.

```
.na
Traditionally dinosaurs have been thought of as being cold-
blooded reptiles. However, contemporary evidence on posture,
skeleton, and eating habits indicates some dinosaurs may have
been warm-blooded. It is a mistake to think that dinosaurs and
cave dwellers lived at the same time.

.ad
Dinosaurs died out 65 million years ago, and the earliest human
dates back to no more than four million years.
It is also a myth that dinosaurs died during the Ice Age.
The last Ice Age, to which the myth presumably refers, ended
10,000 years ago.
```

Here is how this example would be printed:

Traditionally dinosaurs have been thought of as being cold-blooded reptiles. However, contemporary evidence on posture, skeleton, and eating habits indicates some dinosaurs may have been warm-blooded. It is a mistake to think that dinosaurs and cave dwellers lived at the same time.

Dinosaurs died out 65 million years ago, and the earliest human dates back to no more than four million years. It is also a myth that dinosaurs died during the Ice Age. The last Ice Age, to which the myth presumably refers, ended 10,000 years ago.

When you want to stop lines from being joined together, use the `.nf` request. For example, when you put an address in a letter, you don't want the city and state to be added to the end of the street address on the previous line. To prevent `nroff` from filling lines, use `.nf` (no fill). The `.nf` request doesn't justify your text, but stops the filling process and prints your text with line breaks as they appear in the file. To restart line filling, use the `.fi` (fill) request.

Changing Line Spacing

The `nroff` and `troff` programs both use single line spacing as the default. You can easily change the line spacing by adding the number of blank lines you want between each line using the request `.ls` *n*, where *n* is the number of the spaces you want between each line. The following request begins double spacing text then returns to single spacing.

```
.ls 2
A movie theater manager in Seoul, South Korea, decided that the
running time of the movie
I.
The Sound of Music
R.
was too long, so he shortened it by cutting out all the songs.
.ls
```

The double-spaced text when printed appears as follows:

A movie theater manager in Seoul, South Korea, decided

that the running time of the movie *The Sound of Music*

was too long, so he shortened it by cutting out all the songs.

Inserting Blank Lines

You can insert any number of blank lines using the `.sp` *n* request. The letter *n* indicates the number of line spaces you want to insert in the text. For example,

```
Rough draft
.sp 3
It was a dark and stormy night.
```

adds three lines between the first line of text and the text following the .sp 3 request, printed as follows:

Rough draft

It was a dark and stormy night.

Indenting Lines

To indent text from the left margin, use the .in request followed by the number of spaces to indent. You can add spaces to an indent by preceding the number in the argument with a plus (+) sign or decrease spaces with a minus sign (-). For example, .in +5 increases the current indent by five spaces.

Typically, the first line of a paragraph is indented. If you want to temporarily indent a single line of text, use the request .ti *n*, where *n* is the number of spaces you want to indent that one line.

Setting Tabs

Tabs are most frequently used to produce output in columns. The troff tab stops are set by default every half inch from the current indent. The nroff tab stops are set every .8 inch. You can set tabs using the .ta request followed by the tab position you want to set. For example,

```
.ta 1i 1.5i 2i 2.5i 3i 3.5i 4i 4.5i 5i 5.5i 6i
```

sets tabs every $1/2$ inch across a page. You can also set tabs relative to the previous tab stops by preceding the tab number with a plus (+) sign. For example,

```
.ta 1 +.5i +.5i +.5i +.5i +.5i +.5i +.5i +.5i +.5i
```

produces the same results as the previous `.ta` example. You can also create right-adjusted or centered tabs. To right-adjust a tab, add the letter `R` after the tab setting. When you right-adjust a tab, the text following the tab is lined up against the right margin. To center a tab entry, add the letter `C` after the tab setting.

The following shows how to create two columns of text using right-adjusted tabs. It is mandatory that you use the `.nf` (no fill) request at the beginning of this example to stop filling text. The `.fi` (fill) request at the end of this example is optional, depending on whether or not you want to resume filling text.

```
.nf
.ta 3.5iR
Date    Holiday
Jan 1   New Year's Day
Jan 15  Martin Luther King, Jr., Day
Feb 12  Lincoln's Birthday
Feb 14  Valentine's Day
Feb 22  Washington's Birthday
Mar 17  St. Patrick's Day
.fi
```

When printed this looks like this:

Date	Holiday
Jan 1	New Year's Day
Jan 15	Martin Luther King, Jr., Day
Feb 12	Lincoln's Birthday
Feb 14	Valentine's Day
Feb 22	Washington's Birthday
Mar 17	St. Patrick's Day

Centering Lines

The `.ce` request centers a single line of text. You can center multiple lines of text by following `.ce` with the number of lines of text you want centered. Blank lines are not counted when using the `.ce` request.

```
.ce 2
Men have become tools of their tools.
Thoreau
```

When printed, this appears as follows:

Men have become tools of their tools.

Thoreau

Formatting Paragraphs

You can produce several different kinds of paragraphs with the -ms macro package. For example, standard paragraphs begin with an indented first sentence, and left block paragraphs don't indent the first sentence. The following section shows examples of how text would appear using -ms macros for formatting standard, left-block, indented, and quoted paragraphs.

Standard Paragraphs

The standard paragraph is an indented, left-aligned paragraph. Insert the -ms macro .PP to format the following text as a standard paragraph:

```
.PP
Because of the radiant properties of the sun, people believe that
it consists of an entirely different material than earth. The sun
burns because of its size. It consists of the same cosmic matter
from which all of the planets are made.
```

When printed, the paragraph appears with an indent as follows:

Because of the radiant properties of the sun, people believe that it consists of an entirely different material than earth. The sun burns because of its size. It consists of the same cosmic matter from which all of the planets are made.

Left-Block Paragraphs

A left-block paragraph is the same as a standard paragraph, only without an indent. Left block paragraphs are indicated by the macro .LP, as shown here:

```
.LP
The sun contains 99.8 percent mass of the solar system and is a
million times larger than the earth. The effect of its size is to
produce pressure at the center so great that even atoms are
crushed, exploding their nuclei, and allowing them to smash into
each other. These collisions are actually nuclear reactions and
are felt and seen by us from 93 million miles away as heat and
light.
```

When printed the paragraph appears left-aligned, without an indent, as follows:

The sun contains 99.8 percent mass of the solar system and is a million times larger than the earth. The effect of its size is to produce pressure at the center so great that even atoms are crushed, exploding their nuclei, and allowing them to smash into each other. These collisions are actually nuclear reactions and are felt and seen by us from 93 million miles away as heat and light.

If you don't add an .LP or .PP request, all your paragraphs will be unindented with both the left and right margins aligned.

Block Quotes

The .QP (quoted paragraph) macro indents a paragraph on both sides, with blank lines above and below the paragraph.

```
.PP
The giant marlin has towed the old man's boat far off the coast
of Cuba. The old man is exhausted but has outlasted the fish. He
hoists a sail and begins heading for home. Hemingway writes,
.QP
They sailed well and the old man soaked his hands in the salt
water and tried to keep his head clear. There were high cumulus
clouds and enough cirrus above them so that the old man knew the
breeze would last all night. The old man looked at the fish con-
stantly to make sure it was true. It was an hour before the first
shark hit him.
.PP
```

The above example, when printed, appears as follows:

> The giant marlin has towed the old man's boat far off the coast of Cuba. The old man is exhausted but has outlasted the fish. He hoists a sail and begins heading for home. Hemingway writes,
>
> > They sailed well and the old man soaked his hands in the salt water and tried to keep his head clear. There were high cumulus clouds and enough cirrus above them so that the old man knew the breeze would last all night. The old man looked at the fish constantly to make sure it was true. It was an hour before the first shark hit him.

Indented Paragraphs

Indented paragraphs are frequently used for creating bulleted or numbered lists. The syntax for creating an indented paragraph is as follows:

```
.IP label n
```

This command indents a paragraph n spaces after a "hanging" label. If a label is more than one word, the words must be enclosed in double quotation marks. If an indent isn't specified, an indent of five spaces is used. The following is an example of formatting indented paragraphs.

```
.IP (i) 5
Never use a metaphor, simile, or other figure of speech that you
are used to seeing in print.
.IP (ii) 5
Never use a long word where a short one will do.
.IP (iii) 5
If it is possible to cut a word out, always cut it out.
.IP (iv) 5
Never use the passive where you can use the active.
.IP (v) 5
Never use a foreign phrase, a scientific word, or a jargon word
if you can think of an everyday English equivalent.
.IP (vi) 5
Break any of these rules sooner than say anything outright
barbarous.
```

When printed, the above example appears as follows:

When printed, the above example appears as follows:

    (i)   Never use a metaphor, simile, or other figure of speech that you are used to seeing in print.

   (ii)   Never use a long word where a short one will do.

  (iii)   If it is possible to cut a word out, always cut it out.

  (iv)   Never use the passive where you can use the active.

   (v)   Never use a foreign phrase, a scientific word, or a jargon word if you can think of an everyday English equivalent.

  (vi)   Break any of these rules sooner than say anything outright barbarous.

Outline Paragraphs

To create an outline, use the `.IP` (indented) macro with the `.RS` (right-shift) and `.RE` (right-shift end) macros. Each time you use the `.RS` request, the indention moves in another five spaces. The `.RE` request moves the indention back five spaces.

```
.IP I.
Making the Most of Priorities
.RS
.IP A.
The To Do list
.RS
.IP 1.
Setting priorities
.IP 2.
Grouping tasks
.RE
.RE
.IP II.
Tasks Better Left Undone
.RS
.IP A.
The 80/20 rule
.RS
.IP 1.
Skipping less important jobs
```

```
.IP 2.
Coping with information overload
.RE
.RE
```

The above example, when printed, appears as follows:

I. Making the Most of Priorities

   A. The To Do list

      1. Setting priorities

      2. Grouping tasks

II. Tasks Better Left Undone

   A. The 80/20 rule

      1. Skipping less important jobs

      2. Coping with information overload

Changing the Page Layout

You can change the layout of your document, such as margins or page sizing, if the default page-layout settings don't match your needs. Figure 13.1 shows the elements of page layout that you'll work with in this section.

Number Registers

In order to change the default page-layout settings, such as margins, you need to use number registers. *Number registers* are memory locations that store values of page-layout settings. You usually use one or two letters to specify a number register, that is, to say which part of the layout you want to change. Note however, that −ms number registers do not take effect immediately. If you need the effect immediately, use the `troff` command equivalent, which is a period and the lowercase equivalent of the register.

FIGURE 13.1

Elements of page layout

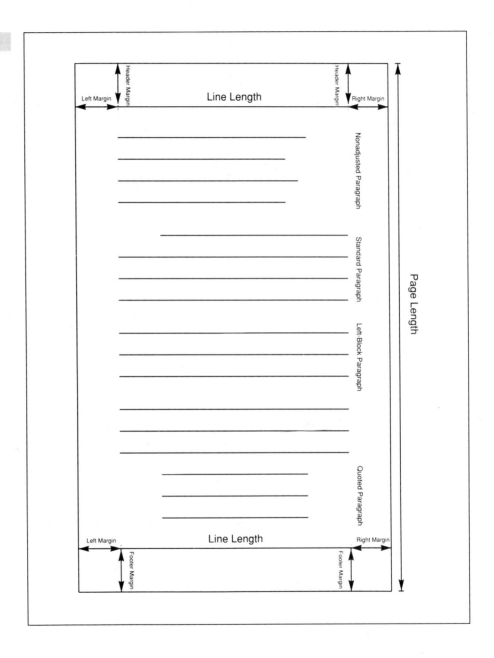

The following shows an example of using .nr to change the default point size to 9 points.

```
.nr PS 9
```

The following lists a summary of -ms number registers.

REGISTER	CONTROLS	TAKES EFFECT	DEFAULT
CW	Column width	The next occurrence of two-column text (next .2C)	$7/15$ of the set line length
FM	Footer margin	The next page	1 inch
GW	Gap width between columns	The next occurrence of two-column text (next .2C)	$1/15$ of the set line length
GM	Header margin	The next page	1 inch
LL	Line length	The next paragraph	6 inches
PD	Paragraph spacing	The next paragraph	0.3 of line spacing
PI	Paragraph indent	The next paragraph	5 spaces
PO	Page offset	The next page	$26/27$ inch
PS	Point size	The next paragraph	10 points
VS	Line spacing	The next paragraph	12 points

Setting Left and Right Margins

Margins are the white spaces at the top, bottom, left, and right of your printed document. By default, the `troff` program initially sets the margins to one inch (the `nroff` program sets the left margins to zero). To specify a one-and-a-half-inch-wide left margin, at the beginning of your text insert the command

```
.nr PO 1.5i
```

The `nr` in this command stands for number register. The `PO` stands for Page Offset; the number `1.5` followed by the letter `i` will offset the page 1.5 inches.

The right margin is determined by the left margin setting and the line length setting. To discover how wide your right margin is, subtract the length of your text line and the width of the left margin from the total width of the page, which is normally 8.5 inches. The result is the size of the right margin. The default line length is 6 inches. If you want one-and-a-half inch margins on both sides of the printout of your document, you need to offset the left margin by one-and-a-half inches and change the line-length setting to 5 inches. To do this, insert these commands above the first line of the file you want to format:

```
.br
.po 1.5i
.ll 5i
```

The `br` is a break that typically precedes the page offset and line length changes. The `.po` is the `troff` equivalent of `.nr Po`, which offsets the left margin. `ll` indicates the line length, which in this example is 5 inches.

Setting Top and Bottom Margins

The `.pl` (page length) request lets you change the number of lines on a page. This request actually specifies how many vertical inches of space the text should fill. At the top of the document, insert `.pl` *n*, where *n* indicates the number of inches the text should fill. The default page length is 11 inches.

For example, to change the page length to 10 inches, use the following command:

```
.pl 10i
```

Determining Page Breaks

Sometimes it is necessary to begin printing information on a new page. The `.bp` (break page) request ends the text at the bottom of a page and begins it at the top of the next page. Here is an example of using the `.bp` request to ensure that a list of paintings begins on a new page.

```
The following page lists the paintings that accompany this
document.
.bp
The List of Paintings

.nf
Old Woman
Old Guitarist
Les Demoiselles d'Avignon
The Three Musicians
Guernica
```

Keeping Text Together

The `nroff` and `troff` programs break pages when the text reaches the bottom margin. You can prevent a page break from occurring in the middle of a block of text by using the `.KS` and `.KE` macros. Suppose you have a paragraph that appears at the bottom of a page and you want it to appear with a paragraph on the next page. Precede the first paragraph with `.KS` and end it with `.KE`, as shown in the following example:

```
.KS
People look for a reflection of their own personalities or the
person they dream of being in the eyes of an animal companion.
That is the reason I sometimes look into the face of my dog Stan
(I have two) and see wistful sadness and existential angst, when
all he is actually doing is slowly scanning the ceiling for flies.
.KE
```

If you need to keep text together on the same page, try using the `.ne n` (need) request, where n is the number of lines to keep on the page. If there is room on the page, `.ne` places all the specified lines on that page.

Headers and Footers

Headers and footers are titles that appear at the top and bottom of a page. Titles that occur at the top of a page are called *headers*. Titles printed at the bottom of a page are called *footers*. If you want to use headers or footers, use `.pl` to change the page length and create space at the top and bottom of your printed pages. These spaces are called the *header margin* and the *footer margin*.

Headers and footers begin printing on the second page of your document. When you use `-ms` with `nroff`, date footers and page number headers are added automatically. Add the `.ND` macro request if you want to eliminate the date when using the `-ms` macro package with `nroff`. When `-ms` is used with `troff`, the date footers are not included. To create the header "Great Prime Time Shows," type the following request on the very first line of your file:

```
.ds CH Great Prime Time Shows
```

The `.ds CH` (define string Center Header) request clears the default setting of `CH`, which is the current page number surrounded by hyphens, and instructs `nroff` to instead center the text "Great Prime Time Shows" as the new header. Note that the quotes are not printed with your header. If you want to add a page number to your header, use the percent sign (`%`). The percent sign tells the automatic page counter to place page numbers in your header. To include page numbers in our previous example, insert

```
.ds CH Great Prime Time Shows %
```

at the top of the file.

You can create headers and footers and specify their location by using the requests listed below.

COMMAND	HEADER AND FOOTER TEXT PLACEMENT
`.ds LH`	Places header text at the left margin.
`.ds CH`	Centers header text.
`.ds RH`	Places header text at the right margin.

COMMAND	HEADER AND FOOTER TEXT PLACEMENT
`.ds LF`	Places footer text at the left margin.
`.ds CF`	Centers footer text.
`.ds RF`	Places footer text at the right margin.

Creating Multiple Columns

In order to get more information on a page, you may want to set your text in multiple columns. Use the following macros with the `col` command to create multiple columns.

MACRO	RESULT
`.2C`	Begins the first column of two-column text.
`.RC`	Begins the second column of two-column text.
`.1C`	Returns to single-column text. Switching from double- to single-column text causes an automatic page break.

The following excerpt from the *Virginia Pilot* shows how to create double columns with the `.2C` request.

```
.2C
.PP
A group calling itself the Partiers League for Christmas Cookie
Liberation kidnapped a Ronald McDonald statue from a Sacramento,
California, McDonald's. They sent a ransom note which read: "Mr.
McDonald is safe, unharmed, and, I assure you, entirely unable to
escape." The note demanded that McDonald's give a free box of
cookies to any child under eight who visited the restaurant on
Christmas Eve.
.PP
"This is not a hoax," said the note. "If any qualified child is
refused cookies, Ronald dies."
.RC
.PP
```

```
The note came with a photo of a blindfolded Ronald McDonald, a
stick of dynamite hanging from his neck. A note on the wall be-
hind the statue read: "Do as they say or I'm McHistory."
.PP
This is not the only case of a crime involving the theft of a res-
taurant statue. In Iron Mountain, Michigan, someone absconded
with a Big Boy restaurant statue and whisked it off to Niagara,
Wisconsin.
```

Entering the command

```
nroff -ms filename | col | lp
```

pipes the file name through the **col** filter to print this example as follows:

A group calling itself the Partiers League for Christmas Cookie Liberation kidnapped a Ronald McDonald statue from a Sacramento, California, McDonald's. They sent a ransom note which read: "Mr. McDonald is safe, unharmed, and, I assure you, entirely unable to escape." The note demanded that McDonald's give a free box of cookies to any child under eight who visited the restaurant on Christmas Eve.

"This is not a hoax," said the note. "If any qualified child is refused cookies, Ronald dies."

The note came with a photo of a blindfolded Ronald McDonald, a stick of dynamite hanging from his neck. A note on the wall behind the statue read: "Do as they say or I'm McHistory."

This is not the only case of a crime involving the theft of a restaurant statue. In Iron Mountain, Michigan, someone absconded with a Big Boy restaurant statue and whisked it off to Niagara, Wisconsin.

Creating Tables

It's easy to create simple tables in SunOS. Below is an example of a table that contains design elements you often use in tables.

	PHONE LIST	
Names	**Phone Numbers**	**Contact**
Sun Support	800-872-4786	Ann
Bookware	415-967-8283	Steve
SYBEX	510-523-8233	George

Here is the combination of formatting entries and text that was used to create this table.

```
.TS
tab(/);
c s s
l l l.
Phone List

Names/Phone Numbers/Contact

Sun Support/800-872-4786/Ann
Bookware/415-967-8283/Steve
SYBEX/510-523-8233/George
.TE
```

The following list explains the formatting entries used to create the table.

OPTION OR MACRO	RESULT
.TS (table start)	Begins the table.
tab (/)	Indicates that / will be used to delimit columns (the delimiting character will not be printed).

OPTION OR MACRO	RESULT
c s s	Specifies a table of three columns beginning with a centered header. (Only the `Phone List` line will be created because it is the only one without column delimiters.) You cannot use the letter **s** in the first column because the **s** indicates entries from a previous column span the following column.
l l l.	Indicates that each column is left aligned (include period).
.TE	Ends the table.

When you want to print a table, use the **tbl** command as follows:

```
tbl tablename | troff | lp
```

Below are some common formatting entries that were not used in the example table.

OPTION	RESULT
r	Right-adjusted column entry.
n	Numerical column entry.
s	Span previous column's text across this column.

The following list contains options you can use to affect the whole table.

OPTION	RESULT
allbox	Boxes each entry in the table in a box.
box	Frames the entire table with a box.
center	Centers the table on the page.
doublebox	Frames the table with a double line box.
linesize(n)	Sets the table text to n point size.
tab(x)	Uses x to separate table entries.

You can combine these options on one line. For example, an option line added after the .TS request might be

```
center allbox tab(/);
```

Be sure to end your option line with a semicolon, otherwise the system will display an error message.

Running Print Jobs

An essential capability of SunOS is to print files. The following section teaches you how to print files, check the status of print jobs, and cancel print jobs. Printers are often in high demand in a networking environment because multiple terminals are often connected to a small number of printers. To keep things running smoothly, SunOS usually feeds printing jobs to printers on a first-come, first-served basis. A *printing job* is a term for a file sent to be printed as hard copy (on paper). Printing jobs are sent to a print *queue*, which stores the printing jobs in memory in the order they're received.

Most networks have multiple printers available for you to choose from. Each printer in a network has a unique name. The **destination** acts as an address for sending your printing jobs to a specific printer. Usually, your system also has a *default printer*. If you don't specify a particular printer when sending a print job, the print job is automatically sent to the default printer. The command syntax for printing a file to the default printer is

```
lp filename
```

If you want to use a different printer than the default printer, you need to specify the printer after the **lp** command using the *-d destination* option. The command syntax for printing a file to a printer other than the default printer is

```
lp -d destination filename
```

The **lp** (line printer) command instructs SunOS to send to the print queue a copy of the file to be printed. The *-d destination* option requests the specific printer by its assigned name. For example, if you wanted to send a copy of the file `report` to the printer at a destination named `laserwriter`, you would type the following:

```
lp -d laserwriter report
```

Printing nroff and troff Files

If you want to print a document formatted using `nroff` and `-ms` macro requests to a line printer, enter

```
nroff -ms | lp
```

As explained earlier in this chapter, the `troff` formatting program is designed to format files for printing on typesetters or laser printers. If you're printing a file to a PostScript printer, you need to run the file through the `dpost` filter. To print a document formatted using `troff` and `-ms` macro requests to a PostScript printer, enter

```
troff -ms filename | dpost | lp -d destination
```

N O T E

The `dpost` filter file is stored in the `/usr/lib/lp/postscript` directory. In most cases, your system administrator will have set up your `.profile` file to include this path. If you cannot access the dpost filter, see Chapter 15, "Customizing Solaris," to add the path to your `.profile` file.

Printing Multiple-Page Files

SunOS provides a handy page formatting and printing utility called `pr`. The `pr` command separates text into pages and adds a left-aligned header to each page. The header starts printing at the second page and includes the current date, time, file name, and page number. The general command syntax for the `pr` command is

```
pr filename(s) | lp -d destination
```

You can print multiple files using the **pr** command by adding a space between each file name. For more information on the **pr** command, see Part IV, "Command Reference."

Printing Multiple Copies of a File

You can easily print multiple copies of the same file adding the **-n#** option to the **lp** command, where **#** is the number of copies you want. For example, suppose you want to use the default printer to print seven copies of the file **ratings**. Type the following:

```
lp -n7 ratings
```

Sending Multiple Files to the Printer

You can specify several files to be printed by separating file names with a space. For example, to print the files **report1** and **report2** on the default printer, type

```
lp report1 report2
```

Printing the Output of a Command

As with most SunOS utilities, you can connect the output of a command to the input of the print command using a pipe (|). For example, you can instruct SunOS to list the contents of a directory using the **ls** command, then send the output of the **ls** command to the printer as follows:

```
ls | lp
```

Getting Notified When a Print Job Is Done

You can instruct the print command to let you know when the printer has finished printing your job. When your print job is finished, at the next system prompt the message `You have mail` is displayed. To be notified that a print job is completed, type the command

```
lp -m filename
```

The `-m` option instructs the print command to send you a mail message at the next system prompt after your printed job has been completed. If you're entering commands in a Shell or Command Tool, you can instruct the print command to send a message to your console window by entering

```
lp -w filename
```

Changing or Suppressing the Banner Page

Each printing job is preceded by a single page called a banner page. The *banner page* contains information about the printer and the user issuing the print job. You can add a title line of up to eight characters to the banner page. Suppose you wanted to add the title "nocharge" to the banner page for the file **case101**. Enter the command

```
lp -t nocharge case101
```

If you want your title to include more than one word (that is, if there is a space between characters), such as "Perry Mason's Pro Bono Publico Case 101," you must place the title in quotes: `lp -t "Perry Mason's Pro Bono Publico Case 101" case101`.

In order to suppress the printing of the banner page, your system administrator must have set up the printer to allow the **-nobanner** option. If your printer is set up to print files without a banner page, enter

```
lp -o nobanner filename
```

to print the file without a banner page.

Checking the Printer Status

The `lpstat` command is used to display the status of the available printers, the status of print jobs, and the print request ID numbers of your print jobs in case you need to cancel a print job. To display a list of the printers that are configured on your system, type

```
lpstat -s
```

This displays a message similar to the following:

```
scheduler is running
system default destination: bedrock
system for dodge: longbranch
system for lapd: dragnet
```

If you want to check to see what printer is set up as the default printer, simply use the -d option. To see which printers are accepting requests, use `lpstat -a`. To list your printing jobs waiting in the default print queue, enter the command

```
lpstat -o
```

To determine how busy a printer is by viewing how many print jobs are waiting in a printer queue, add the *-p printername* option to the `lpstat` command, where *printername* is the name of the printer you want to check on. You can see all the characteristics for a printer by including the -1 option after the *-p printername* option. For example, entering

```
lpstat -p bedrock -1
```

displays the following listing for the PostScript printer named bedrock:

```
printer bedrock is idle. enabled since Thu Jan 23 15:42:01 PDT
1993. available.
    Form mounted:
    Content types: PS
    Printer Types: PS
    Description: Epson EPL-7500 Bldg. #1
    Connection: direct
    Interface: /usr/lib/lp/model/standard
    After fault: continue
```

```
Users allowed:
   (none)
Forms allowed:
   (none)
Banner not required
Character sets
Default pitch:
Default page size: 80 wide 66 long
Default port settings:
```

Removing Printer Jobs

If you decide not to print a job after sending it to the default printer, you can remove it from the queue by typing the `cancel` command, followed by the job number, as shown below:

`cancel jobnumber`

You can find out the job number by first typing the command `lpstat` to list the print jobs and their assigned job numbers. If your printing job is already printing, the printing job isn't terminated. You can remove all your printing jobs from the default printer queue by typing the following:

`cancel -u username`

where *username* is your login ID.

T I P

If you have only one print job in a print queue to remove, it's easier to use cancel *-u username* than to find the job number, and use the command `cancel jobnumber`.

Command Summary

The following lists the commands and requests covered in this chapter and their functions.

COMMAND OR REQUEST	RESULT
.ad	Returns to justified right margin.
.B	Boldfaces text.
.bp	Ends text at the bottom of a page and begins it at the top of the next page.
.ds	Changes the default setting of headers and footers.
.fi	Restarts line filling.
.I	Changes type to italic.
.in *n*	Indents text *n* spaces.
.IP *n*	Indents a paragraph *n* spaces after a hanging indent.
.KE	Signifies end of text to keep on one page.
.KS	Keeps a specified block of text on one page.
.LG	Makes font two points larger.
.LP	Formats text into left-block paragraphs.
lpstat	Lists your print jobs waiting in the default print queue.
lp	Sends a copy of the file to be printed to the print queue.
cancel	Removes a print job from the print queue.

COMMAND OR REQUEST	RESULT
.ls *n*	Inserts *n* spaces between each line.
.na	Produces a nonjustified margin.
.ND	Eliminates date in headers when using the -ms macro package.
.ne *n*	Keeps *n* lines on one page.
.nf	Stops the line-filling process.
.NL	Returns font to normal size.
.nr PO *n*i	Offsets left margin *n* inches.
nroff	Text formatting command used with line printers.
1C	Returns from two-column to single-column text.
pl *n*	Changes the page length to n inches.
.PP	Formats text into standard paragraphs.
pr	Allows user to format and print multiple-page files.
.ps *n*	Changes the size of the font indicated by *n*.
.QP	Formats text into block quotes.
.R	Returns to normal typeface.
RC	Begins the second column of two-column text.
.RE	Moves the indent to the left five spaces.
.RS	Shifts indent five spaces to the right.
.SM	Makes font two points smaller.
.sp *n*	Inserts n line spaces in text.
.ta	Sets tabs.
.TE	Indicates the end of a table.

COMMAND OR REQUEST	RESULT
ti n	Temporarily indents a line n spaces.
troff	Text formatting command used with typesetters and laser printers.
.TS	Indicates the beginning of a table.
.2C	Begins the first column of two-column text.
>UL *word*	Underlines a word in a sentence.
.ul *n*	Underlines *n* words.

Multitasking with SunOS

SUNOS is a multitasking operating system, which means you can run several commands simultaneously. Up until now, all the commands in this book have been run one at a time in the *foreground*, so the results appear directly on your screen. Running jobs in the *background* allows you to run commands on your screen while other commands are being processed in the background. Both SunOS and the Korn shell provide you with a collection of commands for managing commands running in the background. This chapter helps you squeeze the maximum power out of Solaris by explaining how to run and manage commands running in the background.

Running a Command in the Background

Certain commands, such as formatting and printing a long text document with **troff**, take a long time to run. This type of time-consuming program is best run in the background so it doesn't tie up your screen and keep you from doing other work. To run a command as a background job, add the ampersand (**&**) at the end of the command line before you press Return. For example, typing

```
troff -ms schedules | lp &
```

instructs SunOS to format the file **schedules** using the **troff** program and run the job in the background. When you run a command in the background, the Korn shell executes the command and displays a job identification number similar to this:

[1]   183

Redirecting a Background Command's Output

A background job normally sends the result of its processing to the screen unless you redirect its output. Having the output of a background command appear on your screen while you are entering another command can be confusing. To redirect the output of a background command to a file, use the > redirection symbol. For example, entering

```
find . -name "chap*" -print > chapters &
```

redirects the standard output of the `find` command to a file named `chapters`. For more information on redirecting output, see Chapter 10, "Improving Your Command-Line Productivity."

Another way of preventing a background job from sending its output to your screen is to restrict writing to your terminal by entering

```
stty tostop
```

When the `stty tostop` command is activated, the `stty tostop` program suspends any background program that attempts to write to the screen. When the job has output, a message appears. For example, executing the command `find.-name "chap*" -print &` after issuing the `stty tostop` command, displays

```
[1] + Stopped (tty output) find . -name "chap*" -print &
```

To display the find command's output, you need to bring the job back into the foreground by typing

```
fg
```

To remove the screen output restriction, type

```
stty -tostop
```

Keeping Error Messages from Displaying on Your Screen

By default, standard error messages appear on your screen so you can find out immediately if there is a problem with the execution of the background command. For example, if you searched the entire system using the `find` command, error messages appear for directories that you do not have permission to read. To keep error messages from displaying on your screen, redirect the standard error as well as standard output either to the same file or to a different one, as shown in the following example.

```
find / -name "chap*" -print > chapters 2> errors &
```

This command line runs the `find` command in the background and saves standard output in the `chapters` file and any error messages in the file named `errors`.

To eliminate the error output, redirect it to `/dev/null`. The `/dev/null` is a device that acts like a trash can. Sending the information to this device causes the information to disappear. For example, enter

```
find / -name "chap*" > chapters 2> /dev/null &
```

to run the `find` command, send its output to `chapters`, and discard any error messages.

Controlling Your Jobs

The Korn shell provides job control commands for managing commands running in the background. Using the Korn shell you can list, suspend, resume, terminate, and switch jobs between the foreground and background. The Korn shell normally notifies you when background jobs change status, such as when a job terminates.

If you are using the Bourne shell, you will need to start a special shell, known as the job shell, to manage commands running in the background. To start the job shell, enter `jsh -i` at the system prompt.

Checking the Status of a Job

To check the status of jobs placed in the background, use the Korn shell's `jobs` command. The `jobs` command indicates if a job is done, running, or stopped. Typing `jobs` displays a list similar to the following:

```
[2]     Stopped   troff -ms yearend report93 &
```

```
[3]   -  Stopped   find / -name "a*" &
[4]   +  Stopped   vi program1.c &
[5]      Running   lp -t legal fees &
```

The first column identifies the job with a number in brackets. *Job numbers* are assigned by the Korn shell for jobs generated at your terminal. Job numbers are unique and relevant only to your work on the system. The current job is indicated by a plus sign (+), and the next job after that is indicated by a minus sign (–) to the right of the first column. If no jobs are running, entering **jobs** simply returns you to the shell prompt.

Job Names

In most cases, you refer to a job by its job number; however, the Korn shell gives you several alternatives to refer to a job. The Korn shell uses the percent sign to identify jobs. The following lists Korn shell job name equivalents.

% *n*	The letter *n* indicates the job number you want to refer to.
%+ or %%	The current job.
%–	The previous job.
%*string*	Job name that begins with *string*.
%?*string*	Job name matches part or all of *string*.

Suspending and Restarting Jobs

You can suspend a job you're currently working on in the foreground by typing Control-z. Using this command suspends the processing of the program, places the program in the background, and assigns the stopped program a job number. To resume the program in the background, enter **bg** %*n*, where *n* is the job number you want to resume. You can also stop a background job by typing **stop** %*n*, where *n* is the job number you want to stop. The **stop** command, like Control-z, suspends but doesn't terminate the command.

Logging Out of SunOS with Stopped Jobs

If you try to log out of SunOS while a job is stopped in the background, SunOS displays the warning message `There are stopped jobs`. Typing the `exit` command again logs you out and terminates any stopped jobs in the background. All other (unstopped) background jobs will be terminated when you log out. If you want to view which jobs are stopped before you log out, type `jobs`.

Switching Jobs between Foreground and Background

To move a running job from the background to the foreground, use the `fg` command followed by a percent sign and the job number. For example, typing `fg %2` moves job 2 into the foreground. Typing `fg` without a job number brings the current job (marked by the plus sign (+) in the `jobs` list) to the foreground.

Suppose you have a program running in the foreground and need to perform another task on your screen. You can quickly place the foreground command into the background. First, press Control-z, which automatically stops the program and places it in the background. Next, type `bg` to resume running the program in the background. To resume a stopped job in the background, type `bg %n`, where *n* is the job number. For example, typing `bg %4` instructs SunOS to resume running job number 4 in the background.

If a command running in the background needs a response from the user, the job is stopped. You need to use the `fg` command to bring the command to the foreground and respond to the command. For example, if you enter `rm -i backup* &`, the screen displays

```
[1]   375
rm: remove backup1: (y/n)?
```

Press Return to display the Korn shell prompt and enter `fg`. Press Return again and you can answer the `rm` command's prompts.

NOTE Remember, any time you need to know a job number, type jobs for a listing of background jobs and their respective numbers.

If you start a background job from a directory different from your working directory and bring that job to the foreground, SunOS changes your working directory to that directory. SunOS warns you when the system changes your working directory as a result of bringing a background job to the foreground.

Terminating Jobs

Any time you accidentally execute a wrong command or realize you don't want a particular program to run, you can terminate the job using the kill command. To terminate a program running in the background, type kill %*n*, where *n* is the number of the job you want to terminate. For example, typing kill %3 terminates job number three. Some programs need more than the kill command to be terminated. Strengthen the killing power of the kill command with this syntax:

```
kill -9 %n
```

To terminate a program running in the foreground, press Control-c. You can also terminate a foreground program by pressing Control-z to suspend it and move it to the background. Then use the kill command to terminate the program. The following lists essential job control commands.

COMMAND	DESCRIPTION
command &	Creates a background job.
Control-z	Stops the job you're working on.
jobs	Lists both stopped and background jobs, assigning them job numbers in brackets; for example, [1]. The current job is identified with a + and the next job with a -. With the -1 option, the listing includes the PID number. (PID numbers are explained in this chapter.)

COMMAND	DESCRIPTION
`fg`	Brings the current job (marked with a + in the jobs list) into the foreground, starting the job if it's stopped.
`fg %n`	Brings job *n* into the foreground, starting the job if it's stopped.
`bg`	Puts the current job (marked with a + in the jobs list) into the background, starting the job if it's stopped.
`bg %n`	Resumes job *n* in the background.
`stop %`	Stops the current job in the background.
`stop %n`	Stops background job *n*.
`kill %n`	Terminates background job `%n`.
`stty tostop`	Suspends background jobs that write to the screen.
`stty - tostop`	Allows background jobs to write to the screen.

Waiting for a Background Job to Finish Executing

If you need the results of a background command before you can continue working, use the `wait` command to wait for the background job to finish. The Korn shell keeps track of the commands it is performing. By entering

```
wait $1
```

the Korn shell waits until the most recent background job is finished executing. You can specify another background job by entering the job ID after the `wait` command. For example, enter

```
wait %243
```

to wait for the background job with the job ID of 243 to finish executing. If you omit a job number or the $1 argument, the Korn shell waits for all your background jobs to finish executing.

Running Commands in the Background after Exiting

By default, commands running in the background are terminated when you log out. You can ensure that a job is completed even after logging out. To continue running a command in the background even after logging out, use the `nohup` (no hang up) command. The `nohup` command causes standard output and standard error to be sent to `nohup.out`. For example, entering

```
nohup spell folio
```

and issuing the `exit` command to log out ensures that the `spell` command continues checking the `folio` file and redirects any misspellings to the `nohup.out` file. The `nohup` command only works with a single command. If you entered the command line `nohup spell folio > mispelled | sort | lp` then logged out, only the output of the spell command is redirected to the file `mispelled`. In this instance, the `nohup` command does not apply to the `sort` and `lp` commands. However, you can enter multiple `nohup` commands, or you can place all the commands you want to execute in a file and enter

```
nohup ksh filename
```

This executes all the commands in the file you specified and ensures that each command is not terminated when you log out.

Displaying and Terminating Processes

When you execute a command, the command and the data that it is working with are referred to as an active *process*. Just as the Korn shell includes job control commands, SunOS includes a collection of commands for managing processes.

Every command you run using SunOS, whether in the foreground or background, is assigned a unique *process ID* (PID) number. PID numbers are assigned by SunOS for all processes throughout the system. SunOS juggles its time and resources amongst the various processes currently running and uses the PID number to track the progress, current status, amount of time, and percentage of available memory each process uses.

Checking the Status of a Process

To see what processes you have running, type **ps** and press Return. SunOS takes a snapshot of the active processes and displays a list of processes generated from your account, similar to the one below:

```
PID   TTY      TIME   COMD
227   PTS/11   0:11   ksh
229   PTS/11   0:00   ps
```

In addition to showing the PID number for each process generated from your account, the **ps** command also lists the terminal where it originated, its current status, processing time used, and the command it's performing.

If you are using the Korn shell, you can list the PID numbers for running jobs by entering

```
jobs -l
```

Using the -l (long) option displays both job and PID numbers for all your background jobs, similar to the following:

```
[2]      194  Stopped    troff -ms yearend report93
[3]   -  207  Stopped    find / -name "a*"
[4]   +  211  Stopped    vi program1.c
[5]      243  Running    lp -t legal fees
```

Here the PID numbers are given in the third column. Alternatively, you can display the PID numbers of all jobs by entering **jobs -p**.

You can report on all processes that are being run on your system by typing

```
ps -e
```

This displays a listing similar to the following:

```
PID  TTY      TIME   COMD
0    ?        0:03   sched
1    ?        0:01   init
2    ?        0:00   pageout
3    ?        0:01   fsflush
173  ?        0:00   sac
150  ?        0:00   sendmail
174  console  0:01   ksh
110  ?        0:02   inetd
96   ?        0:00   rpcbind
88   ?        0:00   in.route
98   ?        0:00   keyserv
102  ?        0:00   kerbd
113  ?        0:00   statd
115  ?        0:011  ockd
126  ?        0:00   automoun
141  ?        0:011  psched
133  ?        0:00   cron
149  ?        0:001  Net
159  ?        0:00   syslogd
179  console  0:04   ps
176  ?        0:01   ttymon
```

For more information on finding the status of a process, you can add the -1 long option. Entering

```
ps -el
```

displays a listing similar to the following:

```
F   S UID  PID PPID   C PRI  NI  ADDR      SZ  WCHAN      TTY TIME   COMD
39  T 0    0    0     80 0    SYf00b8eb0    0              ?  0:03   sched
28  S 0    1    0     80 1    20ff113800   50ff1139d0      ?  0:01   init
39  S 0         2     01 0    SYff113000   0f00b69a0       ?  0:00   pageout
39  S 0    3    0     80 0    SYff112800   0f00bbbac       ?  0:01 fsflush
28  S 0    173  1     32 1    20ff19f800  224ff28b24e      ?  0:00     sac
28  S 0    150  1     24 1    20ff27a800  300ff1d6d4e      ?  0:00sendmail
28  S5000 174  11    63 1    20ff1a0800  254ff1a0870console0:01    ksh
28  S 0    110  1     80 1    20ff214000  277f00b8c80      ?  0:02   inetd
28  S 0    96   1     47 1    20ff222800  299f00b8c80      ?  0:00 rpcbind
28  S 0    88   1     19 1    20ff213000  240f00b8c80      ?  0:00in.route
28  S 0    98   1      5 1    20ff222000  253f00b8c80      ?  0:00 keyserv
28  S 0    102  1     34 1    20ff21f800  289f00b8c80      ?  0:00   kerbd
28  S 0    113  1     45 1    20ff235000  280f00b8c80      ?  0:00   statd
28  S 0    115  1     80 1    20ff240800  375f00b8c80      ?  0:01   lockd
28  S 0    126  1      8 1    20ff23f000  247f00b8c80      ?  0:00automoun
28  S 0    141  1     80 1    20ff19f000  551f00b8c80      ?  0:01 lpsched
28  S 0    133  1     26 1    20ff26f800  139ff1a6f4e      ?  0:00    cron
```

```
28 S    0 149  141   29   1  20ff27c000 269f00b8c80    ? 0:00   lpNet
28 S    0 159    1    61   1  20ff288000 287f00b8c80    ? 0:00 syslogd
28 05000 180  174   20   1  20ff205000 133        console0:00      ps
28 S    0 176  173   54   1  20ff286000 251ff2861d0    ? 0:01  ttymon
```

The following lists a few key fields, you can check to find processes that may be hogging up your system resources. If necessary, use the kill command to terminate the processes. Killing a process is explained in the following section.

- Check the UID field for lots of processes owned by the same user. This may result from someone running a script that starts a lot of background jobs without waiting for any of the jobs to terminate.

- Check the S column for the letter Z. The letter Z, known as flag Z, stands for a zombie process. A *zombie* process is a process that has been killed but refuses to die. When you notice this, you should either become a superuser and kill the process or let your system administrator know. Be sure to double check this listing because some zombies do die when a device, such as a printer or tape drive, changes status.

- Check the TIME and C field for processes that have accumulated a large amount of CPU time. You can check the start time (STIME) of a process by entering ps -f. Processes with long time entries might be runaway processes that progressively use more and more CPU time. It is also possible that the process might be in an endless loop.

- Check the SZ field for processes that consume a large percentage of memory.

Terminating a Process

Any time you accidentally execute a wrong command or realize you don't want a particular program to run, you can terminate the command using the kill command with the PID number. First type the ps command to determine the PID number. Once you know the PID number, type kill, followed by the PID number. For example, type

```
kill 3193
```

terminates the command running in the background with the assigned PID number 3193. You can kill multiple processes by entering multiple PID numbers as arguments to the `kill` command. For example, type

```
kill 3193 3199 3200
```

to terminate processes 3193, 3199, and 3200.

In order to kill a process, SunOS sends the process a signal. A *signal* is a brief message that SunOS uses to communicate with a process. When you execute the `kill` command, SunOS sends signal 15 to the process you have specified. Depending on the process you are trying to kill, signal 15 may not terminate the process. If the process does not terminate using the `kill` command alone, use the command

```
kill -9 PIDnumber
```

to terminate a process. Signal 9 sends an unconditional kill signal to the process.

Scheduling Processes

Whether you're logged in at the terminal or not, you can execute commands at a time and date you specify, using one of SunOS's scheduling commands. The **at** command executes commands at a time and date you specify and sends the results of the process via electronic mail to whomever you indicate. The syntax of the **at** command is

```
at time date increment
```

NOTE Your system administrator may restrict access to the at command. If you cannot use the at command on your system, check with your system administrator.

You specify the time for the **at** command as a one-, two-, or four-digit number. One- and two-digit numbers specify an hour, while four-digit numbers specify an hour and a minute. The **at** program assumes a 24-hour clock unless you place am or pm immediately after the number, in which case at uses a 12-hour clock. You can also use the word now in place of a time. If you do use now, you must also specify a date or an increment of time. An acceptable increment is a number followed by one of the following (plural or singular): minutes, hours, days, weeks, months, or years. For example, typing

```
at now + 30 minutes
```

means execute the command 30 minutes from the time the command is entered. You can also use the word next to specify when a command will be executed. For example

```
at now next week
```

means execute the command at the current time one week from now.

If you don't specify a date, at executes the job the same day if the hour you specify in time is greater than the current hour. If the hour is less than the current hour, at executes the process the next day. You can abbreviate the days of the week to the first three letters. To specify a date, use the name of the month followed by the number of the day in the month. You can also follow the month and day with a year.

Performing a Process at a Later Time

Suppose you want to send the text file fired.ltr to a user named bfife, but you want to hold its release until 8 a.m. the next morning. The following four steps demonstrate how to send the file at 8 a.m. the following day and let someone else know when the dirty deed has been done.

1. Type at 8am and press Return. If you are using the at command before 8 a.m. on the day before you're sending this file, you need to specify the day.

2. Enter mail -s 'Greetings from Personnel' bfife < fired.let then press Return. This command instructs SunOS to mail the file fired.let to the user bfife.

3. Enter echo 'Message sent' | mail -s Message ihangman then press Return. This command instructs SunOS to send a message to ihangman, confirming the file fired.let was sent to bfife.

4. Press Control-d to end the at command session. SunOS displays <EOT> and ends the at command session, displays a job confirmation message, then returns to the SunOS prompt, as shown in the following example:

```
$ at 8am
mail -s 'Greetings from Personnel' bfife < fired.let
echo 'Message sent' | mail -s Message ihangman
<EOT>
job 31629 at Thu Feb 22 08:00:00 1999
$
```

Displaying the Processes to Be Performed

Any at commands you enter are stored in a queue, a temporary storage file, until it comes time to execute the commands. The atq (at queue) command lists at command jobs that are queued for execution. The atq command lists the at jobs chronologically. You can list another user's at jobs by specifying the user's name after the atq command. By using the -c option you can display the jobs in the order they were created, rather than when the command is scheduled to be executed.

Running a Batch of Commands in the Background

The batch command is similar to the at command, except batch executes multiple commands one after another, waiting for the previous command to complete. Using the batch command ensures that you don't hog up the system's resources by running several background jobs simultaneously. The batch command can take input from a file name or you can specify commands. For example, entering

```
batch
```

```
find / -name "resume" -print
sort employees > colist
troff -ms manuscript
```

and pressing Control-d begins processing the commands. SunOS responds with a message similar to the following:

```
Warning: commands will be executed using /usr/bin/sh
job 715773735.a at Sun Sep 6 03:09:19 1993
```

The commands are then executed in the background and the results are sent to you via mail.

Removing at and batch Commands

The `atrm` (at remove) command removes jobs that were created with the `at` or `batch` command, but have not yet been executed. The `atrm` removes each job number you specify and/or all jobs, provided that you own the indicated jobs. Use the `-a` option to remove all unexecuted `at` jobs that you created. To have `atrm` prompt you before removing a job, use the `-i` (interactive) option. To suppress all information regarding the removal of the specified job, use the `-f` (force) option. The following example prompts for confirmation before removing jobs created using the `at` command for the user `rpetrie`:

```
atrm -i rpetrie
```

Scheduling Repeated Tasks

The `cron` command lets you run programs that you want to execute repeatedly at preset intervals you specify. This command is useful for doing timed backups, file transfers, mail forwarding, or file cleanup and maintenance. The commands that `cron` runs are listed in a file named `crontab`. You don't actually enter the `cron` command. Instead the system administrator activates the `cron` command, which executes the commands listed in the `crontab` file.

To enter the commands and scheduling information into the `crontab` file, use the following format for each command you want to run.

```
Min Hrs Day_of_Month Month Day_of_Week Command
```

The Time options are as follows:

FIELD	OPTIONS
Min	0–59
Hour	0–23 (0 is midnight)
Month	1–12
Day of Month	0–31
Day of Week	0–6 (0 is Sunday)

Each field entry is separated by a space or tab, and individual entries can be combined for repetition and separated by spaces. For example, if you want to remove core files from your home directory at 12:15 p.m. on the first day of every month, in your `crontab` file, type

```
0 12,15 1 * * find I / -name "core" -exec rm {} \;
```

The comma after the hour field specifies minute values past the hour. The asterisk (*) indicates that the schedule is valid for all possible values in the field. If you want to restrict a command to run only between a time interval, such as the hours of 9:00 a.m. and 5:00 p.m., separate the beginning and ending field entries with a hyphen. For example, the `crontab` entry

```
0 9-16  *  *  1-5 find I / -name "core" -exec rm {} \;
```

restricts the command to be run only on Monday through Friday between the hours 9:00 a.m. and 5:00 p.m. Using the `1-5` entry is the same as entering the values as 1,2,3,4,5.

To edit the `crontab` file or to create the entries, enter

```
crontab -e username
```

This starts the `ed` editor and loads or creates your personal `crontab` file for editing. For information on using the `ed` editor, open the Command or Shell Tool and at the prompt, enter `man ed`. Standard output from the timed commands, if it is not redirected to a file, is collected and mailed to you upon completion of the job.

Changing the Priority of a Command

The `nice` command is used to lower the scheduling priority of a command. This command is helpful, especially to other users, when you want to run a command that makes large demands of the system. If you don't need the output of a command right away, change the priority level using the following format:

```
nice -increment command
```

The default priority is set to 10. To lower the priority of a command, enter an increment higher than 10 but less than 20. For example, enter

```
nice -19 grep exam * &
```

to lower the priority of a `grep` command and run the command in the background. The priority of a command can only be increased by a super-user. A higher priority is indicated by a double minus sign. For example, the command

```
nice --10 grep exam * &
```

increases the priority of the `grep` command by 10 units.

Suspending the Execution of a Command

The `sleep` command suspends the execution of a command for a specified number of seconds. For example, entering

```
sleep 600;echo "\007 Call tech support again"
```

suspends the execution of the echo command for 10 minutes.

Command Summary

The following lists the commands covered in this chapter and their functions.

`&`	Executes commands in the background.
`at`	Executes commands at specified time and date.
`atrm`	Removes jobs created using the `at` and `batch` commands.
`batch`	Executes multiple commands in the background.
`bg`	Executes a job in the background (Korn shell).
`exit`	Logs you out and terminates any stopped jobs in the background.
`fg`	Executes a job in the foreground.
`kill`	Terminates the execution of a command.
`nice`	Changes the priority of a command.
`nohup`	Continues executing a command even after logging out.
`ps`	Lists processes currently running.
`sleep`	Suspends the execution of a command.
`wait`	Waits for background jobs to finish.

PART THREE

Personalizing Forms and Reports

CHAPTER

15

Customizing Solaris

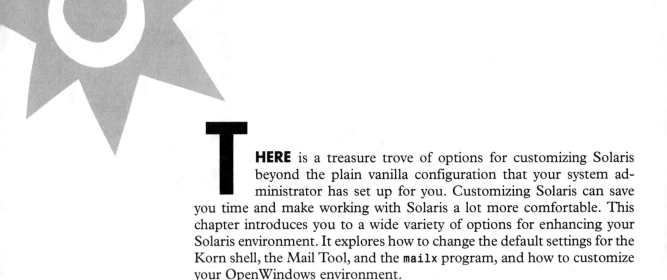

THERE is a treasure trove of options for customizing Solaris beyond the plain vanilla configuration that your system administrator has set up for you. Customizing Solaris can save you time and make working with Solaris a lot more comfortable. This chapter introduces you to a wide variety of options for enhancing your Solaris environment. It explores how to change the default settings for the Korn shell, the Mail Tool, and the `mailx` program, and how to customize your OpenWindows environment.

Working with Variables

A *variable* is a named memory location in which a value is stored. A number of variables provided by the Korn shell allow you to customize your working environment. Variables that affect your Solaris environment are commonly referred to as *environment variables*. For example, `HOME` is an environment variable that keeps track of your home directory. Some variables are automatically set by the Korn shell, some have a default value if not set, while others have no value unless specifically set.

After you log in, the Korn shell looks for the master profile file `/etc/profile`. The `/etc/profile` file contains *predefined variables* settings. Some of these variables are added by your system administrator. For example, a common predefined variable is `noclobber`. The `noclobber` variable ensures that you don't overwrite existing files when you use the `>` ("to") redirection symbol. All the customization options in this chapter can be changed on a temporary basis, so you can test out the option, or you can modify the related initialization file to permanently save your changes.

Storing Variables

If you enter a variable at the command line it is only effective for the current session. In most cases you will store variables in your .profile file. The .profile file is a hidden file stored in your home directory. After executing the master /etc/profile file, the Korn shell reads and executes the .profile file in your home directory. This .profile file contains your local environment settings, such as which directories are searched for commands and your default permissions settings. Modifying or adding a variable to your .profile file changes your Solaris environment for future sessions. You can also create your own variables to avoid repeatedly typing long strings of characters. The following sections explain how to list variable settings and how to change variable settings for a single session or permanently.

Listing Variables

To display your current environment variables, at the prompt, type

```
env
```

and press Return. A listing similar to the following appears:

```
HOME=/export/home/rpetrie
HISTORY=100
HZ=100
IFS=
LOGNAME=rpetrie
MAIL=/var/mail/rpetrie
MAILCHECK=600
MANPATH=/usr/openwin/share/man:/usr/man
MANSECTS=\1:1m:1c:1f:1s:1b:2:\3:3c:3i:3n:3m:3k:3g:3e:3x11:3xt:3w:
3b:9:4:5:7:8
OPTIND=1
OPENWINHOME=/usr/openwin
PATH=/usr/openwin/bin:/usr/bin:/bin:/etc:/usr/lib/lp/postscript
LD_LIBRARY_PATH=/usr/openwin/lib
PS1='$ '
PS2='> '
SHELL=/bin/ksh
TERM=sun
TZ=US/Pacific
XINTRC=/usr/openwin/lib/Xinitrc
```

The `env` command only lists the environment settings that have been set in the master `/etc/profile` file and the `.profile` file in your home directory. You can list all your Korn shell variables using the `set` command.

Changing Variables

A variable is set using a variable name, an equals sign (=), and what you want the variable set to. If you set a variable at the command line, it is only available during the current session. You must change your `.profile` file to make the variable setting effective the next time you log in. You can ignore variables in the `.profile` file by placing a pound (comment) sign (#) at the beginning of the line you want to ignore. You can also indicate multiple commands using the semicolon, just as you do when using the command line.

Before changing your `.profile` file, copy it to a file named `profile.bak` as a backup to ensure that you can return to your default settings. Once you have a backup of your original file, you can experiment with the settings and decide if you want to use the original. Because the `.profile` file is a hidden file, you may need to choose the `Customize` item from the File Manager's `View` menu to change the `Hidden Files` setting to `Show`. You cannot double-click on the `.profile` file to edit the file. Instead use the `Load` item from the Text Editor's `File` menu or drag and drop the `.profile` file into the Text Editor. Of course you can also edit the `.profile` file using the vi editor. Remember the global `profile` file with the file name `profile` is included in the `/etc` directory. The `/etc/profile` file can only be edited by your system administrator. The following lists some typical `.profile` file variable entries along with explanations.

VARIABLE	DESCRIPTION
`HOME=/home/`*`username`*	Sets the HOME variable to your default directory.
`HISTFILE=.`*`filename`*	Sets the file to store your last commands. If the HISTFILE variable is not set, the default `$HOME/` `.sh_history` file is used.

VARIABLE	DESCRIPTION
`HISTORY=25`	Sets the history mechanism to record the last 25 commands entered.
`IFS=`	Defines the internal field separator, normally the space or tab character, that is used to separate command words.
`LOGNAME=`*`username`*	Specifies your login name.
`MAIL=/var/mail/`*`username`*	Sets the path to your mailbox file for receiving mail.
`MAILCHECK=600`	Indicates in seconds how often your mailbox file is checked for mail.
`MANPATH=/usr/openwin/` `share/man:/usr/man`	Specifies which directories to check for online manual page files.

`MANSECTS=\1:1m:1c:1f:1s:1`
`b:2:\3:3c:3i:3n:3m:3k:3g:`
`3e:3x11:3xt:3w:`
`3b:9:4:5:7:8`
	Specifies the available sections of the online manual pages.

`OPENWINHOME=/usr/openwin`	Indicates the location of the OpenWindows directory.
`LD_LIBRARY_PATH=/usr/` `openwin/lib`	Specifies which directories to check for shared library files.
`SHELL=/bin/ksh`	Specifies the shell to use as the default.
`TERM=sun`	Sets your terminal type.

VARIABLE	DESCRIPTION
`TZ=US/Pacific`	Defines the time zone.
`XINITRC=/usr/openwin/` `lib/Xinitrc`	Specifies which initialization script to run when starting OpenWindows.

NOTE

Any variables you don't add to the `.profile` file are lost when you log out of SunOS. In order to store your variables so that you don't have to recreate them each time you log in, add them to the `.profile` file, where SunOS stores your default variable settings.

Displaying and Referencing Variables

In order to display or reference a variable, you need to inform the Korn shell that you are referring to the contents of a variable. The dollar sign ($) indicates that a variable is being referenced. To display an existing variable's current value, enter the **echo** command followed by a $ and the variable name. For example, using the **echo** command on the variable **$OPENWINHOME** as follows,

```
echo $OPENWINHOME
```

displays

```
/usr/openwin
```

or the directory that the **$OPENWINHOME** variable is set to (where your OpenWindows program files reside).

Saving Time with the PATH Variable

The PATH variable is the most important variable in your .profile file. This variable identifies directories that the system should look in for commands you enter at the command line. Regardless of your current directory, SunOS will search through the directories, from left to right, in your PATH variable for the command you are executing. The path statement needs to exist to allow access to SunOS commands. If a command is not found, the following error message is displayed:

```
/bin/ksh: command:  not found
```

The default PATH is /bin:/usr/bin. A colon (:) by itself in the PATH statement specifies to check the current directory. Enter $PATH to display your PATH variable. The following is an example of a typical path statement:

```
PATH=:/bin:/usr/bin:/etc/:usr/lib/lp/postscript
```

This path setting instructs Solaris to check the current directory :, the /bin directory, then /usr/bin, /etc/, and lastly the usr/lib/lp/ postscript. Note that each directory is separated by a space and each directory in the path statement is separated by a colon.

WARNING Adding several directories to your PATH can slow down system performance because each directory is checked each time you execute a command.

By default, the current directory is not checked. If you need to run a program that is in the current directory, use the period (.) to indicate the current directory. For example, if you changed to the /usr/openwin/bin directory to run the openwin command, you need to enter

```
./openwin
```

If you find that you are frequently changing to a directory to run a command, add the directory containing the command to your PATH variable. After adding the directory to your PATH variable, you can have your changes take effect without restarting OpenWindows. Make sure you are in your

HOME directory and at the shell prompt, enter

```
./.profile
```

Then you can execute the program without changing directories.

Simplifying Directory Navigation

The CDPATH variable contains a list of colon-separated directories to check when a full path name is not given to the cd command. Each directory in CDPATH is searched from left to right for a directory that matches the cd argument. A colon (:) alone in CDPATH stands for the current directory. For example, adding the line

```
CDPATH=:/home/ataylor:/usr/openwin
```

indicates to check the current directory first, /home/ataylor, then /usr/openwin, when cd is not given a full path name. Instead of typing cd /usr/openwin/lib, you can type cd lib; or to change directory to /home/ataylor/bin, you can type:

```
cd bin
```

By default the CDPATH variable is not set, so you will have to add it to your .profile file.

WARNING Make sure that only frequently used directories are included. If you add several directories to the CDPATH variable setting, your system's performance slows down because each directory is searched each time you perform the cd command.

Specifying How Long to Wait for Input

The TMOUT variable specifies the number of seconds that the Korn shell will wait for input before displaying a 60-second warning message and exiting. By default, the TMOUT variable is disabled (set to 0) meaning there is no time limit for the Korn shell to wait for input before displaying a 60-second warning message and exiting. This variable is usually set by the system administrator in the /etc/profile file. To set a 5-minute timer, add the following line to your .profile file.

```
TMOUT=300
```

Customizing Your Command Prompt

There are four prompt variables in the Korn shell. The prompt variable begins with PS and is followed by the number of the prompt. Typically you will only use PS1 and PS2; these contain the primary prompts displayed by the Korn shell when it is ready to read a command. If not specified, the default is $ for regular users, and # for superusers. PS2 specifies the secondary prompt string and is displayed whenever the Korn shell needs more input. For example, the PS2 variable is displayed when you press Return before a complete command has been given, or continue a command onto the next line with the \ character. If not specified, the default for PS2 is the > character, as shown in the following example.

```
$ print "This is the first line \
> This is the second"
```

You can change the prompt by assigning a new value to the PS1 variable. For example, entering

```
PS1="Your Wish, Master: "
```

displays a prompt message like this:

```
Your Wish, Master:
```

This is a cute prompt but not very helpful. To customize your prompt to display the current command number so you can easily reexecute commands and display the working directory, use the ! and the PWD variable.

```
PS1='!:${PWD} $ '
```

If you really want to display a ! in the prompt, type two exclamation points instead of one (!!). Using the single exclamation point changes the prompt to display the current history command number. The $PWD variable displays the current working directory. The following shows examples of changing directories using the prompt entry `PS1='!:${PWD} $ '`:

```
67:/home/ataylor $ cd /tmp
68:/tmp $ cd /usr/mail/ataylor
69:/usr/mail/ataylor $
```

Creating Your Own Variables

Besides the Korn shell's predefined variables in the `.profile` file, you can also create your own variables and add them to your `.profile` file. Remember, variables you create are lost when you log out, unless you add them to the `.profile` file. Be sure to make a backup copy of your `.profile` file to ensure that you can return to your default settings. Once you have a backup of your original file, you can experiment with the settings.

To assign the name and value of a variable, follow the variable name you want by an equal sign and the string of characters you want to assign to the variable. An example of setting a variable is to assign an abbreviation to a long path name. For example, the command

```
sounds=/usr/openwin/lib/locale/C/help/handbooks/sounds
```

allows you to type `$sounds` to indicate the `/usr/openwin/lib/locale/C/help/handbooks/sounds` directory.

WARNING

The Korn shell is sensitive to white space in variable settings. Don't add a space on either side of the equal sign. Only add a space in a variable setting that is within the double quotes.

Unsetting a Variable

The `unset` command lets you unset a variable. For example, if you have a variable named X and do not want the variable to be active, you can unset the variable as follows:

```
unset X
```

Storing Commands and Path Names as a Variable

Instead of typing out long, complicated commands or path names, you can store them as array variables. An array variable lets you specify one variable from a list of variables. You store a list of words as array variables by assigning each array variable a value using the following syntax:

```
variable[0]=value variable[1]=value variable[2]=value
variable[3]=value
```

For example, entering

```
opus[0]=frame/chaps opus[1]=frame/notes opus[2]=frame/docs
opus[3]=frame/tmp
```

specifies the directories `frame/chaps`, `frame/notes`, `frame/docs`, and `frame/tmp` as words in a variable list.

You specify a word in a variable list by entering a **$** and inserting the word and word number in curly braces; for instance, using the **opus** variable example above and entering the command

```
echo ${opus[2]}
```

displays the second value in the list of variables, which in the previous example is

```
frame/docs
```

To display the first and last array variable in the previous example, enter

```
echo ${opus[0]} ${opus[3]}
```

This displays `frame/chaps` and `frame/tmp`.

Output Substitution and Variables

Output substitution allows you to use the output of a command as an argument for another command. Using output substitution with other commands, such as echo, can make displaying the output of a command a lot less cryptic. To substitute a variable with command output, use the following format:

```
variable=$(command)
```

You can also surround a command with back quote marks (`); the command within the back quote marks or parentheses is executed and substitutes the resulting output for the variable. For example, suppose you have a list of file names stored in a file called printlist; entering lp `cat printlist` prints each file listed in the file printlist. The following example uses output substitution to assign the current date to a variable named day.

```
day=$(date)
echo The date and time is $day
```

displays

```
The date and time is Sat Jan 22 12:00:00 PDT 1994
```

The set command can be used to set the words of the command line to variables $0 through $9. This lets you extract selected pieces of data from the output of a command. For example, entering

```
set $(date)
```

sets the $0 variable so that it refers to the command. The $1 variable refers to Sat. Each following word is assigned the subsequent variable number. Therefore, by specifying the fifth word ($4) of the date command's output, you can extract the time. For example, entering

```
echo The time is $4 $5
```

displays

```
The time is 12:00:00 PDT
```

Customizing Korn Shell Options

The Korn shell has a number of options that specify your environment and control execution. There are options that cause background jobs to be run at a lower priority, prevent files from being overwritten with redirection operators, disable file name expansion, enable vi-style commands when editing the command line, and more.

Besides variables, the Korn shell lets you use a variety of options. Korn shell options are enabled with the `set -o` *option*, `set -`*option*, or `ksh -o` command. You can disable a command by entering the set `+o` *option* or set `+`*option* command. You can list settings to determine if they are on or off by entering

```
set -o
```

The first column lists the option name, and the second shows if the option is enabled or disabled, as shown in the following:

```
Current option settings
allexport       off
bgnice          on
emacs           off
errexit         off
gmacs           off
ignoreeof       off
interactive     on
keyword         off
markdirs        off
monitor         on
noexec          off
noclobber       off
noglob          off
nolog           off
nounset         off
privileged      off
restricted      off
trackall        off
verbose         off
```

```
vi              off
viraw           off
xtrace          off
```

As with variables, you can temporarily set an option from the command line. To permanently set an option, add it the `.profile` file in your home directory. Before changing your `.profile` file, be sure to copy it to a file named `.profile.bak` as a backup to ensure that you can return to your default settings. Once you have a backup of your original file, you can experiment with the settings and decide if you want to use the original. The following sections explain some common options you can use to customize the Korn shell.

Running Background Jobs at a Reduced Priority

The `bgnice` option runs in the background, saving you from having to run the `nice` command. When you enable the `bgnice` option, all background jobs are automatically run at a reduced priority, as if you had used the `nice` command to start them. To enable the `bgnice` option, enter

```
set -o bgnice
```

Any background jobs you start by adding an `&` at the end of the command line are run at a reduced priority.

Displaying and Changing a Logout Message

Typically, pressing Control-d at the system prompt logs you out or closes the active `Shell Tool` or `Command Tool` window. The `setignoreeof` option disables Control-d. To have the system prompt you to end a session by typing exit rather than using Control-d, enter

```
set -o ignoreeof
```

When you press Control-d, the message `Use 'exit' to logout` appears. If this variable is not set, pressing Control-d is the same as issuing the `exit` command. By default, this option is disabled.

Marking Directories

When enabled, the `markdirs` option appends directory names with a /
and list the contents of each subdirectory. The `markdirs` option is similar
to listing files using the `ls -F`, except that you only see the results when
using wildcard expansion. Enabling the `markdirs` option produces an organized listing of subdirectories and their contents, which makes listing
subdirectories and their contents a breeze. However, the `markdirs` option
is only effective for listing files using wildcard characters. By default, the
`markdirs` option is disabled. This means that entering `ls` displays a listing
similar to this:

```
Application     Document     bin      images      mail
```

enabling the `markdirs` option by entering

```
set -o markdirs
```

and entering `ls *` displays a listing similar to this:

```
Application             Document
bin/:
answerbook              cdplayer            killfish
images/:
book.icon               bricks              force.x
book_glyph_mask.icon    clouds              snapshot.rs
mail/:
letter                  proposal            report
```

Disabling File Name Substitution

The `noglob` option disables file name substitution and can be set using
either of these commands:

```
set -f
```

or

```
set -o noglob
```

Protecting Files

The `noclobber` option prevents redirection from overwriting (*clobbering*) existing files when using the > ("to") redirection symbol. By default, this option is disabled. To enable the `noclobber` option, enter:

```
set -o noclobber
```

If you enter a redirection command that will overwrite an existing file, the system responds with a message informing you that the file already exists. If `noclobber` is enabled, and you really want to overwrite a file, use the >| operator as follows:

```
ls>|out.txt
```

Displaying an Error Message for Unset Variables

The `unset` command lets you unset a variable. The `nounset` option causes the Korn shell to display an error message when it tries to expand a variable that is not set or has been unset. By default, the `nounset` option is disabled. The Korn shell interprets unset variables as if their values were null. To enable the `nounset` option, enter

```
set -o nounset
```

The Korn shell displays an error message when it encounters unset variables and causes the command to abort, as shown in the following example.

```
unset X
print $X
/bin/ksh: X: parameter not set
```

Changing Command Line Editing Modes

If you are familiar with the vi editor, you can make the same commands available for editing the command line. Using the vi editing commands, you can navigate and edit any part of the command line to make changes, just as you would to edit a line in vi. To enable vi command line editing, enter

```
set -o vi
```

You can also substitute the vi argument with either **emacs** or **gmacs** to enable **emacs** or **gmacs** editing commands.

Changing the Default File Permissions

One of the first lines in the master /etc/.profile file contains the **umask** command. The **umask** command sets the default file and directory permissions assigned to the files and directories you create. The syntax for the **umask** command is

```
umask nnn
```

where each *n* is a number that sets the permissions for files and directories for the owner, group, and public. The first number indicates the owner permissions; the second, group permissions; the last, public permissions. The **umask** command uses different values for permissions than the **chmod** command. The default setting for the **umask** command is usually **022**, which assigns *files* with read and write permissions for the owner and read only to other users (-rw-r--r--). The **022** setting assigns *directories* with read, write, and execute permissions for the owner, execute and read permissions for groups, and execute permissions to the public (drwxr-xr-x). The following lists the file and directory permissions used with **umask**.

NUMBER	FILE PERMISSION	DIRECTORY PERMISSION
0	rw-	rwx
1	rw-	rw-
2	r--	r-x
3	r--	r--
4	-w-	-wx

NUMBER	FILE PERMISSION	DIRECTORY PERMISSION
5	-w-	-w-
6	---	--x
7	---	---

Working with Aliases

Aliases give you the power to rename any command with a name you can more easily remember. For example, if you're new to Solaris but familiar with the MS-DOS operating system, you might frequently find yourself entering the DOS command `dir` instead of `ls` to list a directory's contents. Assigning an alias named `dir` to the command `ls` enables you to use the list command by typing either `dir` or `ls`. When Solaris processes your commands, the command line is scanned from left to right to see if it contains an alias. If a command line has an alias, the SunOS command that matches the alias is used. Aliases may already be available to you, depending on how your system administrator has set up your account. Typing the **alias** command by itself displays all defined aliases.

Some aliases may already be predefined by your system administrator. For example, the `cp` (copy) and `mv` (move) commands may have the interactive option (`-i`) added to prevent you from accidentally overwriting files by prompting you when existing files are going to be overwritten. If you want to save your alias for future sessions, simply add the alias to your `.profile` file.

Creating an Alias

To create an alias, type **alias** followed by the name you want to assign as the alias, then type the command you want to match the alias. For example, **alias dir=ls** enables you to type either `dir` or `ls` to obtain a directory listing. Using the **alias** command, you can abbreviate long command lines. To create an alias for multiword strings, enclose the multiword string in quotes. For example, typing **alias lc="ls -l chap*"** causes the system to display a long listing of all the files in the working directory beginning with `chap` whenever you enter `lc`. Note that the asterisk (*) wildcard character is enclosed *inside* the quotation marks. Both single and double quotation marks can be used to indicate multi-word text. If you frequently use the `history` command, try adding the following to your `.profile` file:

```
alias h=history
```

You can now get a `history` listing by simply typing the letter `h`.

Undoing an Alias

You remove an alias by entering the `unalias` command, followed by the alias name. For example, entering

```
unalias dir
```

removes the `dir` alias.

Customizing Mail Program Variables

The `.mailrc` file works similarly to the `.profile` file, except that it stores aliases and variables relating to the mail program for sending and receiving electronic mail. The `.mailrc` file is usually stored in your home directory. While the `.profile` file provides a few variables that allow you to specify how often to check for mail, where to send your mail, what your mail notification message is, and the search path for mailbox files, there are many additional mail variables that affect both the `mailx` program and the DeskSet.

The `.mailrc` file contains many predefined variables. You can turn default mail variable settings off by preceding the predefined variable with `no`. For example, to turn the variable `hold` off, add `no` to the `hold` variable as follows: `set nohold`. If a file is indicated by a variable, it's set with an equal sign; for example, `MBOX=mbox` sets the storage mailbox for your mail to the file named `mbox`. The following is a list of `.mailrc` variables and their default settings.

VARIABLE	PURPOSE	DEFAULT SETTING
append	Adds letters to the end of `mbox`.	off
askcc	Displays the carbon copy prompt `Cc:` when writing a letter.	on
asksub	Prompts for a subject when writing a letter.	on
autoprint	Displays the next letter in the mailbox when one is deleted.	off
DEAD	Stores partial letters in case of interruption, such as a power failure.	Sends the contents to a file called `dead.letter` in your home directory.
dot	Makes a single dot (period) act as the termination character to indicate the end of a letter.	off (set to on in the global start-up file)
EDITOR	Determines which editor to use when composing letters.	`ed`
folder	Determines which directory contains your mail folders.	`mail`

VARIABLE	PURPOSE	DEFAULT SETTING
header	Causes the header list to be displayed when you enter the `mail` command.	on
hold	Holds letters in your mailbox until you save or delete them.	off
ignoreof	Changes the end-of-file character to a period or the tilde character rather than Control-d.	off
keep	Retains your mailbox even if it's empty. When set to `nokeep,` the mailbox is removed until you receive mail.	off
keepsave	Prevents `mail` from deleting a letter from your mailbox when you save the letter in another file or folder.	off
MBOX	Specifies which file letters are stored in after they've been read.	The `mbox` file in your home directory.

VARIABLE	PURPOSE	DEFAULT SETTING
`metoo`	Sends letters to yourself when you send a letter to an alias group of which you're a member.	off
`outfolder`	Keeps a record of every letter you send in a folder named `outfolder`.	off
`page`	Ejects a page after each letter.	off
`prompt`	Sets the mail prompt.	`&;`
`quiet`	Suppresses the initial `mail` program display of its version number and a short sample letter.	off
`save`	Saves partial letters into the file specified in the `DEAD` variable setting.	on
`SHELL`	The name of the command interpreter.	Set from the environment setting.

VARIABLE	PURPOSE	DEFAULT SETTING
showto	Displays the letter's recipient rather than your name when sending copies of letters to yourself or letters to a group of which you're a member.	off

Indicating How Often to Check for Mail

The MAILCHECK variable specifies how often, in seconds, to check for new mail. If not set, or set to zero, new mail is checked before each new prompt is displayed. Otherwise, the default setting is **600** seconds (10 minutes).

Specifying Where to Send Your Mail

The MAIL variable contains the name of the mailbox file to check for new mail. It is not used if MAILPATH is set. The MAILPATH variable contains a colon-separated list of mailbox files to check for new mail and is used if you want to read multiple mailboxes. It overrides the MAIL variable if both are set. This MAILPATH setting specifies to check two mailbox files, /home/ataylor/mbox and /news/mbox.

```
MAILPATH=/home/ataylor/mbox:/news/mbox
```

This only works if you have read permission on the mailbox file. If MAIL-PATH is not set, there is no default.

Changing Your Mail Notification Message

When you get new mail, the Korn shell displays this message on your terminal right before the prompt: you have mail in mailbox-file. You can also create your own mail notification message by appending a ? followed by your message to the mailbox files given in MAILPATH. If you wanted your message to be "Check your mail," then MAILPATH would be set like this:

```
MAILPATH=homeataylor/mbox?'Check your mail'
```

Adding an Alias for Sending Mail to a Group

You can add aliases to your .mailrc file to define a group of user names as a single name. For example, adding the following line to the .mailrc file

```
alias mailist lricardo@desilu sbertrille@santanco
janderson@springfield
```

allows you to send a letter to lricardo, sbertrille, and jandrson at their respective machines via the mail program, using the alias name mailist. The Mail Tool also lets you create and store aliases for sending mail to a group. This is explained in Chapter 3, "The Multimedia Mail Tool Makes Mail Easy."

Customizing Your Terminal Settings

The TERM variable is not used by the Korn shell, but several other programs, such as the vi editor, look for this variable. It specifies your terminal settings, and is usually set in the /etc/profile file by your system administrator. For example, if you start vi and open an existing file and get garbage on your screen, or the vi commands are not working correctly, try resetting the TERM variable. If you are using a Sun terminal, add the following line to your .profile file:

```
TERM=sun
```

If you are using Solaris 2 for x86, add the line

```
TERM=AT386
```

Changing the Backspace and Delete Key Assignment

In most cases, you will not need to change the default key assignment; however, if you find that the Delete or Backspace keys are not set correctly, you can easily change them. The `stty` command lets you set how the Backspace and Delete keys work. On some Sun workstation keyboards the default setting for the Backspace key is # and Delete is sometimes set to @. If your Backspace key doesn't work, try pressing Control-h to delete the previous character and pressing Control-u to delete an entire line. You can change the Backspace key so that you can erase the previous character when you press the Backspace key and erase an entire line by pressing Delete. The `stty` command is normally placed in your `.profile` file. To change the Backspace key setting, enter

        stty erase <Back Space>

The notation `<Back Space>` indicates that you should press the Backspace key. You can also assign the Backspace key by specifying the ASCII code Control-h. Use the caret (^) to indicate the Control key as follows

        stty erase \^H

To change the Delete key to delete the entire line, enter

        stty kill <Delete>

The notation `<Delete>` indicates that you should press the Delete key. If you make an error before typing Return, you can press the Backspace to erase the error or press the Delete key to erase the entire line.

Changing Keyboard Preferences

The `xset` command lets you set how the keyboard bell sounds and the volume of the keyboard clicks, and lets you control the keyboard's auto-repeat feature. The `b` option lets you control the bell volume, pitch, and duration. The syntax for the `xset` option is

        xset b *volume pitch duration*

The *volume* parameter can be any number from 1 to 100. The *pitch* is measured in hertz and can be set from 1 to 1000 hertz. The *duration* can be anywhere from 1 to 1000 milliseconds. If no parameters are given, the system defaults are used. You can turn off the keyboard bell by setting the volume parameter to 0. If only one parameter is given, the bell volume is set to that value. If two values are listed, the second parameter specifies the bell pitch. For example, the command:

```
xset b 50 500 50
```

sets the volume of the keyboard bell to 50 percent of its maximum loudness, the pitch to 500 hertz, and the duration to 50 milliseconds.

The **xset** command's **c** option sets the volume of the keyboard's key click. The syntax for the keyboard click is

```
xset c volume
```

The *volume* can be a value from 1 to 100, indicating a percentage of the maximum volume. For example,

```
xset c 100
```

sets each key to click at the highest volume. You can turn the key click off by using the value 0. Alternatively, you can also use the parameters on or off. If you specify the on parameter, the system default for volume is used.

If you hold a key down and the keystroke is repeated over and over again, the keyboard's auto-repeat feature is enabled. If the auto-repeat feature is not enabled, you can enable the keyboard's auto-repeat feature by entering

```
xset r on
```

Enter **xset -r off** to disable key repeat feature.

Modifying Your OpenWindows Environment

The .Xdefaults file contains the basic properties you set for the Workspace as well as any special settings you might add. To view and edit the .Xdefaults file, open the file from your home directory using any text editor. Figure 15.1 shows an example of an .Xdefaults file. The variables that you can edit appear after the colon on each line.

NOTE   The entries in the .Xdefaults file vary depending upon the type of monitor you have and the settings you choose from the Workspace Properties window. Additionally, the order of the settings varies.

Changing Screensavers

The Lock Screen item found in the Utilities submenu of the Workspace menu displays a screen of randomly appearing Sun logos and locks your screen so that a password needs to be entered to return to OpenWindows. This feature is especially helpful when you will be away from your terminal for an extend period of time. You don't have to use the standard screensaver; you can lock your screen and specify another screensaver feature by using the following syntax.

```
xlock -mode screensaver
```

Adding the nolock argument lets you enable a screensaver without locking your screen.

```
xlock -mode screensaver -nolock
```

FIGURE 15.1

A sample .Xdefaults
file

Substitute the *screensaver* variable with one of the following screensavers.

SCREENSAVER	DESCRIPTION
hop	Shows the "real plane fractals" from the September 1986 issue of *Scientific American*.
life	Displays Conway's Game of Life.

SCREENSAVER	DESCRIPTION
qix	Displays spinning lines similar to those in the video game of the same name.
image	Shows several Sun logos randomly appearing on the screen.
swarm	Shows a swarm of bees following a wasp.
roto	Shows a swirling rotor.
pyro	Shows fireworks.
flame	Shows some interesting fractals.
blank	Shows a blank screen.
random	Picks a random mode of all the above except **blank** mode.

The **xset** command lets you enable a screensaver that makes the screen go blank after a period of no use. To use the **xset** command to enable the screensaver, enter

```
xset s on
```

You can specify how much time to wait before invoking the screensaver. For example, entering

```
xset s 300
```

sets the system to wait 5 minutes (300 seconds) before blanking the screen.

To restore your desktop, move the mouse in any direction. Although input from any keyboard key or mouse button will restore your screen, move the mouse instead. Pressing a key creates system input, so if the pointer is positioned in a text file, you may insert a character in the text. This option is turned off by default.

When you quit OpenWindows, the screensaver feature will be disabled again, and you must enter the **xset** command again to enable it. To disable the screensaver with the command line, enter

```
xset s off
```

Turning On the Screensaver Permanently

The `$OPENWIN/lib/Xinitrc/` file stores the initial OpenWindows startup script (a script is a file containing commands). If you want to turn the screensaver feature on automatically, you must copy and rename the Xinitrc file to .xinitrc in your home directory. To do this, enter

```
cp $OPENWINHOME/lib/Xinitrc $HOME/.xinitrc
```

Open the `.Xinitrc` file using any text editor and add the line

```
xset s on
```

to the end of the file. Save the changes and quit the editor. The next time you start OpenWindows, the screensaver will be active. If you want to disable the screensaver feature, simply add a # in front of the `xset` command line (comment out) or remove the `xset` command from the `.xinitrc` file and restart OpenWindows.

Customizing the Workspace

The `xsetroot` command allows you to tailor the appearance of the Workspace (background) window. The `xsetroot` command includes several options. You can display a solid color background, a pattern, or a tiled bitmap image as your background. The following explains how to change the Workspace using the `xsetroot` command.

To set the Workspace to a solid color, use the `-solid` option followed by the color you want to change the Workspace to. The next section includes a listing of some of the colors you can choose from when you want to change the color of the root window. For example, entering

```
xsetroot -solid lightsteelblue
```

changes the Workspace to a light steel blue color.

The `-bitmap` option followed by the name of the bitmap file lets you display a tiled image as your background. Entering the command line

```
xsetroot -bitmap $OPENWINHOME/share/include/X11/bitmaps/mensetmanus
```

displays the background shown in Figure 15.2.

FIGURE 15.2

A tiled bitmap image background

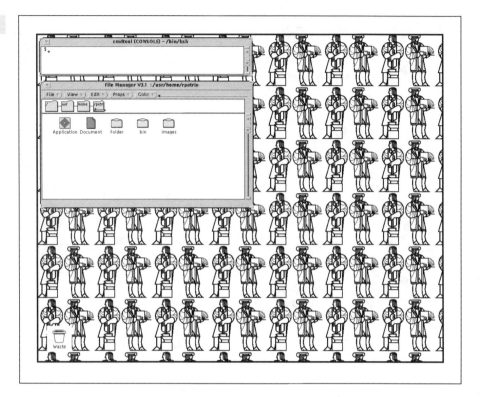

NOTE   Displaying a complex bitmap picture eats up more memory than a solid background. Each time a window is displayed, OpenWindows must repaint the screen. If you are running low on memory, use a solid background rather than a complex bitmap picture.

By default, the background color of a bitmap image is black and the foreground color is white. The **-fg color** option sets the foreground color of the Workspace. The **-bg color** option sets the background color of the Workspace. The following displays a bitmap image named **force.x** with a snow background and a gray foreground, as shown in Figure 15.3. Note

FIGURE 15.3

A bitmap image with
a snow background
and a gray foreground

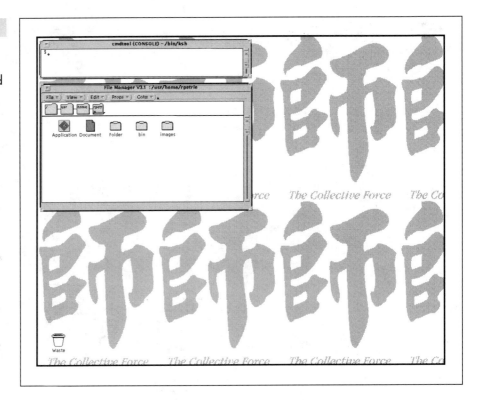

that the `force.x` file is used only as an example of foreground and background colors. It is not a file that comes with Solaris.

```
xsetroot -bitmap $HOME/images/force.x -bg snow -fg gray
```

You can reverse the foreground and background color by adding the `-rv` or `-reverse` option with another option. Using the `-rv` option without another specified option changes the Workspace to the default state. The following reverses the background color of the previous example.

```
xsetroot -bitmap $HOME/force.x -bg snow -fg gray -rv
```

The `-mod x y` option lets you display a grid pattern as your background. The x and y arguments can be any number from 0 to 16. For example, entering

```
xsetroot -mod 3 12
```

displays a plaid pattern as your Workspace background.

T I P

The OpenWindows demo program `realxfishdb` stored in the `$OPENWINHOME/demo` directory lets you create a background of a realistic aquarium with fish that swim behind your windows. You can change the types of fish in the aquarium by using the program `fish_props` in the same directory. A section on how to add a menu of options to display the aquarium background, change the fish, and remove the aquarium background is included at the end of this chapter.

Changing Windows to Display in Inverse Video

Some users find that it reduces eye strain to change windows to display white text on a black background instead of black text on a white background. To change your display, add the following two lines to the `.Xdefaults` file in your home directory using any text editor.

```
window.color.foreground: white
window.color.background: black
```

Save the changes and quit the editor.

In order for your changes to take effect, you need to run the `xrdb` command to read the contents of the `.Xdefaults` resource database. At the system prompt in a Command Tool or Shell Tool, enter

```
xrdb .Xdefaults
```

Any DeskSet applications you open after making this change are displayed in inverse video. To revert to black on white, just remove the `window.color` lines from the `.Xdefaults` file, save the changes, and again type the `xrdb` `.Xdefaults` command in a Command Tool or Shell Tool window.

Specifying a Window's Colors

One of the richest customization features of Solaris is the variety of colors that can be assigned to the Workspace, windows, and icons. There are over 900 colors that you can assign. The following is a list of some of the predefined colors. For a complete listing of the colors, enter the following command

```
showrgb | more
```

This displays the contents of the `rgb.txt` file that stores your color options. The `rgb.txt` file is located in the `/usr/openwin/lib` directory. Although some color names appear in the `rgb.txt` file as two or more words, you must eliminate any spaces when specifying a color. The following lists the primary RGB (Red Green Blue) color settings (0–255) that you can enter when using OpenWindows' Color Chooser (such as in the Icon Editor or the Binder), and the color names for setting colors from the command line.

COLOR CODE	COLOR
255 250 250	snow
248 248 255	ghostwhite
250 235 215	antiquewhite
255 228 196	bisque
255 218 185	peachpuff
255 222 173	navajowhite
255 248 220	cornsilk
255 255 240	ivory
255 250 205	lemonchiffon
255 245 238	seashell
240 255 240	honeydew
240 255 255	azure
230 230 250	lavender
255 240 245	lavenderblush
255 228 225	mistyrose
255 255 255	white
0 0 0	black
47 79 79	darkslategray
105 105 105	dimgray

COLOR CODE	COLOR
112 128 144	slategray
119 136 153	lightslategray
192 192 192	gray
211 211 211	lightgray
25 25 112	midnightblue
0 0 128	navy
100 149 237	cornflowerblue
72 61 139	darkslateblue
106 90 205	slateblue
123 104 238	mediumslateblue
132 112 255	lightslateblue
0 0 205	mediumblue
65 105 225	royalblue
0 0 255	blue
30 144 255	dodgerblue
0 191 255	deepskyblue
135 206 235	skyblue
135 206 250	lightskyblue
70 130 180	steelblue
176 196 222	lightsteelblue
173 216 230	lightblue
176 224 230	powderblue
175 238 238	paleturquoise
0 206 209	darkturquoise
72 209 204	mediumturquoise
64 224 208	turquoise
0 255 255	cyan

COLOR CODE	COLOR
224 255 255	lightcyan
95 158 160	cadetblue
102 205 170	mediumaquamarine
127 255 212	aquamarine
0 100 0	darkgreen
85 107 47	darkolivegreen
143 188 143	darkseagreen
46 139 87	seagreen
60 179 113	mediumseagreen
32 178 170	lightseagreen
152 251 152	palegreen
0 255 127	springgreen
124 252 0	lawngreen
0 255 0	green
127 255 0	chartreuse
0 250 154	mediumspringgreen
173 255 47	greenyellow
50 205 50	limegreen
154 205 50	yellowgreen
34 139 34	forestgreen
107 142 35	olivedrab
189 183 107	darkkhaki
240 230 140	khaki
238 232 170	palegoldenrod
250 250 210	lightgoldenrodyellow
255 255 224	lightyellow
255 255 0	yellow

COLOR CODE	COLOR
255 215 0	gold
238 221 130	lightgoldenrod
218 165 32	goldenrod
184 134 11	darkgoldenrod
188 143 143	rosybrown
205 92 92	indianred
139 69 19	saddlebrown
160 82 45	sienna
205 133 63	peru
222 184 135	burlywood
245 245 220	beige
245 222 179	wheat
210 180 140	tan
210 105 30	chocolate
178 34 34	firebrick
165 42 42	brown
250 128 114	salmon
255 160 122	lightsalmon
255 165 0	orange
255 140 0	darkorange
255 127 80	coral
240 128 128	lightcoral
255 99 71	tomato
255 69 0	orangered
255 0 0	red
255 105 180	hotpink
255 20 147	deeppink

COLOR CODE	COLOR
255 192 203	pink
255 182 193	lightpink
219 112 147	palevioletred
176 48 96	maroon
208 32 144	violetred
255 0 255	magenta
238 130 238	violet
221 160 221	plum
218 112 214	orchid
186 85 211	mediumorchid
138 43 226	blueviolet
160 32 240	purple
147 112 219	mediumpurple
216 191 216	thistle
3 3 3	gray1
127 127 127	gray50
255 255 255	gray100

Changing the Mouse Pointer

Besides customizing your background, the `xsetroot` command also lets you customize the mouse pointer. To change the mouse pointer, use the following syntax

```
xsetroot -cursor_name cursor-fontname
```

Figure 15.4 shows the available cursors and cursor names from which you can choose. To display the different types of cursor fonts and cursor font

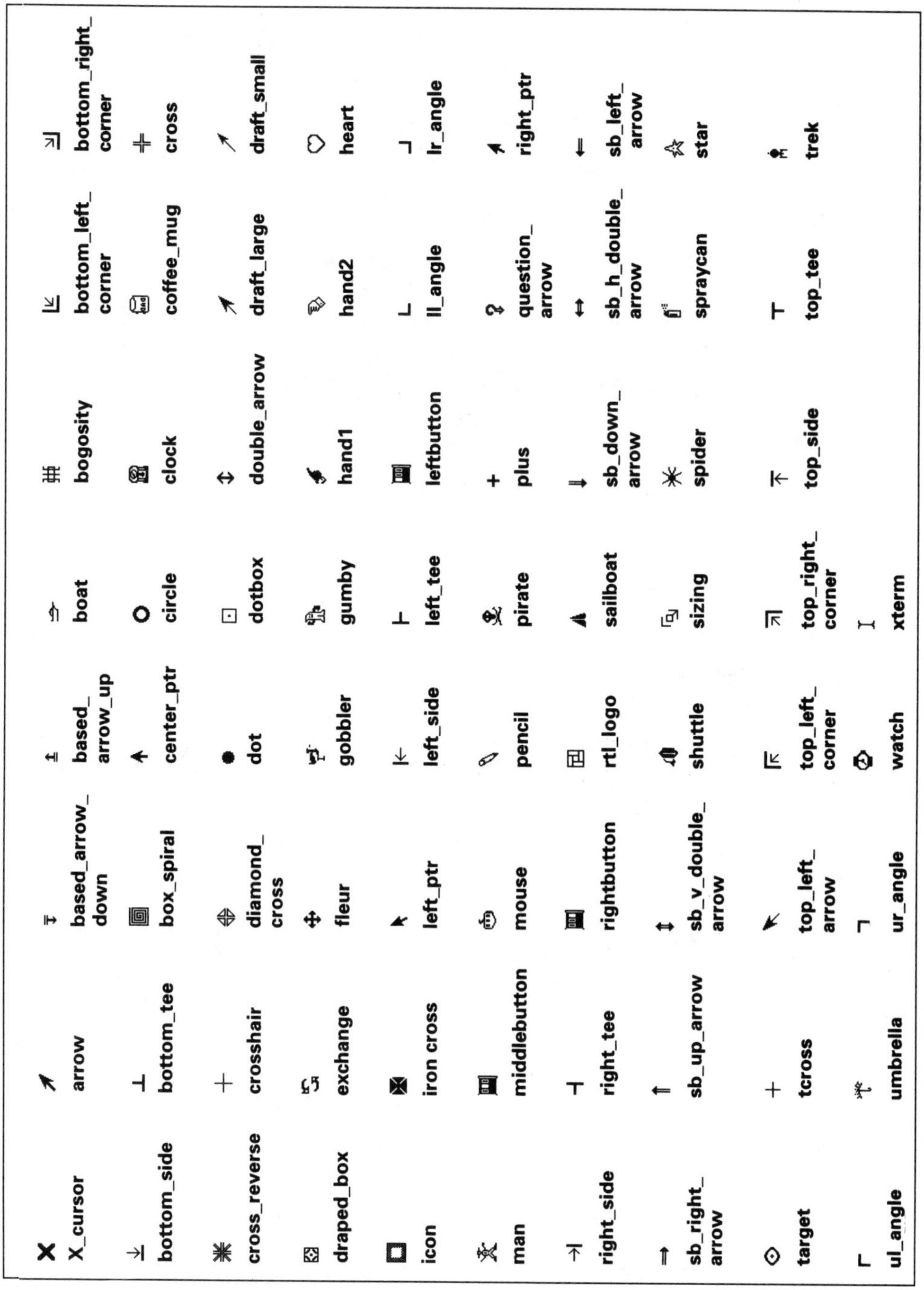
X_cursor
arrow
based_arrow_down
based_arrow_up
boat
bogosity
bottom_left_corner
bottom_right_corner
bottom_side
bottom_tee
box_spiral
center_ptr
circle
clock
coffee_mug
cross
cross_reverse
crosshair
diamond_cross
dot
dotbox
double_arrow
draft_large
draft_small
draped_box
exchange
fleur
gobbler
gumby
hand1
hand2
heart
icon
iron cross
left_ptr
left_side
left_tee
leftbutton
ll_angle
lr_angle
man
middlebutton
mouse
pencil
pirate
plus
question_arrow
right_ptr
right_side
right_tee
rightbutton
rtl_logo
sailboat
sb_down_arrow
sb_h_double_arrow
sb_left_arrow
sb_right_arrow
sb_up_arrow
sb_v_double_arrow
shuttle
sizing
spider
spraycan
star
target
tcross
top_left_arrow
top_left_corner
top_right_corner
top_side
top_tee
trek
ul_angle
umbrella
ur_angle
watch
xterm

FIGURE 15.4

The available cursors and cursor names

background masks on your screen, enter the following in a `Command Tool` or `Shell Tool` window

```
xfd -fn cursor
```

Customizing Fonts

OpenWindows DeskSet applications are set up with default fonts, that is characters available in a particular size, style, and weight, for icons, menus, and windows. However, you can change the default font style and size in windows and window headers. The following explain two methods of customizing fonts: changing the scale of the font (which also affects the window's size), and changing the font style and specifying a different point size. The first method simply increases or decreases the font size (to small, large, or extra large) and the corresponding size of the window, while the second provides greater flexibility in defining the style and specific size.

Specifying the Scale for One Application

You can open a single application with a modified font size from the Shell Tool or Command Tool. You must start a new application to display the new font. To open an application and change the font (and window) scale, type the application name followed by the scale command (-**scale**) and the desired size. The following example opens a Text Editor in the small size:

```
textedit -scale small &
```

Figure 15.5 shows a small and standard Text Editor window.

FIGURE 15.5

A small and standard
Text Editor window

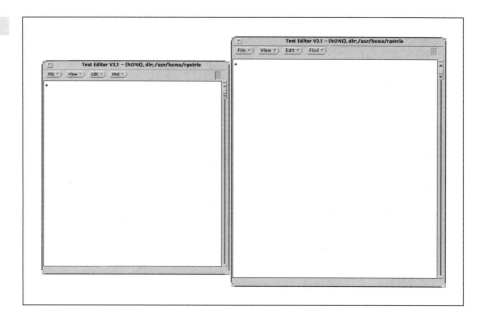

NOTE

The small `Text Editor` window appears open on the Workspace. Adding the ampersand (&) returns the window prompt and enables you to continue using the `Shell Tool` or `Command Tool` window while the `Text Editor` window is running. Otherwise, you would not be able to use the `Shell Tool` or `Command Tool` window until you quit the Text Editor.

The following lists the program names of the DeskSet Tools, which you can use to execute the program from the Shell Tool or Command Tool.

```
audiotool
binder
calctool
clock
cm
cmdtool
filemgr
```

```
iconedit
mailtool
perfmeter
printtool
shelltool
snapshot
tapetool
textedit
```

Choosing a Font Scale

The scale utility enables you to choose from four font sizes for windows. You can make this change for one or more select windows, or you can change the default so that all applications subsequently open in the size you specify. When you scale the font, the window scales with it. Not all font styles and sizes appear on the screen satisfactorily. If the size is too large, some items, such as menu buttons, may be obscured. You can choose from these four sizes:

small

medium (the default)

large

extra_large

Specifying the Font Scale for All Default Applications

If you want to change the default scale of all DeskSet applications, you edit the .Xdefaults file as follows: Open the .Xdefaults file from your home directory using any text editor and add the following line, where size is small, large, or extra_large:

```
Window.Scale: size
```

Because medium is the default, using the medium size does not alter the scale. Save the changes and quit the editor. Type the following at the command line to update the .Xdefaults file's information on the window server:

```
xrdb .Xdefaults
```

Now any new DeskSet or other XView applications that you open from the command line or the Workspace menu appear in the specified scale. To make the changes take effect in existing applications, you can either quit them and restart them or restart the OpenWindows server.

Viewing and Listing Available Fonts

There are two demo programs included for viewing the available font styles and sizes. The Text demo program is available from the Demos submenu of the Workspace menu. It displays lines of text in a font you choose from a list. The Text demo window includes the Text pop-up window menu. Figure 15.6 shows the Show Text and Show All pop-up windows. Figure 15.7 shows a map of the Text demo items.

The Fontview demo is also available from the Demos submenu of the Workspace menu. It lets you see individual characters for any font as well as display a character grid to see the characters available for a font. The Fontview demo window includes the Fontview pop-up window menu. Figure 15.8 shows the Fontview pop-up window. Figure 15.9 shows a map of the Fontview demo items.

FIGURE 15.6

The Show Text and Show All pop-up windows

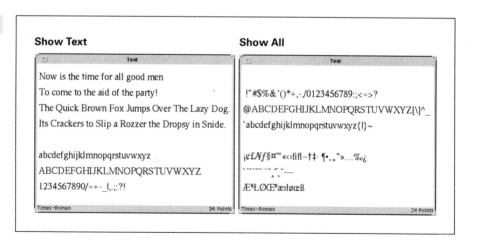

FIGURE 15.7

A menu map of the Text pop-up menu items and pop-up windows

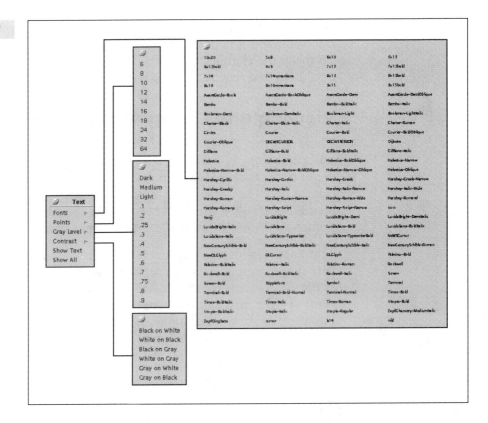

There are over 400 fonts available to OpenWindows applications. You can list the available font names by entering **xlsfonts** at the prompt in a Shell Tool or Command Tool window. To display the listing one screen at a time, enter **xlsfonts | more** or use the Command Tool window to scroll through the font list. Each font has a long name in addition to a shortened version. The full name for **-monotype-gill sans-medium**, is:

```
-monotype-gill sans-medium-i-normal--12-120-75-75-p-52-iso8859-1
```

FIGURE 15.8

Fontview pop-up
window

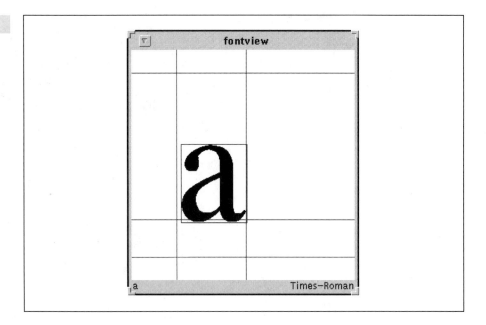

It is easier to reference a font by its short name. The following is a list of the
short names of some popular fonts that you can use to customize windows.

>avantgarde-book
>
>avantgarde-bookoblique
>
>avantgarde-demi
>
>avantgarde-demioblique
>
>bookman-demi
>
>bookman-demiitalic
>
>bookman-light
>
>bookman-lightitalic
>
>charter-black
>
>charter-black-italic
>
>charter-italic
>
>charter-roman

FIGURE 15.9

A map of the Fontview demo items

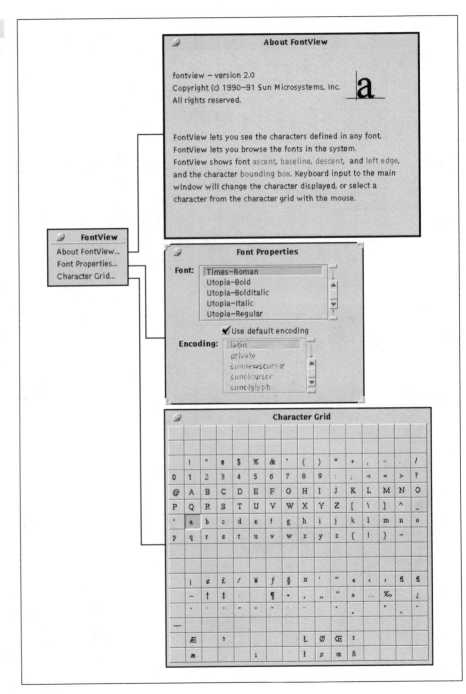

courier

courier-bold

courier-boldoblique

courier-oblique

gillsans

gillsans-bold

gillsans-bolditalic

gillsans-italic

helvetica

helvetica-bold

helvetica-boldoblique

helvetica-narrow

helvetica-narrow-bold

helvetica-narrow-boldoblique

helvetica-narrow-oblique

helvetica-oblique

lucida-bright

lucida-brightdemibold

lucida-brightdemibolditalic

lucida-brightitalic

lucidabright

lucidabright-demi

lucidabright-demiitalic

lucidabright-italic

lucidasans

lucidasans-bold

lucidasans-bolditalic

lucidasans-italic

lucidasans-typewriter

lucidasans-typewriterbold

newcenturyschlbk-bold

newcenturyschlbk-bolditalic

newcenturyschlbk-italic

newcenturyschlbk-roman

palatino-bold

palatino-bolditalic

palatino-italic

palatino-roman

terminal

terminal-bold

terminal-bold-normal

terminal-normal

times-bold

times-bolditalic

times-italic

times-roman

utopia-bold

utopia-bolditalic

utopia-italic

utopia-regular

zapfchancery-mediumitalic

zapfdingbats

Fixed-Width and Proportionally Spaced Fonts

There are two general categories of fonts, *fixed width* and *proportionally spaced*. Each character in a fixed-width font takes up the same amount of space as every other character. By contrast, the characters in a proportionally spaced font require varying amounts of space, depending upon their individual width. Proportionally spaced fonts are more pleasing to the eye.

The default font displayed in Command Tool and Shell Tool is a proportionally spaced font. Although this font is pleasing to the eye, problems occur in character alignment (when spacing and tabbing) with any proportionally spaced font in terminal windows. You may want to choose a fixed-width font for these windows.

Specifying a New Font Style and Size

The default font for windows is Lucida Sans in 12-point (medium); the default font for window headers is Lucida Sans Bold. The term point is a measurement used to indicate the height of a font. A point is approximately $1/72$ inch. You can specify another font style and size for windows and window headers. If the point size is not specified, the default (12-point) is used. You can make the change for a single window, you can make the change in several applications in your submenu, or you can make a permanent change for all your applications by editing your `.Xdefaults` file. Any changes you make do not apply to existing windows; you must start a new application to display the new font. To start a new application, type the application name on a command line followed by the `-fn` (font name) option, and the font style and size. The following changes the font style of the File Manager window.

```
filemgr -fn fontstyle-pointsize &
```

The following command starts a new Command Tool with the proportionally spaced font, Lucida Sans Typewriter Bold.

```
cmdtool -fn lucidasans-typewriter-bold &
```

To start a new Text Editor with the font Helvetica Bold in 14-point, enter:

```
textedit -fn helvetica-bold-14 &
```

Specifying the Font for Applications

If you want to make the font style and size permanent, edit your .Xdefaults file. Note that when you make any changes, the fonts in any applications that you have already started remain as before. Applications you start *after* making the change in your .Xdefaults file appear in the new font and size. Not all font styles and sizes appear the same. If the size is too large, some items, such as menu buttons, may be difficult to read.

To change the font style and size in all DeskSet applications, first, use any text editor to open the .Xdefaults file in your home directory. Insert the line

```
font.name:fontname-size
```

where fontname is the name of the font you want to specify and -size specifies the point size of the font. For example, the following line changes the text in your DeskSet applications to display in Lucida Sans Typewriter Bold font in 14-point. Be sure you press the Tab key when you encounter the <tab> reference in this example.

```
font.name:<tab>lucidasans-typewriter-bold-14
OpenWindows.TitleFont:<tab>lucidasans-typewriter-bold-14
```

Save the changes and quit the editor. Type the following command at the prompt in a Shell Tool or Command Tool to update the window from the .Xdefaults file.

```
xrdb .Xdefaults
```

Customizing OpenWindows Menus

You can customize your OpenWindows Workspace menu by copying and editing the openwin-menu file. The following sections explain how to modify the openwin-menu file to create a submenu in the Workspace menu and indicate the programs you want to start from the submenu. When you modify a menu, you can also customize how a window displays. For example you can change a window to display in inverse video (white type on a black background), or you can change the style and size of the fonts displayed in application windows.

Changing the Workspace Menu

The openwin-menu file specifies the submenus and applications included on the Workspace menu. The location of the system default Workspace menu is $OPENWINHOME/lib. $OPENWINHOME is a variable name for the location of the OpenWindows software (usually /usr/openwin), and lib is the directory that contains OpenWindows' system default files. Before customizing the openwin-menu file, copy the system default files in your home directory. The copy of the openwin-menu file is used to store your personal customizations. The changes you make to the menu file in your home directory override the system default openwin-menu file. To copy the file into your home directory, type the following at the system prompt in a Shell Tool or Command Tool:

```
cp $OPENWINHOME/lib/openwin-menu $HOME/.openwin-menu
```

This creates the file .openwin-menu in your home directory (specified with the variable $HOME). Placing the dot in front of the file name makes it a hidden file. When you open this file it appears as follows:

```
#
# @(#)openwin-menu    23.13 91/07/10 openwin-menu
#
#       OpenWindows default root menu file - top level menu
#

"Workspace" TITLE

"Programs" MENU             $OPENWINHOME/lib/openwin-menu-programs

"Utilities" MENU            $OPENWINHOME/lib/openwin-menu-utilities

"Properties..."             PROPERTIES

SEPARATOR

"Help..."        exec $OPENWINHOME/bin/helpopen
handbooks/top.toc.handbook

"Desktop Intro..."      exec $OPENWINHOME/bin/helpopen
handbooks/desktop.intro.handbook

SEPARATOR

"Exit..."          EXIT
```

Adding a Submenu to the Workspace Menu

Suppose you want to add a submenu of screensavers to the Workspace menu. Open the `.openwin-menu` file with any text editor and add the following line:

```
"Screensavers"       MENU        $HOME/screensavers-menu
```

This word in quotes (`"Screensavers"`) preceding `MENU` indicates the name of the menu that appears in the Workspace menu. You can change the order of any menu item by changing its placement in the `.openwin-menu` file. After adding this line save your changes and quit the editor. The new submenu, `Screensavers`, is not added to your `Workspace` menu until you create the `screensavers-menu`'s file that contains the `Screensavers` menu items.

Adding an Application to a Submenu

The following is an example of how to add a list of screensaver items to the `Screensavers` submenu. Using the text editor of your choice, create a file that contains the following lines:

```
#
# Screensaver Fun!
#

"Screensavers" TITLE PIN

     "Flame" exec xlock -password "Password, Please?" -invalid
"You've made an error, Please try again!" -validate "Validating
Password..." -mode flame -saturation 1
     "Fractals" exec xlock -password "Password, Please?" -invalid
"You've made an error, Please try again!" -validate "Validating
Password..." -mode hop -saturation 1
     "Life" exec xlock -password "Password, Please?" -invalid
"You've made an error, Please try again!" -validate "Validating
Password..." -mode life -saturation 1
     "Logo" exec xlock -password "Password, Please?" -invalid
"You've made an error, Please try again!" -validate "Validating
Password..." -mode image -saturation 1
     "Pyro" exec xlock -password "Password, Please?" -invalid
"You've made an error, Please try again!" -validate "Validating
Password..." -mode pyro -saturation 1
```

```
        "Qix" exec xlock -password "Password, Please?" -invalid
"You've made an error, Please try again!" -validate "Validating
Password..." -mode qix -saturation 1
        "Random" DEFAULT exec xlock -password "Password, Please?" -
invalid "You've made an error, Please try again!" -validate
"Validating Password..." -mode random -saturation 1
        "Rotor" exec xlock -password "Password, Please?" -invalid
"You've made an error, Please try again!" -validate "Validating
Password..." -mode rotor -saturation 1
        "Swarm" exec xlock -password "Password, Please?" -invalid
"You've made an error, Please try again!" -validate "Validating
Password..." -mode swarm -saturation 1
        "Unlocked (Random)" exec $OPENWINHOME/bin/xlock -mode random
-nolock -saturation 1

"Screensavers" END
```

Save the file with the file name **screensavers-menu** and quit the text editor. The root workspace menu will now read this file whenever the **Screensaver** item is chosen. Notice that the word **PIN** after the word **"TITLE"** in the first line indicates that the menu can be pinned to the Workspace. The word **DEFAULT** after the title **"Random"** makes **"Random"** the default item. You can add other screensavers to this menu. Just open a blank line before or after entry, enclose the appropriate screensaver name in quotes, and type in the screensaver's name and options. Figure 15.10 shows the result of adding the above screensavers example to the **Workspace** menu.

Creating Additional Submenus

You can also create additional submenus of items. The following example lets you add a submenu that in turn lets you add an active aquarium as your Workspace background or display a submenu of bitmaps to display as your Workspace background. Use a text editor add the following line to your openwin-menu.

```
"Backgrounds"        MENU        $HOME/backgrounds-menu
```

After adding this line, create a new file named **background-menu** that contains the following lines:

```
#
# Background screens
#
```

FIGURE 15.10

The newly added Screensavers submenu

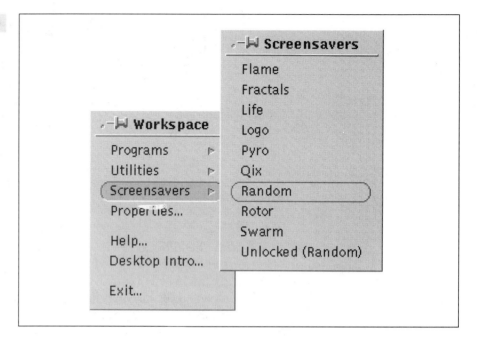

```
"Backgrounds"       TITLE PIN
"Aquarium"       MENU
    "Fish Background"        exec $OPENWINHOME/demo/realxfishdb
    "Fish Props..."            exec $OPENWINHOME/demo/fish_props
    "Kill Fish"            exec $HOME/killfish; REFRESH
"Aquarium"       END PIN
"X-Bitmaps"       MENU
    "Am I Blue"             $OPENWINHOME/bin/xsetroot -solid
lightblue
    "Collective Force" DEFAULT $OPENWINHOME/bin/xsetroot -bg
white -fg grey -bitmap $OPENWINHOME/share/include/X11/bit-
maps/wingdogs
    "Escherknot"            $OPENWINHOME/bin/xsetroot -bg cyan -fg
black -bitmap $OPENWINHOME/share/include/X11/bitmaps/escherknot
    "Hit the Bricks"        $OPENWINHOME/bin/xsetroot -bg firebrick
-fg black -bitmap $OPENWINHOME/share/include/X11/bitmaps/boxes
    "Mensetmanus"          $OPENWINHOME/bin/xsetroot -bg ghostwhite
-fg black -bitmap $OPENWINHOME/share/include/X11/bitmaps/menset-
manus
    "Night Sky"            $OPENWINHOME/bin/xsetroot -bg mid-
nightblue -fg ghostwhite -bitmap
$OPENWINHOME/share/include/X11/bitmaps/star
    "Weave"             $OPENWINHOME/bin/xsetroot -bg black -fg
ghostwhite -bitmap $OPENWINHOME/share/include/X11/bit-
```

```
maps/root_weave
"X-Bitmaps"        END PIN

"Backgrounds"      END
```

Figure 15.11 shows the newly added submenus displayed using the `Fish Background`. The `Aquarium` submenu items appear between the lines `"Aquarium Menu"` and `"Aquarium" End`. The `X-Bitmap` submenu items appear between the lines `"X-Bitmaps" Menu` and `"X-Bitmaps" End`. Notice the line beginning with the title "Kill fish" executes the `killfish` script file (a file containing commands). In order to change the aquarium background to another background, be sure you add and choose the `killfish` item. The `Kill Fish` item runs the Korn shell commands found in the `killfish` file. The following lists the contents of the `killfish` script file:

```
#!/bin/ksh
KILLFISH='ps -e | grep realxfis | cut -c1-6'
kill -9 $KILLFISH > /dev/null
xrefresh &
```

FIGURE 15.11

Newly added submenus displayed using the fish background

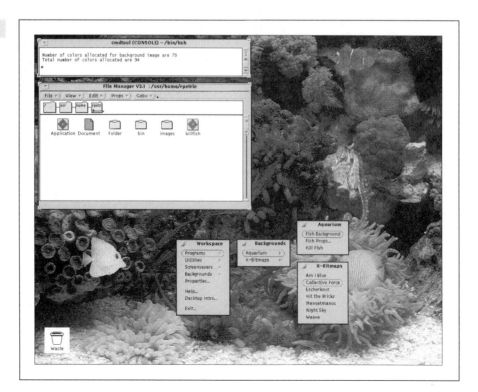

The `killfish` file runs a Korn shell script (a file containing commands) that sets the `KILLFISH` variable. This variable is set to execute a command line that finds the process number of the fish (`realxfis`) background screen, cuts the number of the process, kills the process, and redirects the standard output to a null device.

CHAPTER

16

Networking and Communications

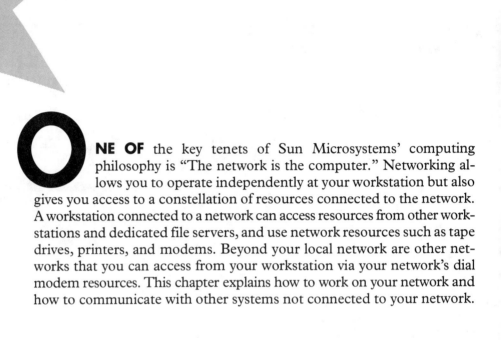

ONE OF the key tenets of Sun Microsystems' computing philosophy is "The network is the computer." Networking allows you to operate independently at your workstation but also gives you access to a constellation of resources connected to the network. A workstation connected to a network can access resources from other workstations and dedicated file servers, and use network resources such as tape drives, printers, and modems. Beyond your local network are other networks that you can access from your workstation via your network's dial modem resources. This chapter explains how to work on your network and how to communicate with other systems not connected to your network.

About Networking Systems

There are two networking systems that are widely used in the UNIX community: Networked File System (NFS) from Sun Microsystems, which runs on most Berkeley UNIX systems, as well as many System V-based UNIX systems, and the Remote File Sharing (RFS) from AT&T, which is part of System V, Release 4. Both of these networking systems are transparent, so the user does not have to know the network is there to use it. The files on the remote system are made available to the users on the local system in such a way that the files appear to be regular files on the local system.

Typically, networks center around a specialized computer, called a *file server*, which includes a powerful computer with large disk capacity that is connected to devices, such as laser printers, modems, and tape backups, that can be shared with other users. Software resources, such as application software that allows multiple users to work on the same file, are also shared on a network.

Different types of computers can communicate on the same network because they share a common language of communications, referred to as *protocols*. There are two primary types of networks: local-area networks (LANs) and wide-area networks (WANS). Local-area networks are networks connected via a coaxial cable or twisted-pair phone wiring. Wide-area networks connect LANs and other computers into a network connected by dial-up or dedicated phone lines, microwave links, or satellite communications.

Networking Solaris

There is a core of commands that allows you to access and use resources on the network. The commands `rlogin`, `rcp`, and `rsh` all allow you to work on other machines remotely from your workstation. To support working remotely on your network, there are several SunOS commands that let you find out information about other users and the network; these include `rusers`, `finger`, `ping`, and `ruptime`.

Logging In Remotely with rlogin

The `rlogin` command enables you to remotely log into other machines on your network. The system you start from is called the *local* system, and the system you want to log into is called the *remote* or *host* system. The `rlogin` command assumes that you have an account and home directory on the remote system. In most cases, you will be prompted for the correct user name and password before you can work on the remote machine. Once you make a connection using the `rlogin` command, you can enter commands on the remote system from your workstation as if you were sitting in front of that machine.

To log into a remote machine, use the following syntax:

```
rlogin hostname
```

where *hostname* is the name of the host (remote) machine. This syntax assumes you have the same login name on both systems. If you have a different login name on each system, you can use the -l option. For example, entering

```
rlogin -l bfife mayberry
```

logs you into the remote machine as the user **bfife**.

To end the **rlogin** session, you can press Control-d or enter

```
exit
```

which returns control back to your workstation.

N O T E

If you forget the name of the host machine, use the rusers or finger command, as explained later in this chapter.

You can set a system up so that you can avoid having to enter your login name and password when you log in remotely by creating a file called .rhosts in your home directory using a text editor. You then add a separate line to the .rhosts file that consists of the host machine name and your login name. For example, if you are **bfife** and want to log in on the **mayberry** machine on the **primetime** system, enter the following in the .rhosts file:

```
primetime bfife
```

When you log in from the **primetime** system, the **mayberry** machine checks **bfife**'s .rhosts file. If the machine name and user name match the machine name and login name typed in from **primetime**, then **mayberry** lets you log in without prompting you for your login name and password.

Transferring Files Remotely with rcp

The `rcp` command enables files to be copied between machines connected to a network. This command works like the `cp` command, except that you need to identify the remote system. You do this by preceding the file path name with the name of the remote system and a colon (:). To copy one or more files from a remote machine to your machine, use the following syntax:

```
rcp hostname:source destination
```

where *hostname* is the name of the remote machine, *source* is the name of the file(s) you want to copy, and *destination* is the path name on your machine where you want the file(s) copied to.

To copy files from your local machine to a remote machine, the syntax is

```
rcp source hostname:destination
```

where *source* is the file(s) you want to copy, *hostname* is the name of the remote machine, and *destination* is the path name on the remote machine where you want the copied files to reside.

You can also copy a file from your machine to a remote machine while you are logged into a third machine. To do this, you must enter the host *name* identifier for both the *source* and *destination* using the following syntax:

```
rcp hostname source:hostname destination
```

For example, entering

```
rcp mayberry:/home/bfife/arrests newrochelle:/home/bfife/records
```

copies the file named **arrests** from bfife's home directory on the **mayberry** machine to the records directory on the **newrochelle** machine. If you omit the full path name for a remote destination, `rcp` assumes the path is relative to your home directory on that system.

If you have a different login name on the remote system than on the host system, you can prefix the remote system name with your login name on that system and an at symbol (@). For example, if your login name on the remote system is **pmason**, you can copy a file as follows:

```
rcp arrests pmason@mayberry:records
```

which copies the `arrests` file to the `records` directory of your home directory on the machine named `mayberry`.

You can copy directories and subdirectories by using the `-r` option. For example, typing

```
rcp -r testdir mayberry: /tmp
```

causes the subdirectory `testdir` and all of its subdirectories and files to be copied into the `/tmp` directory on `mayberry`. You can use normal shorthand commands for specifying directories, such as `$HOME` for your home directory or the period (`.`) for the current directory.

Executing Commands Remotely with rsh

The `rsh` (remote shell) command lets you connect to the specified host machine and execute the specified command. It can be a real timesaver when you only want to perform one task on the remote machine, because it automatically logs into the remote host. However, your user name must be in a list on the host machine in order to use this command. The commands available using the `rsh` command are specified by the system administrator. You cannot run an interactive command such as vi when using the `rsh` command.

To execute a command on a remote machine, type

```
rsh hostname command
```

If you use the `rsh` command without specifying a command, `rsh` logs you into the remote system using the `rlogin` command. Use the `-1 username` option if your user name is different on the remote host machine.

As with the `rlogin` command, you can set up the remote system so that you do not have to enter your password when you remotely log in by creating a file called `.rhosts` (for remote hosts) in your home directory using a text editor, then entering the system name and your user name.

Viewing User Information with rusers

The `rusers` command produces a similar output to the `who` command, but for remote machines. The listing of users is in the order that responses are received after executing the `rusers` command. This default listing does not list a host machine if no users are logged into it. Typing

    rusers

displays the basic report that includes just the names of users logged into all the machines on the network. You can display the basic report for a specific remote host by typing

    rusers *hostname*

Adding the `-1` option to the `rusers` command adds additional information about each user. For example, typing

    rusers -1

displays an output that includes the following information: user ID, host name, terminal, login date, login time, idle time, and login host.

You can use the following options with the `rusers` command.

OPTION	RESULT
-a	Displays idle machines as well as active machines. The `rusers` or `rusers` *hostname* commands by default do not display machines where no users are currently logged on.
-1	Provides more detailed information, including user names, machine and terminal names, the time each user logged in, how long each user's machine has been idle, and the name of the machine that each user logged in from.
-h	Sorts the listing of users alphabetically by the host name.

OPTION	RESULT
-i	Sorts the listing of users by idle time.
-u	Sorts the listing of users by the number of users logged onto a host.

Viewing User Information with finger

The `finger` command is useful for finding out if a user you want to reach is available on the system. It provides information about whether the user has been absent from their system by tracking the last time a keystroke was performed in a shell as well as when the last email message was read. The syntax for the `finger` command is

```
finger [options] username@hostname
```

For example, entering

```
finger bfife@mayberry
```

displays the information about the user **bfife** on the remote **mayberry** machine.

```
mayberry
Login name: bfife
Directory: /home/mayberry/bfife          Shell: /bin/ksh
on since Jan 5 10:10:52 on console
8 hours 40 minutes Idle Time
No unread mail
No plan
```

A **username** can be specified as either a first name, last name, or login name.

You can display information about all the users on a remote machine by using the following syntax:

```
finger [options] hostname
```

which displays the following information about the users on the remote machine:

Login name

Full user name

Terminal name

Idle time

Login time

Location

You can use the following options with the `finger` command.

OPTION	EFFECT
-b	Omits user's home directory and shell from display.
-f	Used with -s to omit the heading that is normally displayed in short format.
-i	Shows idle format, a terse format similar to -s.
-l	Forces long format (the default).
-m	Requires that the name indicated username match exactly, instead of also searching for a match of the first or last names.
-q	Displays a listing in a quick format. The quick format is similar to the short format except that only the login name, terminal, and idle time are printed. Requires an exact match of the user name.
-s	Displays listing in a short format. The short format displays the login name, name, terminal, idle time, when the user logged on, and where the user is located on the network.
-w	Used with -s to omit user's full name, which is normally displayed in short format.

Checking Machine Status with ping

The ping command informs you if another host machine on the network is up and running or not active. If a network is running, it is usually referred to as being up or alive. When you run the ping command, a network message is sent to the specified host machine asking for a response. If the remote machine is up, the message *hostname* is alive is displayed, indicating that the machine responded to the request. If the remote host machine is down or cannot receive the network message, the message no answer from *hostname* is displayed.

The syntax of the ping command is

```
ping hostname
```

Adding the -s (statistics) option to the ping command reports the effectiveness of the data transfer between machines. This is useful if you want to see if the network is running slow. With the -s option, the ping command will continue to send packets until you press Control-c, then it will report the summary statistics. For example, entering

```
ping -s mayberry
```

and then pressing Control-c might generate a report like this:

```
PING mayberry: 56 data bytes
64 bytes from 129.144.50.21: icmp_seq=0  time=80. ms
64 bytes from 129.144.50.21: icmp_seq=1  time=0. ms
64 bytes from 129.144.50.21: icmp_seq=2  time=0. ms
64 bytes from 129.144.50.21: icmp_seq=3  time=0. ms
.
.
.

----mayberry PING Statistics----
4 packets transmitted, 4 packets received, 0% packet loss
round-trip (ms) min/avg/max = 0/20/80
```

Checking Machine Status with rup

The rup command allows you to see the uptime and load average on a remote system. When you execute the rup command, it broadcasts a network message on the local network and displays the responses it receives. To display the uptime and load average for all the machines on your local network, enter

```
rup
```

which displays a table similar to this:

```
mayberry     up   2 days   4:14   load average: 0.00,  0.17,   0.27
newrochelle  up   5 day    2:03   load average: 1.43,  1.39,   1.46
primetime    up   3 days   1:00   load average: 0.00,  0.00,   0.00
```

This table contains the name of each host, whether the host is up or down, the amount of time each host has been up or down, the number of users on that host, and information on the average load on the past minute, 5 minutes, and 15 minutes.

Entering

```
rup hostname
```

displays the same table as the `rup` command for the specified host machine.

Normally the listing is in the order that responses are received, but this order can be changed by specifying one of the following options:

OPTIONS	EFFECT
-h	Sorts the display alphabetically by host machine name.
-l	Sorts the display by the load average values.
-t	Sorts the display by the uptime values.

Modem Communications

The `tip` and `cu` commands allow you to call up using a modem and connect to other UNIX and non-UNIX machines. You can also copy files between your machine and the remote machine with `tip`. The `tip` program, which stands for Telephone Interface Program, is newer and more versatile than cu. The tip and cu programs are not as powerful as many modern telecommunications packages. They do not support Xmodem protocols or transfer binary files. However, they are easy to use, and one or the other is available on most UNIX systems. Both your system and the remote system must have proper hardware installed to make a connection possible using the tip or cu commands, and you must have an account on the remote system.

NOTE   Many system administrators restrict the use of the tip and cu commands for security and to control telephone costs.

Communicating with tip

The tip command establishes a connection to a remote host machine. Once the connection is established, a remote session using tip behaves like an interactive session on a local terminal. The tip command checks the **remote** file in the **/etc** directory for information when making a connection. This file contains all the systems phone lines and modems that tip can work with.

To dial another system using tip, use the following syntax:

```
tip -speed telephonenumber
```

where **-speed-entry** is the baud rate you want to set the modem to for communicating with the remote system. For example, **-9600** establishes the connection at the 9600 baud rate. The *telephonenumber* is the phone number of the other computer you want to access.

If your system administrator maintains an /etcremote file on your system, you can dial another system using the following syntax:

```
tip -speed hostname
```

where the **hostname** entry makes the tip program find the appropriate telephone number in the /etcremote file and dial it.

The tip program displays the prompt **dialing...**, then places the call through your network's modem. When the call is answered by the remote system, `tip` indicates the connection is complete with the prompt `dial-ing...connected`. From this point on, you are connected with the other computer and can proceed to log into the system.

To disconnect from the remote system, enter

~.

The `tip` program responds with an [EOT], meaning end of transmission, and returns you to your local prompt.

Transferring Files with tip

You can send a file from your system to the remote system or vice versa using the `tip` program. Entering

~p

tells `tip` that you want to send a file. Note that the tilde does not appear on the screen. The prompt changes to [put], which notifies you that it is ready for you to specify the file you want to send. Entering

filename

begins the sending of the specified file and displays the number of lines transferred. When the transfer is complete, `tip` will display the total number of lines transferred and an exclamation point (!) indicating the transfer is complete. Transferring a file from the remote machine to your machine is done in a similar manner to sending a file, except you use the ~t command.

The following are common `tip` commands that you can use to perform tasks while connected to the remote machine.

TILDE COMMAND	DESCRIPTION
~p	Puts (sends) a file to the remote machine.
~t	Takes (receives) a file from the remote machine.
~c	Changes directory on your local machine.

TILDE COMMAND	DESCRIPTION
~!	Escapes to a new shell, from which you can return to tip by typing exit. Lets you access your local machine while still being connected to the remote machine.
~Control-z	Suspends tip so you can perform commands on your (local) machine while still being connected to the remote machine. To return to tip, enter the fg command.
~Control-y	Suspends tip locally, but still displays the output of the remote machine.

Setting tip Variables

The tip program maintains a set of variables that can be used in normal operation or can be added to your .tiprc file. To set a variable during a tip session, enter

~s *variable*

To display a particular tip variable setting, enter the ~s, the variable name, and a question mark. For example, entering

~s record?

displays

record=tip.record

To display all the tip program variables, enter

~s all

When the tip program is run, it checks your home directory for a .tiprc file, which is an optional file where you can set tip environment variables. The tip program variables have Boolean, numeric, string, or character values. A tip variable assignment does not include any spaces. Numeric, string, and character values are set with the variable name, an equals sign (=), and a value; for example, entering

~s record=myfile

creates a log file named `myfile` for the current `tip` session. Boolean values are set by entering the variable name. To unset a variable, precede the variable name with an exclamation point (!). For example, to unset the verbose setting, enter

```
~s !verb
```

The following is a list of common `tip` environment variables.

VARIABLE	TYPE	DESCRIPTION
beautify or be, nb	Boolean	Discards unprintable characters so they are not placed into the captured file.
baudrate or ba	Numeric	Displays the baud rate at which the connection was initially established. The `baudrate` variable cannot be changed during a `tip` session.
dialtimeout or dial	Numeric	Displays the number of seconds to wait for a connection to be established. This defaults to 60 seconds. The `dialtimeout` variable cannot be changed during a `tip` session.
disconnect or di	String	Sets the string to send to the remote host when disconnecting. This defaults to the empty string " ". To log out when disconnecting, change the disconnect string to `disconnect=exit`.

VARIABLE	TYPE	DESCRIPTION
echocheck or ec	Boolean	Waits for the remote machine to echo the last character sent in order to synchronize with the remote machine during file transfers.
eofread or eofr	String	Specifies the string of characters that mark the end of transmission during a file transfer (~<). The default is the empty string " ".
eofwrite or eofw	String	Specifies the string that marks the end of transmission during a file transfer (~>). The default is the empty string " ".
eol or el	String	Specifies the string that tip uses to determine the end of a line. The escape character, ~, is recognized only if it is the first character following the end of a line. The default is the empty string " ". The Return key character is always an end-of-line character.
escape or es	Character	Specifies the escape character that informs tip you are entering tip commands rather than communicating with the remote machine. The default escape character is the tilde (~).

VARIABLE	TYPE	DESCRIPTION
exceptions or ex	String	Specifies the string of characters that should not be discarded when **beautify** is turned on. The default is \t\n\f\b for the tab, newline, formfeed, and backspace characters.
framesize or fr	Numeric	Sets the number of characters (bytes) for **tip** to store in a memory buffer when receiving files. When the internal buffer is full or when transfer is complete, **tip** writes the data to disk. The default is 1024 characters (bytes).
halfduplex or hdx	Boolean	Sets **tip** to run in half-duplex mode. In half-duplex mode, **tip** echoes the characters you type. If set off, **tip** will run in full-duplex mode, so the remote machine echoes the characters you type. The default is not set.
localecho or le	Boolean	Sets **tip** to run in half-duplex mode. **localecho** is exactly the same as the **halfduplex** variable.
host or ho	String	Displays the host name that you specified when running **tip**. If you ran **tip** with a phone number, then this will be the name of your local machine. The **host** variable cannot be changed during a **tip** session.

VARIABLE	TYPE	DESCRIPTION
parity or par	String	Specifies the parity setting. Parity is an error-checking procedure in which the number of 1's in transmitted data must match; that is, they must be either even or odd. Parity checking is used to check the accuracy of transmitted data. If the setting is **none**, parity is not checked. **zero** specifies that parity is not checked on input, and the parity bit is set to zero on output. **one** specifies that parity is not checked on input, and the parity bit is set to one on output. **even** specifies that parity of successfully transmitted data must be an even number. **odd** specifies the parity of transmitted data must be odd. The default is **none** (no parity).
phones	String	Specifies the name of the file containing phone numbers. By default, **phones** is set to **/etc/phones**. You can create your own file for system phone numbers by setting the environmental variable **PHONES** to the name of a file containing system names and phone numbers.

VARIABLE	TYPE	DESCRIPTION
`prompt` or `pr`	Char	Specifies the character that marks the end of line for the remote machine. The default is `\n`.
`raise` or `ra`	Boolean	Converts lowercase characters you type to uppercase. Characters you enter in response to the `tip` program's prompts will not be converted. The default is not set.
`rawftp` or `raw`	Boolean	Sends all characters during file transfers. This does not filter out nonprintable characters. Turns off all newline/carriage return pairs that are mapped to newlines. The default is on.
`record` or `rec`	String	Specifies the name of the file to record the current `tip` session when script is turned on. The default file is `tip.record`.
`remote`	String	Specifies the file name that `tip` refers to for descriptions of remote systems. The default is `/etc/remote`. You can change the default by setting the environment variable REMOTE to another file name. The `remote` variable cannot be changed during a `tip` session or in your `.tiprc` file.

VARIABLE	TYPE	DESCRIPTION
`script` or `sc`	Boolean	Records everything you type and everything the remote machine displays appended to the file whose name is defined by record. If **beautify** is turned on, only printable characters are saved. If **beautify** is turned off, everything is saved.
`tabexpand` or `tab`	Boolean	Converts tab characters to eight-space characters. The default is not set.
`tandem` or `ta`	Boolean	Controls data flow. If set to X, the ON/X OFF flow control is used. Control-s stops data flow and Control-q restarts data flow. The default is on.
`etimeout` or `et`	Numeric	Specifies the number of seconds that **tip** should wait for a character to echo when echo check is turned on. The default is 10 seconds.
`verbose` or `verb`	Boolean	Displays messages while dialing and during transfers. The default is on.

Communicating with cu

The **cu** program, like the **tip** program, enables you to connect to another machine using a modem. The **cu** program is not as powerful as the **tip** program. To connect onto another system using the **cu** command, enter

```
cu telephonenumber
```

The cu program's default baud rate is 300, which is excruciatingly slow. The -s option is used with the cu command to specify the baud rate you want. The most common baud rates are 1200, 2400, 9600, 19200, and 38400. For example, entering

```
cu -s9600 5551212
```

dials the number 555-1212 and connects using a 9600 baud rate.

The phone number can include an equal sign (=) as a wait-for-dial-tone code. For example, if you have to dial 9 to get an outside line, enter

```
cu 9=5551212
```

The following options allow you to change various cu default settings.

OPTION	DESCRIPTION
-s *speed*	Sets the baud rate to *speed*.
-e	Sets even parity on outgoing characters.
-o	Sets odd parity on outgoing characters.
-h	Sets half-duplex communications.
-t	Dials a terminal that has been set to autoanswer. The -t option also maps CR (Carriage Return) to CR/LF (Carriage Return/Line Feed) on incoming lines of text.

If the destination system has a name your system recognizes, you can use the system name instead of the phone number. For example, entering

```
cu mayberry
```

establishes a connection with the mayberry system.

To terminate a cu session, first log off the remote system by pressing Control-d, then type

```
~.
```

which terminates the cu connection.

After making the connection to the remote system, enter the commands for the remote machine as you would commands at your machine's command-line prompt. You can enter commands for your machine while still connected to the remote machine by preceding the command with a tilde (~). The following are tilde commands recognized by cu.

COMMAND	DESCRIPTION
~.	Terminates the connection.
~!	Escapes to the local system.
~!*command*	Runs the specified command on the local system.
~$*command*	Runs the specified command on the local system and sends its output to the remote system.
~%cd	Changes the directory on the local system.
~%take *filename1* *filename2*	Copies *filename1* from the remote system to the file *filename2* on the local system. If *filename2* is omitted, the name of *filename1* is used.
~%put *filename1* *filename2*	Copies *filename1* from the local system to the file *filename2* on the remote system. If *filename2* is omitted, the name of *filename1* is used.
~~*line*	Transmits ~*line* to the remote system. This is used when you call system B from system A, then call system C from system B. A single tilde (~) lets you execute commands on system A, and two tildes (~~) can be used to execute commands on system B.
~%break	Transmits a BREAK (Control-c) code to the remote system.

Transferring Files with cu

You can transfer a file from the remote system to your system using the cu program. Entering

```
~%take file
```

transfers *file* from the remote machine to your machine. If you want to copy the transferred file and name it with a different name, enter

```
~%take original copiedfile
```

where *original* is the name of the remote file to transfer and *copiedfile* indicates the name of the transferred file.

To send a file from your system to the remote system using the cu program, enter

```
~%put fromfile tofile
```

which tells cu that you want to send the file named *fromfile* to the file named *tofile* on the remote system. The cu program begins sending *fromfile* and displays the number of lines and characters transferred.

Working with the Internet

The Internet is a huge information superhighway that connects more than 5,000 networks and is used by 5 to 10 million users worldwide. The Internet has mushroomed from its early military-industrial-complex roots into a global system available to any computer user. The Internet uses the TCP/IP (Transport Control Protocol/Interface Program) protocol to allow communication among different operating systems. Three TCP/IP applications, mailx (electronic mail), telnet (remote login), and ftp (file transfer), are basic tools you need to work on the Internet. There are plenty of other applications available on the Internet, but these three programs are the workhorses and are available on nearly all networks connected to the Internet. Working with the mailx program was explained in Chapter 11, "Electronic Mail and Messages." The following sections provide an explanation of the Internet addressing system for sending email and connecting to machines on the Internet, as well as how to work with the telnet and ftp programs.

Internet Addresses

Each computer on the Internet has a name. An Internet computer name is usually several words separated by periods, such as `tyco.usno.navy.mil`. The naming system used by the Internet is known as the Domain Name System (DNS). The DNS is also the worldwide system of distributed databases of names and addresses. DNS names are constructed in a hierarchical fashion.

You can tell the type of network you are connecting to by checking the last part of the address name. For example, in the address `prep.ai.mit.edu`, the `edu` indicates an education domain. This address, by the way, is used for the Free Software foundation at MIT, which you can log into using the `ftp` program and the login name `anonymous`. The main domain-name categories on the Internet are EDU (educational), COM (commercial), GOV (government), MIL (military), ORG (organizations), and NET (networks). In addition, there are also two-letter country codes (like US for the United States and JP for Japan).

Connecting with telnet

The `telnet` program lets you log into host computers in a similar way to using the `rlogin` command, but it can operate with any computer that supports the Telnet protocol, including UNIX and non-UNIX systems. Once connected to a host system, you can usually access a database of on-line information available to any user. Depending on the host system you log into, the commands vary for navigating the host system.

The syntax for using the `telnet` command to connect to a remote system is

```
telnet remotehostname
```

After making the connection, you are prompted for a user name and password on the remote system. In most cases, you can log into a remote host system on the Internet using a public access login user name and password, or you'll know the user name and password before making the connection. For example, entering

```
telnet spacelink.msfc.nasa.gov
```

connects you to the NASA system. When prompted for a login user name and password, enter

`newuser`

You are then presented with a menu of options for reading entries about the history, current state, and future of NASA activities.

You can also make a `telnet` connection by typing `telnet` without a machine name, then at the `telnet` prompt entering

`open` *remotehostname*

Once the connection has been opened, the `telnet` program enters the terminal mode. In this mode, typed text is sent to the remote host system. You can switch from terminal mode to command mode by entering the `telnet` escape character `Control-]`. This returns you to the local machine and the `telnet` program.

The following `telnet` commands are used to start, suspend, and quit a `telnet` session.

COMMAND	DESCRIPTION
`close`	Terminates the connection but allows you to remain in the `telnet` program.
`open` *remotehostname*	Connects to the host machine specified by *remotehostname*.
`bye` or `quit`	Quits the current connection and exits the `telnet` program. You should log out of the remote host, using the `exit` command, before using the `quit` command.
`z`	Temporarily suspends the `telnet` session to allow other commands to be executed on the local system.
`<Return>`	Returns you to the shell at the remote host machine.

Transferring Files with ftp

A tremendous variety of public-domain software is available on the Internet. The most common way that these programs are distributed is via the **ftp** program. The **ftp** command implements the File Transfer Protocol (FTP) that allows files on different systems to be copied back and forth.

To make a connection using **ftp** to an Internet host system, enter

```
ftp remotehostname
```

You can also begin an **ftp** session with a remote host by entering

```
ftp
```

After the **ftp>** program prompt appears, enter

```
open hostname
```

For example, entering

```
open ftp.cs.widener.edu
```

accesses an archive of information about the Simpsons (stored in /pub/simpsons). At the login prompt, enter **anonymous**. Many resources that are accessible using the **ftp** program can be accessed by any user using a generic login name and password.

After the remote system has accepted your login name and password, you are ready to start transferring files. The **ftp** program can transfer files in two directions using the **get** and **put** commands. The **get** command copies files from the remote host machine to your system. The **put** command copies files from your system to the remote host machine. The **get** and **put** commands use the syntax

```
get source-file destination-file
put source-file destination-file
```

The *source-file* is the name of the file you want to copy. The *destination-file* is the name of the copied file. The *destination-file* name is optional; if it is omitted, the copied file is given the same name as the *source-file*.

Before copying a file, you need to make sure the correct transfer type is set. The default transfer type is ASCII. If you want to transfer an application or program file, you need to set the file transfer type to binary. To do this, at the `ftp>` prompt, enter

    `binary`

To set the file transfer type back to ASCII, use the `ascii` command. Once the file transfer type is set, you can use the `get` or `put` command. When you use either the `get` or `put` command, the `ftp` program reports that the transfer has begun, then reports when the file transfer has been completed and tells you how long the transfer took.

You can copy more than one file with the `mget` and `mput` commands, which use the same syntax as the `get` and `put` commands, except you can use metacharacters, such as (?) and (*) to specify multiple files.

To terminate an `ftp` session, at the `ftp>` prompt, enter

    `quit`

The following lists the most commonly used `ftp` commands.

COMMAND	ACTION
`?`	Lists available `ftp` commands.
`append` *localfile* *remotefile*	Appends the local file specified by *localfile* to the file on the remote host specified by *remotefile*.
`ascii`	Sets the file transfer type to ASCII (the default setting).
`bell`	Sounds a bell when a file transfer is completed.
`binary`	Sets the file transfer type to binary.
`bye` or `quit`	Terminates the `ftp` session.
`cd` *remote directoryname*	Changes the current directory on the remote machine to the directory specified.
`close`	Terminates the `ftp` session with the remote machine, but continues the `ftp` session on the local machine.

COMMAND	ACTION
`delete` *`remotefilename`*	Deletes the remote file name specified by *remotefilename*.
`get` *`remotefilename`* *`[localfilename]`*	Copies *remotefile* to the local host. If *localfilename* is not specified, the copy has the same name as the original file (*remotefilename*).
`help`	Lists available `ftp` commands.
`help` *command*	Describes the command specified by *command*.
`lcd` *`[directoryname]`*	Changes the current directory on the local machine to the directory specified by *directoryname*; if no directory is specified, `lcd` changes to the user's home directory.
`mget` *`remotefilenames`*	Copies the files specified by *remotefilenames* to the current directory on the local machine.
`mkdir directory-name`	Makes a directory with the name specified by *directoryname* on the remote host machine.
`mput` *`localfilenames`*	Copies the files specified by *localfilenames* to the current directory on the remote host.
`open` *`[remotehostname]`*	Sets up a connection with the host machine specified; if no host is specified, a prompt appears for entering the host machine name.
`put` *`localfilename`* *`[remotefilename]`*	Copies the file to the remote host with the file name specified.
`pwd`	Displays the name of the current directory on the remote host machine.

System
Administration Basics

THIS chapter explains essential system administration tasks. These tasks may need to be performed if your system administrator is unavailable or as routine tasks if your system administrator has issued you a superuser password. A *superuser* is a privileged user with unrestricted access to all files and commands. While there are some system administration tasks that a nonsuperuser can perform, in most cases you must be a superuser to perform system administration tasks that affect other users on your system or network. Basic system administration tasks include booting up and shutting down your system, accessing devices (such as disk drives), archiving files, and using the OpenWindows Administration Tool to perform the most elementary system administration tasks of adding or deleting a user, workstation, or printer to or from the network.

Working as a Superuser

The superuser is also referred to as a *root* user, and these terms are used interchangeably to describe the same privileged user status. When you have superuser privileges, the shell provides a special pound sign (#) prompt to remind you that you have privileged access to the system. The system keeps a log that records each time someone logs in as root or someone uses the superuser command.

To become a superuser if you are not already logged into the system, at the login prompt enter

```
root
```

To become a superuser if you are already logged into the system as a user other than root, enter

`su`

To exit superuser status, type

`exit`

Communicating with Users on Your Network

An important part of performing system administrator tasks is to make sure you always let users know when you are about to perform a task that will affect them, such as rebooting a system or changing the environment. There are several ways you can communicate with users, such as using the `mailx` and `write` commands. The following sections explain how to create a login message to communicate with users as they log in, and how to use the `wall` and the `rwall` commands to communicate with all the users on your system or on the network.

Creating a Login Message

Each time a user logs into a system, any messages from the system administrator are displayed. These messages are not displayed to users already logged in. Login messages are stored in the file `/etc/motd` (message of the day), which is only accessible to the superuser.

To create a login message for the day, do the following:

1. Become a superuser.

2. Use an editor such as vi to open the `/etc/motd` file.

3. Delete any obsolete messages and type your new login message. Make sure your messages are short. If the message is longer than a screenful of text, users won't be able to read the beginning lines.

4. Save the changes. The message is changed and is displayed the next time a user logs into the system.

Sending a Message to All Users on a System or Network

You can send a message to every user on a system using the `wall` command, or send a message to every user on the network using the `rwall` command. You do not have to be a superuser to use either the `wall` or `rwall` command.

To send a message to all users on your system, do the following:

1. At the system prompt, type `wall` and press Return.

2. Type the message text you want to send.

3. When the message is complete, press Control-d. The message is displayed in the console window of each user or at the command line.

To send a message to all users on your network, do the following:

1. At the system prompt, type `rwall -n` *networkname* and press Return.

2. Type the message you want to send.

3. When the message is complete, press Control-d. The message is displayed in the console window of each user on the system or at the command line.

You can also use the `rwall` command to send a message to all users on a specific remote system by typing `rwall` *hostname*, where *hostname* is the name of the remote system you want to send the message.

N O T E Use the `rwall` command carefully, because it consumes extensive system and network resources.

Booting and Rebooting Your System

Booting is the process of powering up a system, testing to determine which attached hardware devices are running, and bringing up the operating system software. You normally don't have to boot your system because Sun workstations are designed to run continuously, preventing wear on system components. Each time you turn on the power, the machine reboots itself so that you can start using it again. In most cases, the system is set up to boot automatically from a local disk or over the network. In certain uncommon circumstances, such as when your system freezes up, you may have to manually boot or reboot your system to get it running again. The following sections explain how to manually boot and reboot your system.

NOTE If your machine is set up to boot from a tape or diskette, you need to insert the appropriate disk or tape for the boot procedure to work.

Booting Your System

If your system is off, simply turning it on will usually cause the system to boot itself. If when you turn the system on, it displays a prompt similar to this:

```
console login type b (boot), c (continue), or n (new command mode)
>
```

at the boot prompt (>), enter

```
n
```

to enter the new command mode. The prompt changes to display

```
Type help for more information
ok
```

At the ok prompt, enter

> boot

NOTE Solaris 2 for x86 does not start the same way as Solaris for Sun Workstations. It boots off a hard disk or a floppy disk drive, so you cannot use these instructions.

Rebooting Your System

If the system is already running and you need to reboot the system from the command prompt, become a superuser by entering

> su

and enter the superuser password. If you are not logged in, enter root at the login prompt to become a superuser. At the superuser prompt (#), enter

> reboot

If you are adding new hardware to your system, you need to reboot with the −r option to reconfigure your system. To run a reconfiguration script for the new hardware, enter

> boot −r

Emergency Rebooting

If you are using a Sun keyboard and the machine doesn't respond to keystrokes such as Control-c, then press Stop-a. (The Stop key is the accelerator key located in the upper-left corner of the keyboard.) On some Sun keyboards the Stop key is labeled L1. If a special prompt (> or ok) is not displayed, check the cables connecting the components of the system. If the system still doesn't respond, try turning off the power, waiting 60 seconds, and then turning the power back on.

WARNING Always allow 60 seconds between turning off the power and turning it back on again. This pause prevents possible damage to power supply components in your machine.

As a last resort if emergency rebooting does not solve the problem, contact Sun Customer Service (1-800-USA-4SUN). If the > boot prompt is displayed, type n and at the ok boot prompt, type **boot** and press Return to reboot the machine. A system login screen or prompt indicates that the system has booted properly and is awaiting a user to log in.

NOTE If you are using Solaris 2 for x86 and the machine doesn't respond to keystrokes, such as Control-c, you need to press the reset button on your computer to reboot.

Shutting Down Your System

The SunOS system software is designed to be left running continuously so that the network and email software can work correctly. However, there are situations that require the system be shut down, which means intentionally stopping execution of the system software. To shut down your workstation or a system, you must be a superuser. You should always shut down the machine before turning any of the power switches off. When you shut down your machine properly, you protect the machine from damage and prevent the loss of your data. You may need to shut down the system in the following circumstances.

- Turning off system power.
- Performing maintenance on a file system.
- Installing a new release of Solaris.
- Adding new hardware to the system.
- Moving the system to another location.

Shutting Down a System

Shutting down a system with multiple users using the `shutdown` command sends a warning message to all users who are logged in, waits for 60 seconds (the default), then shuts down the system to a single-user state (your workstation). You can choose a different default time to allow more time. You can check the activity before shutting down the network by typing `ps -ef` and pressing Return.

Follow these steps to shut down a multiuser system.

1. Become a superuser and change to the root (/) directory.

2. Enter `/usr/sbin/shutdown`. After a short wait, the system shuts down to a single-user state and you can perform any maintenance tasks. You can specify a longer period to wait before shutting down the system by adding the argument `-g` *time* to the `shutdown` command, where time is the amount of time to wait before shutting down the system.

3. Turn off the power to all units in the following order: monitor, external drive unit (if you have one), and system unit.

To quickly shut down and reboot a multiuser system, follow these steps:

1. Become a superuser and change to the root / directory.

2. Enter `/usr/sbin/shutdown -i6`. This command broadcasts a message to all users that the system is being shut down. After the system is shut down, it is restarted in its multiuser state.

3. Enter y when asked `Do you want to continue? (y or n):`. The system shuts down.

Shutting Down Your Workstation

Shutting down a single-user system is similar to shutting down a multi-user system except you use the `init 0` command instead of the `shutdown` command. The following steps explain how to shut down a single-user system.

1. Save any files you are presently editing with applications running on your machine, and quit any applications that will lose information when the machine shuts down.

2. Become a superuser by entering **su** at the system prompt, then entering the password assigned to a superuser.

3. Enter `init 0` and wait for either the **>** or **ok** prompt.

4. Turn off the power to all units in the following order: monitor, external drive unit (if you have one), and system unit.

To shut down and reboot a single-user system, follow these steps:

1. Change to the root directory by entering **cd /**.

2. Enter the **su** (superuser) command.

3. Enter `init 6`. No warning is displayed. After the system is shut down, it is restarted in its single-user state.

Emergency Shutdown for a Single System

If you need to shut down your system in a hurry, enter **uadmin 2 0**. Information is written to the disk and the system displays the boot prompt. To shut down a system that does not respond properly to the keyboard or to the mouse, follow these steps:

1. If you are using a Sun keyboard, press Stop-a (L1-A on some Sun keyboards). If you are using Solaris 2 for x86, there is no equivalent to Stop-a, so you must use the reset button on your PC.

2. Turn off the power to all units in the following order: monitor, external drive unit (if you have one), and system unit.

Managing Hard Drives and CD ROM Drives on Your Network

The system administrator is responsible for making sure that devices such as disk drives are available to users on the network. In order for a drive to be available, it must be formatted and contain a file system. Solaris allows users to work with different file systems, such as ufs (UNIX file system) and Sun's Network File System (NFS). The process of making a drive and its file system available to the system by attaching it into the directory tree at the specified mount point is called *mounting*. To mount and unmount drives, you must have superuser privileges. The following sections explain what file systems are, and how to identify a drive by its device name, list mounted drives, mount and unmount drives onto your network, and display information about a drive.

Understanding File Systems

A *file system* is a structure of directories used to locate and store files. The ufs (UNIX file system) is the default file system and Sun's network file system (NFS) is the network file system used by Solaris. NFS requests are translated from the UNIX file system to the network file system and sent across the network and translated back to the UNIX file system. *File systems are normally associated with a particular type of media.* File systems exist for floppy diskettes, hard disks, and CD ROMs. You can add the following types of file systems as a super user:

FILE SYSTEM	DESCRIPTION
ufs	UNIX file system. The ufs is the default file system for SunOS.
hsfs	High Sierra is the CD ROM file system. The hsfs is a read-only file system. The hsfs supports Rock Ridge extensions.
pcfs	PC file system, which allows you to read and write data on MS-DOS-formatted diskettes.

Identifying a Drive by Its Device Name

In some cases you will need to specify a disk drive by its device name, such as when you add a drive to your system and want to mount it. At first the device name of a disk may seem a little overwhelming, but if you break down the device name it is fairly easy to follow. The device name of a SCSI disk drive consists of four parts. The disk device name takes the following format:

```
/dev/rdsk/cwtxdysz
```

The following identifies the four parts of a disk device name.

cw   Indicates the controller number. The controller is a device that can be a separate board in your workstation that your drive is connected to or it can be integrated into the SCSI disk drive. The controller is responsible for organizing data on the disk. If you only have one disk controller on your system, the controller identifier will always be 0.

tx   Specifies the target address. To identify the target address, look at the switch that is set on the back of your disk drive.

d*y*   Displays the drive number. If the disk has an embedded controller, the drive number is always 0.

s*z*   Displays the slice (partition) number. The slice number can be a number 0 to 7. The most common assignments for disk slices are: slice 0, which is used by the operating system; slice 1, used for swapping data from memory to disk; slice 2, which indicates the entire disk; and slice 6, which typically contains the /usr directory and its subdirectories.

Mounting a File System

There are three ways that file systems can be mounted. The first method, called automounting, mounts and unmounts file systems shared through the network file system (NFS) automatically by simply changing directories. This method is totally transparent to the user. The second method is to manually mount a drive from the command line. You must be logged in as a superuser in order to manually mount a file system. The third method lets you add an entry into a special file (/etc/vfstab) so that a drive is automatically mounted when the system is booted. Adding an entry in this file also makes it so you can mount a file system by simply referring to its mount point (the directory the file system is mounted on). The following sections explain how to list mounted file systems, mount file systems using each of these three methods, and unmount file systems.

Listing Mounted File Systems

Any user can display which file systems are mounted by entering

```
mount
```

which displays a listing similar to this:

```
/ on /dev/dsk/c0t1d0s0 read/write on Mon Nov 28 15:23:09 1994
/usr on /dev/dsk/c0t1d0s6 read/write on Mon Nov 28 15:23:09 1994
/proc on /proc read/write on Mon Nov 28 15:23:09 1994
/dev/fd on fd read/write on Mon Nov 28 15:23:09 1994
/tmp on swap read/write on Mon Nov 28 15:30:13 1994
/opt on /dev/dsk/c0t1d0s5 setuid on Mon Nov 28 15:30:15 1994
/mnt on /dev/dsk/c0t0d0s6 setuid on Mon Nov 28 15:30:17 1994
```

Mounting Using the Automounter

You can mount file systems shared through the network file system (NFS) using a method called *automounting*. The `automount` program, commonly referred to as the *automounter*, runs in the background and mounts and unmounts remote directories as they are needed. The automounter mounts and unmounts file systems whenever a user changes into or out of a directory that is available through the automounter. The `automount` program mounts the file system on the user's system and remains mounted as long as the user remains in the directory or is using a file in a remote directory. If the remote file system is not accessed for a certain period of time, it is automatically unmounted.

Manually Mounting a File System

To manually mount a disk drive from the command line, you need to specify the disk drive's device name. The `mount` command adds a file system to the root file system to make it available to the network. The file system is attached to an existing directory, which is then considered the *mount point*. If the mount point directory has any files or subdirectories prior to the mount operation, they are hidden until the file system is unmounted. Manually mounting a file system adds an entry to the `/etc/mnttab` file. For example, to mount a disk set up as target disk 1 that is the first disk on the system (0), and mount its sixth slice (s6) and attach the disk drive at the `/disk1` directory, follow these steps:

1. Become a superuser.

2. At the superuser prompt, enter `mkdir /disk1`.

3. Enter `mount /dev/dsk/c0t1d0s6 /disk1` to attach the disk to the file system.

4. Type `exit` to return to exit the superuser privileges.

Adding the `-F filesystemtype` argument specifies the file system type on which to operate. The most common file systems are ufs (UNIX file system), hsfs (High Sierra file system), nfs (network file system), and pcfs (PC file system).

The following list describes generic options commonly supported by most file system types.

-m   Mounts the file system without making an entry in /etc/mnttab.

-r   Mounts the file system read-only.

-o   Specifies the file system type-specific options in a comma-separated (without spaces) list of suboptions. These are the standard ufs mount options:

     n   Mounts the file system without making an entry in the /etc/mnttab `file`.

     rw   Mounts the system as read and write.

     ro   Mounts the system so it is read-only.

To mount target disk 3 (t3) on the sixth partition (s6) on the `/mnt` directory, enter

```
mount /dev/dsk/c0t3d0s6 /mnt
```

Mounting a High Sierra File System

The hsfs (High Sierra file system) is the file system used with Sun CD ROMs. Sun's CD ROM drives are set to SCSI target 6 by default. The following example mounts a CD ROM using the High Sierra file system (hsfs) on the directory `/cdrom`.

```
mount -F hsfs -o ro /dev/dsk/c0t6d0s2 /cdrom
```

If the mount information for a drive is in your `/etc/vfstab/` file, you can mount a drive by just adding the mount point. For example, enter

```
mount /cdrom
```

to mount the `cdrom` drive on the `/cdrom` directory. The `mount` command checks the `/etc/vfstab` for the information it needs to mount the drive.

Mounting a PCFS File System

In order to mount a PC file system (pcfs) to get access to files on a floppy diskette that came from a MS-DOS PC, you first need to create a directory to attach the pcfs file system to. To create the directory /pcfiles for mounting the MS-DOS floppy, enter

```
mkdir /pcfiles
```

You can now mount the floppy disk drive on the directory named /pcfiles by entering

```
mount -F pcfs /dev/diskette /pcfiles
```

The -F option specifies the type of file system to mount.

To unmount the floppy diskette mounted on the /pcfiles directory, first change to a directory in the file system other than the /pcfiles directory, and enter

```
umount /pcfiles
```

Mounting a Device Automatically

The /etc/vfstab (virtual file system table) file contains a list of devices that are automatically made available when booting the system. To see the list of disks that are in your /etc/vfstab file, enter

```
more /etc/vfstab
```

The following is a sample /etc/vfstab file listing.

```
#device             device            mount   FS    fsck mount mount
#to mount           to fsck           point   type  pass atboot options
#
#/dev/dsk/c1d0s2    /dev/rdsk/c1d0s2  /usr    ufs   1    yes    -
/proc               -                 /proc   proc  -    no     -
fd                  -                 /dev/fd fd    -    no     -
swap                -                 /tmp    tmpfs -    yes    -
/dev/dsk/c0t1d0s0   /dev/rdsk/c0t1d0s0 /      ufs   1    no     -
/dev/dsk/c0t1d0s6   /dev/rdsk/c0t1d0s6 /usr   ufs   2    no     -
/dev/dsk/c0t1d0s5   /dev/rdsk/c0t1d0s5 /opt   ufs   3    yes    -
/dev/dsk/c0t1d0s1   -                 -       swap  -    no     -
/dev/dsk/c0t0d0s6   /dev/rdsk/c0t0d0s6 /mnt   ufs   2    yes    -
/dev/dsk/c0t6d0s2   /dev/rdsk/c0t6d0s2 /cdrom hsfs  -    no     ro
```

When you boot up the system, the `mountall` command is performed to mount all the devices that are specified to be mounted in the `/etc/vstab` file. The `fsck` command is also run to check the file systems to be mounted when booting the system.

You can add a device to the `/etc/vfstab` file to have the device mounted automatically when you boot. Each entry in the `/etc/vfstab` file has seven fields that are separated by spaces or a tab. The following briefly explains each of the fields in the `/etc/vfstab` file.

FIELD	DESCRIPTION
device to mount	Identifies the device that you want to mount; for example, entering `dev/dsk/c0t1d0s6` indicates the drive set to target 1 on the sixth slice (partition).
device to fsck	Identifies the raw (character) device that corresponds to the file system you want to mount; for example, `/dev/rdsk/c0t1d0s6` is the raw device name for the `/dev/rdsk/c0t1d0s6` device. This determines that the device to check should be treated as a raw character device rather than a block device. Use a dash (–) when there is no applicable device, such as for a read-only file system or a network-based file system.
mount point	Specifies the directory to use for mounting the device; for example, the /usr directory might be the mount point for `/dev/dsk/c0t1d0s6`, or the `/cdrom` directory might be the mount point for `/dev/dsk/c0t6d0s2`.
FS type	Indicates the type of file system to be mounted. For example, enter ufs for a UNIX file system, `hsfs` for a CD ROM, or `pcfs` for a MS-DOS file system.

FIELD	DESCRIPTION
`fsck pass`	Specifies the pass number used by the fsck command to specify whether to check a file system. A dash (−) indicates that you do not want the file system to be checked. When the field contains a value of 1 or more, the file system is checked. A `ufs` file system with a zero (0) indicates that the file system should not be checked. When the field contains a value of 1, the file system is checked sequentially. Otherwise, the value of the pass number does not have any effect.
`mount at boot`	Specifies whether the file system should be automatically mounted by the `mountall` command when the system is booted. Enter **yes** to mount the file system or **no** *not* to mount the file system automatically. This field has nothing to do with the automounter program.
`mount options`	Specifies the options for mounting the file system. Options are separated by commas with no spaces. These are the same options commonly supported by the file system type (as explained earlier). For example, `ro` stands for read-only device (the default is `rw`). To specify no options, use a dash (−).

Unmounting a File System

To unmount a file system you must change to a directory that is in a file system other than the one to be unmounted, and enter the `umount` com mand followed by the file system's mount point. The `mount` command maintains a table of mounted file systems in `/etc/mnttab`. The `mount` command adds an entry to the mount table; the `umount` command removes an entry from the table.

Unmounting a file system removes it from the system's directory tree and removes the entry from the /etc/mnttab (mount table) file. Once a file is unmounted, any subdirectories and files that existed in the mount point's directory become available. File systems are automatically unmounted when shutting down the system. To unmount a specific disk drive, use the umount command followed by the name of the disk drive you want to remove. The following unmounts the file system mounted on the /add directory.

```
umount /add
```

You can also specify a drive to unmount by adding the device name to the umount command. The following example unmounts the file system for the target disk 3 (t3) mounted on the sixth partition (s6).

```
umount /dev/dsk/c0t3d0s6
```

You cannot unmount a disk that is being used. If the directory or files are being accessed, the message umount: /add busy is displayed.

Displaying Disk Information

To check the amount of space that you have available on a disk, use the du command. The du (disk usage) command reports the number of 512-byte disk blocks used per file or directory. If the directory contains sub-directories, the subdirectories and their files are included in the block count. Entering

```
du
```

displays a listing similar to this:

```
2    ./.wastebasket
16086   ./Folder/frame/chaps
26  ./Folder/frame/notes
226 ./Folder/frame/docs
314 ./Folder/frame/reports
16654   ./Folder/frame
19630   ./Folder
6   ./.cetables
162 ./.Mail
996 ./bin
3470./images
18  ./.menus
24484   .
```

You can display the total amount of allocated space in kilobytes, rather than 512-kilobyte blocks by entering

```
du -k
```

If you use the same disk as in the previous du example, the command du -k displays the following report:

```
1     ./.wastebasket
8043./Folder/frame/chaps
13   ./Folder/frame/notes
113  ./Folder/frame/docs
157  ./Folder/frame/reports
8327./Folder/frame
9815./Folder
3     ./.cetables
81   ./.Mail
498  ./bin
1735./images
9     ./.menus
12245   .
```

The df command reports the amount of occupied disk space, the amount of used and available space, and how much of the file system's storage space has been used. If you use the df command without any argument, the amount of space occupied and files for all mounted file systems are displayed. Entering

```
df -k
```

displays a listing of the amount in kilobytes of used and available space, similar to this:

Filesystem	kbytes	used	avail	capacity	Mounted on
/dev/dsk/c0t0d0s0	24143	15954	5779	73%	/
/dev/dsk/c0t0d0s6	192151	171623	1318	99%	/usr
/proc	0	0	0	0%	/proc
fd	0	0	0	0%	/dev/fd
swap	80180	16	80164	0%	/tmp
/dev/dsk/c0t0d0s5	95167	77279	8378	90%	/opt
/dev/dsk/c0t6d0s2	186723	180697	0	100%	/cdrom

To display a partition map of a disk, use the prtvtoc command. The prtvtoc command displays the volume table of contents for the disk you specify. You must be a superuser to use the prtvtoc command. Keep in mind this command only works when the slice (partition) you specify has space allocated to it. To display information about target disk 1 for the entire disk, become a superuser and enter

```
prtvtoc /dev/rdsk/c0t1d0s2
```

which displays output similar to this:

```
* /dev/rdsk/c0t1d0s2 partition map
*
* Dimensions:
*     512 bytes/sector
*      80 sectors/track
*       9 tracks/cylinder
*     720 sectors/cylinder
*    2500 cylinders
*    1151 accessible cylinders
*
* Flags:
*   1: unmountable
*  10: read-only
*
*                          First   Sector  Last
* Partition  Tag Flags  Sector  Count  Sector  Mount Directory
      0        2   00        0    51840   51839  /
      1        3   01    51840   164160  215999
      2        5   00        0   828720  828719
      5        6   00   216000   203040  419039  /opt
      6        4   00   419040   409680  828719  /usr
```

Working with Floppy Disks

If your workstation has a floppy disk drive, you can perform several tasks using Solaris to work with floppy disks. The following sections explain how to use a formatted disk, format a floppy disk for storing SunOS files, create a file system on a floppy disk, format a floppy disk for MS-DOS files, and write-protect floppy disks.

Using a Floppy Disk

To use a formatted disk, first insert the diskette into the drive, label side up. Push firmly to lock the diskette into place. To eject the diskette from the drive, type `eject` at the command prompt and press Return. If the diskette does not work correctly, it may need to be formatted.

Formatting a Floppy Disk in the SunOS Format

To format a diskette you must first know whether you are using a high-density (1.44Mb) diskette or a double-density (720K) diskette. By default, `fdformat` formats a high-density diskette (1.44 Mb) in the SunOS format. Before you format a diskette, make sure you can't see through the square hole in the upper-right corner of the diskette. If the notch is uncovered, push the plastic tab up to cover the notch. This makes it so you can format or write to the disk.

Remember, the format of your diskette must match the type of diskette you are using. You cannot format a high-density diskette with a double-density format. The `fdformat` command formats and verifies each track on the diskette, and terminates if it finds any bad sectors. All existing data on the diskette is destroyed by formatting.

To format a high-density diskette in the SunOS format, insert the diskette into the drive and at the command prompt enter

```
fdformat
```

The system displays the message

```
Press Return to start formatting floppy.
```

Pressing Return formats the diskette. If you want to abort the format command, type Control-c.

If you are using a double-density diskette, insert the diskette into the drive and enter

```
fdformat -1
```

To automatically eject the disk after formatting, add the −**e** (eject) option. You can only use the −**e** option on a Sun workstation. For example, to format a double-density 3.5" disk in a SunOS format and eject the disk after formatting it, enter

```
fdformat -l -e
```

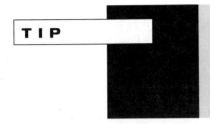

T I P

If you are using a Sun workstation and you cannot eject a diskette from a drive using the eject command, straighten a wire paper clip and insert it into the pinhole under the diskette slot. This manually ejects the floppy diskette.

Creating a File System on a Floppy Disk

As with a hard disk or a CD ROM, you can mount a floppy disk to your network. In order to mount a floppy disk, you must create a file system on it. After formatting the disk, become a superuser by typing **su** and your superuser password at the prompt, and enter

```
newfs /dev/rdiskette
```

This displays the following prompt:

```
newfs: construct a new file system /dev/rdiskette (y/n)?
```

Enter **y** to create the new UNIX file system on the floppy diskette or **n** to abort the **newfs** command. Typing **y** displays output similar to this:

```
/dev/rdiskette:        2880 sectors in 80 cylinders of 2 tracks, 18
sectors
      1.5MB in 5 cyl groups (16 c/g, 0.29MB/g, 128 i/g)
super-block backups (for fsck -F ufs -o b=#) at:
 32, 640, 1184, 1792, 2336,
```

To mount the new file system on the new diskette, make a directory to use as the mount point and enter

```
mount /dev/diskette /floppy
```

Replace /`floppy` with the directory you created as the mount point. If the floppy diskette is not in the drive, the following message appears:

```
fd0: drive not ready
mount: I/O error
mount: cannot /dev/diskette appears.
```

Formatting Disks for Use with MS-DOS

The `fdformat` command also lets you format a disk for use with MS-DOS. To format a high-density (1.44 Mb) diskette that installs an MS-DOS file system and boot sector on the disk after formatting, insert the diskette into the drive, label side up, and at the prompt, enter

```
fdformat -d
```

and press Return to format the floppy diskette. Any diskettes formatted using this option can be read by MS-DOS but are not bootable.

MS-DOS can include a label written to the diskette that identifies the disk when listing files. To add an MS-DOS label on the disk when formatting it, use the following syntax:

```
fdformat -d -b label
```

The text specified by label can be up to eleven characters, but cannot include spaces. For example, enter

```
fdformat -d -b DOS-DISK
```

at the prompt and press Return to format the floppy diskette and add the label **DOS-DISK** to the newly formatted disk.

To format a double-density disk (720K) for use with MS-DOS using a Sun workstation, insert the diskette into the drive, label side up, and enter

```
fdformat -d -1
```

If you're using Solaris 2 for x86, use the −D option instead of the −d −1 options.

Both of these are the equivalent of entering `format a:/f:720` on an MS-DOS PC.

WARNING Do not mix MS-DOS and SunOS files on the same diskette.

Write-Protecting Diskettes

Write-protecting a diskette prevents its contents from being erased or overwritten. To write-protect a diskette, follow the steps below:

1. Turn the diskette upside down and find the write-protect tab. The diskette is upside down when the metal circle at the center of the diskette is showing. If you hold the diskette at the label end, the write-protect notch is in the lower-right corner.

2. Using a ballpoint pen, pull the tab toward the edge until you can see through the notch.

Once you have write-protected a diskette, information cannot be saved on it. When you want to write information on the diskette, you need to change it back to its write-enabled status by pushing the tab back so that the hole is completely covered.

Working with Tapes

Tape drives are used primarily to store backup data on a network system. Solaris provides a number of features for archiving and managing your system backup files. The name for ¼-inch cartridge tape drives found on Sun workstations follows this format:

```
/dev/rmt/n
```

where *n* is the tape drive number for the ¼-inch cartridge tape drive.

Most SCSI drives automatically detect the density or format on the tape and read it accordingly. By default, the tape drive writes at the highest ("preferred") density it supports. If you need to specify the density for a tape drive, add the character that identifies the tape density after the tape drive number. For example, if you are using a tape drive that writes at a medium density, add the letter m after the tape device number (/dev/rmt/0m). The following is a list of characters used to specify different densities for SCSI tape drives.

null	Default, preferred (highest) density.
l	Low (800 bpi).
m	Medium (1600 bpi).
h	High (6250 bpi).
u	Ultra (reserved).

Preparing a Tape for Data

To insert a ¼-inch cartridge tape into an external tape drive unit, hold the cartridge with the label side up. The tape head faces the slide lock on the left side of the slot. Press the cartridge firmly into the slot and pull the slide lock to the right so that it holds the cartridge in place. When a cartridge is first loaded, it is a good idea to perform what is called a tensioning pass. This ensures an even distribution of tension throughout the tape. To run a tensioning pass on the ¼-inch cartridge tape in the first tape drive, insert the tape into the tape drive and enter the following:

```
mt -f /dev/rmt/0 retension
```

To release the cartridge, pull the slide lock to the left.

Backing Up Files and File Systems to Tape

The tar and cpio commands are the ones most commonly used to copy files and file systems to tape. Use the tar command to copy files and directory subdirectories to a single tape. Use the cpio command when you need to copy arbitrary sets of files, special files, or file systems that require multiple tape volumes. The cpio command packs data onto tape more efficiently than the tar command and skips over any bad spots in a tape when restoring data. The cpio command also provides options for writing files with different header formats (such as `tar`, `crc`, `odc`, `bar`), providing better portability between systems of different types.

After performing a backup or a retrieval, the system typically rewinds the tape. To prevent rewinding, the device name should be appended with the letter `n` at the end of the device name, such as `/dev/rmt/0n`.

Copying Files with the tar Command

The `tar` command includes several options for copying files. Adding the `c` option to the tar command instructs the `tar` command to copy files and overwrite any files existing on the tape. You can use wildcard characters to specify files that match a certain pattern. For example, to copy any files in your current directory that begin with the string `chap` to the default tape drive (`dev/rmt/0`), and overwrite any existing files on the tape, enter

```
tar cvf /dev/rmt/0 chap*
```

To display the files archived on a ¼-inch cartridge tape drive, enter

```
tar tvf /dev/rmt/0
```

WARNING The `tar` command stores the path name used when the archive was created. Use relative rather than absolute path names if you later extract files to a different directory. For more information on relative and absolute path names, see Chapter 9, "Navigating Directories and Working with Files."

Retrieving tar Files from a Tape

To extract (copy) all the files created using the `tar` command from a tape into the current directory, perform the following steps:

1. Insert the tape into the tape drive.

2. Change to the directory where you want to store the extracted files. For example, enter **cd** to change to your home directory.

3. Enter **tar xvf /dev/rmt/0**. Be sure to substitute the **0** with the appropriate drive number for your tape drive.

If you want to only extract some of the files on a tape, append the device name with a space and the file names you want to retrieve. You can use wild characters to extract a group of files matching a specified pattern. For example, entering

```
tar xvf /dev/rmt/0 chap*
```

extracts all files beginning with **chap** and copies them to the current directory. You can also list individual file names after the tape drive's name. For example, entering

```
tar xvf /dev/rmt/0 chap1 textfile report
```

extracts (copies) the three files **chap1**, **textfile**, and **report** into the current directory.

Copying Files with cpio

The **cpio** command can copy individual files, groups of files, or complete file systems in from or out to tape or disk. Unlike **tar**, the **cpio** command can create archives that require multiple tapes or diskettes. It also recognizes when the media is full and prompts you to insert another volume. The **cpio** command takes a list of files or path names and writes it to the standard output. Typically, the **cpio** command sends output to the standard output, so you need to redirect the output to a file or a device. You can also feed a command's output to the **cpio** command using the pipe (|). For example, to feed the output of the **ls** command to the **cpio** command to copy all files in the current directory and redirect the output to the first tape drive, enter

```
ls | cpio -oc > /dev/rmt/0
```

To verify a copy operation, list all the files archived on a tape by entering

```
cpio -civt < /dev/rmt/0
```

NOTE For information about the `cpio` command's options, see Part IV, "Command Reference."

Copying and Moving Directory Trees

To copy directory trees between file systems, make sure you are in the directory you want to copy and enter

```
find . -print -depth | cpio -pd /filesystem2
```

Replace `filesystem2` with the directory in the file system where you want the files copied to. The `find` command's `-print` option displays the names of the located files, and the `-depth` option instructs the `find` command to begin at the last subdirectory and search on up to the current directory. The output of the `find` command is sent via the pipe (|) to the `cpio` command. The `cpio` command's `-p` option creates the list of files, and the `-d` option creates the directories.

Moving a directory tree is similar to copying a directory tree, except you need to remove the original directory tree after verifying that the copy operation was successful. To verify a copy operation, change to the directory that you copied the files to and enter the `ls` command. The following explains how to copy and remove a directory tree.

```
find . -print -depth | cpio -pad /newdir
```

Be sure to replace `newdir` with the directory that you want the files moved to. To remove the old directory tree, change to a directory other than the directory you want to remove and enter

```
rm -rf /olddirectory
```

where `olddirectory` is the name of the directory you want to remove.

Retrieving Files

To retrieve all files from a tape and copy them into the current directory, enter

```
cpio -icv < /dev/rmt/0
```

To retrieve only some of the files from a tape, you must specify a pattern to match. The following example retrieves all files beginning with `report` and uses the `d` option to create subdirectories if needed.

```
cpio -icdv "report*" < /dev/rmt/0
```

In previous versions of SunOS, the bar format was frequently used to archive files to floppy disks. The bar format is no longer supported in SunOS 5.x. To restore files on a diskette created with the `bar` command, enter

```
cpio -ivH bar < /dev/diskette
```

Write-Protecting Tapes

To protect a ¼-inch cartridge tape so that it cannot be erased or written to, you will need a screwdriver or a coin. On the top of the tape is the word "SAFE," with an arrow and a notch for rotating the arrow. To write-protect the tape, insert the head of the screwdriver or coin in the notch and rotate the arrow to point to the word "SAFE." To enable writing to the tape, move the arrow so that it is pointing away from the word "SAFE."

Working with the Administration Tool

The Administration Tool is an OpenWindows application that greatly simplifies many common system administration tasks. The Administration Tool provides four separate applications for managing your system: the Database Manager, Printer Manager, Host Manager, and User Account Manager. Figure 17.1 shows the Administration Tool window. The following sections explain how to use the Administration Tool to view system

FIGURE 17.1

The Administration
Tool

database entries, and to add a user, a host, and a printer to your system. To start the Administration Tool, in a Command Tool or Shell Tool, enter

```
admintool &
```

Typically, you should not run the Administration Tool as a superuser or root unless you have root access to every system you need to administer. If you don't have root privileges, you can run the Administration Tool to affect your local machine, but you must be a member of the `sysadmin` group (GID 14). See your system administrator for more information on becoming a `sysadmin` group member.

About Network Naming Services

In order to work with the Database Manager, Printer Manager, Host Manager, and User Account Manager you need to know what type of naming service your network is using. NIS+ (Network Information Service+) is the new networking naming service for Solaris. NIS+ makes use of databases that store much more information than the older version of NIS. NIS is the network-naming service that is shipped with SunOS 4.1. NIS servers refer to NIS files that contain two-column maps that store information about the network, workstations, and users. You cannot add a workstation using the Host Manager if you select the NIS naming service. The Host Manager cannot directly update NIS database maps. If your network uses the NIS naming service, choose **None** rather than **NIS** when the **Select Naming Service** pop-up window appears. You will still need to update the NIS maps after adding the workstation, as explained later in this chapter. If you're not using a naming service, usually one workstation maintains network information files in the /etc directory.

Working with the Database Manager

The Database Manager is used to manage NIS+ tables and ufs files in the /etc directory. It allows you to view, search through, and edit different network databases, such as a database for hosts and groups.

To work with the Database Manager, follow these steps:

1. Click the left mouse button on the Database Manager icon to start the Database Manager. The **Load Database** pop-up window appears, as shown in Figure 17.2.

2. Click the left mouse button on the name of the database you want from the **Databases** scrolling list.

3. Click on the naming service your network is set up for. Check to make sure that the domain or host name is correct. The domain name defaults to the current workstation's domain. In most cases, you will want to use the default domain or host name.

FIGURE 17.2

The Load Database
pop-up window

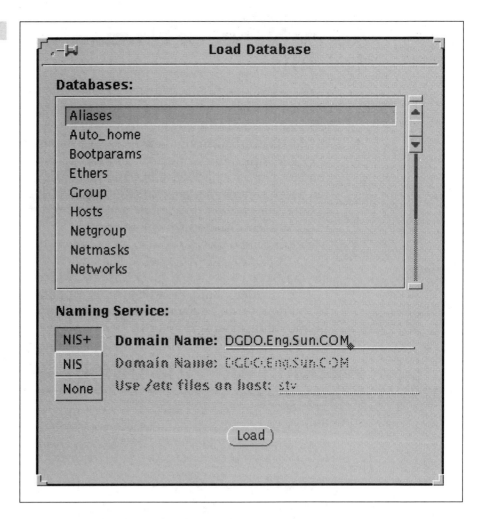

4. Click the left mouse button on the Load button. The window containing the database you selected is displayed. Figure 17.3 shows a sample Passwd (password) database displayed in the **Database Manager** window. Each database has a **File**, **View**, and **Edit** menu button at the top of the window for viewing and modifying system databases.

5. Click the right mouse button on the abbreviated window menu button and click on the **Quit** item to quit the Database Manager.

FIGURE 17.3

Sample Passwd
(password) database
listing in the Database
Manager

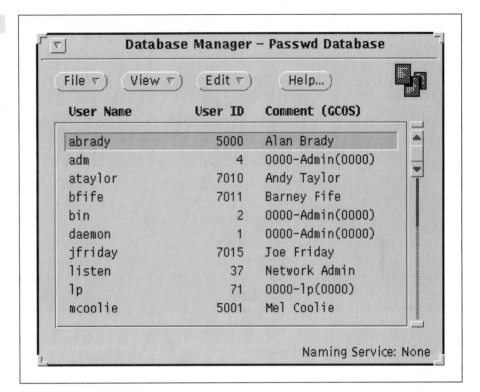

Working with the User Account Manager

The User Account Manager edits the database files that contain user information. It sets password security, creates the user's home directory, and specifies the user's default permission settings. Once you have added a user to the system, you can use the user's settings as a template for additional users.

Adding a User to the System

The following steps explain how to add a user using the User Account Manager.

1. Click the left mouse button on the User Account Manager button to start the User Account Manager. The `Select Naming Service` pop-up window is displayed, as shown in Figure 17.4.

2. Click on the naming service your network is set up for.

3. Check to make sure that the domain or host name is correct. The domain name defaults to the current workstation's domain. In most cases, you will want to use the default domain or host name.

4. Click the left mouse button on the `Apply` button. The `User Account Manager` window appears, as shown in Figure 17.5.

5. Click the left mouse button on the `Edit` button. The `Add User` pop-up window appears.

6. Fill in the fields and choose the settings for each entry in the `Add User` window. The table below describes each of the fields and settings in the `Add User` window, and supplies sample field and setting entries.

FIGURE 17.4

The Select Naming Service pop-up window

User Account Manager: Select Naming Service
Naming Service:
NIS+ **Domain Name:** DGDO.Eng.Sun.COM
NIS Domain Name: DGDO.Eng.Sun.COM
None Use /etc files on host: stv
Show: ▽ All Users
(Apply) (Reset)

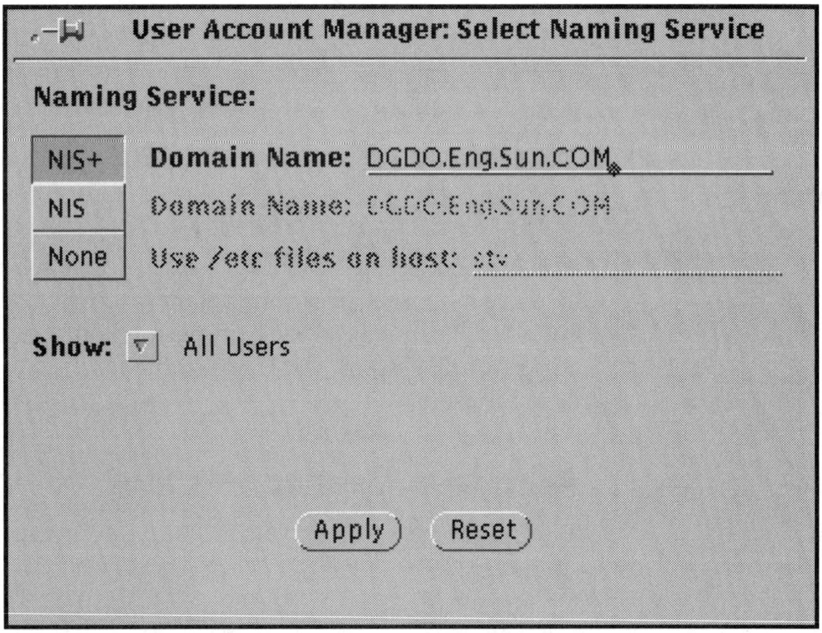

FIGURE 17.5

The User Account
Manager window

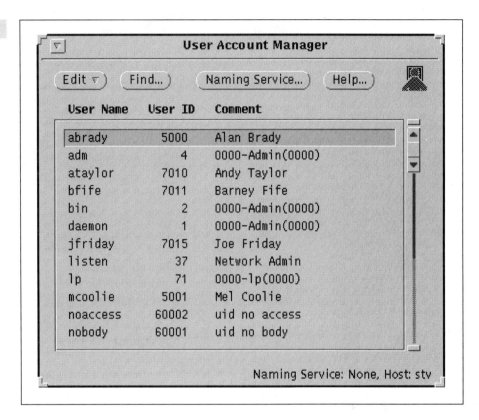

7. Click on the **Add** button to add the new user account to the system.

CONTROL	DESCRIPTION
User Name	Specifies a unique login name consisting of two to eight letters and numerals. The first character must be a letter, and the user name must contain at least one lowercase letter. Remember that the login command is case specific, so in order to log in, the user must enter his or her user name exactly as it is entered in this field.

CONTROL	DESCRIPTION
User ID	Specifies a unique number between 100 and 60000. The user ID number is stored in the **passwd** database file, and identifies the user account throughout the network.
Primary Group	Indicates the name of a preexisting group or a group ID number (GID). The group **other** is the default primary group.
Secondary Groups	Indicates additional names of preexisting groups or group ID numbers that you want the user to belong to. Each secondary group name is separated by a space. **Secondary Groups** is an optional field.
Comment	Identifies the user and includes any pertinent information about the user, such as his or her department and phone extension. **Comment** is an optional field, but typically is at least the user's name. For example, Robert Petrie is the **Comment** entry for the user **rpetrie**, who has been used as an example throughout this book.
Login Shell	Determines which default shell is started when the user logs in. The available shells are the Bourne shell (**/bin/sh**), the C shell (**/bin/csh**), the Korn shell (**/bin/ksh**), or Other (a shell you specify). For example, in this book all users use the Korn shell as the default shell.

CONTROL	DESCRIPTION
Password	Determines whether or not a password is required and how attempts to log in are handled. The `Cleared until first login` setting lets the user specify his or her password when he or she first logs in. The `Account is locked` setting disables the account with an invalid password. This allows a user to own files but not to log into the system. The `No password — setuid only` setting creates an account that cannot be logged into directly. This lets programs such as `lp` run under an account without allowing a user to log in under the account. In almost all cases, you will choose `Cleared until first login`.
Min Change	Specifies the minimum number of days required between password changes. The default is `0`, which lets you change your password any time.
Max Change	Specifies the maximum number of days before which, if the password is not changed, the account is locked. The `Max Change` is an optional field.
Max Inactive	Specifies the number of days the account may remain unaccessed before it is locked. This ensures that a user, such as a temporary employee, doesn't continue to have access to his or her account after termination. The `Max Inactive` is an optional field.
Expiration Date	Specifies the date on which the user account expires. The default is `None`.

CONTROL	DESCRIPTION
Warning	Specifies the number of days to begin warning the user before password expires. No warning is given if this field is left blank. The `Warning` setting is an optional field.
Create Home Dir	Determines whether to have the user's home directory automatically created. If you choose to have the home directory created, the `Yes if checked` box displays a check mark and the `Skeleton Path` field is activated. If this box is checked, you must fill in the `Path` and `Server` fields.
Path	Specifies the path of the user's home directory. For example, for a user named `rpetrie`, you might enter `/export/home/rpetrie`.
Server	Identifies the name of the host machine on which the user's home directory resides.
Skeleton Path	Specifies the path to the directory that stores initialization files. The files in this directory will be copied into the user's home directory. For example, the default home directory initialization files exist in the `/etc/skel` directory. The skeleton path must reside on the same host machine as the user's home directory. The `Skeleton Path` is an optional field.

CONTROL	DESCRIPTION
Auto Home Setup	Determines whether or not you want the user's home directory to be automatically mounted. This makes the user's home directory automatically accessible on any system on the network by entering /home/username, where *username* is the login name of the user.
Permissions	Determines who can read from, write to, and execute files in the user's home directory. Permissions enabled appear with a check mark. To disable a permission setting, click in the check box of the permission you want to change.

Copying a User's Settings

To copy a user's existing settings to create a new account from an already existing account, click on the user name of the account you want to copy and choose Copy User from the Edit menu. The Copy User window appears with most of the original user's settings displayed. The Name, User ID, and Password remain blank so you can change the fields for the new user. Note that the Comment and Path fields still contain the original user's information, which in most cases will need to be changed.

Deleting a User

To delete a user account from a network, in the User Account Manager window, click on the name of the user you want to delete. Next, click the right mouse button on the Edit menu and choose the Delete User item. The Delete User pop-up window is displayed, as shown in Figure 17.6. This pop-up window includes the user's name, ID, and any comments about the user. Two check boxes let you choose whether or not to delete the user's home directory and its contents and the user's mailbox and its

FIGURE 17.6

The Delete User
pop-up window

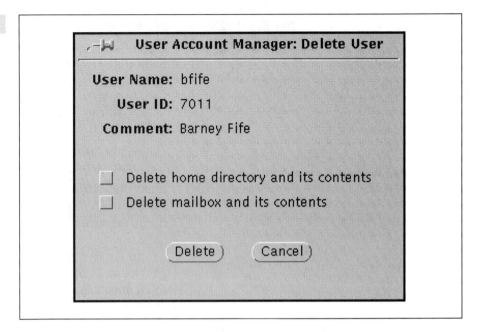

contents. Click on the check boxes to delete the user's home directory and mailbox files. Lastly, click the left mouse button on the **Delete** button to confirm the deletion.

Working with the Host Manager

The Host Manager lets you add or remove a workstation to or from the network. It lets you fill in blank fields to provide all the information that SunOS needs so users can log in. In order to add a host to a network, you need to know the type of naming information service (NIS) your network uses. As explained earlier, a network naming service is a method by which information about workstations is maintained. The three choices for specifying a network naming service are NIS+, NIS, and None.

Adding a Workstation to the Network

When Solaris is installed on a workstation, it prompts for several configuration settings. In order to add a workstation to an existing network, you need to include this information about your workstation in the **Host Manager** window. The following steps explain how to add a host workstation to a network.

1. Click the left mouse button on the **Host Manager** button to start the Host Manager.

2. Click on the naming service your network is set up for. If you are using NIS, be sure to choose **None**, and follow the instructions for updating the NIS maps in the next section.

3. Check to make sure that the domain or host name is correct. The domain name defaults to the current workstation's domain. In most cases, you will want to use the default domain or host name.

4. Click the left mouse button on the **Apply** button. The Host Manager window appears, as shown in Figure 17.7.

5. Click the left mouse button on the **Edit** button. The **Add Host** window appears.

6. Fill in the fields and choose the settings for each entry in the **Add Host** window. The following table describes each of the configuration fields and settings that the Host Manager requires to add a host workstation to the network and gives examples. Keep in mind that your entries will differ from the examples.

7. Click on the **Add** button to add the host account.

8. Click the right mouse button on the abbreviated window menu button and click on the **Quit** item to quit the Host Manager.

FIGURE 17.7

The Host Manager
window

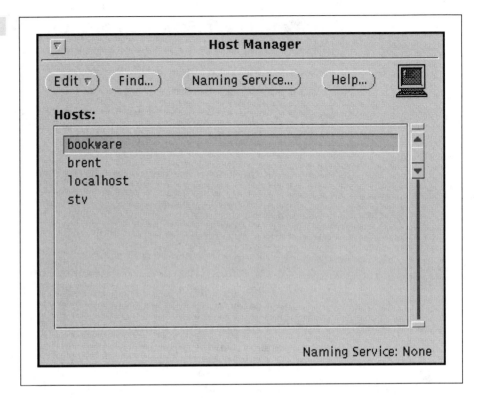

CONTROL	DESCRIPTION
Client Type	Specifies one of three types of client settings: standalone, diskless, and dataless. A standalone client is a computer that keeps all the file systems it needs on its own local disk. A diskless client gets all its file systems from another workstation, called a file server. A dataless client keeps the machine's root and swap file systems on a local disk, and stores the /usr and /home file systems on another workstation.

CONTROL	DESCRIPTION
Host Name	Specifies the unique name by which a workstation is known on the network. Type `uname -n` in a Command Tool or Shell Tool to display any installed system's host names. For instance, two host names used in examples in this book are `mayberry` and `primetime`.
IP Address	Identifies the unique Internet protocol address specified by four fields separated by periods. For example, a sample IP address might be `195.5.2.15`. Each field is a decimal number between 0 and 255. These addresses are required if your machines are connected to the Internet.
Ethernet Address	Indicates the workstation's ethernet address, specified by six fields separated by colons. Each field is a hexadecimal number between 0 and FF. The ethernet address can be obtained from a workstation during its boot sequence. For example, a sample ethernet address might be `02:60:8C:1B:7F:02`.
Timezone Region	Specifies the time zone for the region of the world you live in. SunOS recognizes world time zones and automatically adjusts the system clock for daylight saving time. You supply either the time zone for your area, or an offset from Greenwich mean time (GMT).
Timezone	The time zone for your area. For example, if you live in California choose `Pacific`.

Updating NIS Maps

Unless you are adding a host using the NIS network naming service with the Host Manager, you can skip this section. As previously mentioned, the

Host Manager does not directly support the NIS naming service. If you have added a host that is connected to a network using the NIS naming service by choosing **None** for the naming service, you need to manually add the new /etc entries into the NIS maps. When you use the Host Manager with an NIS network, you specify a workstation whose local /etc files are to be updated by the Host Manager. This workstation is known as a *database server*. The updated files include /etc/hosts, /etc/ethers, /etc/timezone, and /etc/bootparams. After you have finished using the Host Manager, do the following:

1. Write down the entries created in the four /etc files on the database server. For each new machine you added, there will be a new entry in the database server's /etc/hosts, /etc/ethers, /etc/timezone, and /etc/bootparams files.

2. On the NIS workstation that you added, copy each new entry that you noted previously into the corresponding files on the NIS master machine for your domain, so the new entries in the /etc/hosts file of the database server are also in the /etc/hosts file on the NIS master machine.

3. Do the same with each new entry in the /etc/ethers, /etc/timezone, and /etc/bootparams files.

4. At the shell prompt on the NIS master machine, enter the command line **cd** /var/yp to change to the /var/yp directory, then enter the **make** command. This remakes the NIS maps to allow the new workstations full access to the resources of the NIS network.

5. Once you have updated the NIS maps, remove the entries on the database server that were added by the Host Manager.

6. If you are adding a diskless client that is going to run SunOS 4.1.x, then change directories to the diskless client's root file system using the following command syntax: **cd** /export/root/*diskless-client*. Replace *disklessclient* with the diskless client's host name.

7. Enter **mv** /var/yp- var/yp to rename the yp- file to yp in the var directory.

8. Change the entry in the /etc/defaultdomain file to match your network's NIS domain name.

Deleting a Host from the Network

To delete a host from a network, in the `Host Manager` window, do the following:

1. Click on the name of the host you want to delete.

2. Click the right mouse button on the `Edit` menu and choose the `Delete Host` item.

3. Click the left mouse button on the `Delete` button to confirm the deletion.

Working with the Printer Manager

The Printer Manager lets you add printers to a host computer from any system in the network. Once a printer is added to a system, it is referred to as a *printer server*. You can also add access to remote printers (printers attached to a remote workstation), but the Printer Manager must be installed on each remote system you need to access. If you try to use the Printer Manager from your local machine to add or access printers across the network, it won't work.

WARNING The Printer Manager will not help you install printers on workstations running SunOS 4.1 (BSD); however, it does allow you to access remote printers already attached to SunOS 4.1 printer servers.

Adding a Printer

The Printer Manager lets you add a printer either to the local system, the workstation on which you're running the Printer Manager, or to a remote printer server over the network. To add a printer do the following:

1. Click on the Printer Manager icon. The `Printer Manager` window appears, as shown in Figure 17.8.

FIGURE 17.8

The Printer Manager window

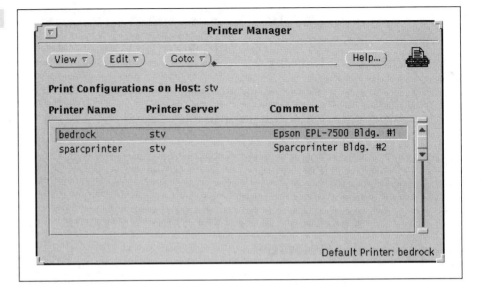

2. Click the right mouse button on the **Edit** button.

3. Choose the **Add Local Printer** item from the **Add Printer** submenu. The **Local Printer** window appears, as shown in Figure 17.9.

4. Fill in the fields in the **Local Printer** window. The following table describes each of the fields and settings, and supplies sample field entries and settings. Remember, your entries and settings may differ from these examples.

5. Click the left mouse button on the **Add** button to finish adding the printer.

6. Click the right mouse button on the abbreviated window menu button and click on the **Quit** item to quit the Printer Manager.

The following table describes each of the fields and settings, and supplies sample field entries and settings.

Printer Manager: Local Printer

Printer Name:

Printer Server: stv

Comment:

Printer Port: ▽ /dev/term/a

Printer Type: ▽ Postscript

File Contents: ▽ Postscript

Fault Notification: ▽ Write to superuser

System Default: Yes No

Print Banner: Required Not required

Register with NIS+: Yes No

User Access List: Edit ▽

(Add) (Reset) (Help...)

CONTROL	DESCRIPTION
Printer Name	Specifies the unique name of the printer you are adding. A printer name can consist of up to 14 alphanumeric characters and underscores. For example, the printer name used in examples in this book is `bedrock`.
Printer Server	Identifies the name of the host workstation to which the printer is attached. For example, the printer server name shown in Figure 17.9 is `stv`.
Comment	Describes the printer or indicates its location. For example, you might enter the make of the printer and its location, `Epson EPL-7500 Bldg. #1`.
Printer Port	Specifies the device name of the port to which the printer is attached. The default is `/dev/term/a`.
Printer Type	Specifies the type of printer you are using. The default is `Postscript`.
File Contents	Determines what types of files can be printed. Common types include `Postscript` and `ASCII`.
Fault Notification	Indicates what action to take in case of printer error or problems. The three choices include writing a message to the root user, sending email, or no notification. The default is `Write to superuser`.
System Default	Determines whether or not the printer will be the default printer for users of the computer to which it is attached. The default is `No`.

CONTROL	DESCRIPTION
`Print Banner`	Specifies whether banner pages are required for each print job. Users still need to use the `-o nobanner` option with the `lp` command so that a banner page is not printed. The default is `Required`.
`Register with NIS+`	Creates a NIS+ table of all registered printers in the network. Unless you specified that you are using the NIS+ network-naming service, this setting is unavailable.
`User Access List`	Specifies, by user name, who will be able to access the printer. The `Edit` button next to the `User Access List` text field lets you insert user names into or delete user names from the scrolling list.

Adding a Remote Printer

The Printer Manager lets you add access to a remote printer. The remote workstation must be running the Printer Manager, or if the remote system is running SunOS 4.1, the printer must already be attached to the remote system. To add access to a remote printer, do the following:

1. Type the name of the remote system in the `Goto` text field.

2. Click the left mouse button on the `Goto` button. This is the same as choosing the `Add Access to Remote Printer` item from the `Edit` menu.

3. Click the left mouse button on the `Edit` item. The `Access to Remote Printer` pop-up window appears, as shown in Figure 17.10.

4. Fill in the fields in the `Access to Remote Printer` window. The following table describes each of the fields and settings and gives examples. Remember, your entries and settings may differ from these examples.

5. Click the left mouse button on the `Add` button.

FIGURE 17.10

The Access to Remote
Printer pop-up window

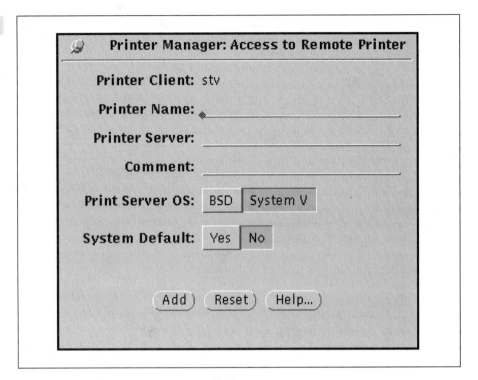

6. Click the right mouse button on the abbreviated window menu button and click on the `Quit` item to quit the Printer Manager.

CONTROL	DESCRIPTION
Printer Name	Specifies the unique name of the printer you are adding. A printer name can consist of up to 14 alphanumeric characters and underscores. For instance, the printer name used in examples in this book is **bedrock**.
Printer Server	Identifies the name of the host workstation to which the printer is attached. For example, the printer server name shown in Figure 17.10 is **stv**.

CONTROL	DESCRIPTION
Comment	Describes the printer or indicates its location. For example, you might enter the make of the printer and its location, `Postscript Bldg. #31`.
Printer Server OS	Specifies whether the workstation that is acting as a printer server is using SunOS 4.1 (`BSD`) or SunOS 5.x (`System V`).
System Default	Determines whether or not the system defaults to the remote printer. The default is `No`.

PART FOUR

Command
Reference

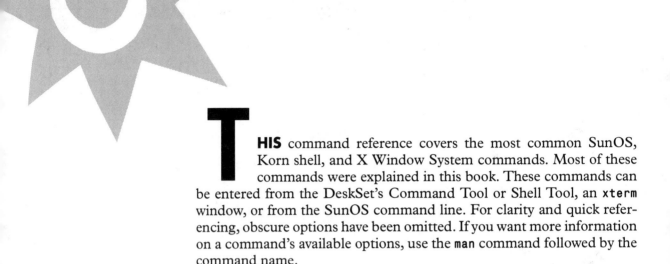

THIS command reference covers the most common SunOS, Korn shell, and X Window System commands. Most of these commands were explained in this book. These commands can be entered from the DeskSet's Command Tool or Shell Tool, an `xterm` window, or from the SunOS command line. For clarity and quick referencing, obscure options have been omitted. If you want more information on a command's available options, use the `man` command followed by the command name.

Making the Transition to SunOS 5.X (SVR4)

If you are making the transition to SunOS 5.x (SVR4) from an earlier version of SunOS or from Berkeley Standard Distribution UNIX (BSD), keep in mind that many BSD commands are still available and are stored in the `/usr/ucb/` directory. Some of these commands have the same name as SunOS 5.x commands. If the PATH variable in your `.profile` file specifies `/usr/ucb` before the `/usr/bin` directory, you will end up running the BSD version of the command. If you are making the transition from System V Release 3 (SVR3), keep in mind that many additional commands are available with SVR4 that did not exist in SVR3. This command reference only explains how to use SunOS 5.x (SVR4) commands.

Command Reference Conventions

The conventions for this command reference are relatively simple. Text that appears in italicized brackets *[ ]* indicates an optional argument. Text that appears in italics indicates a place holder or text that varies; for example, *filename* would be replaced with an actual file name. Keystrokes that you press in the examples appear in angled brackets, for example, <Control-d>.

alias

Syntax

```
alias [name] [definition]
```

Description The `alias` command is a Korn shell command that lets you define shorthand ways to enter commands.

Options The `alias` command has no options.

Example If you want to always be prompted before copying over existing files, enter

```
alias cp="cp -i"
```

into your `.profile` file. This makes `cp` run `cp -i` instead, which prompts you before overwriting files.

Entering

```
alias cp
```

displays any definition in effect for `cp`.

Entering

```
alias
```

displays all `alias` definitions in effect.

See Also unalias, set

at

Syntax

```
at [options] time [date] [+ increment]
```

Description The `at` command runs a command or program from a file at some later time. By using `at`, it is possible to print long files after working hours or send reminders to yourself or others. It is also possible to set up a job to run and reschedule itself every day, week, month, and so on.

When scheduling a job to run at a later time, you have a great deal of latitude in specifying when it is to run. The time may be specified as either one, two, or four digits. One or two digits specifies hours, while four digits specifies hours and minutes. The time may also be specified with a colon separating hours and minutes (hour:minute). Either a 24-hour clock or an appended `am` or `pm` may be used. The special times `noon`, `midnight`, `now`, and `next` are also recognized. If no date is specified, the job runs at the next occurrence of *time*, the same day if *time* is after the current time, or the next day if *time* has already passed that day.

If *date* is included, it may take the form of either a month name followed by a day number or a day of the week. If a day of the week is used, it may be either fully spelled out or abbreviated with the first three letters. If the month given is before the current month, the next year is assumed.

An increment is a number followed by *minutes, hours, days, weeks, months,* or *years* (the singular form is used if appropriate). Thus, `at now + 15 minutes` means 15 minutes from the time the command is entered.

If no script file is specified (a script file is a file that contains SunOS commands, or programs, to be run together), `at` will take its input from the keyboard. If a script file is specified, it should contain the commands you would enter from the keyboard for `at` to run. If the script file named `run.at` contains

```
at -f  run.me 15:00 today
```

```
at -f run.at 08:00 tomorrow
```

and the file `run.me` contains commands that print out memos that need to be routed every evening, then the system will automatically print out the memos every afternoon at 3:00 p.m. and reschedule the job the next morning.

Options

-m	Sends mail after the job has been run, even if the job is successful.
-r [*jobs*]	Removes jobs previously scheduled. The job number is determined by entering `at -l`.
-l [*jobs*]	Lists any jobs at has waiting to run.
-f [*scriptfile*]	Reads commands to be executed from *scriptfile*.

Example Entering

```
at -f atfile -m now + 15 minutes
```

runs commands from the file `atfile` in 15 minutes and displays

```
job 36983.a at Sat Oct 8 17:42:00 1994
```

where 36983 is the job queue entry number. Because the -m option was specified, this command sends mail when completed.

Entering

```
at -f atprint 1:00pm Friday
```

runs commands from the file `atprint` on the next Friday at 1:00 p.m. and displays

```
job 36984.a at Fri Oct 14 13:00:00 1994
```

Again, 36984 is the job queue entry number. To delete Friday's job, enter

```
at -r 36984.a
```

Had you not been sure of the queue entry number, you could have entered

```
at -l
```

which would have displayed

```
user = rpetrie 36983.a at Sat Oct 8 17:42:00 1994
user = rpetrie 36984.a at Fri Oct 14 13:00:00 1994
```

from which you could determine the job queue entry.

See Also atq, atrm, batch

atq

Syntax

```
atq [options] [usernames]
```

Description The atq command displays jobs created by the at command that are still in the job queue. Normally, jobs are sorted by the order in which they will execute. The superuser can display all jobs or specify the users whose jobs are in the queue he or she wants to display. Otherwise, only your jobs are displayed.

Options

-c	Displays the jobs in the queue sorted according to the time the **at** command was given.
-n	Displays the total number of jobs in the queue.

Example The following command displays the total number of jobs in the queue.

```
atq -n
```

See Also at, atrm, batch

atrm

Syntax

```
atrm [options] [users jobIDs]
```

Description The `atrm` command removes jobs that are in the queue by using the `at` command that matches the specified *jobIDs*. A superuser can also specify the users whose jobs are to be removed.

Options

-a	Removes all jobs belonging to the current user. This option lets a superuser remove all jobs.
-f	Removes jobs unconditionally and suppresses all removal information.
-i	Prompts to verify removal of a job. Press y to remove the job or n to leave the job.

Example To confirm that all jobs should be removed, enter

```
atrm -ai
```

See Also at, atq, batch

banner

Syntax

```
banner string
```

Description The banner command displays a string of characters as a poster on the standard output. The *string* can contain up to ten characters.

Options The banner command has no options.

Example

```
banner "Headline"
```

See Also echo

batch

Syntax

```
batch [options]
```

Description The batch command executes commands entered on standard input when the system load level permits. Input for the batch command ends when you press Control-d. Unlike at, which will execute commands at a specific time, batch executes commands one after another (waiting for each one to complete). Using the batch command avoids the high system load caused by running several background jobs at once. The output from commands are mailed to the person that started the batch command, unless it is redirected to a file.

Options The batch command has no options.

Example This is an example of how to run multiple commands from the command line using the batch command.

```
batch
find . -name "*.tmp" -exec rm {} \;
find . -name core -exec rm {} \;
troff -ms report | dpost | lp -Tpostscript
<Control-d>
```

The following example executes multiple commands stored in a file named mycmds and sends the output to another file named mycmds.stats.

```
batch
mycmds >mycmds.stats
<Control-d>
```

See Also at, atg, atrm, mail

bc

Syntax

```
bc [options] [files]
```

Description The **bc** command is an interactive arithmetic language processor and compiler that can also convert numbers from one base to another. Input can be taken from files or read from the standard input. You can use any of the following arithmetic symbols: + for addition, – for subtraction, * for multiplication, and / for division. To exit the **bc** command, type quit or Control-d.

Unless you specify otherwise, **bc** determines how many decimal places it should display. To specify a number of decimal places, after typing in the **bc** command, enter

```
scale=n
```

Where *n* is the number of decimal places you want.

The **bc** command can also convert between decimal, octal, hexadecimal, and any other bases. Special memory locations known as **ibase** and **obase** are used for converting and displaying values. To change how the base of numbers that are typed in are read, use the following format:

```
ibase=n
```

The **obase** location stores the base in which numbers are displayed. To change how the base of numbers are displayed, use the following format:

```
obase=n
```

Typically *n* will be the number 8 (octal), 10 (decimal), or 16 (hex). However, you can make any type of conversion by setting **ibase** to the base you have and **obase** to the base you want. Typing **ibase** or **obase** on a line by itself displays its current value.

Options

-c	Compile only.
-l	Makes available functions from the math library.

Example To use the **bc** command to multiply 3113*60, enter

```
bc
3113*60 <Return>
186780
<Control-d>
```

To set the number of decimals to 5 and divide 73 by 140, enter

```
bc <Return>
scale=5<Return>
73/140<Return>
0.52142
<Control-d>
```

To display the octal equivalent of the decimal number 10, type the following:

```
bc <Return>
ibase=8 <Return>
10<Return>
8
<Control-d>
```

To convert the decimal number 30 to its hexadecimal representation, enter

```
bc
obase=16
30
1E
<Control-d>
```

cal

Syntax

```
cal [month] year
```

Description The cal command by itself displays a calendar for the current month. The cal command followed by *month* and *year* gives a calendar for the month of the year specified. The cal command followed by *year* displays a calendar for the entire year. Note that entering cal 11 displays the year 11 A.D., not November of the current year.

Options The cal command has no options.

Example If today's date is Saturday, October 5, 1999, then entering

    cal

displays

```
    October 1999
 S   M  Tu   W  Th   F   S
                     1   2
 3   4   5   6   7   8   9
10  11  12  13  14  15  16
17  18  19  20  21  22  23
24  25  26  27  28  29  30
31
```

For the more historically minded, entering

    cal 9 1752

displays

```
    September 1752
 S   M  Tu   W  Th   F   S
             1   2  14  15  16
17  18  19  20  21  22  23
24  25  26  27  28  29  30
```

This displays the month of September for the year the calendar changed from Gregorian to Julian.

See Also calendar, date

calendar

Syntax

```
calendar [option]
```

Description The `calendar` command is a reminder service. It looks for the file `calendar` in the current directory and displays lines that have today's or tomorrow's date. The `calendar` command recognizes `Aug. 31`, `august 31`, and `8/31` as valid dates, but not `31 August` or `31/8`. Designating the month as an asterisk (*) in the file `calendar` indicates all months.

Options

-   Allows a superuser to implement calendars for all users, searching each user's login directory for a file named `calendar`. Entries that match are sent to a user via mail.

Example Entering

```
*/15 PAYDAY!
```

in the file `calendar` causes the `calendar` command to display

```
*/15 PAYDAY!
```

if the command is run on the fifteenth (or the day before) of any month. On Fridays the `calendar` command considers tomorrow to be Monday.

See Also cal

cancel

Syntax

```
cancel [options] [printers]
```

Description The `cancel` command cancels requests for print jobs made with the `lp` command. A user can specify one or more *request-IDs* of print jobs to be canceled. The user can specify one or more printers to cancel current printing jobs. The `cancel` command also permits a user to cancel all of his or her own jobs on all printers. When used in this manner, the *printers* option identifies the printers on which the user's jobs will be canceled. When the printers option is used, all jobs queued for those printers will be canceled. Unless your system administrator has granted you special privileges, using the -u option will only allow you to cancel requests associated with your own login ID.

Options

request-ID   Cancels the print request for the print jobs *request-ID* specified.

-u *loginID*   Cancels the print request for the user identified by *loginID*.

Example If there is only one request sent to a printer, entering

```
cancel sparcprinter
```

cancels the print request sent to the printer named `sparcprinter`. To cancel a specific print request, add the *request-ID*; for example, entering

```
cancel sparcprinter-119
```

cancels the print job with the *request-ID* `sparcprinter-119`. Entering

```
cancel -u bsimpson
```

cancels the print request sent by the user `bsimpson`.

See Also `lp`, `lpstat`

cat

Syntax

```
cat [options] [filenames]
```

Description The `cat` command creates, displays, and joins files.

Options

-e	Displays a $ character at the end of each line. The -e option is ignored unless used with the -v option.
-s	Causes cat to suppress error messages if the file does not exist.
-t	Displays tab characters as ^I and formfeed characters as ^L. The -t option is ignored unless it is used with the -v option.
-v	Makes control characters visible (for instance, Control-z appears on-screen as ^Z, Control-d as ^D, and so on). The Delete character prints as ^?. To display tabs and new lines as control characters, you must specify the -t option.

Example Entering

```
cat file1
```

displays the contents of file1 to the screen. Entering

```
cat file1 file2
```

displays the contents of file1 followed by the contents of file2. Entering

```
cat file1 file2 > file3
```

sends the contents of file1 followed by file2 to a new file called file3. Entering

```
cat > file1
```

takes input from the keyboard and sends the input to a new file called file1. Press Control-d to return to the prompt. Entering

```
cat file1 file2 >> file3
```

appends the contents of file1 and file2 to the already existing file3. Entering

```
cat
```

takes input from the keyboard (until a Control-d is entered) and sends its output to the screen.

See Also cp, echo, rm, more, pr, head, tail

cd

Syntax

```
cd [directoryname]
```

Description The cd command changes the working directory to either your home directory (if no directory name is included) or to the directory indicated by *directoryname*. The main purpose of directories is to keep things organized. When working on multiple projects, you might make separate directories for each; thus, if two projects need a document called description, they will not conflict. By changing to the appropriate directory, you can avoid conflicting file names.

A directory is indicated by a relative or absolute path. A relative path references a subdirectory from the current directory when you type in the subdirectory's name, whereas an absolute directory always starts from the root directory. An absolute directory begins with a forward slash (/). A relative path can also use the dot (.) for the current directory or two dots (..) for the parent of the current directory.

Options The cd command has no options.

Example Entering

```
cd
```

changes the current working directory to your home directory.

Entering

```
cd /etc
```

changes the current working directory to the directory /etc. If your current directory is /games/scores, then entering

```
cd ..
```

changes the current working directory to the directory /games.

If you are a DOS user, you may be used to seeing your current path as part of your prompt. However, with Solaris you must reset the prompt string every time you change to another directory. The cd command only changes to the directory without the path. To reset the prompt every time you use the cd command, enter the following example. Note that the > prompt appears after you type the first line and press Return.

```
chdir() { <Return>
cd $* <Return>
PS1="${PWD}> "<Return>
}<Return>
```

After you press the last Return, the $ prompt returns. Now enter

```
alias cd="chdir"
```

To have the current path appear as part of your prompt, every time you use cd to change to another directory for future sessions, enter the previous examples into your .profile file. Adding these lines to your .profile file will cause the system's cd command to reset the prompt to display the current directory every time cd is used.

See Also pwd

chgrp

Syntax

```
chgrp [options] group filename(s)
```

Description The chgrp command changes the group association of a file (or files in the case of the -R option). Because Solaris is a multiuser system, built-in safeguards keep users from accidentally (or even deliberately) deleting one another's files. These safeguards protect against unauthorized reading, writing, copying, and deleting of files (as well as executing of executable files). See your system administrator about setting up groups.

Each file has a set of permissions associated with it: read, write, and execute. These three permissions may be applied to the owner of the file (usually the creator of the file), everyone else on the system, and specific groups of users. Entering the command `ls -lg` displays file names and information about their permission and group settings. The permissions are listed, then the number of links, the group ownership, the block size, the creation date, and finally, the file's name.

```
drwxrwxrwx    8    cntrct      4096    Feb    4    16:40        .
drwxr-xr-x   12    authrs      4122    Aug    7    17:00        ..
-rwxrwxrwx    1    cntrct    159360    Nov    5    11:40    file1
-rwx------    1    cntrct       658    Dec    1    15:30    file2
-r-xr-xr-x    1    cntrct     12555    Aug   13    08:30    archive
drwxrwxrwx   20    cntrct      1536    Oct   15    11:11    public
drwx------   11    cntrct       385    Jul    5    02:40    private
drwx-w--w-    2    cntrct        10    Oct    4    10:01    incoming
drwxr-xr-x    2    cntrct        10    Jul   21    17:32    outgoing
drwxrwx---   17    proj1       3072    Feb   17    09:48    project1
drwxrwx---   04    proj2       4096    May   21    08:45    project2
```

The `chgrp` command sets or changes the groups associated with a file's group permissions. To make the change, you must be the owner of the file as well as a member of the group to which you change the file.

Options

`-h`	Changes the group of a symbolic link.
`-R`	Causes `chgrp` to recursively descend through the directory (that is, into the subdirectories).

Example Entering

```
chgrp groupname filename
```

changes the group associated with *filename* to *groupname*.

See Also `chown`, `ls`, `chmod`

chmod

Syntax

```
chmod [-R] mode filename(s)
```

Description The `chmod` command changes the permissions (*mode*) associated with the file *filename* (or files in the case of the -R option). Built-in SunOS safeguards keep users from accidentally (or even deliberately) deleting one another's files. These safeguards prevent unauthorized reading, writing, copying, and deleting of files (as well as executing of executable files).

Each file has a set of permissions associated with it: read, write, and execute. These three permissions may be applied to the owner of the file (usually the creator of the file), everyone else on the system, and groups of people defined by entries in the file /etc/passwd. Entering the command `ls -l` displays file names and information about their permissions. The permissions are listed, then the number of links, the owner, the block size, the creation date, and finally, the file's name.

```
drwxrwxrwx   8  lgoodman   cntrct      4096  Feb   4  16:40         .
drwxr-xr-x  12  root       authrs      4122  Aug   7  17:00         ..
-rwxrwxrwx   1  lgoodman   cntrct    159360  Nov   5  11:40    file1
-rwx------   1  lgoodman   cntrct       658  Dec   1  15:30    file2
-r-xr-xr-x   1  lgoodman   cntrct     12555  Aug  13  08:30  archive
drwxrwxrwx  20  lgoodman   cntrct      1536  Oct  15  11:11   public
drwx------  11  lgoodman   cntrct       385  Jul   5  02:40  private
drwx-w--w-   2  lgoodman   cntrct        10  Oct   4  10:01incoming
drwxr-xr-x   2  lgoodman   cntrct        10  Jul  21  17:32outgoing
drwxrwx---  17  lgoodman   proj1       3072  Feb  17  09:48project1
drwxrwx---  04  lgoodman   proj2       4096  May  21  08:45project2
```

The first letter indicates the listing is for a directory (**d**) or a file (–). The next three letters are the permissions given the owner of the file: (**r** is read or copy permission, **w** is write or delete permission, **x** is execute or search permission). The next three letters are the permissions for the groups assigned. The last three letters are the permissions for everyone on the system. The listing shows that **file1** may be read, written, or executed by anyone on the system. **file2** may be read, written, or executed only by the owner, **lgoodman**. The file **archive** may be read by anyone, but no one (not even the owner) may overwrite the file. The directory **public** may have files read from, written to, or searched by anyone on the system. The directory `private` may only be written to, read from, or searched by the owner. The directory `incoming` may be written to by anyone, while no one but the owner may read or search it. The directory `outgoing` may be searched or copied from by anyone, but may only be written to by the owner. The directories `project1` and `project2` may be accessed only by the owner and the members of the respective groups `proj1` and `proj2`.

The modes are given in either of two formats for this command. An absolute mode is an octal number formed by summing up the following octal numbers representing the enabled permissions.

`400`	Read by owner allowed
`200`	Write by owner allowed
`100`	Execute (search in directory) by owner allowed
`040`	Read by associated group allowed
`020`	Write by associated group allowed
`010`	Execute (search in directory) by associated group allowed
`004`	Read by everyone allowed
`002`	Write by everyone allowed
`001`	Execute (search in directory) by everyone allowed

Thus a permission mode of **777** enables all to read, write, and execute. A permission of **744** enables the owner to read, write, and execute while allowing everyone else only read permission.

The other format uses letter symbols instead of numbers. The symbolic mode looks like this:

[who] operation permission

where *who* is

`u`	User's permissions
`g`	Group's permissions

o	Other's permissions
a	Permissions for everyone (equivalent to **ugo**)

The *operation* is

+	Adds the permission
-	Removes the permission
=	Explicitly assigns the permission and any permissions not listed will be disallowed

and the *permission* is a combination of

r	Read
w	Write
x	Execute

Options

-R	Sets the mode for all specified files in the current and any other appropriate subdirectories

Example Entering

```
chmod o-w file1
```

denies write permission to others not in your group on the file named **file1**. Entering

```
chmod a+r file1
```

gives everyone (the owner, members of your group, and everyone else) read permission on the file named **file1**. Entering

```
chmod 700 file1
```

gives the owner of **file1** read, write, and execute permission while denying members of the owner's group and the rest of the users any permissions. Entering

```
chmod 222 file1
```

gives everyone write permission only.

See Also chgrp, chown, ls

chown

Syntax

```
chown [options] owner [group] filename
```

Description The chown command changes the owner of the file named *filename* to the user named *owner*. The user *owner* is specified by either the login name or the user identification number (UID). The *group* may likewise be specified as either a group name or group identification number (GID).

Since Solaris is a multiuser system, built-in safeguards keep users from accidentally (or even deliberately) deleting one another's files. These safeguards protect against unauthorized reading, writing, copying, and deleting of files (as well as executing of executable files). Another safeguard is that only someone logged in as a superuser (usually the system administrator) can execute **chown**.

Options

-h	Changes the owner of a symbolic link.
-R	Sets the mode for all specified files in the current and any other appropriate subdirectories.

Example Entering

```
chown ataylor chapter1
```

causes **ataylor** to become the owner of the file called **chapter1**.

See Also chgrp, chmod, ls

clear

Syntax

```
clear
```

Description The clear command clears the screen and returns the cursor to the upper-left corner. This is useful for clearing clutter from the screen.

Options The clear command has no options.

Example Entering

```
clear
```

clears the screen.

See Also set

cmp

Syntax

```
cmp [options] file1 file2
```

Description The cmp command compares *file1* with *file2* and displays the differing byte and line numbers.

Options

-l	For each difference, prints the byte number in decimal and the differing bytes in octal.
-s	Does not display file differences, but returns exit codes.
0	Exit code indicating files are identical.

1	Exit code indicating files are different.
2	Exit code indicating files are inaccessible.

Example This command prints a message if two files are the same (exit code is 0):

```
cmp -s old new && echo 'no changes'
```

See Also comm, diff

comm

Syntax

```
comm [options] file1 file2
```

Description The comm command reads *file1* and *file2* and displays three columns of output: lines unique to *file1*, lines unique to *file2*, and lines common to both files. The comm command is similar to diff in that both commands compare two files. But comm can also be used like uniq; that is, comm selects duplicate or unique lines between sorted files, whereas uniq selects duplicate or unique lines within the same sorted file. Before you run the comm command, sort the files to be compared using the sort command.

Options

–	Reads the standard input.
–1	Suppresses displaying lines unique from *file1* (column 1).
–2	Suppresses displaying lines unique from *file2* (column 2).
–3	Suppresses displaying lines in both *file1* and *file2* (column 3).
–12	Displays only lines common to *file1* and *file2* (displays only column 3).

-13	Displays only lines unique to *file2* (displays only column 2).
-23	Displays only lines unique to *file1* (displays only column 1).

Example To compare two lists of phone numbers, and display lines that appear in both lists, enter:

```
comm -12 blackbk phonelist
```

See Also diff, uniq

compress

Syntax

```
compress [options] [filename]
```

Description The compress command reduces the storage size of the file *filename* by use of a compression algorithm (Lempel-Ziv). The file *filename* is replaced by a file with a .Z extension. The .Z file is about half the size of the source file. The compression depends greatly upon the contents of the input file. To restore a compressed file, use the command uncompress. To view a file without changing the .Z file, use the command zcat.

Options

-c	Writes to the screen (or standard output); does not change any files. The zcat command is equivalent to the -c option.
-f	Forces compression regardless of whether the file actually shrinks (not all files shrink from compress) or the .Z file already exists.
-v	Displays the percentage of reduction attained by running compress.

Example Given a file, `report.text`, with a size of 4608 bytes, entering

```
compress report.text
```

results in a file `report.text.Z` with a size of 2696 bytes. To uncompress `report.text.Z`, enter

```
uncompress report.text
```

Note that with the `uncompress` command the `.Z` extension is optional.

See Also `uncompress`, `zcat`

cp

Syntax

```
cp [options] filename1 filename2
cp [options] directory1 directory2
cp [options] filenames directory
```

Description Entering `cp filename1 filename2` copies `filename1` to `filename2`. If `filename2` already exists, it is overwritten and the old file is lost. You might want to enter **alias cp cp -i** into your .profile file. The `cp -i` command asks for confirmation before overwriting a file.

Entering `cp -r directory1 directory2` copies all the files of `directory1` and any files in any subdirectories of `directory1` into `directory2`, creating `directory2`, if it does not already exist, and any subdirectories of `directory2`.

Entering `cp filenames directory` copies all of the files specified by `filenames` into `directory`. The destination directory must already exist.

For files that are linked (`ln`), `cp` copies the contents pointed to by a link, not the link itself; files that are linked will not have their copies linked.

Options

-i   Prompts for confirmation before overwriting an existing file. Pressing **y** confirms the copy should proceed; any other key aborts the **cp** operation.

-p   Copies the source file(s) and keeps the same modification time and permission modes.

-r   If any of the source files are directories, copies the directory, all its files, any subdirectories, and any files in the subdirectories.

Example Entering

```
cp file1 file2
```

copies the contents of **file1** to **file2**. If **file2** does not already exist, it is created; if it does exist, the old contents are replaced and lost.

Here is an example of using **cp** to copy directories:

```
cp -r rpetrie/part4 rpetrie/archive
```

This copies all of the directory **part4** into the directory **archive**, creating **archive** if necessary.

See Also mv, ln, rename, mkdir

cpio

Syntax

```
cpio -p [options]
cpio -o [options]
cpio -p [options]
```

Description The **cpio** command is an archiving program that can copy individual files, groups of files, or complete file systems in from or out to tape or disk. The `cpio` command can create archives that require multiple tapes or diskettes. It also recognizes when the tape or diskette is full and prompts you to insert another volume. The `cpio` command packs data onto tape more efficiently than the `tar` command.

Options

-i *[options]* *[patterns]*	Matches patterns from standard input to retrieve files. The command syntax cpio-i *[options]* *[patterns]* copies in files whose names match the patterns specified. Each pattern can include the * and ? wildcard characters. Patterns should be quoted or escaped so they are interpreted by `cpio`, not by the shell. If no pattern is used, all files are copied in. During extraction, existing files are not overwritten by older versions in the archive (unless –u is specified).
-o *[options]*	Reads and copies list of files whose names are specified to the standard output. The files are combined into an archive file.
-p *[options]* *directory*	Reads a list of files from the standard input and copies the files to another directory on the same system. Destination path names are interpreted relative to the named directory. This is useful for copying directories and their contents.
-a	Resets the access times of input files after performing the copy operation.
-A	Appends files to an archive (must use with *-o* option).
-b	Reverses the byte order in each word and half-word. Words are 4 bytes (only with –i).
-B	Blocks input or output using 5120 bytes per record (default is 512 bytes per record).

-c	Reads or writes header information as ASCII characters; you must use this option when the source and destination machines are of differing types.
-C *n*	Blocks input or output like -B, but block size can be any positive integer *n*.
-d	Creates directories as needed. This option is useful when some of the files you are copying are directories. (Do not use with the -o option).
-E *filename*	Extracts file names listed in file from the archives.
-f	Copies in all files that do *not* match the *pattern* specified with the -i option.
-H *header*	Reads or writes header information in *header* format. Values for *header* are bar (bar header and format), crc (ASCII header containing expanded device numbers), odc (ASCII header containing small device numbers), ustar (IEEE/P1003 Data interchange Standard header), or tar (tar header). This option is used only with the -i option.
-I *filename*	Reads input from *filename*.
-k	Skips corrupted file headers and I/0 errors.
-l	Links files rather than copies files. This option is used only with the -p option.
-L	Follows symbolic links.
-m	Retains previous file modification time. This option does not work for directories.

-M *string*	Specifies a message (*string*) to use when switching media. To display the sequence number of the next tape or diskette, use the variable %d in the *string*. The -M string option modifier is valid only with -I or -O.
-O *filename*	Sends the output to `filename`. Use only with the -o option.
-r	Lets you interactively rename files as they are copied. When `cpio` copies each file, it waits for you to type a new name. If you press Return, the file is skipped. If you type a period (.), the original path and file name will be used.
-R *ID*	Reassigns owner and group permissions for each file to the user's login ID. (This option is available to superusers only.)
-t	Displays a table of contents of the input only; no files are created. When used with the -v option, the listing output resembles `ls -l`. This option cannot be used with -V.
-u	Copies files unconditionally; old files can overwrite new files.
-v	Displays a list of file names. When used with the -t option, the listing output resembles `ls -l` output.
-V	Prints a dot for each file read or written. This shows that the `cpio` command is working without cluttering the screen.

Example To copy all files in a directory to a tape, enter

```
ls | cpio -oc > /dev/rmt/0
```

To list all the files on tape, enter

```
cpio -civt < /dev/rmt/0
```

To retrieve all files from a tape and copy them to the current directory, enter

```
cpio -icv < /dev/rmt/0
```

To retrieve only some of the files from a tape, you must specify a pattern to match. The following example retrieves all files beginning with **report**, and creates subdirectories if needed.

```
cpio -icdv "report*" < /dev/rmt/0
```

To copy directory trees between file systems, enter

```
cd /filesystem1
find . -print -depth | cpio -pdm /filesystem2
```

To restore files on a diskette created with the **bar** command, enter

```
cpio -ivH bar < /dev/diskette
```

See Also find, tar

crontab

Syntax

```
crontab [filename]
crontab [options]
crontab [options] [username]
```

Description The crontab command allows you to submit a list of commands that the system will run for you at times you specify. You can only work with the crontab program if your name is included in the /usr/sbin/cron.d/cron.allow file. The /usr/sbin/cron.d/cron.deny file contains the list of users not allowed to run crontab. If neither of these two files exist, only the superuser can start crontab. Your list of commands are stored in files that are referred to as crontab files. Numbers are supplied before each command to specify the execution time. The execution time and command to run in the crontab file must be on a new line. The system utility named cron reads your current crontab file and runs the commands in your crontab file. A superuser can run crontab for another user by adding the *username* argument. The format for each entry in the **crontab** file is:

```
minute hour day-of-the-month month day-of-the-week command
```

The range of acceptable numbers for each of these five fields is as follows:

minute	0–59
hour	0–23
day of the month	1–31
month	1–12
day of the week	0–6 (0 = Sunday)

You can use an asterisk (*) to indicate all possible values. Use a comma between multiple values and a hyphen (–) to indicate a range. Standard output and error output is mailed to the person who started the **crontab** command unless it is redirected to a file.

Options

-e	Edits the user's current **crontab** file (or creates one).
-l	Lists the user's file in the **crontab** directory.
-r	Deletes the user's file in the **crontab** directory.

Example The following shows a crontab entry that mails a reminder at noon on the 1st and 15th of each month to **rpetrie**.

```
0 12 1,15 * * echo "Time to submit biweekly report" | mail rpetrie
```

The following example installs a file named **cronfile** as the **crontab** file:

```
crontab cronfile
```

To list the **crontab** entries and send the output to a file named **cronlist**, enter

```
crontab -l >cronlist
```

To edit the `crontab` file using the default editor (`ed`), enter

```
crontab -e
```

For information on the `ed` editor, type `man ed`.

See Also `at`, `atq`, `atrm`, `batch`

cu

Syntax

```
cu [options] telephonenumber
```

Description The `cu` command enables you to call another UNIX system, log in, and use that system while you are still logged into your own system. You can also use the `cu` command to connect to a non-UNIX system. In order for `cu` to operate correctly, your system administrator must have added it when installing Solaris and configured the files in the `/usr/lib/uucp` directory. If `cu` doesn't exist on your system, use the `tip` command. The `cu` command works by using your UNIX system's dial-out capability and connecting your terminal to an outgoing modem. You can use the equal symbol (=) to instruct `cu` to wait for a secondary dial tone before dialing the rest of the phone number. Adding the minus symbol (–) instructs `cu` to pause for four seconds before dialing the rest of the phone number. Once you are connected to another system, you follow normal procedures for logging in. Your terminal then becomes a remote terminal for the system you are connected to. You can also use the `cu` command to transfer files between your system and the remote system.

The `cu` command runs as two processes: transmit and receive. The transmit process reads lines from the standard input and transmits the standard input to the connected system. Lines beginning with a tilde (~) are treated as instructions to the calling system rather than lines to be transmitted. The receive process takes data from the remote system and echoes it on the standard output.

Options

-b*n*	Processes lines using *n*-bit characters; n can be either 7 or 8.
-c*name*	Searches UUCP's **Devices** file and selects the local area network that matches *name*.
-d	Displays diagnostic traces.
-e	Sends even-parity data to remote system.
-h	Sets communications mode to half-duplex. This emulates local **echo** and support calls to other systems expecting terminals to use half-duplex mode.
-l*line*	Specifies a device name to use as the communications line, such as (**/dev/term/a**).
-n	Prompts user for a telephone number.
-o	Uses odd parity.
-s*speed*	Sets transmission speed to *speed*. The standard transmission speeds are 1200, 2400, and 9600. The default is 1200.
-t	Dials an ASCII terminal that has auto-answer set.

The following are tilde commands for performing tasks on your local system while connected to the host system.

~.	Terminates the connection.
~!	Escapes to an interactive shell on the local system.
~!*command*	Runs *command* on local system.
~$*command*	Runs *command* locally and sends output to remote system as a command to be run on the remote system.
~o/%cd	Changes directory on the local system.

~%take file [target]	Copies *file* from remote system to *target* on the local system. If *target* is omitted, *file* is used in both places.
~%put file [target]	Copy *file* from the local system to *target* on the remote system. If *target* is omitted, file is used in both places.
~ ~.	Allows you to pass a line that begins with a tilde. This command lets you issue commands to more than one system in a cu chain.
~%b	Sends a BREAK sequence to remote system.
~%ifc	Turns the DC3/DC1 XON/XOFF control protocol (characters ^S, ^Q) on or off for the remainder of the session.
~ofc	Sets output flow control either on or off.

Example To connect to another system, enter

    cu 5551234

where 5551234 is the modem phone number for the system you want to connect to. This command calls a computer using the first available device (modem).

Entering

    cu -s9600 5551234

calls a computer that has a 9600 baud modem. The local computer will use the first available device supporting the speed.

To dial a 9 and wait for a secondary dial tone, enter

    cu 9=5551234

To connect to a destination system that recognizes your system, you can use the system name instead of the phone number. For example, enter

    cu mayberry

The `uuname` command lists the recognized systems. Systems that are recognized by your system are listed in the `/etc/uucp/Systems` file.

See Also   `rcp`, `rlogin`

cut

Syntax

```
cut options [filename]
```

Description   The `cut` command allows you to extract fields from lines of a file or columns from a table. It has two modes. The `-c` option selects columns from a file. Columns are one character wide and are identified by number. The `-f` option selects fields. Fields are recognized by a field delimiter (the default is tab) and identified by number. In both options, a hyphen is used to indicate a range of numbers and a comma is used to separate individual numbers or ranges. The list of identifying numbers follows the appropriate option without spaces.

Options

`-c`*list*	Cuts the column positions identified in list.
`-d`*c*	Used with `-f` to specify field delimiter as character *c* (default is tab); special characters such as spaces must be quoted.
`-f`*list*	Cuts the fields identified in list.
`-s`	Used with `-f` to suppress lines without delimiters.

Example   Entering

```
cut -c3-6,9 report
```

displays columns three through six and column nine of the file `report`.

Entering

```
cut -f2,5 -d: sales
```

prints fields two and five of the file **sales**, with the fields separated by a colon.

To cut characters in the fourth column of a file named **file1**, and paste them back as the first column in the same file, enter

```
cut -c4 file1 | paste - file1
```

The **cut** command is often used with the pipe (|) to extract text when the characters appear in a fixed-width format, such as the output from the **ls -l** command. The following example cuts and displays the size and name of files from an **ls -l** file listing.

```
ls -l | cut -c33-40,54-
```

The notation **54-** indicates columns 54 through the end of the line.

See Also join, paste

date

Syntax

```
date [+format]
```

Description The **date** command displays this information: **day, month, date, hour:minute:second, time zone, year,** thus giving you access to current time and date information at your workstation. The **date** command is also used by the system administrator to set the system date and time.

Options

%n	Inserts newline character.
%t	Inserts tab character.
%m	Displays month as two digits (**01** to **12**).
%d	Displays day as two digits (**01** to **31**).
%y	Displays last two digits of the year (**00** to **99**).

%D	Displays date in mm/dd/yy format.
%H	Displays hour in 24-hour clock format.
%M	Displays minute as 00 to 59.
%S	Displays seconds as 00 to 59.
%T	Displays time as hour:minute:second.
%j	Displays day of the year as 000-365.
%w	Displays the day of the week as Sunday = 0.
%a	Displays weekday abbreviated to three letters as SUN, MON, TUE...
%h	Displays the month abbreviated to three letters as MAY, JUN, JUL...
%r	Displays hour in 12-hour format as AM/PM

Example If today's date is Saturday, the 5th of October, 1999, and the time is 11:15 a.m., then entering

```
date
```

displays

```
Sat Oct 5 11:15:01 PDT 1999
```

For a gentle reminder every morning, you might add this into the .login file in your home directory:

```
date +'Good Morning! Today is %a %h %d %nThe time is: %r.'
```

which displays

```
Good Morning! Today is Fri Aug 13.
The time is 09:00:00 AM.
```

To change the date to December 25, 1999, 12:01 a.m., become a superuser and enter

```
date 1225001999
```

See Also time

deroff

Syntax

```
deroff [options] [filename(s)]
```

Description The `deroff` command removes all `nroff` and `troff` requests and macros, backslash escape sequences, and `tbl` and `eqn` constructs from the specified files and displays the remaining text on the screen. You can use the wildcard characters ? and * to indicate multiple files, or you can enter a list of file names by separating each name with a space.

Options

-mm	Suppresses text that appears on macro lines; paragraphs will print but headings might be stripped.
-w	Outputs the text as a list, one word per line.

Example To remove formatting instructions from two files named `status` and `text`, and display the text remaining in the two files, enter

```
deroff status text
```

To remove `troff` instructions from the file named `report1` and save the remaining text in a file named `report2`, enter

```
deroff report1 > report2
```

See Also `troff`

df

Syntax

```
df [options] [filesystem]
```

Description The `df` command reports the amount of occupied disk space, the amount of used and available space, and how much of the file system's storage space has been used. If you use the **df** command without any argument, the amount of space occupied and files for all mounted file systems is displayed.

Options

−b	Reports the amount of free disk space in kilobytes.
−F *filesystemtype*	Reports on an unmounted file system specified by *filesystemtype*. Available file system types can be seen by displaying the **/etc/vfstab** file.
−g	Reports the amount of occupied and free disk space, the type of file system, the file system ID, file name length, block size, and fragment size.
−k	Reports the amount of occupied and free disk space in kilobytes, as well as the percent of capacity used.
−t	Reports the total allocated space as well as free space.

Example Entering

```
df -k
```

displays a listing of the amount of used and available space similar to the following:

```
Filesystem         kbytes     used    avail  capacity  Mounted on
/dev/dsk/c0t0d0s0   24143    15954     5779      73%          /
/dev/dsk/c0t0d0s6  192151   171623     1318      99%       /usr
/proc                   0        0        0       0%      /proc
fd                      0        0        0       0%    /dev/fd
swap                80180       16    80164       0%       /tmp
/dev/dsk/c0t0d0s5   95167    77279     8378      90%       /opt
/dev/dsk/c0t6d0s2  186723   180697        0     100%     /cdrom
```

See Also du

diff

Syntax

```
diff [options] filename1 filename2
```

Description The diff command compares *filename1* to *filename2* and identifies which lines to change to make the files identical. All differing lines are displayed, as are commands needed to convert *filename1* into *filename2*. The commands are **a**, **d**, and **c**. An **a** means that lines are added to *filename1* to match *filename2*; a **d** means that lines are deleted from *filename1* to match *filename2*; a **c** means that lines have changed from *filename1* to *filename2*.

Options

-b   Ignores trailing blanks (spaces and tabs) and treats all other strings of blanks as equals.

-i   Ignores the case of letters. Treats A as equivalent to a.

-w   Ignores all blanks (spaces and tabs). Treats 3 + 5 = 8 as equivalent to 3+5=8.

Example Given two files, file1, which contains

```
Anne Addams     111 N 1st St     555-1111
Bill Browne     222 S 2nd St     555-2222
Cher Clarke     333 E 3rd Av     555-3333
Dave Durham     444 W 4th Av     555-4444
```

and file2, which contains

```
Anne Smythe     111 N 1st St     555-1111
Bill Browne     222 S 2nd St     555-2222
Carl Change     777 E 7th Av     555-7777
Dave Durham     444 W 4th Av     555-4444
Eddy Elliot     555 Park Pl      555-5555
```

entering

```
diff file1 file2
```

yields

```
1c1
< Anne Addams      111 N 1st St      555-1111
---
> Anne Smythe      111 N 1st St      555-1111
3c3
< Cher Clarke      333 E 3rd Av      555-3333
---
> Carl Change      777 E 7th Av      555-7777
4a5
> Eddy Elliot      555 Park Pl       555-5555
```

This shows that lines one and three have been changed and line five has been added.

dircmp

Syntax

```
dircmp [options] directory1 directory2
```

Description The `dircmp` command compares the contents of *directory1* and *directory2* and lists information on files that are unique to each directory. It then displays two-column output, listing the word **same** before all files that are the same in both directories. If you are comparing directories containing several files, it is easier to use the **Command Tool** window, because using a Shell Tool causes text to scroll past.

Options

-d	Compares the contents of files with the same name in both directories and outputs a list telling what must be changed in the two files to bring them into agreement.
-s	Suppresses all messages about identical files.
-w*n*	Changes the width of the output line length to *n* characters (the default is 72).

Example Entering

```
dircmp -S docs1 docs2
```

compares the directory *docs1* with *docs2* and returns to the prompt if the files are the same in both directories.

See Also cmp, diff

domainname

Syntax

```
domainname name
```

Description The domainname command sets or displays the name of the current Network Information Service (NIS) domain. Only the superuser can set the name of the domain. The domain name is usually set by your system administrator during the installation. Entering domainname displays the name of the current NIS domain name.

Options There are no options for the domainname command.

Example Entering

```
domainname
```

displays the current domain name.

If you have superuser privileges, entering

```
domainname mayberry
```

sets the domain name as mayberry.

dpost

Syntax

```
dpost [options] [files]
```

Description The `dpost` command translates files formatted by `troff` into PostScript for printing.

Options

−c*n*	Prints n copies of each page. The default is 1.
−e*n*	Sets the text encoding level to *n*. The recognized choices are 0, 1, and 2. The size of the output file and print time should decrease as *n* increases. Level 2 encoding will typically be about 20 percent faster than level 0, which is the default and produces output essentially identical to earlier versions of `dpost`.
−m*n*	Increases (multiplies) the size of logical pages by factor scale. The default is 1.0.
−n*n*	Prints *n* logical pages on each sheet of output. The default is 1.
−o*list*	Prints only pages contained in a comma-separated list.
−p*mode*	Specifies layout to be either portrait (long side is vertical; also the default) or landscape (long side is horizontal). Layout can be abbreviated to **p** or **l**.
−w*n*	Draws troff graphics (e.g., `pic`, `tbl`) using lines that are *n* points thick. The default is 0.3.
−x*n*	Offsets the x-coordinate of the origin *n* inches to the right (if *n* is positive).
−y*n*	Offsets the y-coordinate of the origin *n* inches down (if *n* is positive). Default origin is the upper-left corner of the page.
−F *directory*	Sets the font directory to *directory*. The default is `/usr/lib/font`.

-H *directory*	Sets the host-resident font directory to *directory*. Files there must describe PostScript fonts and have file names corresponding to a two-character **troff** font.
-L *filename*	Sets the PostScript prologue to file. The default is **/usr/lib/postscript/dpost.ps**.
-O	Omits PostScript pictures from output. Useful when running in a networked environment.

Example Entering

```
troff -ms myfile | dpost | lp -Tpostscript
```

formats the file named **myfile** with **troff**, translates the file to PostScript format, and sends the file to be printed on a PostScript printer.

Entering

```
troff file1 | dpost>file1.ps
```

formats the file containing **troff** requests named **file1**, sends the output to the **dpost** filter, and stores the translated output in a file named **file1.ps**.

See Also troff

du

Syntax

```
du [options] [directory]
```

Description The **du** command gives the number of 512K blocks used by a directory and all of its subdirectories. If no directory name is specified, it reports on the current directory and all subdirectories.

Options

-a	Reports on every directory and file instead of just each directory.
-k	Reports usage in kilobytes.
-r	By default, the **du** command ignores files and directories it cannot open. The -r option reports when **du** cannot open a file or directory.
-s	Reports the total disk usage for each specified directory, or the total for the current directory if a directory is not specified.

Example Entering

    du -a

displays disk usage information on all subdirectories and files in the current directory. Entering

    du /usr/

reports the number of 512k blocks contained in all files and all subdirectories under the directory /usr.

See Also df

echo

Syntax

    echo [options] string

Description The echo command displays a string on the screen (or standard output). This command is often used within a script file to display the progress of the file or to request some user input. (A script file is a file that contains SunOS commands, or programs, to be run together.)

Options

-n   Does not output newline characters
                   (carriage return characters).

The following are special options that can be used in the echo command's argument.

\b	backspace
\c	display line without newline
\f	formfeed
\n	newline
\r	carriage return
\t	tab
\v	vertical tab
\n	Displays the ASCII value for the number indicated by *n*. The number *n* can be any 1-, 2-, or 3-digit octal value; for example, \07 rings a bell, because the ASCII value of the bell is octal 07.
\\	backslash

Examples Entering

```
echo "Hi Mom"
```

displays

```
Hi Mom
```

The echo command is useful for displaying the value of a variable, for example, entering

```
echo $OPENWINHOME
```

displays

```
/usr/openwin
```

or the name of the directory that is stored as your OPENWINHOME variable.

The echo command is often used with pipes. The following is an example of sending the output of the echo command so that it is sent to the mail program as a mail message to a user named lpartridge.

```
echo "Don't forget the battle of the bands today" | mail
lpartridge
```

eject

Syntax

```
eject [options] [device | nickname]
```

Description The eject command removes media from disk drives that do not have a manual eject button. The device can be specified by its name or by a nickname; if no device is specified, the default device is used. The default device is /dev/rdiskette. The eject command automatically searches for any mounted file systems that reside on the device and attempts to umount them prior to ejecting the media.

Options

-d	Displays the name of the default drive to be ejected.
-f	Forces the device to eject. The -f option can cause an ejection of a device that currently contains mounted partitions.
-n	Displays an assigned nickname for the device.
-q	Checks to see if the media is present.

Example The following ejects the floppy disk from the disk drive:

```
eject
```

If you have a CD ROM and a floppy diskette, entering

```
eject -n
```

displays a listing similar to this:

```
eject: nicknames are:
     fd -> /dev/rdiskette
     fd0 -> /dev/rdiskette
     floppy -> /dev/rdiskette
     /dev/rdiskette -> /dev/rdiskette
     /dev/fd0 -> /dev/rdiskette
     /dev/fd0a -> /dev/rdiskette
     /dev/fd0b -> /dev/rdiskette
     /dev/fd0c -> /dev/rdiskette
     diskette -> /dev/rdiskette
     /dev/diskette -> /dev/rdiskette
     sr -> /dev/rdsk/c0t6d0s0
     sr0 -> /dev/rdsk/c0t6d0s0
     cd -> /dev/rdsk/c0t6d0s0
     cdrom -> /dev/rdsk/c0t6d0s0
     /dev/sr0 -> /dev/rdsk/c0t6d0s0
     c0t6d0s0 -> /dev/rdsk/c0t6d0s0
```

See Also fdformat, mount

env

Syntax

```
env [option] [variable=value ...] [command]
```

Description The env command displays or alters environment variables. When issued without a command argument, the env command displays all global environment variables. When a command argument is specified, the variable's value is added to the environment.

Options

–	Ignores the current environment. Restricts the environment for command to that specified by the arguments.

name=value   Sets the environment variable file name to value and adds it to the environment before the given command is run.

Example To display your current environment, enter

```
env
```

To temporarily change your time zone setting from Pacific Standard Time to Eastern Standard Time and add it to the environment before running the **date** command, enter

```
env TZ=EST5EDT date
```

After issuing the **date** command, the **TZ** environment variable returns to its previous setting.

See Also set

exit

Syntax

```
exit
```

Description The **exit** command terminates a SunOS session. Entering **exit** is the same as pressing Control-d. The **exit** command is used to log out of the system. If you entered **su** to become a superuser, typing **exit** returns you to the previous shell. By requiring users to exit, the system is protected against unauthorized use and is able to reallocate resources no longer in use (such as memory and CPU time). If you type **exit** in a **Shell Tool** or **Command Tool** window, only the window is terminated.

Options The **exit** command has no options.

See Also login

expand

Syntax

```
expand [-n] [-tab1,tab2,...,tabn] [filename]
```

Description The expand command copies the file specified by *filename* to the standard output, converting tab characters to spaces. This is useful before sorting, looking at specific columns, or printing on some printers (those that have no tab capability, for instance). Specifying --*n* sets the tab width. The default is eight spaces. The -tab1,tab2...tab*n* arguments indicate numbers used to set tabs at columns.

Options The expand command has no options.

Example Enter

```
expand -2,10,18,30 report > report.notab
```

to make a copy of the file report with the tab stops set to the second, tenth, eighteenth, and thirtieth columns (just like setting tab stops on a typewriter).

Enter

```
expand -5 phonelist > phonelist.notab
```

to make a copy of phonelist (named phonelist.notab) with tabs converted to five spaces.

See Also unexpand

fdformat

Syntax

```
fdformat [options]
```

Description The fdformat command formats and verifies each track on the diskette, and terminates if it finds any bad sectors. All existing data on the diskette, if any, is destroyed by formatting. By default, `fdformat` formats high-density diskettes (1.44MB). Options exist to format medium-density diskettes (1.2MB) and double-density diskettes (720K). The `fdformat` command also lets you format a disk for use with MS-DOS.

Options

-d	Installs an MS-DOS file system and boot sector on the disk after formatting. This is equivalent to the MS-DOS FORMAT command. Any diskettes formatted using this option can be read by MS-DOS but are not bootable.
-D	Formats a double-density (720K) diskette on a machine running Solaris 2 for x86.
-e	Ejects the diskette when done. This option doesn't work with drives that require you to manually eject disks.
-f	Starts format without asking for confirmation.
-1	Formats a double-density (720K) diskette on a Sun workstation.
-m	Formats a medium-density (1.2MB) diskette.
-v	Verifies the floppy diskette after formatting.
-b *label*	Puts an MS-DOS *label* on the disk after formatting it. This option is only meaningful when the -d option is also set.

Example Entering

```
fdformat
```

formats a high-density diskette in a SunOS format.

Entering

```
fdformat -1
```

formats a 3.5" double-density disk in a SunOS format.

Entering

```
fdformat -d -b DOS-Disk
```

formats a high-density (1.44MB) diskette for use with MS-DOS and labels the disk **DOS-Disk**.

Entering

```
fdformat -d -l
```

formats a double-density disk (720K) on a Sun workstation for use with MS-DOS.

See Also cpio, tar

fgrep

Syntax

```
fgrep [options] -'string-' [files]
```

Description The fgrep command searches one or more files for a character string and displays all lines that contain that string. The fgrep command searches for a string, instead of searching for a pattern that matches an expression like the grep command does. Because fgrep does not support regular expressions, it is faster than grep. (fgrep stands for fast grep.) Special characters like $, *, [, ^, (,), and \ are interpreted literally, but should be enclosed in quotes.

Options

-c	Displays only a count of matching lines.
-h	Displays matching lines but not file names (inverse of −l).
-i	Ignores case. Searches for both upper- and lowercase letters.

`-l`	Lists file names, but does not list matched lines.
`-n`	Displays lines and their line numbers.
`-s`	Works silently, that is, displays nothing except error messages. This is useful for checking error status.
`-v`	Displays all lines that don't match a pattern.
`-x`	Displays lines only if a *string* matches the entire line.
`-e` *string*	Searches for a string that begins with a hyphen (-).
`-f` *filename*	Gets a list of strings from *filename*.

Example To display the number of lines in a file named `phonefile` that contain (415), enter

```
fgrep -c '(415)' phonefile
```

To display lines in `file1` that don't contain any spaces, enter

```
fgrep -v ' ' file1
```

To display lines in a file named `textfile` that contain the words in the file named `searchme`, enter

```
fgrep -f searchme textfile
```

To display the number of lines in a file named `countfile` that do not contain 13, enter

```
fgrep -c -v '13' countfile
```

See Also find, grep

file

Syntax

```
file [-f namesfile] filename(s)
```

Description The `file` command determines what kind of information a file contains, and whether the file is executable, a text file, or a C program file, and so on. Be aware that the `file` command sometimes mistakenly identifies files.

Options

-f *namesfile*   *namesfile* is a file containing a list of files to identify. *namesfile* must contain only names of files.

Example Entering

```
file old.docs mygrep test.*
```

displays

```
old.docs:    directory
mygrep:      executable /bin/ksh script
test.c:      c program text
test:        ascii text
```

find

Syntax

```
find pathnamelist expression
```

Description The `find` command is an extremely powerful, useful, and adaptable tool. Although it is one of the more difficult commands to master, it is worth the effort. The `find` command searches all files and subdirectories of the directories in *pathnamelist* and checks for files that meet the criteria described by *expression*. *pathnamelist* is a list of directories to be searched. `find` searches all files and subdirectories in *pathnamelist*. *expression* is a list of selection criteria or actions to be taken. The selection criteria in *expression* are checked for each of the files in *pathnamelist*. The criteria are checked until one of them fails, at which point the next file is checked. It is possible to use `find` to perform such tasks as these:

- Check all files under a directory for the occurrence of a word, such as a group member's name.

- Check each file's creation date and list only those files created after or before a particular date.

- List only those files modified between two dates.

The *expression* list is traversed left to right. As long as the test in *expression* evaluates true, the next test is performed. In other words, the expression is evaluated as if the items are connected with logical ANDs. If a test is not met, the processing of the current file is ended, and the next file is checked. It is possible to cause a logical OR to be performed by using the –o argument; just because one check fails, this does not terminate further checking on the file. The criteria to be checked are separated by spaces.

Any action (as opposed to a test or check) in *expression* always counts as a test that is met; an action never causes an end to checking of the current file unless the action is the last item in the expression list.

Options

!	Negates the next argument. `!-name filename` checks true for files whose name is *not filename*.
`-atime` *n*	Indicates the expression is true if the file has been accessed in *n* days. The `find` command itself changes the access time of files in *pathnamelist*.

-ctime *n*	Indicates the expression is true if the file has been changed in *n* days. That is, either the file has been modified or the file's attributes (its owner, group, permissions, and so on) have changed.
-depth	Always yields true. This is an action to be performed, not a check to be made. The depth argument causes the find command to check the contents of subdirectories before any other files in the directory containing the subdirectories +.
-exec *command*	Indicates the expression is true if the executed *command* returns a zero value as an exit status. This usually means a requested command has occurred. (For instance, grep returns a zero if the requested string of characters was found, and returns a nonzero if the requested string of characters was not found.) The specified command must be followed by an escaped semicolon (\;). To specify the current file, use curly braces ({}).
\(expression \)	Indicates the expression is true if the parenthesized expression is true. Used for grouping expressions, usually with the -o operator. Parentheses must be preceded by backslashes, and the expression must be separated from the parentheses by spaces.
-group *groupname*	Indicates the expression is true if the file belongs to *groupname*.
-links *n*	Indicates the expression is true if the file has *n* links.

`-mtime` *n*	Indicates the expression is true if the file has been modified (that is, written to) in the last *n* days.
`-name` *filename*	Indicates the expression is true if `filename` matches the current file name. An `*`, `?`, or `[` and `]` can be used, but must be escaped (that is, put within quotes or preceded by a backslash).
`-newer` *filename*	Indicates the expression is true if the current file has been modified more recently than filename.
`-nogroup`	Indicates the expression is true if the file belongs to a group not in an assigned group in the `/etc/group` file.
`-nouser`	Indicates the expression is true if the file belongs to a user not in the `/etc/passwd` file.
`-o`	If two criteria are separated by spaces, this expression indicates they must both be true to continue checking; that is, both must be true to proceed, because as soon as a check fails, the next file is checked. Using -o between two arguments causes a logical OR to be performed. Thus `-name larry -o -name- brent` will evaluate to true if the current file has a name of either `larry` or `brent`.
`-ok` *command*	Like -exec, except `command` is written to the screen (`< command ... arguments>?`); input from the keyboard is then expected, and `command` is executed only if a `y` is input.

`-perm` `octalnumber`	Indicates the expression is true if the *octalnumber* matches the file permissions of the current file.
`-print`	This expression always yields true. This is an action to be performed, not a check to be made. It prints the current path name.
`-prune`	This expression always yields true. This is an action to be performed, not a check to be made. This is used to keep find from checking into directories—it prunes the search tree.
`-size` *n*	Indicates the expression is true if the file is n blocks long (there are typically 512 characters in a block). If *n* is followed by a c, the size is in characters instead of blocks.
`-type` *typechar*	Indicates the expression is true if the type of the current file is `typechar`, where `typechar` has the following values and associated meanings:

`b`	Block special files (that is, tape drives)
`c`	Character special files (that is, terminals)
`d`	Directories
`f`	Regular files
`l`	Symbolic links
`s`	Sockets
`-user` *username*	True if the file belongs to username

Example Entering

```
find . -print
```

displays the name of all files and all subdirectories under the current directory. Entering

```
find . -name test -print
```

displays the path name of all files or subdirectories under the current directory whose name is **test**. Entering

```
find . -name \*.doc -print
```

displays all files or subdirectories under the current directory whose name has a `.doc` extension. Entering

```
find . -perm 700 -print
```

lists all the files in your home directory with their permissions set to 700 (only the owner has read, write, and execute permissions). Entering

```
find /usr/home/rpetrie -type f -exec grep -l sunspots {} \;
```

displays the names of all files under the directory `/usr/home/rpetrie` (note the use of `-type f` to eliminate anything that is not a file) that contain the word **sunspots**. The **grep** command searches each file for **sunspots** and, since `-l` is specified, prints only the name of the file and not the line containing **sunspots**. Note the use of {} to mean the current file and the `\;`, which must follow any command to **-exec**. Entering

```
find . \( -user ataylor -o -user rpetrie \) -ok cp {} ~/temp \;
```

searches through the working directory and its subdirectories for files belonging to either **rpetrie** or **ataylor** and prompts for confirmation before copying them into the directory `~/temp`. Entering

```
find . -type d -print
```

lists all the subdirectories of the working directory. Entering

```
find . \! -name '.' -type d -print -prune
```

lists all the main subdirectories of the working directory, but does not list the subsubdirectories as the previous example does. Entering

```
find . -type f -size +500c -atime +30 -ok rm {} \;
```

searches through your working directory for files larger than 500 characters that have not been accessed in the last 30 days, and asks whether you want to delete them.

See Also chgrp, chmod, ln, ls, passwd

finger

Syntax

finger [options] *[username]*

Description The finger command, with no user name specified, displays information about each user that is logged in. The information listed is as follows:

- Login name
- Full name
- Terminal name (preceded with an '*' if write permission is denied)
- Idle time
- Login time
- Location (which is taken from the comment field from the file /etc/ttytab)

If a user name is specified, the information is displayed about that user only. The user name can be specified as a first name, last name, or an account (login) name. When a user name is specified, the following information is also displayed:

- The user's home directory and login shell
- The time the user last logged in
- The terminal and terminal information from /etc/ttytab
- The last time the user received and read mail
- The contents of the file named .plan (if it exists) in their home directory
- The projects listed in the file named .project (if it exists) in their home directory

Options

-m	Matches only user name (not first or last name).
-l	Outputs long format.
-s	Outputs short format.

Example Entering

```
finger
```

displays information about all users currently logged in. Entering

```
finger -m lgoodman
```

displays information about user `lgoodman`. Entering

```
finger larry
```

displays information about any user whose first, last, or login name is `larry`.

See Also who, rusers

fold

Syntax

```
fold [-w width] filename
```

Description The `fold` command breaks lines at the maximum width as indicated by *width*. The default width is 80 characters. The *width* should be a multiple of eight if tabs are present; if it is not, you should use the `expand` command before using `fold`. (If you don't, when the tab character is printed, it will move the print head over eight spaces, which will throw off the row widths.) The `fold` command is useful for displaying files on screens with widths less than 80 characters wide, or for setting the width of a file. (For instance, a file's width might be made narrower to set it off from a file it is merged with.)

Options The `fold` command has no options.

Example Entering

```
fold -w 20 filename1 > filename2
```

copies *filename1* into *filename2*, but first adjusts the lines to a width of 20 characters.

ftp

Syntax

```
ftp [options] [hostname]
```

Description The ftp command is your gateway to the Internet's standard File Transfer Protocol (FTP). It allows you to log in and transfer files to and from a remote system. The ftp command is usually used to transfer binary or ASCII files during an Internet connection. If the client host with which ftp is to communicate is specified after the ftp command, ftp immediately attempts to establish a connection to an FTP server on that host; otherwise ftp enters its command interpreter and awaits instructions from the user. When ftp is awaiting commands, it displays the prompt ftp>.

Options

-d	Enables debugging.
-g	Disables file name expansion so that file names are read literally.
-i	Disables interactive prompting during multiple file transfers.
-n	Does not attempt to automatically log in upon initial connection.
-v	Shows all responses from the remote host and transfer statistics.

The following are commands that can be entered at the `ftp` prompt after connecting with another system.

`! [command]`	Runs a shell command on the local system. If the command argument is not added, starts an interactive shell.
`account [passwd]`	Supplies a password required by the remote system. If the passwd argument is not added, the user is prompted to enter a password.
`append local-file [remotefile]`	Appends a local file to a file on the remote system. If the *remotefile* argument is not added, the local-file name is used.
`ascii`	Sets the file type to ASCII for file transfer.
`bell`	Sounds a bell after each command is complete.
`binary`	Sets the file type to binary for file transfer.
`bye`	Exits the `ftp` command.
`cd directory`	Changes the current directory on the remote system to directory.
`cdup`	Changes the remote directory to the parent directory, one level up.
`close`	Terminates the `ftp` session and returns to the command interpreter.
`cr`	Toggles return character stripping during ASCII file transfer.
`delete remotefile`	Deletes the specified *remotefile* from on the remote system.

dir [remotedirec- tory] [localfile]	The dir command without any arguments lists the directory contents of the remote system. If the *localfile* argument is added, dir puts the output in *localfile*.
disconnect	Terminates the ftp session and returns to the command interpreter. This is the same as entering the close command.
get *remotefile* *localfile*	Copies remotefile and stores it on the local system as *localfile*.
help *command*	Displays help messages for all ftp commands if no *command* argument is given. Otherwise, displays help for the specified ftp command.
lcd *[dir]*	Changes the working directory on the local system. The default is $HOME.
ls [remotedirectory] [localfile]	Without a *remotedirectory* or *localfile* argument, ls displays a list of the contents of a remote directory. Otherwise, it puts the listing of the remote directory into the contents of *localfile*. If no *remotedirectory* is given, ls uses the current remote directory.
mdelete [remotefiles]	Deletes remotefiles on a remote system.
mdir *remotefiles* *localfile*	Lists remote files, enabling you to specify multiple files. If the *localfile* argument is added, mdir puts the listing of remotefiles in *localfile*.
mget *remotefiles*	Executes the get command to transfer multiple files, specified by remotefiles, to local directory.

mkdir *directory*	Creates *directory* on the remote system.
mput *localfiles*	Expands the * wildcard in a list of local files and executes the put command to send the localfiles to a remote system.
open *host*	Establishes a connection to a specified *host*.
prompt	Toggles interactive prompting on or off. The default is on.
put *localfile* *[remotefile]*	Sends localfile to a remote system. You can specify a different file name by adding the remotefile argument. The remotefile argument specifies the name of the copied file.
pwd	Displays the remote host's current working directory.
quit	Exits the ftp command. This is the same as the bye command.
recv *remotefile* *[localfile]*	Retrieves a remote file and stores it on the local system. This is the same as the get command.
remotehelp *[command]*	Requests help from the remote ftp host. Displays help messages for all ftp commands if no *command* argument is given. Otherwise, displays help for the specified *command*.
rename *file1* *file2*	Renames *file1* on the remote host to *file2*.
rmdir *directory*	Deletes directory on the remote host.

send *localfile* *[remotefile]*	Sends *localfile* to a remote system. You can specify a different file name by adding the *remotefile* argument. The *remotefile* argument specifies the name of the copied file. This is the same as the `put` command.
status	Displays the current status of the `ftp` command.
type	Sets the representation type to ASCII, binary, image, or tenex (used to talk to TENEX machines).
user *username*	Identifies the user to the remote `ftp` host when autologin is disabled.
verbose	Toggles verbose mode on or off, which echoes the results of `ftp` commands to the screen.
?	Prints help message about `ftp` commands. This is the same as the `help` command.

Example Entering

```
ftp
```

activates the `ftp` program and displays the `ftp>` prompt. To connect to a host on the Internet that contains an archive of the Simpsons cartoon trivia, enter

```
open ftp.cs.widener.edu
```

The `ftp.cs.widener.edu` is the full domain name of the machine you are connecting to. After establishing the connection with the remote system, log in as **anonymous**.

At the `ftp>` prompt, enter the following to change to the directory `/pub/simpsons` and copy all the files beginning with the letter **s**,

```
cd pub/simpsons
mget s*
```

The `mget s*` command line will cause `ftp` to prompt you to confirm each copy operation. If you answer y, the file is copied to the current directory on your machine. Answering n, skips to the next file. To exit your connection, at the `ftp>` prompt, enter

    quit

See Also `rcp`, `rlogin`, `telnet`

grep

Syntax

    grep [options] [-e expression] filename

Description The `grep` command searches the file indicated by *filename* (or the standard input) for lines containing *expression*. If `grep` finds a line containing *expression*, it displays the line. If more than one file is specified by *filename*, the file name precedes the line.

The **grep** command can search a file for the string **word**, for instance. When searching for **word**, it also finds **wordy**, **wordless**, and **words**. If you want to locate **word** by itself, specify **word** in single close quotes, `' word '` (note the beginning and ending spaces inside the quote). To specify the beginning of a line use the caret (^), and use the dollar sign for the end of a line ($). To specify any of several characters, enclose the characters in square brackets. `[Bb]ill` matches **bill** or **Bill**, and `[A-Z]ill` matches any uppercase letter followed by **ill**. `[A-Za-z]ill` matches any letter (upper- or lowercase) followed by **ill**. A period (.) matches any single character (letters and special characters such as !, @, #...). Within a range delineated by square brackets, a caret (^) means any character except those in the brackets, so `[^0-9]` matches any nondigit. An asterisk (*) matches zero or more preceding characters. The string **ab*c** matches **a**, followed by zero or more **b**'s, followed by a **c**. For example, **abc**, **abbc**, and **ac** all match **ab*c** (note that the **ac** has zero occurrences of b). The string **ab.*c** matches **ab**, followed by zero or more of any other character, followed by **c**. For example, **abac**, **abdtzc**, and **abc** all match **ab.*c**.

To specify any special character ($, ^, [,], or \), precede it with a backslash (\). To use any of these special characters, you must enclose the string you are searching for in delimiters. A delimiter is a way to specify the beginning and ending of a string. The delimiter can be any character, such as ~, #, or /, so long as the delimiter does not appear in the string.

Options

-c	Displays a count of matching lines rather than displaying the matching lines.
-h	Inhibits the displaying of file names.
-i	Ignores the case of letters (for example, treats A as a).
-l	Lists only the file names of files with matching lines.
-n	Lists each matching line preceded by its line number from the beginning of the file.
-v	Lists lines that do not match the search string.

Example Entering

```
grep SunOS *
```

lists any files in the current directory that contain the word SunOS (note the capitals). To search for the string SunOS regardless of the case of the letters, enter

```
grep -i sunos *
```

To search for lines in files that contain numbers, enter

```
grep '[0-9]' *
```

Note the use of the single close quote to begin and end the search string; this enables the use of the square brackets ([ ]) to denote the range of zero to nine.

To search C program files for comments, enter

```
grep '/\*' *.c
```

The backslash is used to escape the wildcard usage of the asterisk. Also note the use of the single close quote (') as a delimiter, since this command looks for a slash (/), and needs the backslash (\) to precede the asterisk (*). To search for users on your system who do not have passwords, enter

```
grep '^[^:]*::' /etc/passwd
```

This example searches the /etc/passwd file for any number of characters besides colons followed by a double colon at the beginning of lines.

See Also fgrep, find

groups

Syntax

```
groups [username]
```

Description Shows the groups that the user belongs to. Groups are listed in /etc/passwd and /etc/group. Without arguments, the groups command displays the groups to which the current user belongs. With a user name specified as an argument, the **groups** command displays all the groups to which the user name belongs.

Options The groups command has no options.

Example Entering

```
groups bfife
```

displays the groups that **bfife** belongs to.

See Also newgrp

head

Syntax

```
head [-count] [filename]
```

Description   If you are not sure what is in a file, using **head** shows you; or if you cannot remember which file begins with some particular text, **head** can help you find out without loading many different files into a word processor or editor. The **head** command sends the beginning of a file (or the standard input) to the display (or the standard output). How many lines get sent is determined by count. If *count* is not specified, **head** sends 10 lines. Whether standard input or a file is used depends on whether a file name is added. If a file name is not specified, the standard input is used. If more than one file is specified, **head** begins each file's display with ==>filename<==.

Options   The **head** command has no options.

Example   Entering

```
head -2 file1 file2 file3
```

prints out the first two lines of each file indicated, such as:

```
==> file1 <==
  I. Introduction
For the image coding application, strictly speaking, all
==> file2 <==
The output of a discrete information source is a message
that consists of a sequence of symbols.  The actual message
==> file3 <==
Boolean logic is the logic we are all familiar with, the
logic we all think of when we think of mathematical logic.
```

See Also   cat, more, tail

history

Syntax

```
history [options] [n]
```

Description The history command displays a list of previously entered commands in the order of oldest to most recent. By default, the history command stores the last 128 commands in a file named sh_history. The shell stores a list of commands in the order you enter them. Erroneous commands, such as spelling errors, are stored in the history list as well as correct commands. You can repeat a command by entering r n, where n is the number of the command in the history list that you wish to repeat. Entering r reexecutes the last command.

Options

    -r   Reverses the order of commands listed to most recent first.

Example Entering

```
history -5
```

prints out the five most recent commands plus the history command you just entered. Such a list may look like this:

```
3 cd ./book/pt4
4 ls -al
5 cat log
6 cat log
7 rm log
8 history -5
```

id

Syntax

```
id
```

Description The `id` command displays your user name and ID, and your group name and ID.

Options The `id` command has no options.

Example Entering

    id

might display

    uid=1230(lgoodman) gid=204(cntrcts)

See Also `finger`, `who`, `who am i`

kill

Syntax

    kill [-signal] processIDnumber

Description A program is an executable file. When a program is loaded into memory and executed, it is called a process. If you and a coworker are both running a CAD package, there are two processes—one is yours, the other your coworker's.

A signal is a message sent to a process. For instance, if a program begins execution, and you want to stop it before it's done, you can send it a signal to stop. You may also want to stop a process for just a while, and later resume. Signals are also used when two or more processes are cooperating and need to send messages to each other.

Various system signals are defined within SunOS. Two defined signals are SIGKILL and SIGTERM. SIGKILL is the ninth defined signal (indicated by -9), which tells a program to abort itself. A process must shut itself down if it receives a SIGKILL message. SIGTERM is the fifteenth defined message (-15) and requests that a program shut itself down. A process may ignore a SIGTERM, but it can not ignore a SIGKILL.

The `kill` command terminates a process, as specified by its process ID number. Usually `kill` sends a signal `-15` to the process. Sometimes a process is harder to terminate; then a signal `-9` is needed. To determine the correct process ID number, use the `ps` command.

Options

    -1   Prints a list of symbolic signal names.

Example If you were running a process in the background, such as the following:

```
find / -name "test*" -print &
```

entering

```
ps
```

would display a list similar to this one:

```
PID     TTY     TIME    COMD
15021 PS/08     0:00    ksh
15100 PS/08     0:02    find / -name "test*" -print&
15101 PS/08     0:00    ps
```

Notice the `find` command has a process ID number of 15100.

To terminate this process, enter

```
kill 15100
```

The screen should display this line:

```
[1]    Terminated              find / -name "test*" -print&
```

If the `kill` command did not terminate this process, you would then enter

```
kill -9 15100
```

See Also ps

last

Syntax

```
last [options] user
```

Description The last command reads the /var/adm/wtmp file and reports the last logins by a user or terminal. It is useful as a quick accounting log of who is accessing what systems.

Options

-n *number*	Limits the number of entries displayed to the number specified.
-f *filename*	Uses an alternative file name instead of /var/adm/wtmp.

Example Entering

```
last -n 10 rpetrie
```

displays the last ten times the user named **rpetire** logged in.

See Also login

ln

Syntax

```
ln [-fs] filename1 [filename2]
ln [-fs] filename(s) directory
ln [-fs] sourcefile1 newlink
```

Description When you create a file on disk, SunOS places the file name in the appropriate directory and creates a link (or pointer) that points to the physical file. The ln command creates a link (or pointer) between *filename1* and *filename2*. This makes it possible to refer to the same file by two different names. One person may prefer to name a file **phone.list**, while another prefers to call the file **numbers**. The ln command makes it possible for both names to point to the same file. The ln command can be used to point to the same file from different directories. If you are working on a project, and want to access a file from the proj1 directory as if it were in your home directory, you could create a link from your home directory to the project directory.

There is an important difference between creating a link to a file and copying the file to another directory. With linked files, when one copy of the file is updated, all links to that file are simultaneously updated, whereas with a copy of the file, all copies must be updated individually. If you change the permissions of a file, any links to that file have their permissions changed also. Links are removed with the rm command. As long as a file has at least one link remaining, the file itself is not deleted.

The first form of the ln command creates a link called *filename2* to the existing file *filename1*. If *filename2* is not specified, the link is created in the current directory with the file name *filename1*. In the second form, ln creates a link in *directory* to *filename(s)*. In the last form, a symbolic link is made that may point to directories.

Options

-f	Forces a hard link to a directory. Only a superuser may use this option.
-s	Creates a symbolic link, which is useful for pointing to directories.
-n	Prevents the link file from overwriting the contents of an existing file with same file name.

Example If you are working on a file and want to call it sanitation, while a coworker wants to call the same file garbage, create a link to garbage called sanitation:

```
ln garbage sanitation
```

In your home directory you can link a subdirectory, project, to the already existing proj1 directory by entering

```
ln proj1/* project
```

See Also rm, cp

login

Syntax

```
login [username]
```

Description The login command signs the user identified by *username* onto the system. By requiring users to log in, it is possible to protect the system from unauthorized use and to tailor the system to each user. This command may be used to change from one user to another in the middle of a session. If used without *username*, login will request a user name. In either case, login then prompts for a password.

Options

username   Establishes connection without first being prompted for entering *username*.

Example Enter

```
login pmason
```

to log in as **pmason**. The user indicated by **pmason** must be a valid user on the system in order to log in.

See Also exit, passwd

logname

Syntax

```
logname
```

Description The logname command displays your login name by displaying the contents of the LOGNAME environment variable. The LOGNAME environment variable setting is located in the /etc/profile file.

Options The `logname` command has no options.

Example If the current user logged in as `rpetrie`, entering

```
logname
```

displays

```
rpetrie
```

See Also `last`, `login`

look

Syntax

```
look string
look [options] string filename
```

Description The `look` command finds words in the system dictionary (`/usr/dict/words`) or lines in a sorted list that begin with a specified string.

Options

`-d`	Uses only letters, digits, tab, and space characters in the comparison.
`-f`	Ignores case.

Example Entering

```
look rece
```

displays

```
receipt
receive
recent
receptacle
reception
receptive
receptor
```

```
recess
recession
recessive
```

which are all the words in the dictionary file that begin with the characters "rece."

See Also grep, sort

lp

Syntax

```
lp [options] [files]
```

Description The lp command sends files to the print queue to be printed. This allows you to work on a file, print it out, then continue to work on the file while it is still printing out. The file prints in the same state as when you gave the print command. This command also allows you to print out several files at one time.

Options

-c	Makes copies of files before printing. If the -c option is not specified, any changes made to the named files after the request is made but before it is printed will be reflected in the printed output.
-d *destination*	Chooses the destination (printer) of the print job. By default, *destination* is taken from the environment variable **LPDEST**. Otherwise, the computer system's default destination is used.
-m	Sends a mail message informing you that the files have been printed. By default, no mail is sent upon completion of the print request.

-n *number*	Prints the specified number of copies of the output.
-o *option*	Specifies printer-dependent options. Several options may be specified by repeating the -o *option* (e.g., -o *option1* -o *option2*), or by specifying a list of options enclosed in double quotes (e.g., -o *"option1 option2"*). SunOS recognizes the following -o options: nobanner suppresses the printing of a banner page; nofilebreak suppresses the insertion of a formfeed between files; length=[number][scale] prints request with pages number lines long. The number can be followed by a scale character: i indicates inches and c indicates centimeters. A length setting without a scale indicator indicates lines. For example, length=66 indicates a page length of 66 lines, length=11i indicates a page length of 11 inches, and length=27.94c indicates a page length of 27.94 centimeters. width=[number][scale] prints request with the page width set to number columns wide. A width setting without a scale indicator indicates columns. You can use the same scale indicators as with the length option. lpi=[number][scale] prints request with the line pitch set to number lines per inch. A line pitch setting without a scale indicator indicates lines per inch. You can use the same scale indicators as with the length option. cpi=*number* prints request with the character pitch set to *number* characters per inch. For example, character pitch can be set to pica by entering 10 characters per inch, or elite by entering 12 characters per inch. There is no standard character-per-inch setting.

-P *pagelist*	Prints the pages specified in pagelist in ascending order. The pages specified in *pagelist* may consist of single page numbers, or a combination of both.
-q *priority-level*	Assigns this request a *priority-level* in the printing queue. The values that can be used to specify *priority-level* can range from 0, the highest priority, to 39, the lowest priority. The default priority is set by the system administrator. -t *title*, prints title on the banner page of the output. The default is no title. Enclose *title* in double quotes if it contains blanks.
-w	Writes a message on the user's terminal after the files have been printed. If the user is not logged in, then a mail message is sent instead.

Examples Entering

```
lp text.file
```

prints out the file **text.file** to the default printer. Entering

```
lp -d sparcprinter *.rpt
```

sends all files ending with **.rpt** to the printer named **sparcprinter**.

See Also cancel, lp, lpstat, pr

lpstat

Syntax

```
lpstat [options]
```

Description The lpstat command displays the status of a printer queue. SunOS takes files to be printed and places them into a queue (a storage place in memory). This allows you to print out a file or several files while you continue working on the same file.

For each of the jobs in the queue, the lpstat command reports the user requesting the print job, the job's current position in the queue, the name of the file to be printed, the print request number (needed to remove the job from the queue), and the size of the print job in bytes. If the print request number is specified, lpstat reports on that print job only. If -u *userID* is specified, lpstat reports on all print jobs requested by that user.

Options Several options allow you to enter a list of users and printers. The list can be the login ID of a user or the printer request ID number. The print request ID number is the printer's name followed by a hyphen and a number. A typical printer ID might be sparcprinter-12. When creating a list, separate each item in the list with a comma.

-d	Reports the system default destination for print requests.
-o *[list]*	Reports the status of all output requests. The list is optional and includes printer names and print request ID numbers.
-p *[list]*	Reports the status of printers identified in list.
-t	Reports all status information, including the print request ID numbers, the user who requested the print job, the file size in bytes, and the date and time the request was made.
-u *[userIDs]*	Displays the status of print requests for specific users. Replaces *userIDs* with the user's login IDs.

Example To list the status of all print requests waiting in the print queue, enter

```
lpstat -t
```

which displays output similar to this:

```
scheduler is running
system default destination: sparcprinter
device for sparcprinter: /dev/term/a
sparcprinter accepting requests since Jan 22 10:07
printer sparcprinter now printing sparcprinter-12. enabled since
Jan 22 10:07
sparcprinter-12 jrockford  512          Jul 1920:17 on sparcprinter
sparcprinter-13 jrockford  1024         Jul 1920:20
sparcprinter-14 jrockford  1152         Jul 1920:19
```

See Also cancel, lp, pr

ls

Syntax

```
ls [options] filename
```

Description The ls command lists the files and subdirectories of a directory, as well as additional information about each file. The output is sorted alphabetically. When the *filename* argument is not added, the contents of the current directory are listed.

Options

-a	Lists all entries. Without this option, entries beginning with a dot (.) are not listed.
-c	Lists files sorted by the time of creation.
-d	If the ls argument *filename* is a directory, lists only its name.
-F	Marks directories with a trailing slash (/), executable files with a trailing asterisk (*), and links with a trailing at sign (@).
-g	Shows the group ownership of the file (used with the -l option).

-l   Lists files in long format. This gives the permission modes, number of links to the file, owner of the file, and time of the file's creation or last modification.

-r   Reverses the order of the sort, listing files in reverse alphabetic order.

-R   Recursively lists any subdirectories encountered.

-t   Sorts by time of last modification instead of alphabetically, listing oldest files and directories first.

-u   Sorts by the time of the last access instead of the time of last modification when used with the -t option.

Example Entering

```
ls -altR
```

displays a list of all the files in the current directory and all subdirectories of the current directory, sorted by the time each was last modified.

mail

Syntax

```
mail
mail [options] [users]
```

Description The mail command reads or sends mail. If no user is listed, the mail program checks for and displays existing mail messages. Adding one or more user names after the mail command lets you compose and send mail to the specified user(s). Mail messages are read from standard input until the user presses Control-d or a line containing just a period is entered. For a quick summary of mail commands, after starting the mail command, type a question mark (?).

COMMAND REFERENCE

Options The following are options for reading mail.

-e	Tests to see if mail exists without printing it. Returns an Exit status code 0 if mail exists; otherwise returns an exit status code 1.
-f*mailboxfile*	Reads mail from alternate mailbox file indicated by mailboxfile.
-h	Displays a window of messages rather than the latest message.
-p	Displays all messages without pausing.
-P	Displays all messages with all header lines.
-q	Exits the mail program after an interrupt (Control-c).
-r	Displays mail messages with oldest messages displaying first.

The following are options for sending mail.

m *messagetype*	Adds a "Message-type:" line to the message header with the value of *messagetype*.
-t	Adds a "To:" line at the heading of the letter, listing the names of the recipients.
-w	Sends mail to remote users without waiting for remote transfer program to be completed.

The following are options for forwarding mail.

-F *recipients*	Forwards all incoming mail to recipients.
-F " "	Removes mail forwarding.

Example Entering

```
mail -h
```

displays mail headers for incoming mail messages and displays the **?** mail prompt. To read a message, enter the number at the right of list. To quit the mail program, at the **?** prompt, enter

```
q
```

Entering

```
mail sdrucker <Return>
Do you have Prince Albert in a can? <Return>
<Control-d>
```

sends the mail message "Do you have Prince Albert in a can?" to `sdrucker`.

Entering

```
mail -F fziffel
```

forwards the current user's incoming mail to the user named fziffel.

See Also `mailx, mesg, notify, talk, write`

mailx

Description The `mailx` command provides an interactive interface for reading or sending mail. The `mailx` command's options are covered in detail in Chapter 11, "Electronic Mail and Messages."

man

Syntax

```
man command
```

Description The `man` command displays information about commands from the online reference manuals usually located in the `/usr/share/man` directory. Not all systems have the manuals on line, but for those that do, this is a convenient command.

Options

-a	Displays all pages matching *command*.
-l	Like -a, but only lists the pages.
-f *files*	Displays a one-line summary of one or more reference *files*.
-t	Formats the manual pages with troff.
-k *keywords*	Displays any header line that contains one of the specified *keywords*.

Example Entering

```
man find
```

displays information on the find command.

mesg

Syntax

```
mesg [options]
```

Description The mesg command reports on the status of message posting to your screen.

Options

-n	Disables posting of messages to your screen through the write command.
-y	Enables posting of messages to your screen through the write command.

Example Entering

```
mesg
```

displays

```
is y
```

or

```
is n
```

Entering

```
mesg-n
```

displays just the prompt and disables posting messages to the screen.

See Also `write`, `talk`

mkdir

Syntax

```
mkdir directoryname
```

Description The `mkdir` command makes directories.

Options `-m mode`

Specifies the access mode for new directories. For a listing of available modes, see the `chmod` command.

`-p`   Creates parent directories if they do not exist.

Example Entering

```
mkdir directory1
```

creates a directory named `directory1` in the current directory. If `mkdir` cannot make a requested directory, it displays an error message. For instance, the command

```
mkdir .
```

causes the screen to display the message

```
mkdir:    Failed to make directory "."; File exists
```

The error is that `mkdir .` is telling the computer to make a directory with the name . (dot). Dot already refers to the directory in which you are currently working.

Entering

```
mkdir -m 444 directory2
```

creates a read-only directory named `directory2` in the current directory.

See Also chmod, rm, rmdir

more

Syntax

```
more [options]
```

Description The `more` command displays files one screenful at a time. This is useful when trying to view large files, which `cat` displays too fast to read. Using `more`, the display pauses after each screenful, until you enter either a Return or another command that `more` can interpret.

Options The `more` command interprets various keystrokes as commands. The numerical argument by default is one, but you can repeat any command by preceding it with *n*, the number of times you want that command repeated. The following list explains keystroke commands that can be used with `more`.

h	Displays help for `more` and a description of the `more` commands.
*n*b	Skips back *n* screenfuls, then displays a screenful. **b** alone skips back one screenful.

n/pattern	Searches for the *n*th occurrence of *pattern*. */pattern* alone moves to the first occurrence of *pattern*.
*n*s	Skips *n* lines, then displays a screenful. s alone skips one line.
q or Q	Exits the more command.
<Return>	Displays another line.
<Spacebar>	Displays the next screenful.
*n*z	If *n* precedes z, *n* sets the new default for the number of lines per screen. z alone is the same as a space.

The following are more command options.

-c	Clears the screen before displaying the file.
-d	Displays an error message rather than ringing the terminal bell if an unrecognized more command is used.
-l	Treats formfeeds as any other character, not as a page break. Without this, more treats formfeeds contained within the file as page breaks.
-linecount	Displays the number of lines indicated by *linecount* as a screenful instead of the default (typically 24 lines).
+linenumber	Starts display at the line indicated by linenumber, instead of the beginning of the file.
+/pattern	Starts display at the two lines before the line containing pattern. Note that there is no trailing slash (/). (If one is included, it becomes part of the search pattern.)
-s	Squeezes the output, replacing multiple, consecutive blank lines in the file with a single blank line.

Example Entering

```
more .profile
```

displays your `.profile` file, pausing at the end of each screenful. A good use for `more` is to use it with a pipe at the end of a command line; that way you can slow down the output to allow time to read. For instance, entering

```
ls -R | more
```

displays all directory and file names beginning at the root (/) directory. The `more` command allows you to read each screenful. If you enter the above command, type `q` to quit the `more` command.

See Also cat

mount

Syntax

```
mount [options]
umount mountpoint
```

Description The `mount` command adds a file system to the root file system to make it available to the network. The file system is attached to an existing directory, which is then considered the mount point. If the mount point directory has any files or subdirectories prior to the mount operation, they are hidden until the file system is unmounted. Only a superuser can mount file systems using the `mount` command. However, any user can change to the directory on which the file system is mounted. Any user can list mounted file systems by entering the `mount` command without an argument. If a superuser adds only a partial argument, `mount` will search `/etc/vfstab` for an entry to supply the missing arguments.

To unmount a file system, you must change to a directory that is in a file system other than the one to be unmounted, and enter the `umount` command followed by the file system's mount point. The `mount` command maintains a table of mounted file systems in `/etc/mnttab`. The `mount` command adds an entry to the mount table; the `umount` command removes an entry from the table.

Options

-F *filesystemtype*	Specifies the file system type on which to operate. The most common file systems are ufs (UNIX file system), hsfs (High Sierra file system), nfs (network file system), and pcfs (PC file system).
-V	Echoes the complete command line, but does not execute the command. The command line is generated by using the options and arguments provided by the user and adding to them information derived from /etc/vfstab. This option should be used to verify and validate the command line.
-p	Displays the list of mounted file systems in the /etc/vfstab format. Must be the only option specified.
-v	Displays the list of mounted file systems in verbose format. You cannot specify additional options when using the -v option.

Use -o to specify file system type-specific options. The following are generic options commonly supported by most file system types.

-m	Mounts the file system without making an entry in /etc/mnttab.
-ro	Mounts the file system so it is read-only.
rw	Mounts the system as read and write (the default).

Example Entering

```
mount
```

displays a list of the file systems currently mounted.

To mount target disk 3 (t3) on the sixth partition (s6) on the /mnt directory, enter

```
mount /dev/dsk/c0t3d0s6 /mnt
```

Sun's CD ROM drives are set to SCSI target 6 by default. The following example mounts a CD ROM using the High Sierra file system (hsfs) on the directory /cdrom.

```
mount -F hsfs -o ro /dev/dsk/c0t6d0s2 /cdrom
```

Keep in mind that not all CD ROM disks are in hsfs format. Some CD ROM disks use the standard ufs format. If the mount information for a drive is in your /etc/vfstab/ file, you can mount a drive by just adding the mount point. For example, enter

```
mount /cdrom
```

to mount the cdrom drive on the /cdrom directory. The mount command checks the /etc/vfstab for the information it needs to mount the drive.

To mount a PC file system (pcfs) on the directory /pcfiles to get access to files on a floppy diskette that came from an MS-DOS PC, enter

```
mount -F pcfs /dev/diskette /pcfiles
```

To unmount a file system mounted on the /mnt directory, first change to a directory in the file system other than the one attached at the /mnt directory, and enter

```
umount /mnt
```

You can also specify a drive to unmount by adding the device name to the umount command. The following unmounts the file system for the target disk 3 (t3) mounted on the 6th partition (s6).

```
umount /dev/dsk/c0t3d0s6
```

See Also umount

mv

Syntax

```
mv [options] filename1 filename2
```

or

```
mv [options] directoryname1 directoryname2
```

Description The mv command moves or renames *filename1* to *filename2* (that is, it makes a copy, then deletes the original file). If you are moving or renaming directories, mv moves all of *directoryname1* to *directoryname2;* if *directoryname2* does not exist, mv creates it. The mv command can be used to rename a file. It is also possible to use mv to copy a file over another file, thus deleting the old file. If you copy a .profile file from someone else's home directory into yours, their .profile file will replace yours.

The mv command returns to the system prompt if successful. It is a good idea for new users to use mv -i, as mv by itself does not give feedback to the user, which can lead to unknowingly deleting files. If you always want to use the -i option with mv, enter alias mv='mv -i' into your .profile file. This will cause ~ mv -i to be run whenever mv is entered.

Options

-f	Forces removal even if the file or directory permissions don't allow it.
-i	Asks for confirmation before replacing an existing file or directory.

Example Entering

```
mv /socrates/questions /delphi/answers
```

removes the file named questions in the directory socrates, places it into the delphi directory, and renames the file answers.

See Also rm, cp, alias

newgrp

Syntax

```
newgrp [group]
```

Description The newgrp command changes a user's group identification. Only the group ID is changed; the user remains a member of all groups previously assigned. The user remains logged in and the current directory is unchanged, but the group ID of newly created files is set to the new effective group ID. With no *group* specified, newgrp changes the group identification back to the group specified in the user's password file entry. Before you can use the newgrp command, your system administrator needs to have created the group.

Options The newgrp command has no options.

Example Entering

```
newgrp wildbunch
```

changes your group to the wildbunch group, which must already have been set up by a system administrator. If your group uses a password, you must enter the password to change the user's group identification.

See Also chgrp

nice

Syntax

```
nice [-n] command(s)
```

Description The nice command runs commands at low priority. Since Solaris is a multitasking system, it needs to know which jobs have priority. For instance, a user typing at the keyboard generally deserves priority over a file being printed to a printer. Various jobs are assigned various priorities. So if you decide to search the entire file system for a file you've misplaced, you can tell the operating system to give the command a low priority by using the `nice` command. The `nice` command is especially useful when running jobs in the background.

The *-n* argument tells `nice` how nice to be. The larger the number used for *-n*, the lower the priority the command gets and the slower it runs. *-n* should be in the range of zero to twenty; if no *-n* is present, `nice` defaults to *-10*.

Options The `nice` command has no options.

Example Entering

```
nice -19 grep jabberwocky *
```

executes the `grep` command, which looks for the word jabberwocky in all files indicated by the asterisk with a lower priority than usual.

nohup

Syntax

```
nohup command [arguments]
```

Description The `nohup` command runs a command immune to `hangup` signals and quits. The action of logging out sends a `hangup` signal that terminates all your processes. You can keep a job running after you log out by preceding the command with `nohup`. To execute a pipeline or list of commands, the list or pipeline must be in a script file. `nohup` recognizes only one command per line. Entering `nohup` *command1*; *command2* applies *nohup* only to *command1*. Note that entering nohup (*command1*; *command2*) is syntactically incorrect.

Example If you enter commands into a file named `script`, then enter

```
nohup sh script &
```

the commands are run in the background, and will continue to run even if you log out.

See Also `ps, jobs, kill`

openwin

Syntax

```
openwin [options]
```

Description   The openwin command is the shell script that sets up Open-
Windows, the windowing environment based on the OPEN LOOK
graphical user interface. OpenWindows includes the DeskSet applications that let you perform a wide variety of Solaris tasks using a friendly
graphical environment instead of the command line. To access Open-
Windows, your environment variable OPENWINHOME must be set to the
directory in which the OpenWindows software resides, usually
/usr/openwin. The OpenWindows environment is usually set up automatically, so the openwin command's options are rarely used.

Once the OpenWindows environment is displayed, you can start any of
the DeskSet applications using the Workspace menu's Programs submenu
or by entering the command name for the application you want to start
in the Shell or Command Tool. The following are the command names for
the OpenWindows DeskSet.

APPLICATION	COMMAND NAME
Audio Tool	audiotool
Binder	binder
Calculator	calctool
Clock	clock
Calendar Manager	cm
Command Tool	cmdtool
File Manager	filemgr
Icon Editor	iconedit
Mail Tool	mailtool
Performance Meter	perfmeter
Print Tool	printool
Shell Tool	shelltool

Snapshot	`snapshot`
Tape Tool	`tapetool`
Text Editor	`textedit`

Options The following options are unique to the `openwin` command. The `openwin` command also accepts the same command-line options as the `xnews` command. For more information on `xnews` options, type `man xnews` at the prompt.

`-banner`	Displays the OpenWindows banner screen at startup. This option slightly increases the amount of time it takes to start up Open-Windows.
`-noauth`	By default, the OpenWindows' X11/NeWS server implements the "MIT-MAGIC-COOKIE" security mechanism. The `-noauth` option reverts to the security mode of previous X11/NeWS server versions. Running the server with this option enabled lowers your level of security.
`-includedemo`	Specifies that the path to the demo directory should be included in the user's search path.
`-nobanner`	Causes OpenWindows to start without displaying the banner screen at startup. This option slightly decreases the amount of time that it takes for OpenWindows to start.

Example Entering

```
openwin -nobanner
```

at the command prompt, starts the OpenWindows environment without displaying the banner screen that welcomes you to OpenWindows.

To start the OpenWindows' Text Editor after starting OpenWindows in a Shell Tool, enter

```
textedit &
```

Adding the ampersand (**&**) after the **textedit** command starts the Text Editor program in the background, making the **Shell Tool** window available for entering additional commands.

See Also xrdb

pack

Syntax

```
pack [options] filename(s)
```

Description The **pack** command compacts files and replaces them with compressed files with a .z appended to the file name. To restore the files to their original form, use the **unpack** command.

Options

–	Print number of times each byte is used, relative frequency, and byte code.
–f	Force the file to be compressed even when disk space isn't saved.

Example Entering

```
pack *.ps
```

compacts each file ending with .**ps**, replaces the file with a compressed file, and appends the file name with a .**z**. For example, compressing files **butterfly.ps**, **porsche.ps**, and **tiger.ps** replaces them with files named **butterfly.ps.z**, **porsche.ps.z**, and **tiger.ps.z**.

See Also compress, pcat, unpack, zcat

passwd

Syntax

```
passwd
```

Description The `passwd` command changes your login password. It prompts you for your old password, then for the new password, then for the new password again. Only a system administrator can change your password without knowing your current password.

When changing your password, the new password must be at least six characters and contain at least two alphabetical characters and at least one numeric or special character. The new password must differ by at least three characters from the old password. Remember, case counts, as do spaces and other control characters. You should avoid using names, dates, social security numbers, and so on as passwords, since they are easy to guess.

Options

`-s`	Displays password information (`NP` indicates no password, `PS` indicates an active password, and `LK` indicates a locked password).

Example The following illustrates a sample password changing session. Enter

```
passwd
```

The system responds with

```
Old password:
```

When you enter your old password, it is not displayed on the screen. The screen then displays

```
New password:
```

Enter the new password. Note that it is not displayed. Then you reenter your new password at this prompt:

```
Re-enter new password:
```

and your old password is changed. If you enter a different password the second time, the system responds with this message:

```
Mismatch — They don't match; try again
```

and the prompt `New password` appears. Your password remains unchanged. If you fail to enter enough characters for the new password, the system responds with the message

```
Password is too short—must be at least 6 characters.
```

If you reenter the same password each time this prompt is displayed, on the third try, SunOS responds with `Too many failures — try later`.

paste

Syntax

```
paste [options] filename1 filename2
```

Description The `paste` command merges corresponding lines of several files. Each file is treated as a column, or series of columns, and the columns are concatenated horizontally. The `paste` command performs horizontal merging in a manner similar to the way the `cat` command performs vertical merging. The `paste` command replaces the newline character at the end of the first line in the first file with a tab (or another character with the -d option), then appends the first line in the second file, and so on.

Options

-d*list*

Without this option, the newline characters at the end of each line (in each file) except the last newline character, are replaced with a tab. This option allows the use of characters other than the tab character. The characters in list are substituted for the newlines. *list* is used circularly; when it is exhausted, it is restarted from the beginning. *list* may contain special escape sequences: \n (newline), \t (tab), \\ (backslash), and \0 (an empty string, not a null character).

Example If a file called men contains the following list:

```
Anthony
Othello
Romeo
Larry
```

and a file called women contains this list:

```
Cleopatra
Ophelia
Juliet
Rhonda
```

then entering

```
paste -d"+" men women
```

results in this display:

```
Anthony+Cleopatra
Othello+Ophelia
Romeo+Juliet
Larry+Rhonda
```

See Also cat, pr

pcat

Syntax

    pcat [options]

Description Displays the contents of one or more packed files.

Options The pcat command has no options.

Example Entering

    pcat file1.z file2.z

displays the contents of the packed files file1.z and file2.z.

See Also compress, pack, unpack, zcat

pg

Syntax

    pg [options] [files]

Description The pg command displays the specified files, one screenful at a time. When you enter the pg command, a : prompt appears for you to enter display commands. To display the next page, press the Return key. To get help with the pg command, press h. To quit displaying a file, press q.

Options

-c	Clears the screens before displaying each page.
-e	Does not pause between files.
-f	Does not split lines that are longer than the screen width.

-n	Issues a **pg** command without waiting for you to press Return.
-p *string*	Uses string for the command prompt. If *string* contains the special variable **%d**, the prompt is replaced with the current page number. The default prompt displays a colon (:).
-s	Displays messages in inverse video.
-n	Uses *n* lines for each window. The default is a full screen.
+n	Begins displaying at line number n.
+/*pattern*/	Begins displaying at first line containing *pattern*.

The following are display commands you can enter at the : prompt. To navigate by multiple pages or lines, most commands can be preceded by a number, as in: +1<Return> to move to the next page or -1 <Return> to return to the previous page.

h	Displays help.
q or Q	Quits the **pg** command.
<Return>	Displays the next page.
l	Displays next line.
d	Displays half a page more.
. or <Control-l>	Redisplays the current page.
f	Skips to the next page forward.
n	Moves to the next file.
p	Moves to the previous file.
$	Displays the last page.
*n*w	Sets window size to *n* and displays next page.
s *filename*	Saves the current file in *filename*.

/pattern/	Searches forward for *pattern*.
?pattern? or ^pattern^	Searches backward for *pattern*.
!command	Executes *command*.

Example Entering

```
pg -p 'Page %d : ' file1
```

displays `file1` and sets the prompt to display the page number.

Entering

```
pg -c file2
```

displays `file2`, clearing the screen after each page.

See Also cat, more, pr

ping

Syntax

```
ping [options] host [timeout]
ping [options] IPaddress [timeout]
```

Description The `ping` command is a network utility that tells you if another machine on the network is operational. It uses the ICMP protocol's ECHO_REQUEST datagram to check the specified host. The ICMP protocol is responsible for error handling on a TCP/IP network. If the datagram is sent and received successfully, the network is considered to be alive. Otherwise, `ping` informs you that there is no response from the host.

Options

-I*n*   Specifies the interval between successive transmissions. The number specified by *n* determines the number of seconds between transmissions. The default without the -I option is one second.

-n   Displays network addresses as numbers.

-s   Reports the effectiveness of the data transfer. This option sends packets to the host until you press Control-d or a timeout occurs.

-v   Lists any ICMP packets, other than ECHO_RESPONSE, that are received.

Example Entering

```
ping primetime
```

displays

```
primetime is alive
```

indicating that the host `primetime` responded to the ICMP data. You can also replace the host's name with the IP address. For example, if the host `primetime` has an Internet Protocol address of 192.9.200.1, you could enter the following:

```
ping 192.9.200.1
```

pr

Syntax

```
pr [options] [filename]
```

Description The `pr` command displays files according to options you specify. If no options are specified, the default format is 66 lines per page, with a five-line header and a five-line trailer. By default, each page includes a header containing the page number, file name, and the file's date and time. The pr command can also be used to prepare files for printing. The pr command reads standard input if *filename* is -, or no filename is specified.

Options

+*page*	Begins displaying at the page number indicated by **page**. The default is page one.
-*columns*	Produces output having *n* columns. The default is one column. The columns option does not work with the -m option.
-a	Displays the file in a multicolumn format. Lines that cannot fit in a column are truncated.
-d	Double-spaces the output.
-e*cn*	Expands tabs to positions to every nth position. The default is 8. The c specifies the input tab character. The default field delimeter is a tab.
-f	Separates pages using a single formfeed character instead of a series of blank lines.
-F	Folds input lines to fit in current column width (avoids truncation by -a or -m).
-h *string*	Replaces the default text line of the header with *string*. The -h is ignored when -t is specified or the -1 option is ten lines or less.
-i*cn*	Converts white space to the field delimiter indicated by c set at every *n*th position. The default field delimiter is a tab set at every 8th position.
-1*n*	Sets page length to *n*. The default is 66 lines per page.

-m	Merges up to eight files, displaying all files simultaneously, one per column. If a line is too long to fit in a column, the line is truncated (can't be used with -n and -a).
-n*cn*	Numbers lines with numbers n digits in length (default is 5), followed by the field separator indicated by *c*. The default field separator is tab.
-o*n*	Offsets each line *n* spaces. The default is 0 spaces.
-p	Pauses before displaying each page.
-r	Suppresses error messages for files that can't be found.
-s*c*	Separates columns with c. The default is a tab.
-t	Omits header and trailing blank lines.
-w*n*	Sets the line width to *n* characters. The default width is 72 characters.

Example To format a file named `report` with double spacing and add the header "Monthly Attendance Report" and send the formatted output to the default printer, enter

```
pr -dh "Monthly Attendance Report" report | lp
```

Entering

```
pr -m file1 file2
```

displays a side-by-side list of file1 and file2.

ps

Syntax

```
ps [options]
```

Description The ps command displays information about processes. Informally, processes can be thought of as jobs the system is running. Every job that runs on SunOS has a process ID number (PID) assigned to it. The column headings displayed in a ps listing depend on whether the f (full) or l (long) option is used. The following lists the headers, the option that displays the header, and a brief description of each header:

HEADER	DESCRIPTION
F	Indicates the status word. The status word is a special option associated with a process (represented by 00, 01, 02, 04, 08, and 10). For example, 00 indicates that the process has terminated; 10 indicates the process is currently in memory.
S	Indicates the state of the process. The state of a process is given as a single character. B and W mean that the process is waiting. I stands for idle. O means the process is running on a processor. R means that it is loaded as a runnable process in queue. S means sleeping. T means stopped and being traced. X indicates that the process is waiting for more primary memory. Z stands for Zombie, meaning the process has terminated.
UID (f,l)	User ID of the process owner.
PID (all)	Process ID number.
PPID (f,l)	Process number of the parent process.
C (f,l)	Processor utilization for scheduling.
STIME (f)	Starting time of the process.
PRI (l)	Priority of the process.
NI (l)	The nice value for priority.
ADDR (l)	Memory address or disk address of the process.
SZ (l)	Size of the swappable process in main memory.

WCHAN (l)	The event for which a process is sleeping.
TTY (all)	The controlling terminal ID.
TIME (all)	Cumulative execution time.
COM (all)	The command name.

Options

-e	Prints information about every process.
-f	Generates a full listing.
-l	Generates a long listing.
-p *processlist*	Lists only process data for the process ID numbers given in `processlist`.
-u *IDlist*	Lists only process data for the user ID number or login name given in IDlist. In the listing, the numerical user ID will be listed unless you specify the -f option.

Example Entering

    ps

displays information about processes running on the system, similar to this:

```
PID   TTY   TIME   COMD
9084  p/10  0:00   ksh
9346  p/11  0:00   ps
```

Entering

    ps -l

displays a listing similar to this:

```
F S  UID  PID PPID C PRI  NI   ADDR     SZ  WCHAN     TTY    TIME COMD
8 S 7001  386  384 80  1   20  ff227000 254 ff227070  pts/1 0:00  ksh
8 O 7001  391  386 22  1   20  ff229800 133           pts/1 0:00  ps
8 T 7001  389  386 20  1   24  ff3da800 228           pts/1 0:00  vi
```

See Also kill, nice

pwd

Syntax

```
pwd
```

Description The `pwd` command displays the path name of the current directory.

Options The `pwd` command has no options.

Example Remembering that `cd` changes the current directory to the directory specified, enter

```
cd /usr/lgoodman/book
```

then

```
pwd
```

This displays

```
/usr/lgoodman/book
```

See Also cd

rcp

Syntax

```
rcp [options] hostname:filename1 filename2
rcp [options] hostname:filename(s) directory
```

Description The `rcp` command copies files between systems on a network. The *hostname* can be omitted for a file on the local machine. If a path name is not included when specifying *filename2*, the files are placed in your home directory. If you have a different user name on the remote host, precede *hostname* with your user name and an at symbol (@) (*username@hostname:filename1*).

Options

-p	Preserves in copies the modification times, access times, and modes of the original files.
-r	If target and sources are both directories, -r copies each subtree rooted at *filename*.

Example Entering

```
rcp log.txt memo primetime:/tmp
```

copies the local files **log.txt** and memo to the /**tmp** directory on the system named **primetime**.

To copy the local **bin** directory and all subdirectories to the /**tmp** directory on the machine named primetime with times and modes unchanged, enter

```
rcp -rp /bin primetime:/tmp
```

See Also cp, ftp, rlogin, rsh

rlogin

Syntax

```
rlogin [options] system
```

Description The rlogin command logs users onto a remote system. The user is prompted for a password unless the .rhosts file in their home directory contains the host name and user name of the user.

Options

-8	Allows 8-bit data, instead of 7-bit data, to pass across the network.
-e*c*	Sets the escape character to c. The default is the tilde (~).

-l *username*   Logs into the remote system using *username* instead of the current user's name.

Example Entering

```
rlogin primetime
```

logs into the system with the host name `primetime`.

The -l option is especially useful when you are working on another person's machine and using their user name, and you need to log into your own machine as yourself. For example, entering

```
rlogin -l ataylor primetime
```

logs you onto the host machine named `primetime` as `ataylor`.

See Also ftp, rsh

rm

Syntax

```
rm [options] filename
```

Description The `rm` command deletes one or more files. You must have write permission in the directory that contains the file or files, but you need not have write permission for the file. If you do not have write permission, the permissions are displayed and you are prompted to confirm the deletion. If you have write permission, the `rm` command returns to the system prompt if successful unless the -i option is used. It is a good idea for new users to use this option, as `rm` runs without giving feedback to the user, which can lead to unknowingly deleting files. If you want to always use the -i option with the `rm` command, enter

```
alias rm 'rm -i'
```

into your `.profile` file. This will cause ~ `rm -i` to be run when `rm` is typed in.

Options

-f
Forces removal even if the file or directory permissions don't allow it. A file can have write permission disabled to keep the file from being overwritten or erased. If you try `rm` on a file that has its protection set to disable writing, then `rm` will not delete the file. If the -f option is used, the delete will occur regardless of what permissions are set.

-i
Asks whether to delete each file or to examine each directory if the -r option is used.

-r
Recursively deletes the files and subdirectories associated with a directory, as well as the directory itself.

Example Entering

```
rm lgoodman/temp
```

removes the file **temp** from the directory **lgoodman**. Entering

```
rm -r lgoodman/book
```

removes all the files from all the subdirectories of **book**, as well as the subdirectory **book**.

See Also `mv`, `cp`, `alias`

rmdir

Syntax

```
rmdir directoryname
```

Description The `rmdir` command removes directories. The directory must be empty (not containing any files or subdirectories) before using the `rmdir` command.

Options This command has no options.

Example Entering

```
rmdir tmp
```

removes the directory `tmp` from the current working directory.

See Also `mkdir`, `ls`, `rm`

rsh

Syntax

```
rsh [options] hostname command
```

Description The `rsh` command lets you execute a single command on a remote machine without having to formally log in using the `rlogin` command. Commands available using the `rsh` command are determined by the system administrator for the remote machine. If you omit the *command* argument, `rsh` logs you into the remote host using the `rlogin` command. A remote host may have a file named `/etc/hosts.equiv` that contains a list of trusted hostnames with which it shares usernames, or users can set up a `.rhosts` file in their home directories to use the `rsh` command. The `.rhosts` file contains the *hostname*, a space, and then the *username*. If the names of the local host and user name are not found in the `/etc/hosts.equiv` on the remote host machine, and the local user name and host name are not in the remote user's `.rhosts` file, access is denied.

Options

`-l` *username*	Uses a specific user name as the remote user name.
`-n`	Redirects the input of the `rsh` command to `/dev/null`.

Example Entering

```
rsh mayberry ls
```

executes the `ls` command on the remote machine, `mayberry`.

See Also `rlogin, rcp`

rup

Syntax

```
rup [options] hostname
```

Description The `rup` command shows the host status of local systems.

Options

-h	Sorts alphabetically by host.
-l	Sorts by load average.
-t	Sorts by up time.

Example Entering

```
rup mayberry
```

queries the host machine `mayberry` and displays its status.

See Also `who`

ruptime

Syntax

```
ruptime [options]
```

Description The `ruptime` command displays the status for all systems on the local network. If no options are added, `ruptime` displays the status sorted by host name.

Options

-a	Includes users even if they have been idle for more than an hour.
-l	Sorts the list of systems by load average.
-r	Reverses the sort order.
-t	Sorts the list of systems by the amount of time the system has been up and running.
-u	Sorts the list of systems by the number of users on the system.

Example Entering

```
ruptime -u
```

displays the system list, with the system being used by the most users listed first and the least number of users listed last.

See Also rwho

rusers

Syntax

```
rusers [options] hostname
```

Description The `rusers` command shows who is logged into local systems on the network.

Options

-a	Reports on a host machine even if no users are logged in.

-h	Sorts alphabetically by the host name.
-i	Sorts by idle time.
-l	Gives a long list, similar to that of the who command.
-u	Sorts by the number of users.

Example Entering

    rusers

displays the users logged in on the local system.

Entering

    rusers mayberry

displays the users logged in on the remote system mayberry.

See Also rup, who

rwho

Syntax

    rwho [options]

Description The rwho command displays who is logged on for all machines on the local network.

Options

-a	Includes users even if they have been idle for more than an hour.

Example Entering

    rwho -a

displays all users who are logged onto the local network.

See Also `finger`, `rusers`, `who`

script

Syntax

```
script [option] [filename]
```

Description The `script` command keeps a record of your login session, storing in a file everything that displays on your screen. If a file name is not included after the `script` command, the record is stored in a file named `typescript`. The `script` command records nonprinting characters as control characters and includes prompts. The script ends when Control-d or `exit` is typed.

Option

    `-a`   Appends the script record to *filename*, rather than overwriting it.

Example Entering

```
script mycmds
```

displays the message

```
Script is started, file is mycmds
```

Any commands and output for the session are stored until you press Control-d or type `exit`. When you press Control-d or type `exit`, the message `Script is done, file is mycmds` displays before you are returned to the prompt.

set

Syntax

```
set [variable=value]
```

Description The set command, without `variable` or `value`, displays the values of all shell variables. Shell variables are used from within the shell, as opposed to environment variables, which may be used within programs as well as within the shell. Shell variables are used to save typing in long commands often. For instance, a path variable tells the operating system where to look for executable files or scripts so that you don't have to type a path with each name of a program or script.

The set command followed by `variable` assigns a null value as the current value of `variable`. The set command with `variable` followed by `value` assigns the value indicated by `value` to the variable indicated by `variable`.

Options The set command has no options.

Example Entering

```
set
```

displays the current value of any defined shell variables, with a display similar to this:

```
DISPLAY=:0.0
ERRNO=10
FCEDIT=/bin/ed
FONTPATH=/usr/openwin/lib/fonts:/usr/openwin/lib/fonts/misc
HELPPATH=/usr/openwin/lib/locale:/usr/openwin/lib/help
HOME=/export/home/rpetrie
HZ=100
IFS=
LANG=C
LD_LIBRARY_PATH=/usr/openwin/lib
LINENO=1
LOGNAME=rpetrie
MAIL=/var/mail/rpetrie
MAILCHECK=600
MANPATH=/usr/openwin/share/man:/usr/man
MANSECTS=\1:1m:1c:1f:1s:1b:2:\3:3c:3i:3n:3m:3k:3g:3e:3x11:3xt:3w:
3b:9:4:5:7:8
NOSUNVIEW=0
OPENWINHOME=/usr/openwin
OPTIND=1
PATH=/usr/openwin/bin:/usr/sbin:/sbin:/usr/bin:/bin:/etc:/usr/lib
/lp/postscript:/usr/openwin/demo:
PPID=443
PS1=$
PS2=>
```

```
PS3=#?
PS4=+
PWD=/export/home/rpetrie
RANDOM=21942
SECONDS=89
SHELL=/bin/ksh
TERM=sun-cmd
TERMCAP=sun-cmd:te=\E[>4h:ti=\E[>4l:tc=sun:
TMOUT=0
TZ=US/Pacific
WINDOW_PARENT=/dev/win0
WINDOW_TERMIOS=
WINDOW_TTYPARMS=D,D,13107203,21509,13,13,127,21,1409614040,3,28,1
7,19,4,-1,26,25,18,15
WMGR_ENV_PLACEHOLDER=/dev/win3
XFILESEARCHPATH=/usr/openwin/lib/locale/%L/%T/%N%S:/usr/openwin/l
ib/%T/%N%S
XINITRC=/usr/openwin/lib/Xinitrc
_=/usr/openwin/bin/openwin
```

See Also env

sleep

Syntax

```
sleep time
```

Description The sleep command suspends execution of a process for a specified number of seconds.

Options The sleep command has no options.

Example Using sleep, you can execute a command at some later time, such as the following:

```
(sleep 600; echo try that phone call again ) &
```

which does nothing for 600 seconds (ten minutes), then displays

```
try that phone call again
```

See Also at

sort

Syntax

```
sort [options] [-o outfile] filename
```

Description The `sort` command sorts lines within the specified file and writes its output to either the screen or the file specified with the `-o` `outfile` option. Output lines are sorted character by character, left to right. If more than one file is specified as input, the files are sorted and collated.

Options

`-b`	Ignores leading blanks.
`-d`	Sorts by ascending dictionary order (uppercase letters first, then lowercase). Only letters, digits, and blanks are significant in comparison. The default is to sort using ASCII order, where all ASCII characters are significant.
`-f`	Ignores uppercase and lowercase differences.
`-i`	Ignores characters outside the ASCII range 040 to 0176 in nonnumeric comparisons.
`-n`	Sorts by numeric order.
`-r`	Reverses the collating sequence.

Example Entering

```
sort -o sorted namelist
```

sorts the file **namelist**, and writes the output to the sorted file **sorted**. Entering

```
sort dept[a-f] -o sorted.depts
```

sorts the six files, **depta** through **deptf**, and stores the output into the file **sorted.depts**.

See Also `tr, uniq`

spell

Syntax

```
spell [options] filename
```

Description The `spell` command checks a file for spelling errors. The output is an alphabetized list of all words that cannot be found in, or derived from, the system dictionary file.

Options

−b	Accepts British spellings, such as "centre," "colour," and "travelled."
−v	Displays all the words not literally in the system dictionary. Words that can be derived from the dictionary are displayed, showing the plausible derivation.
−x	Displays every possible stem for each word.

Example Entering

```
spell resume > corrections
```

reads in the file **resume**, checking for spelling errors, and writes any words not in the dictionary to the file **corrections**.

See Also `sort, uniq`

strings

Syntax

```
strings [options] files
```

Description The `string` command searches for ASCII characters in binary files.

Options

`-a`	Searches entire file, not just the initialized data portion of object files. You can also specify this option as -.
`-o`	Displays the string's offset position before the string.
`-n` *n*	Specifies the minimum string length as *n*. The default is to search for a string length of four ASCII characters.

Example Entering

```
strings program1
```

searches for and displays any string of four ASCII characters or more in the binary file program1.

SU

Syntax

```
su username
```

Description The `su` command temporarily switches your user ID to that of *username*. The `su` command prompts for a password, just as if you were logging in, and with a correct password changes your user ID and group ID to that of *username*. The `.profile` file is read. The current directory is not changed, but the HOME variable is changed. If no name is specified, `su` creates a shell for a privileged user.

Example To change to user `bjoy` enter

```
su bjoy
```

then enter the appropriate password for **b'joy** at the prompt

```
password:
```

To become a privileged user, enter

```
su
```

then enter the root password at the **password** prompt.

See Also login

tail

Syntax

```
tail [options] [filename]
```

Description The **tail** command sends the end of *filename* to the screen. The user can specify how many lines are sent. If the number of lines to be sent is not specified, **tail** sends ten lines. Whether standard input or a file is used depends upon whether or not the *filename* argument is used. If the *filename* argument is not specified, the keyboard (or standard input) is used. If you have a file that stores transactions, using **tail** you can quickly review the most recent activity.

Options

+*n* or -*n*	With no number specified, **tail** outputs the last ten lines of the input. If +*n* *present*, **tail** outputs the number of lines, characters, or blocks from the beginning of the input; if -*n* is present, **tail** counts back from the end of the file.
l	Refers to lines when added after +*n* or -*n*.
b	Refers to blocks when added after +*n* or -*n*.
c	Refers to characters when added after +n or -*n*.
r	Outputs the lines in reverse order.

Example Using the file named `phonelist` and entering

```
tail -31 phonelist
```

displays

```
Thomas, Ginger    (408) 555-2323
Williams, Greg    (408) 555-2916
Young, Charles    (415) 555-2380
```

Entering

```
tail -23c phonelist
```

displays

```
Charles (415) 555-2380
```

Note that if options `l`, `b`, or `c` are used, they must immediately follow any `+n` or `-n` with no intervening spaces.

See Also `cat`, `more`, `head`

talk

Syntax

```
talk username [tty]
```

Description The `talk` command establishes a two-way, terminal-to-terminal communication path. It allows users to send messages back and forth by typing them in.

Options The `talk` command has no options.

Example Entering

```
talk lgoodman
```

displays the following on `lgoodman`'s terminal:

```
Message from Talk_Daemon@primetime at 2:03…
talk:  connection requested by rpetrie@primetime
talk:  respond with:  talk rpetrie@primetime
```

where `primetime` is your computer's host name. `2:03` is the current time. `r.petrie` is your login name. The other user (in this case `lgoodman`) should then enter

```
talk yourname
```

This establishes the link between your terminals. To exit, just enter your system's interrupt character (on some systems press Control-o). Note that pressing Control-l redraws the screen while you are using the `talk` command.

See Also `mesg`, `who`, `write`

tar

Syntax

```
tar [key] [options] [tarfilename] [blocksize] [excludefile] [-I
includefile] [filename1] [filename2 ...] [-C directory filename3]
[filename4]
```

Description The `tar` command archives and recovers files. It can create, add to, list, and retrieve files from an archive. The first option following `tar` is the key. The key specifies these actions: create (creates a new tarfile); write (writes the designated files to the end of the tarfile); table of contents (lists the table of contents of the tarfile); update (adds the named files to the tarfile if they are not already present or current); extract (extracts files from an archive file). One of these must be entered. After the key comes any modifiers. An archive file may reside on a system disk, floppy disk, tape unit, or anywhere else SunOS can write or to read a file.

Common places to archive files are tape drives and floppy disks. The `/dev` directory has several files in it that are really devices such as a tape drive, terminal, system disk, or floppy disk drive. `/dev/rdiskette` is really a floppy drive, and `/dev/rmt/0` is really a tape drive.

The `tar` command knows about directory structures and can preserve absolute, relative, or no directory information. If the files specified to archive are given with a full path, that information is preserved, and when the file is recovered, it is placed back into the correct directory. If the files are specified with a relative path at the time of the archive, they are placed in the directory with the same relative path from the current working directory at the time of the recovery. If, at the time of the archive, the files are specified from the current directory with just a file name, they will be placed into whatever the current working directory is at the time of recovery.

The `tar` command keeps track of a great deal of information besides the file's contents. It keeps track of things like a *checksum*, which is a number used to help insure data integrity, the permissions associated with the files, their creation dates, and so on.

Examples of device names commonly found on Sun workstations include:

DEVICE NAME	DEVICE
`/dev/rmt/0`	¼-inch tape cartridge
`/dev/rdiskette`	3½-inch diskette

To specify the density for a tape drive, you need to add a character that identifies the tape density after the tape drive number. For example, if you are using a tape drive that writes at a medium density, add the letter `m` after the tape device number (`/dev/rmt/0m`). The following is a list of characters used to specify different densities for SCSI tape drives.

`null`	Default, preferred (highest) density
`l`	Low (800 bpi)
`m`	Medium (1600 bpi)
`h`	High (6250 bpi)
`u`	Ultra (reserved)

After performing a backup or a retrieval on some devices, the system typically rewinds the tape and resets the file pointers for diskettes. To prevent rewinding, the device name should be appended with an `n` at the end of the device name (`/dev/rmt/0mn`).

Keys

c   Creates a new archive file. This overwrites anything previously stored on the media (it overwrites files on floppies, for instance).

r   Appends the named files to an existing archive file. Any existing files in the archive are not changed. This does not work with ¼-inch tape.

t   Prints the names of any specified files as they appear in the archive file. If no files are specified, this key displays a directory of all files contained in the archive file.

u   Performs an update, appending files to the archive only if they are not already present or if they have been modified since they were last written to the tape. This option runs slowly due to the checking it must perform. This does not work with ¼-inch tape.

x   Extracts files from an archive file. Given a file list, this option only extracts the files specified. With no file list, this option extracts all the files in an archive.

Options

f   Uses the next argument as the name of the file to read or write as the archive file (instead of the default of /dev/rmt/0). If - is used, the standard input or standard output is used; thus tar can be used in a pipe.

FF   Excludes all SCCS directories, all files with .o as their suffix, and all files named errs, core, and a.out.

l   Displays error messages if links to archived
              files cannot be resolved. Without this
              option, error messages about unresolved
              links will not be displayed.

L   Follows symbolic links, which allows linked
              files to be treated as if they were normal
              files or directories. Without this option, `tar`
              does not support symbolic links.

m   Does not extract modification times with
              files. Sets the modification time to the time
              of the extraction.

o   Suppresses information specifying owner
              and permission modes normally placed
              into the archive. Such information makes
              previous versions of `tar` generate error
              messages like `filename: cannot create`.

v   Displays the name of each file archived
              or extracted. When used with the `t` key,
              displays a listing similar to `ls -l`.

w   Waits for user confirmation before taking
              any action. Displays the action to be taken
              followed by the file name and waits for a `y`
              entered from the keyboard. Anything other
              than a `y` causes no action to be taken for
              the named file.

-I   Uses `includefilename`, the next file name,
              as a list of files, one per line, entered on the
              command line for the `tar` command.
              Excluded files take precedence over
              included files. See the `-x` option.

Example To archive the current working directory to the default tape drive (`dev/rmt/0`), and overwrite anything else on the tape, enter

    tar cv.

To list the files on a ¼–inch cartridge tape drive, enter

    tar tvf /dev/rmt/0

To archive the files **memo** and **report** on a floppy disk, enter

    tar cvf /dev/rdiskette memo report

To extract the files from a floppy diskette into the current directory, enter

    tar xvf /dev/rdiskette

See Also chdir, ls, cpio

tee

Syntax

    tee [options] [filename]

Description The **tee** command replicates the standard output. This command is usually used in a pipe. A pipe (I) is a way to connect the output of one command or program to the input of another command or program. The standard input is usually the keyboard, but by using pipes, you can get input from the output of a command or program instead. Sometimes when constructing long pipes, it is desirable to save intermediate results. If you form a **tee** in the pipe, you can siphon off some of the information and direct it to a file.

Options

-a   Appends the output to the specified file
                instead of overwriting the existing contents.

-i   Ignores interrupts.

Example Entering

```
pr final.draft | tee report.printed | lp
```

prepares the file `final.draft` for printing, saves a copy of the formatted file as `report.printed`, and sends a formatted copy to the printer.

See Also `lp`, `ls`, `pr`, `wc`

telnet

Syntax

```
telnet [hostname [port]]
```

Description The `telnet` command allows you to communicate with another machine using the TELNET protocol. If no host name is specified, `telnet` displays the prompt `telnet >`, indicating that it is in command mode. If a *hostname* or *port* is added, `telnet` opens the host indicated. After the connection is established, you are prompted for a user name and password on the remote system.

Commands The `telnet` command contains a command mode that offers many features and options. You can switch from terminal mode to command mode with the telnet escape character, which defaults to Control-]. After pressing Control-], a new prompt appears from the local telnet command mode. At this point you can enter any of several telnet commands. The following lists several `telnet` commands.

COMMAND	EFFECT
`close`	Terminates the connection but remains in the `telnet` program.
`open` *hostname*	Starts a connection to the named host machine.
`quit`	Quits the current connection and exits the telnet program. This command is the same as the `close` command.

COMMAND	EFFECT
z	Temporarily suspends the telnet session to allow other commands to be executed on the local system.
?	Prints help information on available telnet commands.
<Return>	Returns you to the shell at the remote host machine.

Example Entering

```
telnet spacelink.msfc.nasa.gov
```

connects you to the NASA system. When prompted for a login user name and password, enter

```
newuser
```

You are then presented with a menu of options for reading entries about the history, current state, and future of NASA activities.

See Also ftp, rlogin

time

Syntax

```
time [command]
```

Description The time command times how long a command takes to run, or with no command specified, tells how much time has been used for the current process.

Options The time command has no options.

Example Entering

```
time find / -name "*.ps" -print &
```

To transfer the file `macabre` from the remote machine to your machine, enter

    ~t

then press Return and enter

    macabre

touch

Syntax

    touch [options] filename(s)

Description The `touch` command sets the access and modification time of the file *filename* to the current time. The *filename* is created if it does not exist. The `touch` command is often used with the special programming command `make` to force a complete rebuild of a program.

Options

-c   Does not create `filename` if it does not
                         exist.

Example Enter

    touch *.c

to change the access and modification of any files with the .c extension in the current directory.

tr

Syntax

    tr [options] [string1] [string2]

Description The `tr` command copies the standard input to the standard output, translating occurrences from *string1* into corresponding characters in *string2*. A common use of `tr` is to convert a file to all uppercase or lowercase.

Options

`-c`	Complements the set of characters in *string1* with respect to the set of ASCII codes 1-255 (so that `tr -cd 0-9` means to delete everything that's not a number).
`-d`	Deletes all characters in *string1*. For example, `tr -d '^A-^Z' < in.ctrl > out.txt` can be used to strip all control characters from a file (for printing a file, for instance).
`-s`	Squeezes strings of repeated characters from *string2* to single characters.

Example Entering

```
cat mixed.txt | tr "[A-Z]" "[a-z]" > lower.txt
```

translates the file `mixed.txt`, containing both upper- and lowercase, into the file `lower.txt`, containing only lowercase letters. Entering

```
cat infile.txt | tr " " "\012" > outfile.txt
```

translates the file `in.file` into a file, `out.file`, that converts spaces into newlines with one word per line. Note that this example has no effect on the case of the characters contained in any of the files.

Entering

```
tr -d "&" < textfile1 > textfile2
```

deletes the & character from *textfile1* and saves the output in *textfile2*.

See Also expand

tty

Syntax

```
tty [option]
```

Description The `tty` command prints the path name of your terminal's device file.

Options

`-l`	Prints the synchronous line number.
`-s`	Returns only the codes: 0 (a terminal), 1 (not a terminal), 2 (invalid options used).

Example Entering

```
tty
```

displays something similar to

```
/dev/pts/1
```

umask

Syntax

```
umask [mask]
```

Description The `umask` command displays or sets the file creation mode mask. Entering the `unmask` command alone displays the current file recreation mask. The numbers are like the numbers used for `chmod`, except that with `umask`, the numbers represent the permissions that are not granted, whereas with `chmod` the numbers represent the permissions that are granted. Because SunOS is a multiuser system, there are built-in safeguards to keep users from accidentally (or even deliberately) deleting another user's files. These safeguards protect against unauthorized reading, writing, copying, deleting, and executing of files.

The modes are given in either of two formats for this command. An absolute mode is an octal number formed by summing the following octal numbers representing the enabled permissions. There are three fields, one for the owner of the file, one for the group to which the file belongs, and one for everybody else.

0	Grants read and write permission for files, and read, write, and search permission for directories.
1	Grants read and write permission for files and directories.
2	Grants only read permission for files, and grants read and search permission for directories.
3	Grants only read permission for files and directories.
4	Grants only write permission for files, and write and search permission for directories.
5	Grants only write permission for files and directories.
6	Grants no permissions for files, and grants only search permission for directories.
7	Grants no permissions (denies all permissions) for files and directories.

By default, files are given the permissions mode 666 (rw-rw-rw-), which gives everyone read and write access. Directories are given the permissions mode 777 (rwxrwxrwx), which gives everyone read, write, and search permission.

Options The umask command has no options.

Example Entering

```
umask
```

displays the current setting of the file creation mask. Entering

```
umask 002
```

sets the file creation `mask` so the owner and group have all privileges, while the rest of the world has only read permission.

See Also `chgrp, chmod, chown, ls`

unalias

Syntax

```
unalias pattern
```

Description The `unalias` command is a Korn shell command that discards aliases. Any aliases that match *pattern* are discarded, so `unalias *` discards all previous aliases.

Options The `unalias` command has no options.

Example If you have previously aliased `ls` with

```
alias ls="ls -l"
```

which displays a long listing anytime `ls` is entered, you can undo the `alias` with

```
unalias ls
```

See Also `alias`

uname

Syntax

```
uname [options]
```

Description The `uname` command displays information about the operating system. If no options are specified, only the current operating system's name is displayed.

Options

-a	Displays all information about the current system.
-m	Displays the machine name.
-n	Displays the node name. The node name is the name by which the system is known to a network.
-p	Displays the current host's processor type.
-r	Displays the number of the operating system release.
-s	Displays the name of the operating system. This is the default.
-v	Displays the operating system version.

Example Entering

    uname -a

is the same as entering uname -mnprsv, which displays a listing similar to this:

    SunOS primetime 5.1 Generic sun4c sparc

uncompress

Syntax

    uncompress [options] [filename]

Description The uncompress command recovers a compressed file.

Options

-c	Writes to the screen (or standard output). Does not change any files. (The zcat command is equivalent to the -c option.)
-v	Displays the percentage of reduction.

Example Given a file, `report.text`, with a size of 4608 bytes, entering

```
compress report.text
```

results in a file, `report.text.Z`, with a size of 2696 bytes. To uncompress this file, enter

```
uncompress report.text
```

Note that with the `uncompress` command, the `.Z` extension is optional.

See Also `compress`

unexpand

Syntax

```
unexpand [option] filename
```

Description The `unexpand` command is the opposite of the `expand` command. It copies file names (or the standard input) to the standard output, putting tab characters back into the data. By default, only leading space and tab characters are converted to strings of tabs.

Options

`-a`   Inserts tab characters when replacing a run of two or more space characters would produce a smaller output file.

Example Entering

```
unexpand myfile
```

reverses the effect of running the expand command on `myfile`.

See Also `expand`

uniq

Syntax

```
uniq [options] [inputfilename] [outputfilename]
```

Description The `uniq` command is used to remove or report on adjacent duplicate lines within a file. Normally `uniq` removes the second and succeeding repeated lines, passing everything else through to the output. To be removed, duplicate lines must be adjacent.

Options

-c	Precedes each line by a count of the number of times it occurred in the input.
-d	Displays one occurrence of just the repeated lines from the input.
-u	Displays just those lines that were not repeated in the input.
+*n*	Ignores the first *n* characters when comparing lines.
-*n*	Ignores the first n fields, together with any blanks before each field. A field is a string of characters separated by space or tab characters.

Examples Entering

```
cat singers musicians | sort | uniq > talent
```

combines the files **singers** and **musicians**, sorts the combined file, eliminates any duplicates, and stores the results in the file **talent**. Entering

```
cat singers musicians | sort | uniq -d > diverse
```

combines the files, sorts them, and saves only duplicate lines, thus showing entries common to two or more files.

See Also sort

units

Syntax

```
units
```

Description The `units` command converts between units of measure. (Be aware that the money conversions are not current.) For a complete list of known units, look in the file `/usr/share/lib/unittab`. Note that the `units` command only does multiplicative scale changes; thus it can convert Kelvin to Rankine, but not Celsius to Fahrenheit. The `units` command operates interactively.

Options The `units` command has no options.

Example Enter

```
units
```

and the `units` command displays

```
You have:
```

Enter

```
36 inch
```

and the `units` command displays

```
You want:
```

Enter

```
feet
```

and the `units` command displays

```
* 3.000000e+00
/ 3.333333e-01
```

To terminate the program, press Control-d.

unpack

Syntax

    unpack filename(s)

Description Expands one or more files created with the **pack** command to their original form.

Options The unpack command has no options.

Example To unpack a previously packed file, mucho.psz, enter

    unpack mucho.psz

See Also pack

vacation

Syntax

    vacation [options]

Description Automatically return a mail message to sender announcing that you are on vacation. To disable the **vacation** command, type mail -F " ".

-I	Begins forwarding your mail and informing other users sending you mail that you are on vacation. If the -I option and the *username* argument are omitted, the **vacation** command lets you interactively turn **vacation** on or off. If the -I option is omitted but the **username** is included, **vacation** reads from the standard input for a line indicating who the vacation message is from (From *username*).

-a *alias* Indicates that *alias* is one of the valid aliases for the user running the `vacation` command, so that mail addressed to `alias` generates a reply.

-t *n* Specifies the time interval between repeat replies to the same sender. You can specify seconds (-t*n*s), minutes (-t*n*m), hours (-t*n*h), days(-t*n*d), or weeks (-t*n*w). The default is one week.

Example The following is a sample listing of prompts displayed after entering the `vacation` command.

```
This program can be used to answer your mail automatically
when you go away on vacation.
You have a message file in /export/home/rpetrie/.vacation.msg.
Would you like to see it? y
Subject:  I am on vacation
Precedence: junk

Your mail regarding "$SUBJECT" will be read when I return.

If you have something urgent, please contact...
Would you like to edit it? n
To enable the vacation feature a ".forward" file is created.
Would you like to enable the vacation feature? y
Vacation feature ENABLED. Please remember to turn it off when
you get back from vacation. Bon voyage.
```

See Also mail, mailx

vi

Syntax

```
vi [options] [filename(s)]
```

Description The vi editor is a visual text editor. See Chapter 12, "Using the vi Editor" for detailed coverage on working with vi. Chapter 13, "Formatting and Printing" explains how to work with `nroff` and `troff` text-formatting commands.

wall

Syntax

```
wall [options] [filename]
```

Description The `wall` command writes to all logged-in users (as such it is usually used by the system administrator for important messages). The standard input is read until a Control-d is entered. It is then sent to all logged-in users preceded by the message "Broadcast Message." If *filename* is specified, the input is taken from the indicated file instead of from the standard input.

Options

    -a   Writes to all terminals.

Example Entering

```
wall fired
```

broadcasts the file `fired` to all users logged onto the network.

See Also mesg, write

wc

Syntax

```
wc [options] [filename]
```

Description The `wc` command counts the lines, words, and characters in *filename*. If *filename* is not specified, `wc` counts the standard input. Words are separated by spaces, tabs, or newlines (carriage returns). The `wc` command is very useful in piping. You can use the `who` command, which lists the users currently logged in (giving one user per line), and pipe its output to `wc`, which then counts the number of lines by entering `who | wc -l`. This counts and displays the number of currently logged-on users. Combining ls, a command to list the files in a directory, with wc, a command to count lines, as follows

```
ls | wc -l
```

counts the number of files in the current directory.

Options

  -l Counts the lines in the specified file.

  -w Counts the words in the specified file.

  -C Counts characters in the specified file.

  -c Counts bytes in the specified file.

Example Entering the command

```
wc file1
```

displays

```
227   876   6220 file1
```

which means there are 227 lines, 876 words, and 6220 characters in the file file1.

Entering

```
wc -l file1
```

displays

```
227 file1
```

which means there are 227 lines in the file file1.

Entering

```
wc -C file1
```

displays

```
6220 file1
```

which means there are 6220 characters in the file file1.

which

Syntax

which *filename*

Description The `which` command locates a command and displays its path name The `which` command cannot find built-in shell commands such as `history` and `set`.

Options The `which` command has no options.

Example Entering

which vi

displays

/usr/bin/vi

Entering

which set

displays a path similar to this:

no set in /usr/openwin/bin /usr/sbin /sbin /usr/bin /bin /etc
/usr/lib/lp/postscript /usr/openwin/demo .

where everything after the `no set in` is a possible path setting, and the `which` command could not find a command named `set` in the path.

who

Syntax

who

Description The `who` command displays the login name, terminal name, and login time for each user currently logged in on the local host machine.

Options The `who` command has no options.

Example Entering

```
who
```

displays something like

```
nbacon     tty6 Feb 29 09:18  (nbacon_tty)
rgoodman   tty3 Feb 29 13:12  (rgoodman_tty)
egoodman   tty9 Feb 29 08:10  (ecyr_tty)
```

See Also `who am i, rwho`

who am i

Syntax

```
who am i
```

Description The `who am i` command displays your login name.

Options The `who am i` command has no options.

Example Entering

```
who am i
```

displays something like

```
lgoodman
```

See Also `who`

write

Syntax

```
write username
```

Description The `write` command allows you to send a message to another user's terminal (if they have allowed it through the use of the `mesg` command). If the user is logged into more than one terminal, you must specify `tty`, which is a terminal number.

Options The `write` command has no options.

Example Entering

```
write bheslop
lunch in 10 minutes?
<Control-d>
```

displays on bheslop's terminal

```
Message from lgoodman on stv (pts/1) [Mon Dec 27 11:50:03 ...
lunch in 10 minutes?
```

See Also `mesg`, `talk`, `ps`

xfd

Syntax

```
xfd [options] -fn fontname
```

Description The `xfd` command is an X program that creates an X window for displaying all of the characters of the font indicated by the argument *fontname*. The window contains the name of the font being displayed, a grid containing one character per cell, and three buttons (`Prev Page`, `Next Page`, and `quit`). The text above the character grid displays the selected character's metrics. The characters are shown in increasing ASCII order from left to right, and top to bottom.

Options

`-box`	Displays a box filled with the background color (indicated by `-bc`) outlining the area of each character.

-bc *color*	Specifies the color used to make up the grid surrounding displayed characters.
-center	Centers each character in its grid for viewing characters at arbitrary locations in the font. The default is 0.
-columns *n*	Specifies the number of columns to use when creating the grid for displaying characters.
-rows *n*	Specifies the number of rows to use when creating the grid for displaying characters.
-start *n*	Displays as the first character the character that has position n.

Example Entering

```
xfd -fn rockwell &
```

displays all the characters in the Rockwell font.

Entering

```
xfd -columns 40 -rows 25 -start 1568 -fn kanji
```

displays, in a grid 40 columns by 25 rows, the kanji characters starting at character 1568 in the font named Kanji.

See Also xfontsel, xlsfonts

xfontsel

Syntax

```
xfontsel [options]
```

Description The xfontsel command is an X program that creates a window that allows you to show display font names by pointing and clicking. The window lets you display a font by choosing from a variety of menus, including the font foundry (fndry), font family (fmly), font weight (wght), font slant (slant), set width (sWdth), pixels points in tenths of a point (ptSz), horizontal resolution in dots per inch (`resx`), vertical resolution in dots per inch (`resy`), average width in tenths of a pixel (`avgWdth`).

Options

`-pattern` *fontname*	Specifies a subset of available fonts, with names that contain the pattern specified by *fontname*. The pattern can be a partial or full font name, but the pattern must occur somewhere in the full font name.
`-print`	Displays the selected font's name before returning to the command prompt after pressing the `quit` button.
`-sample text`	Displays the text to display the selected font. Be sure to put *text* containing spaces within quotation marks. The default *text* is lower-case and uppercase letters and the digits 0 through 9.

Example Entering

```
xfontsel
```

displays the **xfontsel** window with the alphabet and numbers 0 through 9 in the default display font.

To display the first font that contains "adobe-times" in its font name, enter

```
xfontsel -pattern *adobe-times*&
```

Entering

```
xfontsel -pattern *bitstream-charter*240* -sample "Bitstream
Charter (24 points)"&
```

displays the text "Bitstream Charter (24 points)" for the first font that contains "bitstream-charter" and "240" in its font name.

See Also xfd, xlsfonts

xhost

Syntax

```
xhost [options]
```

Description The xhost command is an X command that adds and deletes hosts from the list of machines that are allowed to make connections to the X host. The xhost command is often required to set up application programs on your machine. If no arguments are added to the xhost command, a message indicates whether or not access control is enabled, and a list of hosts you are allowed to connect to is displayed.

Options

[+]*hostname*	Adds *hostname* to the list of machines that are allowed to connect to the X server.
-*hostname*	Removes hostname from the list of machines that are allowed to connect to the X server. Existing connections are not broken, but new connection attempts will be denied.
+	Grants access to everyone, even if they aren't on the list of allowed hosts. In other words, access control is turned off.
–	Restricts access to only those machines on the list of allowed hosts. In other words, access control is turned on.

Example Entering

```
xhost +tvland +camelot
```

adds the hosts tvland and camelot to the X server access list.

Entering

```
xhost +
```

grants access to everyone on the network.

See Also openwin

xlock

Syntax

```
xlock [options]
```

Description The xlock command is an X command that locks the screen and starts a screen saver until you enter your password. While xlock is running, the screen displays a changing pattern of Sun logos. When you press a key or a mouse button, you are prompted for your password to return to OpenWindows. If the correct password is typed, the screen is unlocked. If you make a mistake when typing your password, press Control-h to backspace over the mistake, or press Control-u to start over. To return to the locked screen, click on the small icon version of the changing pattern.

Options

-mode *screensaver*	There are ten screensavers you can choose from. The following gives a brief description of each screensaver.
hop	Displays the "real plane fractals" from the September 1986 issue of Scientific American.
life	Displays Conway's game of life.

`qix`	Displays the spinning lines similar to the ones in the old video game by the same name.
`image`	Displays several Sun logos appearing randomly on the screen.
`swarm`	Displays a swarm of bees following a wasp.
`rotor`	Displays a swirling rotor.
`pyro`	Displays fireworks.
`flame`	Displays fractals.
`blank`	Displays nothing but a black screen.
`random`	Picks and displays a random screensaver from all of the above except the `blank` screensaver.
`-delay` *users*	Sets the speed at which a screensaver will operate. It sets the number of microseconds to delay between batches of animation. In the `blank` screensaver, it is important to set this to some small number of seconds, because the keyboard and mouse are only checked after each delay; so you cannot set the delay too high, but a delay of zero would needlessly consume CPU time by continuously checking for mouse and keyboard input, since `blank` screensaver has no work to do.

-batchcount *n*	Sets number of things to do for a screensaver to *n*. When you use the hop screensaver, *n* refers to the number of pixels rendered in the same color. When you use the life screensaver, *n* is the number of generations to let each species live. When you use the qix screensaver, *n* is the number of lines rendered in the same color. When you use the image screensaver, *n* is the number of Sun logos to display on the screen at once. When you use the swarm screensaver, *n* is the number of bees. When you use the rotor screensaver, *n* is the number of rotor things that whirr. When you use the pyro screensaver, *n* is the maximum number of flying rockets at one time. When you use the flame screensaver, *n* is the number of levels to recurse (larger numbers are more complex). When you use the blank screensaver, *n* means nothing.
-nice *n*	Sets the nice setting of the xlock process to *n*.
-timeout *seconds*	Sets the number of *seconds* before the password screen will time out.
-saturation *value*	Sets saturation of the color ramp used to *value*. 0 is gray-scale and 1 is very rich color. 0.4 is a nice pastel.
-font *fontname*	Sets the font to be used on the prompt screen.
-fg *color*	Sets the color of the text on the password screen to color.

-bg *color*	Sets the color of the background on the password screen to *color*.
-username *textstring*	The textstring is shown in front of user name, defaults to `Name:`
-password *textstring*	The *textstring* is the password prompt. The default is `Password:`
-info *textstring*	Informs the user what to do to unlock the screen. The default displays `Enter password to unlock; select icon to lock.`
-validate *textstring*	Specifies the message shown while validating the password. The default is `Validating login...`
-invalid textstring	Specifies the message shown when a password is invalid. The default is `Invalid login.`
-mono or +mono	Displays screensaver in monochrome (black and white), rather than the default color.
+nolock or -nolock	Causes `xlock` to only draw the patterns and not lock the display. Pressing a key or clicking a mouse button terminates the screensaver.
-echokeys or +echokeys	Causes `xlock` to echo the question mark (?) for each key typed at the password prompt. The default is to not echo keystrokes.
-usefirst or +usefirst	Causes `xlock` to use the keystroke that got you to the password screen as the first character in the password. The default is to ignore the first key pressed.
-v	Verbose mode; tells what options it is going to use.

Example Entering

```
xlock -mode rotor
```

displays a whirling rotor that saves the screen.

To display a screensaver that does not require you to enter a password, add the -nolock option. For example, to start the **pyro** screensaver without password protection, enter

```
xlock -mode pyro -nolock
```

To change the swarm of bees to include 100 bees in the **swarm** screensaver, enter

```
xlock -batchcount 100 -mode swarm
```

See Also xset

xlsfonts

Syntax

```
xlsfonts [options] -fn [pattern]
```

Description The xlsfonts command lists available fonts that match pattern. *The wildcard characters* * and ? can be used to match characters. If no pattern is given, * is assumed.

Options

-l[l[l]]	Generate medium (-l), long (-ll), and extremely long listings(-lll).
-c	Produces a list using multiple columns. This option is the same as using the argument -n **0**.
-1	Produces a list using a single column. This option is the same as using the argument -n **1**.

-w *width*	Specifies how many characters should appear in a column *width*. The default is a width of 79 characters.
-n *columns*	Uses number of columns in displaying the output. By default, the xlsfonts command attempts to fit as many columns of font names into the number of characters specified by -w *width*.
-u	Specifies not to sort the listing.

Example Entering

```
xlsfonts -fn \*linotype*
```

displays the available linotype fonts.

Entering

```
xlsfonts -l -fn \*monotype*
```

displays a long listing of available monotype fonts.

See Also xfd, xfontsel

xman

Syntax

```
xman [options]
```

Description The xman command displays a window for viewing the X manual pages for X commands. The initial Manual Browser window displays three buttons Help, Manual Page, and Quit. Clicking on the Manual Page or Help buttons displays the initial Manual Page window, containing instructions for displaying X manual pages. At the top of the Manual Page window are two menu buttons (Options and Sections) for displaying X manual pages. To scroll through the introductory text, press the right mouse button on the scrollbar at the left side of the Manual Page window.

Options

-helpfile *filename*	Uses an alternate file indicated by *filename* for help.
-bothshown	Displays both the manual page and manual directory in the same window.
-notopbox	Displays the **Manual Page** window without the displaying the initial **Manual Browser** window with the three buttons in it.

Example Entering

```
xman &
```

displays the initial **Manual Browser** window.

Entering

```
xman -notopbox -bothshown &
```

displays a split window with the directory of user commands at the top and the help manual page in the lower window.

See Also man

xrdb

Syntax

```
xrdb [options]
```

Description The xrdb command reads the .Xdefaults file and sets the basic properties for OpenWindows, such as the Workspace and window colors. The xrdb command also allows you to display or edit the contents of the .Xdefaults file. This program is run each time you start OpenWindows.

Options

`-help`	Displays a usage summary of command-line options. Using any unsupported option has the same effect.
`-query`	Displays the current contents of the `.Xdefaults` file.
`-quiet`	Does not warn about duplicate entries.
`-edit` *filename*	Copies the `.Xdefaults` file into *filename* replacing any values already listed. This allows you to put changes that you have made to your defaults back into your `.Xdefaults` file, preserving any comments.
`-backup` *string*	Generates a backup file appending an extension indicated by *string* to the file name used with the `-edit` option.

Example Entering

```
xrdb
```

reads and executes the `.Xdefaults` file.

To display the contents of your `.Xdefaults` file, enter

```
xrdb -query
```

See Also openwin, xset, xsetroot

xset

Syntax

```
xset [options]
```

Description The xset command lets you customize X environment settings for OpenWindows features, such as the bell, the key click, and the screensaver. Any X settings that you change are lost or reset to their default values when you log out unless you add them to the .xinitrc file in your home directory. If the .xinitrc file does not exist in your home directory, you need to copy and rename the $OPENWINHOME/lib/Xinitrc file to $HOME/.xinitrc.

Options

[-]b [volume [pitch [duration]]] [on | off]	Sets the volume, pitch, and duration of the bell. If no arguments are given, the bell is enabled and the system defaults are used. Unlike most options, preceding the b with a dash (-) turns the bell off. You can also turn the bell off by adding the off argument. If only one number is given, the bell *volume* will be set to that value, as a percentage of its maximum. The second number specifies the bell's *pitch*, in hertz, and the third number specifies the *duration* of the bell in milliseconds.

`[-]c [value][on	off]`	Sets the volume of the key click. The c option accepts an optional *value* from 0 to 100 that indicates the volume as a percentage of maximum. As with the b option, preceding the c with a dash (−) disables the key click. If no arguments are added, the system defaults are used. If the **off** argument is added, the keyclick is disabled.
`fp=path`	Sets the font path used by the server. The path must be a directory or a comma-separated list of directories.
`fp default`	Restores the default font path.
`fp rehash`	Rereads the font databases in the current font path. This is generally used only when adding new fonts to a font directory (after running *mkfontdir* to recreate the font database).
`-fp path` or `fp- path`	Removes elements from the current font path. *path* must be a directory or a comma-separated list of directories.
`+fp path` or `fp+ path`	Inserts or appends elements to the current font path, respectively. The path must be a directory or comma-separated list of directories.

led [*integer*] [*on* | off]

Turns LEDs (the lights on your keyboard) on or off. The *led* option without an argument turns all LEDs on. With a preceding dash or the *off* argument added, turns LEDs off. Adding an *integer* between 1 and 32 turns the respective LED on or off.

m [*acceleration* [*threshold*]] [default]

Sets how far the mouse pointer moves on the screen in relation to how far you move the mouse. The *acceleration* argument is a multiplier that is applied to the pointer motion. In other words, if the acceleration is set to 5, when you move the mouse, it will move 5 times as fast. To keep the mouse pointer from leaping around, you can also set a *threshold*. The *threshold* setting makes it so that the acceleration factor only takes effect if the pointer moves more than the number of pixels indicated by *threshold*. If no arguments are added, the system defaults are used.

`s [time [cycle]]` `[blank	noblank]` `[on	off] [default]`	Sets up the screensaver. If no arguments are added, the system is set to its default screensaver characteristics. The off argument turns the screensaver off. The `blank` argument blanks the video instead of displaying a background pattern, while `noblank` sets the preference to display a pattern rather than blanking the video. The *time* and *cycle* arguments determine how many seconds the keyboard must be inactive for the screen blanker to start, and the period in which to change the background pattern to avoid damage to your screen, respectively.
`q`	Displays information on the current X settings.

Example Entering

    xset s 300

enables a screen blanker that starts after five minutes.

Entering

    xset c 75

sets a fairly loud key click sound.

Entering

    xset m 6 12

speeds up the acceleration of the mouse. This sets the mouse movement so that if you move more than 12 pixels, the mouse moves 6 times as many pixels on the screen as you moved the mouse.

```
xset b 100 1000 80
```

sets the volume of the bell to its maximum setting, the pitch to 1000 hertz, and the duration to 80 milliseconds.

See Also xsetroot

xsetroot

Syntax

```
xsetroot [options]
```

Description The xsetroot command sets the appearance of the Workspace's background. Without any options or if the -def option is added, the Workspace resets to its defaults. If you add the -def option with other options, only the nonspecified options are reset to their defaults.

Options

-help	Displays a summary of command-line options.
-def	Resets unspecified attributes to default values. The background defaults to a gray mesh pattern.
-cursor cursorfile maskfile	Sets cursor shape for the mouse pointer. The default mouse pointer is an arrow cursor.
-cursor_name cursor name	Changes the root window cursor to one of the standard cursors.

`-bitmap` *filename*	Uses the bitmap file specified by `filename` to set the Workspace background. The default is a gray mesh pattern.
`-mod` *x y*	Makes a plaid grid pattern on the screen. The *x* and *y* are integers ranging from 1 to 16. Zero and negative numbers are taken as 1.
`-gray` or `-grey`	Displays a gray background.
`-solid` *color*	Displays the Workspace background as a solid color.

Example Entering

```
xsetroot -solid turquoise3
```

displays a solid turquoise Workspace background.

To display a bitmap image as your background, enter

```
xsetroot -bitmap $OPENWINHOME/share/include/X11/bitmaps/xlogo64
```

which will display the background to a tiled series of X logos.

Entering

```
xsetroot -cursor_name gumby
```

changes the mouse pointer to a gumby figure.

See Also xset

xterm

Syntax

```
xterm [options]
```

Description The `xterm` command starts a terminal emulator for you to enter commands. It provides options for VT100- and Tektronics-compatible terminals. The `xterm` window provides four menus that allow you to manipulate the VT102 and Tektronics windows. To display the menus, press the Control key and one of the three mouse buttons. If you are using Solaris 2 for x86 with a two-button mouse, press both mouse buttons to simulate the middle mouse button. There are numerous options for the `xterm` command. The following section lists some of the most common options.

Options

-bg *color*	Sets the background color of the `xterm` window. The default is white.
-fg *color*	Sets the color of the foreground (text) of the `xterm` window. The default is black.
-fn *font*	Specifies a *font* to use instead of the default font.
-help	Displays a summary of available `xterm` options.
-j or +j	Specifies that the `xterm` window should do jump scrolling. Normally, text is scrolled one line at a time; this option allows the `xterm` window to move multiple lines at a time. Jump scrolling makes `xterm` much faster when you are scanning through large amounts of text. The +j option specifies that `xterm` window not do jump scrolling.

-1 *logname*   Sends xterm input and output into a file called XtermLog.*n*, where *n* represents the process ID number. Logging allows you to keep track of the sequence of commands and output data. The logging option can be turned on and off from the Main Options menu, which is displayed by pressing the Control key and the left mouse button.

-lf
filename   Specifies the file in which the commands and output are written, rather than the default XtermLog.*n* where *n* represents the process ID number. The log file is created in the directory that xterm was started from.

-RV   Reverses the foreground and background colors. This option can also be turned on and off from the VT Options menu.

-sb or +sb   Displays a scroll bar for the xterm window and saves lines that are scrolled off the top of the window so they can be viewed.

Example Entering

    xterm -sb &

displays an xterm window with a scroll bar.

To create an xterm window with a blue background and yellow text, enter

    xterm -bg midnightblue -fg yellow &

If you want to store commands and output from the commands into a log file, named mycmds, enter

    xterm -l -lf mycmds &

See Also openwin

zcat

Syntax

```
zcat filename
```

Description The zcat command is like the cat command except it only displays uncompressed output for the contents of a compressed file (compressed files end with .Z). It leaves the compressed file unchanged.

Options The zcat command has no options.

Example Entering

```
zcat readme.Z
```

displays the compressed contents of the file readme.Z in an uncompressed format.

See Also compress, pack, pcat

INDEX

This index contains certain typographical conventions to assist you in finding information. **Boldface** page numbers are references to primary topics and explanations that are emphasized in the text. *Italics* indicate page numbers that reference figures.

E

GET A FREE CATALOG JUST FOR EXPRESSING YOUR OPINION.

Help us improve our books and get a **FREE** full-color catalog in the bargain. Please complete this form, pull out this page and send it in today. The address is on the reverse side.

Name _____   Company _____

Address _____   City _____ State ____ Zip _____

Phone (____) _____

1. How would you rate the overall quality of this book?

❑ Excellent
❑ Very Good
❑ Good
❑ Fair
❑ Below Average
❑ Poor

2. What were the things you liked most about the book? (Check all that apply)

❑ Pace
❑ Format
❑ Writing Style
❑ Examples
❑ Table of Contents
❑ Index
❑ Price
❑ Illustrations
❑ Type Style
❑ Cover
❑ Depth of Coverage
❑ Fast Track Notes

3. What were the things you liked *least* about the book? (Check all that apply)

❑ Pace
❑ Format
❑ Writing Style
❑ Examples
❑ Table of Contents
❑ Index
❑ Price
❑ Illustrations
❑ Type Style
❑ Cover
❑ Depth of Coverage
❑ Fast Track Notes

4. Where did you buy this book?

❑ Bookstore chain
❑ Small independent bookstore
❑ Computer store
❑ Wholesale club
❑ College bookstore
❑ Technical bookstore
❑ Other _____

5. How did you decide to buy this particular book?

❑ Recommended by friend
❑ Recommended by store personnel
❑ Author's reputation
❑ Sybex's reputation
❑ Read book review in _____
❑ Other _____

6. How did you pay for this book?

❑ Used own funds
❑ Reimbursed by company
❑ Received book as a gift

7. What is your level of experience with the subject covered in this book?

❑ Beginner
❑ Intermediate
❑ Advanced

8. How long have you been using a computer?

years _____

months _____

9. Where do you most often use your computer?

❑ Home
❑ Work

❑ Both
❑ Other _____

10. What kind of computer equipment do you have? (Check all that apply)

❑ PC Compatible Desktop Computer
❑ PC Compatible Laptop Computer
❑ Apple/Mac Computer
❑ Apple/Mac Laptop Computer
❑ CD ROM
❑ Fax Modem
❑ Data Modem
❑ Scanner
❑ Sound Card
❑ Other _____

11. What other kinds of software packages do you ordinarily use?

❑ Accounting
❑ Databases
❑ Networks
❑ Apple/Mac
❑ Desktop Publishing
❑ Spreadsheets
❑ CAD
❑ Games
❑ Word Processing
❑ Communications
❑ Money Management
❑ Other _____

12. What operating systems do you ordinarily use?

❑ DOS
❑ OS/2
❑ Windows
❑ Apple/Mac
❑ Windows NT
❑ Other _____

13. On what computer-related subject(s) would you like to see more books?

_____

_____

_____

_____

14. Do you have any other comments about this book? (Please feel free to use a separate piece of paper if you need more room)

_____

_____

_____

_____

- - - - - - - - - - PLEASE FOLD, SEAL, AND MAIL TO SYBEX - - - - - - - - - -

SYBEX INC.
Department M
2021 Challenger Drive
Alameda, CA
94501

SYBEX®

SunOS 4.1 Command	SunOS 5.x (SVR4) Changes
ls	The −A option, which listed entries whose names began with a ., except the current directory (.) and the parent directory (..), is no longer available. The ls command now defaults to a single column rather than multicolumn output when the output is a terminal.
mach	Use the uname −p command for similar results.
mail	The −i option, which ignored interrupts, is no longer available. Mail forwarding is now accomplished using the −F (forward) option. The n and dq commands, which were used to read mail, are no longer available.
mount	Most mount command options must now be specified after the file system type has been specified (mount −F filesystem), unless the file system is entered in the /etc/vfstab file.
mount_tfs	Use the mount -F filesystem command for similar results.
mountall	Use the mount −a command for similar results.
mv	The - option is no longer available. Instead use the −− option to explicitly mark the end of any command-line options so that mv can recognize file name arguments that begin with a −.
nice	This command now defaults to 10. The + option (nice +n) for the SunOS 5.x command increments the nice priority value by n; the C shell nice command sets the nice value to n. The C shell defaults to 4.
pack/unpack	The pack command's file name argument is no longer restricted to 12 characters; instead, the variable NAME_MAX −2 determines the length of the file name.
passwd	The -F filename (treat filename as the password file) and −y (change the password in the NIS database) options are no longer available. The −f option now forces the user to change the password at the next login. The −s option displays the password attributes for the user's login name, rather than changing the user's login shell.
pr	The −n option now displays balanced columns.
printenv	Use the env command for similar results.
ps	The −C, −k, −n, −r, −S, −U, −v, −w, and −x options are no longer available. The −c option displays six columns of process information, rather than just the associated command's name. The −e option displays information about all processes, instead of displaying the environment as well as the arguments to the command. The −g option is specified as −g idlist and restricts the listing to those processes whose process group IDs appear in idlist. The −u uidlist restricts the listing to processes whose user-ID numbers of login names appear in uidlist.